WHERE TO STAY ENGLAND 1997
CONTENTS

Upfront

A Sign of Quality	2
Finding Your Ideal Accommodation	4
A Look at Some of the Best	6
National Accessible Scheme	8
Key to Regional Sections	10
Tourist Information Centres	12

Places to Stay

London	17
Cumbria	27
Northumbria	57
North West	79
Yorkshire	89
Heart of England	113
Middle England	151
East Anglia	173
West Country	197
South of England	247
South East England	269
Self-Catering Agencies	287

Information Pages

National Grading and Classification Scheme	296
General Advice and Information	297
About the Guide Entries	299
Events for 1997	301
Enquiry Coupons	307

Town Index and Location Maps

Town Index	313
Index to Advertisers	317
Mileage Chart	318
Location Maps	321
Your Quick Guide	336

Key to Symbols

Inside back cover

D1785422

Front cover:
Border Rose Cottage, Akeld,
Wooler, Northumberland.
Back cover: (from top)
Pennine Lodge, St. John's Chapel,
County Durham.
Ciderpress Cottage/Walnut Tree
Cottage, Tonbridge, Kent.
Yeldersley Hall, Ashbourne,
Derbyshire.

i

A SIGN OF QUALITY

Knowing what to expect is vital when choosing a place to stay whether you're planning a self-catering break in an oak-beamed cottage, a bungalow with sea view or city-centre apartment.

Whatever type of accommodation you are looking for, you'll find that properties in *Where to Stay* offer the reassurance provided by the English Tourist Board's official National Quality Grading and Classification Scheme.

The assessment of a self-catering property under the Scheme consists of two parts: the first, using the Key symbol, classifies the range of facilities and equipment provided for guests; the second, from De Luxe to Approved, indicates the overall quality standard of these facilities and equipment.

Classification of facilities

The range of facilities and equipment provided is classified under one of five bands: from **One Key** (clean and comfortable, with adequate facilities and equipment for the number of people accommodated) to **Five Key** (providing full range of facilities and equipment). Quite simply, the more Keys, the wider the range. Please note that a higher number of Keys does not necessarily imply that the quality on offer is superior to that available at an establishment with fewer Keys.

Quality grading

A separate quality grading indicates the overall standard of facilities and equipment. Properties are awarded one of the following quality gradings:

De Luxe (excellent overall standard)
Highly Commended (very good overall standard)
Commended (good overall standard)
Approved (acceptable overall standard)

The Tourist Board's inspectors base their assessment on a wide variety of items, from the appearance of the building and tidiness of the garden to the standard and state of the furnishings, fittings and floor coverings. They give due consideration to the nature and size of the establishment in their overall assessment. You will therefore find that many types of accommodation in *Where to Stay* have been able to achieve a Highly Commended or De Luxe quality grading.

Many self-catering establishments have a range of accommodation units in the building or on the site and in some cases the individual units may have different quality gradings and classifications. In such cases, the entry shows the range available.

Range of facilities

The classification **One** to **Five Key** tells you the range of facilities and equipment provided. The more Keys, the wider the range. Below is an indication of some of the facilities you can expect under each classification.

🔑 Clean and comfortable, with adequate facilities and equipment for the number of people accommodated.

🔑🔑 Accommodation with additional facilities, including colour TV, shaver point or adaptor, easy chairs and/or sofa seats, bedside units/shelves.

🔑🔑🔑 Self-contained and with extra facilities and equipment, including availability of linen and towels, vacuum cleaner, iron and board, payphone on site, bedside lights, dressing table in adult bedrooms.

🔑🔑🔑🔑 Additional facilities and equipment, including washing machine and tumble dryer in unit or on site (unless laundry service available), supplementary lighting in living areas and coffee maker in kitchen.

🔑🔑🔑🔑🔑 All the requirements of the lower classifications plus such enhancements as controlled heating, hairdryer, dishwasher, fridge/ freezer, microwave oven, bath and shower.

Accessible Scheme

If you have difficulty walking or are a wheelchair user, it is important to be able to identify those establishments that will be able to cater for your requirements. If you book accommodation displaying an Accessible symbol, there's no longer any guesswork involved. Establishments can be awarded one of these categories of accessibility:

Category 1 accessible to all wheelchair users including those travelling independently

Category 2 accessible to a wheelchair user with assistance

Category 3 accessible to a wheelchair user able to walk short distances and up at least three steps.

See page 8 for a full list of establishments in this guide who have an Accessible symbol.

FINDING YOUR IDEAL ACCOMMODATION

Whatever your requirements, your preferences or your price range, *Where to Stay* will lead you straight to a selection of fine accommodation in England. From prices, quality and facilities on offer, you can see what's available at a glance.

Regional sections

The guide is divided into eleven regional sections. See the map on page 10. Each section contains an alphabetical listing of the region's cities, towns and villages with their accommodation establishments.

At the beginning of each section is a brief description of the area and a selection of interesting places to visit which may persuade you to stay a little longer - an illustrative map shows where they can be found.

Town index and location maps

The town index on page 313 and the colour location maps at the back of the guide show all the places featuring accommodation in this guide.

If the place you plan to visit is included in the town index, turn to the page number given for accommodation.

If, however, it is not included in the town index - or you just have a general idea of the area in which you wish to stay - use the colour location maps. You will find accommodation in all the places printed in black. Then simply refer back to the town index for the relevant page.

Service and facilities

Each accommodation listing contains detailed information to help you decide if it is right for you. This information has been provided by the proprietors themselves, and our aim has been to ensure that it is as objective and factual as possible.

Below the establishment name you will find the Key classification, One to Five Key, which indicates the range of services and facilities provided. The quality grading, De Luxe, Highly Commended, Commended or Approved tells you the overall standard of services and facilities. Detailed information on classification and gradings can be found on page 296.

At-a-glance symbols at the end of each entry give you additional information on services and facilities - a key to symbols can be found on the back cover flap. Keep this open to refer to as you read.

Accessibility

If you are a wheelchair user or have difficulty walking, look for the Accessible symbol. You will find a full list of entries participating in the National Accessible Scheme on page 8.

Check for changes

Please remember that changes may occur after the guide is printed. When you have found a suitable place to stay we advise you to contact the establishment to check availability, and also to confirm prices and any specific facilities which may be important to you. The coupons at the back of the guide will help you with your enquiries.

Then make your booking and, if you have time, confirm it in writing.

Further information

You may find it useful to read the information pages at the back of this guide (see page 295), particularly the section on cancellations.

Town Name ▶	**GILLAMOOR**
Map reference ▶	North Yorkshire Map Ref 5C3
Town description ▶	Village much admired by photographers for its views of Farndale, including 'Surprise View' from the churchyard.
Establishment name ▶	**Holly Cottage** 🅜
National Key classification and quality grading ▶	🔑🔑🔑 COMMENDED
Address, telephone and fax numbers ▶	Gillamoor, York YO8 3XT ☎ (01751) 0088 Contact Mrs. West
Establishment description ▶	*Delightful old cottage with period furnishings, in beautiful unspoilt village.*
National wheelchair access category ▶	Wheelchair access category 2 ♿ 1 self-contained unit; sleeping max 4
Accommodation, price guide and facilities ▶	

Price per week:	£min	£max
Low season	150.00	200.00
High season	200.00	350.00

At-a-glance symbols - see ▶
flap on back cover

🛥 Ⓜ ⓖ ⏢ ⊙ 🗖 MW 📺 🗖 📠 📧 ∥ P
☉ ▶ ❄ 🆂🅿

A LOOK AT SOME OF THE BEST

Self-catering holiday homes included in this *Where to Stay* guide which have achieved the highest quality grade of DE LUXE for the exceptionally high quality standard of the facilities and equipment they provide are featured on these pages. Please use the Town Index (page 313) to find the page numbers for their full entry listings.

Elterwater Hall, Great Langdale, Cumbria

Abbot's Court Cottages, Evesham, Hereford & Worcester

Folk on the Hill, Sandringham, Norfolk

Abbot's Court Cottages, Evesham, Hereford &
Worcester
Cheese Press Cottage, Hartington, Derbyshire
Ciderpress Cottage/Walnut Tree Cottage,
Tonbridge, Kent
Commonwood Cottages, Looe, Cornwall
The Corbyn, Torquay, Devon
Dove Cottage, Todmorden, West Yorkshire
Elterwater Hall, Great Langdale, Cumbria
Folk on the Hill, Sandringham, Norfolk
Gibbs Hill Farm Cottages, Haltwhistle,
Northumberland
Kennacott Court, Widemouth Bay, Cornwall
La Hogue Cottage, Newmarket, Suffolk
The Lakelands, Ambleside, Cumbria
Little Quarme Country Cottages,
Wheddon Cross, Somerset
Longlands at Cartmel, Cartmel, Cumbria
Melbreak Cottage, Loweswater, Cumbria
Newham Farm Cottages, Lostwithiel, Cornwall
**Old Coach House Riverside & Garden
Cottages,** Ambleside, Cumbria
The Pele Tower, Rothbury, Northumberland

Longlands at Cartmel, Cartmel, Cumbria

The Pump House Apartment, Billericay, Essex
Upper Mytholm Barn, Hebden Bridge,
West Yorkshire
Yeldersley Hall, Ashbourne, Derbyshire
York Lakeside Lodges, York

NATIONAL ACCESSIBLE SCHEME

Throughout Britain, the Tourist Boards are inspecting all types of places to stay, on holiday or business, that provide accessible accommodation for wheelchair users and others who may have difficulty walking.

The Tourist Boards recognise three categories of accessibility:

 Category 1
Accessible to all wheelchair users including those travelling independently.

 Category 2
Accessible to a wheelchair user with assistance.

 Category 3
Accessible to a wheelchair user able to walk short distances and up at least three steps.

If you have additional needs or special requirements of any kind, we strongly recommend that you make sure these can be met by your chosen establishment before you confirm your booking.

The criteria the Tourist Boards have adopted do not, necessarily, conform to British Standards or to Building Regulations. They reflect what the Boards understand to be acceptable to meet the practical needs of wheelchair users.

The following establishments listed in this *Where to Stay* guide had been inspected and given an access category at the time of going to press. Use the Town Index at the

back of the guide to find page numbers for their full entries.

 Category 1

CHESTERFIELD, DERBYSHIRE
- Swallow Cottage, Owl Cottage & Pheasant Croft
COLYTON, DEVON
- Smallicombe Farm
HARTGROVE, DORSET
- Hartgrove Farm
SEDBERGH, CUMBRIA
- Bainbridge Court

 Category 2

ASHWATER, DEVON
- Blagdon Farm Country Holidays
ATHERSTONE, WARWICKSHIRE
- Hipsley Farm Cottages
BAKEWELL, DERBYSHIRE
- Haddon Grove Farm Cottages
BICESTER, OXFORDSHIRE
- Pimlico Farm Country Cottages
BRIDPORT, DORSET
- Rudge Farm
BRUTON, SOMERSET
- Discove Farm
CANTERBURY, KENT
- Old Dairy Farmhouse Annexe
CHEDGRAVE, NORFOLK
- Barn Owl Holidays
COCKERMOUTH, CUMBRIA
- Simonscales Mill Cottage
COLYTON, DEVON
- Smallicombe Farm

CRESSBROOK, DERBYSHIRE
- Cressbrook Hall Cottages
DILHAM, NORFOLK
- Dairy Farm Cottages
EAST WITTERING, WEST SUSSEX
- Doves Flutter
HADLEIGH, SUFFOLK
- Stable Cottages
HARROGATE, NORTH YORKSHIRE
- Dinmore Cottages
HAWORTH, WEST YORKSHIRE
- Westfield Farm Cottages
LITTON CHENEY, DORSET
- Baglake Barn & Brewery Cottage
NAYLAND, SUFFOLK
- Gladwins Farm
TORQUAY, DEVON
- The Corbyn
WHITBY, NORTH YORKSHIRE
- Captain Cook's Haven
YORK
- York Lakeside Lodges

 Category 3

ABBERLEY, HEREFORD & WORCESTER
- Old Yates Cottages
ALNWICK, NORTHUMBERLAND
- Village Farm
ASHDON, ESSEX
- Whitensmere Farm Cottages
BAKEWELL, DERBYSHIRE
- Bolehill Farm Holiday
BAMBURGH, NORTHUMBERLAND
- Point Cottages
BATH, BATH AND NORTH EAST SOMERSET
- Greyfield Farm Cottages

BELLINGHAM, NORTHUMBERLAND
- Conheath Cottage
BOSLEY, CHESHIRE
- The Old Brye
BOURNEMOUTH, DORSET
- Watersedge
BRATTON, SOMERSET
- Woodcombe Lodges
CASTLE ACRE, NORFOLK
- Cherry Tree Cottage
DORKING, SURREY
- Bulmer Farm
EDITH WESTON, LEICESTERSHIRE
- Rutland Water Cottages
FOXLEY, NORFOLK
- Moor Farm Holidays
HAWKSHEAD, CUMBRIA
- Rogerground House
HOLMBRIDGE, WEST YORKSHIRE
- Waterside Cottage
MILTON ABBES, DORSET
- Luccombe Farm

MOSTERTON, DORSET
- Riverside
NEWENT, GLOUCESTERSHIRE
- Windmill Annexe
NEWTON-ON-RAWCLIFFE,
  NORTH YORKSHIRE
- Manor Farm Holidays
NUTLEY, EAST SUSSEX
- White House Farm Holiday
OLNEY, BUCKINGHAMSHIRE
- The Old Stone Barn
ST AUSTELL, CORNWALL
- Poltarrow Farm
STROUD, GLOUCESTERSHIRE
- Whitminster House Cottages
ULLSWATER, CUMBRIA
- Patterdale Hall Estate
WELTON, CUMBRIA
- Green View Lodges & Well
  Cottage

The National Accessible Scheme forms part of the Tourism for All Campaign that is being promoted by all three National Tourist Boards. Additional help and guidance on finding suitable holiday accommodation for those with special needs can be obtained from:
Holiday Care Service
2 Old Bank Chambers,
Station Road,
Horley, Surrey RH6 9HW.
Tel: (01293) 774535.
Fax: (01293) 784647.
Minicom: (01293) 776943.

KEY TO
REGIONAL SECTIONS

This *Where to Stay* guide is divided into 11 regional sections as shown on the map below. To identify each regional section and its page number, please refer to the key opposite. The index lists the counties of England and indicates under which regional section you will find them.

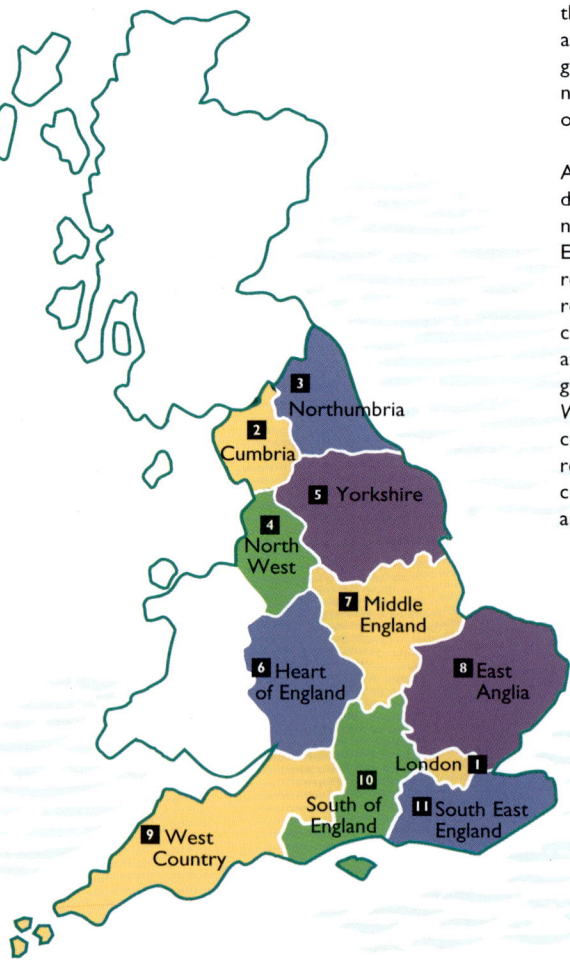

Colour location maps showing all the cities, towns and villages with accommodation listed in this guide, and an index to the place names, can be found at the back of the guide.

As you are probably aware, during 1996 the boundaries and names of a number of counties in England were changed as the result of local government reorganisation. The main county changes that had been announced at the time of compiling the 1997 guide have been reflected in *Where to Stay*, particularly in the county index opposite, the regional section maps, in the colour location maps at the back and in the town descriptions.**

If you want to find out more about what there is to see and do in a particular area, contact the appropriate Regional Tourist Board. Details are given both at the beginning and end of each regional section.

KEY TO MAP

1 London   17

2 Cumbria   27

3 Northumbria   57

4 North West   79

5 Yorkshire   89

6 Heart of England   113

7 Middle England   151

8 East Anglia   173

9 West Country   197

10 South of England   247

11 South East England   269

** This is how you will find the following county changes have been reflected in *Where to Stay*:

Avon is replaced by Bath & North East Somerset, City of Bristol, North Somerset and South Gloucestershire

Cleveland is replaced by Tees Valley

Humberside is replaced by East Riding of Yorkshire, North Lincolnshire and North East Lincolnshire

Although there have been changes to the unitary authority boundaries in the following areas, you will see that the familiar regional names have been retained for: Greater Manchester, Merseyside, South Yorkshire, Tyne & Wear, West Midlands and West Yorkshire

Please note that further changes are planned for 1997 which have yet to be confirmed.

COUNTY INDEX

Bath & North East Somerset:
West Country

Bedfordshire:
East Anglia

Berkshire:
South of England

Buckinghamshire:
South of England

Cambridgeshire:
East Anglia

Cheshire:
North West

City of Bristol:
West Country

Cornwall:
West Country

Cumbria:
Cumbria

Derbyshire:
Middle England

Derbyshire High Peak District:
North West

Devon:
West Country

Dorset (Eastern):
West Country

Dorset (Western):
South of England

Durham:
Northumbria

East Riding of Yorkshire:
Yorkshire

Essex:
East Anglia

Gloucestershire:
Heart of England

Greater London:
London

Greater Manchester:
North West

Hampshire:
South of England

Hereford & Worcester:
Heart of England

Hertfordshire:
East Anglia

Isle of Wight:
South of England

Isles of Scilly:
West Country

Kent:
South East England

Lancashire:
North West

Leicestershire:
Middle England

Lincolnshire:
Middle England

Merseyside:
North West

Norfolk:
East Anglia

North Lincolnshire:
Yorkshire

North East Lincolnshire:
Yorkshire

North Somerset:
West Country

North Yorkshire:
Yorkshire

Northamptonshire:
Middle England

Northumberland:
Northumbria

Nottinghamshire:
Middle England

Oxfordshire:
South of England

Shropshire:
Heart of England

Somerset:
West Country

South Gloucestershire:
West Country

South Yorkshire:
Yorkshire

Staffordshire:
Heart of England

Suffolk:
East Anglia

Surrey:
South East England

Tees Valley:
Northumbria

Tyne & Wear:
Northumbria

Warwickshire:
Heart of England

West Midlands:
Heart of England

West Sussex:
South East England

Wiltshire:
West Country

USE YOUR *i*'S

When it comes to your next England break, the first stage of your journey could be closer than you think. You've probably got a Tourist Information Centre nearby which is there to serve the local community - as well as visitors.

So make us your first stop. We'll be happy to help you, wherever you're heading.

Many Tourist Information Centres can provide you with maps and guides, helping you plan well in advance. And sometimes it's even possible for us to book your accommodation, too.

A visit to your nearest Information Centre can pay off in other ways as well. We can point you in the right direction when it comes to finding out about all the special events which are happening in the local region.

In fact, we can give you details of places to visit within easy reach... and perhaps tempt you to plan a day trip or weekend away.

Across the country, there are more than 550 Tourist Information Centres so you're never far away. You'll find the address of your nearest Tourist Information Centre in your local Phone Book.

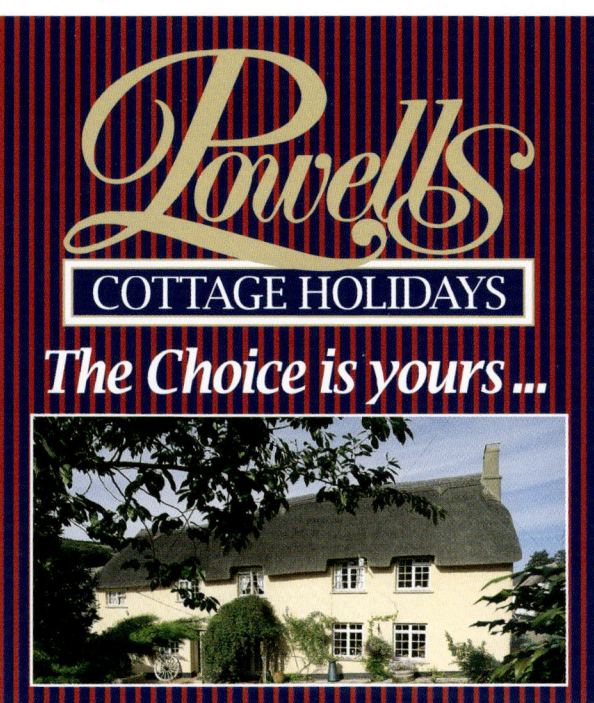

THE ENGLAND FOR EXCELLENCE AWARDS
WINNERS 1995

The England for Excellence Awards were created by the English Tourist Board to recognise and reward the highest standards of excellence and quality in all major sectors of tourism in England. The coveted Leo statuette, presented each year to winners, has become firmly established as the ultimate accolade in the English tourism industry.

Over the past eight years the Leo has been won by all types and sizes of business with one common attribute - excellence in the facilities and services they offer.

Hotel of the Year
Sponsored by Yellow Pages

The Four Seasons Hotel, London
(Five Crown, De Luxe)
London

Bed and Breakfast of the Year
Sponsored by Blackpool Pleasure Beach

Tree Tops
(Two Crown, De Luxe)
Berwick-upon-Tweed,
Northumberland

Holiday Centre of the Year
Sponsored by Senior King

Potters Leisure
Hopton on Sea, Norfolk

Self-Catering Holiday of the Year
Sponsored by Country Holidays Group

The Corbyn Holidays Suites & Villas - Brights of Nettlebe
(Five Key, De Luxe)
Torquay, Devon

Visitor Attraction of the Year
Sponsored by Hilton National

Hampton Court Palace
Surrey

Tourism Town of the Year
Sponsored by Marks & Spencer

Manchester - The City Visitor
Destination

Tourism for All Award
Sponsored by Gould & Portmans

Cheshire County Council
'Tourism for All' Programme

Tourist Information Centre of the Year
Sponsored by Ordnance Survey

Sunderland Tourist Information
Centre
Tyne and Wear

Outstanding Contribution to English Tourism Award
Sponsored by Hilton International

BBC TV / Pride and Prejudice

IS IT ACCESSIBLE?

If you are a wheelchair user or someone who has difficulty walking,
look for the national 'Accessible' symbol when choosing where to stay.

All the places that display a symbol have been checked by a Tourist Board inspector
against standard criteria that reflect the practical needs of wheelchair users.

There are three categories of accessibility:

Category 1 Accessible to all wheelchair users including those travelling independently

Category 2 Accessible to a wheelchair user with assistance

Category 3 Accessible to a wheelchair user able to walk short distances
and up at least three steps

Establishments in this guide which have a wheelchair access category
are listed on pages 8 and 9.

WHERE TO STAY IN ENGLAND

Published by: English Tourist Board,
Thames Tower, Black's Road,
Hammersmith, London W6 9EL.
ISBN 0 86143 200 2
Managing Editor: Jane Collinson
Technical Manager: Marita Sen
Compilation & Production: Guide
Associates, Croydon
Design and illustrations: Jackson Lowe
Marketing, Lewes, East Sussex
Colour Photography: Mike Williams
(front cover)
Cartography: Colin Earl
Typesetting: Reed Technologies and
Information Services, London and
Jackson Lowe Marketing, Lewes
Printing and Binding: Bemrose Security
Printing, Derby
Advertisement Sales: Madison Bell Ltd,
3 St. Peter's Street, Islington Green,
London N1 8JD. (0171) 359 7737.
© English Tourist Board (except
where stated)

The English Tourist Board
The Board is a statutory body
created by the Development of
Tourism Act 1969 to develop and
market England's tourism. Its main
objectives are to provide a welcome
for people visiting England; to
encourage people living in England to
take their holidays there; and to
encourage the provision and
improvement of tourist amenities and
facilities in England. The Board has a
statutory duty to advise the
Government on tourism matters
relating to England and, with
Government approval and support,
administers the national classification
and grading schemes for tourist
accommodation in England.

LONDON

No one can capture the atmosphere of London in words alone. One of the eternally great cities, it remains true that 'if you're tired of London, you're tired of life'.

Buckingham Palace, the Tower and Madame Tussaud's are just the beginning... London has more than 100 museums and galleries, the finest theatres in the world and some of the most exciting shops, restaurants and markets.

Stroll through the many gracious parks, discover Jack the Ripper's East End, explore 'the City', follow in the footsteps of Dickens. Or if you prefer, hop on a red bus or catch a black cab. Whichever way you go, seeing the sights of London is an unforgettable experience.

FOR MORE INFORMATION CONTACT:
London Tourist Board
26 Grosvenor Gardens, London SW1W 0DU

Where to Go in London - see pages 18-20
Where to Stay in London - see pages 23-25

LONDON

Where to Go and What to See

You will find hundreds of interesting places to visit during your stay in London, just some of which are listed in these pages. Contact any Tourist Information Centre in the region for more ideas on days out in London.

■ **Bankside Gallery**
48 Hopton Street,
London SE1 9JH
Tel: (0171) 928 7521
Home of The Royal Watercolour Society and The Royal Society of Painter-Printmakers. Changing exhibitions of watercolours and prints.

■ **British Museum**
Great Russell Street,
London WC1B 3DG
Tel: (0171) 636 1555
One of the great museums of the world, showing the works of man from all over the world from prehistoric times to the present day.

■ **Cabinet War Rooms**
Clive Steps,
King Charles Street,
London SW1A 2AQ
Tel: (0171) 930 6961
The underground headquarters used by Winston Churchill and the British Government during World War II. Includes Cabinet Room,

transatlantic telephone room and Map Room.

■ **Design Museum**
Shad Thames,
London SE1 2YD
Tel: (0171) 403 6933
A study collection showing the development of design in mass production. Review of new products, graphics gallery, and changing programme of exhibitions.

■ **Dickens House**
48 Doughty Street,
London WC1N 2LF
Tel: (0171) 405 2127
Charles Dickens' home from 1837-1839. Collection of letters, pictures, first editions, furniture, memorabilia, restored rooms.

■ **Fan Museum**
12 Crooms Hill,
London SE10 8ER
Tel: (0181) 305 1441
The only venue in the world devoted entirely to the art and craft

of the fan. Changing exhibitions. Beautifully restored 18thC houses. Gift shop.

■ **Guards Museum**
Wellington Barracks,
Birdcage Walk,
London SW1E 6HQ
Tel: (0171) 414 3428
Collection of uniforms, colours and artefacts spanning over 300 years of history of the Foot Guards.

■ **Hampton Court Palace**
Hampton Court,
Surrey KT8 9AU
Tel: (0181) 781 9500
Oldest Tudor palace in England. Tudor kitchens, tennis courts, maze, state apartments and King's apartments.

■ **HMS Belfast**
Morgan's Lane, Tooley Street,
London SE1 2JH
Tel: (0171) 407 6434
11,500 tonne World War II cruiser moored on the Thames. Now a

floating naval museum, with seven decks to explore. Many naval exhibits on show.

■ **Imperial War Museum**
Lambeth Road,
London SE1 6HZ
Tel: (0171) 416 5000
The story of 20thC war from Flanders to Bosnia. Features include the Blitz Experience, Operation Jericho and the Trench Experience.

■ **London Dungeon**
28-34 Tooley Street,
London SE1 2SZ
Tel: (0171) 403 0606
World's first medieval horror museum. Now featuring two major shows: "The Jack the Ripper Experience" and "The Theatre of the Guillotine".

■ **Madame Tussaud's**
Marylebone Road,
London NW1 5LR
Tel: (0171) 935 6861
Wax figures in themed settings, including The Garden Party, 200 Years, Superstars, The Grand Hall, The Chamber of Horrors and The Spirit of London.

■ **Museum of London**
150 London Wall,
London EC2Y 5HN

Tel: (0171) 600 3699
Galleries illustrate over 2000 years of the capital's social history, from prehistoric times to the 20thC. Regular temporary exhibitions, lunchtime lecture programmes.

■ **Museum of the Moving Image**
South Bank, Waterloo,
London SE1 8XT
Tel: (0171) 928 3535
A celebration of cinema and television. 44 exhibit areas offer plenty of hands-on participation, and a cast of actors to tell visitors more.

■ **National Gallery**
Trafalgar Square,
London WC2N 5DN
Tel: (0171) 839 3321
Western painting from 1260-1920, including work by Van Gogh, Rembrandt, Cezanne, Turner, Gainsborough, Leonardo da Vinci, Renoir and Botticelli.

■ **National Maritime Museum**
Romney Road, Greenwich,
London SE10 9NF
Tel: (0181) 858 4422
Britain's maritime heritage illustrated through actual and model ships, paintings, uniforms, navigation and astronomy

instruments, archives and photographs. Queen's House.

■ **National Portrait Gallery**
St Martin's Place,
London WC2H 0HE
Tel: (0171) 306 0055
Permanent collection of portraits of famous men and women from the Middle Ages to the present day.

■ **National Postal Museum**
King Edward Building,
King Edward Street,
London EC1A 1LP
Tel: (0171) 239 5420
One of the most important and extensive collections of postage stamps in the world, including the Phillips and Berne Collections. Temporary exhibitions.

■ **Natural History Museum**
Cromwell Road,
London SW7 5BD
Tel: (0171) 938 9123
Home of the wonders of the natural world, one of the most popular museums in the world, and one of London's finest landmarks.

■ **Old Royal Observatory**
(Flamsteed House),
Greenwich Park,
London SE10 9NF
Tel: (0181) 858 4422

Museum of time and space. Greenwich Meridian, working telescopes, planetarium and timeball. Wren's Octagon Room. Intricate clocks and computer simulations. Restored in 1993.

■ Rock Circus
London Pavilion, Piccadilly Circus,
London W1V 9LA
Tel: (0171) 734 7203
The exhibition is an amazing combination of stereo sound through personal headsets, audio animatronic (moving) and Madame Tussauds (wax) figures of over 50 rock stars.

■ Royal Air Force Museum
Grahame Park Way,
London NW9 5LL
Tel: (0181) 205 2266
Britain's National Museum of aviation features over 70 full size aircraft, Flight Simulator, "Touch & Try" Jet Provost Trainer and Eurofighter 2000 Theatre.

■ Science Museum
Exhibition Road,
London SW7 2DD
Tel: (0171) 938 8000
National Museum of Science and Industry. Full size replica of Apollo 11 Lunar Lander, launch pad, Wellcome Museum of History of Medicine, flight lab, food for thought, optics.

■ Sherlock Holmes Museum
221B Baker Street,
London NW1 6XE
Tel: (0171) 935 8866
Grade 2 listed lodging house. 1st floor Holmes' apartment. Second floor Mrs Hudson's room and Doctor Watson's room. Third floor souvenir shop. Reading room and exhibition room.

■ Thames Barrier Visitors' Centre
Unity Way, London SE18 5NJ
Tel: (0181) 854 1373
Exhibition with 10-min video, a working scale model and a multi-media show. Also riverside walkways, children's play area and Thames Barrier Buffet.

■ Tower Bridge
London SE1 2UP
Tel: (0171) 403 3761
Exhibition explains the history of the bridge and how it operates. Original steam powered engines on view. Panoramic views from fully-glazed walkways. Gift shop.

■ Tower of London
Tower Hill,
London EC3N 4AB
Tel: (0171) 709 0765
Building spans 900 years of British history. The nation's Crown Jewels, regalia and armoury robes on display. Home of the "Beefeaters" and ravens.

■ Victoria and Albert Museum
Cromwell Road,
London SW7 2RL
Tel: (0171) 938 8500
The V & A is the world's finest museum of the decorative arts. Its collection, housed in magnificent Victorian buildings, span 2000 years including sculpture and furniture.

FIND OUT MORE
A free information pack about holidays and attractions in London is available on written request from:
London Tourist Board and Convention Bureau,
26 Grosvenor Gardens,
London SW1W 0DU.

TOURIST INFORMATION

Tourist and leisure information can be obtained from Tourist Information Centres throughout England. Details of centres and other information services in Greater London are given below. The symbol ⊨ means that an accommodation booking service is provided.

Tourist Information Centres

Points of arrival

Victoria Station, Forecourt, SW1 ⊨
Easter-October, daily 0800-1900.
November-Easter, reduced opening hours.
Liverpool Street Underground Station, EC2 ⊨
Monday-Friday 0800-1800.
Saturday-Sunday 0845-17.30.
Heathrow Terminals 1, 2, 3 Underground Station Concourse (Heathrow Airport) ⊨
Daily 0800-1800.
Heathrow Terminal 3 Arrivals Concourse ⊨
0600-2300.
Waterloo International Arrivals Hall ⊨
0830-2100
The above information centres provide a London and Britain tourist information service, offer a hotel accommodation booking service, stock free and saleable publications on Britain and London and sell theatre tickets, tourist tickets for bus and underground and tickets for sightseeing tours.

Inner London

British Travel Centre ⊨
12 Regent Street, Piccadilly Circus, SW1Y 4PQ
Monday-Friday 0900-1830.
Saturday-Sunday 1000-1600
(0900-1700 Saturdays May-September).

Tower Hamlets Tourist Information Centre
107a Commercial Street, E1 6BG
Tel: (0181) 375 2549
Monday-Friday 0930-1630.
Greenwich Tourist Information Centre ⊨
46 Greenwich Church Street, SE10 9BL
Tel: (0181) 858 6376
April-September, daily 1015-1645. October-March, reduced opening hours.
Hackney Museum and Tourist Information Centre
Central Hall, Mare Street, E8
Tel: (0181) 985 9055
Tuesday-Friday 1000-1700.
Saturday 1330-1700.
Islington Tourist Information Centre ⊨
44 Duncan Street, N1 8BW
Tel: (0171) 278 8787
Monday 1400-1600.
Tuesday-Saturday 1000-1700.
Lewisham Tourist Information Centre
Lewisham Library, Lewisham High Street, SE13 6LG
Tel: (0181) 297 8317
Monday 1000-1700.
Tuesday-Friday 0900-1700
Selfridges ⊨
Oxford Street, W1. Basement Services Arcade
Open during normal store hours.
Southwark Tourist Information Centre ⊨
Hay's Galleria,
Tooley Street, SE1 2HD
Tel: (0171) 403 8299

Monday-Friday 1030-1700.
Saturday-Sunday 1100-1700.
(Reduced winter opening).

Outer London

Bexley Tourist Information Centre
Central Library, Townley Road, Bexleyheath DA6 7HJ
Tel: (0181) 303 9052
Monday, Tuesday, Thursday 0930-2000.
Wednesday & Friday 0930-1730.
Saturday 0930-1700.
Also at Hall Place Visitor Centre
Bourne Road, Bexley
Tel: (01322) 558676
June-September, daily 1130-1630.
Croydon Tourist Information Centre ⊨
Katharine Street,
Croydon CR9 1ET
Tel: (0181) 253 1009
Monday-Wednesday & Friday 0900-1800. Thursday 0930-1800.
Saturday 0900-1700.
Sunday 1200-1700.
Foots Cray Tourist Information Centre ⊨
Tesco Store Car Park,
Edgington Way, Sidcup DA14 5AH
Summer only, Monday-Saturday 1000-1800.
Sunday 1000-1600.
Harrow Tourist Information Centre
Civic Centre, Station Road,
Harrow HA1 2XF
Tel: (0181) 424 1103
Monday-Friday 0900-1700.

Hillingdon Tourist Information Centre
Central Library,
14 High Street,
Uxbridge UB8 1HD
Tel: Uxbridge (01895) 250706
Monday, Tuesday
& Thursday 0930-2000.
Friday & Wednesday 0930-1730.
Saturday 0930-1600.

Hounslow Tourist Information Centre
24 The Treaty Centre,
Hounslow High Street,
Hounslow TW3 1ES
Tel: (0181) 572 8279
Monday, Wednesday, Friday
& Saturday 0930-1730.
Tuesday, Thursday 0930-2000.

Kingston Tourist Information Centre
The Market House,
The Market Place,
Kingston upon Thames
KT1 1JS
Tel: (0181) 547 5592
Monday-Friday 1000-1700.
Saturday 0900-1600.

Redbridge Tourist Information Centre
Town Hall, High Road, Ilford,
Essex 1G1 1DD
Tel: (0181) 478 3020
Monday-Friday 0830-1700.

Richmond Tourist Information Centre ⌗
Old Town Hall,
Whittaker Avenue,
Richmond upon Thames
TW9 1TP
Tel: (0181) 940 9125
Monday-Friday 1000-1800.
Saturday 1000-1700.
May-October,
also Sunday 1015-1615.

Twickenham Tourist Information Centre
The Altrium, Civic Centre,
York Street,
Twickenham TW1 3BZ
Tel: (0181) 891 7272
Monday-Friday 0900-1700.

Visitorcall

The London Tourist Board and Convention Bureau's 'Phone Guide to London' operates 24 hours a day. To access a full range of information call 0839 123456. To access specific lines dial 0839 123 followed by:

What's on this week - 400
What's on next 3 months - 401
Sunday in London - 407
Rock and pop concerts - 422
Popular attractions - 480
Where to take children - 424

Museums - 429
Palaces (including Buckingham Palace) - 481
Current exhibitions - 403
Changing the Guard - 411
Popular West End shows - 416
London dining - 485
Calls cost 45p per minute cheap rate, 50p per minute at all other times (as at October '96).
To order a Visitorcall card please call (0171) 971 0026. Information for callers using push-button telephones: (0171) 971 0027.

Artsline

London's information and advice service for disabled people on arts and entertainment.
Call (0171) 388 2227.

CHECK THE MAPS

The colour maps at the back of this guide show all the cities, towns and villages for which you will find accommodation entries.

Refer to the town index to find the page on which it is listed.

WHERE TO STAY (LONDON)

Accommodation entries in this section are listed under **Inner London** (covering the

postcode areas E1 to W14) and **Outer London** (covering the remainder of Greater London)

- please refer to the colour location maps 6 and 7 at the back of this guide.

A contact address is given where it differs from the address of the establishment.

Prices shown are weekly per unit.

At-a-glance symbols at the end of each accommodation entry give useful information

about services and facilities. A key to symbols can be found inside the back cover flap.

Keep this open for easy reference.

INNER LONDON
See colour maps 6 & 7

Ashburn Garden Apartments
COMMENDED

3 Ashburn Gardens, London
SW7 4DG
☎ (0171) 370 2663
Fax (0171) 370 6743
Contact: Mr. A Aresti
*Well-established block of quality
serviced apartments, centrally located
in Kensington. Close to shops, museums
and transport.*
24 self-contained units; sleeping 3–6

Price per week:	£min	£max
Low season	455.00	700.00
High season	490.00	980.00

Belgard
COMMENDED

London
Contact: Mrs. N Reynish, P.O. Box
1026, London W2 1QE
☎ (0171) 262 5273 & (01865)
514199
Fax (0171) 402 7173
*One-bedroom apartments, fully
equipped, superior standard, in quiet
location near Marble Arch. Several
underground and bus routes close by.
Convenient for late shopping and all
amenities.*
4 self-contained units; sleeping 4

Price per week:	£min	£max
Low season	300.00	
High season		450.00

Cards accepted: Access, Visa

7 The Birches
22 Avenue Road, London SE25 4EF
☎ (0181) 653 9197 & (0410)
403627
Contact: Ms C Heffernan
*Two-bedroomed ground floor flat in
quiet area of London, next to a lake.
Recently refurbished kitchen and
bathroom.*
1 self-contained unit; sleeping 2–4

Price per week:	£min	£max
Low season	300.00	400.00
High season	475.00	550.00

Carena Holiday Accommodation
APPROVED

79 St. George's Avenue, Tufnell Park,
London
Contact: Mr M Chouthi, 98 St.
George's Avenue, Tufnell Park,
London N7 0AH
☎ (0171) 607 7453 & Mobile 0860
329802
Fax (0171) 607 7453
*In a quiet road yet close to public
transport. Comfortable and affordable
apartments with a range of quality
facilities and services. Perfectly
positioned for easy access to London's
main attractions. A friendly, family-run
establishment where a warm welcome
awaits all guests.*
3 self-contained units,
1 non-self-contained unit;
sleeping 2–5

Price per week:	£min	£max
Low season	190.00	400.00
High season	200.00	450.00

4 Charlwood Place
APPROVED

London
Contact: Mr. A Singleton, 14 The
Spinneys, Bickley, Bromley, Kent
BR1 2NU
☎ (0181) 467 0369
*Self-contained double-bedroomed flat
with separate bathroom and kitchen.*
1 self-contained unit; sleeping 1–2

Price per week:	£min	£max
Low season	160.00	180.00
High season	180.00	200.00

Chepstow Place
COMMENDED

19 Chepstow Place, Bayswater,
London W2 4TT
☎ (0181) 907 7661
Fax (0181) 907 7661
Contact: Mr. D E Rixon
*Quiet family-run flats in refurbished
Victorian house. Central location near
Queensway, Portobello, shops and
restaurants. Cleaning, linen, heating
inclusive.*
2 self-contained units; sleeping 3–4

Price per week:	£min	£max
Low season	250.00	300.00
High season	300.00	380.00

All accommodation in this
guide has been graded, or is
awaiting a grading, by a trained
Tourist Board inspector.

INNER LONDON
Continued

Clarendon House
COMMENDED

48 Ranelagh Road, Ealing, London
Contact: Mrs Anne Pedley, 21E
Harewood Close, Bexhill-on-Sea,
East Sussex TN39 3LX
☎ (01424) 212954
Fax (01424) 212954

Spacious apartments in Victorian house in a quiet residential area close to tube. Suitable for sightseeing or business purposes. On-road parking is unrestricted.
1 self-contained unit,
2 non-self-contained units;
sleeping 2–4

Price per week:	£min	£max
Low season	235.00	265.00
High season	260.00	300.00

Cards accepted: Access, Visa

24 Combemartin Road
HIGHLY COMMENDED

Southfields, London SW18 5PR
☎ (0181) 789 2663 & 0956 545431
Fax (0181) 265 5499
Contact: Mr & Mrs A Afriat
Garden flat in leafiest suburb within 30 minutes West End. Underground 3 minutes' walk. Close Wimbledon tennis, A3, M4. Easy access M25, Gatwick, Heathrow. Off-street parking. Ideal for business or holiday.
E-mail:afriat@mistral.co.uk
Internet:http://www.mistral.co.uk/afriat
1 self-contained unit; sleeping 4

Price per week:	£min	£max
Low season	200.00	300.00
High season	300.00	450.00

Information on accommodation listed in this guide has been supplied by the proprietors. As changes may occur you are advised to check details at the time of booking.

Ealing Tourist Flats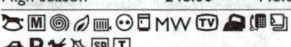
UP TO COMMENDED

94 Gordon Road, and 10 Hastings Road, London
Contact: Mr W G Smith, 94 Gordon Road, Ealing, London W13 8PT
☎ (0181) 566 8187 & (01895) 233365
Fax (0181) 566 7670

Attractive apartments for business or holiday travellers. Close to underground, restaurants and shopping arcades. Ideal location with good parking.
7 self-contained units; sleeping 4–7

Price per week:	£min	£max
Low season	225.00	415.00
High season	248.00	448.00

Map references apply to the colour maps at the back of this guide.

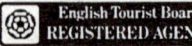

Emperors Gate Short Stay Apartments M

UP TO COMMENDED

8 Knaresborough Place, Kensington,
London SW5 0TG
☎ (0171) 244 8409 & 373 0323
Fax (0171) 373 6455
Contact: Mr R G Arnold
*Centrally located, high-standard suites,
close to Knightsbridge, Olympia and
Earl's Court. Daily rates also available.
Daily maid service.*
18 self-contained units; sleeping 4

Price per week:	£min	£max
Low season	483.00	1015.00
High season	595.00	1015.00

Cards accepted: Access, Visa, Diners,
Amex, Switch/Delta

Orion London M

COMMENDED

7-21 Goswell Road, London
EC1M 7AH
☎ (0171) 566 8000
Fax (0171) 566 8130
Contact: Mr Gus Bakker
*Purpose-built apartment-hotel in the
City of London, very near Barbican
Exhibition Centre. All studios and
apartments are well equipped and
furnished. Excellent value for money.
Prices per night from £79 (2 people) to
£119 (4 people) excluding breakfast.*
129 self-contained units;
sleeping 2–4

Price per week:	£min	£max
Low season	490.00	735.00
High season	490.00	735.00

Cards accepted: Access, Visa, Diners,
Amex, Switch/Delta

Royal Court Apartments M

UP TO HIGHLY COMMENDED

51 Gloucester Terrace, London
W2 3DQ
☎ (0171) 402 5077 & 0800 318798
Fax (0171) 724 0286
Contact: Mr M S Gill

*Close to Hyde Park and tube/bus
routes. Studios to 3-bedroomed
apartments with kitchenette, dining
area, direct-dial telephone, satellite TV.
Serviced daily, 24-hour*

reception/security facility. Breakfast
room, leisure centre. Daily rates
available.
78 self-contained units; sleeping 1–7

Price per week:	£min	£max
Low season	445.00	850.00
High season	525.00	1225.00

Cards accepted: Access, Visa, Diners,
Amex, Switch/Delta

73 Station Road

APPROVED

Hendon, London
Contact: Mr A Herzka, Ashbourne
House, Alberon Gardens, London
NW11 0BN
☎ (0181) 455 9667 & 0850 361777
*Spacious house with all modern
conveniences and large garden. On bus
routes. Close to railway and
underground stations, M1 and Brent
Cross Shopping Centre.*
1 self-contained unit; sleeping max 7

Price per week:	£min	£max
Low season	250.00	300.00
High season	300.00	400.00

The Village Property Services M

APPROVED

98 Dollis Hill Avenue, London
NW2 6QX
☎ (0181) 452 5327
Fax (0181) 452 0903
Contact: Mr M A Abeyakoon
*Self-contained apartment at realistic
weekly rental. Convenient for West End
shops, theatre, cinema, etc.*
1 self-contained unit; sleeping 3–7

Price per week:	£min	£max
Low season	200.00	350.00
High season	350.00	650.00

Cards accepted: Access, Visa, Diners,
Amex

Ad See display advertisement on
page 13

25a Westgrove Lane

COMMENDED

Greenwich, London
Contact: Rev. R C Butler, St.
Margaret's Rectory, Brandram Road,
London SE13 5EA
☎ (0181) 852 0633
Fax (0181) 297 2877
*Ground floor flat in a period house on
the edge of Blackheath, near
Greenwich Park. Easy access to central
London.*
1 self-contained unit; sleeping max 4

Price per week:	£min	£max
Low season	225.00	
High season		250.00

OUTER LONDON

See colour map 6

London Country Apartments Ltd M

UP TO HIGHLY COMMENDED

Amy Johnson House, 15 Cherry
Orchard Road, Croydon
Contact: Mrs. G Mitchell,
Management Office, 161 Brighton
Road, Purley, Surrey CR8 4HE
☎ (0181) 686 8068 & 0850 111074
Fax (0181) 686 0678
*Superbly-appointed apartments at East
Croydon just 15 minutes by rail to
London Victoria station and 17 minutes
to London Gatwick Airport. Ideally
placed for business and holiday stays.
Children welcome.*
24 self-contained units; sleeping 2–7

Price per week:	£min	£max
Low season	280.00	890.00
High season	295.00	995.00

Cards accepted: Access, Visa, Amex,
Switch/Delta

USE YOUR *i*'s

There are more than 550 Tourist Information Centres throughout England offering friendly help with accommodation and holiday ideas as well as suggestions of places to visit and things to do. There may well be a centre in your home town which can help you before you set out. You'll find the address of your nearest Tourist Information Centre in your local Phone Book.

AT-A-GLANCE SYMBOLS

Symbols at the end of each accommodation entry give useful information about services and facilities. A key to symbols can be found inside the back cover flap.

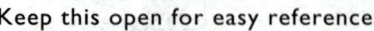

Keep this open for easy reference.

ENQUIRY COUPONS

To help you obtain further information about advertisers and accommodation featured in this guide you will find enquiry coupons at the back. Send these directly to the establishments in which you are interested. Remember to complete both sides of the coupon.

CUMBRIA

Cumbria is simply one of the most extraordinarily beautiful places on earth. Wordsworth lived here among its shimmering lakes and towering crags, and called it 'the loveliest spot that man hath ever found'; a 'spot' which attracts walkers, climbers and watersports enthusiasts, all year round.

But you don't have to be energetic! There are pretty villages, working farms, museums, visitors centres - plus the whole of the Lake District National Park to explore.

To the west of the Lakes lies Cumbria's unspoilt coastline. To the north you'll find the wild North Pennines and Borderlands. To the southeast, the peaceful Eden Valley. And between... paradise.

FOR MORE INFORMATION CONTACT:
Cumbria Tourist Board
Ashleigh, Holly Road, Windermere,
Cumbria LA23 2AQ
Tel: (015394) 44444 **Fax:** (015394) 44041

Where to Go in Cumbria – see pages 28-31
Where to Stay in Cumbria – see pages 32-55

CUMBRIA

Where to Go and What to See

You will find hundreds of interesting places to visit during your stay in Cumbria, just some of which are listed in these pages. The number against each name will help you locate it on the map (page 31). Contact any Tourist Information Centre in the region for more ideas on days out in Cumbria.

1 Linton Tweeds
Shaddon Mills, Shaddon Gate,
Carlisle, Cumbria CA2 5TZ
Tel: (01228) 27569
Shows history of weaving in Carlisle up to Lintons today. Available for visitors to have hands on weaving and other activities.

2 Tullie House Museum and Art Gallery
Castle Street, Carlisle,
Cumbria CA3 8TP
Tel: (01228) 34781
Major tourist complex housing: museum, art gallery, education facility, lecture theatre, shops, herb garden, restaurant and terrace bars.

3 Four Seasons Farm Experience
Sceugh Mire, Southwaite,
Carlisle CA4 0LS
Tel: (016974) 73753
An open farm where you can meet the animals, bottle feed the lambs, make your own butter and bread, plus other farming activities.

4 Senhouse Roman Museum
The Battery, Sea Brows,
Maryport, Cumbria CA15 6JD
Tel: (01900) 816168
Once the headquarters of Hadrian's Coastal Defence system. UK's largest group of Roman altars, stones and inscriptions from a single site. Roman military equipment, stunning sculpture.

5 Lakeland Sheep and Wool Centre
Egremont Road, Cockermouth,
Cumbria CA13 0QX
Tel: (01900) 822673
An all weather attraction with live sheep shows and working dog demonstrations. Includes large screen and other tourism exhibitions on the area, a wool shop and seafood restaurant.

6 The Printing House Museum
102 Main Street, Cockermouth,
Cumbria CA13 9LX
Tel: (01900) 824984
Printing machinery and equipment. Tour of the museum follows the development of printing from the 15thC to the present day.

7 Dalemain Historic House and Gardens
Dalemain Estate Office
Penrith,
Cumbria CA11 0HB
Tel: (017684) 86450
Historic house with Georgian furniture. Westmorland and Cumberland Yeomanry Museum, agricultural bygones, adventure playground, licensed restaurant, famous gardens.

8 Mirehouse
Underskiddaw,
Cumbria CA12 4QE
Tel: (017687) 72287
17thC house with wide ranging literary and artistic connections. Grounds to Bassenthwaite Lake include playgrounds, garden, tearoom.

9 **Dove Cottage & Wordsworth Museum**
Town End, Grasmere,
Ambleside, Cumbria LA22 9SH
Tel: (015394) 35544
*Wordsworth's home 1799-1808.
Poet's possessions, museum with
manuscripts, farmhouse
reconstruction, paintings and
drawings. Special events throughout
the year.*

10 **Rydal Mount**
Ambleside, Cumbria LA22 9LU
Tel: (015394) 33002
*William Wordsworth's home
for 37 years. Family portraits,
furniture, first editions and personal
possessions. Garden landscaped by
the poet. 9thC Norse Mound,
magnificent views.*

11 **Sellafield Visitors Centre**
Sellafield, Seascale,
Cumbria CA20 1PG
Tel: (019467) 27027
*Exhibition of nuclear power and
the nuclear industry.*

12 **Eskdale Corn Mill**
Boot, Holmrook,
Cumbria CA19 1TG
Tel: (019467) 23335
*A historic water-powered corn mill
near Dalegarth Station, approached*
*via packhorse bridge. Early wooden
machinery, milling and farming.
Exhibition and waterfalls.*

13 **Brockhole - Lake District National Park Visitor Centre**
Windermere,
Cumbria LA23 1LJ
Tel: (015394) 46601
*Exhibitions include National Park
Story, slide shows, films, shop,
gardens, grounds, adventure
playground, drystone walling area,
trails, events. Gaddums restaurant,
tearoom, putting.*

14 **Muncaster Castle, Gardens and Owl Centre**
Ravenglass,
Cumbria CA18 1RQ
Tel: (01229) 717614
*14thC pele tower with 15th and
19thC additions. Gardens contain
an exceptional collection of
rhododendrons and azaleas.
Extensive collection of owls.*

15 **Ravenglass and Eskdale Railway**
Ravenglass, Cumbria CA18 1SW
Tel: (01229) 717171
*England's oldest narrow-guage
railway runs for 7 miles through
glorious scenery to the foot of
England's highest hills. Most trains
steam hauled.*

16 **Steam Yacht Gondola**
Pier Cottage, Coniston,
Cumbria LA21 8AJ
Tel: (015394) 41288
*Victorian steam powered vessel now
National Trust owned and
completely renovated with opulently
upholstered saloon.*

17 **Amazonia**
Glebe Road, Bowness-on-
Windermere, Windermere,
Cumbria LA23 3HE
Tel: (015394) 48002
*Large display of exotic reptiles and
insects from around the world
including pythons, crocodiles and
tarantula spiders! Visitors are able
to handle certain animals.*

18 **The World of Beatrix Potter**
The Old Laundry, Crag Brow,
Bowness-on-Windermere,
Windermere, Cumbria LA23 3BX
Tel: (015394) 88444
*The life and works of Beatrix Potter
presented on a 9 screen video wall,
film on her life, and three-
dimensional recreations of some of
the scenes from her popular tales.*

19 **Levens Hall**
Levens, Kendal, Cumbria LA8 0PD
Tel: (015395) 60321
*Elizabethan mansion, incorporating
a pele tower. Famous topiary*

garden laid out in 1694, steam
collection, plant centre, shop, play
and picnic areas.

20 Sizergh Castle
Kendal, Cumbria LA8 8AE
Tel: (015395) 60070
*Strickland family home for 750
years, now National Trust owned.
With 14thC pele tower, 15thC
great hall, 16thC wings. Stuart
connections. Rock garden, rose
garden, daffodils.*

**23 Lakeside & Haverthwaite
Railway**
Haverthwaite Station,
Ulverston,
Cumbria LA12 8AL
Tel: (015395) 31594
*Standard gauge steam railway
operating a daily seasonal service
through the beautiful Leven Valley.
Steam and diesel locomotives
on display.*

**26 South Lakes
Wild Animal Park**
Crossgates,
Dalton-in-Furness,
Cumbria LA15 8JR
Tel: (01229) 466086
*Wild animal park in over 14 acres
with over 120 species of animals
from all over the world. Large
water-fowl ponds.
Miniature railway.*

**21 Heron Corn Mill
and Museum of Papermaking**
Waterhouse Mills,
Beetham, Milnthorpe,
Cumbria LA7 7AR
Tel: (015395) 63363
*Restored working corn mill featuring
14ft high waterwheel. The museum
shows paper-making both historic
and modern with artefacts, displays
and diagrams.*

22 Heron Glass
54 The Gill, Ulverston,
Cumbria LA12 7BL
Tel: (01229) 581121
*A combined visitor centre and
workshop. Traditional glassmaking
demonstrations daily.
Factory shop.*

**24 Phil Cotton's Classic Bikes
Working Museum**
Victoria Road,
Ulverston,
Cumbria LA12 0BY
Tel: (01229) 586099
*Classic motorcycle display, with
video, restoration areas and small
shop.*

25 Holker Hall and Gardens
Cark in Cartmel,
Cumbria LA11 7PL
Tel: (015395) 58328
*Victorian wing, formal and
woodland garden, deer park,
motor museum, adventure
playground and gift shop.
Exhibitions including Timeless Toys
and Teddies.*

27 The Dock Museum
North Road,
Barrow-in-Furness,
Cumbria LA14 2PW
Tel: (01229) 870871
*Presents the story of steel
shipbuilding for which
Barrow is famous.
Interactive displays, nautical
adventure playground.*

28 Furness Abbey
Barrow-in-Furness,
Cumbria LA13 0TJ
Tel: (01229) 823420
*Ruins of a 12C Cistercian abbey.
Extensive remains include
transepts, choir, west tower
of church, canopied seats
and arches.*

Map of Cumbria

SCOTLAND

NORTHUMBERLAND

0 ——— 20 Miles
0 ——— 30 Kms

• Longtown

• Brampton

Carlisle **1** **2**

• Silloth

Southwaite **3**

Maryport **4**

• Bassenthwaite

Broughton • **5** **6**
Cockermouth

CUMBRIA

• Penrith **7**

DURHAM

• Workington

8 Keswick

• Pooley Bridge

• Whitehaven

• Appleby-in-Westmorland

• Cleator Moor

• Egremont

Grasmere **9**

• Brough

Kirkby Stephen •

Seascale

11

10 Ambleside

12 Boot

13 Windermere

Coniston **16**

17 **18** Bowness-on-Windermere

14 **15**
Ravenglass

19 **20** Kendal

• Sedburgh

• Millom

Grange-over-
Sands

Beetham

Kirkby
Lonsdale

NORTH
YORKSHIRE

Ulverston

22 **23**
24

25

Cark in
Cartmel

21

26

Barrow-in-Furness **27** **28** Dalton-in-
Furness

29

LANCS

FIND OUT MORE

Further information about
holidays and attractions in
Cumbria is available from:
Cumbria Tourist Board,
Ashleigh,
Holly Road,
Windermere,
Cumbria LA23 2AQ.
Tel: (015394) 44444

These publications are
available from the
Cumbria Tourist Board:
■ **Cumbria The Lake District
Touring Map** - including tourist
information and touring caravan
and camping parks £3.45.
Laminated poster £2.95.
■ **Days Out in Cumbria -**
Over 200 ideas for a great day
out £1.25.

■ **Short Walks** - Good for
Families - route descriptions,
maps and information for
14 walks in lesser known areas
of Cumbria 95p.
■ **Wordsworth's
Lake District** - folded map
showing major Wordsworthian
sites plus biographical details
60p. Japanese language version
£1. Laminated poster £1.

WHERE TO STAY (CUMBRIA)

Accommodation entries in this region are listed in alphabetical order of place name, and then in alphabetical order of establishment. A contact address is given where it differs from the address of the establishment.

Map references refer to the colour location maps at the back of this guide.

Prices shown are weekly per unit.

At-a-glance symbols at the end of each accommodation entry give useful information about services and facilities. A key to symbols can be found inside the back cover flap. Keep this open for easy reference.

ALSTON

Cumbria
Map ref 5B2

Alston is the highest market town in England, set amongst the highest fells of the Pennines and close to the Pennine Way in an Area of Outstanding Natural Beauty. Mainly 17th C buildings and steep, cobbled streets.

Lorne House

COMMENDED

Overburn, Alston
Contact: Mr J H Kendall, Marsh End, 28 Woolsington Park South, Woolsington, Newcastle upon Tyne NE13 8BJ
☎ (0191) 286 9771
Recently restored early 19th C stone house. Land originally owned by Lord High Admiral of England (1600 AD). 3 bedrooms, 2 bathrooms, mains services, large garden.
1 self-contained unit; sleeping 6

Price per week:	£min	£max
Low season	165.00	200.00
High season	270.00	330.00

Information on accommodation listed in this guide has been supplied by the proprietors. As changes may occur you are advised to check details at the time of booking.

AMBLESIDE

Cumbria
Map ref 5A3

Market town situated at the head of Lake Windermere and surrounded by fells. The historic town centre is now a conservation area and the country around Ambleside is rich in historic and literary associations. Good centre for touring, walking and climbing.
Tourist Information Centre
☎ *(015394) 32582*

Beck Cottage

COMMENDED

5 Busk Cottages, Blue Hill Road, Ambleside
Contact: Mrs N K Morris, 11 Maple Grove, Worsley, Manchester M28 4ED
☎ (0161) 790 8023 & (0585) 655592
18th C beamed character cottage, delightfully furnished, convenient for shops, lake and fells. Warm and cosy in winter. Parking on lane.
1 self-contained unit; sleeping max 4

Price per week:	£min	£max
Low season	135.00	215.00
High season	225.00	335.00

Beeches Chestnuts and Hole House

COMMENDED

High Wray, Ambleside

Contact: Mr and Mrs J R Benson, Tock How Farm, High Wray, Ambleside, Cumbria LA22 0JF
☎ Ambleside (015394) 36481 & 0585 092941

Hole House: charming, secluded 17th C cottage with wonderful views. Chestnuts and Beeches: tastefully converted to form 2 delightful cottages with spectacular views.
3 self-contained units; sleeping max 6

Price per week:	£min	£max
Low season	185.00	450.00
High season	185.00	450.00

Birch Cottage

COMMENDED

8 Edinboro, Ambleside
Contact: Mrs S Birkett, Dale View, Little Langdale, Ambleside, Cumbria LA22 9NY
☎ Langdale (015394) 37329
Comfortable cottage in quiet hamlet on outskirts of village. Views to Wansfell and Loughrigg. Non smoking establishment.
1 self-contained unit; sleeping 4

Price per week:	£min	£max
Low season	180.00	230.00
High season	260.00	310.00

Eden Vale 𝔐
APPROVED

Lake Road, Ambleside LA22 0DB
☎ (015394) 32313
Contact: Mr & Mrs D Irvin
Clean, warm and comfortable - the flatlets and chalets are on a level site close to all Ambleside amenities.
13 self-contained units; sleeping 2

Price per week:	£min	£max
Low season	135.00	135.00
High season	185.00	185.00

The Grove Farm 𝔐
HIGHLY COMMENDED

Stockghyll Lane, Ambleside
LA22 9LG
☎ (015394) 33074
Fax (015394) 31881
Contact: Mrs Zorika Thompson
700-acre mixed farm. Our friendly, family-run working farm lies below Kirkstone Pass, above Lake Windermere yet only one mile from Ambleside. Personal welcome assured.
2 self-contained units; sleeping 2–6

Price per week:	£min	£max
Low season	115.00	200.00
High season	260.00	350.00

Kirkstone Foot Country House Hotel 𝔐
HIGHLY COMMENDED

Kirkstone Pass Road, Ambleside
Contact: Miss Alison Magee,
Kirkstone Foot Country House,
Hotel, Kirkstone Pass Road,
Ambleside, Cumbria LA22 9EH
☎ Ambleside (015394) 32232
Fax (015394) 32232

Self-contained apartments and cottages adjoining a licensed and secluded 17th C manor house hotel in its own grounds.
14 self-contained units; sleeping 2–8

Price per week:	£min	£max
Low season	275.00	775.00
High season	375.00	780.00

Open February–December
Cards accepted: Access, Visa, Diners, Amex, Switch/Delta

The Lakelands 𝔐
UP TO DE LUXE

Lower Gale, Ambleside LA22 0BD
☎ Windermere (015394) 33777
Fax (015394) 31301
Contact: Mrs Catrina Fletcher
Self-catering apartments at The Lakelands, set in a unique position overlooking Ambleside with unspoilt views of the surrounding fells. Furnished with quality in mind. Private leisure centre available for use of guests.
8 self-contained units; sleeping 4–8

Price per week:	£min	£max
Low season	225.00	445.00
High season	445.00	595.00

Little Beck
COMMENDED

Fairview Road, Ambleside
Contact: Mrs I Cook, Raaesbeck,
Fairview Road, Ambleside, Cumbria
LA22 9EE
☎ (015394) 33844
In the older part of Ambleside in an elevated and quiet position. Garden and uninterrupted views of Wansfell Pike, yet only 3 minutes' walk from the village.
1 self-contained unit; sleeping max 4

Price per week:	£min	£max
High season	215.00	295.00

Loughrigg View Cottage 𝔐
COMMENDED

Rydal Road, Ambleside LA22 9PN
☎ (015394) 32193
Contact: Mr Edward Scott
Three-bedroomed cottage-style apartment attached to the hotel. Spectacular views, dogs welcome. Use of hotel facilities, grounds and parking.
1 self-contained unit; sleeping max 6

Price per week:	£min	£max
Low season	160.00	
High season		360.00

Cards accepted: Access, Visa

52 Low Brow 𝔐
COMMENDED

Kirkfield, Ambleside
Contact: Mrs A Smith, 10 Oaks
Field, Ambleside, Cumbria LA22 9EJ
☎ Ambleside (015394) 33288
Three-bedroomed terraced house, 5 minutes from town centre. Ideal base for walking and touring the Lakes. Parking.
1 self-contained unit; sleeping max 6

Price per week:	£min	£max
High season	220.00	275.00

Open June–September and Christmas

Neaum Crag Court

Flats 10,13,14, Loughrigg, Ambleside
Contact: Mr Keiran Taylor-Thomas,
The Operation Ltd, Charter House,
Latham Close, Bredbury, Stockport,
Cheshire SK6 2SD
☎ (0161) 494 1000
Fax (0161) 494 1000

Self-catering apartments in 18 acres, in the heart of the Lake District. Private balconies and superb views of the Langdales.
3 self-contained units; sleeping 4

Price per week:	£min	£max
Low season	320.00	420.00
High season	420.00	560.00

Cards accepted: Access, Visa, Amex, Switch/Delta

Old Coach House, Riverside & Garden Cottages 𝔐
UP TO DE LUXE

Clappersgate, Skelwith Bridge,
Ambleside
Contact: Mr V R Vyner-Brooks,
Middle Barrows Green, Kendal,
Cumbria LA8 0JG
☎ (0151) 526 5451 & 9321 &
Kendal (015395) 60242
Fax (0151) 526 1331
Cottages furnished and equipped to a very high standard. Old Coach House features four-poster bed and shared use of riverside garden with mooring. Riverside Cottage has exposed beams, inglenook with open fire and four-poster bed. Garden Cottage is in idyllic surroundings.
3 self-contained units; sleeping 2–6

Price per week:	£min	£max
Low season	288.00	735.00
High season	294.00	783.00

A key to symbols can be found inside the back cover flap.

AMBLESIDE
Continued

Ramsteads ⋔
⚷⚷ UP TO COMMENDED
Ramsteads, Outgate, Ambleside
LA22 0NH
☎ (015394) 36583
Contact: Mr G Evans
Timber lodges in 25 acres of natural
woodland. Ideal centre for walkers,
naturalists and country lovers.
7 self-contained units; sleeping 4–6

Price per week:	£min	£max
Low season	135.00	240.00
High season	190.00	330.00

Open March–November

Riverside Cottages ⋔
⚷⚷ UP TO HIGHLY COMMMENDED
Rothay Bridge, Ambleside
Contact: Mr & Mrs Rhone, c/o
Riverside Lodge, Rothay Bridge,
Ambleside, Cumbria LA22 0EH
☎ Ambleside (015394) 34208
Recent development of holiday cottages
with every modern amenity. In idyllic
riverside setting near town centre of
Ambleside.
5 self-contained units; sleeping 2–6

Price per week:	£min	£max
Low season	175.00	250.00
High season	290.00	435.00

Cards accepted: Access, Visa

Scandale Bridge Cottage ⋔
⚷⚷⚷ HIGHLY COMMENDED
Rydal Road, Ambleside
Contact: Mr and Mrs Derek
Sweeney, Travellers Rest, Grasmere,
Ambleside, Cumbria LA22 9RR
☎ Grasmere (015394) 35604
Lakeland stone built cottage just on
edge of Ambleside. Private gardens,
river frontage. High standard of fixtures
and fittings. Colour brochure available.
1 self-contained unit; sleeping max 7

Price per week:	£min	£max
Low season	195.00	275.00
High season	350.00	450.00

All accommodation in this
guide has been graded, or is
awaiting a grading, by a trained
Tourist Board inspector.

APPLEBY-IN-WESTMORLAND
Cumbria
Map ref 5B3

Former county town of
Westmorland, at the foot of the
Pennines in the Eden Valley. The
castle was rebuilt in the 17th C,
except for its Norman keep, ditches
and ramparts. It now houses a Rare
Breeds Survival Trust Centre. Good
centre for exploring the Eden Valley.
Tourist Information Centre
☎ (017683) 51177

Ivy Cottage
⚷⚷ COMMENDED
Long Marton,
Appleby-in-Westmorland
Contact: Mrs H Grisdale, Pen-Erin,
Long Marton,
Appleby-in-Westmorland, Cumbria
CA16 6BN
☎ Kirkby Thore (017683) 61233
18th C sandstone cottage, in village.
Recently modernised, tastefully
decorated and very attractive. Under
personal supervision.
1 self-contained unit; sleeping max 4

Price per week:	£min	£max
Low season	190.00	200.00
High season	200.00	210.00

Keisley Coach House ⋔
⚷⚷ COMMENDED
Keisley House, Dufton,
Appleby-in-Westmorland
Contact: Mrs Hall, Keisley House,
Dufton, Appleby-in-Westmorland,
Cumbria CA16 6NF
☎ Appleby in Westmorland
(017683) 51230
Fax (017683) 51230
On Pennine fellside 1.5 miles from
Dufton village. 2 double bedrooms,
large kitchen/dining room, sitting room
with open fireplace. Panoramic views
over Eden Valley.
1 self-contained unit; sleeping max 4

Price per week:	£min	£max
Low season	170.00	220.00
High season	270.00	

Open March–October

The National Grading and
Classification Scheme is
explained in full at the
back of this guide.

Milburn Grange Holiday Cottages ⋔
⚷⚷⚷ − ⚷⚷⚷⚷ COMMENDED
Milburn Grange, Knock,
Appleby-in-Westmorland
CA16 6DR
☎ Kirkby Thore (017683) 61867 &
0836 547130
Fax (017683) 61867
Contact: Mrs Margaret Burke
Quality beamed cottages set in lovely
hamlet at foot of Pennines. Excellent
for Lakes, Borders, dales, walking,
relaxing. Cosy and warm in winter.
9 self-contained units; sleeping 2–7

Price per week:	£min	£max
Low season	150.00	200.00
High season	220.00	360.00

BAILEY
Cumbria
Map ref 5B2

Bailey Mill ⋔
⚷⚷ COMMENDED
Bailey, Newcastleton, Roxburghshire
TD9 0TR
☎ Roadhead (016977) 48617
Fax (016977) 48617
Contact: Mrs P Copeland
18th C grain mill nestling on the
Scottish border, idyllic base for forest
walks and country drives. On-site
sauna, jacuzzi, gym, games room, riding
and fishing.
5 self-contained units; sleeping 3–9

Price per week:	£min	£max
Low season	78.00	128.00
High season	128.00	448.00

Cards accepted: Visa

BASSENTHWAITE
Cumbria
Map ref 5A2

Standing in an idyllic setting, nestled
at the foot of Skiddaw and Ullock
Pike, this village is just a mile from
Bassenthwaite Lake, the one true
"lake" in the Lake District. The area
is visited by many varieties of
migrating birds.

Irton House Farm ⋔
⚷⚷⚷ HIGHLY COMMENDED
Isel, Cockermouth CA13 9ST
☎ (017687) 76380
Contact: Mr & Mrs R W Almond
234-acre mixed farm. Beamed lounge
and bedroom overlooking lake, modern

kitchen. On A591 between Bassenthwaite and Bothel. Wheelchair access.
1 self-contained unit; sleeping 2

Price per week:	£min	£max
Low season	196.00	
High season		298.00

Cards accepted: Access, Visa

🐟 ◎ 🏠 💻 ⊙ 🖥 M W 💺 TV 🗎 📠 ⦅📱⦆ 🖨 ♠ P U ❄ SP

Parkergate ⋒

🔑🔑🔑🔑 HIGHLY COMMENDED

Bassenthwaite, Keswick
Contact: Mrs Jane Phillips, Parkergate, Bassenthwaite, Keswick, Cumbria CA12 4QG
☎ Keswick (017687) 76376
Fax (017687) 76911
Traditional stone barn newly converted to cosy holiday homes. Two have open log fires and patios. All have outstanding views towards Bassenthwaite Lake and/or Skiddaw. Utter tranquillity. Owners live on site.
4 self-contained units; sleeping 2–6

Price per week:	£min	£max
Low season	200.00	300.00
High season	300.00	430.00

🐟 ◎ 🏠 💻 ⊙ 🖥 M W TV 🗎 📠 ⦅📱⦆ 🖨 ♠ P ❄ ⚲ SP 🏵

BORROWDALE

Cumbria
Map ref 5A3

Stretching south of Derwentwater to Seathwaite in the heart of the Lake District, the valley is walled by high fellsides. It can justly claim to be the most scenically impressive valley in the Lake District. Excellent centre for walking and climbing.

Rose Cottage Holiday Flats ⋒

🔑🔑🔑 COMMENDED

Rosthwaite, Borrowdale, Keswick CA12 5XB
☎ (017687) 77678
Contact: Mr Truckle
Two cosy flats above village general stores, each perfect for two. Immediate access to fells. Good eating-out nearby.
2 self-contained units; sleeping max 2

Price per week:	£min	£max
Low season	135.00	155.00
High season	195.00	210.00

Cards accepted: Access, Visa

M ◎ 🏠 ⊙ 🖥 TV 📠 🖨 P ❄ ✂ SP

The Smithy ⋒

🔑🔑🔑 COMMENDED

Leathes Cottage, Borrowdale, Keswick

Contact: Mr A R Patey, Leathes Cottage, Borrowdale, Keswick, Cumbria CA12 5UY
☎ Borrowdale (017687) 77377
Peaceful Borrowdale cottage, near Grange and 3.5 miles from Keswick. Glorious views of Skiddaw and Derwentwater. Comfortably furnished and with well-equipped kitchen.
1 self-contained unit; sleeping max 6

Price per week:	£min	£max
Low season	100.00	150.00
High season	300.00	350.00

🐟 M ◎ 🏠 ⊙ 🖥 💺 TV 🗎 📠 📠 ♠ P ❄ ✂ SP 🐕

BRAITHWAITE

Cumbria
Map ref 5A3

Braithwaite nestles at the foot of the Whinlatter Pass and has a magnificent backdrop of the mountains forming the Coledale Horseshoe.

Barrow View Cottage ⋒

🔑🔑🔑 COMMENDED

Braithwaite, Keswick
Contact: Mr C C Horton, 5 St. Johns Street, Keswick, Cumbria CA12 5AP
☎ Keswick (017687) 74627
Well-equipped beamed country cottage. Stunning views over fields to fells. Separate power shower. Tariff includes towels.
1 self-contained unit; sleeping 4

Price per week:	£min	£max
Low season	200.00	250.00
High season	250.00	350.00

Cards accepted: Access, Visa, Switch/Delta

🐟 M ◎ 🏠 ⊙ 🖥 M W 💺 TV 🗎 📠 🖨 ♠ P ❄ ✂ SP

BRAMPTON

Cumbria
Map ref 5B2

Excellent centre for exploring Hadrian's Wall. Wednesday is market day around the Moot Hall in this delightful sandstone-built town. Wall plaque marks the site of Bonnie Prince Charlie and his Jacobite army headquarters whilst they laid siege to Carlisle Castle in 1745.

Tarnside Cottages ⋒

🔑🔑🔑🔑 HIGHLY COMMENDED

Farlam, Brampton CA8 1LA
☎ (016977) 46675 & mobile 0831 561301
Contact: Mrs Vicky Reed
600-acre mixed farm. Uniquely

designed stone and cedarwood semi-detached cottages on farm, a quarter of a mile from Talkin Tarn. Footpath to the tarn in Farlam village.
2 self-contained units; sleeping max 4

Price per week:	£min	£max
Low season	150.00	267.00
High season	158.00	320.00

🐟 ◎ 🏠 ⊙ 🖥 M W TV 🗎 📠 🖨 ♠ P ▶ ❄ SP

BROUGHTON-IN-FURNESS

Cumbria
Map ref 5A3

Old market village whose historic charter to hold fairs is still proclaimed every year on the first day of August in the market square. Good centre for touring the pretty Duddon Valley.

Cooksons Cottages ⋒

🔑🔑🔑 COMMENDED

Broadgate, Millom
Contact: Mr D R Lewthwaite, Broadgate, Thwaites, Millom, Cumbria LA18 5JY
☎ Broughton in Furness (01229) 716295
Fax (01229) 716976
Two cottages in lovely countryside with good walks and beautiful views. House, sleeping 8, also available.
2 self-contained units; sleeping 2–5

Price per week:	£min	£max
Low season	95.00	
High season		298.00

🐟 M ◎ 🏠 🌿 🍴 ⊙ 🖥 TV 🗎 📠 📠 ♠ P U ✂ 🧦 ❄ SP

Holebeck Farm Cottages

Hole Beck Farm, Woodland, Broughton-in-Furness LA20 6AH
☎ (01229) 716364
Contact: Mrs Sheila Hutchinson
95-acre mixed farm. Recent barn conversion in beautiful situation, outstanding views. High quality accommodation, central heating, all mod cons, ample parking.
2 self-contained units; sleeping 2–6

Price per week:	£min	£max
Low season	250.00	300.00
High season	300.00	395.00

🐟 M ◎ 🏠 ⊙ 🖥 M W 💺 TV 🗎 📠 🖨 ♠ P 🏵

> For ideas on places to visit refer to the introduction at the beginning of this section.

BROUGHTON-IN-FURNESS
Continued

Thornthwaite Farm
APPROVED
Woodland Hall, Woodland,
Broughton-in-Furness LA20 6DF
☎ (01229) 716340
Contact: Mrs J Jackson
Farm cottage amidst beautiful scenery in good walking area. Private fishing lake. A quiet, relaxing holiday with a warm and friendly welcome. Established 29 years.
4 self-contained units; sleeping 4–6

Price per week:	£min	£max
Low season	140.00	180.00
High season	200.00	260.00

Walk Mill Cottage
APPROVED
Ulpha, Duddon Bridge, Millom
Contact: Mr B Basnett, Albion House, Sutton, Pulborough, West Sussex RH20 1PL
☎ (01798) 869244
South-facing cottage set in its own acre of grounds on Logan Beck, providing beautiful views. Electric heating in every room, 2 log/coal fires.
1 self-contained unit; sleeping max 8

Price per week:	£min	£max
Low season	165.00	
High season	375.00	

BUTTERMERE
Cumbria
Map ref 5A3

Small village surrounded by high mountains, between Buttermere Lake and Crummock Water. An ideal centre for walking and climbing the nearby peaks and for touring.

Bridge Hotel Self Catering Apartments
HIGHLY COMMENDED
Bridge Hotel, Buttermere, Cockermouth
Contact: Mrs Catherine Santini, Bridge Hotel, Buttermere, Cockermouth, Cumbria CA13 9UZ
☎ Buttermere (017687) 70252
Fax (017687) 70252

Please mention this guide when making your booking.

Beautifully situated overlooking Buttermere lake. All services inclusive. Sky TV, direct dial telephone, dishwasher, microwave, food processor, hair dryer, furnished patio. Dogs welcome.
7 self-contained units; sleeping 4–6

Price per week:	£min	£max
Low season	285.00	360.00
High season	395.00	495.00

Cards accepted: Access, Visa, Switch/Delta

CALDBECK
Cumbria
Map ref 5A2

Quaint limestone village lying on the northern fringe of the Lake District National Park. John Peel, the famous huntsman who is immortalised in song, is buried in the churchyard. The fells surrounding Caldbeck were once heavily mined, being rich in lead, copper and barytes.

High Greenrigg House
COMMENDED
Caldbeck, Wigton
Contact: Mr & Mrs F&R Jacobs, High Greenrigg House, Caldbeck, Wigton, Cumbria CA7 8HD
☎ Caldbeck (016974) 78430
The cottages, part of a carefully restored 17th C farmhouse, are remotely situated in the northern Lake District National Park.
2 self-contained units; sleeping 4–6

Price per week:	£min	£max
Low season	125.00	240.00
High season	250.00	375.00

Cards accepted: Access, Visa

Manor Cottage
HIGHLY COMMENDED
Fellside, Caldbeck, Wigton
CA7 8HA
☎ (016974) 78214
Contact: Mrs Ann Wade
17th C tastefully converted barn for peaceful, relaxing holidays. Galleried lounge with panoramic views. Unspoilt North Lakes, immediate access to fells.

1 self-contained unit

Price per week:	£min	£max
Low season	120.00	
High season		280.00

Open March–November

Monoleys
COMMENDED
Caldbeck, Wigton
Contact: Mrs S Pigg, Monoleys, The Old Brewery, Caldbeck, Wigton, Cumbria CA7 8EW
☎ Caldbeck (016974) 78420
Fax (016974) 78478

Beautifully maintained converted barn in quiet village within national park. Mostly en-suite. Open fire in honeymoon/anniversary/special occasion apartment. Ideal touring and walking location.
4 self-contained units; sleeping 2–5

Price per week:	£min	£max
Low season	135.00	195.00
High season	220.00	340.00

Cards accepted: Access, Visa, Amex

CARLETON
Cumbria
Map ref 5A2

Newbiggin Hall
UP TO HIGHLY COMMENDED
Carleton, Carlisle CA4 0AJ
☎ Carlisle (01228) 27549
Contact: Mr & Mrs D&J Bates
Historic pele-tower house with 3 charming apartments, modernised to a high standard yet retaining character. Delightful grounds with views to Pennines. Excellent access to North Lakes, Scottish Borders and Roman Wall.
3 self-contained units; sleeping 2–6

Price per week:	£min	£max
Low season	130.00	200.00
High season	225.00	375.00

CARLISLE

Cumbria
Map ref 5A2

Cumbria's only city is rich in history. Attractions include the small red sandstone cathedral and 900-year-old castle with magnificent view from the keep. Award-winning Tullie House Museum and Art Gallery brings 2,000 years of Border history dramatically to life. Excellent centre for shopping.
Tourist Information Centre ☎ (01228) 512444

Meadow View & Burn Cottage ⚹

COMMENDED

New Pallyards, Hethersgill, Carlisle
Contact: Mrs G Elwen, New Pallyards, Hethersgill, Carlisle CA6 6HZ
☎ Carlisle (01228) 577 308
Fax (01228) 577308
Large modern bungalow and stone-built cottage, fully centrally heated. Lovely country setting, woodland walks, home-cooked meals available.
2 self-contained units; sleeping 2–8

Price per week:	£min	£max
Low season	80.00	160.00
High season	180.00	375.00

Cards accepted: Access, Visa, Amex

CARTMEL

Cumbria
Map ref 5A3

Picturesque conserved village based on a 12th C priory with a well-preserved church and gatehouse. Just half a mile outside the Lake District National Park, this is a peaceful base for walking and touring, with historic houses and beautiful scenery.

Longlands at Cartmel ⚹

DE LUXE

Cartmel, Grange-over-Sands LA11 6HG
☎ Grange-over-Sands (015395) 36475
Fax (015395) 36172
Contact: Robert & Judy Johnson
Idyllic cottages in a secret corner of Southern Lakeland offering a unique combination of quality, freedom and tranquillity. Featured in BBC TV's "Holiday" programme and in major magazines and newspapers.

9 self-contained units; sleeping 2–6

Price per week:	£min	£max
Low season	190.00	470.00
High season	300.00	690.00

Cards accepted: Access, Visa, Amex, Switch/Delta

CASTLE CARROCK

Cumbria
Map ref 5B2

Small, tranquil village nestling at the north-western tip of the North Pennines, in an Area of Outstanding Natural Beauty.

Tottergill Farm ⚹

HIGHLY COMMENDED

Castle Carrock, Carlisle CA4 9DP
☎ Hayton (01228) 70615 & 0385 996950
Contact: Mrs Alison Bridges
320-acre livestock farm. Barn converted into self-contained cottages with wood beams and character. Building is in courtyard next to Grade II listed farm building with a tower.
4 self-contained units; sleeping 3–4

Price per week:	£min	£max
Low season	160.00	235.00
High season	210.00	310.00

CLEATOR

Cumbria
Map ref 5A3

6 miles from the Georgian port of Whitehaven with easy access to the western fells. Features a grotto similar to that in Lourdes, France.

Coach House ⚹

APPROVED

Hazel Holme, Cleator CA23 3AF
☎ Cleator Moor (01946) 810436
Contact: Mr & Mrs H Porter
3-bedroomed holiday home with country walks, fishing and riding nearby. Parking. 7-8 miles from the sea.
1 self-contained unit; sleeping max 6

Price per week:	£min	£max
Low season	90.00	115.00
High season	120.00	160.00

COCKERMOUTH

Cumbria
Map ref 5A2

Ancient market town at confluence of Rivers Cocker and Derwent. Birthplace of William Wordsworth in 1770. The house where he was born is at the end of the town's broad, tree-lined main street and is now owned by the National Trust. Good touring base for the Lakes.
Tourist Information Centre ☎ (01900) 822634

Broadings Holiday Cottages ⚹

UP TO HIGHLY COMMENDED

Mockerkin, Cockermouth
Contact: Mrs Christine Greening, Kilndale, Mockerkin, Cockermouth, Cumbria CA13 0ST
☎ Lamplugh (01946) 861672
375-acre dairy farm. Well-equipped self-contained house and cottages, 5.5 miles from Cockermouth. Tennis court.
4 self-contained units; sleeping 4–10

Price per week:	£min	£max
Low season	154.00	226.00
High season	294.00	497.00

Jenkin Cottage ⚹

COMMENDED

Embleton, Cockermouth
Contact: Mrs M E Teasdale, Jenkin Farm, Embleton, Cockermouth, Cumbria CA13 9TN
☎ Bassenthwaite Lake (017687) 76387
Cosy cottage on working family hill farm. Peaceful country setting. Good views. Open fire. Fully equipped. Sorry, no pets.
1 self-contained unit; sleeping 1–6

Price per week:	£min	£max
Low season	220.00	250.00
High season	240.00	350.00

Map references apply to the colour maps at the back of this guide.

Establishments should be open throughout the year, unless otherwise stated.

COCKERMOUTH
Continued

46 Kirkgate
🔑🔑🔑 HIGHLY COMMENDED

Cockermouth
Contact: Mrs P M Livesey, Fawcett House, High Brigham, Cockermouth, Cumbria CA13 0TG
☎ Cockermouth (01900) 825442
Charming listed Georgian cottage in delightful location. Quiet, yet close to town centre. Open log fire. For non-smokers only.
1 self-contained unit; sleeping max 4

Price per week:	£min	£max
Low season	175.00	190.00
High season		275.00

🛇🐕◎🛏☉🗄MW📺📺🗄🛆🍴🌙
🛆P🛇 SP🏮⊤◎

Simonscales Mill Cottage
🔑🔑🔑 COMMENDED

Simonscales Mill, Simonsclaes Lane, Cockermouth CA13 9TG
☎ (01900) 822594 & 0378 312576
Contact: Mrs Sue Lowes
5-acre smallholding. Converted former flax mill on banks of river. Quiet location on outskirts of market town. Suitable for all, including disabled.
Wheelchair access category 2♿
1 self-contained unit; sleeping max 4

Price per week:	£min	£max
Low season	200.00	250.00
High season	250.00	300.00

Open January–October, December
🛇M◎🛏☉🗄MW📺📺🗄🛆🌙
🛆P🍴🛇🌸 SP

West Winds
🔑🔑 COMMENDED

Mockerkin, Cockermouth CA13 0ST
☎ Lamplugh (01946) 861440
Contact: Mr and Mrs David & Marian Beattie
In quiet village, 5.5 miles south west of Cockermouth, 2.5 miles Loweswater, 5 miles Ennerdale. Annexe to modern bungalow, with double bedroom, shower room, modern kitchen, sitting room plus bed-settee.
1 self-contained unit; sleeping max 4

Price per week:	£min	£max
Low season	100.00	140.00
High season	125.00	175.00

🛇◎🛏☉🗄📺🛆🌙🛆P🌸

CONISTON
Cumbria
Map ref 5A3

The 803m fell Coniston Old Man dominates the skyline to the east of this village at the northern end of Coniston Water. Arthur Ransome set his "Swallows and Amazons" stories here. Coniston's most famous resident was John Ruskin, whose home, Brantwood, is open to the public. Good centre for walking.

1 and 2 Ash Gill Cottages ⚅
🔑🔑🔑 HIGHLY COMMENDED

Torver, Coniston
Contact: Mrs Dorothy Cowburn, Lyndene, Pope Lane, Whitestake, Preston, Lancashire PR4 4JR
☎ Preston (01772) 612832
Two houses equipped to the highest standard. Ample parking, gardens and patios. Excellent base for walking, touring, watersports, pony trekking.
2 self-contained units; sleeping 6

Price per week:	£min	£max
Low season	230.00	
High season		360.00

🛇3M◎🧺🛏☉🗄MW📺🛆🌙
🛆P🌸🍴🌙 SP

The Coach House ⚅
🔑🔑 COMMENDED

Brigg House, Torver, Coniston LA21 8AY
☎ (015394) 41592
Contact: Mr Ray Newport
Cosy, 18th C coachman's cottage in secluded rural setting at the foot of Coniston Old Man. Beautiful views. The ideal year-round hideaway. Non-smoking.
1 self-contained unit; sleeping 3

Price per week:	£min	£max
Low season	160.00	210.00
High season	210.00	330.00

🛇4◎🛏☉🗄MW📺📺🗄🛆🍴
🌙🛆P🌸🌙 SP

The Coppermines Coniston ⚅
🔑🔑 COMMENDED

Coppermines Valley, Coniston LA21 8HX
☎ (015394) 41765 & (0421) 584488
Contact: Mr Philip Johnston

Unique cottages in mountain scenery.

Quality, character, log fires, beams, central heating. Get away and unwind.
4 self-contained units; sleeping 2–22

Price per week:	£min	£max
Low season	180.00	800.00
High season	280.00	1600.00

🛇M◎🛏☉🗄📺🗄🛆🌙🍴🛆P
🌙U🌸🌙 SP

Fell View
🔑🔑🔑 HIGHLY COMMENDED

Yewdale Road, Coniston
Contact: Mrs Jean Birkett, Yew Tree Farm, Coniston, Cumbria LA21 8DP
☎ Windermere (015394) 41433
Detached house with large garden, on edge of village. Panoramic views.
1 self-contained unit; sleeping max 5

Price per week:	£min	£max
Low season	195.00	
High season	350.00	350.00

🛇◎🛏☉🗄MW📺🗄🛆🌙🛆P
🌸🍴 SP

Gaythorne Bungalow
🔑🔑 COMMENDED

Coniston
Contact: Mr J E Usher, Dixon House, Coniston, Cumbria LA21 8HQ
☎ (015394) 41217
Stone-built detached bungalow, with own garden, in a private yet convenient position close to the centre of Coniston village.
1 self-contained unit; sleeping max 4

Price per week:	£min	£max
Low season	140.00	180.00
High season	190.00	300.00

🛇◎🛏☉🗄MW📺🗄🛆🌙🛆
PU🌸🌙 SP

10 Green Cottages ⚅
🔑🔑 COMMENDED

Torver, Coniston
Contact: Mr K J Culshaw, 73 Larch Grove, Kendal, Cumbria LA9 6AX
☎ Kendal (01539) 740534 &
Coniston (015394) 41523
Terraced former railway cottage with garden. Quiet setting between lake and Coniston fells. Quality fittings and well heated. Ideal base for walking or touring.
1 self-contained unit; sleeping max 5

Price per week:	£min	£max
Low season	140.00	180.00
High season	180.00	290.00

🛇M◎🛏☉🗄📺🗄🛆🌙🛆PU🌸
🍴 SP

Please check prices and other details at the time of booking.

Map references apply to the colour maps at the back of this guide.

How Head Cottage

🔑🔑🔑🔑 UP TO COMMENDED

East of Lake, Coniston LA21 8AA
☎ (015394) 41594
Fax (015394) 41594
Contact: Mr RMG Rogers
Two self-contained cottages both in an elevated position with outstanding views of lake and mountain.
2 self-contained units; sleeping 3

Price per week:	£min	£max
Low season	125.00	180.00
High season	195.00	250.00

🐕 M © ▥ ☺ 🗋 MW TV 🚗 📷 🚲 P ❄ ✗ SP

Thurston House 🏔

🔑🔑🔑🔑 APPROVED

Tilberthwaite Avenue, Coniston
Contact: Mr and Mrs A Jefferson, 21 Chale Green, Harwood, Bolton BL2 3NJ
☎ Bolton (01204) 419261
Lakeland stone house, converted into spacious, clean, comfortable flats. Quiet location, close to lake and village centre.
5 self-contained units,
2 non-self-contained units;
sleeping 2–5

Price per week:	£min	£max
Low season	65.00	120.00
High season	100.00	225.00

Open February–November and Christmas

🐕 M © ▥ ☺ 🗋 TV 🚗 📷 🚲 P ❄

Wheelgate Country Cottages 🏔

🔑🔑🔑🔑🔑 COMMENDED

Little Arrow, Coniston LA21 8AU
☎ (015394) 41418
Contact: Mr & Mrs R Lupton
17th C farm buildings tastefully converted into character cottages, all equipped to a high standard. Complimentary leisure facilities. Resident, caring owners.
4 self-contained units; sleeping 2–5

Price per week:	£min	£max
Low season	135.00	220.00
High season	190.00	375.00

🐕 M © ▥ ☺ 🗋 ⟮ TV 🗋 🚗 ⟮▤⟯ 🍴 🚲 P U ❄ ✗ SP

Winton Shelt Gill

🔑🔑🔑 APPROVED

Haws Bank, Coniston
Contact: Mrs R Dean, 9 The Fairway, Sheffield, South Yorkshire S10 4LX
☎ Sheffield (0114) 230 8077
Medieval cottage with a view of Lake Coniston from the timbered living room, a stream in the garden and easy access to hill walks.

---

1 self-contained unit; sleeping max 5

Price per week:	£min	£max
Low season	150.00	
High season		325.00

🐕 M © ▥ ☺ 🗋 MW TV 🚗 📷 🚲 P ❄ SP 🏠 T

CROOKLANDS

Cumbria
Map ref 5B3

Village set amid the rolling fields, hedges and hills of England's largest drumlin belt.

Old Farmhouse

🔑🔑 COMMENDED

Crooklands, Milnthorpe LA7 7NW
☎ (015395) 67716
Contact: Mrs J Norman
Tasteful, spacious apartment in traditional farmhouse. Modern kitchen, shared patio and garden areas, parking. Close to Lakes, dales and coast, good views of surrounding countryside.
1 self-contained unit; sleeping max 4

Price per week:	£min	£max
Low season	125.00	
High season		250.00

🐕 M © ▥ ☺ 🗋 TV 🗋 🚗 ⟮▤⟯ 🚲 P ❄ SP

Preston Patrick Hall Cottage

🔑🔑 COMMENDED

Crooklands, Milnthorpe
Contact: Mrs Armitage, Preston Patrick Hall, Milnthorpe, Cumbria LA7 7NY
☎ Crooklands (015395) 67200
Fax (015395) 67200
500-acre mixed farm. Wing of a 14th C farmhouse, set within 250 acres of farmland, between Kendal and Kirkby Lonsdale.
1 self-contained unit; sleeping max 6

Price per week:	£min	£max
Low season	100.00	
High season		300.00

🐕 © ▥ ☺ 🗋 ⟮ 🗋 TV 🚗 📷 🚲 P ⟳ U 🚣 ❄ ✗ ▥ SP 🏠

DENT

Cumbria
Map ref 5B3

Very picturesque village with narrow cobbled streets, lying within the boundaries of the Yorkshire Dales National Park.

Middleton's Cottage and Fountain Cottage 🏔

🔑🔑 COMMENDED

Main Street, Dent, Sedbergh

Contact: Mr & Mrs P M Ayers, The Old Rectory, Litlington, Polegate, East Sussex BN26 5RB
☎ Alfriston (01323) 870032 & 870920
Fax (01323) 870032
Middleton's Cottage - cosy 2-storey village centre cottage, built mid-17th C. Two bedrooms, bathroom/wc, kitchen/dining area, lounge, garden, parking. Fountain Cottage - 3-storey character cottage built mid-17th C.
2 self-contained units; sleeping 4

Price per week:	£min	£max
Low season	140.00	180.00
High season	195.00	250.00

🐕 © ▥ ☺ 🗋 ⟮ TV 🗋 🚗 🚲 P ❄ ✗ ▥ SP

ELTERWATER

Cumbria
Map ref 5A3

Attractive village at the foot of Great Langdale with a small village green as its focal point.

Barnhowe 🏔

🔑🔑🔑🔑 UP TO HIGHLY COMMENDED

Lane Ends, Elterwater, Ambleside LA22 9HW
☎ Langdale (015394) 37346
Fax (015394) 37346
Contact: Mr M Riley
Beautiful 17th C riverside cottage, sleeping 6. Also, small cottage on common, sleeping 4.
2 self-contained units; sleeping 4–6

Price per week:	£min	£max
Low season	125.00	295.00
High season	235.00	495.00

🐕 M © ▥ ☺ 🗋 ⟮ TV 🗋 🚗 ⟮▤⟯ 🚲 P ❄ ✗ SP

The Bushells 🏔

🔑🔑 COMMENDED

2 Main Street, Elterwater, Ambleside
Contact: Mr Eric Bushell, 7 Oakland Vale, Wallasey, Merseyside L45 1LQ
☎ (0151) 639 5401
Fax (0151) 639 5401
Comfortable and well-equipped stone-built cottage, on the outskirts of a picturesque village in Langdale. Central for fell walking, bird-watching and all Lakeland activities.
1 self-contained unit; sleeping max 5

Price per week:	£min	£max
Low season	220.00	260.00
High season	280.00	360.00

🐕 3 M © ▥ ☺ 🗋 MW ⟮ TV 🗋 🚗 🗋 🚲 U ❄ SP

ELTERWATER
Continued

Lane Ends Cottages
UP TO COMMENDED

Elterwater, Ambleside
Contact: Mrs M E Rice, Fellside,
3 and 4 Lane Ends, Elterwater,
Ambleside, Cumbria LA22 9HS
☎ Langdale (015394) 37678
*Family-run stone-built cottages with
open fireplaces. In a peaceful setting in
Great Langdale on the edge of the
common, with views of the surrounding
fells.*
3 self-contained units; sleeping 5–6

Price per week:	£min	£max
Low season	160.00	
High season	260.00	

Wheelwrights ♨
UP TO HIGHLY COMMENDED

Elterwater, Ambleside LA22 9HS
☎ Langdale (015394) 37635 & 0378
170611
Fax (015394) 37618
Contact: Mr I Price
*Very well-equipped properties in fine
situation. Featured by BBC TV and
"Good Housekeeping" magazine.
Supervised by the owners.*
25 self-contained units; sleeping 2–6

Price per week:	£min	£max
Low season	195.00	295.00
High season	285.00	525.00

Cards accepted: Access, Visa

Wistaria Cottage & No. 3 Main Street ♨
COMMENDED

Elterwater, Ambleside
Contact: Mrs D Beardmore, 2 Beech
Drive, Kidsgrove, Stoke-on-Trent
ST7 1BA
☎ Kidsgrove (01782) 783170
*Traditional 18th C cottages near the
village centre. Tastefully renovated,
well-equipped. Cleaned and maintained
by owners. Warm and comfortable,
off-peak heating, open fires. Fell and
valley walking. 1 cottage has vanity
units with hot and cold water in
bedrooms.*
2 self-contained units; sleeping 3–4

Price per week:	£min	£max
Low season	264.00	293.00
High season	290.00	323.00

ENNERDALE
Cumbria
Map ref 5A3

The most western valley of the Lake
District. The small village of
Ennerdale Bridge is an ideal centre
for walking and rock climbing and
lies just one mile west of Ennerdale
Water. Pillar and Pillar Rock, famous
for its rock climbs, towers over the
lake.

Croasdale Farmhouse Cottage and Barn ♨
UP TO COMMENDED

Croasdale, Ennerdale Bridge,
Cleator Moor
Contact: Mr N Stanfield, Hawthorne
Cottage, Chapel Lane, Gentleshaw,
Rugeley, Staffordshire WS15 4ND
☎ Burntwood (01543) 682249
*Traditional 18th C Lakeland farmhouse
sleeps 8, adjoining cottage sleeps 2-3,
barn conversion sleeps 5-6. In peaceful
valley, 1.5 miles from Ennerdale Water.
Pets welcome.*
3 self-contained units; sleeping 3–8

Price per week:	£min	£max
Low season	125.00	270.00
High season	175.00	440.00

ESKDALE
Cumbria
Map ref 5A3

Several minor roads lead to the
west end of this beautiful valley, or it
can be approached via the east over
the Hardknott Pass, the Lake
District's steepest pass. Scafell Pike
and Bow Fell lie to the north and a
miniature railway links the Eskdale
Valley with Ravenglass on the coast.

Fisherground Farm ♨
COMMENDED

Eskdale, Holmrook CA19 1TF
☎ (019467) 23319
Contact: Mrs J E Hall
*100-acre hill farm. Traditional fell farm
in a peaceful Lakeland valley. 2 stone
cottages with open fires. 3 pine lodges
sharing an acre of orchard. Adventure
playground, games room, sports hall.
Pets welcome.*
5 self-contained units; sleeping 6

Price per week:	£min	£max
Low season	160.00	210.00
High season	220.00	430.00

Old Brantrake ♨
COMMENDED

Brant Rake, Eskdale, Holmrook
CA19 1TT
☎ (019467) 23340
Contact: Mr J B Tyson
*Recently restored 17th C listed
farmhouse in rural setting, ideal for
central fells or touring. 3 bedrooms,
wood fire, modern kitchen.*
1 self-contained unit; sleeping max 6

Price per week:	£min	£max
Low season	190.00	
High season		420.00

GARRIGILL
Cumbria
Map ref 5B2

Old lead-mining village high in the
Pennines. Nearby attractions include
the 50-foot Ash Hill Force waterfall
and the heritage centre at Killhope
which details the history of lead
mining in the area.

Brook Cottage ♨
COMMENDED

Garrigill, Alston
Contact: Mr and Mrs Gifford,
Moordale, Garrigill, Alston, Cumbria
CA9 3EB
☎ Alston (01434) 381688
*Stone-built cottage at south end of
Garrigill village. Maintained and
furnished to a high standard. Lots of
stone and beams.*
1 self-contained unit; sleeping max 6

Price per week:	£min	£max
Low season	100.00	150.00
High season	170.00	300.00

GLENRIDDING
Cumbria
Map ref 5A3

Village at southern end of lake
Ullswater. Motor yachts depart and
return from here along the lake.
Footpath to Helvellyn starts here.

Ullswater House Maisonette ♨
COMMENDED

Ullswater House, Glenridding,
Penrith

Contact: Mr Sharman, Sharmans Convenience Store, Ullswater House, Glenridding, Penrith, Cumbria CA10 0PA
☎ Glenridding (017684) 82221 & 82582
Fax (017684) 82122
Comfortably furnished first and second floor flat. Views of Lake Ullswater and surrounding fells.
1 self-contained unit; sleeping max 10

Price per week:	£min	£max
Low season	260.00	410.00
High season	340.00	410.00

Cards accepted: Access, Visa, Switch/Delta

🖥️Ⓜ◎🛏️☺🗂️MW📺📺🗜️🍳🐕‍🦺🐾PU

GRANGE-OVER-SANDS

Cumbria
Map ref 5A3

Set on the beautiful Cartmel Peninsula, this tranquil resort, known as Lakeland's Riviera, overlooks Morecambe Bay. Pleasant seafront walks and beautiful gardens. The bay attracts many species of wading birds.

Cornerways Bungalow 🏔️
🔑🔑 COMMENDED
Field Broughton, Grange-over-Sands
Contact: Mrs Eunice Rigg, Prospect House, Barber Green, Grange-over-Sands, Cumbria LA11 6HU
☎ Grange-over-Sands (015395) 36329
Pleasant bungalow in quiet situation. All-round views, private garden with parking. Ideal base for touring Lake District. Personal supervision.
1 self-contained unit; sleeping 4

Price per week:	£min	£max
Low season	230.00	250.00
High season	250.00	300.00

Open March–October

🖥️4Ⓜ◎🛏️☺🗂️MW📺🗜️🍳🐾🐕‍🦺P

Wycombe Holiday Flats 🏔️
🔑🔑🔑🔑 COMMENDED
The Esplanade, Grange-over-Sands
Contact: Mrs W G Benson, Wycombe, The Esplanade, Grange-over-Sands, Cumbria LA11 7HH
☎ Grange-over-Sands (015395) 32297
Fax (015395) 32297
Beautifully furnished and equipped (including satellite TV). Spectacular views. Seafront location in conservation

area. *Recreational amenities, restaurant and shops 100 metres. Train passengers met.*
3 self-contained units; sleeping 3–5

Price per week:	£min	£max
Low season	120.00	220.00
High season	240.00	340.00

🖥️Ⓜ◎🛏️☺🗂️MW📺📺🗜️🍳🐾PU🐾🐾SP◎

GRASMERE

Cumbria
Map ref 5A3

Described by William Wordsworth as "the loveliest spot that man hath ever found", this village, famous for its gingerbread, is in a beautiful setting overlooked by Helm Grag. Wordsworth lived at Dove Cottage. The cottage and museum are open to the public.

Beck Allans 🏔️
🔑🔑🔑🔑 – 🔑🔑🔑🔑🔑
UP TO HIGHLY COMMENDED
College Street, Grasmere LA22 9SZ
☎ (015394) 35563
Fax (015394) 35563
Contact: Mrs P Taylor
Selection of very comfortable holiday apartments, renovated and redecorated. Log fires, en-suite bathrooms, new kitchens, Sky movies. Timbered grounds in centre of village adjacent to River Rothay. Owners in residence. Swimming pool and jacuzzi.
7 self-contained units; sleeping 2–5

Price per week:	£min	£max
Low season	125.00	285.00
High season	180.00	435.00

Cards accepted: Access, Visa

🖥️Ⓜ◎🛏️☺🗂️📺🗜️🍳🍳🐾P🐾SP📋

Field Foot Holiday Cottages and High Dale Park Barn 🏔️
🔑🔑🔑🔑 – 🔑🔑🔑🔑🔑
UP TO HIGHLY COMMENDED
Broadgate, Grasmere, Ambleside
Contact: Mrs S H Brown, High Dale Park Farm, High Dale Park, Satterthwaite, Ulverston, Cumbria LA12 8LJ
☎ Satterthwaite (01229) 860226
Well-equipped cottages in the centre of Grasmere village. Close to all amenities and many walks. Storage heaters for winter warmth.
5 self-contained units; sleeping 2–8

Price per week:	£min	£max
Low season	170.00	
High season		375.00

🖥️Ⓜ◎🛏️☺🗂️📺📺🗜️🍳🍳🐾PU🐾🐾

Grasmere Lodge
🔑🔑🔑🔑 COMMENDED
Forest Side, Grasmere, Ambleside
Contact: Mr Hugh McLarty, 20 Wellesley Road, Liverpool L8 3SU
☎ (0151) 7271144 & 0850 512346

Secluded fellside lodge located 5 minutes' walk from Grasmere centre. Additional en-suite bedrooms for hire to accommodate larger groups.
5 self-contained units; sleeping 4

Price per week:	£min	£max
Low season	150.00	245.00
High season	224.00	315.00

🖥️Ⓜ◎🛏️☺🗂️MW📺🗜️🍳🐾P🐾🐾SP📋

Lake View Holiday Flats 🏔️
🔑🔑🔑 APPROVED
Lake View Drive, Grasmere, Ambleside LA22 9TD
☎ (015394) 35384
Contact: Mr Peter Mosey
In own grounds, overlooking the lake, with a footpath to the side of the lake. In the village off the main road.
3 self-contained units; sleeping 2–5

Price per week:	£min	£max
Low season	124.00	168.00
High season	232.00	319.00

🖥️10Ⓜ◎🛏️☺🗂️MW📺📺🗜️🍳🍳🐾P🎣🐾🐾SP

Meadow Brow 🏔️
🔑🔑🔑 APPROVED
Grasmere, Ambleside
Contact: Mr J A and Mrs W Wade, Woodvine Cottage, 45 Buxton Old Road, Disley, Cheshire SK12 2AL
☎ Disley (01663) 735089 & 766289
Cottage and flats in the wing of a country house in peaceful surroundings. Only 1 mile from centre of Grasmere, the shops and amenities.
4 self-contained units; sleeping 2–4

Price per week:	£min	£max
Low season	150.00	220.00
High season	175.00	310.00

🖥️8Ⓜ◎🌳🛏️☺🗂️MW📺📺🗜️🍳🍳🐾P🐾🐾SP🏠

Establishments should be open throughout the year, unless otherwise stated.

GRASMERE

Continued

Silvergarth

🔑🔑🔑🔑 COMMENDED

1 Low Riddings, Grasmere, Ambleside
Contact: Mrs Susan Coward, Swan Hotel, Grasmere, Ambleside, Cumbria LA22 9RF
☎ Grasmere (015394) 35624
Cosy Lakeland house on edge of village, furnished to high standard. Three bedrooms, coal fire, attractive garden. Parking. Magnificent views.
1 self-contained unit; sleeping 5

Price per week:	£min	£max
Low season	130.00	225.00
High season	250.00	360.00

🛏🅼◎▥⊙🖰MW💺📺🗄🖨🖼
🔌P∪☼

GRAYRIGG

Cumbria
Map ref 5B3

Village on the A685 north of Kendal. Important in the development of the Quaker church.

Punchbowl House

🔑🔑🔑 HIGHLY COMMENDED

Grayrigg, Kendal LA8 9BU
☎ (01539) 824345
Contact: Mrs D Johnson
Spacious two-storey accommodation attached to a Victorian farmhouse, conveniently situated between the Lakes and Dales. Open fire and all facilities included. Non-smoking.
1 self-contained unit; sleeping max 6

Price per week:	£min	£max
Low season	150.00	
High season		280.00

🛏5◎▥⊙🖰📺🖨🖵🔌P✗SP

GREAT LANGDALE

Cumbria
Map ref 5A3

Picturesque valley at the foot of the Langdale Pikes, popular with walkers and climbers of every ability, with some of the Lake District's loveliest waterfalls.

Elterwater Hall ♈

DE LUXE

The Langdale Estate, Great Langdale, Ambleside

Contact: Mrs Fredericka Johns, Langdale Hotel & Country Club, Great Langdale, Ambleside, Cumbria LA22 9JD
☎ Ambleside (015394) 37302
Fax (015394) 37394
Elterwater Hall is situated in its own grounds and forms part of the award-winning Langdale Estate with its hotel and country club, a short walk away.
6 self-contained units; sleeping 2–6

Price per week:	£min	£max
Low season	525.00	687.00
High season	656.00	1139.00

Cards accepted: Access, Visa, Diners, Amex, Switch/Delta

🛏🅼◎▥⊙🖰MW💺📺🗄🖨🖼
🖵🔌P⸮✎∪♪☼✗

Langdale Estate Chapel Stile Apartments ♈

🔑🔑🔑🔑 HIGHLY COMMENDED

The Langdale Estate, Great Langdale, Ambleside
Contact: Mrs Fredericka Johns, Langdale Hotel & Country Club, Great Langdale, Ambleside, Cumbria LA22 9JD
☎ Ambleside (015394) 37302
Fax (015394) 37394
Chapel Stile is situated next to Wainwrights Inn and forms part of the award-winning Langdale Estate with its hotel and country club, a short walk away.
10 self-contained units; sleeping 2–8

Price per week:	£min	£max
Low season	409.00	582.00
High season	525.00	850.00

Cards accepted: Access, Visa, Diners, Amex, Switch/Delta

🛏🅼◎▥⊙🖰MW💺📺🗄🖨🖼
🖵🔌P⸮✎∪♪☼✗

Langdale Estate Lodges ♈

🔑🔑🔑🔑 HIGHLY COMMENDED

Langdale Estate, Great Langdale, Ambleside
Contact: Mrs Fredericka Johns, Langdale Hotel & Country Club, Great Langdale, Ambleside, Cumbria LA22 9JD
☎ Ambleside (015394) 37302
Fax (015394) 37394
Formerly an old gunpowder mill for the Elterwater Gunpowder Company and now a hotel and lodge complex, with a leisure centre and all facilities attached.
81 self-contained units; sleeping 2–8

Price per week:	£min	£max
Low season	410.00	720.00
High season	720.00	1320.00

Cards accepted: Access, Visa, Diners, Amex, Switch/Delta

🛏🅼◎▥⊙🖰MW💺📺🗄🖨🖼🖵
🔌P⸮✎∪♪☼✗⌫

GREYSTOKE

Cumbria
Map ref 5A2

Some attractive 17th C cottages with cobbled forecourts stand near the village green. The privately-owned castle, which stands on the edge of a vast, wooded park, is remarkable for the follies that were built in the 18th C to enhance the views from its windows.

Brathen Cottage

The Thorpe, Greystoke, Penrith
Contact: Mrs Christine Mole, Brathen Cottage, Brathen the Thorpe, Greystoke, Penrith, Cumbria CA11 0TJ
☎ Greystoke (017684) 83595
Comfortable barn conversion on the edge of the village. Convenient for the motorway and the Lake District National Park.
1 self-contained unit; sleeping max 6

Price per week:	£min	£max
Low season	130.00	150.00
High season	170.00	200.00

🛏🅼◎▥⊙🖰💺📺🗄🖨🖵🔌P
☼SP

HAWKSHEAD

Cumbria
Map ref 5A3

Lying near Esthwaite Water, this village has great charm and character. Its small squares are linked by flagged or cobbled alleys and the main square is dominated by the market house, or Shambles, where the butchers had their stalls in days gone by.

Bridge View

🔑🔑🔑 COMMENDED

Hawkshead, Ambleside
Contact: Mrs S Dewhurst, 2 Bridge View, Hawkshead, Ambleside, Cumbria LA22 0PL
☎ Hawkshead (015394) 36340
Cottage quarter of a mile from the beautiful village of Hawkshead, famous for Beatrix Potter and Wordsworth. Central for all parts of the Lakes. Garden and parking.
1 self-contained unit; sleeping 5

Price per week:	£min	£max
Low season	195.00	
High season		355.00

🛏5🅼◎▥⊙MW💺📺🖨🖵
🔌☼✗

Broomriggs

🦎🦎—🔑 🦎🦎🦎

UP TO HIGHLY COMMENDED

Hawkshead, Ambleside LA22 0JX
☎ (015394) 36280
Contact: Mrs J R Haddow
Broomriggs apartments are located 1 mile from Hawkshead, overlooking Esthwaite Water. Large gardens and lake frontage, boats available. Also cottages, most with lake views.
11 self-contained units; sleeping 2–8

Price per week:	£min	£max
Low season	150.00	280.00
High season	280.00	400.00

🛏️ⓂⓒⓂ🖾⊙Ⓣ MW 🎵 TV 🍳📞🛋️ 🎵 ♿Ⓟ∪❄🚭 SP

The Croft Holiday Flats 🔺

🦎🦎🦎 COMMENDED

North Lonsdale Road, Hawkshead, Ambleside LA22 0NX
☎ (015394) 36374
Fax (015394) 36544
Contact: Mrs R E Barr
Large house with garden, converted into holiday flats. In village of Hawkshead on B5286 from Ambleside.
7 self-contained units; sleeping 4–6

Price per week:	£min	£max
Low season	115.00	145.00
High season	230.00	275.00

🛏️ⓂⓒⓂ⊙Ⓣ TV 🍳🖾 ♿Ⓟ❄ SP

Heron Cottage & Columbine Cottage 🔺

🦎🦎🦎 COMMENDED

13 & 14 Kings Yard, Hawkshead, Ambleside
Contact: Mr & Mrs Rhone, Riverside Lodge, Rothay Bridge, Ambleside, Cumbria LA22 OEH
☎ Ambleside (015394) 34208
New courtyard cottages furnished to a high standard and with every modern amenity. Near the centre of delightful Hawkshead.
2 self-contained units; sleeping 2–6

Price per week:	£min	£max
Low season	175.00	250.00
High season	290.00	435.00

Cards accepted: Access, Visa
🛏️ⓂⓒⓂ⊙Ⓣ MW TV 🍳🛋️📞
♿Ⓟ∪🎵🚭 SP

COLOUR MAPS

Colour maps at the back of this guide pinpoint all places in which you will find accommodation listed.

Rogerground House Hawkshead Holiday Homes 🔺

🦎🦎—🔑 🦎🦎🦎 UP TO COMMENDED

Hawkshead, Ambleside
Contact: Mr I G Mackie, 2 Rowanside, Prestbury, Macclesfield, Cheshire SK10 4BE
☎ Macclesfield (01625) 828624

A Tudor cottage, 17th C farmhouse and converted barn provide holiday homes of distinctive, traditional character with lovely walled gardens and splendid views.
Wheelchair access category 3🚶
6 self-contained units; sleeping 2–8

Price per week:	£min	£max
Low season	135.00	355.00
High season	185.00	515.00

🛏️ⓂⓒⓂ⊙Ⓣ TV 🍳🛋️📞🖾 ♿Ⓟ
∪❄🚭 SP 🏠

HIGH LORTON

Cumbria
Map ref 5A3

On the B5292 between Keswick and Cockermouth. Spectacular views from nearby Whinlatter Pass down this predominantly farming valley.

Holemire House Barn

🦎🦎🦎 HIGHLY COMMENDED

Holemire House, High Lorton, Cockermouth CA13 9TX
☎ (01900) 85225
Contact: Mrs A Fearfield

Traditional Lakeland barn with exposed beams, converted to quality accommodation for two. In beautiful Lorton Vale, overlooking local fells. Close to Keswick and the northern Lakes. Warm in winter, light and sunny in summer.
1 self-contained unit; sleeping 2

Price per week:	£min	£max
Low season	175.00	190.00
High season	225.00	290.00

ⓒⓂ⊙Ⓣ MW 🎵 TV 🍳🛋️🎵❄
✈ SP

A picturesqu[...]
once a thrivi[...]
500 ft above se[...]
outside the Lak[...]
Park. Good views [...]
the surrounding fe[...]

Mid Farm Holiday Cottages 🔺

🦎🦎—🔑 🦎🦎🦎

HIGHLY COMMENDED

Mid Farm, Ruthwaite, Ireby, Carlisle CA5 1HG
☎ Low Ireby (016973) 71547
Contact: Mrs D Darnton
64-acre livestock farm. Three traditional Lakeland cottages created from stone-built 17th C barn on small working farm in historic hamlet of Ruthwaite. Superb views of Skiddaw and Caldbeck Fells, excellent walking.
3 self-contained units; sleeping 4–6

Price per week:	£min	£max
Low season	185.00	205.00
High season	210.00	398.00

🛏️ⓒⓂ⊙Ⓣ TV 🍳🛋️ ♿Ⓟ❄🚭 SP

KENDAL

Cumbria
Map ref 5B3

The "Auld Grey Town" lies in the valley of the River Kent with a backcloth of limestone fells. Situated just outside the Lake District National Park, it is a good centre for touring the Lakes and surrounding country. Ruined castle, reputed birthplace of Catherine Parr.
Tourist Information Centre ☎ (01539) 725758

Field End Barns and Shaw End Mansion 🔺

🦎🦎🦎 🦎🦎 UP TO HIGHLY COMMENDED

Patton, Kendal LA8 9DU
☎ (01539) 824220 & 0378 596863
Contact: Mr E D Robinson
Five award-winning spacious barn conversions and 4 elegant apartments in Georgian manor house. Set on 200-acre estate in beautiful, peaceful location.
9 self-contained units; sleeping 7–9

Price per week:	£min	£max
Low season	110.00	190.00
High season	160.00	325.00

🛏️ⓂⓒⓂ⊙Ⓣ MW TV 🍳🛋️📞
♿∪🎵❄ SP

...h Swinklebank Farm

🔑🔑 COMMENDED

Longsleddale, Kendal LA8 9BD
☎ (01539) 823682
Contact: Mrs O B Simpson
1400-acre hill farm. Self-contained annexe to farmhouse in beautiful fell-walking countryside. Living room, kitchenette, shower room, 2 bedrooms, 1 with bunks.
1 self-contained unit; sleeping max 4

Price per week:	£min	£max
Low season	100.00	
High season		190.00

High Underbrow Cottage

🔑🔑 COMMENDED

Burneside, Kendal
Contact: Mrs Bateman, High Underbrow Farm, Burneside, Kendal, Cumbria LA8 9AY
☎ Kendal (01539) 721927
Mixed farm. Quiet location with lovely views. Ideal for touring Lakes and Dales.
1 self-contained unit; sleeping max 4

Price per week:	£min	£max
Low season	120.00	
High season		180.00

Middle Swinklebank

🔑🔑 COMMENDED

Longsleddale, Kendal
Contact: Mrs Mary Todd, Swinklebank House, Longsleddale, Kendal, Cumbria LA8 9BD
☎ Selside (01539) 823 275 & 823 256
Comfortable cottage, part of 17th C farmhouse, well-equipped, central heating, log fire. Idyllic setting in quiet, unspoilt valley. No additional charges.
1 self-contained unit; sleeping 2–4

Price per week:	£min	£max
Low season	180.00	180.00
High season	180.00	180.00

Plumgarths Holiday Flats ⚑

🔑🔑 — 🔑🔑

HIGHLY COMMENDED

Crook Road, Kendal LA8 8LX
☎ (01539) 720010
Fax (01539) 735367
Contact: Mr and Mrs Wharram

17th C Lakeland house converted to flats. Situated on the edge of the Lake District National Park in 3 acres of peaceful gardens and woods.
5 self-contained units; sleeping 3–7

Price per week:	£min	£max
Low season	150.00	200.00
High season	265.00	450.00

Stable Cottage

🔑🔑 COMMENDED

Natland Mill Beck Farm, Kendal
Contact: Mrs Heather Gardner, Barn House, Natland Mill Beck Farm, Kendal, Cumbria LA9 7LH
☎ Kendal (01539) 729333
Only 1.5 miles from Kendal, stone-built cottage forming part of 17th C farmstead. Quiet and peaceful. Super facilities, beautifully furnished. Ideal for walking and touring Lake District and Yorkshire Dales.
1 self-contained unit; sleeping 4

Price per week:	£min	£max
Low season	195.00	200.00
High season	200.00	300.00

KESWICK

Cumbria
Map ref 5A3

Beautifully positioned town beside Derwentwater and below the mountains of Skiddaw and Blencathra. Excellent base for walking, climbing, watersports and touring. Motor-launches operate on Derwentwater and motor boats, rowing boats and canoes can be hired.
*Tourist Information Centre
☎ (017687) 72645*

Acorn Flats ⚑

🔑🔑 — 🔑🔑

HIGHLY COMMENDED

Acorn House, Ambleside Road, Keswick CA12 4DL
☎ (017687) 72553
Contact: Mr J Miller
Fully contained spacious holiday flats situated 5 minutes' walk from town centre. Recently built and furnished to the highest standards. Cleanliness guaranteed.

2 self-contained units; sleeping 2–5

Price per week:	£min	£max
Low season	150.00	250.00
High season	300.00	380.00

Belle Vue ⚑

🔑🔑 COMMENDED

24 Lake Road, Keswick
Contact: Mrs L G Hartley, Hillside, Portinscale, Keswick, Cumbria CA12 5RS
☎ Keswick (017687) 71065
Lovely detached Lakeland residence, comfortable and well-equipped, close to lake. Felltop views of Catbells/Newlands Valley. Owner maintained.
3 self-contained units; sleeping 4

Price per week:	£min	£max
Low season	90.00	160.00
High season	160.00	310.00

Blencathra ⚑

🔑🔑 COMMENDED

3 Dunkley Court, Helvellyn Street, Keswick
Contact: Mrs M E Khan, 10 Howard Place, Carlisle CA1 1HR
☎ Carlisle (01228) 23635
Modern flat near town centre. Fitted kitchen. King-sized beds. Three-night breaks November to April. Beautiful views of surrounding fells.
1 self-contained unit; sleeping max 6

Price per week:	£min	£max
Low season	75.00	180.00
High season	190.00	275.00

Brigham Farm Flats ⚑

🔑🔑 — 🔑🔑 UP TO HIGHLY COMMENDED

Low Brigham, Keswick
Contact: Mr N Green, Brigham Farm Flats, Fornside House, St Johns-in-the-Vale, Keswick, Cumbria CA12 4TS
☎ Keswick (017687) 79666
Pleasantly secluded spacious apartments, handsomely furnished, with gas CH. Half a mile from Keswick town centre. Ample parking.
6 self-contained units; sleeping 2–4

Price per week:	£min	£max
Low season	75.00	195.00
High season	170.00	275.00

3 Catherine Cottages

🔑🔑 APPROVED

Keswick
Contact: Mrs D Allison, 2 Raven
Lane, Applethwaite, Keswick,
Cumbria CA12 4PW
☎ Keswick (017687) 74153
*Cottage in a quiet area near Fitz Park,
5 minutes' walk from the shops. Owner
maintained. Car park. SAE for
brochure.*
1 self-contained unit; sleeping max 5

Price per week:	£min	£max
Low season	110.00	140.00
High season	160.00	200.00

🛏🍳🔥☀🍴📺🛁📶🅿🚶✕

Chaucer House Hotel M

🔑🔑🔑 HIGHLY COMMENDED

Derwentwater Place, Keswick
CA12 4DR
☎ (017687) 72318 & 73223
Fax (017687) 75551
Contact: Mr K Pechartscheck
*Beautifully furnished flats, quietly
situated a few minutes' walk from town
centre and Lake Derwentwater. Private
parking.*
2 self-contained units; sleeping 4

Price per week:	£min	£max
Low season	202.00	202.00
High season	225.00	315.00

Cards accepted: Access, Visa, Amex
🛏☀🔥☀🍴MW📶📺🛁📶🍽
🅿🚶SP🅣

Derwent House and Brandelhowe M

🔑🔑🔑 COMMENDED

Portinscale, Keswick
Contact: Mr and Mrs Oliver Bull,
Derwent House Holidays, Stone
Heath, Hilderstone, Staffordshire
ST15 8SH
☎ Hilderstone (01889) 505678 &
Stoke-on-Trent (01782) 281321
Fax (01889) 505679

*Traditional stone and slate Lakeland
building converted and renovated to
form 4 comfortable holiday suites at
Portinscale Village on Derwentwater.
1 mile from Keswick.*
4 self-contained units; sleeping 2–6

Price per week:	£min	£max
Low season	95.00	175.00
High season	185.00	280.00

🛏6☀🔥☀🍴MW📶📺🛁🛁
🅿🚫SP☀

Derwentwater Hotel M

🔑🔑🔑 – 🔑🔑🔑

HIGHLY COMMENDED

Portinscale, Keswick CA12 5RE
☎ (017687) 72538
Fax (017687) 71002
Contact: Mr Ian Aston

*In quiet village of Portinscale in 16
acres of lakeside grounds, 1 mile from
Keswick. Fully equipped, self-catering
with style. Cottages now available.
Rates include dinner on arrival and
breakfast on departure.*
18 self-contained units; sleeping 1–6

Price per week:	£min	£max
Low season	185.00	299.00
High season	385.00	550.00

Cards accepted: Access, Visa, Amex,
Switch/Delta
🛏☀🍳🔥☀🍴MW📶📺🛁📶🍽
🍽🅿🚶☀🚫SP🅣
Ad See display advertisement on this
page

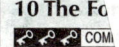

10 The Fo...

🔑🔑 COM...

Keswick
Contact: Mr ...
Harbinger Ro...
E14 9AA
☎ (0171) 515 ...
(017687) 73493...
*Well-appointed h... set on
the outskirts of Ke...ick by the River
Greta, 1 mile from the town centre.*
1 self-contained unit; sleeping max 6

Price per week:	£min	£max
Low season	220.00	250.00
High season	260.00	300.00

🛏☀🔥☀🍴MW📺🛁🛁📶🅿☀
SP

Fountain Cottage and Hideaway Cottage M

🔑🔑 UP TO COMMENDED

Keswick
Contact: Dr and Mrs W E Preston, 5
Mill Bank, Lymm, Cheshire
WA13 9DG
☎ (01925) 756479
*Owner maintained, cosy, well-equipped
cottages. One is centrally positioned, 2
bedrooms, no smoking or pets. The
other is on the edge of town with fell
views, 3 bedrooms, pets accepted,
private parking.*
2 self-contained units; sleeping 3–7

Price per week:	£min	£max
Low season	135.00	185.00
High season	195.00	345.00

🛏Ⓜ☀🔥☀🍴MW📶📺🛁📶🅿

Information on
accommodation listed in this
guide has been supplied by the
proprietors. As changes may
occur you are advised to check
details at the time of booking.

...ney Peak

🔑🔑–🔑🔑🔑 UP TO COMMENDED

Portinscale, Keswick
Contact: Mrs J P Smith, 55
Blythwood Road, Pinner, Middlesex
HA5 3QW
☎ (0181) 429 0402

*Traditional Cumbrian house in
Portinscale. Tastefully converted into
flats with central heating included in
rental. Superb views, ample parking.
Children and dogs welcome.*
11 self-contained units; sleeping 2–6

Price per week:	£min	£max
Low season	109.00	209.00
High season	199.00	439.00

🐕📞◎▥.☉🖥TV🗆🅿🧺(📶🔥P SP

Keswick Timeshare Limited

🔑🔑🔑 HIGHLY COMMENDED

Keswick Bridge, Brundholme Road,
Keswick CA12 4NL
☎ (017687) 73591
Fax (017687) 75811
Contact: Mr David Etherden
*20 self-contained lodges in own
grounds on the River Greta, a few
minutes' walk from the centre of
Keswick. 1, 2 and 3 bedroomed lodges
available.*
20 self-contained units; sleeping 4–8

Price per week:	£min	£max
Low season	250.00	390.00
High season	340.00	620.00

Cards accepted: Access, Visa,
Switch/Delta

🐕M◎▥.☉🖥MW📺TV🗆🅿(📶
🧺♿PU♪⏁❄✈ SP ◎

Kingsfell/Kingstarn

🔑🔑🔑 COMMENDED

16 Blencathra Street, Keswick
Contact: Mr N Gillham, 7 St.
Stephens Close, St Albans,
Hertfordshire AL3 4AB
☎ St Albans (01727) 853531
*Comfortable and well-equipped
Victorian townhouses in central
location. Pleasant views, modern
kitchens. Games room with pool table
at Kingsfell. Inclusive price.*

2 self-contained units; sleeping 8

Price per week:	£min	£max
Low season	175.00	280.00
High season	280.00	460.00

🐕📞▥.☉🖥MW📺TV🗆🅿(📶
U SP

Luxurious Lakeland

COMMENDED

35 Main Street, Keswick CA12 5BL
☎ (017687) 72790
Fax (017687) 72790
Contact: Mr John Mitchell

*Lakeland flats and cottages located in
one of Keswick's most desirable areas.
All with gas CH, some with 2
bathrooms (1 en-suite).*
4 self-contained units; sleeping 4–8

Price per week:	£min	£max
Low season	99.00	199.00
High season	199.00	335.00

🐕📞◎⌀▥.☉🖥MW📺TV🗆🅿🧺
♿❄⚡ SP

Riverside Holiday Flats

🔑🔑🔑 APPROVED

Keswick
Contact: Mr J Stephenson, Burleigh
Mead, The Heads, Keswick, Cumbria
CA12 5ER
☎ Keswick (017687) 72750
Fax (017687) 75435
*Completely self-contained, enjoying
peaceful riverside setting. Overlooking
Lower Fitz Park, yet close to town
centre and shops. Private parking.*
12 self-contained units; sleeping 2–5

Price per week:	£min	£max
Low season	100.00	168.00
High season	185.00	252.00

Open March–November

🐕M◎▥.☉🖥TV🗆🅿🔥P✈

Wren Cottage

🔑🔑 COMMENDED

1 Greta Street, Keswick
Contact: Mrs M Eastop, Wren
Cottage, c/o 1 Victoria Place, Stirling
FK8 2QX
☎ Stirling (01786) 462599
Fax (01786) 462617
*Comfortable, convenient, well-equipped
cottage all on one level. Small enclosed
garden with summerhouse and table
tennis facility.*

1 self-contained unit; sleeping max 4

Price per week:	£min	£max
Low season	160.00	
High season		300.00

Open March–October

🐕📞◎⌀▥.☉🖥MW📺TV🗆🅿(📶
🔥♿❄

Unspoilt Eden Valley village on the
River Lyvennet.

Glenlivet, Glengrant, Well Tree & Hill Top Barn

🔑🔑–🔑🔑 UP TO HIGHLY COMMENDED

King's Meaburn, Penrith
Contact: Mrs D M Addison, Keld,
King's Meaburn, Penrith, Cumbria
CA10 3BS
☎ Morland (01931) 714226
Fax (01931) 714598
*Attractive well-furnished cottages in
quiet village, overlooking the beautiful
Lyvennet Valley and the Lakeland hills.
Log fires in winter. Fishing, fuel and
linen inclusive. Children and pets
welcome.*
4 self-contained units; sleeping 3–6

Price per week:	£min	£max
Low season	160.00	240.00
High season	250.00	400.00

🐕◎▥.☉🖥TV🗆🅿🧺♿PU♪
❄ SP ◎

Charming old town of narrow
streets and Georgian buildings, set
in the superb scenery of the Lune
Valley. The Devil's Bridge over the
River Lune is probably 13th C.
Tourist Information Centre
☎ *(015242) 71437*

Barkin House

Gatebeck, Kendal LA8 0HX
☎ Crooklands (015395) 67277 &
67122
Contact: Mrs Mary Merritt
*100-acre mixed farm. Recently
converted barn in beautifully peaceful
surroundings, between lakes and dales.
5 miles north of Kirkby Lonsdale. Clean,
homely and a warm welcome always.*
1 self-contained unit; sleeping 4

Price per week:	£min	£max
Low season	150.00	200.00
High season	200.00	250.00

M◎▥.☉🖥MW📺TV🗆🅿🧺♿
P❄✈ SP

KIRKBY STEPHEN

Cumbria
Map ref 5B3

Old market town close to the River Eden, with many fine Georgian buildings and an attractive market square. St Stephen's Church is known as the "Cathedral of the Dales". Good base for exploring the Eden Valley and the Dales.

Chestnut Cottage and Swallows Barn

COMMENDED

Augill House, Brough, Kirkby Stephen
Contact: Mrs J Atkinson, Augill House Farm, Brough, Kirkby Stephen, Cumbria CA17 4DX
☎ Brough (017683) 41305
Two charming properties on working farm, ideal for the Lakes and Northern Pennines. Chestnut is great for couples; the Barn, with its en-suite bedrooms and spacious lounge, is ideal for families.
2 self-contained units; sleeping 2–5

Price per week:	£min	£max
Low season	100.00	200.00
High season	100.00	300.00

Dairy Cottage

HIGHLY COMMENDED

Townhead Farm, Brough Sowerby, Kirkby Stephen
Contact: Mr & Mrs Benson, Augill View, Brough Sowerby, Kirkby Stephen, Cumbria CA17 4EG
☎ Kirkby Stephen (017683) 41877
Splendid stone-built cottage offering first-rate accommodation, quality and character. Log fire, exposed beams, rich pine furnishings, exceptional kitchen area, modern bathroom, outstanding rural location and spectacular views.
1 self-contained unit; sleeping 1–6

Price per week:	£min	£max
Low season	200.00	250.00
High season	250.00	340.00

Information on accommodation listed in this guide has been supplied by the proprietors. As changes may occur you are advised to check details at the time of booking.

LANGDALE

Cumbria
Map ref 5A3

The two Langdale valleys (Great Langdale and Little Langdale) lie in the heart of beautiful mountain scenery. The craggy Langdale Pikes are almost 2500 ft high. An ideal walking and climbing area and base for touring.

Oakdene

HIGHLY COMMENDED

Chapel Stile, Ambleside
Contact: Mrs Patricia Locke, 17 Shay Lane, Hale, Altrincham, Cheshire WA15 8NZ
☎ Altrincham (0161) 904 9445
4-bedroomed and 3-bedroomed houses. Large pleasant garden with lovely views of the fells. Shop, pub and river nearby. Prices include membership of Langdale Leisure Club with swimming pool, squash courts, etc.
2 self-contained units; sleeping 6–8

Price per week:	£min	£max
Low season	280.00	410.00
High season	450.00	790.00

Park House

HIGHLY COMMENDED

Skelwith Bridge, Ambleside LA22 9NP
☎ Ambleside (015394) 33648 & 34176
Contact: Mr I Landon
Traditional cottage, part of 17th C farmhouse with walled garden. Unspoilt glorious countryside, overlooking Elterwater and the Langdale Valley.
1 self-contained unit; sleeping max 6

Price per week:	£min	£max
Low season	200.00	
High season		400.00

Open February–November

LAZONBY

Cumbria
Map ref 5B2

Busy, working village of stone cottages, set beside the River Eden amid sweeping pastoral landscape. Good fishing available.

Edengrove Holiday Cottages

COMMENDED

Lazonby, Penrith.

Contact: Mrs E P Bell, The Old Rectory, Lazonby, Penrith, Cumbria CA10 1BX
☎ Penrith (01768) 898242 & 898437
Fax (01768) 898720
These 19th C cottages have modern amenities and a large garden. On the edge of a quiet Eden Valley village. Heated swimming pool close by.
5 self-contained units; sleeping 5–6

Price per week:	£min	£max
Low season	130.00	175.00
High season	195.00	290.00

LONGSLEDDALE

Cumbria
Map ref 5B3

Quiet valley in the south-eastern fells, stretching 6 miles and lying 5 miles north of Kendal. Narrow roads, bordered by rolling hillsides, woodlands and craggy valley head.

The Coach House

COMMENDED

Capplebarrow House, Longsleddale, Kendal LA8 9BB
☎ Selside (01539) 823686
Contact: Mrs J Farmer
Stone-built, converted coach house with ground floor shower room and bedroom and open staircase to first floor kitchen and lounge.
1 self-contained unit; sleeping max 4

Price per week:	£min	£max
Low season	100.00	140.00
High season	140.00	175.00

LORTON

Cumbria
Map ref 5A3

High and Low Lorton are set in a beautiful vale north of Crummock Water and at the foot of the Whinlatter Pass. Church of St Cuthbert is well worth a visit.

Brow Farmhouse

COMMENDED

The Brow, Vale of Lorton, Cockermouth
Contact: Mr & Mrs A E Hudson, 79 Porchfield Square, Manchester M3 4FG
☎ (0161) 834 3888 & Cockermouth (01900) 85638
Converted farmhouse with log fire, full
Continued ▶

LORTON
Continued

central heating, washing machine and microwave. Secluded hillside homestead with grand views across Lorton.

1 self-contained unit; sleeping max 6

Price per week:	£min	£max
Low season	175.00	250.00
High season	250.00	425.00

High Swinside Farm Holiday Cottages ♦♦

UP TO COMMENDED

High Swinside Farm, Lorton, Cockermouth CA13 9UA
☎ Cockermouth (01900) 85206 & 85033
Fax (01900) 85206
Contact: Mr T and Mrs V Cresswell
Former hill farm where the local Jennings Brewery was founded in 1826. Well known and loved for its panoramic views.

3 self-contained units; sleeping 4–9

Price per week:	£min	£max
Low season	180.00	320.00
High season	340.00	690.00

1 2 3 & 4 Midtown Cottages ♦♦

COMMENDED

Lorton, Cockermouth
Contact: Mr & Mrs S Hinde, Yew Tree Cottage, Applethwaite, Keswick, Cumbria CA12 4PN
☎ Keswick (017687) 74440
Fax (017687) 74440
Four warm, well-furnished and decorated country cottages with superb Lakeland fell views. Quiet, unspoilt farming village between Keswick and Buttermere. Good parking. Laundry room. Owner cleaned and managed.

4 self-contained units; sleeping 4

Price per week:	£min	£max
Low season	190.00	230.00
High season	240.00	330.00

All accommodation in this guide has been graded, or is awaiting a grading, by a trained Tourist Board inspector.

LOWESWATER

Cumbria
Map ref 5A3

Scattered village lying between Loweswater, one of the smaller lakes, and Crummock Water. Mountains surround this quiet valley of three lakes, giving some marvellous views.

The Howe ♦♦

COMMENDED

Mosser, Cockermouth CA13 0RA
☎ Cockermouth (01900) 823660
Contact: Mrs M Townson
Hilltop cottage, lovely setting inside national park. Open plan with upstairs lounge and fell views. Thoughtfully prepared for the perfect family holiday. Farmhouse also available.

2 self-contained units; sleeping 4–6

Price per week:	£min	£max
Low season	180.00	200.00
High season	225.00	295.00

Loweswater Holiday Cottages ♦♦

UP TO HIGHLY COMMENDED

Scale Hill, Loweswater, Cockermouth CA13 9UX
☎ Cockermouth (01900) 85232
Contact: Mr M E Thompson
Cottages, nestling among magnificent fells and 3 beautiful lakes. Some serviced daily. Available all year. Open fires, gardens, children and pets welcome. Family-run. Colour brochure available.

9 self-contained units; sleeping 2–6

Price per week:	£min	£max
Low season	130.00	350.00
High season	235.00	675.00

Melbreak Cottage ♦♦

DE LUXE

High Park, Loweswater
Contact: Mr and Mrs D J Edwards, Pickett Howe, Buttermere Valley, Cockermouth, Cumbria CA13 9UY
☎ Lorton (01900) 85444
Fax (01900) 85209

Absolutely no traffic! Lake 5 minutes

across fields, pub half a mile. Stunning mountain and lake views, delightful garden. Oak beams, four-poster, whirlpool bath.

1 self-contained unit; sleeping 6

Price per week:	£min	£max
Low season	350.00	350.00
High season	490.00	670.00

Cards accepted: Access, Visa

MILLOM

Cumbria
Map ref 5A3

Town on the west side of the Duddon Estuary and once a busy centre for iron ore. Birthplace of poet Norman Nicholson, who is celebrated in the town's Folk Museum.

Old Dunningwell ♦♦

COMMENDED

The Green, Millom
Contact: Brigadier R G Lewthwaite, Broadgate, Thwaites, Millom, Cumbria LA18 5JY
☎ Broughton in Furness (01229) 716295
Fax (01229) 716976

Queen Anne house with Victorian addition situated in the country just outside the village of The Green, 4 miles from Millom.

1 self-contained unit; sleeping 8

Price per week:	£min	£max
Low season	100.00	150.00
High season	200.00	400.00

MUNGRISDALE

Cumbria
Map ref 5A2

Set in an unspoilt valley, this hamlet has a simple, white church with a 3-decker pulpit and box pews.

Grisedale View, Howe Top ♦♦

UP TO HIGHLY COMMENDED

Near Howe, Mungrisdale, Penrith CA11 0SH
☎ Threlkeld (017687) 79678
Contact: Mrs C A Weightman
Cottages converted from an old

Cumbria barn with views over the fells. Use of hotel garden and well-stocked bar. Easy access to the Lakes.
4 self-contained units; sleeping 4–7

Price per week:	£min	£max
Low season	170.00	300.00
High season	240.00	480.00

🕿 M ◎ ▥ ⊙ 🗗 MW 🖳 TV 🗄 🖪 🖫 🖳 🚗 ❊ SP

NENTHEAD
Cumbria
Map ref 5B2

Rock House Farm Holidays M
🔑🔑🔑🔑 COMMENDED

Rock House Farm Cottages, Nenthead, Alston
Contact: Mr and Mrs Eric Kite, Rock House Farm Holidays, Rock House Farm, Nenthead, Alston, Cumbria CA9 3NA
🕿 Alston (01434) 382800 & (0191) 4779124
Fax (0191) 4775418
150-acre arable farm. Built circa 1770 on the Cumbrian/Durham Border. Nenthead is 2056 ft high on the A689 road. Rock House offers unparalleled location and accommodation.
3 self-contained units; sleeping 5–12

Price per week:	£min	£max
Low season	118.00	165.00
High season	165.00	228.00

Cards accepted: Access, Visa, Switch/Delta

🕿 M ◎ ▥ ⊙ 🗗 🖳 TV 🖬 ∥ 🚗 P U ❊ 🐾 ▥ SP 🏠

PATTERDALE
Cumbria
Map ref 5A3

Amongst the fells at the southern end of the Ullswater Valley, this village is dominated by Helvellyn and St Sunday Crag. Ideal centre for touring and outdoor activities.

Placefell Cottage M
🔑🔑🔑🔑 HIGHLY COMMENDED

Patterdale, Penrith
Contact: Mrs M Trimble, Hillcote, 80 Gillingate, Kendal, Cumbria LA9 4JB
🕿 Kendal (01539) 726345
Idyllic Lakeland-stone detached cottage with own garden located on hillside. Shop and pub half-mile away. Recently modernised with all modern facilities. Winter short breaks available.
1 self-contained unit; sleeping max 7

Price per week:	£min	£max
Low season	200.00	350.00
High season	350.00	450.00

🕿 M ◎ ▥ ⊙ 🗗 MW 🖳 TV 🖬 🚗 🖫 🖳 🚗 P U ❊ SP

PENRITH
Cumbria
Map ref 5B2

Ancient and historic market town, the northern gateway to the Lake District. Penrith Castle was built as a defence against the Scots. Its ruins, open to the public, stand in the public park. High above the town is the Penrith Beacon, made famous by William Wordsworth.
Tourist Information Centre 🕿 (01768) 867466

Skirwith Hall Cottage and Smithy Cottage M
🔑🔑🔑 – 🔑🔑🔑🔑 UP TO COMMENDED

Skirwith, Penrith
Contact: Mrs L I Wilson, Skirwith Hall, Skirwith, Penrith, Cumbria CA10 1RH
🕿 Penrith (01768) 88241 & Mobile 0836 747320
Fax (01768) 88241
400-acre mixed farm. Character cottages in village east of Penrith. Ideal centre for touring the Lakes and Yorkshire Dales or simply relaxing in idyllic rural surroundings.
2 self-contained units; sleeping 4–9

Price per week:	£min	£max
Low season	105.00	260.00
High season	200.00	350.00

🕿 M ◎ 🖉 ▥ ⊙ 🗗 MW 🖳 TV 🖬 🚗 🖫 🖳 🖬 🚗 P ❊ 🐾 SP 🏠 ◎

Wetheral Cottages M
🔑🔑🔑 HIGHLY COMMENDED

Great Salkeld, Penrith CA11 9NA
🕿 Lazonby (01768) 898779
Contact: Mr C Ranford
Delightful sandstone cottages, peaceful garden setting, in the picturesque village of Great Salkeld, north of Penrith. Comfort and cleanliness assured by resident owners. Prices all-inclusive. Colour brochure.
5 self-contained units; sleeping 3–8

Price per week:	£min	£max
Low season	150.00	240.00
High season	280.00	425.00

🕿 ◎ ▥ ⊙ 🗗 TV 🚗 🖬 🖫 P ❊ 🐾 SP

White Hall Cottage
🔑🔑🔑 HIGHLY COMMENDED

White Hall, Blencarn, Penrith CA10 1TX
🕿 (01768) 88403
Contact: Mrs Margaret May Young

Comfortable, cosy cottage. Lovely beamed sitting/dining room with views of Lakeland hills. Heated throughout. 1 double, 1 single bedroom. Easy access Lakes, dales and Scottish Borders. Brochure available.
1 self-contained unit; sleeping max 3

Price per week:	£min	£max
Low season	110.00	155.00
High season	170.00	210.00

🕿 M ◎ ▥ ⊙ 🗗 MW 🖳 TV 🚗 🖫 🚗 P ❊ 🎯 SP

RYDAL
Cumbria
Map ref 5A3

Small hamlet next to Rydal Water, a small, beautiful lake sheltered by Rydal Fell. Once the home of William Wordsworth, Rydal Mount is open to the public. It is a good centre for walking and touring.

Hall Bank Cottage M
🔑🔑 COMMENDED

Rydal Estate, Rydal, Ambleside
Contact: Fisher Hoggarth, 52 Kirkland, Kendal, Cumbria LA9 5AP
🕿 Kendal (01539) 722592
Fax (01539) 729587
Cottage at Rydal in the heart of the Lake District, providing comfortable accommodation with easy access to main attractions of the area. Central heating, open fire. Large garden.
1 self-contained unit; sleeping 6

Price per week:	£min	£max
Low season	190.00	260.00
High season	260.00	480.00

🕿 M ◎ ▥ 🗗 TV 🚗 🖬 🖫 🚗 P U ❊ SP

SATTERTHWAITE
Cumbria
Map ref 5A3

Secluded village with visitors' centre, set in the heart of the Grizedale Forest. Forest trails, forest sculptures, theatre and pretty waterfalls nearby.

Bobtail Cottage
🔑🔑🔑 COMMENDED

Satterthwaite, Ulverston
Contact: Mrs Eleanor Fletcher, 1 Church Cottage, Satterthwaite, Ulverston, Cumbria LA12 8LP
🕿 Satterthwaite (01229) 860336
Converted barn in Grizedale Forest. Living/dining room with oak beams, colour TV, electric fire and night storage heaters.

Continued ▶

SATTERTHWAITE

Continued

1 self-contained unit; sleeping 4

Price per week:	£min	£max
Low season	160.00	
High season	250.00	

SAWREY

Cumbria
Map ref 5A3

Far Sawrey and Near Sawrey lie near Esthwaite Water. Both villages are small but Near Sawrey is famous for Hill Top Farm, home of Beatrix Potter, now owned by the National Trust and open to the public.

Esthwaite Holidays and Old Barn

COMMENDED

Sawrey, Ambleside
Contact: Mr G Thomason, Cunsey Bridge Cottage, Cunsey Bridge, Ambleside, Cumbria LA22 0LU
☎ Ambleside (015394) 42435

Traditional farm and buildings converted into attractive apartments and cottages in beautiful rural setting. Access to private lakeshore. Free coarse and trout fishing.
11 self-contained units; sleeping 4–7

Price per week:	£min	£max
Low season	140.00	180.00
High season	230.00	335.00

SEATHWAITE

Cumbria
Map ref 5A3

Picturesque hamlet in the Duddon Valley - reputedly Wordsworth's favourite Lakeland valley - between Ulpha and Cockley Beck.

Newfield

APPROVED

Newfield Inn, Seathwaite, Broughton-in-Furness LA20 6ED
☎ Broughton-in-Furness (01229) 716208
Contact: Mr C D Burgess

In the Duddon Valley and next to the Newfield Inn, serving home-cooked food and Theakston's cask-conditioned ales.
2 self-contained units; sleeping 4–6

Price per week:	£min	£max
Low season	130.00	165.00
High season	155.00	200.00

SEDBERGH

Cumbria
Map ref 5B3

This busy market town set below the Howgill Fells is an excellent centre for walkers and touring the Dales and Howgills. The noted boys' school was founded in 1525.

Bainbridge Court, Moss Bank & Weavers Cottage

UP TO HIGHLY COMMENDED

Bainbridge Road, Sedbergh
Contact: Mrs P A Holme, Cobble Country Holidays, 63 Main Street, Sedbergh, Cumbria LA10 5AB
☎ Sedbergh (015396) 21000
Fax (015396) 21710
Quality properties offering a variety of accommodation. Options for parties of 2 to 36 people, low season discounts. Ideal holiday base. Brochure available.
Wheelchair access category 1♿
8 self-contained units; sleeping 6–10

Price per week:	£min	£max
Low season	140.00	262.00
High season	224.00	420.00

SPARK BRIDGE

Cumbria
Map ref 5A3

Small, attractive village beside the River Crake, south of Coniston Water. Cumbria's last bobbin mill recently closed here.

Thurstonville High Lodge

APPROVED

Lowick, Ulverston

Contact: Mr R N Lord, Thurstonville, Lowick, Ulverston, Cumbria LA12 7SX
☎ Greenodd (01229) 861 271

Stone-built gatehouse to Georgian country house. Living room with open fireplace, 2 bedrooms, kitchen/dining room, bathroom, garden. All electric.
1 self-contained unit; sleeping max 4

Price per week:	£min	£max
Low season	115.00	155.00
High season	175.00	200.00

STAVELEY

Cumbria
Map ref 5A3

Large village built in slate, set between Kendal and Windermere at the entrance to the lovely Kentmere Valley.

Brunt Knott Farm

APPROVED

Staveley, Kendal
Contact: Mr and Mrs D Dace, Brunt Knott Farm, Staveley, Kendal, Cumbria LA8 9QX
☎ Staveley (01539) 821030
Fax (01539) 821221
Privately situated hill farm. Elevated position with 40-mile views, 1 mile from Staveley. Backs on to open fells. Each cottage detached and with garden.
4 self-contained units; sleeping 2–4

Price per week:	£min	£max
Low season	135.00	165.00
High season	165.00	240.00

TEBAY

Cumbria
Map ref 5B3

Village lying amongst high fells at the north end of the Lune Gorge.

Fawcett Mill

HIGHLY COMMENDED

Gaisgill, Nr Orton, Tebay

Contact: Mr Alex Hayes, The Operation Ltd, Charter House, Latham Close, Bredbury Park, Stockport, Cheshire SK6 2SD
☎ (0161) 494 1000
Fax (0161) 494 0099

18th C former mill house with 7 bedrooms. Oak beams and open fires throughout. Situated in tranquil valley with easy access to Lakes.
1 self-contained unit; sleeping max 16

Price per week:	£min	£max
Low season	295.00	835.00
High season	425.00	1595.00

Cards accepted: Access, Visa, Amex, Switch/Delta

🛏🐕⊘📠🖥☺🛏MW📻📺🗑🔌🍴📶 🍽🐾P∪☀❄️ SP 🏠

THORNTHWAITE
Cumbria
Map ref 5A3

Small village, west of Keswick, at the southern tip of Bassenthwaite Lake. Forest trails in Thornthwaite Forest.

Beckside Cottage
🔑 🔑 🔑 APPROVED

Thornthwaite, Keswick
Contact: Mrs A M Lawson, Beckside, Thornthwaite, Keswick, Cumbria CA12 5SA
☎ Braithwaite (017687) 78395
Typical Lakeland cottage which is comfortable and well-maintained. In a delightful position on the very edge of Combe Beck within 3 miles of Keswick. Telephone enquiries after 7pm please.
1 self-contained unit; sleeping max 4

Price per week:	£min	£max
Low season	120.00	140.00
High season	150.00	190.00

🛏6 M ◎ 📠🖥☺🛏📺🗑🔌🍽🍴P ∪☀🏠

THRELKELD
Cumbria
Map ref 5A3

This village is a centre for climbing the Saddleback range of mountains, which tower high above it.

1 & 2 Blencathra View
🔑 🔑 🔑 COMMENDED

Threlkeld, Keswick

Contact: Mr Bish, 3 Squires Road, Shepperton, Middlesex TW17 0LQ
☎ Chertsey (01932) 565857
Cottages with superb views, good furnishings and equipment, storage heaters and garden. Pony trekking and golf nearby.
2 self-contained units; sleeping 5

Price per week:	£min	£max
Low season	160.00	
High season		250.00

🛏 M ◎ 📠🖥☺🛏MW📺🗑🔌🍽🍴 ❄️ SP

THURSBY
Cumbria
Map ref 5A2

Meadow Cottage 🎗
🔑 🔑 🔑 🔑 COMMENDED

32 West Park, Crofton, Thursby, Carlisle
Contact: Dr and Mrs Malcolm Quigley, 22 Newby Cross, Wigton Road, Carlisle CA5 6JP
☎ Carlisle (01228) 710180
Fax (01228) 710180
Comfortable 2 bedroomed cottage in quiet farmland. Lake District, Solway Coast and the city of Carlisle are 20 minutes' drive.
1 self-contained unit; sleeping 6

Price per week:	£min	£max
Low season	175.00	200.00
High season	190.00	330.00

🛏 M ◎ 📠🖥☺🛏MW📻📺🗑🔌🍽🍴 🍽🐾P❄️🐕 SP 🏠◎

TROUTBECK
Cumbria
Map ref 5A3

Most of the houses in this picturesque village are 17th C, some retain their spinning galleries and oak-mullioned windows. At the south end of the village is Townend, owned by the National Trust and open to the public, an excellently preserved example of a yeoman farmer's or statesman's house.

Barn Cottage 🎗
🔑 🔑 🔑 🔑 COMMENDED

Troutbeck, Windermere
Contact: Mrs J Cochrane, High Green House, Troutbeck, Windermere, Cumbria LA23 1PN
☎ Ambleside (015394) 34421

For ideas on places to visit refer to the introduction at the beginning of this section.

Very comfortable, modernised traditional Lakeland barn, retaining some ancient features. Outstanding views all round. Sheltered garden. Ideal for family holidays.
1 self-contained unit; sleeping 6

Price per week:	£min	£max
Low season	200.00	300.00
High season	350.00	400.00

🛏 M ◎ 📠🖥☺🛏MW📻📺🗑🔌🍴 🏠🐾P❄️ SP 🏠

Fell Cottage
🔑 🔑 🔑 COMMENDED

Town Head Brow, Troutbeck, Windermere
Contact: Mr Robert Hayward, Riverbank Cottage, Kentmere Road, Staveley, Kendal, Cumbria LA8 9JF
☎ Kendal (01539) 821071 & 0374 776689
Beautifully renovated Lakeland cottage. Patio with barbecue, magnificent views, log fire, oak beams. Excellent walking and riding area. Pubs and shop nearby.
1 self-contained unit; sleeping max 6

Price per week:	£min	£max
Low season	170.00	
High season		335.00

Cards accepted: Access, Visa

🛏 M ◎ 📠🖥☺🛏MW📻📺🔌🍴 🐾P✗ SP T

Rose Cottage 🎗
🔑 🔑 🔑 COMMENDED

Robin Lane, Troutbeck, Windermere
Contact: Mrs A Kelly, 1 Robin Lane, Troutbeck, Windermere, Cumbria LA23 1PF
☎ Ambleside (015394) 32780
18th C cottage and converted barn with gardens and beautiful views over the Troutbeck Valley.
2 self-contained units; sleeping 3–6

Price per week:	£min	£max
Low season	125.00	195.00
High season	250.00	395.00

🛏5 M ◎ 📠🖥☺🛏MW📺🗑🔌🍴 🐾∪☀

The National Grading and Classification Scheme is explained in full at the back of this guide.

ULLSWATER

Cumbria
Map ref 5A3

This beautiful lake, which is over 7 miles long, runs from Glenridding to Pooley Bridge. Lofty peaks ranging around the lake make an impressive background. A steamer service operates along the lake between Pooley Bridge, Howtown and Glenridding in the summer.

Land Ends 🏔

COMMENDED

Watermillock, Ullswater
CA11 0NB
☎ Pooley Bridge (017684) 86438
Fax (017684) 86959
Contact: Mr C R Murphy
Cosy Scandinavian log cabins in the beautiful Ullswater Valley. In 7 acres of woods, fields and trout lakes, 1.5 miles from Ullswater. Quiet location with lovely grounds.
4 self-contained units; sleeping 3–5

Price per week:	£min	£max
Low season	158.00	214.00
High season	180.00	343.00

Patterdale Hall Estate 🏔

UP TO COMMENDED

Glenridding, Penrith
Contact: Mr Stephen Foxall, Estate Office, Patterdale Hall Estate, Glenridding, Penrith, Cumbria CA11 0PJ
☎ Glenridding (017684) 82308
Fax (017684) 82308
300-acre hill farm. A range of comfortable, centrally heated accommodation, set in private estate between Ullswater and Helvellyn. JCB card also available.
Wheelchair access category 3 ♿
16 self-contained units; sleeping 2–6

Price per week:	£min	£max
Low season	116.00	172.00
High season	229.00	392.00

Cards accepted: Access, Visa, Switch/Delta

Ullswater Cottages 🏔

APPROVED

High House, Thackthwaite, Penrith
Contact: Mr & Mrs Cash, Cragside Cottage, Thackthwaite, Ullswater, Penrith, Cumbria CA11 0ND
☎ Pooley Bridge (017684) 86385
Stone cottages in quiet mountain hamlet on the lower slopes of Little
Mell Fell. Own gardens and parking spaces. Brochure available.
4 self-contained units; sleeping 2–6

Price per week:	£min	£max
Low season	90.00	147.00
High season	166.00	280.00

ULVERSTON

Cumbria
Map ref 5A3

Market town lying between green fells and the sea. There is a replica of the Eddystone lighthouse on the Hoad which is a monument to Sir John Barrow, founder of the Royal Geographical Society. Birthplace of Stan Laurel, of Laurel and Hardy.
Tourist Information Centre ☎ *(01229) 587120*

The Falls 🏔

COMMENDED

Mansriggs, Ulverston LA12 7PX
☎ (01229) 583781
Contact: Messrs Cheetham & Unger
17th C farmstead in beautiful surroundings, converted into holiday homes in traditional Lakeland style. Comprehensive food service available. Resident proprietors.
6 self-contained units; sleeping 4–8

Price per week:	£min	£max
Low season	125.00	255.00
High season	200.00	450.00

WASDALE

Cumbria
Map ref 5A3

A very dramatic valley with England's deepest lake, Wastwater, highest mountain, Scafell Pike, and smallest church. The eastern shore of Wastwater is dominated by the 1,500 ft screes dropping steeply into the lake. A good centre for walking and climbing.

Greendale Holiday Apartments 🏔

COMMENDED

Greendale, Wasdale
Contact: Mr and Mrs M D Burnett, Greendale, Wasdale, Cumbria CA20 1EU
☎ Wasdale (019467) 26243

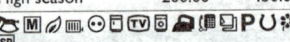

Cosy cottage-style apartments close to Wastwater Lake and 8 miles from the coast. Beautiful scenery and excellent walking facilities.
3 self-contained units; sleeping 4–5

Price per week:	£min	£max
Low season	180.00	220.00
High season	220.00	275.00

Wasdale Head Hall Farm 🏔

APPROVED

Wasdale, Seascale CA20 1EX
☎ (019467) 26245
Contact: Mr Keith Preston
2000-acre mixed farm. Cottage close to lake, Scafell and Great Gable. Warm and comfortable, logs provided. Ideal base for walking, climbing and windsurfing.
1 self-contained unit; sleeping max 7

Price per week:	£min	£max
Low season	140.00	180.00
High season	210.00	240.00

WELTON

Cumbria
Map ref 5A2

Old and new houses spread around a large village green with a tall maypole at Welton, "the place by a spring", between Caldbeck and Carlisle.

Green View Lodges and Well Cottage 🏔

UP TO HIGHLY COMMENDED

Welton, Dalston, Carlisle CA5 7ES
☎ Raughton Head (016974) 76230
Fax (016974) 76523
Contact: Mrs A E Ivinson

Scandinavian lodges in peaceful garden setting, converted chapel and 17th C oak-beamed cottages. Unspoilt views over rolling farmland to Caldbeck Fells. Tiny, picturesque rural hamlet. Golf 5 miles.

Wheelchair access category 3 ♯
6 self-contained units; sleeping 2–7

Price per week:	£min	£max
Low season	145.00	238.00
High season	188.00	460.00

Cards accepted: Access, Visa

⎯M◎▥■☺☐MW☞TV■🔒♨(♫
□➢P✦SP T

WINDERMERE

Cumbria
Map ref 5A3

Once a tiny hamlet before the
introduction of the railway in 1847,
now adjoins Bowness which is on
the lakeside. Centre for sailing and
boating. A good way to see the lake
is a trip on a passenger steamer.
Steamboat Museum has a fine
collection of old boats.
Tourist Information Centre
☎ *(015394) 46499*

Abbey Coach House Ⓜ

⚭⚭ COMMENDED

St. Mary's Park, Windermere
LA23 1AZ
☎ (015394) 44027
Fax (015394) 44027
Contact: Mrs P Bell or Mr C Bell
*Excellent location of ground floor
apartments in quiet, private area.
Ample parking, extensive gardens.*
2 self-contained units; sleeping 4–6

Price per week:	£min	£max
Low season	95.00	195.00
High season	195.00	345.00

⎯M◎▥■☺☐TV■♨(♫➢P
♿✦🏡

Applethwaite Aarons Crag &
Heaning Barn Cottage Ⓜ

⚭⚭⚭ COMMENDED

The Heaning, Heaning Lane,
Windermere LA23 1JW
☎ (015394) 43453
Contact: Mr & Mrs J N Pickup
*Beautifully situated Victorian mansion,
converted into apartments and
cottages, set in 7 acres of grounds.*
14 self-contained units; sleeping 2–6

Price per week:	£min	£max
Low season	75.00	150.00
High season	140.00	430.00

⎯5M◎▥■☺☐TV■♨(♫✦
✕SP

The Ⓜ symbol after an
establishment name indicates
that it is a Regional
Tourist Board member.

Bellman Ground Farm
Cottage

⚭⚭ APPROVED

Bellman Ground,
Bowness-on-Windermere,
Windermere
Contact: Mrs I S Jopson, Bellman
Ground Farm,
Bowness-on-Windermere,
Windermere, Cumbria LA23 3LX
☎ Windermere (015394) 43507
*150-acre dairy farm. Traditional
3-bedroomed farm cottage. Kitchen
with oil fired Aga; sitting-room with
wood-burning stove; bathroom with
bath and shower.*
1 self-contained unit; sleeping max 7

Price per week:	£min	£max
Low season	200.00	225.00
High season	255.00	310.00

Open April–October

⎯◎▥■☺☐MW☞TV■♨(♫
➢P✦SP

Bellman Houses

⚭⚭ COMMENDED

Barker Knott, Winster Road,
Windermere
Contact: Mr and Mrs A Afsari,
Gallowshielorigg Farm, Bardon Mill,
Hexham, Northumberland
NE47 7AR
☎ Haltwhistle (01434) 344338
*17th C whitewashed former farmhouse,
retaining many of its original features.
Recent modernisations provide
comfortable and spacious
accommodation.*
1 self-contained unit; sleeping 6

Price per week:	£min	£max
Low season	275.00	325.00
High season	325.00	375.00

⎯M◎▥■☺☐MW TV■♨(♫
➢P✦✕SP🏡

Birthwaite Edge Ⓜ

⚭⚭⚭ COMMENDED

Birthwaite Road, Windermere
LA23 1BS
☎ (015394) 42861
Fax (015394) 42861
Contact: Mrs Dodsworth
*Peaceful surroundings, 10 minutes'
walk from village and lake. Large
gardens. Resident proprietors.
Cleanliness and comfort guaranteed.
Outdoor pool. Brochure available.*
9 self-contained units; sleeping 2–6

Price per week:	£min	£max
Low season	100.00	150.00
High season	140.00	430.00

⎯M◎▥■☺☐TV■♨(♫□P✦♿
✦✕SP T

Claife Heights Flat Ⓜ

⚭⚭ COMMENDED

Fairfield Country House Hotel,
Brantfell Road,
Bowness-on-Windermere,
Windermere
Contact: Mr and Mrs Ray & Barbara
Hood, Fairfield Country House
Hotel, Brantfell Road,
Bowness-on-Windermere,
Windermere, Cumbria LA23 3AE
☎ Windermere (015394) 46565
Fax (015394) 46565
*Small, friendly, 200-year-old Lakeland
hotel with self-catering apartment, in a
peaceful garden setting close to village,
lake and fells. Private car park, leisure
facilities, bargain breaks.*
1 self-contained unit; sleeping 3

Price per week:	£min	£max
Low season	165.00	220.00
High season	250.00	285.00

Cards accepted: Access, Visa

⎯◎▥■☺☐MW☞TV■(♫
➢PU♪➢✦✕♿SP🏡

Gavel Cottage

⚭⚭⚭ HIGHLY COMMENDED

7 Meadowcroft Cottages, Storrs
Park, Bowness-on-Windermere
Contact: Mr Ian Screeton, Screetons,
25 Bridgegate, Howden, Goole,
North Humberside DN14 7AA
☎ Howden (01430) 431201
Fax (01430) 432114
*Secluded period cottage close to the
marina. Tastefully furnished and well
equipped. Two bedrooms, all modern
facilities. Large garden with summer
house. Member Burnside Leisure
Complex.*
1 self-contained unit; sleeping 4

Price per week:	£min	£max
Low season	220.00	220.00
High season	295.00	440.00

⎯M◎▥■☺☐MW☞TV■♨(
□➢P✦♿SP

Establishments should be
open throughout the year,
unless otherwise stated.

The symbols in each entry
give information about
services and facilities.
A 'key' to these symbols
appears at the back
of this guide.

WINDERMERE

Continued

Lakeview

⚿⚿⚿⚿⚿⚿ HIGHLY COMMENDED

2 Beechwood Close,
Bowness-on-Windermere,
Windermere
Contact: Mrs J F Cuddy,
261 Hadfield Road, Hadfield, Hyde,
Cheshire SK14 8ER
☎ Glossop (01457) 854329

*Detached house in quiet elevated
position, with outstanding views of Lake
Windermere and surrounding fells.
Price includes gas and electricity.*
1 self-contained unit; sleeping max 6

Price per week:	£min	£max
Low season	190.00	290.00
High season	290.00	440.00

Langdale View Holiday Flats ⚑

⚿⚿⚿ COMMENDED

112 Craig Walk,
Bowness-on-Windermere,
Windermere LA23 3AX
☎ (015394) 46655
Contact: Mrs Joan Hannon
*Attractive, comfortable holiday
apartments with car parking. Quiet,
elevated position very close to village
centre, lake, steamers, shops and
restaurants.*
4 self-contained units; sleeping 2–6

Price per week:	£min	£max
Low season	110.00	200.00
High season	160.00	350.00

🍽Ⓜ◎💻⌂·⊙🛏MW📺🛢️🍳🧺🍴
P🚭SP🇹

TOWN INDEX

This can be found at the back
of the guide. If you know
where you want to stay, the
index will give you the page
number listing all
accommodation in your
chosen town, city or village.

Lilac Cottage & Lipwood ⚑

⚿⚿⚿⚿ COMMENDED

Old College Lane, Windermere
Contact: Mrs M Heighton, Lipwood,
Old College Lane, Windermere,
Cumbria LA23 1BY
☎ Windermere (015394) 43494
*Lilac Cottage is an attractive bungalow.
Also, 1 flat in detached Lakeland-stone
house. Both properties are in a quiet
lane close to Windermere village, and
have gardens and parking.*
2 self-contained units; sleeping 4–7

Price per week:	£min	£max
Low season	144.00	188.00
High season	190.00	385.00

Open March–November

🍽Ⓜ◎💻⌂·⊙🛏MW📺🍳🧺🚗
P🌸SP🏠

Lowther Cottage ⚑

⚿⚿⚿ COMMENDED

2 Calgarth View, Troutbeck Bridge,
Windermere
Contact: Mr and Mrs Derek
Sweeney, Travellers Rest, Grasmere,
Ambleside, Cumbria LA22 9RR
☎ Grasmere (015394) 35604
*16th C listed cottage with oak beams
and inglenooks, in a superb central
location. Furnished and equipped to a
high standard, cosy and welcoming.
Colour brochure available.*
1 self-contained unit; sleeping max 4

Price per week:	£min	£max
Low season	95.00	250.00
High season	250.00	325.00

🍽Ⓜ◎💻🛏MW📺🛢️🍳U
🌸SP

Pinethwaite ⚑

⚿⚿⚿⚿⚿⚿ COMMENDED

Lickbarrow Road, Windermere
LA23 2NQ
☎ (015394) 44558
Contact: Mr P A Legge

*Cottages and apartments hidden in a
delightful private woodland (roe deer,
red squirrels) just 1 mile from
Windermere and Bowness villages.
Perfect for families and couples.*
9 self-contained units; sleeping 2–7

Price per week:	£min	£max
Low season	150.00	180.00
High season	250.00	410.00

🍽Ⓜ◎💻⌂·⊙🛏MW📺🛢️🍳🧺🍴
🍳PU🌸🔥🍴🚭SP

Spinnery Cottage Holiday Apartments ⚑

⚿⚿ UP TO HIGHLY COMMENDED

Brantfell Road,
Bowness-on-Windermere,
Windermere LA23 3AE
☎ (015394) 44884
Contact: Mr Ray Hood
*Old spinnery tastefully converted into
apartments. Close to village, lake and
fells but quiet and secluded. Private
parking, leisure facilities, bargain
breaks.*
5 self-contained units; sleeping 2–4

Price per week:	£min	£max
Low season	150.00	210.00
High season	240.00	275.00

Cards accepted: Access, Visa

🍽Ⓜ◎💻⌂·⊙🛏MW📐📺🛢️🍴
🍳🍳PU🎵🌸🚭SP🏠

Windermere Marina Village ⚑

⚿⚿⚿⚿⚿⚿⚿—⚿⚿⚿⚿⚿

HIGHLY COMMENDED

Bowness-on-Windermere,
Windermere LA23 3JQ
☎ (015394) 46551
Fax (015394) 43233
Contact: Ms Suzanne Bateman

*Superbly appointed lakeside cottages
with private leisure club and moorings.
Short breaks and weekly bookings.
Swimming pool, sauna, spas, bistro,
playground.*
3 self-contained units; sleeping 5–8

Price per week:	£min	£max
Low season	300.00	
High season	900.00	

Cards accepted: Access, Visa, Diners,
Amex, Switch/Delta

🍽Ⓜ◎💻⌂·⊙🛏MW📐📺🛢️🍳🍴
〰️🍳🌊U🔥🚭SP🇹

WITHERSLACK

Cumbria
Map ref 5A3

Tranquil village on the east bank of the River Winster, at the south end of the Lyth Valley, famed for its damsons. Good base for touring.

Old Mill Cottages 𝐌
COMMENDED
Millside, Witherslack,
Grange-over-Sands
Contact: Mrs D A Scott, Overleigh House, East Cliff, Preston PR1 3JH
☎ Preston (01772) 253545
Fax (01772) 555354
Architect-owner's restoration of picturesque 18th C cornmill, with Cumbria's largest millwheel. Spacious, detached cottage with every home comfort, lovely walks. Has gained 5 major architectural awards.
2 self-contained units; sleeping 4–7

Price per week:	£min	£max
Low season	160.00	
High season		360.00

COUNTRY CODE

Always follow the Country Code
🍃 Enjoy the countryside and respect its life and work 🍃 Guard against all risk of fire 🍃 Fasten all gates 🍃 Keep your dogs under close control 🍃 Keep to public paths across farmland 🍃 Use gates and stiles to cross fences, hedges and walls 🍃 Leave livestock, crops and machinery alone 🍃 Take your litter home 🍃 Help to keep all water clean 🍃 Protect wildlife, plants and trees 🍃 Take special care on country roads 🍃 Make no unnecessary noise

USE YOUR *i*'s

There are more than 550
Tourist Information Centres
throughout England offering friendly
help with accommodation and
holiday ideas as well as
suggestions of places to visit
and things to do. There may well be
a centre in your home town which
can help you before you set out.
You'll find the address of your
nearest Tourist Information Centre
in your local Phone Book.

CHECK THE MAPS

The colour maps at the back of this guide show
all the cities, towns and villages for which you will
find accommodation entries.

Refer to the town index to find the page
on which it is listed.

ENQUIRY COUPONS

To help you obtain further information
about advertisers and accommodation featured in
this guide you will find enquiry coupons at the back.
Send these directly to the establishments
in which you are interested.
Remember to complete both sides of the coupon.

NORTHUMBRIA

Spectacular countryside awaits the visitor to Northumbria. The high Cheviots and the rugged Pennines leave an indelible impression while the majestic coastline offers sandy beaches, quaint fishing villages and surprisingly lively seaside resorts!

In contrast, Northumbria is also a region with vibrant industrial heritage, cosmopolitan cities and a long tradition of excellence in both the sporting and cultural arenas.

Soak up the history - don't miss Durham Cathedral - explore Catherine Cookson country and visit a traditional Northern pub. Or why not the Metro Centre, Europe's largest shopping city! Wherever you go, you'll be sure of a warm, northern welcome.

FOR MORE INFORMATION CONTACT:
Northumbria Tourist Board
Aykley Heads, Durham DH1 5UX
Tel: (0191) 375 3000 **Fax:** (0191) 386 0899

Where to Go in Northumbria - see pages 58-61
Where to Stay in Northumbria - see pages 62-77

NORTHUMBRIA

Where to Go and What to See

You will find hundreds of interesting places to visit during your stay in Northumbria, just some of which are listed in these pages. The number against each name will help you locate it on the map (page 61). Contact any Tourist Information Centre in the region for more ideas on days out in Northumbria.

1 Lindisfarne Castle
Holy Island,
Berwick-upon-Tweed
Northumberland TD15 2SH
Tel: (01289) 89244
Fort converted into a private home in 1903 for Edward Hudson by the architect Edwin Lutyens.

2 Farne Islands
Seahouses off Northumberland coast,
Northumberland
Tel: (01665) 720651
Bird reserve holding around 55,000 pairs of breeding birds of 21 species. Also home to a large colony of grey seals.

3 Bamburgh Castle
Bamburgh, Northumberland,
NE69 7DF
Tel: (01668) 214208
Magnificent coastal castle completely restored in 1900. Collections of china, porcelain, furniture, paintings, arms and armour.

4 Alnwick Castle
Alnwick,
Northumberland NE66 1NQ
Tel: (01665) 510777
Largest inhabited castle in England after Windsor Castle. Home of the Percys, Dukes of Northumberland since 1309.

5 Cragside House, Gardens and Grounds
Cragside, Rothbury,
Northumberland NE65 7PX
Tel: (01669) 620333
House built 1864-84 for the first Lord Armstrong, Tyneside Industrialist. The first house to be lit by electricity generated by water power.

6 Kielder Water Leaplish Waterside Park
Kielder,
Northumberland NE48 1BX
Tel: (01434) 240395
Largest man made lake in Western Europe. Water sports, fishing, log cabins and caravan site. Cycle hire, crazy golf and restaurant.

7 Wallington House Walled Garden and Grounds
Wallington, Cambo,
Northumberland NE61 4AR
Tel: (01670) 74283
Built 1688 on site of earlier medieval castle. Altered in 1740s. Interior has plasterwork, porcelain, furniture, pictures and needlework.

8 Morpeth Chantry Bagpipe Museum
The Chantry, Bridge Street,
Morpeth,
Northumberland NE61 1PJ
Tel: (01670) 519466
Set in a 13thC church building, this unusual museum specialises in the history and development of Northumbrian small pipes and their music.

9 Sea Life Centre
Grand Parade, Long Sands,
Tynemouth,
Tyne & Wear NE30 4JF
Tel: (0191) 257 6100
Journey beneath the North Sea and

discover thousands of amazing creatures. Over 30 hi-tech displays.

10 Wet 'N Wild
Rotary Way,
North Shields,
Tyne & Wear NE29 6DA
Tel: (0191) 296 1333
Tropical indoor waterpark. A fun water playground providing the UK's wildest and wettest indoor rapid experience.

11 Castle Keep
Saint Nicholas Street,
Castle Garth,
Newcastle upon Tyne NE1 1RQ
Tel: (0191) 232 7938
Built 1168-1178. One of the finest surviving examples of a Norman keep in the country. Panoramic views of the city from the roof. Small museum within keep.

12 Bede's World
Church Bank,
Jarrow,
Tyne & Wear NE32 3DY
Tel: (0191) 489 2106
New museum opened May 1995. Late 18thC hall, excavated finds from Anglo-Saxon and medieval monastery of St Pauls Jarrow nearby. Anglo-Saxon farm with rare breeds.

13 Metroland
Gateshead,
Tyne & Wear NE11 9YZ
Tel: (0191) 493 2048
Europe's only indooor theme park within a large shopping complex. Rollercoaster, dodgems, swinging chairs, pirate ship plus live entertainment.

14 Housesteads Roman Fort
Hadrian's Wall,
Northumberland NE47 6NN
Tel: (01434) 344363
Best preserved and most impressive of the Roman forts. Vercovicium was a 5-acre fort for extensive civil settlement. Only example of a Roman hospital.

15 Wildfowl & Wetlands Trust
Washington,
Tyne & Wear NE38 8LE
Tel: (0191) 416 5454
Collection of 1,250 wildfowl of 108 varieties. Viewing gallery, picnic areas, hides and winter wild bird feeding station. Flamingos, wild grey heron. Food available.

16 Beamish – The North of England Open Air Museum
Beamish, Co Durham DH9 0RG
Tel: (01207) 231811
Visit a town, colliery village, farm

and railway station recreated to show life in the North of England early this century. Pockerley Manor illustrates life in the early 1800s.

17 Durham Castle
Palace Green,
Durham DH1 3RW
Tel: (0191) 374 3863
Fine Bailey castle founded in 1072, Norman chapel dating from 1080. Kitchens and great hall dated 1499 and 1284 respectively.

18 Durham Cathedral
Durham DH1 3EH
Tel: (0191) 386 4266
Widely considered to be the finest example of Norman church architecture in England. Has the tombs of St Cuthbert and The Venerable Bede.

19 Killhope Leadmining Centre
Cowshill,
St John's Chapel,
Co Durham DL13 1AR
Tel: (01388) 537505
Most complete lead mining site in Great Britain. Includes crushing mill with 34ft water wheel, reconstruction of Victorian machinery and miners accommodation.

20 High Force Waterfall

Forest-in-Teesdale,
Middleton-in-Teesdale,
Co Durham DL12
Tel: (01833) 640209
High Force is the most majestic of the waterfalls on the River Tees. The falls are only a short walk from a bus stop, car park and picnic area.

21 Raby Castle

Staindrop,
Co Durham DL2 3AH
Tel: (01833) 660202
Medieval castle in 200-acre park. 600-year-old kitchen and carriage collection. Walled gardens and deer park. Home of Lord Barnard's family for over 350 years.

22 Butterfly World

Preston Park, Yarm Road,
Stockton-on-Tees,
Tees Valley TS18 3RH
Tel: (01642) 791414
An indoor tropical garden populated by exotic free-flying butterflies and complemented by a display of fascinating insects and reptiles.

23 Preston Hall Museum

Yarm Road, Stockton-on-Tees,
Tees Valley TS18 3RH
Tel: (01642) 781184
A Georgian country house set in a park which is a museum of Victoriana. Return to a bygone age, stroll along a high street, explore 100 acres of parkland overlooking the Tees.

24 Captain Cook Birthplace Museum

Stewart Park,
Marton,
Middlesbrough,
Tees Valley TS7 6AS
Tel: (01642) 311211
Early life and voyages of Captain Cook and the countries he visited. Temporary exhibitions.

25 Ormesby Hall

Church Lane,
Ormesby,
Middlesbrough,
Tees Valley TS7 9AS
Tel: (01642) 324188
18thC Palladian mansion with impressive contemporary plasterwork. Magnificent stableblock attributed to Carr of York. Model railway exhibition and children's play area.

26 Hartlepool Historic Quay

Maritime Avenue,
Hartlepool,
Tees Valley TS24 0XZ
Tel: (01429) 860006
An exciting reconstruction of a seaport of the 1800s with buildings and lively quayside.

27 Saltburn Smugglers Heritage Centre

Ship Inn, Saltburn-by-the-Sea,
Tees Valley TS12 1HF
Tel: (01287) 625252
Experience the authentic sights, sounds and smells of Saltburn's smuggling heritage. Listen to tales of John Andrew, "King of the Smugglers".

FIND OUT MORE

Further information about holidays and attractions in Northumbria is available from:
Northumbria Tourist Board,
Aykley Heads,
Durham DH1 5UX.
Tel: (0191) 375 3000

SCOTLAND

Berwick-upon-Tweed

1 Holy Island
2 Farne Islands
Belford
3 Bamburgh
Wooler
Alnwick
4
Amble
Rothbury **5**
6 Keilder
Otterburn
NORTHUMBERLAND
Ashington
Cambo **7**
8
Bellingham
Morpeth
Blyth
Whitley Bay
North Shields
Tynemouth
Haltwhistle
Hexham
Newcastle-upon-Tyne
10 **9**
Housesteads
14
Prudhoe
South Shields
Haydon
Gateshead **13**
Jarrow
Bridge
11 **12**
Stanley
TYNE & WEAR
Beamish
15
Sunderland
Consett
16
Washington
Durham **17** **18**
Peterlee
19
Crook
Cowshill
DURHAM
Hartlepool
20
26
Forest-in-Teesdale
Bishop
HARTLE-
TEES VALLEY
Staindrop **21**
Auckland
POOL
Redcar
Stockton
Middlesbrough
Saltburn-
-on-Tees
27 by-the-Sea
Barnard Castle
22 **23**
25 Ormesby
Darlington
STOCKTON
24
Guisborough
CUMBRIA
-ON-TEES
Marton
MIDDLES-
REDCAR &
BROUGH
CLEEVELAND

NORTH YORKSHIRE

0   20 Miles
0   30 Kms

These publications are available free from the Northumbria Tourist Board:
■ **Northumbria Breaks 1997**
■ **Bed & Breakfast Map - Northumbria and Cumbria**
■ **Great Days Out - regional attraction guide**

■ **Freedom Caravan and Camping Guide - Northumbria, Yorkshire, East Riding, Cumbria and North West**
■ **Schools Out - educational brochure**

Also available are (prices include postage and packaging):
■ **Northumbria Touring Map and Guide £4.75**
■ **Leisure Guide to Northumbria £10.99**
■ **Walk Northumbria £6.**

WHERE TO STAY (NORTHUMBRIA)

Accommodation entries in this region are listed in alphabetical order of place name, and then in alphabetical order of establishment. A contact address is given where it differs from the address of the establishment.

Map references refer to the colour location maps at the back of this guide.

Prices shown are weekly per unit.

At-a-glance symbols at the end of each accommodation entry give useful information about services and facilities. A key to symbols can be found inside the back cover flap. Keep this open for easy reference.

AKELD

Northumberland
Map ref 5B1

Border Rose Cottages

Akeld Manor Cottages, Akeld, Wooler
Contact: Mrs P Allan, Fraggle Rock, 11 Harbour Road, Beadnell, Chathill, Northumberland NE67 5BH
☎ Alnwick (01665) 721035
Fax (01665) 720951
Grade II listed period cottages in lovely national park setting, thoughtfully and tastefully converted to provide luxury accommodation. Splendid leisure complex includes gym, swimming pool, solarium and games room. Short breaks available. A really special experience.
15 self-contained units;

Price per week:	£min	£max
Low season	252.00	
High season		783.00

🐎🛏Ⓜ◎🖵☺🍴MW📺🗄🛋🖥🚲♿P
☂🛗🅿⚙✻✈ SP

WELCOME HOST

This is a nationally recognised customer care programme which aims to promote the highest standards of service and a warm welcome. Establishments who are taking part in this initiative are indicated by the ◎ symbol.

ALLENDALE

Northumberland
Map ref 5B2

Attractive small town set amongst moors, 10 miles south-west of Hexham and claimed to be the geographical centre of Britain. Surrounded by unspoilt walking country, with many well-signposted walks along the East and West Allen Rivers. Traditional Baal ceremony at New Year.

Low Huntwell Cottage

🔑🔑 APPROVED
Sparty Lea, Hexham
Contact: Mr R P Ridley, Low Huntwell Farm, Sparty Lea, Hexham, Northumberland NE47 9UL
☎ Allenheads (01434) 685 223
Set in beautiful rural Northumberland. Peaceful yet with easy access to most leisure facilities.
1 self-contained unit; sleeping max 6

Price per week:	£min	£max
Low season	105.00	130.00
High season	130.00	170.00

🐎Ⓜ◎🖵☺🍴📺🗄🛋🖥🚲
🅿☂🛗⚙✻✈🔪 SP 🏠

Station House Caravan Park

🔑🔑 APPROVED
Catton, Allendale, Hexham
NE47 9QF
☎ Hexham (01434) 683362
Contact: Mrs A G Dodsworth
Flat converted from booking office, station master's office and waiting room of Hexham-Allendale terminal railway station, closed for passengers in 1935 and completely in 1950. Accommodation on ground floor, second bedroom entered via first.

1 self-contained unit; sleeping 6

Price per week:	£min	£max
Low season	100.00	120.00
High season	120.00	160.00

🐎Ⓜ◎🖵☺🍴MW📺🗄🖥
♿🅿☂⚙✻✈🏠

ALNMOUTH

Northumberland
Map ref 5C1

Quiet village with pleasant old buildings, at the mouth of the River Aln where extensive dunes and sands stretch along Alnmouth Bay. 18th C granaries, some converted to dwellings, still stand.

High Buston Hall Cottage and The Hemmel ✣

🔑🔑 - 🔑🔑🔑
UP TO HIGHLY COMMENDED
Alnmouth, Alnwick
Contact: Mr & Mrs Edwards, High Buston Hall, High Buston, Alnmouth, Alnwick, Northumberland NE66 3QH
☎ Alnwick (01665) 830341
Fax (01665) 830341
Wing of elegant Georgian house and stylishly converted range of farm buildings. Commanding coastal views, peaceful village setting close to beach.
2 self-contained units; sleeping 5–10

Price per week:	£min	£max
Low season	150.00	300.00
High season	350.00	750.00

🐎🛏Ⓜ◎🖵☺🍴📺🗄🛋🖥🚲♿P☂⚙
🔪 SP 🏠◎

Wooden Farm Holiday Cottages

APPROVED

Wooden Farm, Lesbury, Alnwick
NE66 2TW
☎ Alnwick (01665) 830342
Contact: Mr W G Farr
Stone-built cottages in a quiet farm setting, overlooking the coast and the picturesque village of Alnmouth.
3 self-contained units; sleeping 7

Price per week:	£min	£max
Low season		150.00
High season		180.00

ALNWICK

Northumberland
Map ref 5C1

Ancient and historic market town, entered through the Hotspur Tower, an original gate in the town walls. The medieval castle, the second biggest in England and still the seat of the Dukes of Northumberland, was restored from ruin in the 18th C.
Tourist Information Centre ☎ (01665) 510665

No 1, No 2 & No 3 Cottages

COMMENDED

Titlington Hall Farm, Alnwick
Contact: Mrs Vera Purvis, Titlington Hall Farm, Alnwick,
Northumberland NE66 2EB
☎ Alnwick (01665) 578 253
Three lovely cottages, spacious, warm and very well equipped. All linen included. Children and pets welcome. Sleeping facilities up to 10.
3 self-contained units; sleeping 4–6

Price per week:	£min	£max
Low season	155.00	195.00
High season	255.00	295.00

WELCOME HOST

This is a nationally recognised customer care programme which aims to promote the highest standards of service and a warm welcome. Establishments who are taking part in this initiative are indicated by the ❀ symbol.

1 Prudhoe Villas ♈

COMMENDED

Prudhoe Street, Alnwick
Contact: Mr S J Brookfield, 1 The Orchard, Prudhoe Street, Alnwick,
Northumberland NE66 1UQ
☎ Alnwick (01665) 602930
Four-bedroomed town house, 3 minutes from town centre and shops. Central heating throughout and comfortable surroundings.
1 self-contained unit; sleeping 8–10

Price per week:	£min	£max
Low season	250.00	300.00
High season	300.00	450.00

Village Farm ♈

UP TO HIGHLY COMMENDED

Shilbottle, Alnwick
Contact: Mrs C M Stoker, Town Foot Farm, Shilbottle, Alnwick,
Northumberland NE66 2HG
☎ Alnwick (01665) 575591
Fax (01665) 575591
17th C farmhouse, Scandinavian chalets and cottages. Own ponies, heated indoor pool, trout pond, tennis court, sauna, sunbed - all free to guests. Sandy beaches 3 miles. Pets welcome. Brochure available.
Wheelchair access category 3
10 self-contained units; sleeping 2–12

Price per week:	£min	£max
Low season	125.00	199.00
High season	199.00	620.00

BAMBURGH

Northumberland
Map ref 5C1

Village with a spectacular red sandstone castle standing 150 ft above the sea. On the village green stands the magnificent Norman church opposite a museum containing mementoes of the heroine Grace Darling.

Blacketts ♈

APPROVED

1 Lucker Road, Bamburgh
Contact: Mr Mark Swearman, Friary House, Friary Farm, Bamburgh,
Northumberland NE69 7BS
☎ Bamburgh (01668) 214387
Purpose-built holiday apartments. Private parking, central heating, tiled kitchen, bath/shower, colour TV, etc.

	£min	£max
2 self-contained units; sleeping 4		
Price per week:		
Low season	70.00	110.00
High season	125.00	230.00

Cards accepted: Access, Visa

Bradford Country Cottages ♈

COMMENDED

Bamburgh NE70 7JT
☎ (01668) 213432
Fax (01668) 213891
Contact: Mr L W Robson
Stone-built cottages in a quiet farm hamlet in peaceful, undulating countryside, halfway between the A1 and Bamburgh. When enquiring please quote reference 1675.
5 self-contained units; sleeping 2–4

Price per week:	£min	£max
Low season	100.00	
High season		300.00

Dukesfield Farm Steading ♈

HIGHLY COMMENDED

Bamburgh
Contact: Mr Eric Robinson, The Glebe, 16 Radcliffe Road, Bamburgh,
Northumberland NE69 7AE
☎ Bamburgh (01668) 214456
Fax (01668) 214354
Rustic farmsteading on coastline with a wealth of dramatic castles and unspoilt beaches. Farne Island birds, fishing, golf nearby.
5 self-contained units; sleeping 4–8

Price per week:	£min	£max
Low season	215.00	350.00
High season	330.00	560.00

Open April–December

Glebe House ♈

HIGHLY COMMENDED

The Glebe, Radcliffe Road, Bamburgh
Contact: Mr Eric Robinson, The Glebe, 16 Radcliffe Road, Bamburgh,
Northumberland NE69 7AE
☎ Bamburgh (01668) 214456
Fax (01668) 214354
On the edge of Bamburgh village, this lovely old vicarage has stunning views of the church and castle. Secluded garden.
1 self-contained unit; sleeping 4–8

Price per week:	£min	£max
Low season	465.00	625.00
High season	625.00	775.00

BAMBURGH
Continued

Greenhill Farm Cottages 🐌
♦♦♦ COMMENDED

Greenhill Farm, Bamburgh
Contact: Mrs S Watson-Armstrong,
Greenhill Farm, Bamburgh,
Northumberland NE69 7AU
☎ Bamburgh (01668) 214415
*500-acre arable farm. Single-storey
farm cottages with fine views of the
Farne Islands and the Cheviot Hills.
300 yards from the beach on the
outskirts of historic Bamburgh. Ideal for
walking, golf, birdwatching.*
4 self-contained units; sleeping 4

Price per week:	£min	£max
Low season	180.00	
High season		260.00

Inglenook Cottage 🐌
♦♦♦ HIGHLY COMMENDED

8 Front Street, Bamburgh
Contact: Mrs A D Moore, 21
Windermere Avenue, Ivanhoe
Grange, Ashby-de-la-Zouch,
Leicestershire LE65 1FA
☎ Leicester (01530) 415920
*3-bedroomed listed cottage beside the
Grove (village green) and only 250
yards from Bamburgh Castle and
beach.*
1 self-contained unit; sleeping max 6

Price per week:	£min	£max
Low season	156.00	240.00
High season	285.00	450.00

Open June–September and
Christmas

No. 16 The Wynding 🐌
♦♦♦ HIGHLY COMMENDED

Bamburgh
Contact: Mr George Bruce, The
Steading, Westburn, Crawcrook,
Ryton, Tyne and Wear NE40 4EU
☎ (0191) 413 2353
*Cottage with 1 twin, 2 double rooms,
bathroom/WC, en-suite shower/WC.
Fully carpeted and equipped. 200 yards
to village and beach. Sorry, no pets.*
1 self-contained unit; sleeping 6

Price per week:	£min	£max
High season	280.00	375.00

Open February–November and
Christmas

Old School House 🐌
♦♦♦ APPROVED

Church Street, Bamburgh
Contact: Mrs E D Stonehouse,
Westwood Farm, Wylam,
Northumberland NE41 8JW
☎ (0191) 413 2135
*Comfortable self-contained houses in
unspoilt, historic Bamburgh. Close to
beaches, golfing, sailing, tennis, bird
sanctuary, Holy Island. Ideal for touring
Northumberland.*
2 self-contained units; sleeping 4–6

Price per week:	£min	£max
Low season	200.00	
High season		380.00

Open May–September

Point Cottages 🐌
♦♦♦♦ HIGHLY COMMENDED

39 The Wynding, Bamburgh
Contact: Mrs E Sanderson, 30 The
Oval, Benton, Newcastle upon Tyne
NE12 9PP
☎ (0191) 266 2800
*Cluster of cottages, with fine sea views,
located next to golf-course. Furnished
to a high standard, log fires, large
garden.*
Wheelchair access category 3
5 self-contained units; sleeping 2–4

Price per week:	£min	£max
Low season	160.00	185.00
High season	325.00	265.00

Saint Oswalds 🐌
♦♦♦ APPROVED

Bamburgh
Contact: Mr A Smith, 10 Aldbourne
Road, London W12 0LN
☎ (0181) 248 9589
Fax (0181) 248 9587
*Large Victorian house, spacious rooms,
garden. Bottom of village, near castle
and beach and opposite the green.*
1 self-contained unit; sleeping 7

Price per week:	£min	£max
Low season	240.00	280.00
High season	325.00	375.00

All accommodation in this
guide has been graded, or is
awaiting a grading, by a trained
Tourist Board inspector.

BARNARD CASTLE
Durham
Map ref 5B3

High over the Tees, a thriving
market town with a busy market
square. Bernard Baliol's 12th C
castle (now ruins) stands nearby.
The Bowes Museum, housed in a
grand 19th C French chateau, holds
fine paintings and furniture. Nearby
are some magnificent buildings.
*Tourist Information Centre ☎ (01833)
690909*

East View
♦♦♦♦ HIGHLY COMMENDED

Barningham, Richmond, North
Yorkshire
Contact: Mr P D Johnson, North
View, Barningham, Richmond, North
Yorkshire DL11 7DU
☎ Teesdale (01833) 621256

*Secluded stone cottage with beams
and gardens in this peaceful village. We
offer traditional style with modern
comfort and convenience in a beautiful
area for touring.*
1 self-contained unit; sleeping 4

Price per week:	£min	£max
Low season	144.00	
High season		306.00

Mount Eff Cottage
♦♦♦ COMMENDED

Westwick, Barnard Castle, County
Durham
Contact: Dales Holiday Cottages,
Carleton Business Centre, Carleton
New Road, Skipton, North
Yorkshire BD23 2DG
☎ Skipton (01756) 799821 &
790919
*Cottage attached to farmhouse, within
walking distance of the Bowes Museum
and the ancient market town of
Barnard Castle.*
1 self-contained unit; sleeping 4

Price per week:	£min	£max
Low season	135.00	
High season		250.00

BARNINGHAM

Durham
Map ref 5B3

Village 4 miles south-east of Barnard Castle.

Rose Cottage Barningham

⚷⚷ COMMENDED

Barningham, Richmond, North Yorkshire
Contact: Mrs N P Millen, 2 Ryton Hall Drive, Ryton, Tyne and Wear NE40 3QB
☎ (0191) 413 2048
Grade II listed dales cottage with open fire, central heating, modern kitchen and appliances. In beautiful, unspoilt village with traditional inn.
1 self-contained unit; sleeping 4

Price per week:	£min	£max
Low season	130.00	170.00
High season	170.00	220.00

⚷🅼◎🖥👁🖥MW🖥📺🚗📷
🚗P❄

BARRASFORD

Northumberland
Map ref 5B2

Lovely village on the North Tyne River, overlooked by the restored 14th C Haughton Castle on the opposite bank.

Barrasford Arms Cottage 🏔

⚷⚷ APPROVED

Barrasford Arms, Barrasford, Hexham
Contact: Mr T Milburn, Barrasford Arms, Barrasford, Hexham, Northumberland NE48 4AA
☎ Humshaugh (01434) 681237
Comfortable cottage adjacent to a small country hotel, only 8 miles from Hexham and the Roman Wall. 15 miles from Kielder, a super centre for touring Northumberland, Lake District and Scottish Borders.
1 self-contained unit; sleeping max 6

Price per week:	£min	£max
Low season	160.00	185.00
High season	185.00	210.00

Cards accepted: Access, Visa
⚷🅼◎🖥👁🖥📺🚗📷🚗P♪
❄SP🅣

> The National Grading and Classification Scheme is explained in full at the back of this guide.

BEADNELL

Northumberland
Map ref 5C1

Charming fishing village on Beadnell Bay. Seashore lime kilns (National Trust), dating from the 18th C, recall busier days as a coal and lime port and a pub is built on to a medieval pele tower which survives from days of the border wars.

Bertonia 🏔

⚷⚷ COMMENDED

7 Longstone Close, Beadnell, Chathill
Contact: Mrs S Beckett, The Farmhouse, Doxford Newhouses, Chathill, Northumberland NE67 5EA
☎ Chathill (01665) 579368
Detached bungalow in quiet location, close to beach and shops. 3 double bedrooms, lounge, kitchen and bathroom plus extra WC and shower. Secluded gardens to rear. Large off-road parking areas and lock-up garage.
1 self-contained unit; sleeping 7

Price per week:	£min	£max
Low season	190.00	
High season		450.00

⚷◎🖥👁MW🖥📺🚗📷🚗P
❄SP

BEAMISH

Durham
Map ref 5C2

Village made famous by the award-winning Beamish, North of England Open Air Museum, which covers every aspect of the life, buildings and artefacts of the North East of 1913. Also in the area are Causey Arch and Tanfield Railway.
Tourist Information Centre ☎ *(0191) 370 2533*

Papermill Cottages 🏔

⚷⚷ UP TO COMMENDED

Beamish Woods, Beamish, Stanley, County Durham
Contact: Mrs Pamela Bovill, Mount Escob, Beamish Woods, Stanley, County Durham DH9 0SA
☎ (0191) 370 0289 & 370 2568
Workers' cottages from Urpeth Papermill c1792. Renovated, retaining traditional open fire ranges, but with modern kitchens and central heating. Idyllic, peaceful setting by river, 6 minutes from A1M.

3 self-contained units; sleeping 3–8

Price per week:	£min	£max
Low season	120.00	170.00
High season	210.00	320.00

⚷◎🖥👁🖥🖥📺🚗📷🚗P
❄SP🏛

BELFORD

Northumberland
Map ref 5B1

Small market town on the old coaching road, close to the coast, the Scottish border and the north-east flank of the Cheviots. Built mostly in stone and very peaceful now that the A1 has by-passed the town, Belford makes an ideal centre for excursions to the moors and coast.

Bricksheds 🏔

⚷⚷ COMMENDED

Station Road, Belford NE70 7DT
☎ (01668) 213605
Contact: Mr & Mrs D Bell
Comfortable, fully-equipped 19th C semi-detached cottage with fitted carpets throughout. All modern facilities, including kitchen and CH. Close to A1.
1 self-contained unit; sleeping max 6

Price per week:	£min	£max
Low season	140.00	170.00
High season	170.00	210.00

Open February–November
⚷🅼◎🖥👁🖥📺🚗📷🚗PU♪
❄

No 4 Easington Demesne 🏔

⚷⚷⚷ COMMENDED

Belford
Contact: Mr P Brewis, Easington Grange, Belford, Northumberland NE70 7EJ
☎ Belford (01668) 213223
Spacious farm cottages on mixed farm, away from public road. Within easy reach of beaches, castles, golf courses, Northumberland National Park, Holy Island and Farne Islands.
1 self-contained unit; sleeping 6

Price per week:	£min	£max
Low season	200.00	250.00
High season	250.00	350.00

Open April–October
Cards accepted: Access, Visa, Diners, Amex
⚷◎🏛👁🖥MW📺🚗📷🚗🦆🚗P
✖

BELFORD

Continued

Outchester & Ross Farm Cottages ⚔

🗝 🗝 🗝 🗝 | UP TO HIGHLY COMMENDED |

Ross Farm, Belford
Contact: Mrs H Sutherland, Ross Farm, Belford, Northumberland NE70 7EN
☎ Belford (01668) 213336

1150-acre mixed farm. Attractive farm and coastguard cottages, modernised to provide comfortable accommodation in unspoilt countryside. 1 mile from the sea, between Bamburgh and Holy Island.
13 self-contained units; sleeping 1–11

Price per week:	£min	£max
Low season	118.00	255.00
High season	270.00	630.00

🐕 🅼 ◎ 🏠 ⊙ 🛏 MW 📺 📷 🖥 🍽 🏄
P ♪ ❋ ✕ SP

BELLINGHAM

Northumberland
Map ref 5B2

Set in the beautiful valley of the North Tyne close to the Kielder Forest, Kielder Water and lonely moorland below the Cheviots. The church has an ancient stone wagon roof fortified in the 18th C with buttresses.
Tourist Information Centre ☎ *(01434) 220616*

Castle Hill View ⚔

🗝 🗝 🗝 | HIGHLY COMMENDED |

Front Street, Bellingham, Hexham
Contact: Mr & Mrs Batey, Highsteads, Front Street, Bellingham, Hexham, Northumberland NE48 2AA
☎ Hexham (01434) 220263
Beautifully modernised terraced cottage, centrally situated not far from Hadrian's Wall. Pleasant views over unspoilt valley at rear. Leisure activities: golf, fishing, walking, swimming, cycling and watersports.
1 self-contained unit; sleeping 4–6

Price per week:	£min	£max
Low season	115.00	
High season	225.00	

Open April–September
🐕 ◎ 🏠 ⊙ 🛏 MW 📧 📺 📷 🍽 🖥
🏄 ▶ ❋

Conheath Cottage ⚔

🗝 🗝 | COMMENDED |

Bellingham, Hexham
Contact: Mrs Zaina Riddle, Blakelaw Farm, Bellingham, Hexham, Northumberland NE48 2EF
☎ Hexham (01434) 220 250
1146-acre hill farm. Quiet, semi-detached cottage. High standard of comfort, very well equipped. Open fire, large garden with furniture and barbecue.
Wheelchair access category 3 ♿
1 self-contained unit; sleeping 5

Price per week:	£min	£max
Low season		160.00
High season		300.00

🐕 🅼 ◎ 🏠 ⊙ 🛏 MW 📧 📺 📷 🍽 🖥
🏄 P ♪ ▶ ❋ ✕

Riverdale Apartments ⚔

🗝 🗝 | COMMENDED |

The Square, Bellingham, Hexham
Contact: Mr J P Cocker, Riverdale Hall Hotel, Bellingham, Hexham, Northumberland NE48 2JT
☎ Bellingham (01434) 220254
Fax (01434) 220457
Apartments comprising lounge (with wardrobe beds), bedroom, bathroom and kitchen. Free use of indoor pool and all facilities at nearby Riverdale Hall Hotel. Short breaks for 2 or more nights from £69.
4 self-contained units; sleeping 4

Price per week:	£min	£max
Low season	120.00	165.00
High season	195.00	245.00

Cards accepted: Access, Visa, Diners, Amex, Switch/Delta
🐕 🅼 ◎ 🏠 ⊙ 🛏 📧 📺 🍽 🖥 🏄 ✎
🖥 ▶ ❋ ❄ SP T

BERWICK-UPON-TWEED

Northumberland
Map ref 5B1

Guarding the mouth of the Tweed, England's northernmost town with the best 16th C city walls in Europe. The handsome Guildhall and barracks date from the 18th C. Three bridges cross to Tweedmouth, the oldest built in 1634.
Tourist Information Centre ☎ *(01289) 330733*

Felkington Farm Cottages ⚔

🗝 🗝 | UP TO COMMENDED |

Felkington Farm, Berwick-upon-Tweed
Contact: Mrs M J Martin, Felkington Farm, Berwick-upon-Tweed, Northumberland TD15 2NR
☎ Berwick-upon-Tweed (01289) 387220
1000-acre mixed farm. Comfortable stone-built farm cottages 6 miles from the coast and in an ideal centre for touring the Borders and Northumberland. Log fire if desired. Children's playground, table tennis, pool table, woodland walk.
2 self-contained units; sleeping 6

Price per week:	£min	£max
Low season	115.00	
High season		260.00

🐕 🅼 ◎ 🏠 ⊙ 🛏 MW 📺 📷 🍽 🖥 🏄
P U ❋ ❄ SP

BISHOP AUCKLAND

Durham
Map ref 5C2

Busy market town on the bank of the River Wear. The Bishop's Palace, a castellated Norman manor house altered in the 18th C, stands in beautiful gardens. Entered from the market square by a handsome 18th C gatehouse, the park is a peaceful retreat of trees and streams.
Tourist Information Centre ☎ *(01388) 604922*

Meadow View

🗝 🗝 🗝 | APPROVED |

38 High Lands, Cockfield, Bishop Auckland, County Durham
Contact: Dales Holiday Cottages, Carleton Business Park, Carleton New Road, Skipton, North Yorkshire BD23 2DG
☎ Skipton (01756) 799821 & 790919
On the edge of Raby Moor, close to Raby Castle, this property provides a welcoming base for holidaymakers wishing to tour this historic region. Within easy reach of all amenities.
1 self-contained unit; sleeping 4–5

Price per week:	£min	£max
Low season		135.00
High season		255.00

🐕 ◎ 🏠 🛏 MW 📧 📺 📷 🍽 🖥 🏄 P

Information on accommodation listed in this guide has been supplied by the proprietors. As changes may occur you are advised to check details at the time of booking.

BLANCHLAND

Northumberland
Map ref 5B2

Beautiful medieval village rebuilt in the 18th C with stone from its ruined abbey, for lead miners working on the surrounding wild moors. The village is approached over a stone bridge across the Derwent or, from the north, through the ancient gatehouse.

4 Boltsburn Terrace ♠

APPROVED

Ramshaw, Blanchland, Consett, County Durham
Contact: Mr C E Davison, "Bolts Brae", 10 Watergate Road, Consett, County Durham DH8 9QS
☎ Consett (01207) 583076 & 506194
Self-contained cottages in picturesque countryside, 2 miles Blanchland, 10 miles Hexham. Hadrian's Wall, Beamish Museum, Durham Cathedral all within driving distance.
1 self-contained unit; sleeping 5

Price per week:	£min	£max
Low season	160.00	160.00
High season	160.00	160.00

Open April–October

Boltslaw Cottage ♠

COMMENDED

Ramshaw, Blanchland, Consett, County Durham
Contact: Mrs N Smith, 6 Selborne Avenue, Gateshead, Tyne and Wear NE9 6ET
☎ Tyneside (0191) 487 9456
Fax (01670) 510300
Two-bedroomed stone cottage with log fire and pine kitchen. Peaceful situation with moorland views. Central heating, telephone, garden with barbecue. Midweek breaks. Reductions for OAPs.
1 self-contained unit; sleeping 5

Price per week:	£min	£max
Low season	125.00	175.00
High season	175.00	225.00

Buckshott Farm Cottage ♠

COMMENDED

Blanchland, Consett, County Durham
Contact: Mrs L P Bainbridge, Buckshott Farm, Blanchland, Consett, County Durham DH8 9PL
☎ Hexham (01434) 675227 & 675296
873-acre livestock farm. Cottage

overlooking the beautiful Derwent Valley. Fitted kitchen, central heating and private garden. Good touring area.
1 self-contained unit; sleeping max 6

Price per week:	£min	£max
Low season	120.00	180.00
High season	180.00	235.00

Open April–October

BOLAM

Durham
Map ref 5C3

Tiny, peaceful hamlet in an agricultural area, 2 miles south of St Helen Auckland near the Roman road Dere Street.

Brackenbury Leazes Farm

APPROVED

Bolam, Darlington, County Durham
Contact: Mrs R P Pickering, Brackenbury House, Bildershaw, West Auckland, Bishop Auckland, County Durham DL14 9PL
☎ Bishop Auckland (01388) 832484
215-acre mixed farm. Adjacent to the A68, in a quiet and secluded setting with good access to the dales and Durham, Darlington and Teesside.
1 self-contained unit; sleeping 7

Price per week:	£min	£max
Low season	120.00	140.00
High season	170.00	190.00

CASTLESIDE

Durham
Map ref 5B2

Village on the edge of the North Pennines on the A68, one of the main routes from England to Scotland.

Allansford Mill Farm Cottage ♠

HIGHLY COMMENDED

Allansford, Castleside, Consett, County Durham
Contact: Anne Broome, The Mill, Allansford, Castleside, Consett, County Durham DH8 9BA
☎ Consett (01207) 591328 & 0374 131108

A warm Northumbrian welcome awaits you in this 16th C farmhouse. Full of

history, character and comfort. On the border of Durham and Northumberland and an ideal base for Newcastle, Durham, Hexham, Beamish Museum and MetroCentre. Sorry, no pets.
1 self-contained unit; sleeping max 10

Price per week:	£min	£max
Low season	200.00	350.00
High season	300.00	600.00

Cards accepted: Visa

CHATHILL

Northumberland
Map ref 5C1

Rural hamlet with mainline station. Preston Tower, a border pele tower, is nearby.

Doxford Farm Holiday Cottages ♠

UP TO HIGHLY COMMENDED

Doxford, Chathill
Contact: Mr A D Turnbull, Doxford Farm, Chathill, Northumberland NE67 5DY
☎ Charlton Mires (01665) 579235
Fax (01665) 579215

400-acre mixed farm. Selection of cottages on beautiful wooded country estate, well off the main road. Five miles of woodland trails with a guided walk every Sunday.
10 self-contained units; sleeping 2–10

Price per week:	£min	£max
Low season	100.00	150.00
High season	150.00	400.00

The symbols in each entry give information about services and facilities. A 'key' to these symbols appears at the back of this guide.

CHATHILL

Continued

Newstead Cottage ⚑

APPROVED

Newstead Farm, Chathill
Contact: Mrs M Riddell, Newstead
Farm, Chathill, Northumberland
NE67 5LH
☎ Chathill (01665) 589263
*Cottages on a mixed farm 4 miles from
beautiful beaches, ideal for touring the
Borders and Cheviot Hills.*
2 self-contained units; sleeping 5

Price per week:	£min	£max
Low season	150.00	180.00
High season	190.00	190.00

Open April–October

⚑Ⓜ◎🖥⊙📺📺🔌🗻🛏♣P∪
🌿❋✕

CONSETT

Durham
Map ref 5B2

Former steel town on the edge of
rolling moors. Modern development
includes the shopping centre and a
handsome Roman Catholic church,
designed by a local architect. To the
west, the Derwent Reservoir
provides water sports and pleasant
walks.

The Cottage, Derwent Grange Farm

APPROVED

Castleside, Consett, County
Durham DH8 9BN
☎ (01207) 508358
Contact: Mr & Mrs Elliot
*Farm cottage, comfortable. Two
bedrooms, TV, large garden area. Near
Durham City, MetroCentre, easy reach
of Northumbria. Wonderful touring
area.*
1 self-contained unit; sleeping 4

Price per week:	£min	£max
Low season	150.00	200.00
High season	175.00	250.00

⚑◎▥⊙📺MW📺🔌🗻🛏
🔌P🌿❋✕♣SP

CORBRIDGE

Northumberland
Map ref 5B2

Small town on the River Tyne. Close
by are extensive remains of the
Roman military town Corstopitum,
with a museum housing important
discoveries from excavations. The
town itself is attractive with shady
trees, a 17th C bridge and
interesting old buildings, notably a
14th C vicarage.

Riversbank

COMMENDED

3 Front Street, Corbridge
Contact: Dr J R Backhurst, Uplands,
Newcastle Road, Corbridge,
Northumberland NE45 5LN
☎ Hexham (01434) 632073
Fax (01434) 632073
*Totally refurbished, attractive stone
cottage with outstanding river views, in
the centre of historic Corbridge.*
1 self-contained unit; sleeping max 4

Price per week:	£min	£max
Low season	145.00	190.00
High season	215.00	315.00

⚑🌿▥⊙🖥MW📺📺🔌🗻🛏
🔌∪❋

Riverview

COMMENDED

Market Place, Corbridge
Contact: Mrs E Lonsdale, 13 Market
Place, Corbridge, Northumberland
NE45 5AW
☎ Hexham (01434) 633027
Fax (01434) 633027
*18th C cottage in the centre of this old
Roman village. It faces the Market
Place and church, with tranquil views at
the rear overlooking the Tyne Valley.*
1 self-contained unit; sleeping 4

Price per week:	£min	£max
Low season	130.00	170.00
High season	170.00	290.00

⚑5◎▥🖥MW📺📺🔌🗻🛏
🔌❋✕

West Fell Cottage

APPROVED

Ladycutter Lane, Corbridge
NE45 5RZ
☎ Hexham (01434) 632044
Contact: Mrs E J Smith
*Two-bedroomed farm cottage near
Dilston Castle and convenient for
Corbridge and the Roman Wall.*
1 self-contained unit; sleeping max 6

Price per week:	£min	£max
Low season	75.00	140.00
High season	150.00	180.00

⚑Ⓜ◎▥⊙🖥📺🗻🔌P∪❋

COTHERSTONE

Durham
Map ref 5B3

Village with remains of Norman
castle, 3 miles north-west of
Barnard Castle. Home of
Cotherstone cheese.

Farthings ⚑

COMMENDED

Cotherstone, Barnard Castle,
County Durham
Contact: Mr C J Bainbridge, Glen
Leigh, Cotherstone, Barnard Castle,
County Durham DL12 9QW
☎ Teesdale (01833) 650331
*Stone-built bungalow on village green.
Two bedrooms, bath and shower. Gas
central heating and fire. Well equipped
and decorated.*
1 self-contained unit; sleeping 4–6

Price per week:	£min	£max
Low season	75.00	110.00
High season	110.00	225.00

⚑◎▥⊙🖥📺📺🗻🛏🔌P
∪❋

Thwaite Hall ⚑

HIGHLY COMMENDED

Cotherstone, Barnard Castle,
County Durham
Contact: Mrs A Wickham, Hillcrest,
Front Street, Whitburn, Tyne and
Wear SR6 7JD
☎ (0191) 529 3793

*Well furnished cottages on outskirts of
the village. In an ideal situation, with
views over the surrounding countryside.*
3 self-contained units; sleeping 2–6

Price per week:	£min	£max
Low season	130.00	190.00
High season	180.00	280.00

⚑Ⓜ◎▥⊙🖥📺📺🗻🛏
🔌P∪❋🗻SP🎣

Self-catering agencies
which have a selection of
holiday homes to let
are listed in a special section
towards the back
of this guide.

Woden Croft Cottage

COMMENDED

Cotherstone, Barnard Castle, County Durham
Contact: Mrs L J Horsley, 42 Station Road, South Cave, Brough, North Humberside HU15 2AA
☎ Brough (01430) 422562
Upper Teesdale cottage on working farm, 5 minutes' drive from Cotherstone and adjacent to River Tees. Off B6277. All modern conveniences. Fishing available.
1 self-contained unit; sleeping 4–6

Price per week:	£min	£max
Low season	150.00	250.00
High season	150.00	250.00

CROOKHAM

Northumberland
Map ref 5B1

Pretty hamlet taking its name from the winding course of the River Till which flows in the shape of a shepherd's crook. Three castles - Etal, Duddo and Ford - can be seen, and nearby the restored Heatherslaw Mill is of great interest.

Askew Cottage

COMMENDED

34 Crookham Village, Cornhill-on-Tweed
Contact: Mrs H Pentland, 32 Crookham Village, Cornhill-on-Tweed, Northumberland TD12 4SY
☎ Crookham (01890) 820201
Comfortable cottage in historic Border country, convenient for Cheviot Hills, Tweed Valley and magnificent coast.
1 self-contained unit; sleeping max 4

Price per week:	£min	£max
Low season	90.00	150.00
High season	150.00	300.00

CULLERCOATS

Tyne and Wear
Map ref 5C2

Former fishing village between Tynemouth and Whitley Bay.

Everitt House

APPROVED

46 Beverley Terrace, Cullercoats, North Shields NE30 4NU
☎ (0191) 252 1568
Contact: Mrs G E Aitken
On seafront, close to Metro station and bus service. 3 flats overlook pretty Cullercoats Bay. For business or holiday use. Ground floor flats suitable for partially disabled persons and chairlift available to 1st and 2nd floors.
5 self-contained units; sleeping 2–6

Price per week:	£min	£max
Low season	95.00	195.00

Forty Five

APPROVED

45 Beverley Terrace, Cullercoats, North Shields NE30 4NU
☎ (0191) 252 5247
Contact: Mr & Mrs Tully
Facing the sea and delightful bays. All modern amenities in flexible self-catering rooms with every comfort and personal supervision.
4 non-self-contained units; sleeping 2–4

Price per week:	£min	£max
Low season	70.00	155.00
High season	90.00	195.00

DURHAM

Durham
Map ref 5C2

Ancient city with its Norman castle and cathedral, now a World Heritage site, set on a bluff high over the Wear. A market and university town and regional centre, spreading beyond the market-place on both banks of the river.
Tourist Information Centre ☎ (0191) 384 3720

Arbour House Bungalow

COMMENDED

Arbour House Farm, Crossgate Moor, Durham, County Durham DH1 4TQ
☎ (0191) 384 2418
Fax (0191) 386 0738
Contact: Mrs R Hunter
Superior bungalow on working farm, with panoramic view over countryside. 5 minutes to Durham City. Suitable for wheelchairs.
1 self-contained unit; sleeping 6

Price per week:	£min	£max
Low season	180.00	320.00
High season	225.00	350.00

EDMUNDBYERS

Durham
Map ref 5B2

Small village in hilly country beneath Muggleswick Common. A winding, man-made lake on the River Derwent just north complements smaller reservoirs southward across the common, offering fishing and picnic areas.

The Burnside

COMMENDED

Edmundbyers, Consett, County Durham DH8 9NG
☎ (01207) 255257
Contact: Mrs B Brown
Apartments in grounds of owner's house and tea room. 10 acres with gardens, stream, fields and pond, at the north end of the Pennines.
4 self-contained units; sleeping 2–4

Price per week:	£min	£max
Low season	150.00	194.00
High season	260.00	371.00

EGGLESTON

Durham
Map ref 5B3

Small village between Barnard Castle and Middleton-in-Teesdale on the edge of the moors. Once a smelting centre for the North Pennines lead industry but no trace of it remains today.

The Granary

APPROVED

Eggleston, Barnard Castle, County Durham
Contact: Mrs R Gray, Eggleston Hall, Barnard Castle, County Durham DL12 0AG
☎ Teesdale (01833) 650378 & 650403
Fax (01833) 650378
Comfortable cottage on a country estate, with superb views over parkland and Upper Teesdale.
1 self-contained unit; sleeping max 6

Price per week:	£min	£max
Low season	160.00	
High season	230.00	

Please mention this guide when making your booking.

You are advised to confirm your booking in writing.

EMBLETON

Northumberland
Map ref 5C1

Coastal village beside a golf-course spread along the edge of Embleton Bay. The old church was extensively restored in the 19th C. The vicarage incorporates a medieval pele tower.

2a Front Street
APPROVED

Embleton, Alnwick
Contact: Mrs Mary Axelby, 86 Crimicar Lane, Sheffield S10 4FB
☎ Sheffield (0114) 230 5090
Spacious, modernised holiday home in the heart of this popular seaside village. Free electricity. The area offers many activities and attractions.
1 self-contained unit; sleeping max 9

Price per week:	£min	£max
Low season	205.00	235.00
High season	325.00	325.00

FOURSTONES

Northumberland
Map ref 5B2

Village 4 miles north-west of the market town of Hexham.

6 Kiln Cottages
APPROVED

Fourstones, Hexham
Contact: Mrs M Bell, 9 Kiln Cottages, Fourstones, Hexham, Northumberland NE47 5DH
☎ Hexham (01434) 674635
Comfortable, ground level, self-contained flat, within a row of stone-built cottages. Fully equipped, 2 double bedrooms. In pleasant rural surroundings, lovely views. Hexham 4 miles, Hadrian's Wall 3 miles.
1 self-contained unit; sleeping max 4

Price per week:	£min	£max
Low season	70.00	110.00
High season	110.00	160.00

FROSTERLEY

Durham
Map ref 5B2

Old quarrying village on the limestone slopes of Weardale. The rich Frosterley marble, black when polished, graces the fonts and columns of many local churches, including Durham Cathedral.

East Cottage
HIGHLY COMMENDED

Holroyd Place, Frosterley, Bishop Auckland, County Durham
Contact: Mrs B Walters, 11 Arlington Road, Middlesbrough, Cleveland TS5 7RD
☎ (01642) 812425
19th C stone-built cottage with exposed beams, antiques, open-fire range, central heating. Close to river and Hamsterley Forest. 1 double and 1 twin bedroom.
1 self-contained unit; sleeping max 6

Price per week:	£min	£max
Low season	90.00	145.00
High season	160.00	190.00

HALTWHISTLE

Northumberland
Map ref 5B2

Small market town with interesting 12th C church, old inns and blacksmith's smithy. North of the town are several important sites and interpretation centres of Hadrian's Wall. Ideal centre for archaeology, outdoor activity or touring holidays.
Tourist Information Centre ☎ (01434) 322002

Ald White Craig Farm Cottages
HIGHLY COMMENDED

Ald White Craig Farm, Near Hadrian's Wall, Haltwhistle
Contact: Mrs J I Laidlow, Ald White Craig Farm, Near Hadrian's Wall, Haltwhistle, Northumberland NE49 9NW
☎ Haltwhistle (01434) 320565
Fax (01434) 320565
50-acre livestock farm. In magnificent countryside on working farm, half a mile from A69. Returning guests recommend these attractive award-winning holiday cottages.

4 self-contained units; sleeping 3–8

Price per week:	£min	£max
Low season	110.00	
High season		400.00

Folding Steads
HIGHLY COMMENDED

Oaky Knowe Farm, Haltwhistle
Contact: Mrs Patricia Murray, Oaky Knowe Farm, Haltwhistle, Northumberland NE49 0NB
☎ Haltwhistle (01434) 320648
300-acre mixed farm. Small farmhouse in own grounds, with panoramic views over Tyne Valley. Surrounded by public footpaths and within easy reach of Roman Wall. Situated halfway up the Shield Hill, turning right past Pyke Dyke Nook.
1 self-contained unit; sleeping 9

Price per week:	£min	£max
Low season	150.00	190.00
High season	190.00	400.00

Gibbs Hill Farm Cottages
UP TO DE LUXE

Bardon Mill, Hexham NE47 7AP
☎ Hexham (01434) 344030
Fax (01434) 344030
Contact: Mrs Valerie Gibson

520-acre hill farm. Delightful stone cottages on working farm/nature reserve in National Park. In sight of Hadrian's Wall. Log fires and gas central heating.
3 self-contained units; sleeping 2–4

Price per week:	£min	£max
Low season	150.00	220.00
High season	220.00	390.00

3 Oakwell Terrace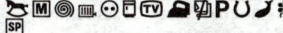

🔑 COMMENDED

Haltwhistle
Contact: Miss Helen Mitchell, 2
Oakwell Terrace, Haltwhistle,
Northumberland NE49 9LR
☎ Haltwhistle (01434) 321939
Fax (01434) 321939
*One of 8 ex-miners' cottages in country
setting. Within walking distance of
heated pool, sports facilities, shops,
pubs and Hadrian's Wall.*
1 self-contained unit; sleeping 6

Price per week:	£min	£max
High season	150.00	250.00

🐕🖊🏭☺🍴📺📺🔌🤍🎯P✤

Small village near Bedburn Beck, at
the edge of the North Pennines. Just
westward lies moorland country of
Hamsterley Common and the
beautiful Hamsterley Forest with
picnic areas and nature trails.

Edge Knoll Farm Cottages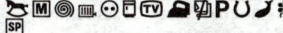

🔑🔑🔑 COMMENDED

Edge Knoll Farm, Hamsterley, Bishop
Auckland, County Durham
DL13 3PF
☎ Witton Le Wear (01388) 488537
Contact: Mr G Edmonds
*Tastefully converted farm buildings,
around a cobbled courtyard. In
beautiful open countryside between the
villages of Witton-le-Wear and
Hamsterley.*
2 self-contained units; sleeping 4

Price per week:	£min	£max
Low season	125.00	200.00
High season	200.00	285.00

🐕Ⓜ◎🏭☺🍴MW📺🤍🎯🍴🤍🍴
PU🖊✤✖🏵 SP 🏠 T

HAMSTERLEY FOREST

Durham
Map ref 5B2

*See also Barnard Castle, Bishop
Auckland, Frosterley, Hamsterley, Tow
Law, Wolsingham*

Grove Cottage

🔑🔑🔑 HIGHLY COMMENDED

Grove House, Hamsterley Forest,
Bishop Auckland, County Durham
Contact: Mrs H P Close, Grove
House, Redford, Hamsterley Forest,
Bishop Auckland, County Durham
DL13 3NL
☎ Witton-le-Wear (01388) 488203

*Idyllic recently renovated cottage in
heart of Hamsterley Forest. Walking,
rivers, birds, pony trekking. A68, follow
signs to forest, 3 miles inside forest.*
1 self-contained unit; sleeping 6

Price per week:	£min	£max
Low season	200.00	285.00
High season	285.00	300.00

🐕◎🏭☺🍴MW🔌📺🤍🎯PU
✤✖🏠🏡

HARWOOD

Durham
Map ref 5B2

The highest settled part of Teesdale,
about 1700 ft above sea level, with
whitewashed 18th C farmhouses
and buildings. An area noted for rare
plants.

Honey Pot Cottage & Frog Hall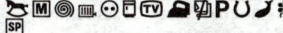

🔑🔑 APPROVED

Harwood-in-Teesdale, Barnard
Castle, County Durham
Contact: The Agent, Raby Estates
Office, Upper Teesdale Estate,
Middleton-in-Teesdale, Barnard
Castle, County Durham DL12 0QH
☎ Teesdale (01833) 640209
Fax (01833) 640963
*Stone-built cottages with original
stone-slate roofs, in open country with
delightful views of Upper Teesdale.*
2 self-contained units; sleeping 4–6

Price per week:	£min	£max
Low season	100.00	110.00
High season	225.00	240.00

🐕Ⓜ◎🏭☺🍴📺🤍🎯PU🖊✤
SP

HAYDON BRIDGE

Northumberland
Map ref 5B2

Small town on the banks of the
South Tyne with an ancient church,
built of stone from sites along the
Roman Wall just north. Ideally
situated for exploring Hadrian's
Wall and the Border country.

Hadrian Lodge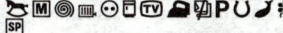

🔑🔑🔑 COMMENDED

Hindshield Moss, North Road,
Haydon Bridge, Hexham NE47 6NF
☎ Tynedale (01434) 688688
Contact: Mr M Chaplin
*Conversion into cottages of large,
stone-built hunting/fishing lodge. Near
Housesteads and Hadrian's Wall.
Games room. Free fishing. Brochure
available.*
3 self-contained units; sleeping 6

Price per week:	£min	£max
Low season	130.00	130.00
High season	200.00	250.00

🐕Ⓜ◎🏭☺🍴MW🔌📺🤍🎯
🍴PJ✖ SP

HEXHAM

Northumberland
Map ref 5B2

Old coaching and market town near
Hadrian's Wall. Since pre-Norman
times a weekly market has been
held in the centre with its
market-place and abbey park, and
the richly-furnished 12th C abbey
church has a superb Anglo-Saxon
crypt.
*Tourist Information Centre ☎ (01434)
605225*

Stotsfold Hall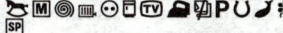

🔑🔑 COMMENDED

Steel, Hexham
Contact: Mrs K J Wootton, Stotsfold
Hall, Steel, Hexham,
Northumberland NE47 0HP
☎ Hexham (01434) 673270
*Cottages set in beautiful grounds of an
old manor house, 6 miles south of
Hexham. Fully-equipped and
double-glazed.*
3 self-contained units;
sleeping max 4

Price per week:	£min	£max
Low season	84.00	105.00
High season	215.00	240.00

🐕Ⓜ◎🏭☺🍴📺🤍🎯🍴P✤✖
✖

HOLY ISLAND

Northumberland
Map ref 5B1

Still an idyllic retreat, tiny island and fishing village and cradle of northern Christianity. It is approached from the mainland at low water by a causeway. The clifftop castle (National Trust) was restored by Sir Edwin Lutyens.

Winn Cottage
🔑🔑 APPROVED

Marygate, Holy Island, Berwick-upon-Tweed
Contact: Mrs K M Winn, 11 Newtons Croft Crescent, Barlborough, Chesterfield, Derbyshire S43 4WA
☎ (01246) 810767
Pleasant, modernised holiday cottage in centre of village. Sheltered garden. Central heating and colour TV. No pets please.
1 self-contained unit; sleeping max 5

Price per week:	£min	£max
Low season	180.00	190.00
High season	190.00	210.00

Open April–November
🎖◎🅿⊙🖸MW🗄TV🖥🧺💼🗘
🚗P❋🍴

KIELDER FOREST

Northumberland

See under Bellingham, West Woodburn

LOFTUS

Tees Valley
Map ref 5C3

Liverton Lodge
🔑🔑🔑 APPROVED

Loftus, Saltburn-by-the-Sea, Cleveland
Contact: Dales Holiday Cottages, Property No.1778, Carleton Business Park, Skipton, North Yorkshire BD23 2DG
☎ Skipton (01756) 799821
Fax (01756) 797012
Lovely farmhouse, retaining many original features, with splendid beams and woodwork. 2 sitting rooms, 4 bedrooms, 2 bathrooms. Grand piano available on request for musical family.
1 self-contained unit; sleeping max 7

Price per week:	£min	£max
Low season		245.00
High season		490.00

Open March–November
Cards accepted: Access, Visa, Diners, Amex

🎖◎🅿🖸⊙🖸MW🗄TV🖥🧺💼🗘
🚗P❋

LOWICK

Northumberland
Map ref 5B1

Inland from Holy Island and near the A1, Lowick has a long, wide main street with a few shops and inns and is in agricultural land between the foothills of the Cheviots and the coast.

Laburnum Cottage 🏵

🔑🔑🔑 APPROVED

South Road, Lowick, Berwick-upon-Tweed
Contact: Mr & Mrs J E Hardy, 41 Longcram, Haddington, East Lothian EH41 4NS
☎ Haddington (01620) 822113
In a quiet village near sea and hills. Spacious detached cottage with private, south-facing garden. Well appointed.
1 self-contained unit; sleeping max 2

Price per week:	£min	£max
Low season	150.00	190.00
High season	240.00	285.00

Open March–October
🎖🍴◎🅿⊙🖸🗄TV🖥🧺💼🗘🚗U❋
🍴

MICKLETON

Durham
Map ref 5B3

Village 2 miles south-east of Middleton-in-Teesdale.

Pennine View and Waters Edge Cottages 🏵

🔑🔑🔑 COMMENDED ✗

Grassholme Water, Grassholme, Mickleton, County Durham
Contact: Dales Holiday Cottages, Carleton Business Centre, Carleton New Road, Skipton, North Yorkshire BD23 2DG
☎ Skipton (01756) 799821
Stone-built cottages sitting on the edge of Grassholme Reservoir. Ideal for walking, fishing and sailing.
2 self-contained units; sleeping max 6

Price per week:	£min	£max
Low season	168.00	168.00
High season	320.00	320.00

🎖◎🅿🖸⊙🖸MW TV🖥🧺💼🗘🚗P
❋🗑SP

MIDDLETON-IN-TEESDALE

Durham
Map ref 5B3

Small stone town of hillside terraces overlooking the river, developed by the London Lead Company in the 18th C. Five miles up-river is the spectacular 70-ft waterfall, High Force.

Castle Cottage
🔑🔑 COMMENDED ✗

Holwick, Middleton-in-Teesdale, Barnard Castle, County Durham
Contact: Mrs J Lynch, Pikestone House, Holwick, Middleton-in-Teesdale, Barnard Castle, County Durham DL12 0NR
☎ Teesdale (01833) 640474
Situated at the top of the hamlet of Holwick, 3 miles from Middleton-in-Teesdale. Commanding views, variety of walks directly outside cottage door.
1 self-contained unit; sleeping 2

Price per week:	£min	£max
Low season	130.00	165.00
High season	165.00	200.00

🎖◎🅿🖸⊙🖸MW🗄TV🖥🧺💼🚗
P❋SP

Country Cottage
🔑🔑 COMMENDED

Newbiggin-in-Teesdale, Middleton-in-Teesdale
Contact: Mr R B Burman, 26 Princes Road, Heaton Moor, Stockport, Cheshire SK4 3NQ
☎ (0161) 442 9566 & 860 7123
200-year-old cottage in quiet and peaceful location and with superb views, surrounded by farmland. Excellent walking countryside.
1 self-contained unit; sleeping max 6

Price per week:	£min	£max
Low season	163.00	
High season		295.00

🎖◎🅿🖸⊙🖸🗄TV🖥🧺💼🍴SP

WELCOME HOST

This is a nationally recognised customer care programme which aims to promote the highest standards of service and a warm welcome. Establishments who are taking part in this initiative are indicated by the 🏵 symbol.

Holiday Cottage Balmar House 𝄞

APPROVED

Balmar Lane, Eggleston, Barnard Castle, County Durham
Contact: Mr C J Robinson, Balmar Cottage, Balmar Lane, Eggleston, Barnard Castle, County Durham DL12 0AN
☎ Teesdale (01833) 650567
Self-contained 2-storey house with enclosed garden, overlooking Tees Valley on quiet no-through road. Many local attractions, and 1 hour from Lake District.
1 self-contained unit; sleeping 5

Price per week:	£min	£max
Low season	127.00	142.00
High season	170.00	255.00

3 Parkin Row and 33 Town End

UP TO COMMENDED

Middleton-in-Teesdale, Barnard Castle, County Durham
Contact: Mrs J Thompson, Cutbush Farmhouse, Hardingham Road, Hingham, Norwich NR9 4LY
☎ Hingham (01953) 850 364
Stone-built lead miners' cottages, 1 up/1 down, flagstone floor, traditional rag rugs, kitchen range, outhouses.
2 self-contained units; sleeping max 2

Price per week:	£min	£max
Low season	90.00	95.00
High season	95.00	120.00

Teesdale Hotel Mews Cottages 𝄞

COMMENDED

c/o Teesdale Hotel, Middleton-in-Teesdale, Barnard Castle, County Durham
Contact: Mr and Mrs D Streit, Teesdale Hotel, Middleton-in-Teesdale, Barnard Castle, County Durham DL12 0QG
☎ Teesdale (01833) 640264
Fax (01833) 640651
Comfortable mews cottages in hotel courtyard, with all the services of the hotel available. Dogs welcome free of charge.
3 self-contained units; sleeping 4–6

Price per week:	£min	£max
Low season	95.00	150.00
High season	184.00	300.00

Cards accepted: Access, Visa

MINDRUM

Northumberland
Map ref 5B1

Hamlet 4 miles south of Cornhill on Tweed by banks of Bowmont Water.

Bowmont Cottage

COMMENDED

Bowmont Hill, Mindrum
Contact: Mr and Mrs S Orpwood, Bowmont Hill, Mindrum, Northumberland TD12 4QW
☎ Mindrum (01890) 850266 & Mobile 0836 513155
Fax (01890) 850245
464-acre arable & livestock farm. Two-bedroomed cottage with bathroom and separate shower room. Large sitting-room with log fire, large kitchen/dining-room with oil-fired Raeburn. Carpeted throughout. Cots, high chair. Dogs by arrangement. Fishing available.
1 self-contained unit; sleeping 4

Price per week:	£min	£max
Low season	130.00	210.00
High season	210.00	275.00

NEASHAM

Durham
Map ref 5C3

Pretty village pleasantly set on the River Tees, south of Darlington.

Cottages at the Newbus Arms 𝄞

COMMENDED

Newbus Arms Hotel and Restaurant, Newbus Arms, Neasham, Darlington, County Durham
Contact: Mr and Mrs Kenny Beagle, Newbus Arms Hotel and, Restaurant, Newbus Arms, Neasham, Darlington, County Durham DL2 1PE
☎ Darlington (01325) 721071
Fax (01325) 721770
These cottages have been carefully converted from courtyard buildings to provide a high standard of comfort, making a perfect base for touring both Northumbria and North Yorkshire.
2 self-contained units; sleeping 5

Price per week:	£min	£max
Low season	145.00	160.00
High season	255.00	285.00

Cards accepted: Access, Visa, Diners, Amex

NEWCASTLE UPON TYNE

Tyne and Wear
Map ref 5C2

Commercial and cultural centre of the North East, with a large indoor shopping centre, Quayside market, museums and theatres which offer an annual 6 week season by the Royal Shakespeare Company. Norman castle keep, medieval alleys, old Guildhall.
Tourist Information Centre ☎ (0191) 261 0610 or 230 0030

135 Audley Road

APPROVED

South Gosforth, Newcastle upon Tyne
Contact: Miss Linda Wright, 137 Audley Road, South Gosforth, Newcastle upon Tyne NE3 1QH
☎ (0191) 285 6374
Self-contained flat, close to shops and Metro. All amenities.
1 self-contained unit; sleeping 6

Price per week:	£min	£max
Low season	140.00	170.00
High season	170.00	210.00

Walbottle House (West)

HIGHLY COMMENDED

Walbottle, Newcastle upon Tyne
Contact: Mrs S E Kent, Walbottle House, Walbottle, Newcastle upon Tyne NE15 8JD
☎ (0191) 264 1108
West wing of 250-year-old listed house, with large garden. Close to Hadrian's Wall, Northumberland and 5 miles from Newcastle.
1 self-contained unit; sleeping 4–6

Price per week:	£min	£max
Low season	180.00	270.00
High season	270.00	350.00

TOWN INDEX

This can be found at the back of the guide. If you know where you want to stay, the index will give you the page number listing all accommodation in your chosen town, city or village.

NEWTON-BY-THE-SEA

Northumberland
Map ref 5C1

Attractive hamlet at the south end of Beadnell Bay with a sandy beach and splendid view of Dunstanburgh Castle. In a designated Area of Outstanding Natural Beauty, Low Newton, part of the village, is now owned by the National Trust.

Keyholes M

COMMENDED

Newton-by-the-Sea, Alnwick
Contact: Mr Owen Sutherland, Dunstan Steads, Embleton, Alnwick, Northumberland NE66 3DT
☎ Alnwick (01665) 576221
Cottages near the beach, all with modern facilities, colour TV and some with central heating. Golf, sailing, fishing and bird-watching nearby.
4 self-contained units; sleeping 6

Price per week:	£min	£max
Low season	180.00	260.00
High season	380.00	500.00

OVINGTON

Northumberland
Map ref 5B2

Quiet village on the north bank of the River Tyne, linked to the adjacent village of Ovingham which has a 17th C packhorse bridge and was the birthplace of the famous artist and engraver Thomas Bewick.

Westgarth Cottage M

COMMENDED

Old Brewery Square, Ovington
Contact: Mrs C Graham, Stonecroft, Ovington, Northumberland
NE42 6EB
☎ Prudhoe (01661) 832202
Attractive stone-built cottage in a small, peaceful village surrounded by beautiful countryside, near the historic towns of Hexham and Corbridge.
1 self-contained unit; sleeping 4

Price per week:	£min	£max
Low season	195.00	225.00
High season	195.00	225.00

A key to symbols can be found inside the back cover flap.

ROTHBURY

Northumberland
Map ref 5B1

Old market town on the River Coquet near the Simonside Hills. It makes an ideal centre for walking and fishing or for exploring this beautiful area from the coast to the Cheviots. Cragside House and Gardens (National Trust) are open to the public.

Alexandra House Holiday Flat M

HIGHLY COMMENDED

High Street, Rothbury, Morpeth
Contact: Mrs L Nicholls, Alexandra House, High Street, Rothbury, Morpeth, Northumberland
NE65 7TE
☎ Rothbury (01669) 621463
Newly converted first floor flat in 18th C house/shop. All amenities, quiet position, warm and cosy. Ideal for walking and touring. No smoking.
1 self-contained unit; sleeping max 2

Price per week:	£min	£max
Low season	130.00	180.00
High season	170.00	220.00

Cards accepted: Access, Visa, Amex, Switch/Delta

The Cottage Well Close

COMMENDED

Townfoot, Rothbury, Morpeth
Contact: Mrs I A Wilbie-Chalk, Well Close, Townfoot, Rothbury, Morpeth, Northumberland
NE65 7HZ
☎ Rothbury (01669) 620430
Fax (01669) 621234

Comfortable wood and stone cottage in 2-acre garden with wood. Bookings Friday-Friday. Late night arrivals accepted. On-site parking.
1 self-contained unit; sleeping max 4

Price per week:	£min	£max
Low season	100.00	150.00
High season	165.00	210.00

High Trewhitt Cottages

APPROVED

Thropton, Rothbury, Morpeth
Contact: Mrs P Younger, High Trewhitt, Thropton, Rothbury, Morpeth, Northumberland
NE65 7ES
☎ Rothbury (01669) 630250
Comfortable country cottages 5 miles from the picturesque village of Rothbury. Within easy reach of the Scottish Borders, Hadrian's Wall and the beautiful Northumberland coast.
2 self-contained units; sleeping 6

Price per week:	£min	£max
Low season	150.00	
High season	180.00	

Open June–October

The Pele Tower M

DE LUXE

Whitton, Rothbury NE65 7RL
☎ (01669) 620410
Fax (01669) 621006
Contact: Mr & Mrs J D Malia

19th C wing of Northumbrian pele tower, origins 1380. Includes whirlpool bath, dishwasher, satellite TV and video. Mountain bikes. Sorry, no smoking and no pets.
1 self-contained unit; sleeping max 4

Price per week:	£min	£max
Low season	245.00	
High season		470.00

Cards accepted: Visa

Sunnyville M

HIGHLY COMMENDED

Backcroft, Rothbury, Morpeth
NE65 7XY
☎ (01669) 620981
Contact: Mr Peter Dawson
3-bedroomed house adjoining proprietor's residence. Fully-equipped kitchen, full gas fired central heating. Bed linen and fuel included. Sorry no pets.
1 self-contained unit; sleeping max 5

Price per week:	£min	£max
Low season	125.00	150.00
High season	220.00	275.00

Whitton Lodge ⚠

🔑🔑🔑 COMMENDED

Rothbury, Morpeth
Contact: Mr R E Thorn, Whitton
Grange, Rothbury, Morpeth,
Northumberland NE65 7RL
☎ Rothbury (01669) 620929

*Listed building in 3 acres of gardens.
Stunning views over Rothbury,
Coquetdale and Simonside, all within
walking distance.*
1 self-contained unit; sleeping 7

Price per week:	£min	£max
Low season	200.00	
High season		400.00

🗝📺⊙🔥MW🎞📺🔦🍴📻
🍴🖊🅰️P∪🌊❄️SP🏠

Set on fine cliffs just north of the
Cleveland Hills, a gracious Victorian
resort with later developments and
wide, firm sands. A handsome
Jacobean mansion at Marske can be
reached along the sands.
Tourist Information Centre ☎ *(01287)
622422*

The Zetland

🔑🔑🔑 COMMENDED

Apartment 17, Marine Parade,
Saltburn-by-the-Sea, Cleveland
Contact: Mr D Carter, Carter Steel
Ltd., Yarm Road, Stockton-on-Tees,
Cleveland TS18 3SA
☎ Middlesbrough (01642) 679831
Fax (01642) 670346
*Apartment in the most famous building
in Saltburn, the old Zetland Hotel, an
imposing Victorian building over 100
years old. Second floor 2 bedroom
apartment with spectacular views of
the sea, cliffs and surrounding
countryside.*
1 self-contained unit; sleeping 4

Price per week:	£min	£max
Low season	125.00	150.00
High season	175.00	250.00

🗝📺⊙🔥MW🎞📺🔦🍴📻
🅰️P📻🌊SP🏠

Small modern resort developed
around a 19th C herring port. Just
offshore, and reached by boat from
here, are the rocky Farne Islands
(National Trust) where there is an
important bird reserve. The bird
observatory occupies a medieval
pele tower.

Brockburn ⚠

🔑🔑 HIGHLY COMMENDED

Monkshouses, Seahouses
Contact: Mrs P Thompson, Highfield
House, Woodhill Farm, Ponteland,
Newcastle upon Tyne NE20 0JA
☎ Ponteland (01661) 860165

*Large 700-year-old house, which still
retains its full character and charm
although thoroughly refurbished.
Positioned directly on the beach,
amongst the sand dunes, with splendid
views of the Farne Islands.*
1 self-contained unit; sleeping 9

Price per week:	£min	£max
Low season	250.00	470.00
High season	470.00	650.00

🗝📺⊙🔥MW🎞📺🔦🍴📻📻
🅰️P❄️🏠

Cliff House Cottages ⚠

🔑🔑 COMMENDED

Seahouses
Contact: Mr S Holford, 88A Fenham
Hall Drive, Newcastle upon Tyne
NE4 9XA
☎ (0191) 232 7983 & 275 0854
Fax (0191) 261 4948

*Cottages in their own courtyard,
overlooking the harbour. Within yards
of the village and the country's most
beautiful beaches and castles.*
4 self-contained units; sleeping 2–5

Price per week:	£min	£max
Low season	145.00	165.00
High season	195.00	225.00

Cards accepted: Access, Visa
🗝M📺⊙🔥MW🎞📺🔦🍴📻
🅰️P∪🌊❄️SP🏠

Small hamlet, now a major golfing
venue, south of Corbridge near the
Derwent Reservoir.

Clairmont Cottage

🔑🔑 COMMENDED

Slaley, Hexham
Contact: Mrs E Allsop, Clairmont,
Slaley, Hexham, Northumberland
NE47 0AD
☎ Hexham (01434) 673686
*Modern bungalow in centre of village
with outstanding view. All amenities
including snooker table. Ideal
walking/touring/golfing base.*
1 self-contained unit; sleeping max 4

Price per week:	£min	£max
Low season	180.00	200.00
High season	260.00	320.00

🗝📺⊙🔥MW🎞📺🔦🍴📻
P❄️✂️SP🕐

Lawn Cottage

🔑 APPROVED

Slaley, Hexham
Contact: Mrs P Wilson, Lawn House,
Slaley, Hexham, Northumberland
NE47 0AS
☎ Hexham (01434) 673388
*Tastefully modernised 18th C
Northumbrian Bastle cottage in a quiet
setting. Within easy reach of
Blanchland, Hadrian's Wall and
Beamish Museum.*
1 self-contained unit; sleeping max 4

Price per week:	£min	£max
Low season	140.00	140.00
High season	140.00	140.00

🗝12M📺⊙🔥📺🔦🍴📻P✂️SP
🏠

TOW LAW

Durham
Map ref 5B2

Old industrial town set on a hilltop 8 miles north-west of Bishop Auckland.

Butsfield Abbey Farm

🔑🔑🔑 APPROVED

Satley, Tow Law, Bishop Auckland, County Durham DL13 4JD
☎ Bishop Auckland (01388) 730509
Contact: T&J Proctor
210-acre mixed farm. Situated 2.5 miles from A68 in peaceful countryside. Central for Hexham, Durham and Newcastle. Farm signposted from main A68. Horse and pony trekking available.
1 self-contained unit; sleeping 2–4

Price per week:	£min	£max
Low season	140.00	150.00
High season	160.00	170.00

🛇🍴📶♿☀🗄🍳📺🖥🧺 SP 🏠

WARKWORTH

Northumberland
Map ref 5C1

A pretty village overlooked by its medieval castle. A 14th C fortified bridge across the wooded Coquet gives a superb view of 18th C terraces climbing to the castle. Upstream is a curious 14th C Hermitage and in the market square is the Norman church of St Lawrence.

Warkworth Station Cottage

🔑🔑🔑 COMMENDED

2 Station Cottages, Warkworth, Morpeth
Contact: Mr B T Arthur, Warkworth Station Cottage, The Old Station House, Warkworth, Morpeth, Northumberland NE65 0YH
☎ Alnwick (01665) 712532
Victorian, stone-built station master's cottage with garage and well-maintained, secluded garden. Situated in the rural outskirts of Warkworth.
1 self-contained unit; sleeping 5

Price per week:	£min	£max
Low season	130.00	
High season		275.00

🛇Ⓜ🍴📶♿☀📺🧺📷♿P✿🚭 SP

WEARHEAD

Durham
Map ref 5B2

Little Allercleugh 🏔

🔑🔑🔑🔑🔑 HIGHLY COMMENDED

Wearhead, Bishop Auckland, County Durham
Contact: Mr J H Rowe, Phillippa Ross & Co, 1G Castle Gardens, Stanhope, County Durham DL13 2FJ
☎ Bishop Auckland (01388) 526111
Fax (01388) 526333
Cosy, well-equipped 2-bedroomed cottage, surrounded by sheep farm. High in the North Pennines Area of Outstanding Natural Beauty.
1 self-contained unit; sleeping max 4

Price per week:	£min	£max
Low season	205.00	245.00
High season	235.00	340.00

🛇🍴📶♿☀🗄MW📺🧺📷♿P✿🚭 SP

WEST WOODBURN

Northumberland
Map ref 5B2

Small hamlet on the River Rede in rolling moorland country.

The Hollow 🏔

🔑🔑🔑🔑 COMMENDED

East Chesterhope, West Woodburn, Hexham
Contact: Mrs Marlene Robson, Wittonstone, Longwitton, Morpeth, Northumberland NE61 4JQ
☎ Morpeth (01670) 772246

Comfortable 19th C 2-bedroomed cottage in peaceful unspoilt wooded valley on the edge of the National Park. 15 miles north of Corbridge, quarter of a mile from A68, 1 mile south-west of West Woodburn village.
1 self-contained unit; sleeping 4

Price per week:	£min	£max
Low season	130.00	
High season		280.00

Open March–November

🛇🍴📶♿☀🗄🍳📺🧺📷♿P♿🚿✿ SP

WOLSINGHAM

Durham
Map ref 5B2

Gateway to the moors of Upper Weardale, small town set at the confluence of the Wear and Waskerley Beck. The moors abound in old lead-workings and quarries; on Waskerley Beck, Tunstall Reservoir is the haunt of bird-watchers. Well placed for exploring the fells and dales.

7 Melbourne Place

🔑🔑 COMMENDED

Wolsingham, Bishop Auckland, County Durham
Contact: Mrs M Gardiner, 3 Melbourne Place, Wolsingham, Bishop Auckland, County Durham DL13 3EQ
☎ Bishop Auckland (01388) 527538
Cosy, 2-bedroomed terraced cottage, with open fire, overlooking small village green in old part of Wolsingham. Excellent walking and touring centre.
1 self-contained unit; sleeping max 4

Price per week:	£min	£max
Low season	120.00	
High season		198.00

🛇Ⓜ🍴📶♿☀🗄MW📺🧺📷♿P✿🚿

Whitfield House Cottage

🔑🔑🔑 APPROVED

23 Front Street, Wolsingham, Bishop Auckland, County Durham
Contact: Mrs M E Shepheard, 25 Front Street, Wolsingham, Bishop Auckland, County Durham DL13 3DF
☎ Weardale (01388) 527466
Spacious accommodation in part of an attractive Queen Anne period house near the centre of this small former market town, which has a pleasant recreation park and indoor swimming pool.
1 self-contained unit; sleeping 7

Price per week:	£min	£max
Low season	175.00	230.00
High season	230.00	330.00

🛇🍴📶♿🗄📺🧺📷📷♿P♿ SP 🏠

National gradings and classifications were correct at the time of going to press but are subject to change. Please check at the time of booking.

You are advised to confirm your booking in writing.

WOOLER

Northumberland
Map ref 5B1

Old grey-stone town, market-place for foresters and hill farmers, set at the edge of the north-east Cheviots. This makes a good base for excursions to Northumberland's loveliest coastline, or for angling and walking in the Borderlands.

Byram House

APPROVED

High Humbleton, Wooler NE71 6SU
☎ (01668) 281647
Contact: Mrs C Easton
Fully self-contained granny flat with own entrance. Beautiful views. Straight out of door into the hills.
1 self-contained unit; sleeping 2

Price per week:	£min	£max
High season	120.00	120.00

Open March–November

Castle Hill Cottage

COMMENDED

West Lilburn, Wooler
Contact: Lord A Hill, Lilburn Cottage, West Lilburn, Alnwick, Northumberland NE66 4PJ
☎ Wooler (01668) 217234
Fax (01668) 281113
Comfortable semi-detached cottage in spectacular rural countryside, 4 miles south of Wooler. Fine views, easy access to coast and hills. 3 bedrooms, 2 bathrooms, garden.
1 self-contained unit; sleeping 5

Price per week:	£min	£max
Low season	235.00	282.00
High season	282.00	305.00

COUNTRY CODE

Always follow the Country Code

Enjoy the countryside and respect its life and work Guard against all risk of fire Fasten all gates Keep your dogs under close control Keep to public paths across farmland Use gates and stiles to cross fences, hedges and walls Leave livestock, crops and machinery alone Take your litter home

Help to keep all water clean

Protect wildlife, plants and trees

Take special care on country roads

Make no unnecessary noise

USE YOUR *i*'s

There are more than 550 Tourist Information Centres throughout England offering friendly help with accommodation and holiday ideas as well as suggestions of places to visit and things to do. There may well be a centre in your home town which can help you before you set out. You'll find the address of your nearest Tourist Information Centre in your local Phone Book.

AT-A-GLANCE SYMBOLS

Symbols at the end of each accommodation entry give useful information about services and facilities. A key to symbols can be found inside the back cover flap.

Keep this open for easy reference.

CHECK THE MAPS

The colour maps at the back of this guide show all the cities, towns and villages for which you will find accommodation entries.

Refer to the town index to find the page on which it is listed.

NORTH WEST

The legacy of the Industrial Revolution can be seen in the North West's fine Victorian architecture, magnificent mill buildings and miles of canals - once used for transportation but today, navigated for pleasure.

Manchester and Liverpool are vibrant centres of popular and 'high' culture while stylish Lytham St Anne's, Southport or glittering Blackpool are among Britain's most famous coastal resorts.

Explore elegant Chester, the historic city of Lancaster or, in total contrast, the pretty villages of the Wirral and the unspoilt border country of Cheshire. From birdlife to nightlife, markets to music festivals, the North West has it all.

FOR MORE INFORMATION CONTACT:
North West Tourist Board
Swan House, Swan Meadow Road,
Wigan Pier, Wigan WN3 5BB
Tel: (01942) 821222 **Fax:** (01942) 820002

Where to Go in the North West -
see pages 80-83
Where to Stay in the North West -
see pages 84-88

NORTH WEST

Where to Go and What to See

You will find hundreds of interesting places to visit during your stay in the North West, just some of which are listed in these pages. The number against each name will help you locate it on the map (page 83). Contact any Tourist Information Centre in the region for more ideas on days out in the North West.

1 Frontierland Western Theme Park
Marine Road, Morecambe,
Lancashire LA4 4DG
Tel: (01524) 410024
Over 40 thrill rides and attractions including the Texas Tornado, the Polo Tower Perculator and Stampede Roller Coaster.

2 Lancaster Castle
Shire Hall, Castle Parade,
Lancaster, Lancashire
Tel: (01524) 64998
Collection of coats of arms, dungeons, crown court, Jane Scott's chair. Grand Jury Room. External tour of castle walls.

3 Blackpool Pleasure Beach
Ocean Boulevard,
Blackpool, Lancashire FY4 1EZ
Tel: (01253) 341033
Amusement park with rides including Space Invader, Big Dipper and Revolution. Funshineland for children. Summer season ice show, Mystique illusion show in Horseshoe Bar.

4 Blackpool Sea Life Centre
The Promenade,
Blackpool,
Lancashire FY1 5AA
Tel: (01253) 22445
Tropical sharks up to 8 feet in length housed in a 100,000 gallon display with underwater walk-through.

5 Blackpool Tower
Promenade,
Blackpool,
Lancashire FY1 4BJ
Tel: (01253) 22242
Tower Ballroom, Bug World, Jungle Jim's playground. Out of this World. Children's entertainment in Hornpipe Galley, Undersea World. Tower Circus, Laser fantasy and Lift Ride.

6 Ribchester Museum of Childhood
Church Street,
Ribchester,
Lancashire PR3 3YE
Tel: (01254) 878520

Large 10-room building contaning childhood toys, dolls and dolls' houses, 20-piece model fairground, Tom Thumb replica, collectors' toy shop.

7 Pleasureland Amusement Park
Marine Drive,
The Fun Coast,
Southport,
Merseyside PR8 1RX
Tel: (01704) 532717
Traditional amusement park with wide variety of thrilling and family rides.

8 Astley Hall
Astley Park,
Chorley,
Lancashire PR7 1NP
Tel: (01257) 262166
Hall dates from 1580 with subsequent additions. Unique collection of furniture including a fine Elizabethan bed and the famous shovel board table in the Long Gallery.

9 Camelot Theme Park and Rare Breeds Farm

Park Hall Road, Charnock Richard,
Lancashire PR7 5LP
Tel: (01257) 453044
Magical kingdom offering over 100 thrilling rides, attractions and medieval entertainment.

10 Wildfowl and Wetland Centre

Martin Mere, Burscough,
Lancashire L40 0TA
Tel: (01704) 895181
45 acres of gardens with over 1600 ducks geese and swans of 120 different kinds. Two flocks of flamingos. 300-acre wild area with 20-acre lake.

11 East Lancashire Railway

Bolton Street Station,
Bury, Lancashire BL9 0EY
Tel: (0161) 764 7790
Eight-mile-long preserved railway operated principally by steam traction, transport museum nearby.

12 Rufford Old Hall

Rufford, Ormskirk,
Lancashire L40 1SG
Tel: (01704) 821254
Fine 15thC building with a magnificent Great Hall, particularly noted for its immense moveable screen.

13 Wigan Pier

Wallgate, Wigan,
Lancashire WN3 4EU
Tel: (01942) 323666
The Way We Were – life in Wigan in 1900. World's largest steam mill engine, cotton machinery hall, shops, picnic gardens, cafeteria, waterbuses and Victorian classroom.

14 Granada Studios Tour

Water Street, Manchester,
Greater Manchester M60 9EA
Tel: (0161) 832 9090
Major television theme park providing an insight into the fascinating world behind the TV screen. Visit three of the most famous streets in Britain.

15 Museum of Science and Industry in Manchester

Liverpool Road, Castlefield,
Manchester,
Greater Manchester M3 4JP
Tel: (0161) 832 2244
The Museum of Science and Industry in Manchester based in the world's oldest passenger railway station, with 15 galleries that amaze, amuse and entertain.

16 Knowsley Safari Park

Prescot,
Merseyside L34 4AN
Tel: (0151) 430 9009

Five-mile drive through game reserves, set in 400 acres of parkland containing lions, tigers, elephants, rhinos, etc. Large picnic areas and children's amusement park.

17 Albert Dock

The Colonnades,
Albert Dock,
Liverpool, L3 4AA
Tel: (0151) 708 8854
Britain's largest Grade I listed historic building. Restored 4-sided dock, including shops, bars, restaurants, entertainment, marina and maritime museum.

18 Croxteth Hall and Country Park

Off Muirhead Avenue East,
Liverpool,
Merseyside L12 0HB
Tel: (0151) 228 5311
500 acre country park and hall with displays, furnished rooms and walled garden. Farm with rare breeds, miniature railway, gift shop, picnic area, riding centre, adventure playground.

19 Tate Gallery Liverpool

Albert Dock, Liverpool L3 4BB
Tel: (0151) 709 3223
The national collection of modern art in the North of England.

20 Dunham Massey Hall and Park

Altrincham, Cheshire WA14 4SJ
Tel: (0161) 941 1025
Historic house, garden and park with restaurant and shop.

21 Lyme Park

Disley, Cheshire SK12 2NX
Tel: (01663) 762023
Country estate within 1377 acres of moorland, woodland and park. Magnificent house with 17 acres of historic gardens.

22 Quarry Bank Mill

Styal, Cheshire SK9 4LA
Tel: (01625) 527468
Georgian water-powered cotton-spinning mill. Four floors of displays and demonstrations, 284 acres of parkland.

23 Norton Priory Museum and Gardens

Tudor Road, Runcorn,
Cheshire WA7 1SX
Tel: (01928) 569895
Excavated Augustinian priory, remains of church, cloister and chapter house. Later site of Tudor mansion and Georgian house. Walled garden and woodland.

24 Boat Museum

Dock Yard Road, Ellesmere Port,
Cheshire L65 4FW
Tel: (0151) 355 5017
Over 50 historic craft, largest floating collection in the world with restored buildings, traditional cottages, workshops, steam engines, boat trips, shop and cafe.

25 Arley Hall and Gardens

Arley, Northwich,
Cheshire CW9 6NA
Tel: (01565) 777353
Early Victorian building set in 12 acres of magnificent gardens. 15thC Tythe barn. Unique collection of water colours of the area.

26 Macclesfield Silk Museum

The Heritage Centre,
Roe Street, Macclesfield,
Cheshire SK11 6UT
Tel: (01625) 613210
Information centre, town history exhibition, silk museum, Sunday school, history exhibition, guided trails.

27 Jodrell Bank Science Centre and Arboretum

Lower Withington,
Macclesfield, Cheshire SK11 9DL
Tel: (01477) 571339
Exhibition and interactive exhibits on astronomy, space, satellites, energy and the environment. Planetarium and the world-famous Lovell telescope and 35 acre arboretum.

28 Cheshire Oaks Designer Outlet Village

Ellesmere Port,
The Wirral L65 9JJ
Over 60 individual stores selling famous branded goods.

29 Chester Zoo

Upton-by-Chester,
Chester, Cheshire CH2 1LH
Tel: (01244) 380280
Penguin pool with underwater views, tropical house, spectacular displays of spring and summer bedding plants. Chimpanzee house and new monorail.

FIND OUT MORE

Further information about holidays and attractions in the North West is available from:
North West Tourist Board,
Swan House,
Swan Meadow Road,
Wigan Pier,
Wigan WN3 5BB.
Tel: (01942) 821222

These publications are available free from the North West Tourist Board:

■ **North West Welcome Guide**
■ **Discover England's North West**
■ **Attraction Map**
■ **Group Travel Guide**
■ **Bed & Breakfast Map**
■ **Caravan and Camping Parks Guide**

CUMBRIA

0   20 Miles

0   30 Kms

NORTH YORKSHIRE

1 Morecambe
2 Lancaster

Fleetwood

LANCASHIRE

Clitheroe

Blackpool **3 4**
5

Ribchester

Nelson

6

Burnley

Lytham St Annes

Preston

Blackburn

Accrington

WEST YORKSHIRE

Darwen

Rawtenstall

Southport

7 Burscough

9 8 Chorley
Charnock
Richard

Ramsbottom

Ormskirk **12**

10

Bolton

Bury **11**

Rochdale

Formby

Skelmersdale

13
Wigan

GREATER MANCHESTER

Oldham

Kirkby

Salford

MERSEYSIDE

St Helens

14 15 Manchester

New Brighton

17

16 Prescot

Stockport

Hoylake

18 19 Huyton

Warrington

Altrincham

Cheadle

Birkenhead

Liverpool

20

21 Disley

DERBY-SHIRE

Styal **22**

23 Runcorn

Arley

Knutsford

Wilmslow

Ellesmere Port

24 28

25

Alderley Edge

26 Macclesfield

Northwich

29 Chester

Winsford

27 Lower Withington

WALES

CHESHIRE

Congleton

Sandbach

Crewe

Alsager

Nantwich

Kidsgrove

STAFFORDSHIRE

WHERE TO STAY (NORTH WEST)

Accommodation entries in this region are listed in alphabetical order of place name, and then in alphabetical order of establishment. A contact address is given where it differs from the address of the establishment.

Map references refer to the colour location maps at the back of this guide.

Prices shown are weekly per unit.

At-a-glance symbols at the end of each accommodation entry give useful information about services and facilities. A key to symbols can be found inside the back cover flap. Keep this open for easy reference.

ALTHAM

Lancashire
Map ref 4A1

The Courtyard

COMMENDED

Moorside House, Burnley Road, Altham, Accrington
Contact: Mrs Elizabeth Parkinson, Red Rose Cottages, 16 Shawbridge Street, Clitheroe, Lancashire BB7 1LY
☎ Clitheroe (01200) 427310
Fax (01200) 428929
First floor apartment with chair lift access in Grade II listed country house. Lovely views. Lounge, twin bedroom, bathroom with shower, fitted kitchen. Private walled garden.
1 self-contained unit; sleeping max 2

Price per week:	£min	£max
Low season	125.00	160.00
High season	180.00	200.00

Cards accepted: Access, Visa

BAY HORSE

Lancashire
Map ref 4A1

Wyresdale and Bowland Lodges

COMMENDED

Wyreside Lakes Fishery, Sunnyside Farmhouse, Bay Horse, Lancaster
Contact: Duchy of Lancaster, Forton, Preston PR3 0AD
☎ Forton (01524) 791494
Two pine lodges overlooking fish lakes and with views to Forest of Bowland hills. Well equipped to sleep four and

six. Verandahs, lawned area for recreation. Laundry room and payphone on site.
2 self-contained units; sleeping 4–6

Price per week:	£min	£max
Low season	160.00	260.00
High season	260.00	340.00

Cards accepted: Access, Visa

BOSLEY

Cheshire
Map ref 4B2

The Old Byre

COMMENDED

Pye Ash Farm, Leek Road, Bosley, Macclesfield
Contact: Mrs D Gilman, Pedley House Farm, Pedley Lane, Congleton, Cheshire CW12 3QD
☎ Congleton (01260) 273650

110-acre mixed farm. Old beamed shippon in beautiful walking area, edge of Peak District and moorlands, 15 miles from Alton Towers. Heating and linen included.
Wheelchair access category 3
2 self-contained units; sleeping 4–6

Price per week:	£min	£max
Low season	150.00	250.00
High season	350.00	400.00

BURY

Greater Manchester
Map ref 4B1

Famous for its black puddings, huge open market and East Lancashire Steam Railway. Birthplace of Sir Robert Peel, founder of the police force and Prime Minister. Bury Art Gallery has an important collection of Turner and Constable paintings.
Tourist Information Centre ☎ (0161) 705 5111

Harcles Hill Farm

COMMENDED

Holcombe, Bury, Lancashire BL8 4NT
☎ Ramsbottom (01706) 823467
Contact: Mrs J Hilditch
10-acre livestock & horses farm. Open plan studio flat on working hill farm. Featuring stone mullion windows, well-equipped kitchen area, double bed and bed settee. Separate shower room with basin and toilet. 10 minutes from M66.
1 self-contained unit; sleeping 2–4

Price per week:	£min	£max
Low season	126.00	175.00
High season	126.00	210.00

All accommodation in this guide has been graded, or is awaiting a grading, by a trained Tourist Board inspector.

CHESTER

Cheshire
Map ref 4A2

Roman and medieval walled city rich in treasures. Black and white buildings are a hallmark, including "The Rows" - two-tier shopping galleries. The racecourse is the only one in the country where horses race anti-clockwise. 900-year-old cathedral, zoo.
Tourist Information Centre ☎ (01244) 317962 or 351609 or 322220

Little Mayfield

APPROVED

Mayfield House, Warrington Road, Hoole Village, Chester CH2 4EX
☎ Mickle Trafford (01244) 300231
Contact: Mr M J Cullen
Self-contained wing of William IV house set in 3 acres of garden with hard tennis court. Spacious rooms. 7 minutes from Chester city centre.
1 self-contained unit; sleeping max 6

Price per week:	£min	£max
Low season	135.00	135.00
High season	195.00	195.00

Open April–December

Tattersall Gate

COMMENDED

1 & 3 Nuns Road, Chester
Contact: Mrs R A Randle, The Thatched Cottage, School Lane, Aldford, Chester CH3 6HY
☎ Chester (01244) 620377
Charming Grade II listed properties, within 4 minutes' walk of Chester city centre, some with spectacular views. Garden, parking.
3 self-contained units; sleeping 4–8

Price per week:	£min	£max
Low season	250.00	375.00
High season	375.00	375.00

Cards accepted: Access, Visa

Woodfield

COMMENDED

Birchenfields Farm, Sealand Road, Chester CH1 6BS
☎ (01244) 880560
Fax (01244) 880560
Contact: Mrs K Cottle
300-acre dairy farm. Three-bedroomed bungalow, sleeping up to 8 plus cot, in rural setting 2.5 miles from Chester city centre. Private parking. Pets welcome.

1 self-contained unit; sleeping max 8

Price per week:	£min	£max
Low season	195.00	
High season		350.00

CHIPPING

Lancashire
Map ref 4A1

Delightful small village with 3 pubs, teashop, ancient church and ghost.

Fell View

HIGHLY COMMENDED

Outlane Head Cottage, Chipping, Preston
Contact: Mrs Elizabeth Parkinson, Red Rose Cottages, 16 Shawbridge Street, Clitheroe, Lancashire BB7 1LY
☎ Clitheroe (01200) 427310
Fax (01200) 428929
First floor apartment with wonderful views over Forest of Bowland fells. Living room with woodburning stove, fitted kitchen, bathroom, twin bedroom, parking, garden area, electric heating all rooms.
1 self-contained unit; sleeping 2

Price per week:	£min	£max
Low season	125.00	155.00
High season	180.00	200.00

Cards accepted: Access, Visa

Rakefoot Barn

HIGHLY COMMENDED

Rakefoot Farm, Chaigley, Clitheroe BB7 3LY
☎ (01995) 61332 & Mobile (0589) 279063
Contact: Mrs P M Gifford
100-acre dairy farm. Recently converted traditional stone barn. A warm welcome awaits you on working farm in beautiful Forest of Bowland. 3 miles from Chipping, 12 miles M6 junctions 31/32. Panoramic views. Units can be linked to sleep 16. Home-cooked meals can be provided. B & B also available in farmhouse.
4 self-contained units; sleeping 2–16

Price per week:	£min	£max
Low season	70.00	
High season		360.00

Please mention this guide when making your booking.

CLITHEROE

Lancashire
Map ref 4A1

Ancient market town with an 800-year-old castle keep and a wide range of award-winning shops. Good base for touring Ribble Valley, Trough of Bowland and Pennine moorland. Country market on Tuesdays and Saturdays.
Tourist Information Centre ☎ (01200) 25566

Dairy Cottage

HIGHLY COMMENDED

23 De Lacy Street, Clitheroe
Contact: Mrs Elizabeth Parkinson, Red Rose Cottages, 16 Shawbridge Street, Clitheroe, Lancashire BB7 1LY
☎ Clitheroe (01200) 427310
Fax (01200) 428929
Modern cottage-style property close to historic town centre. Gas central heating, fitted kitchen, lounge, 2 bedrooms, modern bathroom. Garden with furniture. Open aspect to rear. Off-road parking for 2 cars.
1 self-contained unit; sleeping max 4

Price per week:	£min	£max
Low season	175.00	210.00
High season	250.00	275.00

Cards accepted: Access, Visa

Ingledene

COMMENDED

Rimington Lane, Rimington, Clitheroe
Contact: Mrs B L Lund, Fernlea, Rimington, Clitheroe, Lancashire BB7 4DS
☎ Gisburn (01200) 445640
Super views of fields and hills from all windows. Nice walks, tennis courts, playground, pub serving food, all 2 minutes away.
1 self-contained unit; sleeping max 6

Price per week:	£min	£max
Low season	80.00	100.00
High season	100.00	140.00

Information on accommodation listed in this guide has been supplied by the proprietors. As changes may occur you are advised to check details at the time of booking.

CROSTON

Lancashire
Map ref 4A1

Cockfight Barn

🗝🗝🗝🗝 HIGHLY COMMENDED

Manor House Farm, Carr Lane,
Croston, Preston
Contact: Mrs Elizabeth Parkinson,
Red Rose Cottages, 16 Shawbridge
Street, Clitheroe, Lancashire
BB7 1LY
☎ Clitheroe (01200) 427310
Fax (01200) 428929
*250-year-old barn conversion, in a
conservation area in attractive village. 3
bedrooms, one with en-suite bathroom.
Spacious living area with views over
countryside. Fitted kitchen, orchard and
garden for guests' use.*
1 self-contained unit; sleeping max 6

Price per week:	£min	£max
Low season	260.00	300.00
High season	350.00	400.00

Cards accepted: Access, Visa

🐎🗗🏧☉🖵MW 📺🖬🎦🛢📞🖼🚗
P🌼 SP

GARSTANG

Lancashire
Map ref 4A2

Picturesque country market town.
The gateway to the fells, it stands on
the Lancaster Canal and is a popular
cruising centre. Close by are the
remains of Greenhalgh Castle (no
public access) and the Bleasdale
Circle. Discovery Centre shows
history of Over Wyre and Bowland
fringe areas.
*Tourist Information Centre ☎ (01995)
602125*

Cleveley Mill Flat

Forton, Garstang, Preston PR3 1BY
☎ Forton (01524) 792050
Contact: Mrs P Roberts
*Spacious, modern, first-floor,
self-contained flat in converted
watermill. Idyllic lakeside setting in
beautiful gardens with panoramic views
of Bowland Fells. Fishing.*
1 self-contained unit; sleeping max 4

Price per week:	£min	£max
Low season	160.00	200.00
High season	180.00	220.00

M🗗🏧☉🖵🎦📺🖬🛢📞🖼PU♪
🌼🖼 SP 🞖

A key to symbols can be
found inside the back
cover flap.

GREENFIELD

Greater Manchester
Map ref 4B1

Clifton Cottage

🗝🗝🗝🗝 HIGHLY COMMENDED

111 Chew Valley Road, Greenfield,
Oldham
Contact: Mrs J Wood, 113 Chew
Valley Road, Greenfield, Oldham
OL3 7JJ
☎ Saddleworth (01457) 872098 &
875601
Fax (01457) 870760
*Fully modernised country terraced
cottage. One double and 1 single
bedroom plus double bed-settee in
lounge. Heating, electricity, linen
included.*
1 self-contained unit

Price per week:	£min	£max
Low season	150.00	180.00
High season	170.00	210.00

🐎🗗🏧☉🖵MW 🎦📺🛢📞🖼🚗
🚗P🌼🞖 SP

KETTLESHULME

Greater Manchester
Map ref 4B2

New Hey Cottage

Kishfield Lane, Kettleshulme,
Stockport, Cheshire SK12 7RB
☎ Whaley Bridge (01663) 734354
Contact: Ms Jemima Lawrence
*Traditionally furnished stone-built
cottage in secluded rural position,
surrounded by fields, hills, woods and
stream. Half a mile from village.*
1 self-contained unit; sleeping max 2

Price per week:	£min	£max
Low season	170.00	180.00
High season	190.00	200.00

🐎M🏧☉🖵🎦📺🛢📞🖼🚗P
🞖🞖 SP

The National Grading and
Classification Scheme is
explained in full at the
back of this guide.

Information on
accommodation listed in this
guide has been supplied by the
proprietors. As changes may
occur you are advised to check
details at the time of booking.

KNUTSFORD

Cheshire
Map ref 4A2

Delightful town with many buildings
of architectural and historic interest.
The setting of Elizabeth Gaskell's
"Cranford". Annual May Day
celebration and decorative "sanding"
of the pavements are unique to the
town. Popular Heritage Centre.
*Tourist Information Centre ☎ (01565)
632611 or 632210*

Danebury Gardens Serviced Apartments

🗝🗝🗝🗝 HIGHLY COMMENDED

8 Tabley Road, Knutsford
Contact: Mr Stephen West,
Longview Hotel and Restaurant,
Manchester Road, Knutsford,
Cheshire WA16 0LX
☎ Knutsford (01565) 632119
Fax (01565) 652402
*Properties of character. Tastefully
converted with care to provide fully
serviced apartments of quality, all with
modern amenities.*
5 self-contained units; sleeping 2–6

Price per week:	£min	£max
Low season	325.00	450.00
High season	350.00	475.00

Cards accepted: Access, Visa, Amex

🐎M🏧🗗🏧☉🖵MW 🎦📺🛢📞
🖼📞🚗P🌼

MACCLESFIELD

Cheshire
Map ref 4B2

Cobbled streets and quaint old
buildings stand side by side with
modern shops and three markets.
Centuries of association with the
silk industry; museums feature
working exhibits and social history.
Stunning views of the Peak District
National Park.
*Tourist Information Centre ☎ (01625)
504114*

Mill House Farm Cottage

🗝🗝🗝🗝 COMMENDED

Bosley, Macclesfield
Contact: Mrs L Whittaker, Mill
House Farm, Bosley, Macclesfield,
Cheshire SK11 0NZ
☎ Rushton Spencer (01260)
226265
*130-acre dairy farm. Cottage on
working farm in east Cheshire, on the
border of the Peak District.*

1 self-contained unit; sleeping max 6

Price per week:	£min	£max
Low season	125.00	150.00
High season	150.00	195.00

🖕Ⓜ◎▦.☉🛏MW📭📺🗑🏧🎐
🖼🏕P🖊❄️SP🏵️Ⓣ

MANCHESTER AIRPORT

See under Knutsford, Stockport

NANTWICH

Cheshire
Map ref 4A2

Old market town on the River
Weaver made prosperous in Roman
times by salt springs. Fire destroyed
the town in 1583 and many buildings
were rebuilt in Elizabethan style.
Churche's Mansion (open to the
public) survived the fire.
Tourist Information Centre ☎ *(01270)
610983 or 610880*

Fields Farm

🔑🔑🔑 APPROVED
Off Queens Drive, Edleston,
Nantwich CW5 5JL
☎ (01270) 625769 & 611391
Fax (01270) 625769
Contact: Mr D W Heys
*57-acre livestock farm. Farm building
conversion on working farm. 5 minutes'
walk historic and architectural
Nantwich. Horse-riding and fishing on
premises. No smoking, no dogs. Well
situated for North Wales, Shropshire,
Peak District and historic Cheshire.*
2 self-contained units; sleeping 6

Price per week:	£min	£max
Low season	120.00	180.00
High season	180.00	260.00

🖕◎💧.☉🛏MW📺🗑🏧🎐🖼
🖼P🖖🖊❄️🗡️SP

NESTON

Cheshire
Map ref 4A2

Tumblehome

🔑🔑🔑 HIGHLY COMMENDED
Neston
☎ (0151) 336 1597
Fax (0151) 336 1597
Contact: Mrs J Kennedy
*Old miner's cottage, extensively
restored and modernised to high
standards. Sleeps 4 non-smokers in 2
pine bedrooms. Sorry, no pets.*
1 self-contained unit; sleeping 4

Price per week:	£min	£max
Low season	210.00	265.00
High season	280.00	280.00

🖕5💧▦.🛏MW📺🗑🏧🎐🖼❄️
🗡️SP🏕️

Scene of decisive Royalist defeat by
Cromwell in the Civil War and later
of riots in the Industrial Revolution.
Local history exhibited in Harris
Museum. Famous for its Guild and
the celebration that takes place
every 20 years.
Tourist Information Centre ☎ *(01772)
253731*

Church View Cottage 🏔

🔑🔑🔑 COMMENDED
2 Church View, Water Street,
Brindle, Chorley
Contact: Mrs P E McDade,
Hollyfield, 2 Smithy Close, Brindle,
Chorley, Lancashire PR6 8NW
☎ Hoghton (01254) 852913
Fax (01254) 853400
*Cottage in excellent village location in
the heart of Lancashire countryside.
Beamed ceilings, attractive wall-lighting
and pictures, warm in winter.*
1 self-contained unit; sleeping max 4

Price per week:	£min	£max
Low season	180.00	190.00
High season	200.00	230.00

🖕◎💧.☉🛏MW📭📺🗑🏧🎐
🖼🏕️U❄️🗡️SP

The stone-built villages of
Saddleworth are peppered with old
mill buildings and possess a unique
Pennine character. The superb
scenery of Saddleworth Moor
provides an ideal backdrop for canal
trips, walking and outdoor pursuits.
Tourist Information Centre ☎ *(01457)
870336 or 874093*

The Barn Grove Farm

🔑🔑🔑 COMMENDED
Harrop Court, Diggle, Oldham
OL3 5LN
☎ (01457) 870573
Contact: Mrs V Stocker
*Semi-detached converted barn in quiet
part of Saddleworth. Superb views and
excellent walking. Non-smokers only,
please. Pets welcome.*
1 self-contained unit; sleeping max 3

Price per week:	£min	£max
Low season	110.00	130.00
High season	160.00	210.00

🖕◎▦.☉🛏MW📺🏧🎐🖼P❄️
🗡️SP

Delightful Victorian resort noted for
gardens, sandy beaches and 6
golf-courses, particularly Royal
Birkdale. Attractions include the
Atkinson Art Gallery, Southport
Railway Centre, Pleasureland and
the annual Southport Flower Show.
Excellent shopping, particularly in
Lord Street's elegant boulevard.
Tourist Information Centre ☎ *(01704)
533333*

Martin Lane Holiday Cottages

🔑🔑🔑 HIGHLY COMMENDED
Martin Lane Farmhouse, Burscough,
Ormskirk, Lancashire L40 8JH
☎ Burscough (01704) 893527
Fax (01704) 893527
Contact: Mrs Stubbs

*Self-contained cottages comfortably
furnished to a high standard and fully
equipped, yet still retaining original
features - beams, arches and boskin.
Southport, Liverpool, Preston and
Manchester are all within easy reach.*
2 self-contained units; sleeping 5–7

Price per week:	£min	£max
Low season	229.00	269.00
High season	319.00	375.00

🖕◎▦.☉🛏MW📭📺🗑🏧🎐🖼
🖖P❄️🗡️SP Ⓣ

Sandy Brook Farm

52 Wyke Cop Road, Scarisbrick,
Southport
Contact: Mrs W Core, Sandy Brook
Farm, 52 Wyke Cop Road,
Scarisbrick, Southport, Merseyside
PR8 5LR
☎ Scarisbrick (01704) 880337
*27-acre arable farm. Newly converted
barn offering 5 self-catering
apartments furnished in traditional
style and offering all modern amenities.
3.5 miles from Southport in rural area
of Scarisbrick. One apartment adapted
for disabled.*
5 self-contained units; sleeping 4–6

Price per week:	£min	£max
Low season	100.00	130.00
High season	220.00	250.00

🖕Ⓜ◎▦.☉🛏📺🗑🏧🎐🖼🖖P
🗡️SP

SOUTHPORT

Continued

Stutelea Apart Hotel

COMMENDED

Alexandra Road, Southport
PR9 0NB
☎ (01704) 544220
Fax (01704) 500232
Contact: Mr G Gottig
*Guests have the use of main hotel's
facilities, including bars and restaurant,
lounge, library, jacuzzi, gymnasium,
steam room, solarium and sauna,
heated swimming pool and games
room. Garden.*
7 self-contained units; sleeping 1–6

Price per week:	£min	£max
Low season	120.00	300.00
High season	120.00	450.00

Cards accepted: Access, Visa, Diners,
Amex, Switch/Delta

STOCKPORT

Greater Manchester
Map ref 4B2

Once an important cotton-spinning
and manufacturing centre, Stockport
has an impressive railway viaduct, a
shopping precinct built over the
River Mersey and a new leisure
complex. Lyme Hall and Vernon
Park Museum nearby.
Tourist Information Centre ☎ *(0161)*
474 3320 or 474 3321

Lake View

COMMENDED

Ernocroft Farm, Marple Bridge,
Stockport, Cheshire
Contact: Mrs M Sidebottom, Shire
Cottage, Benches Lane, Chisworth,
Hyde, Cheshire SK14 6RU
☎ Glossop (01457) 866536
*180-acre mixed farm. Well-equipped
bungalow with magnificent views, in
peaceful setting overlooking Etherow
Country Park near Peak District. Cot
available. Restaurant 5 minutes away.*
1 self-contained unit; sleeping max 6

Price per week:	£min	£max
Low season	150.00	220.00
High season	250.00	300.00

WIRRAL

Merseyside

See under Neston

YORKSHIRE

Yorkshire encompass an area of vastly differing landscapes and moods. The wildness of the Yorkshire Moors and 'Brontë Country' soften into the mellow valleys of the Yorkshire Dales, contrasted by the coastline of towering cliffs, lively resorts and pleasant fishing ports.

Many of the grandest gardens in Britain are here. It's also where you can taste fish and chips at their best, sample ale straight from the brewery or go down a coalmine!

Don't miss historic York with its world-famous Minster. You'll also find some of the best museums and industrial heritage sites in England.

FOR MORE INFORMATION CONTACT:
Yorkshire Tourist Board
312 Tadcaster Road, York YO2 2HF
Tel: (01904) 707961 or 707070 (24 hour brochure line)
Fax: (01904) 701414

Where to Go in Yorkshire - see pages 90-93
Where to Stay in Yorkshire - see pages 94-112

YORKSHIRE

Where to Go and What to See

You will find hundreds of interesting places to visit during your stay in Yorkshire, just some of which are listed in these pages. The number against each name will help you locate it on the map (page 93). Contact any Tourist Information Centre in the region for more ideas on days out in Yorkshire.

1 Sea Life Centre
Scalby Mills,
Scarborough,
North Yorkshire YO12 6RP
Tel: (01723) 376125
At the Sea Life Centre you have the opportunity to meet creatures that live in and around the oceans of the British Isles, ranging from starfish and crabs to rays and seals.

2 North Yorkshire Moors Railway
Pickering Station,
Pickering,
North Yorkshire YO18 7AJ
Tel: (01751) 472508
Operates the route between Grosmont and Pickering, through some of the most magnificent scenery of the North York Moors National Park.

3 Flamingo Land Theme Park, Zoo and Holiday Village
Kirby Misperton,
North Yorkshire YO17 0UX
Tel: (01653) 668287
One price family funpark with over 100 attractions, nine shows and Europe's largest privately owned zoo. Large lake, children's and thrill rides.

4 Fountains Abbey and Studley Royal
Ripon,
North Yorkshire HG4 3DZ
Tel: (01765) 608888
Largest monastic ruin in Britain, founded by Cistercian monks in 1132. Landscaped garden laid out 1720-40 with lake, formal watergarden, temples and deer park.

5 Lightwater Valley Theme Park
North Stainley, Ripon,
North Yorkshire HG4 3HT
Tel: (01765) 635321
175 acres of country park featuring range of white-knuckle rides (including the world's biggest rollercoaster), skill testing activities, leisurely pursuits, live entertainment.

6 Castle Howard
Malton,
North Yorkshire YO6 7DA
Tel: (01653) 648444
Set in 1,000 acres of magnificent parkland with nature walks, scenic lake and stunning rose gardens. Attractions include important furniture and works of art.

7 Sewerby Hall and Gardens
Sewerby, Bridlington,
East Riding of Yorkshire
YO15 1EA
Tel: (01262) 673769
Children's zoo, aviary, old English walled garden, bowls, putting, golf, children's corner, museum, art gallery, Amy Johnson collection, novel train from park to North Beach.

8 Yorkshire Dales Falconry & Conservation Centre
Crows Nest, Giggleswick,
North Yorkshire LA2 8AS
Tel: (01729) 825164
Falconry centre with many species

of birds of prey from around the world including vultures, eagles, hawks, falcons and owls. Free flying displays, lecture room and aviaries.

9 Ripley Castle
Ripley,
North Yorkshire HG3 3AY
Tel: (01423) 770152
Ingilby family home since 1345, fine armour, furniture, chandeliers, panelling, priests hiding hole. Langley Castle in Barbara Taylor Bradford's book "Voice from the Heart".

10 Beningbrough Hall
Shipton-by-Beningbrough,
York YO6 1DD
Tel: (01904) 470666
Handsome Baroque house built 1716, nearly 100 pictures from the National Portrait Gallery. Victorian laundry, potting shed, garden, adventure playground, National Trust shop.

11 Skipton Castle
Skipton,
North Yorkshire BD23 1AQ
Tel: (01756) 792442
One of the most complete and well-preserved medieval castles in England. Beautiful Conduit Court with famous yew.

12 Archaeological Resource Centre
St Saviourgate, York YO1 2NN
Tel: (01904) 654324
Visitors can "touch the past", handling ancient finds of pottery and bone, stitching Roman sandals and picking a Viking padlock. A/V display and exploration of dig by computer.

13 Jorvik Viking Centre
Coppergate, York YO1 1NT
Tel: (01904) 643211
Visitors travel back in time in a timecar to a recreation of Viking York. They will see excavated remains of Viking houses and a display of objects found.

14 National Railway Museum
Leeman Road, York YO2 4XJ
Tel: (01904) 621261
Experience nearly 200 years of technical and social history on the railways and see the way they shaped the world.

15 York Castle Museum
The Eye of York, York YO1 1RY
Tel: (01904) 653611
England's most popular museum of everyday life including reconstructed streets and period rooms, Edwardian park, costume and jewellery, arms and armour, craft workshops.

16 York Minster
Deangate, York YO1 2JA
Tel: (01904) 624426
The largest Gothic cathedral in England. Museum of Saxon and Norman remains, chapter house and crypt. Unrivalled views from Norman tower.

17 Hornsea Freeport
Hornsea,
East Riding of Yorkshire
HU18 1UT
Tel: (01964) 534211
Brand names such as Laura Ashley and Alexon all at discount prices. Birds of prey, Butterfly World, Neptunes Kingdom and more.

18 Harewood House
Harewood, Leeds LS17 9LQ
Tel: (0113) 288 6225
18thC Carr/Adam house, Capability Brown landscape, fine Sevres and Chinese porcelain, English and Italian paintings, Chippendale furniture. Exotic bird garden.

19 National Museum of Photography, Film and Television
Pictureville, Bradford,
West Yorkshire BD1 1NQ
Tel: (01274) 727488
This free museum houses the largest cinema screen (Imax) in

Britain. Fly on a magic carpet, operate a TV camera, become a newsreader for a day.

20 Transperience
Transperience Way,
Low Moor,
Bradford,
West Yorkshire BD12 7HQ
Tel: (01274) 690909
With historic vehicle rides and state of the art interactive technology. Travel on a unique journey through the past, present and future of public transport.

21 Royal Armouries Museum
Leeds LS10 1LT
Tel: (0113) 220 1999
History in action at Britain's newest museum. The thrill of jousting tournaments and terror of battlefield recaptured. See one of the world's finest collections of arms and armour.

22 Tetley's Brewery Wharf
The Waterfront,
Leeds LS1 1QG
Tel: (0113) 242 0666
A unique new development which

brings to life the story through the ages of one of the greatest British traditions – the pub.

23 Museum of Army Transport
Beverley,
East Riding of Yorkshire
HU17 0NG
Tel: (01482) 860445
Army road, rail, sea and air exhibits excitingly displayed in two huge indoor exhibition halls, plus the last remaining Blackburn Beverly aircraft. D-Day exhibition.

24 Eureka! The Museum for Children
Discovery Road, Halifax,
West Yorkshire HX1 2NE
Tel: (01422) 330069
Eureka! is the first museum of its kind designed especially for children up to the age of 12. Wherever you go in Eureka! you can touch, listen, feel and smell, as well as look.

25 Piece Hall
Halifax, West Yorkshire HX1 1RE
Tel: (01422) 358087
Historic, colonnaded cloth hall, surrounding open-air courtyard and

comprising 40 speciality shops, art gallery, Tourist Information Centre, three weekly markets and Calderdale Kaleidoscope display.

26 National Coal Mining Museum for England
Caphouse Colliery,
New Road, Overton,
Wakefield,
West Yorkshire WF4 4RH
Tel: (01924) 848806
Exciting, award-winning museum of the Yorkshire coalfield including guided underground tour in authentic old workings, surface displays, working steam winder.

27 Yorkshire Sculpture Park
Bretton, Wakefield,
West Yorkshire WF4 4LG
Tel: (01924) 830302
Beautiful parkland containing regular exhibitions of contemporary sculpture. Permanent collection includes sculpture by Barbara Hepworth and Henry Moore.

28 National Fishing Heritage Centre
Alexandra Dock, Grimsby,
North East Lincolnshire
DN31 1UZ
Tel: (01472) 344867
Spectacular 1950's steam trawler experience. See, hear, smell and touch a series of recreated environments. Museum displays, shop, aquarium and historic fishing vessels.

29 Pleasure Island Theme Park
Kings Road, Cleethorpes,
North East Lincolnshire
DN35 0PL
Tel: (01472) 211511
The East Coast's newest outdoor theme park with great rides, slides and attractions including the Big Splash, Boomerang, Giant Wheel, Mini Mine Train, Terror Rack and Octopus rides.

Further information about holidays and attractions in Yorkshire, East Riding and Northern Lincolnshire is available from
Yorkshire Tourist Board,
312 Tadcaster Road,
York YO2 2HF.
Tel: (01904) 707961 or 707070 (24 hour brochure line)

These publications are available free from the Yorkshire Tourist Board:

■ **Main Holidays and Shortbreaks guide** - information on the region, including hotels, self-catering and caravan and camping parks

■ **Days Out in Yorkshire** (available Easter '97) - information on attractions, major events, getting around the region, etc.

■ **Bed & Breakfast Touring Map**

■ **What's On** - 3 issues per year

■ **Overseas Brochure** - French, Dutch, German

■ **'Freedom'** - caravan and camping guide

■ **Getting Around Yorkshire** - guide to public transport

WHERE TO STAY (YORKSHIRE)

Accommodation entries in this region are listed in alphabetical order of place name, and then in alphabetical order of establishment. A contact address is given where it differs from the address of the establishment.

Map references refer to the colour location maps at the back of this guide.

Prices shown are weekly per unit.

At-a-glance symbols at the end of each accommodation entry give useful information about services and facilities. A key to symbols can be found inside the back cover flap. Keep this open for easy reference.

AMOTHERBY

North Yorkshire
Map ref 5C3

One of a string of villages on the Malton to Hovingham stretch of an old Roman road, which follows the northern ridge of the Howardian Hills.

The Old School House ▲▲

♪♪♪♪ HIGHLY COMMENDED

Church Lane, Amotherby, Malton
Contact: Mrs R Heneage, Hainton Hall, Hainton, Lincoln, Lincolnshire LN3 6LS
☎ Louth (01507) 313223
Fax (01507) 313443
1744 listed house in a tranquil position by the church. Very comfortable. Ideally situated for York, Castle Howard and the moors.
1 self-contained unit; sleeping max 6

Price per week:	£min	£max
Low season	230.00	250.00
High season	300.00	400.00

Open March–September and Christmas

☎ ▥ ☉ ▯ MW 🄴 TV ▯ ▱ 🖳 🚗 ❄ ⌂

AMPLEFORTH

North Yorkshire
Map ref 5C3

Stone-built village in Hambleton Hills. Famous for its abbey and college, a Benedictine public school, founded in 1802, of which Cardinal Hume was once abbot.

Hillside Cottage ▲▲

♪♪♪♪ COMMENDED

Hillside, West End, Ampleforth, York Y06 4DY
☎ (01439) 788303 & 0374 181181
Contact: Mrs P Noble
Attractive converted stone cottage on the edge of national park, enjoying splendid views. Ideally situated for walking, moors, coast. 20 miles York, 10 miles Castle Howard. Personal attention by resident owners.
1 self-contained unit; sleeping max 4

Price per week:	£min	£max
Low season	165.00	165.00
High season	275.00	275.00

☎ 5 ◎ ▥ ☉ ▯ 🄴 TV ▯ ▱ 🖳 ❄ ✗

A key to symbols can be found inside the back cover flap.

All accommodation in this guide has been graded, or is awaiting a grading, by a trained Tourist Board inspector.

APPLETON-LE-MOORS

North Yorkshire
Map ref 5C3

A charming, unspoilt village in the North York Moors National Park. 23 miles inland from Scarborough and 33 miles north of York, it is an excellent centre for the coast, Herriot country, the North Yorkshire Moors Railway and many delightful walks and places of historic interest.

Bluebell Cottage

♪♪♪♪ HIGHLY COMMENDED

Appleton-le-Moors, York
Contact: Mrs J Benson, Burnley House Hotel, Hutton-le-Hole, York Y06 6UA
☎ Lastingham (01751) 417548 & Mobile (0585) 288666
Fax (01751) 417548
Listed, beamed cottage with rustic brick fireplace. Hand-made furniture by local craftsman. Fully fitted kitchen with dining area. Twin bedded room and single room. Bathroom with WC and shower.
1 self-contained unit; sleeping 4

Price per week:	£min	£max
Low season	230.00	250.00
High season	300.00	325.00

☎ ◎ ▥ ☉ ▯ MW 🄴 TV ▯ ▱ 🖳 🚗 P ✗ ⬞ SP ⌂

Information on accommodation listed in this guide has been supplied by the proprietors. As changes may occur you are advised to check details at the time of booking.

For ideas on places to visit refer to the introduction at the beginning of this section.

AYSGARTH

North Yorkshire
Map ref 5B3

Famous for its beautiful Falls - a series of 3 cascades extending for half a mile on the River Ure in Wensleydale. There is a coach and carriage museum at Yore Mill and a National Park Centre.

Kelspring Cottage

APPROVED

Kelspring Farm, Aysgarth, Leyburn DL8 3AJ
☎ Wensleydale (01969) 663467
Contact: Mrs M H Watson
Comfortable, well-appointed cottage with panoramic views over Wensleydale. Please send stamped addressed envelope for further details.
1 self-contained unit; sleeping max 6

Price per week:	£min	£max
Low season	160.00	
High season	195.00	

BARTON-LE-WILLOWS

North Yorkshire
Map ref 5C3

Pretty village 5 miles north of Stamford Bridge.

The Old Granary ⚜

HIGHLY COMMENDED

Green Farm, Barton-le-Willows, York YO6 7PD
☎ Whitwell-on-the-Hill (01653) 618387
Contact: Mrs J R Hudson
250-acre mixed farm. Fully modernised converted granary with large garden, on a working farm in pretty village. 15 minutes' drive to York, with easy access to Castle Howard, moors and coast. Two bedrooms, very spacious, cot, snooker table. Sorry no pets. Price is fully inclusive.
1 self-contained unit; sleeping max 6

Price per week:	£min	£max
Low season	150.00	
High season		300.00

BENTHAM

North Yorkshire
Map ref 5B3

Bentham is said to mean "Home on the Common". A weekly market has been held here since the 14th C. Good walking country.

Holmes Farm Cottage ⚜

COMMENDED

Holmes Farm, Low Bentham, Bentham, Lancaster LA2 7DE
☎ (015242) 61198
Contact: Mrs. L J Story
127-acre livestock farm. Well-equipped converted stone cottage with gas central heating. Adjoining the farmhouse, in a secluded position in beautiful pastureland.
1 self-contained unit; sleeping max 4

Price per week:	£min	£max
Low season	150.00	160.00
High season	160.00	205.00

BOLTON ABBEY

North Yorkshire
Map ref 4B1

This hamlet is best known for its priory situated near a bend in the River Wharfe. It was founded in 1151 by Alicia de Romilly and before that was site of Anglo-Saxon manor. Popular with painters, amongst them Landseer.

Waterfall Cottage ⚜

COMMENDED

Hazlewood, Bolton Abbey, Skipton
Contact: Mrs A Kellett, Trustees of the Chatsworth Settlement, Estate Office, Bolton Abbey, Skipton, North Yorkshire BD23 6EX
☎ Skipton (01756) 710227
Fax (01756) 710535
Delightful detached cottage set in the Wharfe Valley with panoramic views of wooded valleys and surrounding hill pastures.
1 self-contained unit; sleeping max 6

Price per week:	£min	£max
Low season	240.00	255.00
High season	350.00	400.00

Open April–October

BROMPTON-BY-SAWDON

North Yorkshire
Map ref 5D3

William Wordsworth, the renowned Lakeland poet, was married in the parish church in 1802 to Mary Hutchinson of Gallows Hill.

Headon Farm Holiday Cottages ⚜

COMMENDED

Headon Granary, Wydale, Brompton-by-Sawdon, Scarborough YO13 9DG
☎ Scarborough (01723) 859019
Contact: Mr & Mrs C D Proctor
Spacious character stone cottages in quiet wooded setting close to moors and heritage coast. Winner White Rose Award for Tourism 1991.
5 self-contained units; sleeping max 5

Price per week:	£min	£max
Low season	150.00	200.00
High season	210.00	350.00

CARLTON-IN-COVERDALE

North Yorkshire
Map ref 5B3

Attractive village in the secluded valley of Coverdale.

Hollinside & Little Hollin ⚜

COMMENDED

Carlton, Leyburn
Contact: Mr & Mrs P&A Wright, Hollinside, 6 Garden Lane, Southsea, Hampshire PO5 3DP
☎ Portsmouth (01705) 736651

Charming, comfortable local stone cottages in Dales National Park. Ideal central base for walking or for day visits to castles, stately homes, ancient abbeys, theme parks, etc, throughout northern England.
2 self-contained units; sleeping 3–8

Price per week:	£min	£max
Low season	110.00	120.00
High season	195.00	270.00

CLOUGHTON

North Yorkshire
Map ref 5D3

Village close to the East Coast and North York Moors.

Gowland Farm Cottages M

HIGHLY COMMENDED

Gowland Farm, Gowland Lane, Cloughton, Scarborough YO13 ODU
☎ Scarborough (01723) 870924
Contact: Mrs M A Martin
Four charming, converted stone barns overlooking Harwood Dale, 2 miles from the coast, north of Scarborough. Well-furnished, double glazed and centrally heated with all linen provided. White Rose Award 1993: "Self-catering Holiday of the Year" - runner up.
4 self-contained units; sleeping max 7

Price per week:	£min	£max
Low season	90.00	220.00
High season	220.00	395.00

CRAKEHALL

North Yorkshire
Map ref 5C3

One of the prettiest of the lower dales villages, with its 5-acre green dominated by Crakehall Hall and enclosed by stone-built cottages dating back to the 1750s.

St Edmund Country Cottages

COMMENDED

St Edmunds, Crakehall, Bedale DL8 1HP
☎ Bedale (01677) 423584
Contact: Mrs S E Cooper

Renovated cottages in courtyard behind house, overlooking green in pretty dales village. Ideal base for exploring dales and moors.
4 self-contained units; sleeping 2–7

Price per week:	£min	£max
Low season	115.00	215.00
High season	215.00	295.00

CROPTON

North Yorkshire
Map ref 5C3

Moorland village at the top of a high ridge with stone houses, some of cruck construction, a Victorian church and the remains of a 12th C moated castle. Cropton Forest nearby.

Hobbits Hideaway, Stable Cottage & Rue Crofts View M

HIGHLY COMMENDED

High Farm, Cropton, Pickering YO18 8HL
☎ Lastingham (01751) 417461
Contact: Mrs R M Feaster
Well-equipped single storey stone cottages, with fully fitted oak kitchens and large gardens. Ideal base for exploring moor, coast and York.
3 self-contained units; sleeping 4–6

Price per week:	£min	£max
Low season	140.00	
High season		450.00

Open January, March–December

DENHOLME

West Yorkshire
Map ref 4B1

Small West Yorkshire town overlooking moorland. Near "Bronte country".

Blacksmith's Cottages

APPROVED

Forge End, 2 Edge Bottom, Denholme, Bradford BD13 4JW
☎ Bradford (01274) 832850
Contact: Mrs Janet Nella Ackroyd
On the edge of moor, leading to Oxenhope and Haworth.
2 self-contained units; sleeping 3–6

Price per week:	£min	£max
Low season	65.00	85.00
High season	85.00	130.00

Open February–December

EAST BUTTERWICK

North Lincolnshire
Map ref 4C1

Trent House

HIGHLY COMMENDED

East Butterwick, Scunthorpe, South Humberside

Contact: Mrs Doreen Hurley, 20 Lakeside Drive, Silica Lodge, Scunthorpe, South Humberside DN17 2AG
☎ Scunthorpe (01724) 858850
Fax (01724) 858850
Riverside farmhouse with 4 double and 2 twin-bedded rooms plus cot. Electricity included. Short break visitors welcome. Brochure available.
1 self-contained unit; sleeping 12

Price per week:	£min	£max
Low season	250.00	350.00
High season	350.00	500.00

EBBERSTON

North Yorkshire
Map ref 5D3

Picturesque village with a Norman church and hall, overlooking the Vale of Pickering.

Cliff House Self Catering & Leisure Complex M

UP TO HIGHLY COMMENDED

Cliff House, Ebberston, Scarborough YO13 9PA
☎ Scarborough (01723) 859440
Contact: Mr & Mrs D C Wilcock
Comfortable cottages in the grounds of an historic former manor house. Heated indoor pool, jacuzzi, hard tennis court, games room and satellite TV. Colour brochure available on request.
8 self-contained units; sleeping 2–6

Price per week:	£min	£max
Low season	170.00	280.00
High season	240.00	630.00

FILEY

North Yorkshire
Map ref 5D3

Resort with elegant Regency buildings along the front and 6 miles of sandy beaches bounded by natural breakwater, Filey Brigg. Starting point of the Cleveland Way.

The Cottages M

COMMENDED

Muston Grange Farm, Muston Road, Filey YO14 OHU
☎ Scarborough (01723) 516620
Contact: Mr & Mrs David Teet
Situated between Muston and Filey on east coast. The cottages are a range of converted traditional farm buildings providing quality accommodation in a private courtyard setting.

5 self-contained units; sleeping 5

Price per week:	£min	£max
Low season	195.00	285.00
High season	285.00	365.00

Orchard Farm Cottages ᴀᴧ
COMMENDED

143 Stonegate, Hunmanby, Filey
YO14 OPU
☎ Scarborough (01723) 891582
Contact: Mr & Mrs A Hunneybell

Well-appointed 2 and 3-bedroomed cottages with a landscaped courtyard and open fields to the rear. Ideal for touring and visiting surrounding beauty spots. Heated indoor pool, play area, private lake, bar, entertainment, miniature steam railway, during peak season.
8 self-contained units; sleeping 1–7

Price per week:	£min	£max
Low season	150.00	200.00
High season	395.00	480.00

Cards accepted: Access, Visa, Diners, Amex, Switch/Delta

Saint Kitts Self Catering Holiday Flats
APPROVED

2 The Beach, Filey YO14 9LA
☎ Scarborough (01723) 512141
Contact: Mr & Mrs D H Midgley
All flats have lounges facing the sea with views over the beach and bay. The ground floor flat has central heating.
3 self-contained units,
1 non-self-contained unit;
sleeping 5–8

Price per week:	£min	£max
Low season	90.00	120.00
High season	280.00	390.00

The symbols in each entry give information about services and facilities. A 'key' to these symbols appears at the back of this guide.

FOXHOLES
North Yorkshire
Map ref 5D3

Pretty wolds village 10 miles north of Driffield.

Manor Farm Cottage
COMMENDED

Manor Farm, Foxholes, Driffield, East Yorkshire YO25 OQH
☎ Thwing (01262) 470255
Fax (01262) 470555
Contact: Mrs M Lamplough
660-acre mixed farm. Detached brick cottage with its own garden and garage. 3 double bedrooms and an open fire in the living room. Ideal for touring.
1 self-contained unit; sleeping max 7

Price per week:	£min	£max
Low season		180.00
High season		220.00

Open May–October

FYLINGDALES MOOR
North Yorkshire
Map ref 5D3

Where the moorland of the North York Moors National Park meets the sea. An open area of natural beauty between the seaside towns of Scarborough and Whitby.

Billira Cottage ᴀᴧ
COMMENDED

Fylingdales Moor, Whitby
Contact: Mr & Mrs J L Thornton, 6 Flock Leys, Scalby, Scarborough, North Yorkshire YO13 0RG
☎ Scarborough (01723) 362682

Secluded, modernised, detached 3-bedroomed gamekeeper's cottage, comfortably sleeping up to 5 plus a baby. In the North York Moors National Park, near the sea between Scarborough and Whitby. Regret no dogs.
1 self-contained unit; sleeping max 5

Price per week:	£min	£max
Low season	235.00	325.00
High season	345.00	425.00

Open April–October

GLAISDALE
North Yorkshire
Map ref 5C3

Set in a wooded valley with the 350-year-old shingle stone arch "Beggars Bridge" spanning the River Esk. Often described as the "Queen of the dales", central for the North York Moors National Park and close to Whitby. Numerous lovely walks and bridle paths.

Red House Farm
HIGHLY COMMENDED

Glaisdale, Whitby YO21 2PZ
☎ Whitby (01947) 897242
Contact: Mr T J Spashett

12-acre smallholding. Holiday cottages in a Grade II listed barn conversion, on a quiet smallholding. Friendly farm animals, pond and magnificent views. Lovely walks.
1 self-contained unit; sleeping 4

Price per week:	£min	£max
Low season	231.00	339.00
High season	236.00	372.00

GOATHLAND
North Yorkshire
Map ref 5D3

Spacious village has several large greens grazed by sheep and is an ideal centre for walking the North York Moors. Nearby are several waterfalls, among them Mallyan Spout. Plough Monday celebrations held in January. Location for filming of TV "Heartbeat" series.

Abbot's Farm Cottage
APPROVED

Abbot's House, Goathland, Whitby YO22 5NH
☎ Whitby (01947) 896270
Contact: The Proprietor

Continued ▶

GOATHLAND
Continued

50-acre beef farm. Secluded, self-contained farm cottage with a garden and part central heating. An ideal retreat in the heart of the North York Moors. Cots provided. Steam railway nearby. TV's "Heartbeat" country.
1 self-contained unit; sleeping max 6

Price per week:	£min	£max
Low season	160.00	200.00
High season	200.00	260.00

Open March–November

Eskholme ♙
COMMENDED

2 Darnholme Road, Goathland, Whitby
Contact: Mrs J M Hodgson, Woodlands, 31 Shillbank View, Mirfield, West Yorkshire WF14 0QG
☎ Mirfield (01924) 498154
4-bedroomed house with gardens tucked away in this delightful moorland village in the heart of the national park. Good walking country, regular steam trains to Pickering. Only 8 miles from Whitby and its beach.
1 self-contained unit; sleeping 8

Price per week:	£min	£max
Low season	185.00	
High season		400.00

GREAT AYTON

North Yorkshire
Map ref 5C3

Village famous for its strong connections with Captain Cook. His family are buried in the graveyard and there is the Captain Cook Schoolroom Museum.

Rosemary Cottage ♙
COMMENDED

21 Mill Terrace, Great Ayton, Middlesbrough, Cleveland
Contact: Mr L M Juckes, Rosemary Cottage, Cliffe House, Great Ayton, Middlesbrough, Cleveland TS9 6EY
☎ Great Ayton (01642) 723504
Cosy stone-built terraced cottage in charming village beside the scenic North York Moors. Excellent centre for walking, touring or relaxing. Sorry, no smokers, no pets.

---

1 self-contained unit; sleeping max 3

Price per week:	£min	£max
Low season	150.00	200.00
High season	150.00	230.00

Cards accepted: Switch/Delta

GREWELTHORPE

North Yorkshire
Map ref 5C3

Attractive village on the edge of Grewelthorpe Moor, enhanced by the village pond. Four centuries ago a dispute over the rights to the moor led to the "Battle of the Amazons" between wives of Grewelthorpe and Kirkby - thankfully long since resolved!

Sunnyside Cottage ♙
HIGHLY COMMENDED

Grewelthorpe, Ripon
Contact: Mrs Jane Shuttleworth, 224 Bradway Road, Bradway, Sheffield S17 4PE
☎ Sheffield (0114) 235 2783

Delightful, spacious, character cottage in attractive village. Furnished and equipped to highest standards. Cosy sitting room with beamed ceiling and open fire. Full heating. Four bedrooms. Enclosed patio.
1 self-contained unit; sleeping max 7

Price per week:	£min	£max
Low season	180.00	270.00
High season	270.00	370.00

WELCOME HOST

This is a nationally recognised customer care programme which aims to promote the highest standards of service and a warm welcome. Establishments who are taking part in this initiative are indicated by the ⊛ symbol.

HARROGATE

North Yorkshire
Map ref 4B1

A major conference, exhibition and shopping centre, renowned for its spa heritage and award winning floral displays, spacious parks and gardens. Famous for antiques, toffee, fine shopping and excellent tea shops, also its Royal Pump Rooms and Baths.
Tourist Information Centre ☎ (01423) 525666

Ashness Apartments ♙
HIGHLY COMMENDED

15 St Mary's Avenue, Harrogate
Contact: Mrs B Batty, 15 St Mary's Avenue, Harrogate, North Yorkshire HG2 0LP
☎ Harrogate (01423) 526894
Fax (01423) 700038
Lovely, comfortable apartments in elegant Victorian town houses, just a short walk from the gardens, shops and restaurants of beautiful Harrogate.
22 self-contained units; sleeping 3–4

Price per week:	£min	£max
Low season	185.00	245.00
High season	255.00	340.00

Dinmore Cottages ♙
HIGHLY COMMENDED

Dinmore House, Burnt Yates, Harrogate HG3 3ET
☎ (01423) 770860
Fax (01423) 770860
Contact: Mrs Jeanne Townend
Four award-winning dales cottages managed by resident owners. In Nidderdale, near Harrogate and York. Peaceful, magical place with breathtaking views.
Wheelchair access category 2 ♿
4 self-contained units; sleeping 3–5

Price per week:	£min	£max
Low season	201.00	273.00
High season	347.00	507.00

Hillside Mews ♙
HIGHLY COMMENDED

13 Otley Road, Harrogate
Contact: Mr S Hamilton, 16 Otley Road, Harrogate, North Yorkshire HG2 0DN
☎ Harrogate (01423) 566890
Fax (01423) 526057
Detached cottage, superbly situated close to the town centre yet with easy

access to the dales. Renovated to provide accommodation of high standard.

1 self-contained unit; sleeping max 5

Price per week:	£min	£max
Low season	250.00	300.00
High season	330.00	395.00

Cards accepted: Access, Visa

Rudding Holiday Park

UP TO HIGHLY COMMENDED

Rudding Park, Follifoot, Harrogate HG3 1JH
☎ (01423) 870439
Fax (01423) 872286
All properties nestle in and around the beautiful grounds of Rudding Park, close to the picturesque village of Follifoot, 3 miles south of Harrogate. Facilities include shop, swimming pool, children's playground, games room, 18-hole golf course and driving range.
12 self-contained units; sleeping 2–9

Price per week:	£min	£max
Low season	120.00	250.00
High season	250.00	560.00

Cards accepted: Access, Visa

HAWES

North Yorkshire
Map ref 5B3

The capital of Upper Wensleydale on the famous Pennine Way, renowned for great cheeses. Popular with walkers. Dales National Park Information Centre and Folk Museum. Nearby is spectacular Hardraw Force waterfall.

Beckside Cottage

APPROVED

Dyers Garth, Hawes
Contact: Mr & Mrs N Wiseman, 605 Lytham Road, Blackpool, Lancashire FY4 1RG
☎ Blackpool (01253) 343471
Traditional Yorkshire stone cottage in a quiet village, by a river and overlooking a waterfall.
1 self-contained unit; sleeping max 5

Price per week:	£min	£max
Low season	148.00	196.00
High season	196.00	251.00

Open April–October, December

Gaudy Farmhouse

APPROVED

Gayle, Hawes DL8 3NA
☎ Wensleydale (01969) 667231
Contact: Graham & Mary Watts
Imaginatively converted, traditional stone barns, warm and generously equipped. Adjoining the owners' farmhouse in 25 acres beside the Pennine Way, 1 mile from Hawes. Magnificent views overlooking Wensleydale. Unique situation.
4 self-contained units; sleeping 4–6

Price per week:	£min	£max
Low season	115.00	125.00
High season	245.00	260.00

Cards accepted: Access, Visa

Mile House Farm Country Cottages

HIGHLY COMMENDED

Mile House Farm, Hawes DL8 3PT
☎ Wensleydale (01969) 667481
Contact: Mrs Anne Fawcett
Traditional old dales stone cottages with beamed ceilings and open fires, at Sedbusk near Hawes and West Burton, near Aysgarth Falls. Both peaceful locations with spectacular views. Well-equipped, warm and comfortable. Free trout fishing on farm.
2 self-contained units; sleeping 4–8

Price per week:	£min	£max
Low season	155.00	200.00
High season	250.00	350.00

Yorkshire Dales Country Cottages

UP TO HIGHLY COMMENDED

Shaw Ghyll, High Shaw, Simonstone, Hawes DL8 3LY
☎ Wensleydale (01969) 667359
Fax (01969) 667894
Contact: Mrs B Stott
60-acre livestock farm. Stone-built cottages situated in beautiful Wensleydale. Fully equipped and warm, offering comfort and quality at reasonable prices. Free trout fishing.
7 self-contained units; sleeping 1–10

Price per week:	£min	£max
Low season	98.00	228.00
High season	228.00	498.00

Please mention this guide when making your booking.

HAWORTH

West Yorkshire
Map ref 4B1

This Pennine town is famous as home of the Bronte family. The Parsonage is now a Bronte Museum where furniture and possessions of the family are displayed. Moors and Bronte waterfalls nearby and steam trains on the Keighley and Worth Valley Railway pass through.
Tourist Information Centre ☎ (01535) 642329

2 Adam Croft

COMMENDED

Cullingworth, Bradford
Contact: Mr D Ginley, 12 Westfield Drive, Lightcliffe, Halifax, West Yorkshire HX3 8AW
☎ Halifax (01422) 203247
Recently built and well-appointed 3-bedroomed town house on a small development in pleasant village near Haworth. Convenient for National Museum of Photography.
1 self-contained unit; sleeping max 5

Price per week:	£min	£max
Low season	120.00	150.00
High season	160.00	250.00

Heather & Bilberry Cottages

HIGHLY COMMENDED

Hole Farm, Dimples Lane, Haworth, Keighley BD22 8QS
☎ Keighley (01535) 644755
Contact: Mrs J Milner
8-acre mixed farm. Barn conversions backing on to moors. Ten minutes' walk Bronte Museum. See the calves and foals, let your children feed the peacocks and play in the playground.
2 self-contained units; sleeping 4–9

Price per week:	£min	£max
Low season	150.00	
High season		500.00

Westfield Farm Cottages

HIGHLY COMMENDED

Westfield Farm, Tim Lane, Haworth, Keighley BD22 7SA
☎ Keighley (01535) 644568
Fax (01535) 646686
Contact: Mr & Mrs W Carr
100-acre livestock farm. Comfortable, imaginatively converted cottages on hill-farm adjacent to owners'

Continued ▶

HAWORTH

Continued

farmhouse. Lovely views. Cottage for 2 for disabled visitors. Short breaks available.
Wheelchair access category 2&
5 self-contained units; sleeping 2–6

Price per week:	£min	£max
Low season	143.00	198.00
High season	242.00	352.00

Cards accepted: Access, Visa

Woolcombers Cottage

HIGHLY COMMENDED

30 Main Street, Haworth, Keighley
Contact: Mr & Mrs A Johnson, 83 Main Street, Haworth, Keighley, West Yorkshire BD22 8DA
☎ Keighley (01535) 643921
Tastefully restored to a high standard whilst retaining its traditional old world charm, beamed ceilings, etc. 2 double bedrooms, both en-suite.
1 self-contained unit; sleeping max 4

Price per week:	£min	£max
Low season	150.00	175.00
High season	175.00	220.00

HEBDEN BRIDGE

West Yorkshire
Map ref 4B1

Originally a small town on packhorse route, Hebden Bridge grew into a booming mill town in 18th C with rows of "up-and-down" houses of several storeys built against hillsides. Ancient "pace-egg play" custom held on Good Friday. *Tourist Information Centre* ☎ *(01422) 843831*

3 Birks Hall Cottage

APPROVED

Cragg Vale, Hebden Bridge
Contact: Mrs H Wilkinson, 1 Birks Hall, Cragg Vale, Hebden Bridge, West Yorkshire HX7 5SB
☎ Halifax (01422) 882064 & 884509
Country cottage with two bedrooms, bathroom, kitchen and lounge with Georgian windows. In a small, picturesque village near the Pennine centre of Hebden Bridge.
1 self-contained unit; sleeping max 4

Price per week:	£min	£max
Low season	80.00	100.00
High season	100.00	120.00

Great Burlees Farm

UP TO COMMENDED

Hebden Bridge HX7 8PS
☎ (01422) 843382
Contact: Mr & Mrs B Wells
Cottages in 17th C farmhouse and barn conversion. Secluded location on south-facing hillside, spacious gardens. Outstanding Pennine views.
4 self-contained units; sleeping 4–6

Price per week:	£min	£max
Low season	115.00	150.00
High season	230.00	310.00

Upper Mytholm Barn

DE LUXE

Upper Mytholm, Booth, Luddenden, Halifax HX2 6XB
☎ Halifax (01422) 882240 & 886450
Contact: Mrs Dorothy Denton
18th C listed barn attached to owner's house in beautiful Luddenden Dean. 3 bedrooms, log fire, whirlpool bath. Large gardens.
1 self-contained unit; sleeping 6

Price per week:	£min	£max
Low season	270.00	
High season		460.00

HELMSLEY

North Yorkshire
Map ref 5C3

Pretty town on the River Rye at the entrance to Ryedale and the North York Moors, with large square and remains of 12th C castle, several inns and All Saints' Church.

Townend Cottage

COMMENDED

High Lane, Beadlam, Nawton, York YO6 5SY
☎ (01439) 770103
Contact: Mrs M Begg

Very warm and comfortable stone cottage with oak beams. Central heating and log fire included in price. Quiet village near Helmsley, ideal for walking or touring moors, coast and York.

1 self-contained unit; sleeping max 4

Price per week:	£min	£max
Low season		140.00
High season	220.00	275.00

HOLMBRIDGE

West Yorkshire
Map ref 4B1

Pennine village 2 miles south-west of Holmfirth.

Waterside Cottage

HIGHLY COMMENDED

Upper Waterside Farm, Royd Lane, Holmbridge, Holmfirth, Huddersfield HD7 1RL
☎ Holmfirth (01484) 683082
Fax (01484) 638082
Contact: Mrs Pamela Robinson
Set in 11 acres, 300-year-old renovated barn property on edge of Pennines, 2 miles from Holmfirth.
Wheelchair access category 3&
2 self-contained units; sleeping 6

Price per week:	£min	£max
Low season	200.00	300.00
High season	300.00	400.00

HORTON-IN-RIBBLESDALE

North Yorkshire
Map ref 5B3

On the River Ribble and an ideal centre for pot-holing. The Pennine Way runs eastward over Pen-y-ghent, one of the famous "Three Peaks". *Tourist Information Centre* ☎ *(01729) 860333*

1 Rock View

HIGHLY COMMENDED

Horton-in-Ribblesdale, Settle
Contact: Mrs J B Morgan, Ashurst, Links Drive, High Bentham, Lancaster LA2 7BJ
☎ (01524) 261406
Comfortable, modern, well-equipped semi-detached cottage. Yorkshire Dales National Park, on Pennine Way, close to the Settle/Carlisle Railway.
1 self-contained unit; sleeping max 4

Price per week:	£min	£max
Low season	150.00	200.00
High season	210.00	280.00

Cards accepted: Access, Visa, Diners, Amex

HOVINGHAM

North Yorkshire
Map ref 5C3

Peaceful village of golden stone cottages, below Hambleton Hills, clustering around Hovingham Hall, home of Duchess of Kent's family. Hall, built by Sir Thomas Worsley in 1760, is open to the public by appointment.

Lime and Rose Cottage

COMMENDED

Hovingham, York
Contact: Mrs J M James, The Cottage, Gilling East, York YO6 4JG
☎ Ampleforth (01439) 788241
Fax (01439) 788241
Select cottage, ideal for national park, moors, York, dales and coast. Large garden, patio, private parking. Fishing, riding, golf and sports hall nearby. Short breaks available low season. Brochure available.
2 self-contained units; sleeping 4–6

Price per week:	£min	£max
Low season	200.00	250.00
High season	240.00	330.00

HUTTON-LE-HOLE

North Yorkshire
Map ref 5C3

Listed in Domesday Book, this pretty village of red-tiled stone cottages situated around Hutton Beck became a refuge for persecuted Quakers in 17th C. Ryedale Folk Museum.

Moorcroft

COMMENDED

Beck Garth, Hutton-le-Hole, York
Contact: Mr Ian Dobson, Frogs Hall Farm, Takeley, Bishop's Stortford, Hertfordshire CM22 6PE
☎ Bishop's Stortford (01279) 870320
Fax (01279) 870320
Stone-built dormer bungalow overlooking the village green in a picturesque village. Quiet and private.
1 self-contained unit; sleeping max 6

Price per week:	£min	£max
Low season	230.00	250.00
High season	250.00	380.00

INGLEBY GREENHOW

North Yorkshire
Map ref 5C3

Perched on the edge of Cleveland Hills, the village boasts the Norman church of St Andrew's with well-preserved carving and effigies of a priest and a knight. Ingleby Moor rises 1300 ft above village.

Ingleby Manor

HIGHLY COMMENDED

Ingleby Greenhow, Great Ayton TS9 6RB
☎ Great Ayton (01642) 722170
Fax (01642) 722170
Contact: Mrs C Bianco

Exceptionally peaceful, spacious apartments in Grade II* Tudor manor house. Set on edge of moors in 55 acres of gardens and woodland in the national park.
3 self-contained units; sleeping 4–8

Price per week:	£min	£max
Low season	210.00	312.00
High season	296.00	563.00

KIRKBY FLEETHAM

North Yorkshire
Map ref 5C3

Village close to the A1 between dales and moors. Spacious village green has big lime trees and there is the interesting church of St Mary, some remains of moat and walling of a castle and the Hall.

Wren Cottage

COMMENDED

25 Forge Lane, Kirkby Fleetham, Northallerton
Contact: Mrs J R Pybus, Old Street House Farm, Little Holtby, Northallerton, North Yorkshire DL7 9LN
☎ Northallerton (01609) 748622
On a picturesque village green within easy reach of the dales, coast, many sites of historic interest and sporting attractions.
1 self-contained unit; sleeping max 4

Price per week:	£min	£max
Low season		105.00
High season		203.00

KNARESBOROUGH

North Yorkshire
Map ref 4B1

Picturesque market town on the River Nidd, famous for its 11th C castle ruins, overlooking town and river gorge. Attractions include oldest chemist's shop in country, prophetess Mother Shipton's cave, Dropping Well and Court House Museum. Boating on river.

Acorn Cottage

COMMENDED

Oakwood Farm, York Road, Knaresborough
Contact: Mr & Mrs L J Webster, Oak Ridge, Briggate, Knaresborough, North Yorkshire HG5 8BQ
☎ Harrogate (01423) 861083
Fully modernised cottage with own garden in peaceful surroundings. Towels available for hire.
1 self-contained unit; sleeping 6

Price per week:	£min	£max
Low season	150.00	200.00
High season	200.00	275.00

Pebble Cottage

HIGHLY COMMENDED

1 Belmont Avenue, Forest Moor Road, Knaresborough
Contact: Mr & Mrs P A Snowden, Hawthorne House, Dunkeswick, Harewood, Leeds LS17 9LP
☎ Leeds (0113) 288 6254
Delightful, compact cottage, modernised with emphasis on standards. 2 double bedrooms plus studio with 2 singles. Small, enclosed garden and patio. In quiet rural setting, close to Knaresborough. Personal welcome by the owners.
1 self-contained unit; sleeping 6

Price per week:	£min	£max
Low season	195.00	260.00
High season	260.00	320.00

Map references apply to the colour maps at the back of this guide.

LEALHOLM

North Yorkshire
Map ref 5C3

Pretty moorland village on the River Esk below Lealholm Moor.

Greenhouses Farm Cottages ⚲

HIGHLY COMMENDED

Greenhouses Farm, Lealholm, Whitby YO21 2AD
☎ Whitby (01947) 897486
Contact: Mr & Mrs Nick Eddleston
Stone and pantile cottages converted from traditional farm buildings, providing well-equipped, comfortable, centrally heated accommodation. In a beautiful, moorland hamlet within the North York Moors National Park, 9 miles from Whitby.
3 self-contained units; sleeping 3–6

Price per week:	£min	£max
Low season	174.00	231.00
High season	312.00	475.00

LEYBURN

North Yorkshire
Map ref 5B3

Attractive dales market town where Mary Queen of Scots was reputedly captured after her escape from Bolton Castle. Fine views over Wensleydale from nearby.
Tourist Information Centre ☎ (01969) 623069 or 622773

Dales View Holiday Homes ⚲

UP TO COMMENDED

Jenkins Garth, Leyburn DL8 5AZ
☎ Wensleydale (01969) 623707 & 622808
Contact: Messrs J&M Chilton
Spacious apartments with panoramic views and stone-built cottages, all in a secluded position away from traffic yet close to the market place.
5 self-contained units; sleeping 3–6

Price per week:	£min	£max
Low season	105.00	
High season		215.00

Thorney Cottage Holiday Homes

COMMENDED

Spennithorne, Leyburn DL8 5PR
☎ Wensleydale (01969) 622496
Contact: Mrs A Gaines
Converted coach houses situated in 1 acre of grounds overlooking the River Ure to Middleham Castle.
3 self-contained units; sleeping 2–7

Price per week:	£min	£max
Low season	120.00	
High season		320.00

LOCKTON

North Yorkshire
Map ref 5D3

Typical moorland village close to the route of the North Yorkshire Moors Railway.

Barn Cottage

COMMENDED

Lockton, Pickering
Contact: Mrs G A Grant, Barn Cottage, East Farm, Buslingthorpe, Lincoln, Lincolnshire LN3 5AQ
☎ Market Rasen (01673) 842283
Stone and pantile bungalow in a delightful, unspoilt village on the edge of the moors. Off-road parking, enclosed garden. Excellent centre for exploring the North York Moors.
1 self-contained unit; sleeping 6

Price per week:	£min	£max
Low season	180.00	250.00
High season	260.00	330.00

MASHAM

North Yorkshire
Map ref 5C3

Famous market town on the River Ure, with a large market square. St Mary's Church has Norman tower and 13th C spire. Theakston's "Old Peculier" ale is brewed here.

Swan Cottages

COMMENDED

Black Swan, Fearby, Ripon
Contact: Mr John McCourt, Swan Cottage, Black Swan Hotel, Fearby, Ripon, North Yorkshire HG4 4NF
☎ Ripon (01765) 689477
Built in Yorkshire stone and tastefully decorated to a high standard. Double glazed, gas CH, fitted carpets.
2 self-contained units; sleeping 5

Price per week:	£min	£max
Low season	130.00	175.00
High season	175.00	250.00

MYTHOLMROYD

West Yorkshire
Map ref 4B1

Situated in the Calder Valley, the meaning of the name originates from "a clearance of woodland where streams join".

W H Franklin Estates

APPROVED

George Street, Mytholmroyd, Hebden Bridge HX7 5DT
☎ Halifax (01422) 882060 & 882098
Fax (01422) 882060
Contact: Mr W H Franklin
Modernised, stone-built terraced house with dining room/living room, kitchen, 2 first floor bedrooms, bath/WC and 2 second floor bedrooms. Adjacent to shops and transport.
2 self-contained units; sleeping 6–8

Price per week:	£min	£max
Low season	80.00	95.00
High season	95.00	190.00

NEWTON UPON DERWENT

East Riding of Yorkshire
Map ref 4C1

Newton Lodge Cottages ⚲

COMMENDED

Newton Lodge, Newton upon Derwent, York YO4 5DD
☎ Pocklington (01759) 380237
Contact: Mr T J Sherbourne
435-acre arable farm. High quality cottage conversions, well furnished, 2 en-suite bedrooms each with patio area. Ample parking. Open countryside with free lake fishing.
2 self-contained units; sleeping 4

Price per week:	£min	£max
Low season	141.00	189.00
High season	193.00	303.00

Open February–November and Christmas

National gradings and classifications were correct at the time of going to press but are subject to change. Please check at the time of booking.

NEWTON-ON-RAWCLIFFE

North Yorkshire
Map ref 5D3

Pretty village on the edge of the North York Moors National Park.

Manor Farm Holidays ⋔
🗝🗝🗝🗝 UP TO HIGHLY COMMENDED

Manor Farm, Newton-on-Rawcliffe, Pickering YO18 8QA
☎ Pickering (01751) 472601
Contact: Lady Kirk
Stone-built farm courtyard and granary, recently converted to a high standard. In a quiet, attractive village in the North York Moors National Park.
Wheelchair access category 3⟨⟩
4 self-contained units; sleeping 4–8

Price per week:	£min	£max
Low season	130.00	150.00
High season	260.00	375.00

🗏Ⓜ◎⌕🖩.⊙🖵🅣🆅◎🖴📞🔥🚗 PU❀⚬ SP🏮

NORTHALLERTON

North Yorkshire
Map ref 5C3

Formerly a staging post on coaching route to the North and later a railway town. Today a lively market town and administrative capital of North Yorkshire. Parish church of All Saints dates from 1200.
Tourist Information Centre ☎ (01609) 776864

The Byre
🗝🗝🗝🗝 HIGHLY COMMENDED

Hill View Farm, Bullamoor, Northallerton DL6 3QW
☎ (01609) 776072
Contact: Mrs M Crowe
20-acre mixed farm. Converted cow byre with 2 double bedrooms, bathroom, kitchen/dining room, lounge plus additional WC. Double glazed throughout, night storage heating. Located 1.5 miles from Northallerton town centre.
1 self-contained unit; sleeping max 4

Price per week:	£min	£max
Low season	150.00	180.00
High season	200.00	250.00

🗏◎🖩.⊙🖵MW📢🅣🆅◎🖴🖵🔥 🚗P🐾 SP

PATELEY BRIDGE

North Yorkshire
Map ref 5C3

Small market town at centre of Upper Nidderdale. Flax and linen industries once flourished in this remote and beautiful setting.

Rivulet Court ⋔
🗝🗝🗝🗝🗝 HIGHLY COMMENDED

26 High Street, Pateley Bridge, Harrogate
Contact: Mrs Anne Rack, Blazefield, Bewerley, Harrogate, North Yorkshire HG3 5BS
☎ Harrogate (01423) 711001 & 712305
Large self-contained 3-bedroom apartment on 2 floors in own quiet secluded courtyard in the centre of Pateley Bridge. Children and pets welcome.
1 self-contained unit; sleeping 8

Price per week:	£min	£max
Low season	195.00	240.00
High season	320.00	380.00

🗏◎🖩.⊙🖵MW📢🅣🆅◎🖴📞🖵 🚗PU❀ SP🏮

Spinney Cottage and Mistal Cottage
🗝🗝🗝🗝 COMMENDED

Dodd Hill Farm, Dyke Lane, Dacre, Harrogate HG3 4EY
☎ Harrogate (01423) 780643
Contact: Mr & Mrs C D Huby
Holiday cottages attached to owner's home. Two miles from Dacre on the Heyshaw road.
2 self-contained units; sleeping 6–8

Price per week:	£min	£max
Low season	130.00	185.00
High season	190.00	335.00

🗏◎🖩.⊙🖵🅣🆅◎🖴🖵🚗P❀ SP

PICKERING

North Yorkshire
Map ref 5D3

Market town and tourist centre on edge of North York Moors. Parish church has complete set of 15th C wall paintings depicting lives of saints. Part of 12th C castle still stands. Beck Isle Museum. The North York Moors Railway begins here.
Tourist Information Centre ☎ (01751) 473791

Keld Head Farm Holiday Cottages ⋔
🗝🗝🗝🗝 HIGHLY COMMENDED

Keld Head, Pickering YO18 8LL
☎ (01751) 473974
Contact: Mr J I Fearn

Courtyard with 7 individually designed cottages with beamed ceilings and stone fireplaces, extensively equipped and tastefully furnished. Large gardens with playground. Speciality catering, babysitting and bike hire available.
7 self-contained units; sleeping 4–7

Price per week:	£min	£max
Low season	186.00	212.00
High season	445.00	583.00

🗏Ⓜ◎🖩.⊙🖵MW🅣🆅◎🖴📞 🖵PU❀⚬✖⚬ SP◎

REETH

North Yorkshire
Map ref 5B3

Once a market town and lead-mining centre, Reeth today serves holiday-makers in Swaledale with its folk museum and 18th C shops and inns lining the green at High Row.

Burton House, Greystones & Turbine House ⋔
🗝🗝🗝🗝 UP TO HIGHLY COMMENDED

Reeth, Richmond
Contact: Mrs P R Procter, Hill Cottage, Reeth, Richmond, North Yorkshire DL11 6SQ
☎ Richmond (01748) 884273
South-facing, stone-built properties in a quiet location beside the River Arkle,
Continued ▶

REETH
Continued

only 5 minutes' walk to the village centre. All comforts provided at an all-inclusive tariff.
3 self-contained units; sleeping 3–7

Price per week:	£min	£max
Low season	170.00	240.00
High season	275.00	385.00

Swaledale Cottages

UP TO HIGHLY COMMENDED

Thiernswood Hall, Healaugh, Richmond DL11 6UJ
☎ Richmond (01748) 884526
Fax (01748) 884834
Contact: Mrs J T Hughes

Modernised cottages of character with oak beams, climbing roses and mullioned windows. Warm and cosy in winter. Peaceful, rural settings in the Yorkshire Dales, with beautiful views.
6 self-contained units; sleeping 2–10

Price per week:	£min	£max
Low season	119.00	315.00
High season	304.00	672.00

RIPPONDEN
West Yorkshire
Map ref 4B1

Main Calderdale village on the River Ryburn with walks to Ryburn Reservoir and Blackstone Edge Roman road where part of the Roman pavement is still visible. A pleasant main street of traditional houses leads down to the stocks and there is a spired church and a 16th C packhorse bridge.

Thurst House Farm

COMMENDED

Lighthazles Road, Soyland, Ripponden, Sowerby Bridge
Contact: Mrs Judith Marriott, 21 Imperial Road, Edgerton, Huddersfield, West Yorks HD3 3AF
☎ Huddersfield (01484) 531232 & Halifax (01422) 822820
Pretty, 17th C farmhouse close to Bronte district, Hebden Bridge.

Furnished with chintz, antiques. Attractive garden, panoramic pastoral views. Good walks and motoring.
1 self-contained unit; sleeping max 6

Price per week:	£min	£max
Low season	60.00	100.00
High season	185.00	200.00

ROBIN HOOD'S BAY
North Yorkshire
Map ref 5D3

Picturesque village of red-roofed cottages with main street running from clifftop down ravine to seashore. Scene of much smuggling and shipwrecks in 18th C. Robin Hood reputed to have escaped to continent by boat from here.

South View

APPROVED

Fylingthorpe, Whitby
Contact: Mrs B E Reynolds, Gilders Green, Raw, Whitby, North Yorkshire YO22 4PP
☎ Whitby (01947) 880025
Comfortable and well-equipped detached house with a car space. In its own garden, with sea and country views. SAE for details.
1 self-contained unit; sleeping max 6

Price per week:	£min	£max
Low season	110.00	
High season		260.00

SCARBOROUGH
North Yorkshire
Map ref 5D3

Large, popular East Coast seaside resort, formerly a spa town. Beautiful gardens and two splendid sandy beaches. Castle ruins date from 1100; fine Georgian and Victorian houses. Scarborough Millennium depicts 1,000 years of town's history. Sea Life Centre.
Tourist Information Centre ☎ (01723) 373333

Forge Valley Cottages

HIGHLY COMMENDED

East Ayton, Scarborough
Contact: Mr D R Beeley, Barn House, 8a Westgate, Old Malton, Malton, North Yorkshire YO17 0HE
☎ Malton (01653) 698251
Stone-built cottages in lovely village of East Ayton. Gateway to North York Moors, 10 minutes from Yorkshire coast. Fully equipped, cosy and comfortable. Pets welcome, private garden and parking. Open all year.

---

3 self-contained units; sleeping max 5

Price per week:	£min	£max
Low season	95.00	95.00
High season	95.00	395.00

Ivy Cottage

HIGHLY COMMENDED

Castlegate, East Ayton, Scarborough
Contact: Mr & Mrs K Hilton, 1 Ivy Cottage, Castlegate, East Ayton, Scarborough, North Yorkshire Y013 9EJ
☎ Scarborough (01723) 864407
18th C stone-built, beamed cottage in Forge Valley, overlooking the River Derwent. Picturesque countryside, 4 miles from Scarborough.
1 self-contained unit; sleeping max 4

Price per week:	£min	£max
Low season	175.00	245.00
High season	245.00	300.00

Open March–October

Wansbeck Holiday Flats

UP TO COMMENDED

26 Albemarle Crescent, Scarborough YO11 1XX
☎ (01723) 367701
Contact: Mr P Gott
Tastefully decorated and well-equipped flats. Quiet central location with private car park. Caring resident proprietors. Short breaks available off-season.
5 self-contained units; sleeping 2–6

Price per week:	£min	£max
Low season	65.00	100.00
High season	125.00	260.00

Open January–October, December

White Acre

APPROVED

15 Victoria Park, Scarborough
Contact: Mr J G Squire, 54 Falsgrave Road, Scarborough, North Yorkshire YO12 5AX
☎ Scarborough (01723) 374220 & 360542
Fax (01723) 366693
Lovely, large self-contained flats, ideally situated near the beach, overlooking Peasholm. Clothes washer and dryer, cot and high chair. Off-street parking.
2 self-contained units; sleeping 6

Price per week:	£min	£max
Low season	100.00	220.00
High season	220.00	390.00

Open March–October

Wrea Head House Ⓜ

HIGHLY COMMENDED

Wrea Head Farm, Barmoor Lane,
Scalby, Scarborough YO13 0PG
☎ (01723) 375844
Fax (01723) 500274
Contact: Mr & Mrs C J Wood
*Winners of Yorkshire and Humberside
Tourist Board Holiday Cottages of the
Year 1995 and 1992, runner-up in
1994. Superb indoor heated swimming
pool, sauna and jacuzzi. Beautiful
countryside with panoramic sea views.
En-suite B & B available.*
9 self-contained units; sleeping 2–8

Price per week:	£min	£max
Low season	165.00	363.00
High season	267.00	867.00

Cards accepted: Access, Visa

SCOTCH CORNER

North Yorkshire
Map ref 5C3

Famous milestone at the junction of
the A1 and A66 near Richmond.
*Tourist Information Centre ☎ (01325)
377677*

5 Cedar Grove Ⓜ

COMMENDED

Barton, Richmond
Contact: Mr J P Lawson, The Close,
Mill Lane, Cloughton, Scarborough,
North Yorkshire YO13 0AB
☎ Scarborough (01723) 870455
*Two storey semi-detached family house,
situated near village green and local
shops. Five miles south of Darlington
and central location for touring the
Yorkshire Dales, North York Moors,
Northumberland, Durham and Lake
District.*
1 self-contained unit; sleeping max 4

Price per week:	£min	£max
Low season	125.00	175.00
High season	175.00	250.00

Map references apply to
the colour maps at the
back of this guide.

A key to symbols can be
found inside the back
cover flap.

SEDBUSK

North Yorkshire
Map ref 5B3

Wensleydale village where hand
knitting was once a local industry.
Pony trekking centre.

Jasmine Cottage Ⓜ

HIGHLY COMMENDED

Sedbusk, Hawes
Contact: Mrs A D Moore, 79
Cookridge Lane, Leeds LS16 7NE
☎ Leeds (0113) 267 9332
*Modernised 4-bedroomed, detached,
south-facing cottage on the sunny side
of the dale. Pleasant, secluded garden
and a lane leading on to the moor
behind.*
1 self-contained unit; sleeping 6–8

Price per week:	£min	£max
Low season	150.00	285.00
High season	234.00	348.00

SETTLE

North Yorkshire
Map ref 5B3

Town of narrow streets and
Georgian houses in an area of great
limestone hills and crags. Panoramic
view from Castleberg Crag which
stands 300 ft above town.
*Tourist Information Centre ☎ (01729)
825192*

Primrose Cottage Ⓜ

COMMENDED

12 Victoria Street, Settle
Contact: Mr A Diggens, Three Peaks
Cottages, 19 Rectory Road,
Wivenhoe, Colchester, Essex
CO7 9EP
☎ Colchester (01206) 827348
Fax (01206) 827348
*17th C Grade II listed, stone-built
cottage with exposed beams, in a quiet
location 250 yards from the market
square.*
1 self-contained unit; sleeping 5

Price per week:	£min	£max
Low season	145.00	235.00
High season	295.00	295.00

For ideas on places to visit
refer to the introduction at
the beginning of this section.

SHEFFIELD

South Yorkshire
Map ref 4B2

Local iron ore and coal gave
Sheffield its prosperous steel and
cutlery industries. The modern city
centre has many interesting
buildings - cathedral, Cutlers' Hall,
Crucible Theatre, Graves and
Mappin Art Galleries - and
Meadowhall Shopping Centre
nearby.
*Tourist Information Centre ☎ (0114)
273 4671 or 273 4672*

Hangram Lane Farmhouse

HIGHLY COMMENDED

Hangram Lane Grange, Hangram
Lane, Ringinglow, Sheffield S11 7TQ
☎ (0114) 230 3570
Contact: Mrs J Clark
*Comfortable, modernised farmhouse
comprising large kitchen, dining room,
lounge, 1 double bedroom, 2
twin-bedded rooms, bathroom and
toilet. 2 minutes' drive from the Peak
District and shops.*
1 self-contained unit; sleeping 6

Price per week:	£min	£max
Low season	235.00	270.25
High season	282.00	293.75

Lingholme Cottage

HIGHLY COMMENDED

Lingholme Farm, Bradfield Dale,
Sheffield
Contact: Miss G M Shepherd,
Lingholme Cottage, Lingholme Farm,
Smallfield Lane, Bradfield Dale,
Sheffield S6 6LJ
☎ Sheffield (0114) 232 5937 & 285
1347
*Self-contained cottage, renovated to
high standard. Fully-equipped fitted
kitchen, comfortable lounge with TV.
North-west of Sheffield, in the Peak
National Park.*
1 self-contained unit; sleeping 4

Price per week:	£min	£max
Low season	190.00	
High season	250.00	

The Ⓜ symbol after an
establishment name indicates
that it is a Regional
Tourist Board member.

SHEFFIELD

Continued

Moor Royd House ⚏

[🔑 🔑 — 🔑 🔑] HIGHLY COMMENDED

Manchester Road, Millhouse Green,
Sheffield S30 6FG
☎ Barnsley (01226) 763353
Fax (01226) 763353
Contact: Mrs J M Hird
*Northern edge of Peak Park, 1 mile
Langsett Reservoir, off the A628 in
small hamlet. Views over Pennine
Yorkshire. "The Other Side" is studio
apartment for 2; "The Old Farmhouse"
is cottage for 4/5. Additional sleeping
capacity available for further 2 people.
2 self-contained units; sleeping 2–5*

Price per week:	£min	£max
Low season	150.00	300.00
High season	150.00	300.00

Cards accepted: Access, Visa

◎ 🖦 🛏 ⊙ 🗍 M W 📟 TV 🔌 🍳 ⚓ P ❋
SP

SINNINGTON

North Yorkshire
Map ref 5C3

Delightful village with the River
Seven flowing through its broad
greens. A tall maypole and the
spired school overlook a curious
packhorse bridge.

Low Hall Cottage ⚏

[🔑 🔑 🔑] COMMENDED

Low Hall, Sinnington, York
Contact: Mr W A Slowther, Low
Hall, Sinnington, York YO6 6RY
☎ Kirkbymoorside (01751) 431474
*In North York Moors National Park,
wing of country house sleeps 4 plus
cot. Central heating, log fires inclusive,
garage, garden. Pets welcome. Linen
hire, electricity meter.
1 self-contained unit; sleeping max 4*

Price per week:	£min	£max
Low season	100.00	140.00
High season	150.00	240.00

🐄 M ◎ 🖦 ⊙ 🗍 M W 📟 TV 🍳 🔦
⚓ ∪ ❋

ACCESSIBILITY

Look for the ♿ 🦽 🚶 symbols
which indicate accessibility for
wheelchair users. These are
described in detail at the
front of this guide.

SKIPTON

North Yorkshire
Map ref 4B1

Pleasant market town at gateway to
dales, with farming community
atmosphere, a Palladian Town Hall,
parish church and fully roofed castle
at the top of the High Street.
*Tourist Information Centre ☎ (01756)
792809*

Maypole Cottage ⚏

[🔑 🔑 🔑] HIGHLY COMMENDED

Thorpe, Skipton
Contact: Mrs E M Gamble,
Blackburn House, Thorpe, Skipton,
North Yorkshire BD23 6BJ
☎ Burnsall (01756) 720609
*180-acre mixed farm. Stable converted
to a delightful, well-equipped cottage in
the hamlet of Thorpe near Burnsall.
Exposed beams and stonework. Open
fire. Large garden.
1 self-contained unit; sleeping 4*

Price per week:	£min	£max
Low season	190.00	190.00
High season	320.00	320.00

🐄 M ◎ 🖦 ⊙ 🗍 M W TV 🔌 🍳 🍴 ⚓
P ❋ ✕ 🔦 SP

SLINGSBY

North Yorkshire
Map ref 5C3

Large, attractive village with ruined
castle and village green, on Castle
Howard estate.

The Barn ⚏

[🔑 🔑 🔑] COMMENDED

Banchory Cottage, Railway Street,
Slingsby, York YO6 7AH
☎ Hovingham (01653) 628409
Contact: Mrs M E Hood
*Cosy, well-equipped stone cottage with
lovely large gardens. Near Castle
Howard and ideal for York, coast and
moors. Village shops and pub nearby.
1 self-contained unit; sleeping max 4*

Price per week:	£min	£max
Low season	99.00	
High season		265.00

🐄 ◎ 🖦 ⊙ 🗍 M W TV 🔌 🍳 ⚓ P ❋
🐾

All accommodation in this
guide has been graded, or is
awaiting a grading, by a trained
Tourist Board inspector.

STAITHES

North Yorkshire
Map ref 5C3

Busy fishing village until growth of
Whitby, Staithes is a maze of steep,
cobbled streets packed with tall
houses of red brick and bright
paintwork. Smuggling was rife in
18th C. Cotton bonnets worn by
fisherwomen can still be seen.
Strong associations with Captain
Cook.

Streonshalh

[🔑 🔑] APPROVED

Slippery Hill, Staithes,
Saltburn-by-the-Sea, Cleveland
Contact: Mr & Mrs A S George, 36
Tardrew Close, Beverley, North
Humberside HU17 7QH
☎ Hull (01482) 860915
*Fisherman's cottage in a historic village,
40 yards from the sea. Sea views from
the bedrooms. Open fire. Pets welcome.
1 self-contained unit; sleeping max 6*

Price per week:	£min	£max
Low season	120.00	150.00
High season	190.00	250.00

🐄 M ◎ 🖦 ⊙ 🗍 TV 🔌 🍳 ❋ 🔦 SP

STAMFORD BRIDGE

East Riding of Yorkshire
Map ref 4C1

Village 7 miles east of York, site of
battle in September 1066 at which
Harold of England defeated Harald
of Norway and Tostig.

Sparrow Hall Holiday Cottages ⚏

[🔑 🔑 🔑 🔑] COMMENDED

Church Cottage, Scrayingham, York
YO4 1JD
☎ (01759) 371305
Contact: Mrs H Milner
*260-acre dairy farm. Well-equipped
character cottages on working farm.
Heated indoor swimming pool. Peaceful,
rural location. Log fires, gardens,
payphone. Fishing, riding 1 mile.
Convenient Yorkshire Moors and coast.
5 self-contained units; sleeping 4–6*

Price per week:	£min	£max
Low season	170.00	200.00
High season	320.00	400.00

🐄 ◎ 🖦 ⊙ 🗍 M W TV 🔌 🍳 🍴 🔦 P
⛲ ∪ ✎ ❋ ✕ SP

Please check prices and other
details at the time of booking.

STUTTON

North Yorkshire
Map ref 4C1

Small village on the outskirts of Tadcaster.

Cocksford Cottages ⋒
🔑🔑🔑🔑🔑 UP TO HIGHLY COMMENDED

Cocksford Farm, Stutton, Tadcaster LS24 9NG
☎ Tadcaster (01937) 530344 & 834253
Contact: Mrs S Watkinson
Attractive well-appointed cottages with log fires, in picturesque valley. Close to York, convenient for Harrogate, dales, moors and coast. Adjacent to golf club and superb restaurant.
2 self-contained units; sleeping 6–8

Price per week:	£min	£max
Low season	195.00	280.00
High season	295.00	375.00

⌖🐕◎🖥📺🖨➡📺MW📺🖥➡(📺📡P U📍🌣🚭 SP 🎏

SUMMER BRIDGE

North Yorkshire
Map ref 5C3

In Nidderdale. The timbered sloping footpath through Braisty Wood leads to Brimham Rocks.

Dougill Hall ⋒
🔑🔑🔑🔑– UP TO COMMENDED

Summer Bridge, Harrogate HG3 4JR
☎ Harrogate (01423) 780277
Contact: Mrs J Hollings

Delightful, top floor flat in a Georgian manor house on a working farm overlooking the River Nidd. Also available is the Old Cooling House flat.
2 self-contained units; sleeping 4–6

Price per week:	£min	£max
Low season	130.00	155.00
High season	175.00	200.00

⌖🐕M◎🖥🖨📺🖥➡📡🔥➡U🌙🌣🎏

The National Grading and Classification Scheme is explained in full at the back of this guide.

SUTTON-IN-CRAVEN

North Yorkshire
Map ref 4B1

Daisy Cottage ⋒
🔑🔑🔑🔑 COMMENDED

Daisy Place, Sutton-in-Craven, Keighley, West Yorkshire
Contact: Mrs C Barrows, Daisy Cottage, 6 Daisy Place, Sutton-in-Craven, Keighley, West Yorkshire BD20 7LX
☎ Keighley (01535) 634740
Located between Skipton (and the dales) and Haworth. Quiet, cobbled courtyard, private garden and parking. Sleeps 4/5 (1 double and 1 twin). Gas CH.
1 self-contained unit

Price per week:	£min	£max
Low season	150.00	190.00
High season	210.00	260.00

⌖🐕◎🖥📺➡(📺➡P🌣🗡 SP

THIRSK

North Yorkshire
Map ref 5C3

Thriving market town with cobbled square surrounded by old shops and inns and also with a local museum. St Mary's Church is probably the best example of Perpendicular work in Yorkshire.

The Drays ⋒
🔑🔑🔑🔑 HIGHLY COMMENDED

Lilac Cottage, Knayton, Thirsk
Contact: Mr & Mrs C T Duree, The Drays, Lilac Cottage, Knayton, Thirsk, North Yorkshire YO7 4AZ
☎ Thirsk (01845) 537358
Stable conversion with 2 bedrooms in owner's private grounds. Village location. Furnished, decorated and equipped with an emphasis on standards. Short breaks available.
1 self-contained unit; sleeping 4

Price per week:	£min	£max
Low season	180.00	230.00
High season	230.00	285.00

⌖🐕M◎🖥🖨📺📺MW📺🖥➡➡ P🌙🌣🗡 SP

The Old School House
🔑🔑🔑 COMMENDED

Catton, Thirsk
Contact: Mrs G Readman, School House, Catton, Thirsk, North Yorkshire YO7 4SG
☎ Thirsk (01845) 567308
Formerly the village school, attached to the owner's residence at the School House. Comprises 2 bedrooms, 1

double with a single bed and 1 twin-bedded room, all on ground floor.
1 self-contained unit; sleeping max 5

Price per week:	£min	£max
Low season	105.00	140.00
High season	140.00	175.00

⌖🐕M◎🖥🖨📺📺MW📺🖥➡📡(📺🔥➡P🌣 SP 🎏

Poplars Holiday Cottages ⋒
🔑🔑🔑🔑 COMMENDED

The Poplars, Carlton Miniott, Thirsk YO7 4LX
☎ (01845) 522712
Fax (01845) 522712
Contact: Mrs C M Chilton
Pretty cottages in large garden. Village shop and pub. Enjoy Yorkshire's moors, dales and York city. Friendly welcome with afternoon tea on arrival.
3 self-contained units; sleeping 3–4

Price per week:	£min	£max
Low season	120.00	145.00
High season	180.00	250.00

⌖🐕M◎🍃🖥📺📺MW📺📺🖥➡🖥➡P🌣 SP 🎏

THORNTON DALE

North Yorkshire
Map ref 5D3

Picturesque village with Thorntondale Beck, traversed by tiny stone footbridges at the edge of pretty cottage gardens.

Brookwood ⋒
🔑🔑🔑🔑 HIGHLY COMMENDED

Brook Lane, Thornton Dale, Pickering
Contact: Mrs G Balderson, Brookwood, Welcome Cafe, Thornton Dale, Pickering, North Yorkshire YO18 7RW
☎ Pickering (01751) 474272 & 474218
Large detached house in quiet part of the village yet close to the centre. Beautifully furnished throughout. Scarborough, Whitby and Heartbeat country 30 minutes' drive. Sorry, no pets or children under 8.
1 self-contained unit; sleeping max 5

Price per week:	£min	£max
Low season	180.00	350.00
High season	180.00	350.00

Open March–October

⌖🐕8◎🖥🖨📺📺MW📺🖥➡🖥➡ P🌣🗡

You are advised to confirm your booking in writing.

THORNTON DALE

Continued

Easthill House and Gardens ♙

🔑🔑🔑—🔑🔑🔑
HIGHLY COMMENDED

Wilton Road, Thornton Dale,
Pickering YO18 7QP
☎ Pickering (01751) 474561
Contact: Mrs Jennie Green

Scandinavian-style A-frame chalets with magnificent views, nestling in a pine wood in the private grounds of Easthill House. Also apartments in house.
3 self-contained units; sleeping 1–8

Price per week:	£min	£max
Low season	130.00	235.00
High season	270.00	550.00

🦅◎🖥️�🖿🌐☺🗂️MW📺🖵🖵🗑️🛢️🗒️📺
🐕🅿🌸✿🐾🐾⊠ SP

Green Loaning ♙

🔑🔑🔑 COMMENDED

6 Castle Road, Thornton Dale,
Pickering
Contact: Mrs F Boardman, Green
Loaning, 10 Green Gables Close,
Heald Green, Cheadle, Cheshire
SK8 3QT
☎ Manchester (0161) 4988605

Detached bungalow with extras, magnificent views. Sleeps 2-8 plus cot/high chair. No meters. Suitable for disabled. Magnificent 26ft conservatory. No pets. Centrally heated.
1 self-contained unit; sleeping max 8

Price per week:	£min	£max
Low season	235.00	295.00
High season	325.00	435.00

🦅◎🖥️�🖿☺🗂️MW📺🖵🖵🗑️🛢️🗒️📺
🐕🅿⋃🌸✿🐾⊠ SP

Establishments should be open throughout the year, unless otherwise stated.

TODMORDEN

West Yorkshire
Map ref 4B1

In beautiful scenery on the edge of the Pennines at junction of 3 sweeping valleys. Until 1888 the county boundary between Yorkshire and Lancashire cut this old cotton town in half, running through the middle of the Town Hall.
Tourist Information Centre ☎ *(01706) 818181*

The Cottage

🔑🔑🔑 COMMENDED

Causeway East Farmhouse, Lee
Bottom Road, Todmorden,
Lancashire OL14 6HH
☎ (01706) 815265
Contact: Mr & Mrs A Bentham
Part of a 17th C farmhouse beneath the Pennine Way. Ideal for walking and touring.
1 self-contained unit; sleeping max 4

Price per week:	£min	£max
Low season		110.00
High season		140.00

🦅🖚 M ◎🖥️�🖿☺🗂️MW📺🖵🖵🗑️🛢️🗒️
🐕🅿🌸✿🐾⊠ SP 🎠

Dove Cottage

🔑🔑🔑🔑 DE LUXE

Hartley Royd, Bluebell Lane,, Shore,
Todmorden, Lancashire OL14 8SE
☎ (01706) 816111 & 874487
Fax (01706) 878343
Contact: Mr & Mrs David James
Pilling

Luxuriously refurbished 17th C detached cottage with oak beams. Warm and cosy, with wood burning stove and storage heaters. Fully equipped kitchen with dishwasher, abundant hot water, linen and towels included. Gardens, fields and moors.
1 self-contained unit; sleeping 4

Price per week:	£min	£max
Low season	180.00	295.00
High season	295.00	350.00

🦅◎🖥️�🖿☺🗂️MW📺🖵🖵🗑️🛢️🗒️
🐕🅿🌸✿🐾⊠ SP 🎠

Map references apply to the colour maps at the back of this guide.

WAKEFIELD

West Yorkshire
Map ref 4B1

Thriving city with cathedral church of All Saints boasting 247-ft spire. Old Bridge, a 9-arched structure, has fine medieval chantry chapels of St Mary's. Fine Georgian architecture and good shopping centre (The Ridings). National Coal Mining Museum for England nearby.
Tourist Information Centre ☎ *(01924) 305000 or 305001*

Upper Midgley Farm ♙

Midgley, Wakefield WF4 4JH
☎ (01924) 830294
Fax (01924) 830294
Contact: Mr & Mrs Greenwood

80-acre dairy farm. Newly refurbished 300-year-old farm cottage situated on working dairy farm with extensive rural views. Convenient for numerous tourist attractions. Six miles south-west of Wakefield.
1 self-contained unit; sleeping max 8

Price per week:	£min	£max
Low season	150.00	250.00
High season	250.00	350.00

🦅◎🖥️�🖿☺🗂️MW📺🖵🖵🗑️🛢️🗒️📺
🐕🅿⋃🌸✿🐾 SP

WELBURY

North Yorkshire
Map ref 5C3

Village in the Vale of Mowbray with views towards the Hambleton Hills.

Summerfield Cottage ♙

🔑🔑🔑 COMMENDED

Welbury, Northallerton
Contact: Mrs S H Holmes,
Summerfield House Farm, Welbury,
Northallerton, North Yorkshire
DL6 2SL
☎ Northallerton (01609) 882393
Fax (01609) 882393
Enjoy the peaceful surroundings of this modern, well-appointed 3-bedroomed farm cottage, with superb views over open countryside. Central for the dales, North York Moors, coast, Herriot country and York.

1 self-contained unit; sleeping max 5

Price per week:	£min	£max
Low season	110.00	150.00
High season	150.00	200.00

🖤Ⓜ◎🏠⊙🏠📧🎁📺📷📧📧🚗P
♿❄️SP

WEST SCRAFTON

North Yorkshire
Map ref 5B3

Amongst the farmhouses are several cottages once occupied by quarrymen and colliers. In the deep limestone gill below the village are several caverns, one of which, known as Tom Hunter's Parlour, is named after a highwayman supposed to have been captured there.

Hill Top Farm Cottage Holidays

🔑🔑 HIGHLY COMMENDED

West Scrafton, Middleham, Leyburn DL8 4RU
☎ Wensleydale (01969) 640663
Contact: Mr & Mrs B Harrison

180-acre mixed farm. Relax in this recently converted stone barn on working hill farm. Peace and tranquillity, panoramic views. Join in the daily routines.
1 self-contained unit; sleeping 6

Price per week:	£min	£max
Low season	190.00	
High season		399.00

🖤◎🏠⊙🏠MW📺📷📧📧🚗P
♿🎣❄️SP🏠

The Ⓜ symbol after an establishment name indicates that it is a Regional Tourist Board member.

Information on accommodation listed in this guide has been supplied by the proprietors. As changes may occur you are advised to check details at the time of booking.

WHITBY

North Yorkshire
Map ref 5D3

Quaint holiday town with narrow streets and steep alleys at the mouth of the River Esk. Captain James Cook, the famous navigator, lived in Grape Lane. 199 steps lead to St Mary's Church and St Hilda's Abbey overlooking harbour. Dracula connections. Sandy beach.
Tourist Information Centre ☎ (01947) 602674

Asp House

🔑🔑 COMMENDED

Asp House Farm, Stainsacre, Whitby YO22 4LR
☎ (01947) 603997
Contact: Mrs P Ward
70-acre livestock farm. Charming and spacious beamed cottage with beautiful views and a delightful garden. Between the coast, moors and dales, between Whitby and Robin Hood's Bay. Ideal for walking or relaxing. Log fire and storage heaters for winter breaks.
1 self-contained unit; sleeping max 6

Price per week:	£min	£max
Low season	150.00	200.00
High season	250.00	330.00

🖤Ⓜ◎🏠⊙🏠MW📺📷📧📧🚗
P❄️🐾SP◎

Captain Cook's Haven Ⓜ

🔑🔑— UP TO COMMENDED

Larpool Lane, Whitby YO22 4JE
☎ (01947) 601396
Fax (01947) 893573
Contact: Mrs A Barrowman
Tastefully designed and well-equipped, recently-built cottages in a riverside setting only 1 mile from Whitby. Indoor heated pool, children's playground.
Wheelchair access category 2♿
44 self-contained units; sleeping 4–7

Price per week:	£min	£max
Low season	165.00	220.00
High season	200.00	520.00

Open February–October
Cards accepted: Access, Visa
🖤◎🏠⊙🏠MW📧📺📷📧📧
🚗P🎣❄️SP◎

Primrose & Bluebell Cottages Ⓜ

🔑🔑 HIGHLY COMMENDED

Low Newbiggin North Farm, Aislaby, Whitby YO21 1TQ
☎ (01947) 810948
Fax (01947) 810948
Contact: Mr & Mrs K Morton
Farmhouse cottages with full facilities. 4 miles from Whitby in riverside location. Mini golf-course and own helipad.

---

2 self-contained units; sleeping 4–5

Price per week:	£min	£max
Low season	160.00	
High season		300.00

🖤◎🏠⊙🏠MW📧📺📷📧📧
🚗PU🎣❄️🍴SP

Swallow Holiday Cottages Ⓜ

🔑🔑—🔑🔑 COMMENDED

The Farm, Stainsacre, Whitby YO22 4NT
☎ (01947) 603790
Fax (01947) 603790
Contact: Mr & Mrs McNeil

Mews of converted farm cottages in a private courtyard, in a small village close to the moors and the sea. Ideal for couples or family groups. Part weeks available low season.
5 self-contained units; sleeping 3–5

Price per week:	£min	£max
Low season	95.00	130.00
High season	155.00	280.00

Cards accepted: Visa
🖤Ⓜ◎🏠⊙🏠MW📺📷📧🚗P
❄️SP

Swan Cottage Ⓜ

🔑🔑 APPROVED

High Hawsker, Whitby
Contact: Mrs M A Smith, Swan Farm, High Hawsker, Whitby, North Yorkshire YO22 4LH
☎ Whitby (01947) 880682
Country cottage in Hawsker village, 3 miles from Robin Hood's Bay and Whitby. Two double bedrooms and one twin-bedded room. Ideal for beach and North York Moors National Park.
1 self-contained unit; sleeping max 6

Price per week:	£min	£max
Low season	150.00	150.00
High season	200.00	300.00

🖤◎🏠⊙🏠MW📺📷📧📧🚗P
U❄️

The symbols in each entry give information about services and facilities. A 'key' to these symbols appears at the back of this guide.

WHITBY
Continued

White Rose Holiday Cottages ⚏
🔑🔑🔑 UP TO COMMENDED

Rambler's Court, Sleights, Whitby
Contact: Mrs J E Roberts,
Greenacres, 5 Brook Park, Sleights,
Whitby, North Yorkshire YO21 1RT
☎ Whitby (01947) 810763
Relax in superior village house and cottages, all tastefully decorated and well-equipped. Personally supervised by owners. Ideal for coast and country. Short or long breaks in winter.
3 self-contained units; sleeping 4–7

Price per week:	£min	£max
Low season	140.00	205.00
High season	205.00	395.00

🛏📺🟦📖☺🗄📼🏴🍴🚗P Ṳ✿✎SP◎

YORK
Map ref 4C1

Ancient walled city nearly 2000 years old containing many well-preserved medieval buildings. Its Minster has over 100 stained glass windows. Attractions include Castle Museum, National Railway Museum, Jorvik Viking Centre and York Dungeon.
Tourist Information Centre ☎ (01904) 621756 or 621756 or 620557

Abbey House & Intermain Leisure Self Catering Holidays ⚏
🔑🔑🔑 – 🔑🔑🔑 UP TO COMMENDED

7 St Mary's, York
Contact: Mrs J H Lee, Carlton House, 7 St Mary's, York Y03 7DD
☎ York (01904) 636154 & Ripon (01765) 605133
Fax (01904) 612340
Self-contained apartments with 1 or 2 bedrooms, in a quiet residential cul-de-sac in the heart of historic York.
28 self-contained units; sleeping 1–6

Price per week:	£min	£max
Low season	110.00	190.00
High season	190.00	375.00

🛏📺🟦📖☺🗄MW📺🏴🍴🗓🚗 P✎SP🏠📞
Ad See display advertisement on this page

Abbeygate House ⚏
🔑🔑🔑🔑 HIGHLY COMMENDED

2A Bishopgate Street, York
Contact: Mr C Halliday, Abbeygate House, 3 Grange Drive, Horsforth, Leeds LS18 5EQ
☎ Leeds (0113) 258 4947 & 258 9833
Interior-designed Georgian-style town house with 5 bedrooms, overlooking city walls. Fully equipped, garden/patio, parking for 2-3 cars. 5 minutes' walk from city centre. Short breaks available.
1 self-contained unit; sleeping 8

Price per week:	£min	£max
Low season	250.00	295.00
High season	300.00	595.00

Cards accepted: Access, Visa
🛏6◎🟦☺🗄MW📼📺🏴🍴 📖🚗P✿✎SP

Baile Hill Cottage ⚏
🔑🔑🔑 COMMENDED

5 Baile Hill Terrace, Bishophill, York
Contact: Mr & Mrs P&S Hodgson, Baile Hill Cottage, Avalon, North Lane, Wheldrake, York, North Yorkshire YO1 4AY
☎ York (01904) 448670
Fax (01904) 448908
Victorian town cottage with 2 bedrooms, dining room, lounge and modern fitted kitchen. Many original features, plus a four-poster bed. Peaceful, central location overlooking the city walls. Private patio garden, car parking at door.

1 self-contained unit; sleeping max 6

Price per week:	£min	£max
Low season	110.00	239.00
High season	229.00	329.00

🛏◎⊘🟦☺🗄MW📼📺🏴🍴🗓 🚗P✿✎🐾SP

Baille Hill House ⚏
🔑🔑🔑🔑 HIGHLY COMMENDED

2 Bishopgate Street, York
Contact: Mr M F Halliday, 2 Grange Drive, Horsforth, Leeds LS18 5EQ
☎ Leeds (0113) 258 4212

Georgian-style 5-bedroomed town house, adjacent Bishop's Wharf and overlooking medieval city walls. Interior-designed elegance, with co-ordinated Skopos fabrics and furnishings. Private parking. Short breaks available.
1 self-contained unit; sleeping 8

Price per week:	£min	£max
Low season	250.00	400.00
High season	400.00	560.00

Cards accepted: Access, Visa
🛏6◎🟦☺🗄MW📼📺🏴🍴 📖🚗P🍴SP

Bishophill Holidays
🔑🔑🔑 APPROVED

5 Kyme Street, Bishophill, York
Contact: Mrs L A Shimmin, 49 Moorgate, Acomb, York YO2 4HP
☎ York (01904) 796118
Comfortable Victorian artisan's terraced house in a quiet residential conservation area within the City walls. Family-run. Parking available. No extras.
1 self-contained unit; sleeping 1–6

Price per week:	£min	£max
Low season	110.00	160.00
High season	170.00	290.00

Bootham Terrace Apartments

UP TO COMMENDED

6 Bootham Terrace, York
Contact: Mrs S M Harrand, Hedley House, 3-4 Bootham Terrace, York YO3 7DH
☎ York (01904) 637404
City centre apartments next to owner's hotel. Car parking available. Easy 10-minute walk to centre. Quiet location.
3 self-contained units; sleeping 4–6

Price per week:	£min	£max
Low season	100.00	200.00
High season	190.00	305.00

Cedar Lodge

APPROVED

Elvington Grange, Elvington, York Y04 5AZ
☎ (01904) 608340
Contact: Mrs L Brabbs
160-acre mixed farm. On a working farm 6 miles from York. Ideal touring base for York and the surrounding areas. Pubs and shops 1.5 miles away.
1 self-contained unit; sleeping max 6

Price per week:	£min	£max
Low season	170.00	200.00
High season	200.00	260.00

1 Cloisters Walk

COMMENDED

St Maurice's Road, Monkgate, York
Contact: Mrs McManus, 1 Cloisters Walk, Homefinders Holidays, Fossgate Chambers, 47 Fossgate, York YO1 2TF
☎ York (01904) 632660 & 655200
Fax (01904) 651388

Comfortable, modern house, beautifully placed 500 yards from York Minster. Excellent views, tranquil and spacious garden. Your "corner shop" is Sainsbury's (200 yards).
1 self-contained unit; sleeping 6

Price per week:	£min	£max
Low season	180.00	265.00
High season	275.00	330.00

Five Pennies

HIGHLY COMMENDED

Broad Lane, Appleton Roebuck, York YO5 7DS
☎ (01904) 744562
Fax (01904) 744562
Contact: Mrs M B Wilson
Modern, newly constructed self-contained studio unit. In peaceful country area just south of York. Ideal base for touring the city, moors and coastal regions.
1 self-contained unit; sleeping 3

Price per week:	£min	£max
Low season	105.00	
High season		170.00

Grafton House Apartments

COMMENDED

13 Bootham Terrace, York YO3 7DH
☎ (01904) 625902
Contact: Mrs A Harrand
Spacious apartments in Victorian town house with walled garden. Quiet residential area within easy walking distance of city centre. No meters.
4 self-contained units; sleeping 2–5

Price per week:	£min	£max
Low season	150.00	165.00
High season	260.00	280.00

15 Postern Close

COMMENDED

Bishop's Wharfe, York
Contact: English Country Cottages, Grove Farm Barns, Fakenham, Norfolk NR21 9NB
☎ (01328) 851155
Ground floor apartment in the centre of historic York. Part of the award-winning Bishop's Wharfe development on the River Ouse. Within easy walking distance of York city centre, tourist attractions and restaurants. Fully furnished.
1 self-contained unit; sleeping 3

Price per week:	£min	£max
Low season	250.00	350.00
High season	270.00	400.00

84 Postern Close

HIGHLY COMMENDED

Bishop's Wharfe, York
Contact: Mrs B Harris, Angel House Farm, Wistow Common, Selby, North Yorkshire YO8 ORW
☎ Selby (01757) 268250
Fax (01757) 268210
Recently built, fully-equipped town house on a riverside complex less than 5 minutes from the city centre, bus and rail station. Lock-up garage. Sorry, no pets or cot.
1 self-contained unit; sleeping max 6

Price per week:	£min	£max
Low season	250.00	
High season		440.00

A key to symbols can be found inside the back cover flap.

CHECK THE MAPS

The colour maps at the back of this guide show
all the cities, towns and villages for which you will
find accommodation entries.

Refer to the town index to find the page
on which it is listed.

YORK
Continued

Priory Apartment
🗝🗝🗝🗝 COMMENDED

19A Priory Street, York
Contact: Mrs McManus,
Homefinders of York, Fossgate
Chambers, 47 Fossgate, York
YO1 2TF
☎ York (01904) 632660 & 655200
Fax (01904) 651388
Newly-built, 2-bedroomed flat in the centre of York. Fully equipped and heated.
1 self-contained unit; sleeping 4

Price per week:	£min	£max
Low season	190.00	275.00
High season	275.00	330.00

Riverside Holiday Flat ⚶
🗝🗝🗝🗝 HIGHLY COMMENDED

61 Postern Close, York
Contact: Mr P A Jackson, 17 Great
Close, Cawood, Selby, North
Yorkshire YO8 0UG
☎ Selby (01757) 268207 & Mobile
(0585) 921691
Fax (01757) 268122
Double-bedroomed, first floor apartment with a patio balcony.

Overlooking the river and with fine views of the city. Own parking space.
1 self-contained unit; sleeping max 3

Price per week:	£min	£max
Low season	175.00	195.00
High season	230.00	300.00

Swallow Hall
🗝🗝🗝–🗝🗝🗝🗝 COMMENDED

Crockey Hill, York YO1 4SG
☎ (01904) 448219
Contact: Mrs C Scutt

Single-storey cottages of character in a converted stable block overlooking farmland and forestry, 5 miles from York city centre. Open fires. Own 18-hole golf course and driving range.
3 self-contained units; sleeping 4

Price per week:	£min	£max
Low season	140.00	
High season		270.00

York Lakeside Lodges ⚶
🗝🗝🗝🗝 UP TO DE LUXE

Moor Lane, York YO2 2QU
☎ (01904) 702346 & 0831 885824
Fax (01904) 701631
Contact: Mr N Manasir
Well-equipped Scandinavian pine lodges in secluded parkland surrounding private fishing lake, yet within the city of York. Winner White Rose Award.
Wheelchair access category 2♿
16 self-contained units; sleeping 2–7

Price per week:	£min	£max
Low season	180.00	300.00
High season	360.00	580.00

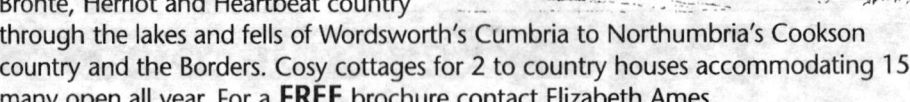

HEART OF ENGLAND

The heart of England is a pot pourri of rural charm and urban vitality. From the spa town of Cheltenham to the busy streets of Birmingham, from the remote grandeur of the Western Marches to the gentle beauty of tiny Cotswold villages, the area will appeal to culture buffs and country lovers alike.

Visit Shakespeare country and Stratford with its world-famous theatre. Discover the craftsmanship of the Potteries and explore the rich industrial heritage of the Black Country. Or simply escape to the Staffordshire peaks, the Malvern Hills, or the gently meandering byways of the Severn Valley.

FOR MORE INFORMATION CONTACT:
Heart of England Tourist Board
Lark Hill Road, Worcester WR5 2EZ
Tel: (01905) 763436 or 763439
Fax: (01905) 763450

Where to Go in the Heart of England -
see pages 114-117
Where to Stay in the Heart of England -
see pages 118-150

HEART OF ENGLAND

Where to Go and What to See

You will find hundreds of interesting places to visit during your stay in the Heart of England, just some of which are listed in these pages. The number against each name will help you locate it on the map (page 117). Contact any Tourist Information Centre in the region for more ideas on days out in the Heart of England.

1 Spode
Spode Works, Church Street,
Stoke-on-Trent,
Staffordshire ST4 1BX
Tel: (01782) 744220
Visitors are shown the various processes in the making of Bone China. Samples can be bought at the Spode Shop.

2 Wedgwood Visitor Centre
Barlaston, Stoke-on-Trent,
Staffordshire ST12 9ES
Tel: (01782) 204141
Located in the Wedgwood Factory which lies within a 500 acre country estate. See potters and decorators at work. Museum and shop.

3 Alton Towers Theme Park
Alton, Staffordshire ST10 4DB
Tel: (0990) 204060
Theme Park with over 125 rides and attractions including Nemesis, Haunted House, Runaway Mine Train, Congo River Rapids, Log Flume, Thunderlooper and Toyland tours.

4 Shugborough Estate
Shugborough, Milford, Stafford,
Staffordshire ST17 0XB
Tel: (01889) 881388
18thC mansion house with fine collection of furniture. Gardens and park contain beautiful neo-classical monuments.

5 The Shrewsbury Quest
193 Abbey Foregate,
Shrewsbury,
Shropshire SY2 6AH
Tel: (01743) 243324
12thC Shrewsbury historical site. Visitors are invited to solve three mysteries, creating manuscripts and playing medieval garden games.

6 Ironbridge Gorge Museum
Ironbridge, Telford,
Shropshire TF8 7AW
Tel: (01952) 433522
Worlds first cast iron bridge, Museum of the River Visitor Centre, Tar Tunnel, Jackfield Tile Museum, Coalport China Museum, Rosehill House, Blists Hill Museum and Museum of Iron.

7 Walsall Arboretum
Lichfield Street,
Walsall, West Midlands
Tel: (01922) 653141
Picturesque Victorian park with over 79 acres of gardens, lakes and parkland, just 5 minutes walk from Walsall town centre. The arboretum is home to the Walsall illuminations.

8 Black Country Museum
Tipton Road, Dudley,
West Midlands DY1 4SQ
Tel: (0121) 557 9643
Midlands open air museum with shops, chapel, canal trip into limestone cavern houses, underground mining display and electric tramway.

9 Birmingham Botanical Gardens and Glasshouses
Westbourne Road,
Edgbaston, Birmingham,

West Midlands B15 3TR
Tel: (0121) 454 1860
Fifteen acres of ornamental gardens and glasshouses. Tropical plants of botanical interest. Aviaries with exotic birds and children's play area.

10 National Sea Life Centre
The Water's Edge, Brindleyplace,
Birmingham B1 2HL
Tel: (0121) 633 4700
Over 55 fascinating displays. The opportunity to come face-to-face with literally 100's of fascinating sea creatures from sharks to shrimps.

11 Cadbury World
Linden Road, Bournville,
Birmingham,
West Midlands B30 2LD
Tel: (0121) 451 4180
Story of Chocolate from Aztec times to present day includes chocolate-making demonstration and children's fantasy factory.

12 National Motorcycle Museum
Coventry Road, Bickenhill,
Solihull, West Midlands B92 0EJ
Tel: (01675) 443311
Museum with a collection of 650 British machines from 1898-1993, housed in a new high architectural standard building.

13 Museum of British Road Transport
St Agnes Lane,
Hales Street, Coventry,
West Midlands CV1 1NN
Tel: (01203) 832425
Museum with a collection of over 400 cars, commercial vehicles, cycles and motorcycles from 1818 to present day.

14 Rugby School Museum
10 Little Church Street,
Rugby, Warwickshire CV21 3AW
Tel: (01788) 574117
Tells the story of the School, scene of Tom Brown's Schooldays, and contains early memorabilia of the game of rugby invented on the School Close.

15 Severn Valley Railway
The Railway Station, Bewdley,
Worcestershire DY12 1BG
Tel: (01299) 403816
Preserved standard gauge steam railway running 16 miles between Kidderminster, Bewdley and Bridgnorth. Collection of locomotives and passenger coaches.

16 Warwick Castle
Warwick,
Warwickshire CV34 4QU
Tel: (01926) 406600
Set in 60 acres of grounds with state rooms, armoury, dungeon, torture chamber, clock tower. Exhibits include a Royal Weekend Party 1898, a preparation for battle scene and Kingmaker Feasts.

17 Ragley Hall
Alcester,
Warwickshire B49 5NJ
Tel: (01789) 762090
17thC Palladian House, home of the Earl and Countess of Yarmouth, restored with French furnishing. Also 3D maze, woodland walk and lakeside picnic area.

18 Heritage Motor Centre
Banbury Road,
Gaydon,
Warwick,
Warwickshire CV35 0BJ
Tel: (01926) 641188
Purpose-built transport museum containing collection of historic British cars. 63 acre site including 4 wheel drive circuit, playground, picnic area and nature reserve.

19 Elgar's Birthplace Museum
Crown East Lane,
Lower Broadheath,
Worcester,
Worcestershire WR2 6RH
Tel: (01905) 333224
The cottage in which Edward Elgar was born, now houses a museum of photographs, musical scores, letters and records.

20 **Shakespeare's Birthplace**
Henley Street,
Stratford-upon-Avon
Warwickshire CV37 6QW
Tel: (01789) 204016
Evoking the busy market town into which he was born, the exhibition covers Shakespeare's home background, schooling, marriage and theatre career in London.

21 **Worcester Cathedral**
10A College Green
Worcester, WR1 2LH
Tel: (01905) 611002
Norman crypt and chapter house. King John's Tomb. Prince Arthur's Chantry, medieval cloisters and buildings.

22 **Malvern Hills Children's Zoo**
Solitaire, Danemoor Cross,
Welland, Malvern,
Worcestershire WR13 6NJ
Tel: (01684) 310016
Tropical animals, pets corner and creepy-crawly house. Visitors can handle the animals, reptiles and see snake demonstrations daily.

23 **The New Mappa Mundi & Chained Library Museum**
Hereford Cathedral,
5 The Cloister, Hereford,
Herefordshire HR1 2NG
Tel: (01432) 359880
The New Library of Hereford Cathedral is open to visitors. See also the unique Mappa Mundi, the largest and most complete map in the world, drawn in 1289.

24 **The National Birds of Prey Centre**
Newent, Gloucestershire GL18 1JJ
Tel: (01531) 820286
Large collection of birds of prey. Flying demonstrations daily, weather permitting, with eagles, falcons, hawks, owls and vultures. Also breeding aviaries.

25 **Three Choirs Vineyards**
Baldwins Farm, Newent,
Gloucestershire GL18 1LS
Tel: (01531) 890555
Home of internationally awarded Three Choirs wine. Visitors are welcome to look round the vineyards and taste the wines at no charge.

26 **National Waterways Museum**
Llanthony Warehouse,
Gloucester Docks,
Gloucester GL1 2EH
Tel: (01452) 318054
Three floors of dockside warehouse with lively displays telling the story of Britain's canals. Outside craft area with demonstrations. Cafe and shop.

27 **Soldiers of Gloucestershire Museum**
Custom House,
Gloucester Docks,
Gloucester GL1 2HE
Tel: (01452) 522682
Listed Victorian building in historic docks. The story of Gloucestershire's foot and horse soldiers in the last 300 years.

FIND OUT MORE

Further information about holidays and attractions in the Heart of England is available from: **Heart of England Tourist Board,**
Lark Hill Road,
Worcester WR5 2EZ.
Tel: (01905) 763436 (24 hours)

These publications are available free from the Heart of England Tourist Board:
■ **Bed & Breakfast Touring Map**
■ **Great Escapes - short breaks and leisure holidays for all seasons**
■ **Events list**

Also available are:
Places to Visit in the Heart of England - a comprehensive guide to over 750 varied attractions and things to see, also great ideas for where to go in winter, (over £40 in discount vouchers included). £3.99
■ **Cotswolds Map** £2.95
■ **Cotswold/Wyndean Map** £3.25
■ **Shropshire/Staffordshire Map** £3.25
Please add 60p postage for up to 3 items, plus 25p for each additional 3 items.

CHESHIRE

DERBYSHIRE

- Leek

Newcastle-
under-Lyme
Stoke-on-Trent
1 **2** Alton **3**
Barlaston
Uttoxeter

Whitchurch

Market Drayton

Oswestry

STAFFORDSHIRE

SHROPSHIRE

Stafford **4**

Newport

Wellington

Rugeley

Cannock

Lichfield

Shrewsbury **5**

Telford

Tamworth

**LEICESTER-
SHIRE**

Ironbridge **6**

Wolverhampton

Walsall

Atherstone

7

Much Wenlock

Bridgnorth

Wombourne

**WEST
MIDLANDS**

Nuneaton

Bishop's Castle

Dudley **8**

Birmingham
9 **10**
Bickenhill

13 Coventry

12

Kidderminster

Bournville

11

Solihull

Rugby **14**

15 Bewdley

Bromsgrove

Hatton

Kenilworth

Ludlow

Stoke Heath

Redditch

Warwick **16**

Royal
Leamington
Spa

Leominster

Droitwich

17 Alcester

18 Gaydon

Kington

19 Lower Broadheath

Bromyard

Stratford-
upon-Avon **20**

Wellesbourne

**HEREFORD
& WORCESTER**

Worcester **21**

WARWICKSHIRE

22 Pershore

Evesham

Welland

Upton upon
Severn

Hereford **23**

Ledbury

Broadway

Tewkesbury

24 **25**

Winchcombe

Newent

Stow on the Wold

Gloucester

Cheltenham

26 **27**

GLOUCESTERSHIRE

WALES

Coleford

Painswick

Northleach

OXFORDSHIRE

Stroud

0   20 Miles

0   30 Kms

Berkeley

Nailsworth

Cirencester

Tetbury

**SOUTH
GLOUCS**

WILTSHIRE

WHERE TO STAY (HEART OF ENGLAND)

Accommodation entries in this region are listed in alphabetical order of place name, and then in alphabetical order of establishment. A contact address is given where it differs from the address of the establishment.

Map references refer to the colour location maps at the back of this guide.

Prices shown are weekly per unit.

At-a-glance symbols at the end of each accommodation entry give useful information about services and facilities. A key to symbols can be found inside the back cover flap. Keep this open for easy reference.

ABBERLEY

Hereford and Worcester
Map ref 4A3

Village with some interesting buildings including a pre-Reformation rectory and a Gothic clock tower with 20 bells. At Great Witley nearby is a magnificent 18th C church with rich plasterwork, paintings and carving and the gardens and ruins of Witley Court.

Old Yates Cottages ⋀

COMMENDED

Old Yates Farm, Abberley, Worcester
Contact: Mr & Mrs R M Goodman, Old Yates Farm, Abberley, Worcester WR6 6AT
☎ Great Witley (01299) 896500
90-acre livestock farm. Cosy, individual cottages in tranquil surroundings amidst beautiful countryside. A personal welcome awaits you. Convenient for exploring the Midlands and Welsh Borders - so much to see and do.
Wheelchair access category 3⚹
6 self-contained units; sleeping 2–8

Price per week:	£min	£max
Low season	115.00	230.00
High season	210.00	370.00

ALCESTER

Warwickshire
Map ref 2B1

Town has Roman origins and many old buildings around the High Street. It is close to Ragley Hall, the 18th C Palladian mansion with its magnificent baroque Great Hall.

Dorset House Cottage and Dorset House

HIGHLY COMMENDED

Meeting Lane, Alcester
Contact: Mrs G Plummer, Dorset House, Church Street, Alcester, Warwickshire B49 5AJ
☎ Stratford-upon-Avon (01789) 762856
Detached quiet cottage and Georgian town house facing the church, each with antique furnishings and modern facilities. Pleasant location 7 miles from Stratford-upon-Avon.
2 self-contained units; sleeping 4–8

Price per week:	£min	£max
Low season	170.00	
High season		500.00

ALDERTON

Gloucestershire
Map ref 2B1

Hillside village with wide views of Evesham Vale. The restored church has a 15th C tower, a broken Saxon font and some medieval glass. Some stone from the previous Norman church has been incorporated into its structure.

Rectory Farm Cottages ⋀

HIGHLY COMMENDED

Alderton, Tewkesbury GL20 8NW
☎ (01242) 620455
Fax (01242) 620455
Contact: Mr & Mrs P Burton
Pretty half-timbered and stone cottages in the centre of the village. Shared use of swimming pool and snooker room.
6 self-contained units; sleeping 3–7

Price per week:	£min	£max
Low season	210.00	450.00
High season	380.00	800.00

The map references refer to the colour maps towards the end of the guide. The first figure is the map number; the letter and figure which follow indicate the grid reference on the map.

A key to symbols can be found inside the back cover flap.

Information on accommodation listed in this guide has been supplied by the proprietors. As changes may occur you are advised to check details at the time of booking.

ALDSWORTH

Gloucestershire
Map ref 2B1

Village near many interesting places such as Northleach with its beautiful church, Burford, one of the finest Cotswold towns, Chedworth Roman Villa and Bibury with its trout farm and famous row of cottages.

Aldsworth Place 🎵
COMMENDED

Aldsworth, Cheltenham
Contact: Mr & Mrs Munson-Kingham, Aldsworth Place, Aldsworth, Cheltenham, Gloucestershire GL54 3RE
☎ Cotswold (01451) 844461
Fax (01451) 844461
Between Burford and Bibury, 1-bedroomed cottages (1 single storey) in converted stableyard in river valley. Comfortably furnished and fully equipped.
3 self-contained units; sleeping 2

Price per week:	£min	£max
Low season	125.00	
High season		250.00

ALSTONEFIELD

Staffordshire
Map ref 4B2

Peaceful village well situated for exploring the pleasant countryside of Dovedale, much of which is owned by the National Trust.

Kitchen Cottage 🎵
COMMENDED

The Old Vicarage, Alstonefield, Ashbourne, Derbyshire
Contact: Ms C Osborne, The Old Vicarage, Alstonefield, Ashbourne, Derbyshire DE6 2FX
☎ Alstonefield (01335) 310453
Fax (01335) 310459
Ground floor flat, part of an 18th C former vicarage, situated in a picturesque village in the Peak District National Park.
1 self-contained unit; sleeping 4

Price per week:	£min	£max
Low season	130.00	250.00
High season	220.00	290.00

ATHERSTONE

Warwickshire
Map ref 4B3

Pleasant market town with some 18th C houses and interesting old inns. Every Shrove Tuesday a game of football is played in the streets, a tradition which dates from the 13th C. Twycross Zoo is nearby with an extensive collection of reptiles and butterflies.

Hipsley Farm Cottages 🎵
HIGHLY COMMENDED

Hipsley Lane, Hurley, Atherstone
Contact: Mrs A Prosser, Waste Farm, Hurley, Atherstone, Warwickshire CV9 2LR
☎ Tamworth (01827) 872437
Fax (01827) 872437
340-acre arable farm. Beautifully converted farm buildings in very quiet countryside, yet only 3 miles from junction 10 M42/A5. Fully equipped, with putting green and barbecue on site.
Wheelchair access category 2 ♿
6 self-contained units; sleeping 2–4

Price per week:	£min	£max
Low season	220.00	280.00
High season	265.00	330.00

BARLASTON

Staffordshire
Map ref 4B2

Wedgwood Memorial College 🎵
APPROVED

Station Road, Barlaston, Stoke-on-Trent ST12 9DG
☎ Stoke-on-Trent (01782) 372105 & 373427
Fax (01782) 372393
Contact: Dr D Tatton
Tastefully decorated detached bungalow and lodge in grounds of adult residential college with relaxed, homely ambience. In quiet village yet close to National Trust downs and Potteries. Convenient for Peak District, Alton Towers. Good quality, home-cooked food with an imaginative repertoire of vegetarian dishes available by arrangement. Limited facilities for disabled.
2 self-contained units; sleeping 4–5

Price per week:	£min	£max
Low season	150.00	
High season	165.00	

Cards accepted: Access, Visa

BAYTON

Hereford and Worcester
Map ref 4A3

A north-west Worcestershire village on a hill, with some pretty cottages of half-timber and with fine distant views into Shropshire from the sloping field in which the church is set.

Broad Meadows Farmhouse 🎵
COMMENDED

Bayton, Clows Top, Kidderminster, Worcestershire DY14 9LP
☎ Clows Top (01299) 832608
Fax (01299) 832608
Contact: Mrs J Chance

Oak-beamed farmhouse apartment plus 16th C timber-framed stable wing. On village edge with superb views. Character accommodation with CH throughout. Units can be interconnected for parties of 10-12.
2 self-contained units; sleeping 4–8

Price per week:	£min	£max
Low season	150.00	250.00
High season	190.00	350.00

BEWDLEY

Hereford and Worcester
Map ref 4A3

Attractive town on the River Severn, approached by a bridge designed by Telford. The town has many elegant buildings and an interesting craft and folk museum. On the Severn Valley Steam Railway. *Tourist Information Centre ☎ (01299) 404740*

Peacock Coach House 🎵
HIGHLY COMMENDED

Lower Park, Bewdley, Worcestershire

Continued ▶

BEWDLEY

Continued

Contact: Mrs P Hall, Peacock Coach House, Lower Park, Bewdley, Worcestershire DY12 2DP
☎ Bewdley (01299) 400149
Fax (01299) 401082
Restored 17th C oak-beamed coach house, 5 minutes from Bewdley town centre and River Severn. Private walled garden with patio and barbecue.
1 self-contained unit; sleeping max 5

Price per week:	£min	£max
Low season	230.00	275.00
High season	275.00	380.00

BIBURY

Gloucestershire
Map ref 2B1

Village on the River Coln with stone houses and the famous 17th C Arlington Row, former weavers' cottages. Arlington Mill is now a folk museum. Trout farm and Bansley House Gardens nearby are open to the public.

Bibury Holiday Cottages

COMMENDED

Coln Cottage, Arlington, Bibury, Cirencester GL7 5NL
☎ Cirencester (01285) 740314
Contact: Mr and Mrs A R Binns
Delightful 17th C Cotswold cottages in lovely gardens, set in the beautiful riverside village of Bibury.
3 self-contained units; sleeping 3–4

Price per week:	£min	£max
Low season	140.00	170.00
High season	180.00	300.00

Cotteswold Court

HIGHLY COMMENDED

Arlington, Bibury, Cirencester
Contact: Mrs Judith Underwood, Cotteswold House, Arlington, Bibury, Cirencester, Gloucestershire GL7 5ND
☎ Cirencester (01285) 740609
Fax (01285) 740609
Ideally situated for touring the Cotswolds, this spacious two-bedroomed apartment has been tastefully furnished and equipped to a high standard. Garage. Central heating, electricity, linen included. No smoking or pets.

1 self-contained unit; sleeping 4

Price per week:	£min	£max
Low season	185.00	
High season		285.00

BIRMINGHAM

West Midlands
Map ref 4B3

Britain's second city, whose attractions include Centenary Square and the ICC with Symphony Hall, the NEC, the City Art Gallery, Barber Institute of Fine Arts, 17th C Aston Hall, science and railway museums, Jewellery Quarter, Cadbury World, 2 cathedrals and Botanical Gardens.
Tourist Information Centre ☎ (0121) 693 6300 or 780 4321

Sandon Properties Ltd

UP TO COMMENDED

385 Hagley Road, Edgbaston, Birmingham
Contact: Ms V Price, Sandon Properties Ltd, 385 Hagley Road, Edgbaston, Birmingham B17 8DL
☎ (0121) 420 2301
Fax (0121) 429 5155
Self-catering serviced apartments with breakfast and grocery service available. "Home from Home". A smart cost-effective alternative to hotels.
8 self-contained units; sleeping 1–8

Price per week:	£min	£max
Low season	150.00	210.00
High season	175.00	245.00

Cards accepted: Access, Visa, Diners, Amex

BIRMINGHAM AIRPORT

West Midlands

See under Birmingham, Coventry

WELCOME HOST

This is a nationally recognised customer care programme which aims to promote the highest standards of service and a warm welcome. Establishments who are taking part in this initiative are indicated by the ✿ symbol.

BISHOP'S CASTLE

Shropshire
Map ref 4A3

A 12th C Planned Town with a castle site at the top of the hill and a church at the bottom of the main street. Many interesting buildings with original timber frames hidden behind present day houses. On the Welsh border close to the Clun Forest in quiet, unspoilt countryside.

Claremont

COMMENDED

Bishop's Castle SY9 5BW
☎ Bishops Castle (01588) 638170
Fax (01588) 638170
Contact: Mrs A Price
A pair of coach house conversions and garden wing of Victorian house, close to the centre of this small market town. Ideally situated for exploring rural Shropshire and the Welsh Borderlands.
3 self-contained units; sleeping 2–6

Price per week:	£min	£max
Low season	90.00	150.00
High season	140.00	260.00

Cards accepted: Access, Visa, Amex, Switch/Delta

Oakeley Mynd

6 Oakeley Mynd, Bishop's Castle
Contact: Mrs C M Kinsey, Coppers End, The Crescent, Bomere Heath, Shrewsbury SY4 3PQ
☎ Bomere Heath (01939) 290710
Spacious, modernised, 3-bedroomed cottage on a hillside overlooking the peaceful town of Bishop's Castle.
1 self-contained unit; sleeping max 6

Price per week:	£min	£max
Low season	220.00	220.00
High season	260.00	260.00

BLOCKLEY

Gloucestershire
Map ref 2B1

This village's prosperity was founded in silk mills and other factories but now it is a quiet, unspoilt place. An excellent centre for exploring pretty Cotswold villages, especially Chipping Campden and Broadway.

Brookdale

HIGHLY COMMENDED

Brook Lane, Blockley, Moreton-in-Marsh

Contact: Mrs A Taylor, The Stables, Mill Lane, Broom, Alcester, Warwickshire B50 4HS
☎ Bidford (01789) 778674 & Mobile 0860 679483

Modernised cottage, retaining original features. Two open fires, large, south-facing garden. Good for walking or touring. Quiet location by a stream. 2 bedrooms. Sorry, no pets or young children.
1 self-contained unit; sleeping 5

Price per week:	£min	£max
Low season	160.00	180.00
High season	200.00	280.00

☎ 8 Ⓜ 🖉 ▥ ☉ 🖵 TV 🖻 🖵 🖈 P ❊ 🖈

Cinquefoil Cottage
🗝 🗝 COMMENDED
54 Park Road, Blockley, Moreton-in-Marsh
Contact: Mrs Patricia Hinksman, 45 Brookmans Avenue, Brookmans Park, Hatfield, Hertfordshire AL9 7QH
☎ Potters Bar (01707) 652485
Cotswold-stone silk worker's cottage, with beamed kitchen, wonderful views, small garden with patios. Crown Inn and village stores 5 minutes' walk. Chipping Campden, Hidcote Manor Gardens and Snowshill nearby.
1 self-contained unit; sleeping 4

Price per week:	£min	£max
Low season	140.00	200.00
High season	220.00	260.00

☎ Ⓜ ◎ ▥ 🖵 TV 🖻 🖲 ❊ 🖈

Honeysuckle Cottage ⋀
🗝 🗝 COMMENDED
44 Park Road, Blockley, Moreton-in-Marsh
Contact: Miss P Street, Wood Blewit, Abbots Morton, Worcester WR7 4NA
☎ (01386) 793287
Fax (01386) 792608
Cotswold stone cottage with lovely views, completely renovated yet retaining original character. Tastefully furnished. Situated on edge of peaceful village. Ideal base for walking/touring.
1 self-contained unit; sleeping 4

Price per week:	£min	£max
Low season	195.00	
High season		285.00

☎ ◎ ▥ ☉ 🖵 MW 🖵 TV 🖻 🖻 🖟
🖈 ❊ 🖈 SP

Lower Farm Cottages ⋀
🗝 🗝 🗝 🗝 UP TO HIGHLY COMMENDED
Blockley, Moreton-in-Marsh
Contact: Mrs K Batchelor, Lower Farmhouse, Blockley, Moreton-in-Marsh, Gloucestershire GL56 9DP
☎ Blockley (01386) 700237
Fax (01386) 700237

Attractively furnished, well-equipped cottages, in tranquil streamside setting on edge of picturesque village, deep within the Cotswolds.
11 self-contained units; sleeping 2–6

Price per week:	£min	£max
Low season	140.00	273.00
High season	280.00	546.00

☎ ◎ ▥ ☉ 🖵 MW 🖵 TV 🖻 🖲 P U ❊ 🖈 🖈 SP 🅜

BOURTON-ON-THE-WATER

Gloucestershire
Map ref 2B1

The River Windrush flows through this famous Cotswold village which has a green, and cottages and houses of Cotswold stone. Its many attractions include a model village, Birdland, a Motor Museum and the Cotswold Perfumery.

Chilverstone Cott, The Cottage Broadlands, Bow Cott & Well Cott
🗝 🗝 🗝 HIGHLY COMMENDED
Sherborne Street, Bourton-on-the-Water, Cheltenham
Contact: Mrs J Fracasso, Chilverstone House, Sherborne Street, Bourton-on-the-Water, Cheltenham, Gloucestershire GL54 2BY
☎ evenings (01451) 820691
Tastefully presented 2 and 3 bedroomed cottages in excellent decorative order. All within 5 minutes' walk of village centre and amenities. Gas, electricity and bed linen included. Sorry, no pets. Short winter breaks available.
4 self-contained units; sleeping 4–5

Price per week:	£min	£max
Low season	155.00	175.00
High season	295.00	325.00

☎ ◎ 🖉 ▥ ☉ 🖵 MW TV 🖻 🖻 🖲 🖈 P ❊ 🖈 SP

Farncombe Flat
🗝 🗝 COMMENDED
Clapton, Bourton-on-the-Water, Cheltenham GL54 2LG
☎ Cotswold (01451) 820120
Contact: Mrs J M Wright
Well appointed apartment. Centrally heated, telephone, inglenook fireplace, laundry, linen provided, dishwasher, colour TV and microwave. Superb views. Telephone for brochure.
1 self-contained unit; sleeping 4

Price per week:	£min	£max
Low season	110.00	
High season		280.00

☎ Ⓜ ◎ ▥ ☉ 🖵 MW 🖵 TV 🖻 🖲 🖟 🖲 🖈 P U ❊ 🖈 🖈 SP

Magnolia Cottage Apartment ⋀
🗝 🗝 COMMENDED
Lansdowne, Bourton-on-the-Water, Cheltenham
Contact: Mr & Mrs M Cotterill, Magnolia Cottage, Lansdowne, Bourton-on-the-Water, Cheltenham, Gloucestershire GL54 2AR
☎ Cotswold (01451) 821841

First-floor apartment, tastefully furnished and fully carpeted. Two twin-bedded rooms. Easy walk to all village amenities. Not suitable for children under 10 and, sorry, no pets. Short breaks in low season.
1 self-contained unit; sleeping 1–4

Price per week:	£min	£max
Low season	220.00	275.00
High season	275.00	325.00

Cards accepted: Access, Visa

☎ 10 ◎ ▥ ☉ 🖵 MW 🖵 TV 🖻 🖲 🖟 🖲 🖈 P ❊ 🖈 🖈 SP

Pheasant Walk and The Retreat
🗝 🗝 🗝 COMMENDED
Grove Farm, Cold Aston, Cheltenham
Contact: Mrs P R Avery, Grove Farm, Cold Aston, Cheltenham, Gloucestershire GL54 3BJ
☎ Cotswold (01451) 810942
Fax (01451) 810942
600-acre mixed farm. A very rural setting in pretty village close to Bourton-on-the-Water. Glorious views across the Coln Valley. An excellent pub within walking distance.

Continued ▶

BOURTON-ON-THE-WATER

Continued

2 self-contained units; sleeping 2–6

Price per week:	£min	£max
Low season	175.00	280.00
High season	295.00	420.00

☆ⓂⓄ▥☉▯MW◖📺🄷🄰🄻🄾
🄰P✎❀✈ SP

South Lawn Holiday Cottage M

🔑🔑🔑 COMMENDED

South Lawn, Victoria Street, Bourton-on-the-Water, Cheltenham Contact: Mrs R Norman, South Lawn, Victoria Street, Bourton-on-the-Water, Cheltenham, Gloucestershire GL54 2BT
☎ Cotswold (01451) 820813
2-bedroomed cottage, supervised by owners, in beautiful quiet surroundings close to village centre.
1 self-contained unit; sleeping 4

Price per week:	£min	£max
Low season	160.00	210.00
High season	210.00	270.00

☆Ⓞ▥☉▯◖📺🄷🄰🄸🄻🄰P
❀✈

BRIDGNORTH

Shropshire
Map ref 4A3

Red sandstone riverside town in 2 parts - High and Low - linked by a cliff railway. Much of interest including a ruined Norman keep, half-timbered 16th C houses, Midland Motor Museum and Severn Valley Railway.
Tourist Information Centre ☎ (01746) 763358

Eudon Burnell Cottages M

🔑🔑🔑–🔑🔑🔑
COMMENDED

Eudon Burnell Farm, Bridgnorth Contact: Mrs M A Crawford Clarke, Eudon Burnell, Bridgnorth, Shropshire WV16 6UD
☎ Middleton Scriven (01746) 789235
Fax (01746) 789550

330-acre arable & dairy farm. Well-equipped 3-bedroomed Victorian country cottages on working farm.

Lovely peaceful location, 3 miles from Bridgnorth. Ideal centre for exploring Shropshire.
3 self-contained units; sleeping 4–5

Price per week:	£min	£max
Low season	170.00	270.00
High season	180.00	310.00

☆Ⓞ▥☉▯MW◖📺🄷🄰🄸🄻
🄰P❀✎ SP 🅃

The Granary

🔑 COMMENDED

The Old Vicarage, Ditton Priors, Bridgnorth WV16 6SQ
☎ (01746) 712272
Fax (01746) 712288
Contact: Mrs S Allen
Farm granary in unspoilt South Shropshire countryside. Bridgnorth 8 miles, Ludlow 16 miles. Studio sitting room, bedroom, kitchen, bathroom. Excellent walking.
1 self-contained unit; sleeping max 4

Price per week:	£min	£max
Low season	140.00	140.00
High season	140.00	140.00

☆Ⓞ▥☉▯🄻◖📺🄷🄰🄹🄰❀

Tudor Cottage

🔑 APPROVED

16 High Street, Claverley, Bridgnorth Contact: Mrs J B Henshaw, The White Cottage, 17 High Street, Claverley, Bridgnorth, Shropshire WV5 7DR
☎ Claverley (01746) 710262
Charming old cottage with beautiful garden in the old world village of Claverley. All amenities. Many places of interest within easy distance.
1 self-contained unit; sleeping max 6

Price per week:	£min	£max
Low season	145.00	145.00
High season	175.00	175.00

Open May–September
☆ⓂⓄ▥☉▯🄻◖📺🄷🄰🄸🄹∥
🄰❀

Wheelwright Cottage

🔑🔑🔑 HIGHLY COMMENDED

Aston Eyre, Bridgnorth Contact: Mrs M A Cosh, Church House, Aston Eyre, Bridgnorth, Shropshire WV16 6XD
☎ Morville (01746) 714248
Beautifully appointed barn conversion with 2 bedrooms. Peaceful situation in rolling hill country. Ideal base for walking and visiting Shropshire's many attractions.
1 self-contained unit; sleeping 7

Price per week:	£min	£max
Low season	100.00	180.00
High season	180.00	350.00

☆Ⓞ▥☉▯MW◖📺🄷🄰🄸🄹
🄰P❀ SP

BRIMFIELD

Hereford and Worcester
Map ref 4A3

Village of thatched and timbered houses near the River Teme, close to Ludlow and looking out towards the Clee Hills of Shropshire.

The Coppice at Stanshawes M

🔑🔑🔑 HIGHLY COMMENDED

Brimfield, Ludlow, Shropshire Contact: Mrs L D Davidson, Stanshawes, Brimfield, Ludlow, Shropshire SY8 4NX
☎ Ludlow (01584) 711028
Comfortable well-appointed oak-beamed barn conversion completed in 1996, standing in 18.5 acres of land near owner's 17th C house. Beautiful hillside location with spectacular views on Shropshire-Herefordshire border.
1 self-contained unit; sleeping max 6

Price per week:	£min	£max
High season	80.00	225.00

Open April–September
☆5Ⓞ▥☉▯🄻◖📺🄷🄰🄸🄹🄰P
❀✈ SP

BROAD CAMPDEN

Gloucestershire
Map ref 2B1

Lion Cottage

🔑🔑🔑 COMMENDED

Broad Campden, Chipping Campden GL55 6UR
☎ Evesham (01386) 840077
Contact: Mrs B L Rawcliffe
Cotswold stone-built cottage with beamed ceilings and open fireplace. Open plan living room with sitting, dining and kitchen areas; 1 double, 1 twin and 1 single bedroom; bathroom and shower room.
1 self-contained unit; sleeping 5

Price per week:	£min	£max
Low season	140.00	180.00
High season	200.00	270.00

☆11Ⓞ∅▥☉▯🄻◖📺🄷🄰🄸🄰
P❀✈

The symbols in each entry give information about services and facilities. A 'key' to these symbols appears at the back of this guide.

BROADWAY

**Hereford and Worcester
Map ref 2B1**

Beautiful Cotswold village called the "Show village of England", with 16th C stone houses and cottages. Near the village is Broadway Tower with magnificent views over 12 counties and a country park with nature trails and adventure playground.

Broadway Court ⚑
HIGHLY COMMENDED

89 High Street, Broadway,
Worcestershire WR12 7AL
☎ (01386) 852237
Fax (01386) 852237
Contact: Mr & Mrs I Woodward
Grade II listed 16th C cottages with delightful and spacious accommodation. Furnished with antiques and paintings. Everything included to ensure the perfect holiday. Two minutes' walk to village centre. Short breaks available.
3 self-contained units; sleeping 4–6

Price per week:	£min	£max
Low season	180.00	300.00
High season	385.00	385.00

The Cottage
HIGHLY COMMENDED

Church Street, Willersey, Broadway,
Worcestershire
Contact: Mrs G D Taylor, Church View, Willersey, Broadway,
Worcestershire WR12 7PN
☎ Broadway (01386) 852591
Located in a cul-de-sac leading to village church. Small enclosed garden and garage. One double, 1 twin and 1 child's bedroom. General stores, Post Office and hairdressing salon next door.
1 self-contained unit; sleeping 5

Price per week:	£min	£max
Low season	170.00	185.00
High season	200.00	310.00

Hesters House ⚑
COMMENDED

86 High Street, Broadway,
Worcestershire
Contact: Mrs L Dungate, Inglenook,
Brokengate Lane, Denham,
Uxbridge, Middlesex UB9 4LA
☎ Denham (01895) 834357
Fax (01895) 832904
Charming, oak-beamed end of terrace cottage with small courtyard, fronting Broadway High Street, surrounded by fields a few minutes' walk away. A

delightful cosy home from which to tour the Cotswolds. Prices include gas and electricity.
1 self-contained unit; sleeping 2

Price per week:	£min	£max
Low season	130.00	130.00
High season	180.00	180.00

BROMSGROVE

**Hereford and Worcester
Map ref 4B3**

This market town near the Lickey Hills has an interesting museum and craft centre and 14th C church with fine tombs and a Carillon tower. The Avoncroft Museum of Buildings is nearby where many old buildings have been re-assembled, having been saved from destruction.
Tourist Information Centre ☎ (01527) 831809

East View Apartment ⚑
COMMENDED

Little Shortwood, Brockhill Lane,
Tardebigge, Bromsgrove,
Worcestershire
Contact: Mr & Mrs J Westwood,
Little Shortwood, Brockhill Lane,
Tardebigge, Bromsgrove,
Worcestershire B60 1LU
☎ Redditch (01527) 63180
Modernised flat in beamed 17th C cottage, on smallholding in open countryside near canal. 10 minutes M5/M42 junctions. Private half-mile drive.
1 self-contained unit; sleeping 4

Price per week:	£min	£max
Low season	100.00	
High season		185.00

BROMYARD

**Hereford and Worcester
Map ref 2B1**

Market town on the River Frome surrounded by orchards, with black and white houses and a Norman church. Nearby at Lower Brockhampton is a 14th C half-timbered moated manor house owned by the National Trust. Heritage Centre.
Tourist Information Centre ☎ (01885) 482038

Old Bell Inn
COMMENDED

15 Church Street, Bromyard,
Herefordshire

Contact: Mr & Mrs J Bancroft,
Fiddlers Nook, Longley Green,
Suckley, Worcester WR6 5DU
☎ Suckley (01886) 884341
Attractive 17th C double-fronted stone cottage with original exposed internal beams and feature fireplaces. Was an inn until c1930s.
1 self-contained unit; sleeping 8

Price per week:	£min	£max
Low season		90.00
High season		200.00

Park House Holiday Flat ⚑
APPROVED

28 Sherford Street, Bromyard,
Herefordshire
Contact: Mrs E M Whiteley, Park House, 28 Sherford Street,
Bromyard, Herefordshire HR7 4DL
☎ (01885) 482294
An ideal centre for touring, run by resident owner. Within easy reach of shops, restaurants and pubs. Ample parking.
1 self-contained unit; sleeping max 5

Price per week:	£min	£max
Low season	100.00	
High season	140.00	150.00

Open May–October

BURWARTON

**Shropshire
Map ref 4A3**

Stately village between Ludlow and Bridgnorth, with the magnificent park of Burwarton Hall, an attractive Georgian inn and the ruin of an old Norman church.

The Wicket ⚑
HIGHLY COMMENDED

Burwarton, Bridgnorth
Contact: Mr R S Tindall, Brown Clee Holidays, Estate Office, Burwarton,
Bridgnorth, Shropshire WV16 6QQ
☎ Burwarton (01746) 787207
Fax (01746) 787422
Peace and seclusion - fully equipped spacious 3-bedroomed cottage on a beautiful private estate. Dogs/horses allowed. Fishing. Suitable for 2 families.
1 self-contained unit; sleeping 8

Price per week:	£min	£max
Low season	230.00	230.00
High season	330.00	330.00

CANON FROME

Hereford and Worcester
Map ref 2B1

This village in the Frome Valley has a modest Victorian church within the shadow of the 18th C Frome Court.

The Swiss Chalet

HIGHLY COMMENDED

Mill Cottage, Canon Frome, Ledbury, Herefordshire
Contact: Mr J N Rutherford, The Swiss Chalet, Mill Cottage, Canon Frome, Ledbury, Herefordshire HR8 2TD
☎ Trumpet (01531) 670506
Victorian Swiss chalet in lovely setting overlooking waterfall on River Frome. Watch kingfishers or catch trout from balcony.
1 self-contained unit; sleeping 2

Price per week:	£min	£max
Low season	143.00	
High season		295.00

CHARLTON KINGS

Gloucestershire
Map ref 2B1

Coxhorne Farm

COMMENDED

London Road, Charlton Kings, Cheltenham
Contact: Mr & Mrs J Close, Coxhorne Farm, London Road, Charlton Kings, Cheltenham, Gloucestershire GL52 6UY
☎ Cheltenham (01242) 236599
96-acre dairy farm. Self-contained studio apartment, attached to farmhouse on working farm. Consisting of kitchen/diner, bathroom and lounge.
1 self-contained unit; sleeping 4

Price per week:	£min	£max
Low season	120.00	140.00
High season	140.00	160.00

The map references refer to the colour maps towards the end of the guide. The first figure is the map number; the letter and figure which follow indicate the grid reference on the map.

CHEDWORTH

Gloucestershire
Map ref 2B1

Village situated in beautiful countryside with a church dating from Norman times. Chedworth Roman Villa is nearby, one of the best preserved in England, with mosaic pavements, bath-house, visitor centre and museum.

Hill Farm Cottage

COMMENDED

Chedworth, Cheltenham
Contact: Mrs E R Edelsten, Hill Farm House, Chedworth, Cheltenham, Gloucestershire GL54 4AG
☎ Cirencester (01285) 720421
2-bedroomed period detached cottage in a secluded position overlooking the village of Chedworth. Ideal for touring the Cotswolds.
1 self-contained unit; sleeping 5

Price per week:	£min	£max
Low season	80.00	130.00
High season	130.00	190.00

Postcombe Cottage

COMMENDED

Chedworth, Cheltenham
Contact: Mrs I B Finch, Woodlands Farm Ltd, Chedworth, Cheltenham, Gloucestershire GL54 4NT
☎ Withington (01242) 890270
Cotswold cottage in a delightfully secluded position on the edge of extensive woods.
1 self-contained unit; sleeping 6

Price per week:	£min	£max
Low season	110.00	120.00
High season	120.00	230.00

CHELMARSH

Shropshire
Map ref 4A3

An unspoilt village near the River Severn, with old timbered cottages and an imposing 14th C church.

Tail End Cottage

COMMENDED

Chelmarsh, Bridgnorth
Contact: Mr D Baxter, The Bulls Head, Chelmarsh, Bridgnorth, Shropshire WV16 6BA
☎ Highley (01746) 861469
Fax (01746) 862646

Superbly furnished cottage with stone featured walls. Fully equipped. Quiet location near owner's 17th C inn. Second cottage also available.
2 self-contained units; sleeping 7

Price per week:	£min	£max
Low season	215.00	290.00
High season	260.00	360.00

Cards accepted: Access, Visa, Switch/Delta

CHELTENHAM

Gloucestershire
Map ref 2B1

Cheltenham was developed as a spa town in the 18th C and has some beautiful Regency architecture, in particular the Pittville Pump Room. It holds international music and literature festivals and is also famous for its race meetings and cricket.
Tourist Information Centre ☎ (01242) 522878

Balcarras Farm Holiday Cottages

COMMENDED

Balcarras Farm, London Road, Charlton Kings, Cheltenham
Contact: Mr & Mrs D Ballinger, Balcarras Farm, London Road, Charlton Kings, Cheltenham, Gloucestershire GL52 6UT
☎ Cheltenham (01242) 584837
Built in 1992 around three sides of paved courtyard at rear of owner's former farmhouse. Single storey cottages, incorporating materials from original stables and cider press. Three stables and grazing available.
5 self-contained units; sleeping 2–4

Price per week:	£min	£max
Low season	138.00	210.00
High season	176.00	300.00

Brook House & Barn

HIGHLY COMMENDED

Brook House, Woolstone, Cheltenham
Contact: Mrs J Foster, The Grange, Woolstone, Cheltenham, Gloucestershire GL50 4RG
☎ Cheltenham (01242) 674471

Period Grade II listed farmhouse of Cotswold stone and Elizabethan Grade II listed thatched barn.
2 self-contained units; sleeping 2–10

Price per week:	£min	£max
Low season	280.00	640.00
High season	720.00	840.00

The Garden Flat

COMMENDED

20 Lansdown Parade, Cheltenham
Contact: Mr R Bradbeer, 20
Lansdown Parade, Cheltenham,
Gloucestershire GL50 2LH
☎ Cheltenham (01242) 577151

Set within a listed Regency terrace built around 1840. Pleasant setting opposite Lansdown Park. Fully self-contained with pretty private courtyard at rear. Within 10 minutes' walk of the town centre and railway station. Convenient for all amenities in Cheltenham and ideal Cotswold touring base.
1 self-contained unit; sleeping 4

Price per week:	£min	£max
Low season	175.00	230.00
High season	230.00	295.00

Holmer Cottages

COMMENDED

Haines Orchard, Woolstone,
Cheltenham GL52 4RG
☎ (01242) 672848
Contact: Mrs J Collins

Late 19th C semi-detached brick cottages, each with own separate sun terrace and private garden, overlooking old apple orchard. Situated in a small rural hamlet convenient for Cotswolds, Malverns, Severn Valley and racing at Cheltenham.
2 self-contained units; sleeping max 3

Price per week:	£min	£max
Low season	200.00	400.00
High season	300.00	400.00

Manor Farm Cottages ⚑

COMMENDED

26 Elkstone, Cheltenham GL53 9PB
☎ (01242) 870418 & 870414
Fax (01242) 870344
Contact: Mrs J Court
Delightful village setting, cosy cottages with open plan living areas, spacious galleried bedrooms, log fires, CH, videos, pretty patio gardens. Pets welcome.
2 self-contained units; sleeping max 2

Price per week:	£min	£max
Low season	130.00	160.00
High season	190.00	200.00

Cards accepted: Access, Visa

Old Rectory Cottages ⚑

UP TO HIGHLY COMMENDED

Woolstone, Cheltenham GL52 4RG
☎ Bishops Cleeve (01242) 673766
Contact: Mr & Mrs P Taylor
Self-catering cottages tastefully converted from old stables and coach house, in a tranquil setting four miles north of Cheltenham.
6 self-contained units; sleeping 2–6

Price per week:	£min	£max
Low season	180.00	250.00
High season	250.00	410.00

Priory Cottage ⚑

COMMENDED

Southam Lane, Southam,
Cheltenham
Contact: Mr I S Mant, Church Gate,
Southam Lane, Southam,
Cheltenham, Gloucestershire
GL52 3NY
☎ Cheltenham (01242) 584693

Old Cotswold-stone cottage with modern facilities, in own garden overlooking orchard. Two bedrooms, dining room, sitting room, kitchen and bathroom. Within walking distance of Area of Outstanding Natural Beauty.
1 self-contained unit; sleeping 4

Price per week:	£min	£max
Low season	140.00	180.00
High season	180.00	250.00

Ullenwood Court Cottages ⚑

HIGHLY COMMENDED

Ullenwood, Cheltenham GL53 9QS
☎ (01242) 236770
Fax (01242) 254680
Contact: Mrs P J Cuttell
Well-equipped, comfortable cottages set in landscaped gardens in the heart of the Cotswolds. 500 yards from Cotswold Hills golf club and 2 miles from Cheltenham.
3 self-contained units; sleeping 4–7

Price per week:	£min	£max
Low season	160.00	190.00
High season	200.00	350.00

The Vergus

COMMENDED

Staverton Village, Cheltenham
Contact: Mrs R M Preen, Ashley,
Staverton Village, Cheltenham,
Gloucestershire GL51 0TW
☎ Cheltenham (01242) 680511 &
Mobile 0973 419613
Detached cottage in small village, with a traditional apple and plum orchard at the bottom of the garden.
1 self-contained unit; sleeping 6

Price per week:	£min	£max
Low season	150.00	230.00
High season	195.00	275.00

Wimble Cottage ⚑

COMMENDED

8 Clare Place, Cheltenham
Contact: Mrs H J Beardsell, Crane
Hill, Oxenton, Cheltenham,
Gloucestershire GL52 4SE
☎ Cheltenham (01242) 673631
Charmingly furnished period cottage in a quiet cul-de-sac in the spa town of Cheltenham. Ideal for touring the Cotswolds and Forest of Dean. Discount for repeat visitors. Italian spoken.
1 self-contained unit; sleeping max 3

Price per week:	£min	£max
Low season	170.00	
High season		310.00

All accommodation in this guide has been graded, or is awaiting a grading, by a trained Tourist Board inspector.

CHIPPING CAMPDEN

Gloucestershire
Map ref 2B1

Outstanding Cotswold wool town with many old stone gabled houses, a splendid church and 17th C almshouses. Nearby are Kiftsgate Court Gardens and Hidcote Manor Gardens (National Trust).

Little Thatch
🔑🔑🔑 HIGHLY COMMENDED
Westington, Chipping Campden
Contact: Mrs D Gadsby, Catbrook Furlong, Chipping Campden, Gloucestershire GL55 6DE
☎ Evesham (01386) 840234
Beautifully restored 17th C thatched character cottage. Ideally situated for touring the Cotswolds and Shakespeare country.
1 self-contained unit; sleeping 3

Price per week:	£min	£max
Low season	210.00	250.00
High season	290.00	360.00

🏕️ Ⓜ ⊙ 🛢️ ⊙ 🗂️ MW 🔌 TV 🖨 🍽️ 🧺 🚗 🌸 ✕ SP

Walkers Retreat 🔼
🔑🔑🔑 COMMENDED
Weston Park Farm, Dovers Hill, Chipping Campden
Contact: Mrs J Whitehouse, Weston Park Farm, Dovers Hill, Chipping Campden, Gloucestershire GL55 6UW
☎ Evesham (01386) 840835
Secluded coach house apartment half a mile from Chipping Campden. Also well-equipped cottage, sleeping 5, quietly situated near town centre. Ideal for walking.
1 self-contained unit; sleeping 2

Price per week:	£min	£max
Low season	150.00	
High season	300.00	

 P 🔍 ✕

CHURCH STRETTON

Shropshire
Map ref 4A3

Church Stretton lies under the eastern slope of the Longmynd surrounded by hills. It is ideal for walkers, with marvellous views, golf and gliding. Wenlock Edge is not far away.

The Acorn 🔼
🔑🔑🔑 COMMENDED
Oaklands, Marshbrook, Church Stretton

Contact: Mr & Mrs J Cooper, Oaklands, Marshbrook, Church Stretton, Shropshire SY6 6RQ
☎ Marshbrook (01694) 781448
Detached chalet-type cottage with stabling/grazing and access to Long Mynd. Situated 2 miles south of Church Stretton.
1 self-contained unit; sleeping 4

Price per week:	£min	£max
Low season	150.00	200.00
High season	195.00	250.00

🏕️ ⊙ 🌿 🛢️ ⊙ 🗂️ 🔌 TV 🖨 🍽️ 🚗 P Ⓤ 🌸 SP T

Fairway 🔼
🔑🔑🔑 COMMENDED
Trevor Hill, Church Stretton
Contact: Miss L Powell, Oaker, 43 Shrewsbury Road, Church Stretton, Shropshire SY6 6EU
☎ (01694) 723159
Delightful, well-equipped detached bungalow, 5 minutes' walk from amenities. Situated on Longmynd. 18-hole golf course. Ideal for walkers and cyclists.
1 self-contained unit; sleeping 6

Price per week:	£min	£max
Low season	160.00	200.00
High season	200.00	260.00

🏕️ Ⓜ ⊙ 🛢️ ⊙ 🗂️ MW TV 🖨 🍽️ 🧺 🖼️ 🚗 P 🌸

Parkgate Cottages
🔑🔑🔑 COMMENDED
Parkgate Farmhouse, Pulverbatch, Shrewsbury
Contact: Mrs E A Hill, Parkgate Farmhouse, Pulverbatch, Shrewsbury SY5 8DH
☎ Church Stretton (01694) 751303
A warm welcome in beautiful Shropshire. Single-storey barn conversion. Numerous tourist attractions locally. Two cottages, each sleeping 2 people.
2 self-contained units; sleeping 2

Price per week:	£min	£max
Low season	120.00	
High season	180.00	

Open January, March–December
Ⓜ ⊙ 🛢️ ⊙ 🗂️ TV 🖨 🍽️ 🧺 🚗 P Ⓤ 🌸 ⊠ SP

Redwood Heights
🔑🔑🔑 HIGHLY COMMENDED
Watling Street South, Church Stretton SY6 7BJ
☎ (01694) 724332 & mobile 0378 920773
Contact: Mrs M Bond
Spacious wing of large modern house, built on a hill in Church Stretton. Private entrance off own sun-terraced lounge. Beautiful views.

1 self-contained unit; sleeping 2

Price per week:	£min	£max
Low season	160.00	160.00
High season	160.00	175.00

🏕️ ⊙ 🛢️ ⊙ 🗂️ MW 🔌 TV 🖨 🍽️ 🧺 🚗 P 🌸 ✕ SP

CIRENCESTER

Gloucestershire
Map ref 2B1

"Capital of the Cotswolds", Cirencester was Britain's second most important Roman town with many finds housed in the Corinium Museum.
Tourist Information Centre ☎ (01285) 654180

Glebe Farm Holiday Lets 🔼
🔑🔑🔑 HIGHLY COMMENDED
Glebe Farm, Barnsley Road, Cirencester GL7 5DY
☎ (01285) 659226 & 740682
Fax (01285) 740638
Contact: Mrs P Handover

Four converted stone barns in peaceful surroundings, with exposed beams and timbers, furnished with pine and antiques. Patio, barbecue and garden.
4 self-contained units; sleeping 2–6

Price per week:	£min	£max
Low season	110.00	195.00
High season	170.00	320.00

🏕️ ⊙ 🛢️ ⊙ 🗂️ MW TV 🖨 🍽️ 🧺 🖼️ 🚗 P Ⓤ 🌸 ⊠ SP

Lake View 🔼
🔑🔑🔑 COMMENDED
9 Blake Road, Abbey Grounds, Cirencester
Contact: Mrs H Kolb, 57 The Whiteway, Cirencester, Gloucestershire GL7 2HQ
☎ Cirencester (01285) 654781
Fax (01285) 654781
Comfortable well-equipped 3-bedroomed town house in the centre of Cirencester. Faces south overlooking landscaped parkland of Abbey Grounds and lake.
1 self-contained unit; sleeping max 6

Price per week:	£min	£max
Low season	123.00	159.00
High season	169.00	269.00

🏕️ ⊙ 🛢️ ⊙ 🗂️ 🔌 TV 🖨 🍽️ 🧺 🖼️ 🚗 P 🌸 ✕ SP 🔵

Mayfield Cottage ⚲

🔑🔑 🔑🔑 APPROVED

Cheltenham Road, Perrotts Brook, Cirencester
Contact: Mrs J I Hutson, Mayfield House, Cheltenham Road, Perrotts Brook, Cirencester, Gloucestershire GL7 7BH
☎ Cirencester (01285) 831301
Semi-detached, part Cotswold-stone cottage, overlooking open fields and the Churn Valley. On A435, 2 miles north of Cirencester. Ideal for touring the Cotswolds. In Area of Outstanding Natural Beauty. No pets please.
1 self-contained unit; sleeping 4

Price per week:	£min	£max
Low season	140.00	
High season		198.00

Old Mill Cottages ⚲

🔑🔑 🔑🔑 COMMENDED

Old Mill Farm, Poole Keynes, Cirencester
Contact: Mrs Catherine Hazell, Ermin House Farm, Syde, Cheltenham, Gloucestershire GL53 9PN
☎ Cirencester (01285) 821255 & Mobile 0831 774611
Fax (01285) 821531
110-acre mixed farm. Well-equipped, superior barn conversions, 4 miles from Cirencester. Quiet rural situation beside Thames. Adjacent Cotswold Water Park. Ideal touring centre.
4 self-contained units; sleeping 2–7

Price per week:	£min	£max
Low season	135.00	225.00
High season	195.00	500.00

CLEARWELL

Gloucestershire
Map ref 2A1

Attractive village in the Forest of Dean, noted for its castle, built in 1735 and one of the oldest Georgian Gothic houses in England. The old mines in Clearwell Caves are open to the public.

4 Temperance Cottages ⚲

🔑🔑 COMMENDED

Pingry Lane, Clearwell, Coleford
Contact: Mrs J S Bond, 3 Post Office Lane, Wantage, Oxfordshire OX12 8DR
☎ Wantage (01235) 767577
Sympathetically restored cottage with modern facilities, garden and peaceful situation in the medieval village of

Clearwell. Further cottage in Coalway, near Forest of Dean, also available.
1 self-contained unit; sleeping 6

Price per week:	£min	£max
Low season	100.00	150.00
High season	160.00	210.00

COBERLEY

Gloucestershire
Map ref 2B1

Upper Coberley Farm

🔑🔑 🔑🔑 COMMENDED

Upper Coberley, Cheltenham GL53 9RB
☎ Cheltenham (01242) 870306
Contact: Mrs A Allen
Wing of 18th C Cotswold-stone farmhouse in idyllic setting in an Area of Outstanding Natural Beauty. Log fires. Meals available. Ideal walking and touring centre.
1 self-contained unit; sleeping 4

Price per week:	£min	£max
Low season	160.00	180.00
High season	180.00	260.00

COLEFORD

Gloucestershire
Map ref 2A1

Small town in the Forest of Dean with the ancient iron mines at Clearwell Caves nearby, where mining equipment and geological samples are displayed. There are several forest trails in the area.
Tourist Information Centre ☎ (01594) 812388

Coach House Cottage

🔑🔑 COMMENDED

Buckstone Lodge, Staunton, Coleford
Contact: Mr & Mrs J Richards, Buckstone Lodge, Staunton, Coleford, Gloucestershire GL16 8PD
☎ (01594) 833122 & 0836 552188
Situated in an Area of Outstanding Natural Beauty and providing quality accommodation for a relaxing holiday or a more energetic break. Panoramic views, woodland walks from cottage.
1 self-contained unit; sleeping 6

Price per week:	£min	£max
Low season	130.00	200.00
High season	250.00	300.00

COLWALL

Hereford and Worcester
Map ref 2B1

Village on the slopes of the Malvern Hills close to the famous Herefordshire Beacon, site of a large Iron Age camp. The area offers excellent walks with the Worcestershire Beacon to the north.

The Ridings Holiday Flat

🔑🔑 🔑🔑 HIGHLY COMMENDED

Evendine, Colwall, Malvern, Worcestershire
Contact: Mrs Judith Slocombe, The Ridings, Evendine, Colwall, Malvern, Worcestershire WR13 6DT
☎ Colwall (01684) 540158
Fax (01684) 540838
Self-contained furnished holiday flat with CH, open fire, beams. Idyllic spot with panoramic views of the hills.
1 self-contained unit; sleeping 2–4

Price per week:	£min	£max
Low season	150.00	
High season	150.00	185.00

COMPTON ABDALE

Gloucestershire
Map ref 2B1

Spring Hill Stable Cottages ⚲

🔑🔑 — 🔑🔑 🔑 COMMENDED

Spring Hill House, Compton Abdale, Cheltenham GL54 4DU
☎ Cheltenham (01242) 890263
Contact: Mrs M L Smail
Charming fully-equipped cottages situated in open countryside, close to the Cotswold village of Compton Abdale.
2 self-contained units; sleeping 2–4

Price per week:	£min	£max
Low season	110.00	145.00
High season	170.00	260.00

Map references apply to the colour maps at the back of this guide.

For ideas on places to visit refer to the introduction at the beginning of this section.

COTSWOLDS

See under Aldsworth, Bibury, Blockley, Bourton-on-the-Water, Broad Campden, Broadway, Chedworth, Cheltenham, Chipping Campden, Cirencester, Coberley, Compton Abdale, Daglingworth, Lechlade, Minchinhampton, Miserden, Moreton-in-Marsh, Naunton, Nympsfield, Owlpen, South Cerney, Stanton, Stow-on-the-Wold, Stroud, Tetbury, Tewkesbury, Winchcombe, Witcombe, Wotton-under-Edge

See also Cotswolds in South of England region

COVENTRY

West Midlands
Map ref 4B3

Modern city with a long history. It has many places of interest including the post-war and ruined medieval cathedrals, art gallery and museums, some 16th C almshouses, St Mary's Guildhall, Lunt Roman fort and the Belgrade Theatre.
Tourist Information Centre ☎ (01203) 832303 or 832304

Cheshire Farm Barns ♪♪

COMMENDED

Cheshire Farm, Church Lane, Corley, Coventry
Contact: Mrs S Sykes, Cheshire Farm, Church Lane, Corley, Coventry CV7 8BA
☎ Fillongley (01676) 540289 & 542269
Pair of 2-bedroomed apartments converted from 300-year-old barns, with lounge/kitchen plus shower room.
2 self-contained units; sleeping 4–5

Price per week:	£min	£max
High season	150.00	295.00

CRASWALL

Hereford and Worcester
Map ref 2A1

Hamlet close to the Welsh border on the east side of the Black Mountains. It lies high up amid wooded countryside with splendid views over Golden Valley. The remains of a small Benedictine priory are nearby.

Rose Cottage ♪♪

APPROVED

Craswall, Hereford
Contact: Mrs M J Howard, The Three Horse Shoes, Craswall, Hereford HR2 0PL
☎ Michaelchurch (01981) 510631
Modernised stone cottage at the foot of the Black Mountains, in an Area of Outstanding Natural Beauty.
1 self-contained unit; sleeping 5

Price per week:	£min	£max
Low season	130.00	
High season	150.00	

DAGLINGWORTH

Gloucestershire
Map ref 2B1

Delightful village in the valley of the River Dunt near Cirencester, with a church which has remnants of Saxon work as well as 3 well-preserved sculptures. There is a medieval dovecote at the manor house.

Corner Cottage ♪♪

COMMENDED

21 Farm Court, Church Lane, Daglingworth, Cirencester
Contact: Mrs V M Bartlett, Brook Cottage, 23 Farm Court, Daglingworth, Cirencester, Gloucestershire GL7 7AF
☎ Cirencester (01285) 653478

Tastefully furnished, well-equipped, traditional Cotswold cottage in small village in tranquil valley. Cosy base for walking or touring. Non-smokers only, please.
1 self-contained unit; sleeping 2

Price per week:	£min	£max
Low season	154.00	154.00
High season	154.00	154.00

DROITWICH

Hereford and Worcester
Map ref 2B1

Old town with natural brine springs, now incorporated into the Brine Baths Health Centre, developed as a spa at the beginning of the 19th C. Of particular interest is the Church of the Sacred Heart with splendid mosaics. Fine parks and a Heritage Centre.
Tourist Information Centre ☎ (01905) 774312

Nunnery Farm ♪♪

HIGHLY COMMENDED

Westwood Park, Droitwich, Worcestershire WR9 0AE
☎ Worcester (01905) 771352
Contact: Mrs A F O'Riordan
15-acre livestock farm. Set in beautiful countryside and close to an historic Elizabethan manor house near Droitwich Spa. Ideal centre for touring. No bookings over Christmas. A non-smoking establishment.
1 self-contained unit; sleeping 4

Price per week:	£min	£max
Low season	130.00	150.00
High season	180.00	240.00

DYMOCK

Gloucestershire
Map ref 2B1

Village with one of the most interesting churches in the area, which has extensive Norman work and a fragment of a manuscript copy of St John's Gospel of the 8th C.

Stable Flat
🔑 🔑 🔑 COMMENDED

Hillgrove, Marcle Road, Dymock
Contact: Mrs J C Napier, Hillgrove, Marcle Road, Dymock, Gloucestershire GL18 2AR
☎ Dymock (01531) 890495
Extensive views overlooking Malvern Hills and Gloucestershire's May Hill. Property is adjacent to country house standing in 7 acres of peaceful countryside.
1 self-contained unit; sleeping 2

Price per week:	£min	£max
Low season	130.00	170.00
High season	170.00	240.00

◎ 🏠 ⊙ 🗑 MW 🔌 📺 🖥 🛄 🚗 P ► ❋

EARDISLEY

Hereford and Worcester
Map ref 2A1

Charming, picturesque village on the Black and White Trail. Ideal touring base for the Borders and the area's many historic buildings and attractions.

Arboyne House
🔑 🔑 🔑 COMMENDED

Church Road, Eardisley, Hereford
Contact: Mr & Mrs C Bysouth, Arboyne House, Church Road, Eardisley, Hereford HR3 6NH
☎ Eardisley (01544) 327058

Grade II listed black and white house. First floor lodge dates from 17th C, detached bakehouse with original oven. In centre of working village. Garden and fields to rear.
2 self-contained units; sleeping 2–6

Price per week:	£min	£max
Low season	100.00	150.00
High season	150.00	225.00

🛏 🕯 🏠 ⊙ 🗑 MW 🔌 📺 🖥 🛄 🚗 P ❋ ✕ SP 🏠 ◎

ECKINGTON

Hereford and Worcester
Map ref 2B1

Large and expanding village in a fruit growing and market gardening area beside the Avon, which is crossed here by a 15th C bridge. Half-timbered houses are much in evidence.

Orchard Cottage 🏍
🔑 🔑 🔑 COMMENDED

Upper End, Eckington, Pershore, Worcestershire
Contact: Mrs M M Lewis, Hadley Farm, Hadley, Droitwich, Worcestershire WR9 0AT
☎ Worcester (01905) 620460
Half-timbered thatched cottage in tranquil village in Vale of Evesham. Easy access to Cotswolds and Shakespeare country.
1 self-contained unit; sleeping 2

Price per week:	£min	£max
Low season	90.00	90.00
High season	90.00	115.00

M ◎ 🏠 ⊙ 🗑 🔌 📺 🖥 🛄 🚗 P ❋ SP 🏠

ELLESMERE

Shropshire
Map ref 4A2

Small market town with old streets and houses and situated close to 9 lakes. The largest, the Mere, has many waterfowl and recreational facilities and some of the other meres have sailing and fishing.

Colemere Farm Cottages 🏍
🔑 🔑 🔑 COMMENDED

Colemere, Ellesmere
Contact: Mr & Mrs C Wilson-Clarke, Greenbanks, (Re: Colemere Farm Cottages), Coptiviney, Ellesmere, Shropshire SY12 0ND
☎ Ellesmere (01691) 623420
Fax (01691) 623420
Cottages skilfully created from fine old brick and slate buildings. Set peacefully in the heart of Shropshire's lake district, 2 miles from Ellesmere.
4 self-contained units; sleeping 2–6

Price per week:	£min	£max
Low season	110.00	160.00
High season	200.00	330.00

🛏 M ◎ 🏠 ⊙ 🗑 📺 🖥 🛄 🚗 P 🎣 SP 🏠

The Stable House 🏍
🔑 🔑 🔑 HIGHLY COMMENDED

Gannow Hill, Welsh Frankton, Whittington, Oswestry
Contact: Mr & Mrs N A Powell, The Villa, Gannow Hill, Welsh Frankton, Whittington, Oswestry, Shropshire SY11 4NX
☎ Ellesmere (01691) 622276
Unique former stables, set in spacious grounds with panoramic views to Welsh borders. Two sitting-rooms and kitchens provide ideal facilities for 2 families sharing.
1 self-contained unit; sleeping 10

Price per week:	£min	£max
Low season	453.00	
High season	462.00	880.00

🛏 M ◎ 🕯 🏠 ⊙ 🗑 MW 🔌 📺 🖥 🛄 📞 🍴 🚗 P ❋ ✕ ⬗ SP 🏠

ELMLEY CASTLE

Hereford and Worcester
Map ref 2B1

Attractive black and white village at the foot of Bredon Hill. No castle exists but this is a popular place to start a walk over Bredon.

Manor Farm House 🏍
🔑 🔑 🔑 APPROVED

Main Street, Elmley Castle, Pershore, Worcestershire
Contact: Mr B D Lovett, Manor Farm House, Main Street, Elmley Castle, Pershore, Worcestershire WR10 3HS
☎ Evesham (01386) 710286 & Mobile 0850 505040
Fax (01386) 710286
Self-contained flatlet with patio, overlooking beautiful garden in village. Excellent base for touring Cotswolds and Malverns.
1 self-contained unit; sleeping 3

Price per week:	£min	£max
Low season	85.00	110.00
High season	120.00	145.00

🛏 10 ◎ 🏠 ⊙ 🗑 MW 🔌 📺 🖥 🛄 🚗 P ❋ ✕

The map references refer to the colour maps towards the end of the guide. The first figure is the map number; the letter and figure which follow indicate the grid reference on the map.

EVESHAM

Hereford and Worcester
Map ref 2B1

Market town in the centre of a fruit-growing area. There are pleasant walks along the River Avon and many old houses and inns. A fine 16th C bell tower stands between 2 churches near the medieval Almonry Museum.
Tourist Information Centre ☎ (01386) 446944

Abbey Gate House ⚫
⚿⚿⚿ HIGHLY COMMENDED

1 Abbey Mews, Evesham, Worcestershire
Contact: Mr & Mrs L J Robinson, 11 Aldridge Road, Walsall WS4 2JN
☎ Walsall (01922) 613355
Character house set in Evesham Abbey grounds, adjacent to shops and river, with 3 double bedrooms, 2 en-suite, 3 toilets. Car parking. Colour TV. No dogs and no children under 10 please.
1 self-contained unit; sleeping max 6

Price per week:	£min	£max
Low season	195.00	
High season		350.00

⌂ 10 ⊚ ⊘ ⊞ ⊙ 🖥 MW 📺 📺 🔲 🔳 🔲 ➡ P ✕ ⊠

Abbot's Court Cottages ⚫
⚿⚿⚿⚿ — ⚿⚿⚿⚿ DE LUXE

Vale of Evesham, Evesham, Worcestershire
Contact: Mr & Mrs A Umbers, Beehive Cottage, Church Lench, Evesham, Worcestershire WR11 4UH
☎ Evesham (01386) 870520
Fax (01386) 871557

Romantic award-winning character cottages in peaceful village setting. Tastefully furnished, mainly with antiques and four-poster beds. Ideal for exploring the Cotswolds and Shakespeare country. Short breaks available all year, from £155. Romantic Breaks (including champagne, flowers, candlelit dinners), golfing and tennis breaks.
12 self-contained units; sleeping 2–8

Price per week:	£min	£max
Low season	316.00	525.00
High season	379.00	895.00

Cards accepted: Access, Visa
⌂ ⊚ ⊞ ⊙ 🖥 MW 📺 📺 🔲 🔳 🔲 🔲 // ➡ P ⚲ ∪ ↑ ✕ ❄ ⊠ SP 🏠 Ⓣ

17 Mortimers Quay ⚫
⚿⚿ HIGHLY COMMENDED

Port Street, Evesham, Worcestershire
Contact: Miss J Bouette, Cinnibar Cottage, 45 Bury End, Broadway, Worcestershire WR12 7AF
☎ Broadway (01386) 858623
Beautifully situated modern apartment overlooking the River Avon, close to centre of Evesham and all amenities. Non-smokers only, welcome.
1 self-contained unit; sleeping max 3

Price per week:	£min	£max
Low season	160.00	
High season		265.00

⌂ 8 ⊚ ⊞ ⊙ 🖥 📺 🔲 🔳 🔲 ➡ P ❄ ✕ SP

Thatchers End ⚫
⚿⚿⚿ HIGHLY COMMENDED

64 Pershore Road, Evesham, Worcestershire
Contact: Mr & Mrs Wilson, 60 Pershore Road, Evesham, Worcestershire WR11 6PQ
☎ Evesham (01386) 446269
Fax (01386) 446269
Delightful Grade II listed thatched black and white cottage with many original features. Tastefully furnished. Enclosed garden, privately and peacefully situated. Parking.
1 self-contained unit; sleeping 6

Price per week:	£min	£max
Low season	275.00	300.00
High season	300.00	500.00

⌂ ⊚ ⊞ ⊙ 🖥 MW 📺 📺 🔲 🔳 🔲 ➡ P ❄ ✕ ⊠ SP 🏠

EWYAS HAROLD

Hereford and Worcester
Map ref 2A1

Attractive village, set in the beautiful scenery of the Golden Valley, which has an interesting church with a 13th C tower. The village of Abbey Dore is nearby with its famous Cistercian church and there are other fine churches in the locality.

The Greig Farm ⚫
⚿ APPROVED

Ewyas Harold, Hereford
Contact: Mrs J C Wright, Lower House Farm, Ewyas Harold, Hereford HR2 OES
☎ Golden Valley (01981) 240488
112-acre livestock farm. Black and white 17th C cottage in beautiful hilltop position. All rooms beamed, old

baking oven in hall, large lawned garden. Gas cooker. Storage heaters. Suitable for large or small parties. Private drive.
1 self-contained unit; sleeping 1–6

Price per week:	£min	£max
Low season	140.00	150.00
High season	150.00	300.00

Open March–December
⌂ ⊘ ⊞ ⊙ 🖥 MW 📺 🔲 🔳 ➡ P ∪ ↑ ❄ ✕ SP 🏠

FOREST OF DEAN

See under Clearwell, Coleford, Gatcombe, Newent, Parkend, Tidenham

FRAMPTON-ON-SEVERN

Gloucestershire
Map ref 2B1

Clair Cottage ⚫
⚿⚿⚿ HIGHLY COMMENDED

Church End, Frampton-on-Severn, Gloucester
Contact: Mrs A Cullen, Church Court Cottage, Church End, Frampton-on-Severn, Gloucester GL2 7EH
☎ Gloucester (01452) 740289
16th C beamed cottage, Grade II listed, in peaceful rural setting. Private garden in summer, open fire in winter.
1 self-contained unit; sleeping max 5

Price per week:	£min	£max
High season	225.00	300.00

⌂ ⊚ ⊞ ⊙ 🖥 MW 📺 📺 🔲 🔳 🔲 ➡ P ❄ ✕ ⊠ SP 🏠

GATCOMBE

Gloucestershire
Map ref 2B1

Pretty village on the banks of the River Severn where there is a building still called "Drake's House" because it is said that he came here to consult with Admiral Wynter at Lydney.

Oatfield Farmhouse & Cottages ⚫

Gatcombe, Blakeney
Contact: Mrs Liz Hoinville, Oatfield Farmhouse & Cottages, Gatcombe, Blakeney, Gloucestershire GL15 4AY
☎ Dean (01594) 510372
Fax (01594) 517040
Award-winning cottages very secluded in 6 acres. Heated. Freezer meals. Gift hamper. Tennis court. Games room. Woodland and clifftop river walks. Short breaks all year.

3 self-contained units; sleeping 2–4

Price per week:	£min	£max
Low season	210.00	290.00
High season	290.00	490.00

🐾🐾📷💻☺️📺 MW 📟📺🅾️ 🛏️📠
✈️P☎️♨️❄️ SP �

HEREFORD

Hereford and Worcester
Map ref 2A1

Agricultural county town, its cathedral containing much Norman work and a large chained library. Among the city's varied attractions are several museums including the Cider Museum and the Old House. *Tourist Information Centre* ☎ *(01432) 268430*

Anvil Cottage

🔑🔑🔑 HIGHLY COMMENDED

Grafton Villa Farm, Grafton, Hereford
Contact: Mrs Jennie Layton, Grafton Villa Farm House, Grafton, Hereford HR2 8ED
☎ Hereford (01432) 268689
200-acre mixed farm. Beautifully converted wainhouse, natural wood and lovely fabrics. Two spacious en-suite bedrooms, open-plan lounge leading to secluded patio.
1 self-contained unit; sleeping 5

Price per week:	£min	£max
Low season	160.00	180.00
High season	240.00	300.00

🐾☺️📺 MW 📟📺🅾️🍽️P❄️✈️🚫
SP �📷

Breinton Court 🅰️

🔑🔑🔑🔑 UP TO COMMENDED

Lower Breinton, Hereford
Contact: Mrs G Hands, Breinton Court, Lower Breinton, Hereford HR4 7PG
☎ Hereford (01432) 268156 & Tewkesbury (01684) 293293
Fax (01684) 295938
Splendid homes with all modern facilities set in 11 acres of wooded grounds, which include 9 hole mini golf, hard tennis court and swimming pool. In country 200 yards from River Wye but only 2 miles from Hereford.
5 self-contained units; sleeping 4–9

Price per week:	£min	£max
Low season	200.00	400.00
High season	425.00	695.00

Open April–October and Christmas
🐾📷📷☺️💻 MW 📺🛏️P🔄
☎️♨️🎵❄️SP

Buttercup Cottage 🅰️

🔑🔑 COMMENDED

Upper Lyde Court, Upper Lyde, Hereford
Contact: Mrs A White, 9 Kingsley Park Avenue, Millhouses, Sheffield S7 2HG
☎ (0114) 236 4357
Barn converted into 3-bedroomed country cottage. Farmhouse kitchen, master bedroom en-suite, central heating. Quiet, rural location between Hereford and Leominster.
1 self-contained unit; sleeping 5

Price per week:	£min	£max
Low season	125.00	160.00
High season	180.00	275.00

Open March–October and Christmas

🐾📷💻☺️🛒 MW 📺🛏️æ✈️P❄️
✈️ SP

Flat 2

🔑 APPROVED

16 St Martins Avenue, Hereford
Contact: Mr & Mrs B Matthews, 16 St Martins Avenue, Hereford, Herefordshire HR2 7RQ
☎ Hereford (01432) 272259
Within walking distance of city centre, overlooking playing fields with river and a selection of leisure activities: swimming, tennis, putting green.
1 self-contained unit; sleeping 2

Price per week:	£min	£max
Low season	75.00	90.00
High season	90.00	125.00

📷💻☺️🛒📟📺🛏️🚗🚙🛞☎️▶️❄️

The Garden House 🅰️

🔑🔑🔑🔑 HIGHLY COMMENDED

Belmont Lodge & Golf Course, Belmont, Hereford
Contact: Miss Louise Nicholson, Belmont Lodge & Golf Course, Belmont, Hereford HR2 9SA
☎ Hereford (01432) 352666
Fax (01432) 358090
Beautifully appointed 5-bedroomed house, accommodating up to 11 people. Set within a lovely walled garden, offering superb views over Hereford and surrounding countryside.
1 self-contained unit; sleeping max 11

Price per week:	£min	£max
Low season	1500.00	
High season		2500.00

Cards accepted: Access, Visa, Diners, Amex

🐾📷💻☺️🛒 MW 📟📺🛏️🖼️æ
P☎️🎵▶️❄️🚫SP

Rushford

🔑🔑🔑 COMMENDED

Belle Bank Avenue, Holmer, Hereford HR4 9RL
☎ (01432) 273380
Contact: Mrs M W Roberts
Much praised wing of owner's detached house. Pretty garden. City fringe, open country views. Services nearby. SAE for brochure. Non-smokers only, please.
1 self-contained unit; sleeping 3

Price per week:	£min	£max
Low season	110.00	140.00
High season	160.00	190.00

🐾📷📷💻☺️🛒 MW 📟📺🅾️🛏️🖼️
✈️P❄️✈️SP

HOARWITHY

Hereford and Worcester
Map ref 2A1

Attractive village on the River Wye which is famous for fishing. Its church was built in the 19th C in Italianate style with the help of Italian workers. The interior contains gold mosaics and marble.

Aspen Cottage

🔑🔑🔑 COMMENDED

Hoarwithy, Hereford
Contact: Mr & Mrs M Gardner, Aspen House, Hoarwithy, Hereford HR2 6QP
☎ Hereford (01432) 840353 & Mobile 0860 709924
Fax (01432) 840353
Single storey sandstone cottage, dating back to the 1700s. Set in attractive village alongside the River Wye, amidst the beautiful countryside of the Wye Valley.
1 self-contained unit; sleeping max 4

Price per week:	£min	£max
Low season	150.00	175.00
High season	200.00	250.00

🐾5📷📷💻☺️💻 MW 📟📺🅾️🛏️
🍽️✈️P🎵▶️❄️🚫SP🇹

Establishments should be open throughout the year, unless otherwise stated.

The 🅰️ symbol after an establishment name indicates that it is a Regional Tourist Board member.

HUNTLEY

Gloucestershire
Map ref 2B1

The Vineary

🔑🔑 COMMENDED

Vinetree Cottage, Solomons Tump,
Huntley, Gloucester
Contact: Mrs A Snow, Vinetree
Cottage, Solomons Tump, Huntley,
Gloucester GL19 3EB
☎ Gloucester (01452) 830006
*2-acre smallholding. The Vineary is a
self-catering annexe to Vinetree
Cottage, in quiet country lane with
open views. Easy access to shop, Post
Office and country inns.*
1 self-contained unit; sleeping 6

Price per week:	£min	£max
Low season	155.00	170.00
High season	200.00	230.00

🛏️Ⓜ◎🖥️⊙🍴MW�📼📺🖼️🔌🖥️
🅿️P✿🍴

ILMINGTON

Warwickshire
Map ref 2B1

Village at the foot of a small hill
close to the Roman Fosse Way,
within a couple of miles of Hidcote
and Kiftsgate Gardens.

Featherbed Cottage 𝕄

🔑🔑🔑 COMMENDED

Featherbed Lane, 8 Nellands Close,
Ilmington, Shipston-on-Stour
Contact: Mr S D Price, Featherbed
Lane, 8 Nellands Close, Ilmington,
Shipston-on-Stour, Warwickshire
CV36 4NF
☎ Ilmington (01608) 682215
*Comfortable, well-equipped
2-bedroomed house in village on the
edge of Cotswolds overlooking open
country. Small garden.*
1 self-contained unit; sleeping 4

Price per week:	£min	£max
Low season		155.00
High season	178.00	210.00

🛏️◎🖥️⊙🍴MW📼📺🖼️🔌🖥️
🅿️P✿🍴🗞️ SP

Self-catering agencies
which have a selection of
holiday homes to let
are listed in a special section
towards the back
of this guide.

IRONBRIDGE

Shropshire
Map ref 4A3

Small town on the Severn where the
Industrial Revolution began. It has
the world's first iron bridge built in
1779. The Ironbridge Gorge
Museum, of exceptional interest,
comprises a rebuilt
turn-of-the-century town and sites
spread over 6 square miles.
*Tourist Information Centre ☎ (01952)
432166*

Dale End Cottages

🔑🔑🔑 COMMENDED

18-19 Buildwas Road, Ironbridge,
Telford
Contact: Mr D W Gibson, St Lukes
House, St Lukes Road, Doseley,
Telford, Shropshire TF4 3BD
☎ Telford (01952) 507107 & Mobile
0802 396289

*Beautifully converted 18th C cottages
and coach house flats, offering superb
family accommodation on the edge of
Dale End Park, Ironbridge.*
2 self-contained units; sleeping 3–6

Price per week:	£min	£max
Low season	100.00	200.00
High season	150.00	300.00

🛏️🖥️◎🖥️⊙🍴MW📺🔌🖥️🖼️🅿️P
✿

Music Masters House & Timmins Cottage 𝕄

57 & 57a Madeley Hill, Ironbridge,
Telford
Contact: Mr D Phillips, Hundred
House Hotel, Norton, Shifnal,
Shropshire TF11 9EE
☎ Telford (01952) 730354
Fax (01952) 730355

*Historic cottages just 10 minutes' walk
from Ironbridge and overlooking the
Gorge. Accommodation includes linen,
electricity, gas heating, colour TV, radio,
washing machine and dryer. Children
and dogs welcome. Ideal for exploring
local museums and outstanding natural
beauty of the Shropshire hills.*

2 self-contained units; sleeping 4–8

Price per week:	£min	£max
Low season	100.00	240.00
High season	180.00	470.00

Cards accepted: Access, Visa, Amex,
Switch/Delta

🛏️🖥️◎🖥️⊙🍴MW📼📺🖼️🔌🖥️
🅿️PU✿🏠Ⓣ

Toll House Flat 𝕄

🔑🔑🔑 COMMENDED

Toll House, Ironbridge, Telford
Contact: Mrs P Gillott, Ironbridge
Gorge Museum Trust, The
Wharfage, Ironbridge, Telford,
Shropshire TF8 7AW
☎ Telford (01952) 433522
Fax (01952) 432204
*Small apartment within the original
tollhouse of the famous iron bridge of
1779, overlooking the River Severn at
the heart of this World Heritage Site.
Storage heating, open fire. Sleeps 2
adults plus a child and a baby.*
1 self-contained unit; sleeping 2

Price per week:	£min	£max
Low season	100.00	120.00
High season	120.00	150.00

Cards accepted: Access, Visa

🛏️◎🖥️⊙🍴📼📺🔌🖥️P✿🏠

KINGTON

Hereford and Worcester
Map ref 2A1

Market town on the Welsh border,
with Offa's Dyke close by. The
Hergest Croft Gardens are
well-known for their beautiful
displays of azaleas and
rhododendrons during May and
June.

Bradnor Farm Cottage 𝕄

🔑🔑🔑 APPROVED

Bradnor Hill, Kington, Herefordshire
Contact: Mrs J E Burgoyne, Nash's
Oak, Lyonshall, Kington,
Herefordshire HR5 3LT
☎ Lyonshall (01544) 340272
*Beautiful, Welsh border, stone farm
cottage with panoramic views,
comfortable and well equipped. 100
yards from golf and Offa's Dyke.*
1 self-contained unit; sleeping max 6

Price per week:	£min	£max
Low season	140.00	160.00
High season	180.00	205.00

🛏️Ⓜ◎🖥️⊙🍴📺🖼️🖼️🔌✿ SP

A key to symbols can be
found inside the back
cover flap.

The Nursery

COMMENDED

Ridgebourne, Kington, Herefordshire
Contact: Mrs E Banks, Hergest Estate, Ridgebourne, Kington, Herefordshire HR5 3EG
☎ (01544) 230160 & (0171) 624 5740
Fax (01544) 230160
Self-contained wing of a Georgian house, set within the 50-acre Hergest Croft Gardens in stunning countryside.
1 self-contained unit; sleeping 7–8

Price per week:	£min	£max
Low season	200.00	300.00
High season	350.00	550.00

LEAMINGTON SPA

Warwickshire
Map ref 4B3

18th C spa town with many fine Georgian and Regency houses. Tea can be taken in the 19th C Pump Room. The attractive Jephson Gardens are laid out alongside the river and there is a museum and art gallery.
Tourist Information Centre ☎ (01926) 311470

Blackdown Farm Cottages

APPROVED

Blackdown Farm, Sandy Lane, Blackdown, Leamington Spa
Contact: Mrs R Solt, Blackdown Farm, Sandy Lane, Leamington Spa, Warwickshire CV32 6QS
☎ Leamington Spa (01926) 422522
Fax (01926) 450996
Cottages converted from farm buildings, in the countryside between Leamington Spa and Kenilworth. Convenient for Shakespeare country, Warwick, Coventry and the Cotswolds.
2 self-contained units; sleeping 3–4

Price per week:	£min	£max
Low season	110.00	
High season		300.00

Furzen Hill Farm

COMMENDED

Cubbington Heath, Leamington Spa CV32 6QZ
☎ (01926) 424791
Contact: Mrs C M Whitfield
185-acre mixed farm. Three cottages at Cubbington. Furzen Hill Cottage sleeps 7 and shares a large garden with the farmhouse and The Barn Cottage which sleeps 4. Dairy Cottage also sleeps 4 and has its own small garden. Cubbington is within easy reach

of Warwick, Stratford-upon-Avon and the National Exhibition Centre.
3 self-contained units; sleeping 4–7

Price per week:	£min	£max
Low season	110.00	
High season		300.00

LECHLADE

Gloucestershire
Map ref 2B1

Attractive village on the River Thames and a popular spot for boating. It has a number of fine Georgian houses and a 15th C church. Nearby is Kelmscott Manor, with its William Morris furnishings, and 18th C Buscot House (National Trust).

Langford House Cottages

HIGHLY COMMENDED

Little Faringdon, Lechlade GL7 3QN
☎ Faringdon (01367) 252210
Fax (01367) 252577
Contact: Lady H A de Mauley
Two beautifully equipped cottages on owner's private estate between Burford and Lechlade, off A361.
2 self-contained units; sleeping 2–4

Price per week:	£min	£max
Low season	175.00	325.00
High season	295.00	476.00

LEDBURY

Hereford and Worcester
Map ref 2B1

Town with cobbled streets and many black and white timbered houses, including the 17th C market house and old inns. Nearby is Eastnor Castle with an interesting collection of tapestries and armour.
Tourist Information Centre ☎ (01531) 636147

Garden Cottage

APPROVED

Westhill, Ledbury, Herefordshire
Contact: Miss U Palairet, Yew Tree Cottage, Westhill, Ledbury, Herefordshire HR8 1JF
☎ Ledbury (01531) 632516
Quiet, modernised, fully-equipped country house with superb views and garden, 1 mile from Ledbury. An excellent touring centre in lovely countryside.
1 self-contained unit; sleeping 6

Price per week:	£min	£max
Low season	90.00	
High season		200.00

Hazelcroft

HIGHLY COMMENDED

Bradlow, Ledbury, Herefordshire
Contact: Mrs R W Moy, Lynden Lea, Bradlow, Ledbury, Herefordshire HR8 1JF
☎ Ledbury (01531) 632804
Fully-appointed bungalow in a peaceful rural location 1 mile from Ledbury, with large garden and commanding views. Excellent touring centre.
1 self-contained unit; sleeping 4

Price per week:	£min	£max
Low season	125.00	155.00
High season	165.00	295.00

Homend Bank Cottage

COMMENDED

Stretton Grandison, Ledbury, Herefordshire
Contact: Mrs E M Segrave, R H & R W Clutton, The Estate Office, Leighton Court, Ledbury, Herefordshire HR8 2UN
☎ Bosbury (01531) 640262
Fax (01531) 640719
Isolated black and white cottage with views over parkland and the Malvern Hills. Surrounded by farmland and woodland.
1 self-contained unit; sleeping 5

Price per week:	£min	£max
Low season	175.00	175.00
High season	225.00	225.00

Open April–October

Netherhall Cottage

COMMENDED

Church Street, Ledbury, Herefordshire
Contact: Mrs P M Harrison, Netherhall, Church Street, Ledbury, Herefordshire HR8 1DJ
☎ Ledbury (01531) 632748
Fax (01531) 635570
Detached early 19th C cottage with enclosed garden, 2 minutes' walk from town centre down historic Church Lane. Modern amenities.
1 self-contained unit; sleeping 3

Price per week:	£min	£max
Low season	115.00	150.00
High season	170.00	220.00

LEDBURY
Continued

Somers Arms House
COMMENDED

Ledbury Road, Eastnor, Ledbury, Herefordshire
Contact: Mrs F Morgan-Oates, Somers Arms House, Ledbury Road, Eastnor, Ledbury, Herefordshire HR8 1EL
☎ Ledbury (01531) 631622
Fax (01531) 631361
Restored designer's cottage, part of old coaching inn. Comfortable sitting room, well-equipped kitchen/dining room, 2 pretty bedrooms. Dogs welcome. Non-smoking. Splendid walking country. Deer park, apple orchard and garden.
1 self-contained unit; sleeping max 3

Price per week:	£min	£max
Low season	180.00	220.00
High season	260.00	290.00

LEEK
Staffordshire
Map ref 4B2

Old silk and textile town, with some interesting buildings and a number of inns dating from the 17th C. Its art gallery has displays of embroidery. Brindley Mill, designed by James Brindley, has been restored as a museum.
Tourist Information Centre ☎ (01538) 381000

Bank End Farm Cottage
COMMENDED

Leek Old Road, Longsdon, Stoke-on-Trent ST9 9QJ
☎ (01538) 383638
Contact: Mrs B Robinson
62-acre mixed farm. Accommodation in 15th C barn. Good views, swimming pool, laundry and restaurant facilities. Walks and fishing.
1 self-contained unit; sleeping max 4

Price per week:	£min	£max
Low season	150.00	160.00
High season	320.00	350.00

Cards accepted: Access, Visa

For ideas on places to visit refer to the introduction at the beginning of this section.

LEOMINSTER
Hereford and Worcester
Map ref 2A1

The town owed its prosperity to wool and has many interesting buildings, notably the timber-framed Grange Court, a former town hall. The impressive Norman priory church has 3 naves and a ducking stool. Berrington Hall (National Trust) is nearby.
Tourist Information Centre ☎ (01568) 616460

The Buzzards
COMMENDED

Kingsland, Leominster, Herefordshire
Contact: Ms E Povey, The Buzzards, Kingsland, Leominster, Herefordshire HR6 9QE
☎ Kingsland (01568) 708941

16-acre smallholding. Relax in 16 quiet acres of woodlands, fields and ponds. Good value, warm welcome. Access for disabled.
1 self-contained unit; sleeping 2–5

Price per week:	£min	£max
Low season	160.00	200.00
High season	200.00	270.00

Puddlecroft
COMMENDED

Lucton, Leominster, Herefordshire HR6 9PH
☎ Yarpole (01568) 780537
Contact: Mrs S M Sampson

Situated in a quiet hamlet, the "black and white" first floor detached flat lies in the private grounds of our house, a 17th C restored and converted barn.
1 self-contained unit; sleeping max 2

Price per week:	£min	£max
Low season	120.00	140.00
High season	120.00	160.00

LEYSTERS
Hereford and Worcester
Map ref 2A1

Tiny village hidden in a remote corner of Herefordshire, with ancient farms scattered in the hills about. A field path leads to Wordsworth's Stone, marking the spot which the poet used to visit when staying nearby.

Mill House Flat
COMMENDED

Woonton Court Farm, Leysters, Leominster, Herefordshire
Contact: Mrs E M Thomas, Woonton Court Farm, Leysters, Leominster, Herefordshire HR6 0HL
☎ Leysters (01568) 750232
300-acre mixed farm. Tastefully converted self-contained first floor flat. 1 large double room and 1 smaller twin-bedded room. Farm produce and freedom to walk the farm. Short breaks available. Children welcome.
1 self-contained unit; sleeping 4

Price per week:	£min	£max
Low season	160.00	200.00
High season	195.00	250.00

LONGTOWN
Hereford and Worcester
Map ref 2A1

In the Black Mountains close to Offa's Dyke Path. The ruined Norman castle once dominated this quiet countryside.

Moody Farm Cottage
COMMENDED

Moody Farm, Longtown, Hereford
Contact: Mr R H Stone, Moody Farm, Longtown, Hereford HR2 0LW
☎ Longtown Castle (01873) 860685
50-acre livestock farm. Well-equipped wing of barn conversion in peaceful valley at foot of Black Mountains. Superb views, garden, stream, private lake-fishing. Wood-burning stove.
1 self-contained unit; sleeping max 5

Price per week:	£min	£max
Low season	125.00	180.00
High season	200.00	280.00

LUDLOW

Shropshire
Map ref 4A3

Outstandingly interesting border town with a magnificent castle high above the River Teme, 2 half-timbered old inns and an impressive 15th C church. The Reader's House, with its 3-storey Jacobean porch, should also be seen. *Tourist Information Centre ☎ (01584) 875053*

Church Bank 🏍

🔑 🔑 🔑 APPROVED

Burrington, Ludlow SY8 2HT
☎ Wigmore (01568) 770426
Contact: Mrs K R Laurie
Stone cottage with large garden, in tiny village near River Teme. Hills and forest for walkers and naturalists.
1 self-contained unit; sleeping max 5

Price per week:	£min	£max
Low season	130.00	
High season		180.00

Open March–October
🔣 ⊚ 🗑 ⊙ 🗂 📺 ⛟ 🔒 🚶 P ∪ ❋

Coldoak Cottage

Snitton Lane, Knowbury, Ludlow SY8 3LB
☎ (01584) 890334
Contact: Miss H Morris
Beamed stone cottage set in meadowland. Quiet situation with panoramic views, large garden. On route of "The Shropshire Way".
1 self-contained unit; sleeping max 5

Price per week:	£min	£max
Low season	190.00	
High season		220.00

🔣 5 ⊚ 🗑 ⊙ 🗂 M W ⛟ 📺 🗄 🔒 📨 🚶 P ❋

The Flat 🏍

🔑 🔑 🔑 APPROVED

13 Broad Street, Ludlow
Contact: Mr & Mrs R Mercer, Tana Leas Farm, Clee St Margaret, Craven Arms, Shropshire SY7 9DZ
☎ Ludlow (01584) 823272
Fax (01584) 823272
Town centre, 2-storey modernised flat. A Tudor building in Ludlow's historic Broad Street.
1 self-contained unit; sleeping 5

Price per week:	£min	£max
Low season	155.00	160.00
High season	160.00	175.00

🔣 M ⊚ 🗑 ⊙ 🗂 ⛟ 📺 🗄 🗄 📨 🚶 ✗ 🏠

The Flat

🔑 🔑 🔑 COMMENDED

The Avenue, Ashford Carbonell, Ludlow SY8 4DA
☎ Richards Castle (01584) 831616
Contact: Mr R E Meredith
Second floor of large, attractive, peaceful country residence set in 6 acres. Completely independent access with fine views and very comfortable accommodation.
1 self-contained unit; sleeping 6

Price per week:	£min	£max
Low season	100.00	160.00
High season	160.00	290.00

🔣 M ⊚ 🗑 ⊙ 🗂 M W ⛟ 📺 🗄 🔒 🚶 P ∪ ❋

The Granary 🏍

🔑 🔑 COMMENDED

Tana Leas Farm, Clee St Margaret, Craven Arms
Contact: Mr & Mrs R Mercer, Tana Leas Farm, Clee St Margaret, Craven Arms, Shropshire SY7 9DZ
☎ Ludlow (01584) 823272
Fax (01584) 823272
45-acre mixed farm. Converted first floor granary situated in Area of Outstanding Natural Beauty. Ideal for a quiet and secluded holiday. 6 miles north east of Ludlow.
1 self-contained unit; sleeping 4

Price per week:	£min	£max
Low season	155.00	160.00
High season	160.00	175.00

🔣 M ⊚ 🗑 ⊙ 🗂 ⛟ 📺 🗄 📨 🗄 🚶 P ∪ ❋ ✗ SP

Hazel Cottage 🏍

🔑 🔑 🔑 HIGHLY COMMENDED

Duxmoor, Onibury, Craven Arms
Contact: Mrs R E Sanders, Duxmoor Farm, Onibury, Craven Arms, Shropshire SY7 9BQ
☎ Bromfield (01584) 856342

Period cottage, retaining all its original features and furnished with antiques throughout. Set in its own "cottage" garden with panoramic views of the countryside, 5 miles north of historic Ludlow and one and a half miles off A49.
1 self-contained unit; sleeping max 4

Price per week:	£min	£max
Low season	140.00	
High season		315.00

🔣 M ⊚ 🗑 ⊙ 🗂 ⛟ 📺 🗄 📨 🗄 (📨) 🔒 🚶 ∪ ❋ ✗ SP 🗄

Post Horn Cottage

🔑 🔑 APPROVED

Palmers Guild Court, Broad Street, Ludlow
Contact: Ms H Davis, 32 Leamington Drive, Chilwell, Beeston, Nottingham
☎ (0115) 922 2383
Charming two-storey cottage in historic town centre building with exposed beams and small private patio. In quiet courtyard off Broad Street.
1 self-contained unit; sleeping 4

Price per week:	£min	£max
Low season	120.00	140.00
High season	175.00	210.00

🔣 ⊚ 🗑 ⊙ 🗂 ⛟ 📺 🗄 📨 ❋ ✗ SP

MADLEY

Hereford and Worcester
Map ref 2A1

At the heart of this village in the meadows stands a glorious church with a remarkable medieval crypt with impressive stonework and a 14th C roof.

Canon Bridge House 🏍

🔑 🔑 COMMENDED

Canon Bridge, Madley, Hereford HR2 9JF
☎ (01981) 251104
Fax (01981) 251412
Contact: Mrs Alison Anscomb

Wing of Georgian country house set above the River Wye. Three acres of gardens, private fishing. Peaceful location. Grade II listed building.
1 self-contained unit; sleeping max 5

Price per week:	£min	£max
High season	195.00	250.00

Open March–October
🔣 ⊚ 🗑 ⊙ 🗂 M W ⛟ 📺 🗄 🗄 🚶 P 🎵 ❋ ✗

MALVERN

**Hereford and Worcester
Map ref 2B1**

Spa town in Victorian times, its water is today bottled and sold worldwide. 6 resorts, set on the slopes of the hills, form part of Malvern. Great Malvern Priory has splendid 15th C windows. It is an excellent walking centre.
Tourist Information Centre ☎ (01684) 892289

Annexe to Blue Cedars

COMMENDED

Blue Cedars, Peachfield Close, Malvern, Worcestershire
Contact: Mrs P M Longmire, Blue Cedars, Peachfield Close, Malvern Wells, Malvern, Worcestershire WR14 4AN
☎ Malvern (01684) 566689
One-bedroomed flat adjoining owners' house, separate entrance. Beautiful views of Malvern Hills. Convenient for walking in the hills, Cotswolds and Wales.
1 self-contained unit; sleeping 2

Price per week:	£min	£max
Low season	100.00	140.00
High season	140.00	165.00

The Coach House

COMMENDED

Como Road, Malvern, Worcestershire
Contact: Mrs J Jones, 58 North Malvern Road, Malvern, Worcestershire WR14 4LX
☎ Malvern (01684) 569562
Detached, turn of the century coach house conversion in the heart of Great Malvern. Set in a secluded garden.
1 self-contained unit; sleeping 4

Price per week:	£min	£max
Low season	150.00	
High season		325.00

The Cottages at Westwood House

HIGHLY COMMENDED

Park Road, West Malvern, Malvern, Worcestershire WR14 3DS
☎ (01684) 892308
Fax (01684) 892882
Contact: Mrs J Wright

Traditional cottages and a spacious garden flat in fine Regency house. Spectacular views over Herefordshire and the Black Mountains.
4 self-contained units; sleeping 2–6

Price per week:	£min	£max
Low season	195.00	350.00
High season	290.00	490.00

End Cottage

COMMENDED

Malvern, Worcestershire
Contact: Mr & Mrs Wight, The Rectory, Fish House Lane, Stoke Prior, Bromsgrove, Worcestershire B60 4JT
☎ Bromsgrove (01527) 832501
Comfortable, fully-equipped home, 1 mile from Great Malvern. Gardens, superb views, excellent walking on the hills nearby. Close to amenities.
1 self-contained unit; sleeping 4

Price per week:	£min	£max
Low season	150.00	250.00
High season	250.00	250.00

Greenbank House Garden Flat

COMMENDED

236 West Malvern Road, West Malvern, Malvern, Worcestershire WR14 4BG
☎ (01684) 567328
Contact: Mrs S M Matthews
On the Malvern Hills, close to shops and on a bus route. Excellent walking and touring centre. Fine outlook.
1 self-contained unit; sleeping 2–4

Price per week:	£min	£max
Low season	100.00	100.00
High season	160.00	160.00

Oakwood Annex

HIGHLY COMMENDED

Oakwood, Blackheath Way, West Malvern, Malvern, Worcestershire
Contact: Mr D B Pereira, Oakwood, Blackheath Way, West Malvern, Malvern, Worcestershire WR14 4DR
☎ Malvern (01684) 574335
Self-contained cottage-styled wing of beautiful Victorian residence, with

superb views and spacious gardens. Ideal for walking or visits to local historic towns such as Worcester, Ledbury, Upton-upon-Severn. Quiet location.
1 self-contained unit; sleeping 4

Price per week:	£min	£max
Low season	150.00	200.00
High season	200.00	300.00

MAYFIELD

**Staffordshire
Map ref 4B2**

Village on the border between Staffordshire and Derbyshire marked by the River Dove which is crossed by the Hanging Bridge. Alton Towers and Dovedale are nearby.

The Coach House

HIGHLY COMMENDED

Lichfield Guest House, Bridge View, Mayfield, Ashbourne, Derbyshire
Contact: Mr & Mrs K Mellor, Lichfield House, Bridge View, Mayfield, Ashbourne, Derbyshire DE6 2HN
☎ Ashbourne (01335) 344422
Fax (01335) 344422
Former old coach house, rebuilt to high standards, standing in the 2 acres of grounds of Lichfield Guest House. Well-equipped and tastefully furnished. Non-smoking.
1 self-contained unit; sleeping 3

Price per week:	£min	£max
Low season	150.00	150.00
High season	250.00	275.00

MILWICH

**Staffordshire
Map ref 4B2**

Village midway between Stone and Uttoxeter. The oldest dated bell in Staffordshire, purported to have rung for Agincourt, is here.

Summerhill Farm

HIGHLY COMMENDED

Milwich, Stafford ST18 0EL
☎ Hilderstone (01889) 505546
Fax (01889) 505692
Contact: Mrs P A Milward
Two-bedroomed fully-equipped cottage, close to Alton Towers, Peak District, Shugborough Hall and Wedgwood. Riding and golf-course close at hand.

1 self-contained unit; sleeping 4

Price per week:	£min	£max
Low season	94.00	110.00
High season	110.00	205.00

🐾 3 Ⓜ 🗔 ⊙ 🗖 MW 📺 🗖 🖥 📠
🖳 🚗 P U ⚡ ❄ SP

MINCHINHAMPTON

Gloucestershire
Map ref 2B1

Stone-built town, with many 17th/18th C buildings, owing its existence to the wool and cloth trades. A 17th C pillared market house may be found in the town square, near which is the Norman and 14th C church.

Vine House ⋀

🐾🐾🐾 COMMENDED

Friday Street, Minchinhampton, Stroud
Contact: Mrs V M Finn, Vine House, Friday Street, Minchinhampton, Stroud, Gloucestershire GL6 9JL
☎ Stroud (01453) 884437
Self-catering flat attached to a family house in the heart of the old Cotswold wool town of Minchinhampton. Wonderful walks.
1 self-contained unit; sleeping 2

Price per week:	£min	£max
Low season	120.00	150.00
High season	150.00	200.00

Open January–November

🐾 6 🖉 🗔 ⊙ 🗖 MW 📺 📺 🗖 🖥 🖳
🚗 P ❄ ✈ SP

MINSTERLEY

Shropshire
Map ref 4A3

Village with a curious little church of 1692 and a fine old black and white hall. The lofty ridge known as the Stiperstones is 4 miles to the south.

Coronation Cottage ⋀

🐾🐾🐾 COMMENDED

Drury Lane, Hope, Minsterley, Shrewsbury
Contact: Mr & Mrs David Stacey, Leigh Manor, Minsterley, Shrewsbury, Shropshire SY5 0EX
☎ Worthen (01743) 891210
2500-acre mixed farm. In breathtaking Marches hills, charming and spacious period cottage tastefully modernised and furnished. 100 metres from 17th C Stables Inn. Own garden, open fire and heating. Leaflet available.

1 self-contained unit; sleeping 5

Price per week:	£min	£max
Low season	135.00	
High season		275.00

🐾 🗔 🗔 📺 ☎ 🖥 🗲 🚗 P U ❄ ⚲
SP

Luckley Cottage ⋀

🐾🐾🐾 COMMENDED

Bromlow, Minsterley, Shrewsbury
Contact: Mr M Johnson, Oakern, Bromlow, Minsterley, Shrewsbury, Shropshire SY5 0ED
☎ Shrewsbury (01743) 891469

9-acre mixed farm. Tastefully converted, fully-equipped cottage on small hill farm in Area of Outstanding Natural Beauty. Ideal for those who wish to get away from it all. On-site horse riding, local golf, fishing and walking.
1 self-contained unit; sleeping 4–5

Price per week:	£min	£max
Low season	145.00	180.00
High season	185.00	250.00

🐾 Ⓜ 🗔 🗔 ⊙ 🗖 📺 📺 🖥 📠 🖳 🗲
🚗 P U ❄

The Woodlands

🐾🐾🐾 COMMENDED

Drury Lane, Minsterley, Shrewsbury
Contact: Mrs S Evans, The Bungalow, Drury Lane, Minsterley, Shrewsbury SY5 0EL
☎ Shrewsbury (01743) 791255
Spacious, fully centrally heated bungalow in secluded location with beautiful country views and looking on to the Stiperstones Hills. 1.5 miles from Minsterley.
1 self-contained unit; sleeping 1–5

Price per week:	£min	£max
Low season	175.00	185.00
High season	185.00	195.00

🐾 🖉 🗔 ⊙ 🗖 MW 📺 📺 🖥 🖺 🚗
P ❄ ✈ SP

Please check prices and other details at the time of booking.

Establishments should be open throughout the year, unless otherwise stated.

MISERDEN

Gloucestershire
Map ref 2B1

Village in wooded valley country with a church of late Saxon origin. The Camp is a hamlet with an interesting group of old houses. and Miserden Park Gardens can be visited between April and September.

Sudgrove Cottages ⋀

🐾🐾🐾 COMMENDED

Miserden, Stroud GL6 7JD
☎ Cirencester (01285) 821322
Contact: Mr M G Ractliffe
Original Cotswold-stone cottages in secluded hamlet. Ideal walking country and central for Cirencester, Stroud, Cheltenham and Gloucester.
3 self-contained units; sleeping 4–6

Price per week:	£min	£max
Low season	135.00	220.00
High season	220.00	310.00

🐾 Ⓜ 🗔 🗔 ⊙ 🗖 📺 📺 🖥 📠 🖳
🚗 P U ❄ SP

MORETON-IN-MARSH

Gloucestershire
Map ref 2B1

Attractive town of Cotswold stone with 17th C houses, an ideal base for touring the Cotswolds. Some of the local attractions include Batsford Park Arboretum, the Jacobean Chastleton House and Sezincote Garden.

Broadmoor Farm Cottage

🐾🐾🐾 COMMENDED

Broadmoor Farm, Little Wolford, Shipston-on-Stour, Warwickshire
Contact: Mrs R M Warriner, Broadmoor Farm, Little Wolford, Shipston-on-Stour, Warwickshire CV36 5LZ
☎ Long Compton (01608) 684223
Fax (01608) 684261
1500-acre mixed farm. Modernised period stone cottage on farm in a tiny hamlet. Comfortable and quiet, with 2 bedrooms, living room, kitchen, bathroom and garden.
1 self-contained unit; sleeping 3

Price per week:	£min	£max
Low season	120.00	
High season		180.00

🐾 Ⓜ 🗔 🗔 ⊙ 🗖 MW 📺 🖥 📠 🖺 🚗
P ❄ ✈ SP

MORETON-IN-MARSH
Continued

The Laurels
COMMENDED

9 St. James Court,
Moreton-in-Marsh
Contact: Mrs S I Billinger, Blue
Cedar House, Stow Road,
Moreton-in-Marsh, Gloucestershire
GL56 0DW
☎ Moreton-in-Marsh (01608)
650299
*Modern well-furnished bungalow with
private garden in the North Cotswolds.
Ideal touring centre, convenient for
shops and services. Central heating and
double glazing.*
1 self-contained unit; sleeping 4

Price per week:	£min	£max
Low season	150.00	200.00
High season	200.00	330.00

MUCH COWARNE
Hereford and Worcester
Map ref 2A1

*Village of scattered farms and
cottages, a solid 13th C church and
a medieval dovecote.*

Cowarne Hall Cottages
HIGHLY COMMENDED

Much Cowarne, Bromyard,
Herefordshire
Contact: Mr & Mrs M Bradbury,
Cowarne Hall, Much Cowarne,
Bromyard, Herefordshire HR7 4JQ
☎ Hereford (01432) 820317
Fax (01432) 820093
*Historic cottages between Malvern
Hills and Wye Valley. Quiet and rural
yet convenient for nearby historic
towns. Free county guides sent after
enquiry.*
3 self-contained units; sleeping 2–8

Price per week:	£min	£max
Low season	175.00	425.00
High season	235.00	680.00

Old Bridgend Cottage
COMMENDED

Much Cowarne, Bromyard,
Herefordshire
Contact: Mrs A M Morgan, 32
Chestnut Grove, New Malden,
Surrey KT3 3JN
☎ (0181) 942 0702

*Picturesque, 17th C, Grade II listed,
black and white cottage in a delightful
position in glorious countryside.
Half-acre garden with large pond. Ideal
centre for touring, walking, cycling. One
double and one single bedroom.*
1 self-contained unit; sleeping 3

Price per week:	£min	£max
Low season	115.00	250.00
High season	115.00	250.00

MUCH WENLOCK
Shropshire
Map ref 4A3

*Small town close to Wenlock Edge
in beautiful scenery and full of
interest. In particular there are the
remains of an 11th C priory with
fine carving and the black and white
16th C Guildhall.*

The Coach House
APPROVED

The Grange, Much Wenlock
Contact: Mrs K.V. Dower, The
Grange, Much Wenlock, Shropshire
TF13 6DD
☎ Much Wenlock (01952) 727152
*Finely restored early Victorian coach
house adjoining country house, set in
24 acres of unspoilt Shropshire
countryside.*
1 self-contained unit; sleeping 4

Price per week:	£min	£max
Low season	100.00	145.00
High season	150.00	200.00

MUNSLOW
Shropshire
Map ref 4A3

*Village on the B4368 between
Craven Arms and Much Wenlock
whose main charm lies in the
ancient church and attractive lawned
rectory.*

Palas Cottage
COMMENDED

Broadstone Farm, Munslow, Craven
Arms SY7 9HQ
☎ (01584) 841240
Contact: Mrs J Williams

*420-acre mixed farm. Delightful
half-timbered cottage set in its own
large garden. Within easy reach of
Ironbridge Gorge and historic towns of
Ludlow and Bridgnorth. Ideal for
walking, cycling and touring.*
1 self-contained unit; sleeping max 5

Price per week:	£min	£max
Low season	100.00	
High season		240.00

NAUNTON
Gloucestershire
Map ref 2B1

*A high place on the Windrush,
renowned for its wild flowers and
with an attractive dovecote.*

Mill Barn Annexe
APPROVED

Mill Barn, Naunton, Cheltenham
GL54 3AF
☎ Cotswold (01451) 850417
Contact: Mrs M Hindley
*Well-appointed flat adjoining converted
barn in peaceful Cotswolds village.
Twin-bedded room, shower room,
sitting/dining room with sofa bed,
kitchenette.*
1 self-contained unit; sleeping 4

Price per week:	£min	£max
Low season	90.00	
High season	165.00	

Open January–November

NEWENT
Gloucestershire
Map ref 2B1

*Small town with the largest
collection of birds of prey in Europe
at the Falconry Centre. Flying
demonstrations daily. Glass
workshop where visitors can watch
glass being blown. There is a
"seconds" shop. North of the village
is the Three Choirs Vineyard.*
*Tourist Information Centre ☎ (01531)
822145*

Windmill Annexe
HIGHLY COMMENDED

Castle Fruit Farm, Castle Tump,
Newent
Contact: Mrs G Sivak, Castle Fruit
Farm, Castle Tump, Newent,
Gloucestershire GL18 1LS
☎ Dymock (01531) 890428

Overlooking Georgian country house, unique windmill, putting green, peaceful gardens and orchards. Private lakes for fishing, swimming. On working fruit farm with farm shop. Lots to see and do locally.
Wheelchair access category 3 ♿
1 self-contained unit; sleeping 4

Price per week:	£min	£max
Low season	125.00	235.00
High season	265.00	300.00

🛏🔟◎▥⊙🛢MW🎻📺🛢🚗🖼
🚗P🎿⚙✳🔌 SP

Gloucestershire
Map ref 2B1

Pretty village high up in the Cotswolds, with a simple mid-Victorian church and a prehistoric long barrow nearby.

Crossways
🔑🔑🔑 COMMENDED
Tinkley Lane, Nympsfield, Stonehouse GL10 3TU
☎ Stroud (01453) 860309
Contact: Mr & Mrs F J Bowen
Annexe to village house. Fully self-contained, own garden, patio, entrance. Fully fitted kitchen, large living room. Twin bedded room, bathroom. Extra beds if necessary.
1 self-contained unit; sleeping 2–4

Price per week:	£min	£max
Low season	110.00	110.00
High season	130.00	130.00

🛏◎▥⊙🛢🎻📺🛢🚗🖼🚗✳

Shropshire
Map ref 4A3

Town close to the Welsh border, the scene of many battles. To the north are the remains of a large Iron Age hill fort. An excellent centre for exploring Shropshire and Offa's Dyke.
Tourist Information Centre ☎ (01691) 662488 or 662753

The Cross Keys
🔑—🔑 UP TO COMMENDED
Selattyn, Oswestry

Contact: Mr & Mrs P J Rothera, The Cross Keys, Selattyn, Oswestry, Shropshire SY10 7DN
☎ Oswestry (01691) 650247
Converted shop and granary attached to pub, regularly featured in the "Good Beer Guide". In beautiful walking country. Accessible to Oswestry, Shrewsbury and Chester.
2 self-contained units; sleeping 5–8

Price per week:	£min	£max
Low season	100.00	140.00
High season	140.00	175.00

🛏▥◎🌊▥⊙🛢MW📺🚗🖼🚗
P🎿🔌 SP

The Hay Loft 🏔
🔑🔑 COMMENDED
White House, Middleton, Oswestry
Contact: Mrs J A Johnson, White House, Middleton, Oswestry, Shropshire SY11 4LT
☎ Oswestry (01691) 657370
5-acre mixed farm. Well equipped converted farm building 2 miles from Oswestry. Pleasant views, ample parking, washer, TV, telephone, snooker. Available for short breaks.
1 self-contained unit; sleeping 4–7

Price per week:	£min	£max
Low season	110.00	130.00
High season		150.00

Open April–October
🛏🌊▥⊙🛢▥📺🛢🚗🖼🚗P
✳ SP

Gloucestershire
Map ref 2B1

Near the Severn Estuary, the 15th C Owlpen Manor (open to visitors April–September) together with its outbuildings and church form a delightful group of Cotswold stone buildings. The weaving village of Uley with its 17th C houses is close by.

Owlpen Manor 🏔
🔑🔑—🔑🔑🔑
UP TO HIGHLY COMMENDED
Owlpen, Uley, Dursley GL11 5BZ
☎ Dursley (01453) 860261
Fax (01453) 860819
Contact: Mrs M Keevil
Period cottages in romantic Cotswold setting, on historic manorial estate in private wooded valley. Fully serviced, licensed restaurant, log fires, four-poster beds, antiques.
9 self-contained units; sleeping 2–9

Price per week:	£min	£max
Low season	165.00	405.00
High season	260.00	730.00

Cards accepted: Access, Visa, Diners, Switch/Delta
🛏▥◎⊙🛢▥🎻📺🛢🚗🖼🚗
🚗P🛢🎿🎻⚙✳🔌 SP🏠T

Gloucestershire
Map ref 2A1

Village in the Forest of Dean, once an important industrial and railway centre, but now quiet and peaceful and a good base for exploring the forest.

The Coach House 🏔
🔑🔑🔑🔑 HIGHLY COMMENDED
Royal Forest of Dean, Parkend, Lydney
Contact: Mrs C Yeatman, Deanfield, Royal Forest of Dean, Parkend, Lydney, Gloucestershire GL15
☎ Dean (01594) 562256
Superbly converted accommodation set in heart of Forest of Dean. Backs on to RSPB reserve and cycle trail. Small village, local pubs, steam trains. Short breaks from £150.
1 self-contained unit; sleeping 2–7

Price per week:	£min	£max
Low season	250.00	300.00
High season	280.00	450.00

🛏▥◎▥⊙🛢MW🎻📺🛢🚗🖼
🛢🚗P🔍🎿✳🔌 SP

Hereford and Worcester
Map ref 2A1

Delightful village close to the Welsh border with many black and white half-timbered cottages, some dating from the 14th C. There is a market hall supported by 8 wooden pillars in the market place, also old inns and a 14th C church with interesting separate bell tower.

Rowena Cottage & Nurse's Cottage 🏔
🔑🔑🔑 APPROVED
2 East Street, Pembridge, Leominster, Herefordshire
Contact: Mrs D Malone, The Cottage, Holme, Newark, Nottinghamshire NG23 7RZ
☎ Newark (01636) 72914

Continued ▶

PEMBRIDGE
Continued

Two black and white beamed cottages, with storage heaters and open fires, in picturesque village. Ideal touring centre for the Marches.
2 self-contained units; sleeping 5–6

Price per week:	£min	£max
Low season	140.00	
High season		230.00

ROSS-ON-WYE

Hereford and Worcester
Map ref 2A1

Attractive market town with a 17th C market hall, set above the River Wye. There are lovely views over the surrounding countryside from the Prospect and the town is close to Goodrich Castle and the Welsh border.
Tourist Information Centre ☎ (01989) 562768

The Ashe ♠
COMMENDED

Bridstow, Ross-on-Wye, Herefordshire HR9 6QA
☎ (01989) 563336
Contact: Mrs T L Green
Spacious, oak-beamed converted granary, mill and stable in each. Also, cottage with 3 bedrooms. Total sleeping capacity 18, plus extra beds and cots. 18-hole par 3 golf-course, fishing and tennis on the farm.
4 self-contained units; sleeping 5–10

Price per week:	£min	£max
Low season	100.00	300.00
High season	200.00	500.00

Bill Mill Cottages ♠
UP TO HIGHLY COMMENDED

Pontshill, Ross-on-Wye, Herefordshire HR9 5TH
☎ Hereford (01432) 840390 & (01989) 750525
Fax (01989) 750760
Contact: Mr I R Jenkins

Owner-supervised converted cottages

set around a listed watermill in the heart of the country. Wild flower gardens, mill pond and large lawns. Central heating and open fires.
5 self-contained units; sleeping 5–6

Price per week:	£min	£max
Low season	175.00	240.00
High season	280.00	395.00

Cider Cottage ♠
COMMENDED

Glewstone, Ross-on-Wye, Herefordshire
Contact: Mrs H A Jackson, Lowcop, Glewstone, Ross-on-Wye, Herefordshire HR9 6AN
☎ Ross-on-Wye (01989) 562827
Fax (01989) 563877
800-acre arable & fruit farm. Cider house converted to character cottage with oak beams and antiques, overlooking apple orchards. Warm in winter with wood burning stove. Convenient for Wye Valley and Forest of Dean.
1 self-contained unit; sleeping 1–5

Price per week:	£min	£max
Low season	150.00	170.00
High season	170.00	250.00

Coughton House
COMMENDED

Coughton, Ross-on-Wye, Herefordshire
Contact: Mr R Balchin, Coughton House, Coughton, Ross-on-Wye, Herefordshire HR9 5SF
☎ Ross-on-Wye (01989) 562612
Fax (01989) 567322

Charming oak-beamed apartment in Georgian country house. Large entrance hall, lounge/bedroom, kitchen/dining room and bathroom. Access to landscaped gardens.
1 self-contained unit; sleeping max 2

Price per week:	£min	£max
Low season	145.00	170.00
High season	180.00	225.00

The Game Larders and The Old Bakehouse
APPROVED

Wythall, Walford, Ross-on-Wye, Herefordshire HR9 5SD
☎ (01989) 562688
Contact: Miss A McIntyre
Two self-contained cottages in wing of a 16th C manor house in secluded setting.
2 self-contained units; sleeping 2–4

Price per week:	£min	£max
Low season	130.00	180.00
High season	190.00	250.00

Holly Cottage & Valley View ♠
APPROVED

The Nurseries, Llangrove, Ross-on-Wye, Herefordshire
Contact: Mrs A C Williams, The Nurseries, Llangrove, Ross-on-Wye, Herefordshire HR9 6ET
☎ Ross-on-Wye (01989) 770252
Holly Cottage is a peaceful cottage in a small village between Ross-on-Wye and Monmouth. Valley View is a bungalow with delightful views in the same village.
2 self-contained units; sleeping 5–6

Price per week:	£min	£max
Low season	99.00	
High season		270.00

Langstone Cottage ♠
APPROVED

Llangarron, Ross-on-Wye, Herefordshire
Contact: Mrs P Amos, Oaklands, Llangarron, Ross-on-Wye, Herefordshire HR9 6NZ
☎ Llangarron (01989) 770277
Cottage with large, enclosed private garden, double-glazing, central heating and conservatory. Set in beautiful countryside yet within 2 miles of Ross-on-Wye/Monmouth dual carriageway. Second cottage has view of 5 counties.
2 self-contained units; sleeping 2–7

Price per week:	£min	£max
Low season	75.00	95.00
High season	125.00	310.00

The ♠ symbol after an establishment name indicates that it is a Regional Tourist Board member.

Man of Ross House

🔑🔑🔑 APPROVED

Ross-on-Wye, Herefordshire
Contact: Mr D Campkin, 8 Maitland
Road, Reading RG1 6NL
☎ Reading (01734) 572561 &
Guildford (01483) 466201
*Spacious, self-contained apartment
with 5 bedrooms in historic, listed
building overlooking market place.
Comfortable, beamed accommodation
retaining period features. Heating
included. Short breaks available (except
July/August).*
1 self-contained unit; sleeping 6

Price per week:	£min	£max
Low season	80.00	240.00
High season	110.00	330.00

🐕◎🖩🗂MW TV 🖨🎞🛏🅿🚫 SP 🏠

2 Pot Acre Cottage 🏔

🔑🔑🔑 APPROVED

Llangarron, Ross-on-Wye,
Herefordshire
Contact: Mrs J Scudamore,
Llangarron Court, Llangarron,
Ross-on-Wye, Herefordshire
HR9 6NP
☎ Ross-on-Wye (01989) 770243
*3-bedroomed cottage with sitting room
and diner/kitchen, enjoying lovely views
in peaceful countryside. Ideally situated
for touring the Wye Valley, Forest of
Dean and Black Mountains.*
1 self-contained unit; sleeping 5

Price per week:	£min	£max
Low season	100.00	225.00
High season	200.00	260.00

Open March–October

🐕🅼◎🖩🗂⊙🗂TV🖨🎞🚐∪❂

Woodfields Coach House and Barn 🏔

🔑🔑🔑 COMMENDED

Woodfields, Llangarron,
Ross-on-Wye, Herefordshire
Contact: Mrs R M Tarry, Woodfields,
Llangarron, Ross-on-Wye,
Herefordshire HR9 6PW
☎ Ross-on-Wye (01989) 770221
*Old traditional coach house and barn,
converted into spacious cottages with
their own garden. Set in beautiful
countryside, 6 miles from Ross-on-Wye.*
2 self-contained units; sleeping 4–6

Price per week:	£min	£max
Low season	150.00	175.00
High season	250.00	295.00

🐕🅼◎🖩🗂⊙🗂MW 🖨TV🛏🖨🎞
🖃🚐🅿∪❂SP🏠

Hereford and Worcester
Map ref 2B1

*Village on the edge of the Vale of
Evesham, with Bredon Hill to the
east and westward views of the
Cotswold hills.*

Hall Farm Country Holidays 🏔

🔑🔑🔑🔑 UP TO HIGHLY COMMENDED

Sedgeberrow, Evesham,
Worcestershire
Contact: Mrs D Stow, Lower
Portway Farm, Sedgeberrow,
Evesham, Worcestershire
WR11 6UB
☎ Evesham (01386) 881298 &
Mobile 0973 682376
Fax (01386) 881298

*Attractive award-winning converted
cottages, well-furnished and equipped.
Also, elegant apartments in Georgian
farmhouse. Set in lawned gardens in
peaceful village location. Ideal for
exploring Cotswolds and other places
of interest. Heated outdoor pool.*
7 self-contained units; sleeping 2–6

Price per week:	£min	£max
Low season	125.00	250.00
High season	210.00	480.00

Open April–October

🐕◎🖩🗂⊙🗂MW TV🖨🎞🖃🅿⚡
🔍❂✈SP🏠

Shropshire
Map ref 4A3

*Beautiful historic town on the River
Severn retaining many fine old
timber-framed houses. Its
attractions include Rowley's
Museum with Roman finds, remains
of a castle, Clive House Museum, St
Chad's 18th C round church, rowing
on the river and the Shrewsbury
Flower Show in August.
Tourist Information Centre ☎ (01743)
350761*

Adcote Barn Cottage 🏔

🔑🔑🔑 COMMENDED

Little Ness, Shrewsbury
Contact: Mrs J L Giles, Adcote Barn,
Little Ness, Shrewsbury SY4 2JZ
☎ Baschurch (01939) 260565
Three-bedroomed barn conversion in a

*quiet rural location, with spacious
gardens and grounds. 6 miles from
Shrewsbury.*
1 self-contained unit; sleeping 5

Price per week:	£min	£max
Low season	120.00	160.00
High season	200.00	275.00

🐕◎🖩🗂⊙🗂🖨TV🛏🖨🎞🚐🅿❂
✈SP

The Flat

🔑🔑🔑 COMMENDED

23A Wyle Cop, Shrewsbury
Contact: Mrs S Arthur, Worldwide
Enterprises Limited, Property
Division, 24A Wyle Cop,
Shrewsbury SY1 1XB
☎ Shrewsbury (01743) 231984
Fax (01743) 231984
*Georgian apartment in a fine old
building with exposed beams, in old
world street in town centre. Lounge,
kitchen, bathroom, 4 bedrooms.*
1 self-contained unit; sleeping 6

Price per week:	£min	£max
Low season	210.00	330.00
High season	210.00	330.00

🐕🅼◎🖉🖩🗂⊙🗂MW🖨TV🛏🖨
🖃🖃🅿∪✈SP🏠

Gloucestershire
Map ref 2B1

*The 15,000 acres of lakes and ponds
and several Country Parks are being
developed at South Cerney as the
Cotswold Water Park, for sailing,
fishing, bird-watching and other
recreational activities.*

Lodge 62, Spring Lakes

🔑🔑🔑 COMMENDED

The Watermark Club, Station Road,
South Cerney, Cirencester
Contact: Mrs J Cooke, 23 Copse
End, Camberley, Surrey GU15 2BP
☎ Camberley (01276) 25540
*Lakeside 3-bedroomed timber lodge
with sun-deck, well equipped and
comfortably furnished. Shower-room in
addition to bathroom. Children
welcome. No smoking establishment.*
1 self-contained unit; sleeping 7

Price per week:	£min	£max
Low season	245.00	
High season		440.00

🐕◎🖩🗂⊙🗂MW🖨TV🛏🖨🎞
🎵🏷❂SP

Map references apply to
the colour maps at the
back of this guide.

STANTON

Gloucestershire
Map ref 2B1

Unspoilt Cotswold village with picturesque stone houses built around 1600. The church dates from Norman times but has 20th C furnishings and glass. Nearby is Stanway House, a Jacobean manor, open to summer visitors, and ruins of Hailes Abbey (English Heritage).

Charity Cottage

COMMENDED

Stanton, Broadway, Worcestershire
Contact: Mrs V Ryland, Charity Farm, Stanton, Broadway, Worcestershire WR12 7NE
☎ Stanton (01386) 584339
180-acre livestock farm. Spacious Cotswold cottage with pretty garden, quietly situated in village, opposite church. Log fire. Close to Cheltenham and Stratford-upon-Avon.
1 self-contained unit; sleeping 6

Price per week:	£min	£max
Low season	200.00	260.00
High season	260.00	385.00

Pax Cottage

COMMENDED

Stanton, Broadway, Worcestershire
Contact: Mr F Smoothy, North Lodge, North Road, Havering-atte-Bower, Romford RM4 1QB
☎ Ingrebourne (01708) 340635
Fax (01708) 340635
Thatched, modernised cottage in a conservation area, listed Grade II. Adjacent to riding school and Cotswold Way. Colour brochure available.
1 self-contained unit; sleeping 6

Price per week:	£min	£max
Low season	210.00	280.00
High season	280.00	330.00

Stanton Court Cottages

UP TO HIGHLY COMMENDED

Stanton Court, Stanton, Broadway, Worcestershire WR12 7NE
☎ (01386) 584551
Fax (01386) 584682
Contact: Mrs S Campbell

Map references apply to the colour maps at the back of this guide.

Cottages in grounds of historic house. Exposed stone walls and timbers, furnished with antiques and country pine. Beautiful gardens.
8 self-contained units; sleeping 2–7

Price per week:	£min	£max
Low season	260.00	460.00
High season	430.00	700.00

Cards accepted: Access, Visa

STIPERSTONES

Shropshire
Map ref 4A3

Below the spectacular ridge of the same name, from which superb views over moorland, forest and hills may be enjoyed.

The Old Granary Cottages

COMMENDED

Middle Farm, Shelve, Minsterley, Shrewsbury
Contact: Mrs A Wyke, Middle Farm, Shelve, Minsterley, Shrewsbury SY5 0JF
☎ Shrewsbury (01743) 891268
460-acre mixed & dairy farm. Recently converted cottages nestling in quiet hamlet of Shelve amongst the south Shropshire hills. Private lake and walks. All facilities. Linen and heating provided.
3 self-contained units; sleeping 4–6

Price per week:	£min	£max
Low season	170.00	210.00
High season	220.00	260.00

The Resting Hill

COMMENDED

46 Snailbeach, Minsterley, Shrewsbury
Contact: Mrs M Rowson, Resting Hill, 46 Snailbeach, Minsterley, Shrewsbury, Shropshire SY5 0LT
☎ Shrewsbury (01743) 791219
The old weighbridge office from a lead mining company which operated in the area.
2 self-contained units; sleeping 2–4

Price per week:	£min	£max
Low season	100.00	125.00
High season	150.00	150.00

Open February–November

STOKE-ON-TRENT

Staffordshire
Map ref 4B2

Famous for its pottery. Factories of several famous makers, including Josiah Wedgwood, can be visited. The City Museum has one of the finest pottery and porcelain collections in the world.
Tourist Information Centre ☎ (01782) 284600

Bank End Farm Cottages

COMMENDED

Hammond Avenue, Brown Edge, Stoke-on-Trent
Contact: Mr & Mrs K E Meredith, Bank End Farm, Hammond Avenue, Brown Edge, Stoke-on-Trent ST6 8QU
☎ Stoke-on-Trent (01782) 502160
Set in pleasant countryside, with village amenities 5 minutes' walk away. Ideal for visiting Potteries and Peak District. Children welcome. Ample parking.
2 self-contained units; sleeping 6

Price per week:	£min	£max
Low season	150.00	185.00
High season	185.00	230.00

STOW-ON-THE-WOLD

Gloucestershire
Map ref 2B1

Attractive Cotswold wool town with a large market-place and some fine houses, especially the old grammar school. There is an interesting church dating from Norman times. Stow-on-the-Wold is surrounded by lovely countryside and Cotswold villages.
Tourist Information Centre ☎ (01451) 831082

Broad Oak Cottage

HIGHLY COMMENDED

Lower Park Street, Stow-on-the-Wold, Cheltenham
Contact: Mrs R Wilson, The Counting House, Stow-on-the-Wold, Cheltenham, Gloucestershire GL54 1AL
☎ Cotswold (01451) 830794
Semi-detached Georgian cottage quietly situated near centre. Great character,

open fire, two bedrooms, dining and sitting rooms, all beautifully equipped.
1 self-contained unit; sleeping max 4

Price per week:	£min	£max
Low season	160.00	300.00
High season	300.00	450.00

🐾 ✂ ◎ ▥ ⊙ ♨ MW 📢 📺 ⊿ 🕮 🍴
🚗 🐾 SP ♨

Greystones ⋀
🔑🔑🔑 HIGHLY COMMENDED

5 Yew Tree Cottages, Mount Pleasant Close, Stow-on-the-Wold
Contact: Mr I James, 30A Albemarle Road, Beckenham, Kent BR3 5HJ
☎ (0181) 658 8267
Fax (0181) 658 1804

Sympathetically refurbished and well-equipped 18th C stone cottage with large patio and garden. Lovely views. Two bathrooms (1 en-suite). Exposed beams, Cotswold fireplace.
1 self-contained unit; sleeping 5

Price per week:	£min	£max
Low season		305.00
High season		410.00

Horseshoe Cottage
🔑🔑🔑 HIGHLY COMMENDED

Forge House, Lower Oddington, Moreton-in-Marsh
Contact: Mr & Mrs M R McHale, Forge House, Lower Oddington, Moreton-in-Marsh, Gloucestershire GL56 0UP
☎ Cotswold (01451) 831556

Former village forge. This listed, detached, stone cottage for 2 adults is set in 1.5 acres of private Cotswold countryside.
1 self-contained unit; sleeping 2

Price per week:	£min	£max
Low season	150.00	
High season		250.00

◎ ▥ ⊙ ♨ MW 📢 📺 ⊿ 🍴 🚗 P
❄ 🍴 SP ♨

The Martins
🔑🔑 HIGHLY COMMENDED

Broadwell, Moreton-in-Marsh
Contact: Mr & Mrs J H Reed, 107 Wyatts Drive, Thorpe Bay, Southend-on-Sea, Essex SS1 3DA
☎ Southend on Sea (01702) 582666
& Cotswold (01451) 821281

Prettily furnished cottage. Both bedrooms with bathroom en-suite. Ideal position on the green in village 1.5 miles from Stow-on-the-Wold. Attractive garden overlooking countryside.
1 self-contained unit; sleeping 4

Price per week:	£min	£max
Low season	325.00	350.00
High season	375.00	475.00

🐾 12 ◎ ▥ ⊙ ♨ 📺 ⊿ 🚗 P ❄ 🍴
🐕 SP

Maugersbury Manor
🔑🔑 COMMENDED

Stow-on-the-Wold, Cheltenham GL54 1HP
☎ Cotswold (01451) 830581
Contact: Mr C S Martin

Quiet, comfortable apartment in old manor house, in a sunny position with pleasant garden and grounds. Ideal for children. Ample parking. Short breaks available and B & B sometimes available.
1 self-contained unit; sleeping 6

Price per week:	£min	£max
Low season	120.00	250.00
High season	120.00	250.00

🐾 M ◎ ▥ ⊙ ♨ MW 📢 📺 ⊿ 🍴
🍴 🚗 P U ❄ SP ♨ T

Park House Cottage ⋀
🔑🔑 COMMENDED

Park House, 8 Park Street, Stow-on-the-Wold, Cheltenham
Contact: Mr & Mrs G Sutton, Park House, 8 Park Street, Stow-on-the-Wold, Cheltenham, Gloucestershire GL54 1AQ
☎ Cotswold (01451) 830159
Fax (01451) 830159

Secluded, cosy cottage for non-smoking couple. Modern kitchen, spacious rooms, patio, gas central heating. Central position. Sorry, no pets.
1 self-contained unit; sleeping 2

Price per week:	£min	£max
Low season	150.00	200.00
High season	200.00	260.00

Cards accepted: Access, Visa, Diners, Amex

◎ ▥ ⊙ ♨ MW 📢 📺 ⊿ 🍴 ❄ 🍴

Quarwood Cottages ⋀
🔑🔑 COMMENDED

Fleurs Cottage, Quarwood, Fosseway, Stow-on-the-Wold, Cheltenham
Contact: Mr J Carthew, Fleurs Cottage, Quarwood, Fosseway, Stow-on-the-Wold, Cheltenham, Gloucestershire GL54 1JU
☎ Cotswold (01451) 830879
Fax (01451) 831918

Charming Cotswold-stone cottages with open log fires. In the picturesque grounds of a private woodland estate in an Area of Outstanding Natural Beauty. Half a mile from Stow-on-the-Wold.
2 self-contained units; sleeping 6–8

Price per week:	£min	£max
Low season	140.00	200.00
High season	200.00	350.00

🐾 ◎ ⊘ ▥ ⊙ ♨ MW 📢 📺 ⊿ 🍴
🍴 🚗 P ❄ 🍴 🐕 SP

Rose's Cottage
🔑🔑🔑 HIGHLY COMMENDED

The Green, Broadwell, Moreton-in-Marsh
Contact: Mr & Mrs R Drinkwater, Rose's Cottage, The Green, Broadwell, Moreton-in-Marsh, Gloucestershire GL56 0UF
☎ Cotswold (01451) 830007

Delightful cottage overlooking the green of charming Cotswold village, in an Area of Outstanding Natural Beauty, 1.5 miles from Stow-on-the-Wold. Ideal for touring.
1 self-contained unit; sleeping 2

Price per week:	£min	£max
Low season	175.00	200.00
High season	200.00	280.00

🐾 ◎ ▥ ⊙ ♨ MW 📢 📺 ⊿ 🚗 🍴 P
❄ SP

Vintners Cottage
🔑🔑🔑 COMMENDED

Broadwell, Moreton-in-Marsh
Contact: Mrs Taylor, 12 Dale Bank, Oakdale, Harrogate, North Yorkshire HG1 2LP
☎ Harrogate (01423) 502355

Delightful 17th C cottage, overlooking the green in a very pretty, unspoilt village. Fully modernised but retaining

Continued ▶

STOW-ON-THE-WOLD
Continued

all original features, fireplace, beams, exposed walls, etc. Can sleep further 2.
1 self-contained unit; sleeping 4

Price per week:	£min	£max
Low season	175.00	195.00
High season	255.00	340.00

☎ M ⓜ ⌨ ⊙ 🛈 M W 🎦 TV 🔲 🍺 (📢 🖫 🚗 P ❀ ✄ SP

STRATFORD-UPON-AVON
Warwickshire
Map ref 2B1

Famous as Shakespeare's home town, Stratford's many attractions include his birthplace, New Place where he died, the Royal Shakespeare Theatre and Gallery, "The World of Shakespeare" 30 minute theatre and Hall's Croft (his daughter's house).
Tourist Information Centre ☎ (01789) 293127

Blythe Lodge
🔑 🔑 HIGHLY COMMENDED

Grange Road, Bidford-on-Avon, Alcester
Contact: Mrs R P Ball, Blythe House, Grange Road, Bidford-on-Avon, Alcester, Warwickshire B50 4BY
☎ Stratford-upon-Avon (01789) 778015
Fax (01789) 778015

Charming detached cottage in riverside village near historic Stratford-upon-Avon and Cotswolds. Three bedrooms, sitting/dining room, delightful antique furnishings, attractive kitchen.
1 self-contained unit; sleeping 6

Price per week:	£min	£max
Low season	319.00	416.00
High season	477.00	673.00

☎ ⓜ 🥚 ⌨ ⊙ 🛈 M W 🎦 TV 🔲 🍺 (📢 🖫 🚗 P ❀ ✄

The 🅼 symbol after an establishment name indicates that it is a Regional Tourist Board member.

Chestnut Cottage
🔑 🔑 COMMENDED

Gospel Oak House, Bishopton, Stratford-upon-Avon
Contact: Mrs J Rush, Gospel Oak House, Bishopton, Stratford-upon-Avon, Warwickshire CV37 0JA
☎ Stratford-upon-Avon (01789) 292764

Set in splendid secluded grounds by woodland, with far reaching views. Well-appointed, attractively furnished, ample parking. 2.5 miles from Stratford-upon-Avon.
1 self-contained unit; sleeping 3

Price per week:	£min	£max
Low season	160.00	180.00
High season	190.00	210.00

☎ M ⓜ ⌨ ⊙ 🛈 M W 🎦 TV 🔲 🍺 (📢 🖫 🚗 P ❀ SP 🚂

---

1 College Mews
🔑 🔑 🔑 COMMENDED

Stratford-upon-Avon
Contact: Mr I R Reid, Inwood House, New Road, Alderminster, Stratford-upon-Avon, Warwickshire CV37 8PE
☎ Stratford-upon-Avon (01789) 450266 & Mobile 0956 602915
Fax (01789) 450266
Quietly situated ground floor apartment in "Old Town", within easy walking distance of theatres, shops and riverside parks. Owner supervised.
1 self-contained unit; sleeping max 2

Price per week:	£min	£max
Low season	190.00	225.00
High season	225.00	260.00

ⓜ 🥚 ⌨ ⊙ 🛈 M W TV 🔲 🍺 🖫 🚗 P ✗ SP

The Cottage - Fosbroke House 🅼
🔑 🔑 🔑 COMMENDED

4 High Street, Bidford-on-Avon, Alcester
Contact: Mr D Newbury, Fosbroke House, 4 High Street, Bidford-on-Avon, Alcester, Warwickshire B50 4BU
☎ Stratford-upon-Avon (01789) 772327
Grade II listed cottage attached to guest house. Modern comforts and facilities combined with original period features. 10 minutes from Stratford.

---

1 self-contained unit; sleeping 4–5

Price per week:	£min	£max
Low season	180.00	200.00
High season	230.00	270.00

Open February–December

☎ 2 🥚 ⌨ ⊙ 🛈 M W 🎦 TV 🔲 🍺 🚗 P ❀ SP 🚂

Honeysuckle Cottage
🔑 🔑 APPROVED

12 New Cottages, Shottery Road, Stratford-upon-Avon
Contact: Mr & Mrs C Deer, Little Orchard House, 84 Shottery Road, Stratford-upon-Avon, Warwickshire CV37 9QQ
☎ Stratford-upon-Avon (01789) 205319
Cosy 3-bedroomed cottage with pretty garden opening on to parkland. Half a mile to town centre and Shottery village. Spacious interior. Winter breaks. Gas central heating.
1 self-contained unit; sleeping 5

Price per week:	£min	£max
Low season	150.00	180.00
High season	240.00	270.00

☎ 5 🥚 ⌨ ⊙ 🛈 M W 🎦 TV 🔲 🍺 🖫 🚗 P ❀ ✄ SP T

King's Lodge 🅼
🔑 🔑 APPROVED

Long Marston, Stratford-upon-Avon
Contact: Mr & Mrs G H Jenkins, King's Lodge, Long Marston, Stratford-upon-Avon, Warwickshire CV37 8RL
☎ Stratford-upon-Avon (01789) 720705
Fax (01789) 720705

Holiday homes in historic country house set in 4.5 acres of garden and parkland, within easy reach of Stratford-upon-Avon and the Cotswolds.
3 self-contained units; sleeping 2–7

Price per week:	£min	£max
Low season	140.00	
High season	270.00	

☎ M ⓜ ⌨ ⊙ 🛈 TV 🍺 🖫 ❀ SP 🚂

All accommodation in this guide has been graded, or is awaiting a grading, by a trained Tourist Board inspector.

Luscombe Farm Cottage ⋀

COMMENDED

Snitterfield, Stratford-upon-Avon
Contact: Mr J R Burrows, Luscombe
Farm, Snitterfield,
Stratford-upon-Avon, Warwickshire
CV37 0PP
☎ Stratford-upon-Avon (01789)
731262
*Comfortable 3-bedroomed cottage, fully
equipped and furnished, with central
heating throughout. 5 miles from
Stratford-upon-Avon, near Snitterfield.*
1 self-contained unit; sleeping 6

Price per week:	£min	£max
Low season	210.00	210.00
High season	210.00	310.00

The Sextons Cottage

HIGHLY COMMENDED

60 Waterside, Stratford-upon-Avon
Contact: Mrs J Nattrass, 27 Beech
Hill Road, Sutton Coldfield, West
Midlands B72 1BY
☎ (0121) 373 6032
Fax (0121) 333 3090
*Grade II listed period cottage
overlooking Shakespeare's Theatre
gardens and River Avon in central
Stratford. Attractively furnished
throughout, one double and one
twin-bedded room. Secluded rear
garden.*
1 self-contained unit; sleeping 4

Price per week:	£min	£max
Low season	270.00	
High season		355.00

42 Shakespeare Street ⋀

COMMENDED

Stratford-upon-Avon
Contact: Mr K D Field, Avon House,
Mulberry Street,
Stratford-upon-Avon, Warwickshire
CV37 6SD
☎ Stratford-upon-Avon (01789)
298141
Fax (01789) 262272
*Grade II listed cottage built 1840, in
quiet back street in town centre, 300m
from Shakespeare's birthplace. Very
cosy. Private parking.*
1 self-contained unit; sleeping 6

Price per week:	£min	£max
Low season	350.00	475.00
High season	350.00	475.00

This old town, surrounded by
attractive hilly country, has been
producing broadcloth for centuries
and the local museum has an
interesting display on the subject.
Many of the mills have been
converted into craft centres and for
other uses.
*Tourist Information Centre ☎ (01453)
765768*

Beulah ⋀

APPROVED

Randwick, Stroud GL6 6HL
☎ (01453) 757577
Contact: Mrs M Davis

*Semi-detached cottage with 3
bedrooms, lounge, kitchen and
bathroom. Fully furnished. Garden with
panoramic views over lake and fields. In
friendly village. Near National Trust
woods and Cotswold Way.*
1 self-contained unit; sleeping max 5

Price per week:	£min	£max
Low season	140.00	180.00
High season	180.00	210.00

Folly Acres

APPROVED

11 Shepherds Croft, Stroud
Contact: Mr R Sanders,
11 Shepherds Croft, Stroud,
Gloucestershire GL5 1US
☎ Stroud (01453) 766822
*7-acre smallholding. Cedarwood chalet
set in an Area of Outstanding Natural
Beauty above the Slad Valley of Laurie
Lee's "Cider with Rosie" fame.*
1 self-contained unit; sleeping 4

Price per week:	£min	£max
Low season	120.00	150.00
High season	150.00	200.00

Westley Farm ⋀

APPROVED

Chalford, Stroud GL6 8HP
☎ Cirencester (01285) 760262
Contact: Mr J Usborne
*80-acre livestock farm. Secluded
Cotswold hill farm with fantastic views*

over Golden Valley. Superb walking
country. Peace and quiet guaranteed.
6 self-contained units; sleeping 2–6

Price per week:	£min	£max
Low season	120.00	190.00
High season	150.00	290.00

Open April–October

Whitminster House Cottages ⋀

UP TO COMMENDED

Whitminster House, Whitminster
Contact: Mrs A R Teesdale,
Whitminster House, Whitminster,
Gloucestershire GL2 7PN
☎ Gloucester (01452) 740204
Fax (01452) 740204

*Picturesque country cottages, ideally
situated near Cotswolds. Fully furnished
and equipped, linen included. Pets
accepted in some units. One specially
adapted for accompanied disabled
guests.*
Wheelchair access category 3♿
8 self-contained units; sleeping 3–10

Price per week:	£min	£max
Low season	175.00	395.00
High season	295.00	615.00

Yew Tree Cottage

COMMENDED

Jacobs Ladder, Leys Hill, Walford,
Ross-on-Wye, Herefordshire
Contact: Mrs M Davies, 82
Tamworth Road, Ashby-de-la-Zouch,
Leicestershire LE6 2PX
☎ (01283) 550321 (day) & (01530)
414200 (evening)
*Cottage with 3 bedrooms, 1 en-suite.
On a wooded hill and approached from
the road by a woodland track.
Woodland paths right up to the kitchen
door.*
1 self-contained unit; sleeping 6

Price per week:	£min	£max
Low season	200.00	300.00
High season	300.00	450.00

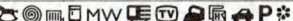

SYMONDS YAT WEST

**Hereford and Worcester
Map ref 2A1**

Jubilee Maze and Exhibition was created here in 1977 to commemorate Queen Elizabeth II's Jubilee, and there are other attractions beside the river. The area of Symonds Yat is a world-renowned beauty spot.

Woodlands

COMMENDED

Ferry Lane, Symonds Yat West, Ross-on-Wye, Herefordshire
Contact: Mrs C Blows, 14 Honeycroft Hill, Uxbridge, Middlesex UB10 9NH
☎ Uxbridge (01895) 236227
Cosy detached stone cottage by River Wye. Terrace with panoramic views of Wye Valley and Royal Forest of Dean. Open fire and exposed beams.
1 self-contained unit; sleeping 6

Price per week:	£min	£max
Low season	150.00	225.00
High season	275.00	275.00

TELFORD

**Shropshire
Map ref 4A3**

New Town named after Thomas Telford, the famous engineer who designed many of the country's canals, bridges and viaducts. It is close to Ironbridge with its monuments and museums to the Industrial Revolution, including restored 18th C buildings.
Tourist Information Centre ☎ (01952) 291370

Old Stables Cottage

COMMENDED

9a Church Street, Madeley, Telford
Contact: Mrs M Ferriday, 4 Laburnum Drive, Madeley, Telford, Shropshire TF7 5SE
☎ Telford (01952) 684238
Cosy and well-equipped listed cottage on the edge of Ironbridge Gorge, 3 minutes' walk from museums and shops. All linen provided, microwave. Holiday/company/short lets available.
1 self-contained unit; sleeping 4

Price per week:	£min	£max
Low season	120.00	160.00
High season	180.00	220.00

TETBURY

**Gloucestershire
Map ref 2B2**

Small market town with 18th C houses and an attractive 17th C Town Hall. It is a good touring centre with many places of interest nearby including Badminton House and Westonbirt Arboretum.

Folly Farm Cottages ᴍ

UP TO COMMENDED

Tetbury
Contact: Mr J Benton, Folly Farm, Tetbury, Gloucestershire GL8 8XA
☎ Tetbury (01666) 502475
Fax (01666) 502358

220-acre dairy farm. Five minutes' walk Tetbury, 18th C superior Cotswold cottages. Games room/function rooms, natural gardens, barbecues. Ideal family reunion venue, all sports facilities nearby. Easy access to motorways.
10 self-contained units; sleeping 2–10

Price per week:	£min	£max
Low season	150.00	390.00
High season	260.00	615.00

Cards accepted: Access, Visa

TEWKESBURY

**Gloucestershire
Map ref 2B1**

Tewkesbury's outstanding possession is its magnificent church, built as an abbey, with a great Norman tower and beautiful 14th C interior. The town stands at the confluence of the Severn and Avon and has many medieval houses, inns and several museums.
Tourist Information Centre ☎ (01684) 295027

Anchor House

HIGHLY COMMENDED

34 Twixtbears, Tewkesbury
Contact: Mrs J Gascoyne, The Stone House, High Street, Twyning, Tewkesbury, Gloucestershire GL20 6DE
☎ Tewkesbury (01684) 295407
Fax (01684) 292572
Modern 4-bedroomed house within

walking distance of rivers and town amenities. Close to Cotswolds and Malverns.
1 self-contained unit; sleeping 7

Price per week:	£min	£max
Low season	180.00	220.00
High season	190.00	395.00

77 High Street

HIGHLY COMMENDED

Tewkesbury
Contact: Mrs P M Last, 15 Abbots Court Drive, Church End, Twyning, Tewkesbury, Gloucestershire GL20 6JJ
☎ Tewkesbury (01684) 292731
Well-timbered, 17th C Grade II listed building on three floors, close to all amenities.
1 self-contained unit; sleeping 4

Price per week:	£min	£max
Low season	125.00	200.00
High season	155.00	235.00

TIDENHAM

**Gloucestershire
Map ref 2A2**

Overlooking the tidal reaches of the mouth of the River Severn. The church tower on the hill once served as a navigation beacon in the Severn estuary.

Tidenham House Lodge

HIGHLY COMMENDED

Tidenham, Chepstow, Gwent
Contact: Mr T S Thomas, T S Thomas & Sons (Lydney) Ltd, Albion Chambers, Hill Street, Lydney, Gloucestershire GL15 5HN
☎ Dean (01594) 842333
Fax (01594) 841180
Lodge adjoining country house in small village. Near Wye Valley Area of Outstanding Natural Beauty and Forest of Dean.
1 self-contained unit; sleeping 5

Price per week:	£min	£max
Low season	125.00	175.00
High season	200.00	300.00

The ᴍ symbol after an establishment name indicates that it is a Regional Tourist Board member.

UPTON-UPON-SEVERN

Hereford and Worcester
Map ref 2B1

Attractive country town on the banks of the Severn and a good river cruising centre. It has many pleasant old houses and inns, and the pepperpot landmark is now the Heritage Centre.
Tourist Information Centre ☎ (01684) 594200

The Pent House ♏

⚷⚷⚷⚷ HIGHLY COMMENDED

Welland Court, Upton-upon-Severn, Worcester
Contact: Mr P Archer, Welland Court, Upton-upon-Severn, Worcester WR8 0ST
☎ Upton-upon-Severn (01684) 594426 & 594413
Fax (01684) 594426
Converted stable. Four en-suite double bedrooms, 2 kitchens, large sitting room, TV, billiard table. Free fishing in the lake.
1 self-contained unit; sleeping 8

Price per week:	£min	£max
Low season	250.00	350.00
High season	400.00	500.00

Cards accepted: Access
☎ ◎ ▥ 🖥 ⊙ 🍽 MW ▣ TV ▣ 🗲 🍳 📠 ▣
🐾 P 🎣 ✻ ✗ ⚲ SP

WARWICK

Warwickshire
Map ref 2B1

Castle rising above the River Avon, 15th C Beauchamp Chapel attached to St Mary's Church, medieval Lord Leycester's Hospital almshouses and several museums. Nearby is Ashorne Hall Nickelodeon and the new National Heritage museum at Gaydon.
Tourist Information Centre ☎ (01926) 492212

Copes Flat ♏

⚷⚷⚷⚷ COMMENDED

Brook Street, Warwick
Contact: Mrs E Draisey, Forth House, 44 High Street, Warwick CV34 4AX
☎ Warwick (01926) 401512
Fax (01926) 490809
Secluded town centre self-contained first floor flat. Sitting room/dining room, bedroom, bathroom, kitchen, telephone. Close to shops and restaurants. Large roof garden.

1 self-contained unit; sleeping 3

Price per week:	£min	£max
Low season	150.00	
High season		275.00

☎ ◎ ▥ 🖥 ⊙ 🍽 MW ▣ TV ▣ 🗲 🍳 📠 ▣
🐾 ✻ ✗ ⚲ SP 🏛

Whitley Elm Cottages ♏

⚷⚷⚷⚷ HIGHLY COMMENDED

Case Lane, Mousley End, Rowington CV35 7JG
☎ Haseley Knob (01926) 484577
Contact: Mr & Mrs C Bevins

Converted barn in the grounds of the owner's Elizabethan manor house, offering high quality service in a very pretty rural area.
4 self-contained units; sleeping 4–6

Price per week:	£min	£max
Low season	215.00	300.00
High season	260.00	450.00

☎ M ◎ ▥ ⊙ 🖥 MW TV ▣ 🗲 🍳 ▣ P
U ✻ SP 🏛 T ◎

WELLESBOURNE

Warwickshire
Map ref 2B1

Picturesque village with several noteworthy inns. The River Dene, which divides the place in two, once separated Wellesbourne Hastings from Wellesbourne Mountford, but now both parts are regarded as one village.

Walton Hall

⚷⚷⚷⚷ HIGHLY COMMENDED

Walton, Wellesbourne, Warwick
Contact: Mr F Staples, Walton Hall Members Ltd, Walton Hall, Walton, Wellesbourne, Warwick CV35 9HU
☎ Stratford upon Avon (01789) 842424
Fax (01789) 470418

Victorian country mansion only 7 miles from Stratford-upon-Avon. Superbly appointed apartments. Many sports and leisure facilities.

40 self-contained units; sleeping 4–6

Price per week:	£min	£max
Low season	525.00	665.00
High season	665.00	840.00

Cards accepted: Access, Visa, Diners, Amex
☎ 1 M ◎ ▥ ⊙ 🖥 MW ▣ TV ▣ 🗲
▣ ∥ 🐾 P 🎿 ⚲ U 🎵 🏊 ✻ ✗
⚲ SP 🏛 T

WELLINGTON

Shropshire
Map ref 4A3

On the west side of Telford district, under the Wrekin and with easy access to Shrewsbury and Ironbridge.

The Coach House ♏

⚷⚷⚷⚷ HIGHLY COMMENDED

Wrockwardine, Wellington, Telford
Contact: Mr & Mrs A E Fellows, Old Vicarage, Wrockwardine, Wellington, Telford, Shropshire TF6 5DG
☎ Telford (01952) 244859 & (0121) 212 2131
Fax (0121) 212 1249

Detached private house providing centrally heated two-bedroomed accommodation. Pleasant location, surrounded by farms yet close to Ironbridge, Shrewsbury and the Welsh Marches.
1 self-contained unit; sleeping 4

Price per week:	£min	£max
Low season	200.00	220.00
High season	250.00	290.00

☎ ◎ ▥ ⊙ 🖥 MW ▣ TV ▣ 🗲 🍳 ▣
🐾 P U ✻ ✗

WEM

Shropshire
Map ref 4A3

Small town connected with Judge Jeffreys who lived in Lowe Hall. Well known for its ales.

Soulton Hall Cottages M

Soulton Hall, Wem, Shrewsbury SY4 5RS
☎ (01939) 232786
Fax (01939) 234097
Contact: Mrs A P Ashton

560-acre mixed farm. Cottages scattered around country estate, with 50 acres of oak woodland and river-brook. All cottages are fully equipped. Ideal for walking, bird-watching or simply relaxing.
3 self-contained units; sleeping max 8

Price per week:	£min	£max
Low season	173.00	220.00
High season	220.00	385.00

Cards accepted: Access, Visa, Diners

WEST FELTON

Shropshire
Map ref 4A3

Rectory Cottage M

COMMENDED

West Felton, Oswestry
Contact: Mrs C Gale, Rectory Coach House, West Felton, Oswestry, Shropshire SY11 4LE
☎ Oswestry (01691) 610229
Detached stone 18th C coachman's cottage, in a listed cobbled courtyard. Two bedrooms, central heating and open fire.
1 self-contained unit; sleeping 4

Price per week:	£min	£max
Low season	150.00	200.00
High season	200.00	225.00

WESTON RHYN

Shropshire
Map ref 4A2

Agricultural parish close to the River Ceiriog and the Chirk Valley. The Druids Temple is a folly built by a local landowner in the last century.

Mill Cottage M

COMMENDED

Mill House, The Wern, Weston Rhyn, Oswestry SY10 7ER
☎ Oswestry (01691) 659738
Contact: Mr & Mrs H Brannick
Converted 18th C barn, set in peaceful, rural surroundings with stream, 4 miles from Oswestry and the Welsh border.
1 self-contained unit; sleeping 5

Price per week:	£min	£max
Low season	150.00	
High season		190.00

WINCHCOMBE

Gloucestershire
Map ref 2B1

Ancient town with a folk museum and railway museum. To the south lies Sudeley Castle with its fine collection of paintings and toys and an Elizabethan garden.

3 The Coates M

COMMENDED

Winchcombe, Cheltenham
Contact: Cottage in the Country, Forest Gate, Frog Lane, Milton-under-Wychwood, Oxfordshire OX7 6JZ
☎ (01993) 831495
Fax (01993) 831095
Spacious, semi-detached house in quiet cul-de-sac. Sitting/dining room, kitchen and cloakroom on ground floor. One twin and 2 double bedrooms, bathroom and WC on first floor. Gas CH, washing machine, fridge/freezer.
1 self-contained unit; sleeping 6

Price per week:	£min	£max
Low season	210.00	
High season		300.00

Open February–October

Manor Farm M

HIGHLY COMMENDED

Greet, Winchcombe, Cheltenham GL54 5BJ
☎ Cheltenham (01242) 602423
Contact: Mr & Mrs Day
480-acre mixed farm. Old Cotswold tithe house on working farm, fully modernised. Close to Sudeley Castle and steam railway. Two smaller cottages and B & B also available.
3 self-contained units; sleeping 3–6

Price per week:	£min	£max
Low season	120.00	150.00
High season	220.00	540.00

North Farmcote Cottage M

APPROVED

Farmcote, Winchcombe, Cheltenham
Contact: Mrs D Eayrs, North Farmcote, Winchcombe, Cheltenham, Gloucestershire GL54 5AU
☎ Cheltenham (01242) 602304
Fax (01242) 603988
Small, semi-detached stone cottage with magnificent views, set in a quiet hamlet in beautiful Cotswold countryside. Ideal centre for touring.
1 self-contained unit; sleeping max 4

Price per week:	£min	£max
Low season	175.00	190.00
High season	205.00	225.00

Postlip House Cottages M

HIGHLY COMMENDED

Postlip House, Winchcombe, Cheltenham GL54 5AH
☎ Cheltenham (01242) 602390
Fax (01242) 602390
Contact: Mr W P Sparks
Beautifully converted cottages in 7 acres of wooded gardens and grounds. Resident proprietors give personal attention. Meal service if required.
5 self-contained units; sleeping 2–6

Price per week:	£min	£max
Low season	175.00	260.00
High season	340.00	470.00

A key to symbols can be found inside the back cover flap.

The M symbol after an establishment name indicates that it is a Regional Tourist Board member.

All accommodation in this guide has been graded, or is awaiting a grading, by a trained Tourist Board inspector.

Stoneways, Millers Barn & The Granary ⚐

HIGHLY COMMENDED

Greet Road, Winchcombe, Cheltenham
Contact: Mr & Mrs Wilson, 60 Pershore Road, Evesham, Worcestershire WR11 6PQ
☎ Evesham (01386) 446269
Fax (01386) 446269
Large converted barn divided into 2 units, also detached stone cottage. All furnished and equipped to a very high standard. Parking, gardens, open views, privately and peacefully situated.
3 self-contained units; sleeping 2–5

Price per week:	£min	£max
Low season	180.00	295.00
High season	220.00	500.00

WITCOMBE

Gloucestershire
Map ref 2B1

Combination of villages scattered south-west of Gloucester on the lower slopes of the Cotswold escarpment up to Birdlip Hill. Remains of a Roman villa.

Witcombe Park Holiday Cottages ⚐

COMMENDED

Great Witcombe, Gloucester
Contact: Mr Hicks-Beach, Witcombe Farm, Great Witcombe, Gloucester GL3 4TR
☎ Gloucester (01452) 863591
On 300-year-old family estate of 1,500 acres. In Area of Outstanding Natural Beauty on the edge of Cotswold Escarpment and Cotswold Way running through beautiful beech woodlands. Witcombe Park Holiday Cottages are a converted barn. Church Farm, old farmhouse built about 1600-1650. Hillview Cottage, similar age.
5 self-contained units; sleeping 2–10

Price per week:	£min	£max
Low season	125.00	220.00
High season	200.00	400.00

COLOUR MAPS

Colour maps at the back of this guide pinpoint all places in which you will find accommodation listed.

WOLVERLEY

Hereford and Worcester
Map ref 4B3

Famous as the birthplace of John Baskerville, innovator in the art of printing, the expanded village lies in the Stour Valley just north of Kidderminster.

The Log House ⚐

COMMENDED

Bodenham Farm, Wolverley, Kidderminster, Worcestershire
Contact: Mrs J Binnian, Bodenham Farm, Wolverley, Kidderminster, Worcestershire DY11 5SY
☎ Kidderminster (01562) 850382
134-acre mixed farm. Holiday home set in landscaped arboretum. Lakes, punting, walking, scenic nature reserve. 1994 winner of Forestry Authority England "Centre of Excellence" award. Newly awarded Heritage Status.
1 self-contained unit; sleeping 6

Price per week:	£min	£max
Low season	120.00	145.00
High season	170.00	220.00

WOOTTON

Staffordshire
Map ref 4B2

A quiet stone village in the shelter of the Weaver Hills, with a fine Jacobean mansion, Wootton Lodge, built c1611. A claim to fame in 1766 was the year-long stay by Jean Jacques Rousseau in the now non-existent Wootton Hall.

Home Farm Cottages ⚐

HIGHLY COMMENDED

Hall Lane, Wootton, Ashbourne DE6 2GW
☎ Ellastone (01335) 324433
Contact: Mrs A Thompson
Stone barn on a small farm, converted sympathetically into attractive cottage-style apartments with every modern comfort. Games room. Farming hamlet in the Peak District, 6 miles from Ashbourne, 3 miles from Alton Towers. Dogs by arrangement.
5 self-contained units; sleeping 2–6

Price per week:	£min	£max
Low season	80.00	240.00
High season	190.00	450.00

WORCESTER

Hereford and Worcester
Map ref 2B1

Lovely riverside city dominated by its Norman and Early English cathedral, King John's burial place. Many old buildings including the 15th C Commandery and the 18th C Guildhall. There are several museums and the Royal Worcester porcelain factory.
Tourist Information Centre ☎ (01905) 726311 or 723471

Noken Farm Cottage ⚐

APPROVED

Noken Farm, Sinton Green, Hallow, Worcester
Contact: Mrs M E Pritchard, Noken Farm, Sinton Green, Hallow, Worcester WR2 6NW
☎ Worcester (01905) 640531
Fax (01905) 640531
200-acre mixed farm. Modern farm cottage, 4 miles north-west of Worcester. Splendid views. Market gardening and sheep.
1 self-contained unit; sleeping 5

Price per week:	£min	£max
Low season	105.00	160.00
High season	160.00	220.00

WOTTON-UNDER-EDGE

Gloucestershire
Map ref 2B2

Small town in the southern Cotswolds. Berkeley Castle is within easy reach.

Gate Cottage ⚐

COMMENDED

Alderley, Wotton-under-Edge
Contact: Dr M P Rowlands, The Gate House, Alderley, Wotton-under-Edge, Gloucestershire GL12 7QT
☎ Dursley (01453) 845356 & 844804
Converted Cotswold stone stable cottage set in 2 acres of lawns and garden with beautiful open panoramic views.
1 self-contained unit; sleeping 6

Price per week:	£min	£max
Low season	160.00	200.00
High season	200.00	300.00

WOTTON-UNDER-EDGE

Continued

Hill Mill Cottage

HIGHLY COMMENDED

Hill Mill House, Ozleworth,
Wotton-under-Edge
Contact: Mrs P Nash, Hill Mill
House, Ozleworth,
Wotton-under-Edge,
Gloucestershire GL12 7QR
☎ Dursley (01453) 842401
*Pretty cottage in beautiful, peaceful
valley in the South Cotswolds. Lounge
with dining area, kitchen, bathroom. 1
double and 1 twin bedroom. Shared
games room. Lake with rowing boat in
6 acres. One mile from Cotswold Way.*
1 self-contained unit; sleeping 4

Price per week:	£min	£max
Low season	160.00	250.00
High season	190.00	280.00

WYE VALLEY

*See under Hereford, Ross-on-Wye,
Symonds Yat, Symonds Yat West*

WYTHALL

**Hereford and Worcester
Map ref 4B3**

On the southern outskirts of
Birmingham heading towards
Evesham.

Inkford Court

UP TO HIGHLY COMMENDED

Alcester Road, Wythall, Birmingham
B47 6DL
☎ (01564) 822304 & Mobile Phone
0831 462451
Contact: Mr J S Bedford

*Four cottages, part of a restoration and
conversion of 18th C period farm
buildings set in 6.5 acres. Ideally
located for Heart of England.*
5 self-contained units; sleeping 5–6

Price per week:	£min	£max
Low season	195.00	275.00
High season	195.00	325.00

COUNTRY CODE

Always follow the Country Code

🌳Enjoy the countryside and respect its life and work 🌳Guard against all risk of fire 🌳Fasten all gates 🌳Keep your dogs under close control 🌳Keep to public paths across farmland 🌳Use gates and stiles to cross fences, hedges and walls 🌳Leave livestock, crops and machinery alone 🌳Take your litter home 🌳Help to keep all water clean 🌳Protect wildlife, plants and trees 🌳Take special care on country roads 🌳Make no unnecessary noise

MIDDLE ENGLAND

Middle England can be enjoyed on foot, by car - and in some places, by canal boat.

From the heights of the High Peaks to the tranquil shire countryside, this region is as rich in history as it is in colour and contrast.

The English Civil War began in Middle England; the tapestry of history is closely woven - with historic houses, heritage centres and museums bearing witness.

Don't miss Lincoln or the Lace-making city of Nottingham, elegant Buxton spa or Skegness by the sea! And then there's Sherwood Forest, haunt of the legendary Robin Hood...

FOR MORE INFORMATION CONTACT:
East Anglia Tourist Board *(Lincolnshire)*
Toppesfield Hall, Hadleigh, Suffolk IP7 5DN
Tel: (01473) 822922 **Fax:** (01473) 823063

Heart of England Tourist Board *(Derbyshire, Nottinghamshire, Leicestershire, Northamptonshire)*
Lark Hill Road, Worcester WR5 2EZ
Tel: (01905) 763436 or 763439
Fax: (01905) 763450

Where to Go in Middle England -
see pages 152-155
Where to Stay in Middle England -
see pages 156-171

MIDDLE ENGLAND

Where to Go and What to See

You will find hundreds of interesting places to visit during your stay in Middle England, just some of which are listed in these pages. The number against each name will help you locate it on the map (page 155). Contact any Tourist Information Centre in the region for more ideas on days out in Middle England.

1 Gainsborough Old Hall
Parnell Street, Gainsborough,
Lincolnshire DN21 2NB
Tel: (01427) 612669
Late medieval timber-framed manor house built c1460, with fine medieval kitchen. Displays on the building and its restoration.

2 World Of Robin Hood
Haughton, Retford,
Nottinghamshire DN22 8DZ
Tel: (01623) 860210
A hands-on medieval experience including The Crusaders, Medieval Market Place, Sherwood Forest, Castle Dungeons Armoury and the Great Hall.

3 Chatsworth House and Garden
Bakewell, Derbyshire DE45 1PP
Tel: (01246) 582204
Built 1687-1707. Collection of fine pictures, books, drawings, furniture. Garden laid out by Capability Brown with fountains and cascade. Farmyard and adventure playground.

4 Lincoln Cathedral
Lincoln LN2 1PZ
Tel: (01522) 544544
Medieval Gothic cathedral of outstanding historical and architectural merit.

5 Museum of Lincolnshire Life
Burton Road,
Lincoln LN1 3LY
Tel: (01522) 528448
The region's largest social history museum. Agricultural, industrial and social history of Lincolnshire from a teapot to a World War I tank. Victorian room setting.

6 The Heights of Abraham
Matlock Bath,
Matlock,
Derbyshire DE4 3PD
Tel: (01629) 582365
Cable car ride across Derwent Valley gives access to Alpine Centre with refreshments, superb views, woodland, prospect tower and two show caves.

7 The National Tramway Museum
Crich, Matlock,
Derbyshire DE4 5DP
Tel: (01773) 852565
Collection of 50 trams from Britain and overseas built 1873-1957. Tram rides on one-mile route, period street scene, depots, power station, workshops, exhibitions.

8 Midland Railway Centre
Butterley Station, Ripley,
Derby DE5 3QZ
Tel: (01773) 747674
Over 25 locomotives and 80 items of historic rolling stock of Midland and LMS origin. Steam-hauled passenger service, museum site. Country and farm parks.

9 American Adventure
Pit Lane, Ilkeston,
Derbyshire DE7 5SX
Tel: (01773) 531521
American theme park with more than 100 rides including Nightmare Niagara Log Flume, Rocky

Mountain, Rapids Ride, The Missile, Motion Master Simulator Cinema and many other attractions.

10 Southwell Minster
Bishop's Drive,
Southwell,
Nottinghamshire NG25 0JP
Tel: (01636) 812649
Building begun c1108. Saxon tympanum, Norman nave and crossing, early English choir. Outstanding foliage carving in Chapter House. Archbishop's Palace ruins.

11 The Galleries of Justice
Shire Hall,
High Pavement,
Nottingham NG1 1HN
Tel: (0115) 952 0555
Condemned! is the visitor attraction at the Galleries of Justice which offers a major crime and punishment experience. Based in and around former 19thC courthouse.

12 Newstead Abbey
Linby, Nottingham NG15 8GE
Tel: (01623) 793557
800-year-old remains of priory church, converted into country house in 16thC. Home of Lord Byron with possessions and manuscripts. Parkland, lake, gardens.

13 Nottingham Industrial Museum
Courtyard Buildings,
Wollaton Park,
Nottingham NG8 2AE
Tel: (0115) 928 4602
18thC stables presenting history of Nottingham's industries: printing, pharmacy, hosiery and lace. Victorian beam engine, horse gin, transport.

14 Belvoir Castle
Belvoir, Lincolnshire NG32 1PD
Tel: (01476) 870262
The present castle is fourth to be built on this site and dates from 1816. Art treasures including works by Poussin, Rubens, Holbein and Reynolds. Museum of Queen's Royal Lancers.

15 Belton House, Park & Gardens
Belton, Grantham,
Lincolnshire NG32 2LS
Tel: (01476) 66116
The crowning achievement of Restoration country house architecture, built in 1685-88 for Sir John Brownlow. Alterations by James Wyatt in 1777.

16 Sudbury Hall
Sudbury, Derbyshire DE6 5HT
Tel: (01283) 585305
Grand 17thC house. Plasterwork ceilings, ceiling paintings, carved staircase and overmantel. Museum of Childhood in old servants' wing.

17 Great Central Railway
Great Central Station,
Great Central Road,
Loughborough,
Leicestershire LE11 1RW
Tel: (01509) 230726
Preserved main line steam railway operating over 8.5 miles from Loughborough to Leicester North.

18 Ye Olde Pork Pie Shoppe
Dickinson & Morris Ltd,
10 Nottingham Street,
Melton Mowbray,
Leicestershire LE13 1NW
Pork pie shop and bakery in 17C building. History of shop and Melton Mowbray Pork Pie industry. Demonstrations of traditional craft of hand raising pork pies.

19 Spalding Tropical Forest
Glenside North,
Pinchbeck,
Spalding,
Lincolnshire PE11 3SD
Tel: (01775) 710882
One half-acre glass house enclosing a tropical environment. Four zones including tropical rain forest, Japanese and Australian tropical plants and Mediterranean temperate zone.

20 Oakham Castle

Market Place, Oakham,
Leicestershire
Tel: (01572) 723654
Splendid 12thC Great Hall of fortified manor house. Unique horseshoe forfeits left by peers of the realm.

21 Newarke Houses Museum

The Newarke, Leicester LE2 7BY
Tel: (0116) 247 3222
Local history and crafts from 1485. Toys and games, clocks, mechanical instruments. 19thC street scene, early 20thC shop. Feature on 19thC giant Daniel Lambert.

22 Twycross Zoo

Twycross, Near Atherstone,
Warwickshire CV9 3PX
Tel: (01827) 880250
Gorillas, orangutans, chimpanzees, modern gibbon complex, elephants, lions, cheetahs, giraffes, reptile house. Pets corner. Rides.

23 Rockingham Castle

Rockingham,
Leicestershire LE16 8TH
Tel: (01536) 770240
Elizabethan house within walls of Norman castle. Fine pictures. Extensive views and gardens with roses and ancient yew hedge.

24 Lamport Hall

Lamport,
Northampton NN6 9HD
Tel: (01604) 686272
17th/18thC house, home of Isham family, mainly John Webb and Francis Smith. Beautiful high room (1655) fine library (1732). Garden home to the 1st Gnome in England.

25 Holdenby House and Gardens

Holdenby,
Northampton NN6 8DJ
Tel: (01604) 770074
Remains of Elizabethan palace and gardens. Fragrant border, falconry centre, armoury, 17thC homestead, tea room and shop.

26 National Dragonfly Museum

Ashton Mill, Ashton,
Northampton PE8 5LB
Tel: (01832) 272427
Discover the wonder and plight of dragonflies. See also the Victorian diesel hydro-electric generating pumping hall and craft exhibitions. Gift shop.

27 Sulgrave Manor

Sulgrave, Near Banbury,
Oxfordshire OX17 2SD
Tel: (01295) 760205
Small manor house of Shakespeare's time, with furniture of period. Fine kitchen. Early English home of ancestors of George Washington.

FIND OUT MORE

Further information about holidays and attractions in Middle England is available from either:
East Anglia Tourist Board,
Toppesfield Hall,
Hadleigh,
Suffolk IP7 5DN.
Tel: (01473) 822922
or **Heart of England Tourist Board**,
Lark Hill Road,
Worcester WR5 2EZ
Tel: (01905) 763436 or 763439

These publications are available free from the East Anglia Tourist Board:
■ **Great Escapes** - short breaks
■ **Touring Map**

These publications are available free from the Heart of England Tourist Board:
■ **Places to Visit** (chargeable)
■ **Peak District and Derbyshire Guide**
■ **Rutland, Rockingham Forest and Stamford Guide**

WEST YORKSHIRE

EAST RIDING OF YORKSHIRE

NORTH LINCOLNSHIRE

N.E. LINCS

SOUTH YORKSHIRE

Glossop

Worksop
Retford
1 Gainsborough

Mablethorpe

Chesterfield
NOTTINGHAM-SHIRE
2

Ingoldmells

Bakewell **3**
Matlock **6**
Butterley
Mansfield
Ollerton
4 **5** Lincoln

Skegness

Crich **7**
8
Ripley
Ashbourne
Ilkeston **9**
Southwell **10**
Newark
LINCOLNSHIRE

Sleaford

Boston

DERBYSHIRE
Derby
11 **12** **13**
Nottingham
14
Belvoir
15 Belton
Grantham

16 Sudbury

STAFFORD-SHIRE
Swadlincote
17 Loughborough
Bourne
19 Spalding

Ashby de la Zouch
18 Melton Mowbray
Stamford
Market Deeping

NORFOLK

LEICESTERSHIRE
20
Oakham

WEST MIDLANDS
22 Twycross
21 Leicester

Hinckley

Foxton
23 Rockingham
Corby
Oundle
Kettering

CAMBRIDGESHIRE

Market Harborough

24 Lamport

NORTHAMPTONSHIRE
Holdenby **25**
Wellingborough
Daventry
Northampton

WARWICKSHIRE

Ashton **26**
27 Sulgrave

BEDFORDSHIRE

OXFORDSHIRE
BUCKS

0   20 Miles
0   30 Kms

WHERE TO STAY (MIDDLE ENGLAND)

Accommodation entries in this region are listed in alphabetical order of place name,

and then in alphabetical order of establishment. A contact address is given where it differs

from the address of the establishment.

Map references refer to the colour location maps at the back of this guide.

Prices shown are weekly per unit.

At-a-glance symbols at the end of each accommodation entry give useful information

about services and facilities. A key to symbols can be found inside the back cover flap.

Keep this open for easy reference.

ALFORD

Lincolnshire
Map ref 4D2

Busy market town with attractive Georgian houses and shops and a Folk Museum in the thatched manor house. A craft market is held on Fridays in the summer months and there is a restored and working 5-sailed tower mill.

Park Farm Holidays

UP TO COMMENDED

Withern, Alford LN13 0DF
☎ Withern (01507) 450331
Fax (01507) 450331
Contact: Mrs E M Burkitt
Self-catering cottages on private road and log cabins in wooded area. Central heating. Secluded area 6 miles from the coast.
6 self-contained units; sleeping 4–6

Price per week:	£min	£max
Low season	110.00	150.00
High season	150.00	260.00

ALKMONTON

Derbyshire
Map ref 4B2

At the end of a 5-mile stretch of straight Roman road, Alkmonton has fantastic views of the surrounding countryside as far as Staffordshire.

Dairy House Farm

HIGHLY COMMENDED

Alkmonton, Longford, Ashbourne DE6 3DG
☎ Ashbourne (01335) 330359
Fax (01335) 330359
Contact: Mr A Harris
82-acre livestock farm. Converted Victorian loose boxes, tastefully furnished and finished, retaining beams and other original features. Non-smokers only and no pets please.
1 self-contained unit; sleeping 3–5

Price per week:	£min	£max
Low season	120.00	200.00
High season	120.00	200.00

ASHBOURNE

Derbyshire
Map ref 4B2

Market town on the edge of the Peak District National Park and an excellent centre for walking. Its impressive church with 212-ft spire stands in an unspoilt old street. Ashbourne is well-known for gingerbread and its Shrovetide football match.
Tourist Information Centre ☎ *(01335) 343666*

Alstonefield Holiday Homes

COMMENDED

Alstonefield, Ashbourne
Contact: Mr & Mrs E R Allen, Alstonefield Holiday Homes, Post Office House, Alstonefield, Ashbourne, Derbyshire DE6 2FX
☎ Alstonefield (01335) 310201

Choice of 5 high quality properties in quiet picturesque village of Alstonefield, 5 times winners of best kept village award. Situated between Dovedale and Manifold Valleys. Ideal for exploring Peak District National Park. Near Alton Towers and Chatsworth. Perfect for winter breaks.

TOWN INDEX

This can be found at the back of the guide. If you know where you want to stay, the index will give you the page number listing all accommodation in your chosen town, city or village.

The map references refer to the colour maps towards the end of the guide. The first figure is the map number; the letter and figure which follow indicate the grid reference on the map.

5 self-contained units; sleeping 4–6

Price per week:	£min	£max
Low season	95.00	175.00
High season	175.00	450.00

Atlow Mill Centre

COMMENDED

Atlow, Ashbourne DE6 1PX
☎ (01335) 370494 & 370279
Contact: Mrs Annie Sutherland
Atlow Mill is approximately 200 years old. It stands in its own secluded valley. Trout stream with private fishing rights.
1 self-contained unit; sleeping max 5

Price per week:	£min	£max
Low season	200.00	240.00

Cards accepted: Access, Visa

Bentley Hall

HIGHLY COMMENDED

Fenny Bentley, Ashbourne DE6 1LE
☎ (01335) 344405
Contact: Mrs Laura Bissell
Bentley Hall is a delightful and convenient base from which to explore the Peak District. Near Ashbourne and Dovedale.
4 self-contained units; sleeping 2–4

Price per week:	£min	£max
Low season	145.00	190.00
High season	180.00	275.00

Dove Barn Cottage

HIGHLY COMMENDED

Church Lane, Church Mayfield, Ashbourne
Contact: Mrs Kayte Alcock, Dove Barn, Church Lane, Church Mayfield, Ashbourne, Derbyshire DE6 2JR
☎ Ashbourne (01335) 300087
15th C refurbished barn conversion with oak beams and galleried bedroom. Good centre for walking, cycling, Alton Towers, Chatsworth, Dovedale, Carsington Water. Short or long breaks.
1 self-contained unit; sleeping 4

Price per week:	£min	£max
Low season	100.00	150.00
High season	200.00	250.00

Fiddlers Barn

COMMENDED

Petthills Lane, Kniveton, Ashbourne
Contact: Mrs E J Hopkin, Brook Cottage, Kniveton, Ashbourne, Derbyshire DE6 1JN
☎ Ashbourne (01335) 342243
Tastefully converted, light and airy first floor flat in red brick barn, adjacent to owner's 17th C home. Own entrance.
1 self-contained unit; sleeping max 5

Price per week:	£min	£max
Low season	150.00	
High season		270.00

Moore's Cottage Farm

COMMENDED

Slack Lane, Upper Mayfield, Ashbourne DE6 2JX
☎ (01335) 300272
Fax (01335) 300668
Contact: Mr David Restrick
40-acre beef farm. Home of Thomas Moore, Irish Georgian poet and friend of Byron, between 1811 and 1817.
3 self-contained units; sleeping 3–5

Price per week:	£min	£max
Low season	125.00	160.00
High season	175.00	270.00

Sunnyside

COMMENDED

Alstonefield, Ashbourne
Contact: Mr John Reavy, 11 Blackthorne Road, Boley Park, Lichfield, Staffordshire WS14 9YJ
☎ Lichfield (01543) 257227
Grade II listed cottage with 4 double bedrooms, log fire and beamed ceilings. Overlooking village green with large, secluded garden and log fire.
1 self-contained unit; sleeping max 8

Price per week:	£min	£max
Low season	290.00	340.00
High season	380.00	475.00

Map references apply to the colour maps at the back of this guide.

A key to symbols can be found inside the back cover flap.

For ideas on places to visit refer to the introduction at the beginning of this section.

Thorpe Cloud View

HIGHLY COMMENDED

Thorpe House, Thorpe, Ashbourne
Contact: Mr Philip Ramsbottom, Gallery Interiors, 11 Victoria Square, Ashbourne, Derbyshire DE6 1GG
☎ Ashbourne (01335) 346099
Tastefully converted cottage with beautiful views, retaining its rural character yet providing the comfort of a modern dwelling. Near Dovedale.
1 self-contained unit; sleeping max 2

Price per week:	£min	£max
Low season	175.00	200.00
High season	200.00	225.00

Woodhead Farm

APPROVED

Agnes Meadow Lane, Kniveton DE6 1JR
☎ (01335) 342274
Contact: Mrs N Short
Spacious cottage on a working beef and sheep farm 750 feet above sea level. 3 miles from Ashbourne. Near Dovedale and the Peak District.
1 self-contained unit; sleeping max 5

Price per week:	£min	£max
Low season	130.00	140.00
High season	150.00	160.00

Open May–September

Yeldersley Hall

UP TO DE LUXE

Ashbourne, DE6 1LS
☎ Ashbourne (01335) 343432
Contact: Mrs Joan Bailey

Two self-contained flats (to sleep 2) equipped to a high standard in stable block. Also fabulous 5 key first floor apartment (to sleep 4) in east wing of historic Georgian country house. 2 miles from Ashbourne.
3 self-contained units; sleeping 2–4

Price per week:	£min	£max
Low season	140.00	265.00
High season	230.00	410.00

ASHFORD IN THE WATER

Derbyshire
Map ref 4B2

Limestone village in attractive surroundings of the Peak District approached by 3 bridges over the River Wye. There is an annual well-dressing ceremony and the village was well-known in the 18th C for its black marble quarries.

Gritstone Cottage

COMMENDED

c/o Gritstone House, Greaves Lane, Ashford in the Water, Bakewell
Contact: Mrs A Lindsay, Gritstone House, Greaves Lane, Ashford in the Water, Bakewell, Derbyshire DE45 1QH
☎ Bakewell (01629) 813563
Fax (01629) 813566
18th C holiday cottage adjacent to owner's house. Price includes heat, light and bed-linen. Good base for stately homes and open country. No smoking, please.
1 self-contained unit; sleeping max 2

Price per week:	£min	£max
Low season	123.00	
High season		210.00

Open March–October

Little Batch

HIGHLY COMMENDED

Church Street, Ashford in the Water, Bakewell
Contact: Mrs J Stephens, 1 Hall End Lane, Ashford in the Water, Bakewell, Derbyshire DE45 1QJ
☎ Bakewell (01629) 813909
Bungalow situated in the grounds of Great Batch Hall, near amenities and close to Bakewell and Chatsworth. Ideal walking and touring centre.
1 self-contained unit; sleeping max 4

Price per week:	£min	£max
Low season	145.00	225.00
High season	275.00	285.00

Nanny Peggys Cottage

COMMENDED

1 Court Lane, Ashford in the Water, Bakewell
Contact: Mr J McGoverne, Willow Croft, Station Road, Great Longstone, Bakewell, Derbyshire DE45 1TS
☎ Bakewell (01629) 640576
Newly renovated throughout, this 400-year-old cottage is ideally placed

for pubs, walking, fishing, cycling or just relaxing. Sleeps 2 adults and 2 children.
1 self-contained unit; sleeping 1–4

Price per week:	£min	£max
Low season	135.00	165.00
High season	180.00	225.00

ASLOCKTON

Nottinghamshire
Map ref 4C2

Pretty village on the edge of the beautiful Vale of Belvoir. Racing horses are trained nearby and can often be seen around the village.

Aslockton Grange Cottage

COMMENDED

Aslockton Grange, Aslockton, Nottingham NG13 9AJ
☎ Whatton (01949) 850204 & 0860 599946
Contact: Mr or Mrs Thompson
Converted 18th C granary surrounded by 5 acres of land. Convenient for touring and near Belvoir Castle and Holme Pierrepont Water Sports Centre. Approximately 9 miles from Grantham, Newark and Nottingham.
1 self-contained unit; sleeping max 5

Price per week:	£min	£max
Low season	180.00	200.00
High season	220.00	240.00

BAKEWELL

Derbyshire
Map ref 4B2

Pleasant market town, famous for its pudding. It is set in beautiful countryside on the River Wye and is an excellent centre for exploring the Derbyshire Dales, the Peak District National Park, Chatsworth and Haddon Hall.
Tourist Information Centre ☎ (01629) 813227

Bolehill Farm Holiday Cottages

COMMENDED

Monyash Road, Bakewell DE45 1QW
☎ (01629) 812359
Fax (01629) 812359
Contact: Mr A J Staley

Charming stone cottages in courtyard setting overlooking Lathkill Dale. Bakewell 2 miles. Games room, sauna, solarium. Past winners of East Midlands Tourist Board Self-Catering Holiday of the Year Award.
Wheelchair access category 3
8 self-contained units; sleeping 2–6

Price per week:	£min	£max
Low season	175.00	290.00
High season	230.00	450.00

Carter's Mill Cottage

HIGHLY COMMENDED

Mill Farm, Haddon Grove, Over Haddon, Bakewell
Contact: Mrs S J Marsden, Mill Farm, Haddon Grove, Over Haddon, Bakewell, Derbyshire DE45 1JF
☎ Bakewell (01629) 812013
Fax (01629) 814734
240-acre livestock farm. Tasteful barn conversion in the beautiful Lathkill Dale, within the curtilage of a working farm.
1 self-contained unit; sleeping max 5

Price per week:	£min	£max
Low season	220.00	320.00
High season	300.00	460.00

2 Coach Cottages

COMMENDED

Bagshaw Hill, Bakewell
Contact: Mrs Caroline Hinchliffe, Brew House, Buxton Road, Bakewell, Derbyshire DE45 1DA
☎ Bakewell (01629) 814102
Fax (01629) 815077
Delightful 17th C cottage providing spacious accommodation in peaceful location with superb views. Just minutes' walk from Bakewell's many facilities. Off-season short breaks available.
1 self-contained unit; sleeping 1–4

Price per week:	£min	£max
Low season	180.00	200.00
High season	210.00	250.00

Edge View

🔑🔑🔑 COMMENDED

Monyash Road, Bakewell
Contact: Mrs G P Rogers, Penylan,
Monyash Road, Bakewell, Derbyshire
DE45 1FG
☎ Bakewell (01629) 813336
*3 bedroomed dormer bungalow, with
kitchen and lounge/dining room. Two
ground floor bedrooms adjacent to
bathroom. Lawn, garden, ample
parking.*
1 self-contained unit; sleeping max 6

Price per week:	£min	£max
Low season	200.00	250.00
High season	250.00	300.00

🛏3 Ⓜ ◎ 🏚 ⊡ ☷ MW ⓉⓋ 🗄 🛋 🔒
🔊P ❀ ✕ SP

Haddon Grove Farm Cottages 𝕄

🔑🔑🔑 COMMENDED

Haddon Grove Farm, Monyash Road,
Bakewell DE45 1JF
☎ (01629) 813551
Contact: Mr J H Boxall

*Attractive collection of converted stone
cottages overlooking Lathkill Dale and
close to Bakewell. Facilities include
recreation room and heated indoor
swimming pool.*
Wheelchair access category 2 ♿
10 self-contained units; sleeping 3–7

Price per week:	£min	£max
Low season	170.00	325.00
High season	295.00	675.00

🛏Ⓜ ◎ 🏚 ⊡ ☷ MW ⓉⓋ 🗄 🛋 (🖦🖳P 🔊
❀ SP Ⓣ

Derbyshire
Map ref 4B2

Village in the Peak District near the
Upper Derwent Reservoirs of
Ladybower, Derwent and Howden.
An excellent centre for walking.

Shatton Hall Farm 𝕄

🔑🔑🔑 UP TO HIGHLY COMMENDED

Bamford, Sheffield S30 2BG
☎ Hope Valley (01433) 620635
Fax (01433) 620635
Contact: Mrs A H Kellie

*110-acre livestock farm. Comfortable
pine furnished cottages, each with
private garden or terrace and ample
parking. Hard tennis court. Superb
setting with woodland and stream-side
walks.*
3 self-contained units;
sleeping max 6

Price per week:	£min	£max
Low season	150.00	175.00
High season	200.00	300.00

🛏Ⓜ ◎ 🏚 ⊡ ☷ MW ⓉⓋ 🗄 🛋 (🖦🖳
🔊P ⚲ ∪ ❀ SP 🎠 ◎

Derbyshire
Map ref 4B2

Pleasant old market town in the
valley of the River Derwent.
Attractive scenery and a wealth of
industrial history.

33 Belper Lane 𝕄

🔑🔑🔑 COMMENDED

Belper
Contact: Mrs S Chadwick,
Tikhi-Dom, Queens Drive, Belper,
Derby, DE56 2TJ
☎ Belper (01773) 823044
19th C mill worker's cottage.
1 self-contained unit; sleeping 4

Price per week:	£min	£max
Low season	125.00	150.00
High season	170.00	210.00

🛏3 🥛 🏚 ⊡ ☷ MW 🍴 ⓉⓋ 🗄 🛋 (🖦
🖳 🔊P SP 🎠

Chevin Green Farm 𝕄

🔑🔑🔑 − 🔑🔑🔑 COMMENDED

Chevin Road, Belper, Derby
DE56 2UN
☎ (01773) 822328
Contact: Mr C A Postles
*Carefully converted 2 and
3-bedroomed self-catering cottages in
beautiful Derbyshire, overlooking the
Derwent Valley.*
5 self-contained units; sleeping 4–6

Price per week:	£min	£max
Low season	95.00	115.00
High season	250.00	295.00

🛏Ⓜ ◎ 🏚 ⊡ ☷ MW ⓉⓋ 🗄 🛋 (🖦🖳P∪
🔊 ✕ Ⓣ

Derbyshire
Map ref 4B2

Small Peak District village set
around gritstone crags with 2 high
rocking stones.

1 Eagle Terrace 𝕄

🔑🔑🔑 COMMENDED

Birchover, Matlock
Contact: Mrs M E Prince, Haresfield
House, Birchover, Matlock,
Derbyshire DE4 2BL
☎ Winster (01629) 650634
*Cottage in the centre of a Peak District
village surrounded by a network of
public footpaths in an Area of
Outstanding Natural Beauty.*
1 self-contained unit; sleeping max 5

Price per week:	£min	£max
Low season	180.00	200.00
High season	190.00	210.00

🛏◎ 🏚 ⊡ ☷ MW ⓉⓋ 🗄 🛋 🔒 🔊P
❀ ✕ SP

BLANKNEY

Lincolnshire
Map ref 4C2

Blankney Golf Club 𝄞

🗝🗝🗝 COMMENDED

Blankney, Lincoln LN4 3AZ
☎ (01526) 320263
Fax (01526) 322521
Contact: Mr D Priest
High quality detached bungalow in the heart of rural Lincolnshire, 1 hour's drive from the coast. Linen provided. Golf available 200 yards by prior booking.
1 self-contained unit; sleeping max 6

Price per week:	£min	£max
Low season	150.00	150.00
High season	250.00	250.00

Cards accepted: Access, Visa

🗝🝰◎▦.⊙🗂MW 📲 TV🗄📠🖥
🏧P🅿❄ SP

BOURNE

Lincolnshire
Map ref 3A1

Market town with remains of a Norman abbey incorporated into the parish church. The birthplace of Lord Burghley.

Stocksfield 𝄞

🗝🗝🗝 COMMENDED

1 Bakers Way, Morton, Bourne
Contact: Mrs G Marsh, Gills Cottage, 23 High Street, Morton, Bourne, Lincolnshire PE10 0NR
☎ Bourne (01778) 570601
Village location. Modern, detached bungalow with 1 double and 1 twin bedroom. Linen, electricity and heating included. Washing machine/dryer. Nice garden.
1 self-contained unit; sleeping max 4

Price per week:	£min	£max
Low season	155.00	
High season		175.00

🝰⊘▦.🗂MW 📲 TV🗄📠🖥🖥🏧
P❄✗

TOWN INDEX

This can be found at the back of the guide. If you know where you want to stay, the index will give you the page number listing all accommodation in your chosen town, city or village.

BRACKLEY

Northamptonshire
Map ref 2C1

Historic market town of mellow stone, with many fine buildings lining the wide High Street and Market Place. Sulgrave Manor (George Washington's ancestral home) and Silverstone Circuit are nearby.
Tourist Information Centre ☎ (01280) 700111

Stowaway 𝄞

🗝🗝🗝 COMMENDED

7 Herrieffs Farm Road, Brackley
Contact: Mrs R Shahani, Lyttelton House, Stowe, Buckingham MK18 5EH
☎ Buckingham (01280) 822391
Fax (01280) 822769
Modern, well-equipped semi-detached house with pretty garden in quiet lane, yet near town centre. Ideal for touring Cotswolds, Stratford-upon-Avon, Oxford, London.
1 self-contained unit; sleeping max 5

Price per week:	£min	£max
Low season	175.00	210.00
High season	210.00	263.00

🝰▦◎▦.⊙🗂MW 📲 TV🗄📠🖥
🖥🏧P❄ SP

Walltree House Farm 𝄞

🗝🗝🗝 UP TO HIGHLY COMMENDED

Steane, Brackley NN13 5NS
☎ Banbury (01295) 811235 & 0860 913399
Fax (01295) 811147
Contact: Mr and Mrs Harrison
350-acre arable farm. Comfortable, quiet cottages in a courtyard overlooking lawns, woodland and a farm with nature trail. Near local sporting activities, historic towns, stately homes, shopping and Silverstone.
2 self-contained units; sleeping 2–6

Price per week:	£min	£max
Low season	185.00	370.00
High season	220.00	460.00

Cards accepted: Access, Visa

🝰◎▦.⊙🗂MW 📲 TV🗄📠🖥
P∪🎣❄✗ SP

Self-catering agencies which have a selection of holiday homes to let are listed in a special section towards the back of this guide.

BROXHOLME

Lincolnshire
Map ref 4C2

Friendly cluster of cottages and barns among the flat pastures by the River Till.

Pingles Cottage 𝄞

🗝🗝🗝 COMMENDED

Grange Farm, Broxholme, Saxilby, Lincoln LN1 2NG
☎ Lincoln (01522) 702441
Contact: Mrs P A Sutcliffe

100-acre mixed farm. Well-equipped cottage with private garden and river fishing, in the hamlet of Broxholme, 6 miles from historic Lincoln. Quiet and secluded but not isolated.
1 self-contained unit; sleeping max 4

Price per week:	£min	£max
Low season	170.00	180.00
High season	225.00	350.00

🝰◎▦.⊙🗂MW 📲 TV🗄📠🖥
🏧P🎣❄ SP◎

BUXTON

Derbyshire
Map ref 4B2

The highest market town in England and one of the oldest spas, with an elegant Crescent, Poole's Cavern, Opera House and attractive Pavilion Gardens. An excellent centre for exploring the Peak District.
Tourist Information Centre ☎ (01298) 25106

Cold Springs Farm 𝄞

🗝🗝🗝 COMMENDED

Manchester Road (A5004), Buxton SK17 6SS
☎ (01298) 22762
Fax (01298) 72005
Contact: Mr S B Millward
100-acre dairy farm. 1 mile from Buxton's town centre, adjacent to the farmhouse on a 100-acre dairy farm overlooking hills. Ideal centre for touring the beautiful Peak District.
2 self-contained units; sleeping 5–6

Price per week:	£min	£max
Low season	85.00	120.00
High season	100.00	150.00

Open May–October

🝰▦◎▦.⊙🗂MW TV🗄📠🖥🖥
P∪🎣

Hargate Hall

🗝🗝🗝🗝🗝 UP TO HIGHLY COMMENDED

Wormhill, Buxton SK17 8TA
☎ (01298) 872591
Contact: Mr Jackson
A country house, 5 miles from Buxton, with many free facilities.
11 self-contained units; sleeping 2–8

Price per week:	£min	£max
Low season	110.00	205.00
High season	240.00	420.00

Sittinglow Farm

🗝🗝 COMMENDED

Dove Holes, Buxton SK17 8DA
☎ Chapel-En-Le-Frith (01298) 812271
Contact: Mrs A S Buckley
250-acre dairy & livestock farm. Cottage adjoining farmhouse. Peaceful surroundings and magnificent views. One mile from village, 4 miles from Buxton. Storage radiators and linen inclusive, other electricity metered.
1 self-contained unit; sleeping max 2

Price per week:	£min	£max
Low season	80.00	120.00
High season	120.00	170.00

CALVER

Derbyshire
Map ref 4B2

Attractive Peak District village beside the River Derwent.

Cliffe View

🗝🗝 APPROVED

The Cross, Main Street, Calver, Sheffield
Contact: Mrs S Ridgeway, 4 Rock View, Miller's Dale, Buxton, Derbyshire SK17 8SN
☎ Tideswell (01298) 872607
There is an open plan living/kitchen area with a galleried bedroom having exposed beams and a shower room with toilet and washbasin.
1 self-contained unit; sleeping max 2

Price per week:	£min	£max
Low season	150.00	
High season	180.00	

CARSINGTON

Derbyshire
Map ref 4B2

The visitor centre at Britain's newest reservoir, Carsington Water, allows visitors to learn about the surrounding countryside and wildlife. Around the reservoir many activities are available including cycling, sailing and horse riding.

Owslow Farm

🗝🗝 COMMENDED

Owslow, Carsington, Matlock DE4 4DD
☎ (01629) 540510 & 540254
Contact: Mr P N Oldfield
230-acre dairy & livestock farm. Farmhouse with open fired sitting room and 2 dining rooms with log burners. Fully equipped kitchen. 2 double, 2 twin bedrooms. Bathrooms up and down.
1 self-contained unit; sleeping max 8

Price per week:	£min	£max
Low season	300.00	400.00
High season	400.00	750.00

CHAPEL-EN-LE-FRITH

Derbyshire
Map ref 4B2

Small market town and a good base for climbing and walking. Close to the show caverns at Castleton.

Hawthorn Cottage

🗝🗝 APPROVED

Bagshaw, Chapel-en-le-Frith, Stockport, Cheshire
Contact: Mrs Olive Fraser, Rose Cottage, Bagshaw, Chapel-en-le-Frith, Stockport, Cheshire SK12 6QU
☎ Chapel-en-le-Frith (01298) 813294
300-year-old detached stone cottage with oak beams and open fire. Lawned garden with patio/barbecue.
1 self-contained unit; sleeping max 6

Price per week:	£min	£max
Low season	130.00	160.00
High season	180.00	250.00

CHESTERFIELD

Derbyshire
Map ref 4B2

Famous for the twisted spire of its parish church, Chesterfield has some fine modern buildings and excellent shopping facilities, including a large, traditional open-air market. Hardwick Hall and Bolsover Castle are nearby.
Tourist Information Centre ☎ (01246) 207777 or 207778

Faversham House

🗝🗝🗝🗝 COMMENDED

145 Somersall Lane, Somersall, Chesterfield
Contact: Mrs J Mullan, Flat One, Faversham Court, Somersall Lane, Somersall, Chesterfield, Derbyshire S40 3LZ
☎ Chesterfield (01246) 566382
The house has secluded gardens with a large, outdoor, heated swimming pool and sun lounge. Overlooks the countryside, near Peak District National Park.
1 self-contained unit; sleeping max 6

Price per week:	£min	£max
Low season	200.00	270.00
High season	270.00	350.00

Swallow Cottage, Owl Cottage and Pheasant Croft

🗝🗝🗝🗝🗝🗝 HIGHLY COMMENDED

Oxton Rakes Hall Farm, Barlow, Sheffield
Contact: Mrs J S Hill, Oxton Rakes Hall Farm, Barlow, Sheffield S18 5SE
☎ Sheffield (0114) 289 0268
Fax (0114) 289 9016
18th C barn conversion. Children very welcome. Heated outdoor swimming pool and indoor games room. Set in 30 acres of beautiful Derbyshire countryside.
Wheelchair access category 1♿
3 self-contained units; sleeping 4–6

Price per week:	£min	£max
Low season	210.00	250.00
High season	250.00	300.00

Cards accepted: Diners

A key to symbols can be found inside the back cover flap.

The National Grading and Classification Scheme is explained in full at the back of this guide.

Map references apply to the colour maps at the back of this guide.

CRESSBROOK

Derbyshire
Map ref 4B2

Delightful dale with stone hall and pleasant houses, steep wooded slopes and superb views.

Cressbrook Hall Cottages ⋀⋀

COMMENDED

Cressbrook Hall, Cressbrook, Buxton SK17 8SY
☎ Tideswell (01298) 871289 & Free Phone 0500 121248
Fax (01298) 871845
Contact: Mrs B H Bailey

Accommodation with a difference! Self-cater or B&B in magnificent surroundings. Special catering services, leisure facilities and the Beauty Room ensure a carefree holiday. Colour brochure.
Wheelchair access category 2⅃
3 self-contained units; sleeping 2–11

Price per week:	£min	£max
Low season	105.00	380.00
High season	225.00	825.00

Cards accepted: Access, Visa

CRICH

Derbyshire
Map ref 4B2

Home of the National Tramway Museum where visitors can ride on trams along a 1 mile scenic route past reconstructed 19th C buildings. There are also workshops, a power station, an exhibition and a lead-mining display to be seen.

Ivy Dene Cottage ⋀⋀

COMMENDED

1 Sandy Lane, Crich, Matlock
Contact: Mrs M Holtam, Market Place, Crich, Matlock, Derbyshire DE4 5DD
☎ Ambergate (01773) 852416
Modernised stone cottage with a comfortable atmosphere. Close to Crich village shops, 1 mile from the Tram Museum, and near Matlock Bath and Chatsworth.

1 self-contained unit; sleeping 1–5

Price per week:	£min	£max
Low season	180.00	200.00
High season	200.00	250.00

CUTTHORPE

Derbyshire
Map ref 4B2

Small, sleepy village, 4 miles north-west of Chesterfield. Rich traditional history including secret passages and the custom of well-dressing which is still carried out today.

The Cottage & The Saltings

APPROVED

Cow Close Farm, Overgreen, Cutthorpe, Chesterfield
Contact: Mr & Mrs D Sutton, Cow Close Farm, Overgreen, Cutthorpe, Chesterfield, Derbyshire S42 7BA
☎ Chesterfield (01246) 232055
7-acre livestock farm. Both cottages have magnificent views and are single-storey conversions of outbuildings surrounding the courtyard of the 17th C farmhouse. A country inn across the road provides excellent meals.
2 self-contained units; sleeping 2–4

Price per week:	£min	£max
Low season	110.00	120.00
High season	170.00	170.00

DERBY

Derbyshire
Map ref 4B2

Modern industrial city but with ancient origins. There is a wide range of attractions including several museums (notably Royal Crown Derby), a theatre, a concert hall, and the cathedral with fine ironwork and Bess of Hardwick's tomb.
Tourist Information Centre ☎ (01332) 255802

Bank Cottage

HIGHLY COMMENDED

3 The Hollow, Mickleover, Derby
Contact: Mrs P K Pym, 2 The Hollow, Mickleover, Derby DE3 5DG
☎ Derby (01332) 515607
Attractive 18th C oak-beamed cottage in a quiet conservation area of Derby, with easy access to the Derbyshire Dales and many other places of interest.

1 self-contained unit; sleeping max 4

Price per week:	£min	£max
Low season	180.00	180.00
High season	180.00	180.00

DIGBY

Lincolnshire
Map ref 4C2

The church in this village has been added to over time giving it many layers of history.

The Lodge

APPROVED

Bloxholm, Dorrington, Lincoln
Contact: Mrs H Gillatt, Allens Farm, Digby Fen, Billinghay, Lincoln LN4 4DT
☎ Billinghay (01526) 860347
Cosy lodge overlooking parkland in a quiet village. All amenities. Scenic walks. Linen and log fire included. Good pub food 2 miles. Central for Lincoln, Sleaford, Boston.
1 self-contained unit; sleeping max 4

Price per week:	£min	£max
Low season	130.00	150.00
High season	140.00	170.00

Cards accepted: Access, Visa, Diners, Amex, Switch/Delta

DONINGTON ON BAIN

Lincolnshire
Map ref 4D2

Encompassed by the high wolds, pretty village with a tiny 700-year-old church.

Mill Lodge

COMMENDED

Benniworth House Farm, Donington on Bain, Louth LN11 9RD
☎ Stenigot (01507) 343265
Contact: Mrs P Cade
189-acre arable and mixed farm. Comfortable warm cottage on lovely farm/nature reserve, good footpaths, near Viking Way. Warm welcome from Ezra and Pamela Cade.
1 self-contained unit; sleeping max 6

Price per week:	£min	£max
Low season	180.00	220.00
High season	180.00	250.00

You are advised to confirm your booking in writing.

DORRINGTON

Lincolnshire
Map ref 4C2

Small village with several pretty cottages and an interesting church.

Dorrington Cottages ⋀⋀

COMMENDED

86-88 Main Street, Dorrington, Lincoln
Contact: Janet Crafer, 12 Church Lane, Timberland, Lincoln LN4 3SB
☎ Martin (01526) 378222
Semi-detached Victorian cottages, beautifully modernised. Central heating. Secluded garden, patio furniture, barbecue. Private parking. Unspoilt village with duck pond. Lincoln 15 miles, Sleaford 6 miles.
2 self-contained units; sleeping 1–5

Price per week:	£min	£max
Low season	150.00	205.00
High season	205.00	275.00

EARL STERNDALE

Derbyshire
Map ref 4B2

Ringed by beautiful hills and steeped in tradition and legend including its unusually named pub "Quiet Woman Inn", which tells the story of a landlady who had her head cut off for talking too much.

Cottage

APPROVED

Earl Sterndale, Buxton
Contact: Mr P Hardwick, Moorland, Earl Sterndale, Buxton, Derbyshire SK17 0BS
☎ Buxton (01298) 83833 & Bakewell (01629) 815185
Traditional cottage for 2, very cosy. Beautifully scenic small village location. Living room with wood-burning stove, kitchen, 1 bedroom, shower room.
1 self-contained unit; sleeping max 2

Price per week:	£min	£max
Low season	105.00	
High season		175.00

The ⋀⋀ symbol after an establishment name indicates that it is a Regional Tourist Board member.

EDITH WESTON

Rutland
Map ref 3A1

Attractive village with thatched and slate-roofed houses built around a green. Close to the largest man-made lake in England - Rutland Water - with a nature reserve and facilities for sailing and fishing.

Rutland Cottage Holidays ⋀⋀

HIGHLY COMMENDED

Stone Cottage, 34 Weston Road, Edith Weston, Rutland LE15 8HQ
☎ Stamford (01780) 720087
Contact: Mr Brian Stuart Wallis
19th C stone cottages, fully renovated, furnished and equipped. In centre of Edith Weston village, on south shore of Rutland Water.
4 self-contained units; sleeping 2–6

Price per week:	£min	£max
Low season	200.00	275.00
High season	300.00	450.00

Rutland Water Cottages ⋀⋀

HIGHLY COMMENDED

Edith Weston, Rutland
Contact: Mrs K S Walmsley, Dormer Cottage, Ryhall, Stamford, Lincolnshire PE9 4JA
☎ Stamford (01780) 64001 & 0385 548356
Fax (01780) 482808
Four period stone country cottages in peaceful village on south shore of Rutland Water, offering great charm with antiques and log fires. 1992 winners of Self Catering Holiday of the Year Award by East Midlands Tourist Board.
Wheelchair access category 3♿
4 self-contained units; sleeping 2–5

Price per week:	£min	£max
Low season	170.00	240.00
High season	220.00	375.00

ACCESSIBILITY

Look for the ♿👤👤 symbols which indicate accessibility for wheelchair users. These are described in detail at the front of this guide.

ELKESLEY

Nottinghamshire
Map ref 4C2

Railway Coach

COMMENDED

Jockey Lane, Elkesley, Retford
Contact: Ms S F Wiltshire, Norwood Cottage, Church Street, East Markham, Newark, Nottinghamshire NG22 0SA
☎ Retford (01777) 872446 & 838097
Fax (01777) 838098
Completely refurbished railway coach with full central heating, lounge, kitchen, bathroom and two double bedrooms. A complimentary food package will await visitors: bacon, eggs, milk, tea, sugar, bread and butter.
1 self-contained unit; sleeping max 4

Price per week:	£min	£max
Low season	260.00	280.00
High season	280.00	310.00

EPPERSTONE

Nottinghamshire
Map ref 4C2

The settlement here was mentioned in the Domesday Book. Its medieval church stands high above the village and there is a manor house and an old dovecote.

The Dovecote ⋀⋀

HIGHLY COMMENDED

Starling Hall, Hagg Lane, Epperstone, Nottingham
Contact: Mrs Christine Knowles, Starling Hall, Hagg Lane, Epperstone, Nottingham NG14 6AX
☎ Nottingham (0115) 966 4435

Tastefully converted barn with quality fittings and some antiques. In a tranquil setting with unspoilt views on a private part of Hagg Lane.
1 self-contained unit; sleeping max 4

Price per week:	£min	£max
Low season	160.00	
High season		260.00

EPPERSTONE
Continued

The Loft House 🅰
🔑 🔑 🔑 🔑 HIGHLY COMMENDED

Criftin Farm, Epperstone, Nottingham
Contact: Mrs J Esam, Criftin Farm, Epperstone, Nottingham NG14 6AT
☎ Nottingham (0115) 965 2039

17th C converted granary with original oak beams, log fire and antiques, equipped to a high standard. Heated swimming pool (open May-September). Ideal base for seeing Robin Hood country. Woodland walks at the back of the farm.
1 self-contained unit; sleeping max 4

Price per week:	£min	£max
Low season	250.00	250.00
High season	285.00	285.00

🔣 🔣 🔣 🔣 🔣 🔣 MW 🔣 TV 🔣 🔣 🔣 🔣
🔣 P 🔣 🔣 🔣 🔣 🔣

The Mistal 🅰
🔑 🔑 🔑 🔑 HIGHLY COMMENDED

Ricketwood Farm, Chapel Lane, Epperstone, Nottingham
Contact: Mr and Mrs Peake, Ricketwood Farm, Chapel Lane, Epperstone, Nottingham NG14 6AR
☎ Nottingham (0115) 965 2086

250-acre arable & livestock farm. Amid rolling countryside, 2 miles from Epperstone. A secluded, 18th C farm building conversion with oak beams, log burner and antiques. Private walled garden, panoramic views.
1 self-contained unit; sleeping max 2

Price per week:	£min	£max
Low season	160.00	190.00
High season	190.00	210.00

🔣 🔣 🔣 🔣 🔣 🔣 MW 🔣 TV 🔣 🔣 🔣
🔣 P 🔣 🔣 🔣

EYAM
Derbyshire
Map ref 4B2

Attractive village famous for the courage it showed during the plague of 1665. The church has several memorials to this time and there is a well-dressing ceremony in August. The fine 17th C manor house of Eyam Hall is open in summer, and Chatsworth is nearby.

Dalehead Court Cottages 🅰
🔑 🔑 🔑 🔑 HIGHLY COMMENDED

The Square, Eyam
Contact: Mrs D M Neary, Laneside Farm, Hope, Derbyshire S30 2RR
☎ Eyam (01433) 620214
Fax (01433) 620214
Choice of newly-restored delightfully appointed cottages in the heart of Derbyshire's most historic village or cosy, beamed riverside farm cottages.
2 self-contained units; sleeping 2–6

Price per week:	£min	£max
Low season	140.00	175.00
High season	160.00	310.00

🔣 🔣 🔣 🔣 🔣 🔣 MW 🔣 TV 🔣 🔣 🔣 🔣
🔣 🔣 P 🔣 🔣 🔣 🔣

GRATTON DALE
Derbyshire
Map ref 4B2

Dale End Farm
🔑 🔑 🔑 COMMENDED

Gratton Dale, Bakewell DE45 1LN
☎ Winster (01629) 650453
Contact: Mrs E M Hague
Delightful period cottage, sleeps up to 4, and 3-bedroomed bungalow, sleeps up to 7. Picturesque, peaceful surroundings. Parking, tennis. Ideal for walking. Weekend breaks available.
3 self-contained units; sleeping 4–7

Price per week:	£min	£max
Low season	135.00	
High season		295.00

🔣 🔣 M 🔣 🔣 🔣 🔣 🔣 TV 🔣 🔣 🔣 🔣 P
🔣 🔣 🔣 🔣 🔣 🔣

GREAT CARLTON
Lincolnshire
Map ref 4D2

Willow Farm 🅰
🔑 🔑 🔑 COMMENDED

Great Carlton, Louth LN11 8JP
☎ Saltfleetby (01507) 338540
Contact: Mr J Clark
Comprising 2 double and 1 single bedrooms. Fly and coarse fishing available on site. Touring caravans welcome by arrangement.

2 self-contained units; sleeping max 5

Price per week:	£min	£max
Low season	100.00	150.00
High season	150.00	250.00

🔣 🔣 🔣 🔣 🔣 🔣 MW 🔣 TV 🔣 🔣 🔣
🔣 P 🔣 🔣 🔣 🔣 🔣 SP

GREAT HUCKLOW
Derbyshire
Map ref 4B2

Small village in the Peak District. Headquarters of the Derbyshire and Lancashire Gliding Club.

South View Cottage
🔑 🔑 🔑 🔑 HIGHLY COMMENDED

Windmill, Great Hucklow, Buxton
Contact: Mrs M Waterhouse, Holme Cottage, Windmill, Great Hucklow, Buxton, Derbyshire SK17 8RE
☎ Tideswell (01298) 871440 & 0831 289289
Modernised country cottage in the hamlet of Windmill in the middle of the Peak District. 2 bedrooms, lounge with stone fireplace, dining room, kitchen and utility room. Small garden and garage. No smoking, please.
1 self-contained unit; sleeping max 4

Price per week:	£min	£max
Low season	180.00	190.00
High season	190.00	220.00

🔣 🔣 M 🔣 🔣 🔣 🔣 MW TV 🔣 🔣 🔣 🔣
P 🔣 🔣

Stanley House Farm
🔑 🔑 🔑 🔑 HIGHLY COMMENDED

Great Hucklow, Buxton SK17 8RL
☎ Tideswell (01298) 871044
Contact: Mrs Margot Darley
Charming, well-equipped conversion of stone barn. Quiet location, offering comfort, convenience and privacy.
1 self-contained unit; sleeping max 4

Price per week:	£min	£max
Low season	95.00	180.00
High season	195.00	230.00

🔣 🔣 6 M 🔣 🔣 🔣 🔣 🔣 TV 🔣 🔣 P U
🔣 SP 🔣

The map references refer to the colour maps towards the end of the guide. The first figure is the map number; the letter and figure which follow indicate the grid reference on the map.

HARTINGTON

Derbyshire
Map ref 4B2

Village with a large market-place set in fine surroundings near the River Dove, well-known for its fishing and Izaak Walton, author of "The Compleat Angler".

Cheese Press Cottage ⋔

🔑 🔑 🔑 DE LUXE

Biggin Grange, Biggin-by-Hartington, Buxton
Contact: Mrs S A Flower, Biggin Grange, Biggin-by-Hartington, Buxton, Derbyshire SK17 0DJ
☎ Buxton (01298) 84772

Charming 18th C romantic hideaway. Gritstone cheese press still in situ. Luxuriously equipped. Woodburning stove. Victorian four-poster. Walled garden/terrace with superb views. Walks into Dovedale. Non-smoking. Winner 1995 East Midlands Tourist Board self-catering holiday of the year award.
1 self-contained unit; sleeping 2

Price per week:	£min	£max
Low season	160.00	240.00
High season	240.00	385.00

🛏 Ⓜ ◎ 🖥 ⊙ 🗑 MW 📺 📺 🖐 🔔 🖐
🍽 🖐 🎵 ✒ ❊ 🗡 SP 🎐

Church View ⋔

🔑 🔑 🔑 APPROVED

Hartington, Buxton
Contact: Miss K Bassett, Digmer, Hartington, Buxton, Derbyshire SK17 0AQ
☎ Hartington (01298) 84660
Three-bedroomed cottage with part central heating. Open fire optional. Patio and lawned garden, lock-up garage.
1 self-contained unit; sleeping max 5

Price per week:	£min	£max
Low season		150.00
High season		200.00

Open April–December
🛏 Ⓜ ◎ 🖥 ⊙ 🗑 MW 📺 📺 🖐 🔔 🖐
🍽 P ❊ 🗡 SP

Map references apply to the colour maps at the back of this guide.

Cotterill Farm Cottages ⋔

🔑 🔑 🔑 — 🔑 🔑 🔑

HIGHLY COMMENDED

Cotterill Farm, Biggin-by-Hartington, Buxton SK17 0DJ
☎ (01298) 84447
Contact: Mrs Francis Skemp
Three cottages, just outside village, in glorious location. Exposed beams. Extensive footpath network. Tissington Trail three-quarters of a mile, River Dove 1 mile.
3 self-contained units; sleeping 4–6

Price per week:	£min	£max
Low season	150.00	220.00
High season	230.00	320.00

🛏 3 ◎ 🖥 ⊙ 🗑 MW 📺 📺 🖐 🔔 🖐
🍽 P ❊ 🗡

1 Staley Cottage ⋔

🔑 🔑 🔑 COMMENDED

Hartington, Buxton
Contact: Mr and Mrs J Oliver, Carr Head Farm, Penistone, Sheffield S30 6GA
☎ Barnsley (01226) 762387
Spacious cottage with 3 bedrooms, dining room, lounge, ground floor bathroom, upstairs shower room/WC and garden. In a pretty village near amenities, shops and restaurants.
1 self-contained unit; sleeping max 5

Price per week:	£min	£max
Low season	200.00	250.00
High season	250.00	300.00

🛏 ◎ 🖥 ⊙ 🗑 MW 📺 📺 🖐 🔔 🖐
🍽 P ❊

Information on accommodation listed in this guide has been supplied by the proprietors. As changes may occur you are advised to check details at the time of booking.

WELCOME HOST

This is a nationally recognised customer care programme which aims to promote the highest standards of service and a warm welcome. Establishments who are taking part in this initiative are indicated by the ◉ symbol.

HATHERSAGE

Derbyshire
Map ref 4B2

Hillside village in the Peak District, dominated by the church with many good brasses and monuments to the Eyre family which provide a link with Charlotte Bronte. Little John, friend of Robin Hood, is said to be buried here.

Derwent Cottage

🔑 🔑 🔑 🔑 HIGHLY COMMENDED

Sheffield Road, Hathersage, Sheffield
Contact: Mr and Mrs R Stewart, Booths Farm, Sheffield Road, Hathersage, Sheffield S30 1DA
☎ Hathersage (01433) 650667
Fully furnished country cottage with delightful garden, patio and views. Ample parking.
1 self-contained unit; sleeping max 4

Price per week:	£min	£max
Low season	150.00	200.00
High season	200.00	250.00

🛏 12 ◎ 🖥 ⊙ 🗑 MW 📺 🔔 🖐 🖐
P ❊ 🗡 SP

HAYFIELD

Derbyshire
Map ref 4B2

Village set in spectacular scenery at the highest point of the Peak District with the best approach to the Kinder Scout plateau via the Kinder Downfall. An excellent centre for walking. Three reservoirs close by.

The Old Wheelwright Cottage ⋔

🔑 🔑 🔑 🔑 COMMENDED

Mill Street, Hayfield, Stockport, Cheshire
Contact: Mr and Mrs C Hadfield, 2 Oaks Avenue, Hayfield, Stockport, Cheshire SK12 5JU
☎ New Mills (01663) 745293 & 743590
Converted barn in picturesque Peak District village, ideal for walking, sightseeing. Two bedrooms, lounge, kitchen area, central heating, parking. Sorry, no smoking and no pets.
1 self-contained unit; sleeping 4

Price per week:	£min	£max
Low season	170.00	
High season		280.00

🛏 ◎ 🖥 🖥 ⊙ 🗑 MW 📺 🔔 🍽 P 🗡
SP

HOLBEACH

Lincolnshire
Map ref 3A1

Small town, mentioned in the Domesday Book, has a splendid 14th C church with a fine tower and spire. The surrounding villages also have interesting churches, and the area is well-known for its bulbfields.

Poachers Den 🅜
🗝🗝 COMMENDED
34 Fen Road, Holbeach, Spalding
Contact: Mr B Flynn, 34 Fen Road, Holbeach, Spalding, Lincolnshire PE12 8QA
☎ Holbeach (01406) 423625
Fax (01406) 423625
Converted coach house in owner's garden on edge of attractive Fenland town. 1 double, 1 twin, both en-suite. Large private woodland garden.
1 self-contained unit; sleeping 2–8

Price per week:	£min	£max
Low season	150.00	200.00
High season	200.00	350.00

☎🅜◎🗐📻☺🗗MW📪📺🖥🔌📼
🍴🔌🅿❄🔌SP◎

HOPE

Derbyshire
Map ref 4B2

Village in the Hope Valley which is an excellent base for walking in the Peak District and for fishing and shooting. There is a well-dressing ceremony each June and its August sheep dog trials are well-known. Castleton Caves are nearby.

Crabtree Cottages 🅜
🗝🗝🗝 HIGHLY COMMENDED
Crabtree Meadow, Aston Lane, Hope, Sheffield
Contact: Mrs P M Mason, Crabtree Meadow, Hope, Sheffield S30 2RA
☎ Hope Valley (01433) 620291
Fax (01433) 620291
Unique cottages in a garden setting, with direct access to the countryside and within easy reach of shops and pubs. Linen and fuel included.
4 self-contained units; sleeping 2–6

Price per week:	£min	£max
Low season	140.00	220.00
High season	180.00	340.00

☎◎🗐📻☺🗗MW📪📺🖥🔌📼
🔌🅿P U❄🗡🔪SP

The Old Bell and Ebenezer Barn 🅜
🗝🗝🗝– 🗝🗝 COMMENDED
Edale Road, Hope, Sheffield

Contact: Mr and Mrs M Davis, Bennetts Grange, Harrison Lane, Fulwood, Sheffield S10 4PA
☎ Sheffield (0114) 230 3463

Listed building, carefully restored, with well-fitted kitchen, central heating, TVs, payphone, laundry facilities, garden games, parking. Linen/towels included. Open all year, short lets welcome. Cots available.
2 self-contained units; sleeping 6–8

Price per week:	£min	£max
Low season	278.00	
High season		636.00

☎📻🗐📻☺🗗MW📪📺🖥🔌📼🔌
🍴🅿❄

Twitchill Farm Cottages 🅜
🗝🗝🗝 HIGHLY COMMENDED
Edale Road, Hope, Sheffield S30 2RF
☎ Hope Valley (01433) 621426
Contact: Mrs S Atkin

Four stone-built cottages surrounded by beautiful scenery. Well equipped, high level of comfort. Horse riding, golf and walking close by.
4 self-contained units; sleeping 6–8

Price per week:	£min	£max
Low season	120.00	
High season		425.00

☎📻◎🗐📻☺🗗MW📪📺🖥🔌
🔌🅿P U❄🔪SP

HORNCASTLE

Lincolnshire
Map ref 4D2

Pleasant market town near the Lincolnshire Wolds, which was once a walled Roman settlement. It was the scene of a decisive Civil War battle, relics of which can be seen in the church. Tennyson's bride lived here.

Southolme Cottage 🅜
Church Lane, Thornton, Horncastle
Contact: Mr David Gresham, 38 Woodlands Road, Moseley, Birmingham B11 4HE
☎ (0121) 449 5666

Detached period cottage in hamlet of Thornton near Horncastle, surrounded by grazing meadows and delightful cottage gardens with views over the wolds, providing a very beautiful home for your holiday.
1 self-contained unit; sleeping max 5

Price per week:	£min	£max
Low season	110.00	250.00
High season	250.00	400.00

☎◎🗐📻☺🗗MW📪📺🖥🔌📼🔌P❄
SP🏠

HORSLEY WOODHOUSE

Derbyshire
Map ref 4B2

Amber Court 🅜
🗝🗝🗝 COMMENDED
Wood Lane, Horsley Woodhouse, Ilkeston
Contact: Mr Nicholas Mitchell, Linkwood Farm, Wood Lane, Horsley Woodhouse, Derby DE7 6BN
☎ Derby (01332) 881811 & (0589) 520232
Fax (01332) 881811

Courtyard conversion with full gas CH, laundry, games room and safe parking. Close to Denby Pottery, American Adventure, golf-courses.
5 self-contained units; sleeping 4–8

Price per week:	£min	£max
Low season	150.00	200.00
High season	280.00	500.00

Cards accepted: Access, Visa, Switch/Delta

☎◎🗐📻☺🗗MW📪📺🖥🔌📼🔌
🔌🅿P U🔪🔪SP

National gradings and classifications were correct at the time of going to press but are subject to change. Please check at the time of booking.

KIRK IRETON

Derbyshire
Map ref 4B2

Stone-built village within easy reach of Dovedale and Matlock.

Pebble Cottage
🔑🔑🔑🔑🔑 HIGHLY COMMENDED

Kirk Ireton, Ashbourne
Contact: Mrs Jenny Holmes, View Cottage, Hemp Lane, Kirk Ireton, Ashbourne, Derbyshire DE6 3JW
☎ (01335) 370571
200-year-old cottage with exposed beams and woodburning stove, warm and cosy in winter. Mature garden. Convenient for Derbyshire Dales, Peak District and Alton Towers.
1 self-contained unit; sleeping max 4

Price per week:	£min	£max
Low season	182.00	214.00
High season	258.00	324.00

⏰🐕©🖥☺🗄 MW 📧 TV🗄 🛋🎒(📞💬 🚗P❄ SP

LAMBLEY

Nottinghamshire
Map ref 4C2

Dickman's Cottage
🔑🔑🔑🔑 COMMENDED

4 Mill Lane, Lambley, Nottingham
Contact: Mrs Rosamond Marshall Smith, Springsyde, Birdcage Walk, Otley, West Yorkshire LS21 3HB
☎ Otley (01943) 850925
Fax (01943) 850925

Beamed cottage with garden. 2 bedrooms - 1 double/1 twin. TV/video, dishwasher, washer/dryer. Owner's second home.
1 self-contained unit; sleeping max 4

Price per week:	£min	£max
Low season	150.00	170.00
High season	200.00	220.00

⏰🐕©🖥☺🗄 MW 📧 TV🗄 🛋🎒(📞💬 🚗P❄✂🏠 SP

All accommodation in this guide has been graded, or is awaiting a grading, by a trained Tourist Board inspector.

LEADENHAM

Lincolnshire
Map ref 3A1

Village on the Lincoln Edge, noted for its fine church spire.

Daisy Cottage 𝕄
🔑🔑🔑🔑 COMMENDED

Leadenham
Contact: Mrs M Booth, Stocks House, Leadenham, Lincolnshire LN5 0PN
☎ Loveden (01400) 272862 & 272226
Old limestone character cottage with garden, comfortably modernised and furnished. Pleasantly situated in quiet country village. Tennis available.
1 self-contained unit; sleeping max 5

Price per week:	£min	£max
Low season	135.00	180.00
High season	195.00	270.00

⏰🐕©🖥☺🗄 MW 📧 TV🗄 🛋📖 🏮🚗P🔍❄ SP ⊚

LINCOLN

Lincolnshire
Map ref 4C2

Ancient city dominated by the magnificent 11th C cathedral with its triple towers. A Roman gateway is still used and there are medieval houses lining narrow, cobbled streets. Other attractions include the Norman castle, several museums and the Usher Gallery. Tourist Information Centre ☎ (01522) 529828

Manor Farm Flat 𝕄
🔑🔑🔑🔑 HIGHLY COMMENDED

Manor Farm, Brattleby, Lincoln LN1 2SQ
☎ (01522) 730475
Contact: Mrs R M Marris

Charming farmhouse wing overlooking garden and countryside. Situated in small village, 6 miles north of historic Lincoln. Convenient East Midlands and Yorkshire. "Home from home" comforts.
1 self-contained unit; sleeping max 4

Price per week:	£min	£max
Low season		170.00
High season		230.00

⏰©🖥☺🗄📧 TV🗄 🛋🎒✂ 🏠 SP⊚

Martingale Cottage
🔑🔑🔑 COMMENDED

17 East Street, Nettleham, Lincoln
Contact: Mrs P A Pate, 19 East Street, Nettleham, Lincoln LN2 2SL
☎ Lincoln (01522) 751795
Comfortable and well-equipped 18th C stone cottage with private parking, near centre of attractive village. Good local facilities including shops and pubs.
1 self-contained unit; sleeping max 2

Price per week:	£min	£max
Low season	80.00	
High season	120.00	

⏰𝕄©🖥☺🗄 MW 📧 TV🗄 🛋🎒🚗❄ 🏠 SP🏮

Old Vicarage Cottage
🔑🔑🔑🔑 COMMENDED

East Street, Nettleham, Lincoln
Contact: Mrs S Downs, The Old Vicarage, East Street, Nettleham, Lincoln LN2 2SL
☎ Lincoln (01522) 750819
18th C stone-built property with original exposed beams in the living area. In a quiet position close to shops, pubs and the centre of this attractive village. Lettings are from Friday to Friday.
1 self-contained unit; sleeping 2–3

Price per week:	£min	£max
Low season	90.00	
High season	120.00	

⏰𝕄✎🖥☺ MW 📧 TV🗄 🛋💬 🚗P❄✂🏠

Self-catering agencies which have a selection of holiday homes to let are listed in a special section towards the back of this guide.

ACCESSIBILITY

Look for the ♿ symbols which indicate accessibility for wheelchair users. These are described in detail at the front of this guide.

LITTON

Derbyshire
Map ref 4B2

Ashleigh Cottage

HIGHLY COMMENDED

Ashleigh, Litton, Buxton
Contact: Mrs S A Maxted, Ashleigh,
Litton, Buxton, Derbyshire
SK17 8QU
☎ Buxton (01298) 872505
*Charming stone cottage in a quiet
village within the Peak District National
Park. Good views, walking and
bird-watching. Local old-world pub has
reputation for quality home-cooked
meals.*
1 self-contained unit; sleeping 1–3

Price per week:	£min	£max
Low season	130.00	150.00
High season	150.00	210.00

LOUTH

Lincolnshire
Map ref 4D2

Attractive old market town set on
the eastern edge of the Lincolnshire
Wolds. St James's Church has an
impressive tower and spire and
there are the remains of a
Cistercian abbey. The museum
contains an interesting collection of
local material.
Tourist Information Centre ☎ *(01507)
609289*

Ashwater House

UP TO HIGHLY COMMENDED

Willow Drive, Louth LN11 0AH
☎ (01507) 609295
Contact: Mrs Y Mapletoft
*A Potton timber-framed cottage in the
country, only 20 minutes' walk from
Louth. Also, log cabin and self-contained
flat. Two acres and coarse fishing lake.*
3 self-contained units; sleeping 4–6

Price per week:	£min	£max
Low season	160.00	180.00
High season	200.00	275.00

LOWER BENEFIELD

Northamptonshire
Map ref 3A1

Granary Cottage

COMMENDED

Lower Benefield, Peterborough
Contact: Mrs R C Singlehurst, Brook
Farm, Lower Benefield,
Peterborough PE8 5AE
☎ Benefield (01832) 205215

*764-acre mixed farm. Converted farm
granary off the A427 between Corby
and Oundle. Set in picturesque
Northamptonshire countryside, with
appealing walks and local attractions
for all the family.*
1 self-contained unit; sleeping max 4

Price per week:	£min	£max
Low season	150.00	150.00
High season	200.00	200.00

LULLINGTON

Derbyshire
Map ref 4B3

In the extreme south of Derbyshire,
near the Staffordshire border.
Beautiful flowers and plants fill the
village green, churchyard and
gardens of the Great House.

Aubrietia Cottage

HIGHLY COMMENDED

Lullington, Swadlincote
Contact: Mrs R Cooper, The
Grange, Lullington, Swadlincote,
Derbyshire DE12 8ED
☎ Tamworth (01827) 373219
Fax (01283) 515885
*Tastefully furnished cottage in
Lullington, several times winner of the
best kept village award. Pleasant
outlook with many places of interest
only a short drive away.*
1 self-contained unit; sleeping max 5

Price per week:	£min	£max
Low season	95.00	115.00
High season	125.00	200.00

MATLOCK

Derbyshire
Map ref 4B2

The town lies beside the narrow
valley of the River Derwent
surrounded by steep wooded hills.
Good centre for exploring
Derbyshire's best scenery.

The Fold

COMMENDED

31 Main Road, Darley Bridge,
Matlock DE4 2JY
☎ (01629) 734333
Contact: Mr Jack Hinman
*Tastefully-appointed, well-equipped, first
floor flat in a converted stable block.
On the fringe of the Peak District
National Park, 10 miles from M1
motorway. Ideal for walking, riding and
fishing. Many local places of interest.*
1 self-contained unit; sleeping 2

Price per week:	£min	£max
Low season	90.00	
High season		150.00

MIDDLETON-BY-YOULGREAVE

Derbyshire
Map ref 4B2

Small hamlet nestling on the River
Bradford, a mile from Youlgreave.

Chapel Cottage

APPROVED

Middleton-by-Youlgreave, Derby
Contact: Miss Jenny Aston, Chapel
House, Middleton-by-Youlgreave,
Derby DE4 1LS
☎ Youlgreave (01629) 636665
*Stone cottage with a private garden
and patio in a small, quiet, unspoilt
village surrounded by delightful
countryside and walks.*
1 self-contained unit; sleeping max 5

Price per week:	£min	£max
Low season	160.00	220.00
High season	220.00	280.00

NORTH SCARLE

Lincolnshire
Map ref 4C2

Red House Farm

COMMENDED

North Scarle, Lincoln LN6 9HB
☎ Lincoln (01522) 778224 & (0585) 818111
Contact: Mr and Mrs Jones
80-acre beef farm. Red brick and pantile cottage. Lounge, kitchen, 2 bedrooms and shower room. Oil central heating. Fishing free of charge. Colour brochure available.
1 self-contained unit; sleeping max 6

Price per week:	£min	£max
Low season	160.00	184.00
High season	228.00	260.00

🖥Ⓜ◎🏠⊙🛋📺🖨🧺⚓P♪❄ 🐾🚫SP

OAKHAM

Leicestershire
Map ref 4C3

Pleasant former county town of Rutland. Fine 12th C Great Hall, part of its castle, with a historic collection of horseshoes. An octagonal Butter Cross stands in the market-place and Rutland County Museum, Rutland Farm Park and Rutland Water are of interest.
Tourist Information Centre ☎ (01572) 724329

Normanton Gardens ₥

UP TO COMMENDED

Normanton, Oakham LE15 8RP
☎ Stamford (01780) 720071
Contact: Mrs B Watt
In private grounds, within walking distance of Rutland Water. Transport is necessary as the nearest village shop is 1 mile away.
3 self-contained units; sleeping 2–4

Price per week:	£min	£max
Low season	100.00	125.00
High season	140.00	175.00

Open April–October
◎🏠⊙🛋MW📺🖨🏬⚓P❄

> Please check prices and other details at the time of booking.

> For ideas on places to visit refer to the introduction at the beginning of this section.

OUNDLE

Northamptonshire
Map ref 3A1

Historic town situated on the River Nene with narrow alleys and courtyards and many stone buildings, including a fine church and historic inns.
Tourist Information Centre ☎ (01832) 274333

Oundle Cottage Breaks ₥

UP TO HIGHLY COMMENDED

30 Market Place, Oundle, Peterborough PE8 4BE
☎ (01832) 273531
Fax (01832) 274938
Contact: Mr and Mrs Simmonds
Self-contained units in the curtilage of a listed building in the centre of historic market town.
3 self-contained units; sleeping 1–5

Price per week:	£min	£max
Low season	100.00	250.00
High season	125.00	275.00

Cards accepted: Access, Visa, Amex, Switch/Delta

📞◎🏠⊙🛋MW📣📺🖨🏬🖥P ❄SP🏠

PEAK DISTRICT

See under Ashbourne, Ashford in the Water, Bakewell, Bamford, Birchover, Buxton, Calver, Chapel-en-le-Frith, Cressbrook, Earl Sterndale, Eyam, Gratton Dale, Great Hucklow, Hartington, Hathersage, Hayfield, Hope, Litton, Thorpe, Tideswell, Winster

POTTERHANWORTH

Lincolnshire
Map ref 4C2

Small, compact village on the edge of a fen. A line of elms on the village high street add a picturesque touch.

The Pantiles ₥

COMMENDED

Church Lane, Potterhanworth, Lincoln
Contact: Mrs S Battle, The Old Hall, Potterhanworth, Lincoln LN4 2DS
☎ Lincoln (01522) 791338 & 791202
Fax (01522) 794888
Fully-equipped, oak-beamed cottage, with fitted carpets, central heating, terrace, garage and gardens, in rural surroundings.

1 self-contained unit; sleeping max 5

Price per week:	£min	£max
Low season	170.00	220.00
High season	200.00	260.00

📞◎🏠⊙🛋📣📺🖨⚓🖥🖥⚓P❄ SP

REDMILE

Leicestershire
Map ref 4C2

Vale of Belvoir village, overlooked by the hilltop castle.

Peacock Farm Guest House and Country Restaurant ₥

COMMENDED

Redmile, Nottinghamshire
Contact: Miss Nicky Need, Peacock Farm Guesthouse and, Country Restaurant, Redmile, Nottingham NG13 0GQ
☎ (01949) 842475
Fax (01949) 43127
Bungalow apartment in the village of Redmile. 10 minutes' walk from Peacock Farm Guesthouse. Peaceful position with views of fields and Belvoir woods.
1 self-contained unit; sleeping max 2

Price per week:	£min	£max
Low season	100.00	150.00
High season	150.00	250.00

Cards accepted: Access, Visa, Diners, Amex, Switch/Delta

◎🏠⊙🛋MW📣📺🖨🏬🖥⚓P ❄🐾

ROPSLEY

Lincolnshire
Map ref 3A1

Situated 6 miles to the east of Grantham, the birthplace of Richard Fox, the Bishop of Winchester.

Appletree Cottage ₥

HIGHLY COMMENDED

Stone House, Church Lane, Ropsley,
Contact: Mr and Mrs Hogan, Stone House, Church Lane, Ropsley, Grantham Grantham, Lincolnshire NG33 4DA
☎ Ingoldsby (01476) 585620
Early 18th C oak-beamed stone cottage with log fire and central heating. In a quiet village surrounded by unspoilt countryside.
1 self-contained unit; sleeping 2

Price per week:	£min	£max
Low season	140.00	140.00
High season	175.00	175.00

Open April–September
📞◎🏠⊙🛋MW📣📺🖨🖥🖥 ⚓P❄🏠

SELSTON

Nottinghamshire
Map ref 4C2

Cottages in the Square 🅜

🗝🗝🗝 ⟷ 🗝🗝🗝 COMMENDED

Nottingham Road, Selston,
Nottingham NG16 6DE
☎ Ripley (01773) 812029
Fax (01623) 559849
Contact: Mrs Janice Hill

Three beautifully appointed period cottages in pretty mews setting on Notts/Derbys border - 2 miles junction 27 M1. Weekend and daily rates available.
3 self-contained units; sleeping 1–3

Price per week:	£min	£max
Low season	225.00	
High season		400.00

Cards accepted: Access, Visa, Amex
🗝🕾⊚⌔💷⊙🖥🏧📺🖬🛋🍽〰 🐾P❄SP T

SHERWOOD FOREST

See under Epperstone

SPILSBY

Lincolnshire
Map ref 4D2

Market town in attractive countryside on the edge of the Lincolnshire Wolds and the Fens. Birthplace of explorer Sir John Franklin and has associations with the poet Tennyson, born in nearby Somersby. It has a medieval market cross.

Northfields Farm Cottages

🗝🗝 🗝 COMMENDED

Northfields Farm, Mavis Enderby,
Spilsby PE23 4EW
☎ Winceby (01507) 588251
Contact: Mrs C A Miller
Cosy, well-equipped farm cottages in unspoilt rural area. Within easy reach of coast and interesting towns with lots to do.
2 self-contained units; sleeping 4–8

Price per week:	£min	£max
Low season	140.00	160.00
High season	150.00	290.00

🕾⊚⌔💷⊙🖥MW📟📺🖬🛋🍽 🐾P🐾❄SP

STANTON-ON-THE-WOLDS

Nottinghamshire
Map ref 4C2

Foxcote Cottage 🅜

🗝🗝 🗝 COMMENDED

Hill Farm, Melton Road,
Stanton-on-the-Wolds, Keyworth
NG12 5PJ
☎ Nottingham (0115) 9374337
Fax (0115) 9375193
Contact: Mrs Joan Hinchley
300-acre arable farm. Cottage overlooking open countryside, fully equipped to a high standard. One double and 2 twin bedrooms, bathroom with separate shower, downstairs shower and WC, private patio and garden with barbecue. Cot and high chair available. All linen and towels included.
1 self-contained unit; sleeping max 6

Price per week:	£min	£max
Low season		300.00
High season		300.00

🕾⊚⌔💷⊙🖥MW📺🖬🛋🍽🐾P ❄🐾

SUTTON ON THE HILL

Derbyshire
Map ref 4B2

Rural community, although only 8 miles west of Derby. The church is slightly elevated and provides excellent views of the Peak District.

The Chop House 🅜

🗝🗝 🗝 COMMENDED

Windle Hill Farm, Sutton on the Hill,
Ashbourne
Contact: Mr and Mrs Lennard,
Windle Hill Farm, Sutton on the Hill,
Ashbourne, Derbyshire DE6 5JH
☎ Etwall (01283) 732377
10-acre smallholding. Converted beamed barn on small working farm with traditional and rare breeds of livestock and poultry. Pleasant views. Ideal base for exploring the Derbyshire Peak District.
1 self-contained unit; sleeping max 8

Price per week:	£min	£max
Low season	130.00	240.00
High season	280.00	350.00

🕾⊠⊚⌔💷⊙🖥MW📟📺🖬🛋🍽 🖵🐾P❄SP

TEMPLE NORMANTON

Derbyshire
Map ref 4B2

Rocklea Private House

🗝🗝 APPROVED

48 Birkin Lane, Temple Normanton,
Chesterfield
Contact: Mr and Mrs R Stirling, 8
Ranworth Road, Bramley,
Rotherham, South Yorkshire
S66 0SN
☎ Rotherham (01709) 543108
In a country lane, this house with large gardens and car parking space is only 3 miles from both the M1 and Chesterfield.
1 self-contained unit; sleeping max 7

Price per week:	£min	£max
Low season	150.00	200.00
High season	200.00	300.00

🕾⊚⌔💷⊙🖥📺🖬🛋🍽PU❄🐾SP

TETFORD

Lincolnshire
Map ref 4D2

Grange Farm Cottages 🅜

🗝🗝 🗝 COMMENDED

The Grange, Salmonby, Tetford,
Horncastle
Contact: Mr A C Parker, Avenue
House, 11 Church Street, Spilsby,
Lincolnshire PE23 5EG
☎ Spilsby (01790) 753187
Well furnished, 2-bedroomed cottages, with central heating, in old barn conversion. Children's play area, nature trail and fishing lakes.
3 self-contained units; sleeping 4

Price per week:	£min	£max
Low season	140.00	160.00
High season	190.00	220.00

🕾⊠⊚⌔💷⊙🖥MW📺🖬🛋🍽🐾 P🐾❄🐾SP

Establishments should be open throughout the year, unless otherwise stated.

The symbols in each entry give information about services and facilities. A 'key' to these symbols appears at the back of this guide.

The 🅜 symbol after an establishment name indicates that it is a Regional Tourist Board member.

THEDDLETHORPE ALL SAINTS

Lincolnshire
Map ref 4D2

Horsleys Cottage
🔑🔑🔑🔑 COMMENDED

Horsleys, Theddlethorpe All Saints,
Mablethorpe
Contact: Mrs J W Stringer, Horsleys,
Theddlethorpe All Saints,
Mablethorpe, Lincolnshire LN12 1PE
☎ Saltfleetby (01507) 338797
Fax (01507) 338797
*Spacious modernised coach house, part
of country house set in three and a
half acres of grass, gardens and
paddocks.*
1 self-contained unit; sleeping 4

Price per week:	£min	£max
Low season	120.00	150.00
High season	160.00	250.00

Ⓜ◎🖥☉Ⓤ MW 📺🗄🍳🚪🔔
♨️P∪🔗✿🗡 SP 🏤◎

THORPE

Derbyshire
Map ref 4B2

Attractive village of limestone
cottages at the foot of Thorpe
Cloud and Bunster Hill at the
entrance to Dovedale. Excellent
centre for walking.

Rosebriar Cottage
🔑🔑🔑🔑 HIGHLY COMMENDED

3 Digmire Lane, Thorpe, Ashbourne
Contact: Mr or Mrs Smithson, The
Gables, Lower Street, Doveridge,
Ashbourne, Derbyshire DE6 5NS
☎ Uttoxeter (01889) 568237
*Delightful 3-bedroomed cottage, very
comfortable and homely
accommodation. Fabulous situation in
beautiful countryside. Private parking
and garden.*
1 self-contained unit; sleeping max 6

Price per week:	£min	£max
Low season	220.00	280.00
High season	330.00	350.00

🍳🐕Ⓜ◎🖥☉Ⓤ MW 📺🗄🍳🚪
🔔♨️P✿🗡 SP

TIDESWELL

Derbyshire
Map ref 4B2

Small town with a large 14th C
church known as the "Cathedral of
the Peak". There is a well-dressing
ceremony each June with Morris
dancing, and many choral events
throughout the year.

Sunnyside
🔑🔑 APPROVED

Gordon Road, Tideswell, Buxton
Contact: Mrs Joan Wain, 11 Pine
Bank, Hindhead, Surrey GU26 6SR
☎ Hindhead (01428) 605442 &
Tideswell (01298) 871030
*Modernised pre-1850 semi-detached
limestone cottage in quiet position.
Bedroom 1 has king-size bed, bedroom
2 has 3ft bunk beds suitable for
children.*
1 self-contained unit; sleeping max 4

Price per week:	£min	£max
Low season	80.00	
High season		175.00

🍳Ⓜ◎🖥☉Ⓤ📺🗄🚪🍳♨️🐕🗡🐈
SP

UPPINGHAM

Leicestershire
Map ref 4C3

Quiet market town dominated by
its famous public school which was
founded in 1584. It has many stone
houses and is surrounded by
attractive countryside.

4 Stockerston Road
🔑 COMMENDED

Uppingham, Oakham LE15 9UD
☎ (01572) 823478 & 823955
Contact: Mr or Mrs Lloyd
*Comfortably appointed flat with its
own private walled garden. Designed
for a couple, but can accommodate a
third person.*
1 self-contained unit; sleeping max 3

Price per week:	£min	£max
Low season	130.00	130.00
High season	130.00	130.00

🍳◎🖥☉Ⓤ MW 📺🗄🚪🍳♨️
∪✿ SP

WHATSTANDWELL

Derbyshire
Map ref 4B2

Standing on the steep hillside above
Derwent Valley, 7 miles south of
Matlock, tiny village with the bridge
over the river as its main feature.

Hill Top Cottage
🔑🔑 COMMENDED

Top Lane, Whatstandwell, Matlock
Contact: Peak Cottages, Strawberry
Lee Lane, Totley Bents, Sheffield
S17 3BA
☎ Sheffield (0114) 262 0777
Fax (0114) 262 0666
*Cosy stone cottage, restored and
tastefully decorated and retaining many
original features, with woodburning
stove. Views across the Derwent Valley.*
1 self-contained unit; sleeping max 4

Price per week:	£min	£max
Low season	160.00	190.00
High season	190.00	280.00

◎🖥☉🗄🍳📺🚪🍳✿ SP

WINSTER

Derbyshire
Map ref 4B2

Village with some interesting old
gritstone houses and cottages,
including the 17th C stone market
hall now owned by the National
Trust. It is a former lead mining
centre.

Rock Cottage ♨️
🔑🔑 HIGHLY COMMENDED

West Bank, Winster, Matlock
Contact: Mr M J Byrne, Bradley
House, Eastbank, Winster, Matlock,
Derbyshire DE4 2DT
☎ Derby (01629) 650687 & (0421)
648377
*Character hillside cottage situated in
the popular Peak District village of
Winster. Panoramic views towards
Lathkill Dale. Superbly modernised and
equipped.*
1 self-contained unit; sleeping max 4

Price per week:	£min	£max
Low season	155.00	200.00
High season	200.00	290.00

🍳⊘🖥☉Ⓤ MW 📺🗄🚪🍳P
SP

USE YOUR *i*'s

There are more than 550 Tourist Information Centres throughout England offering friendly help with accommodation and holiday ideas as well as suggestions of places to visit and things to do. There may well be a centre in your home town which can help you before you set out. You'll find the address of your nearest Tourist Information Centre in your local Phone Book.

AT-A-GLANCE SYMBOLS

Symbols at the end of each accommodation entry give useful information about services and facilities. A key to symbols can be found inside the back cover flap.

Keep this open for easy reference.

COUNTRY CODE

Always follow the Country Code ☙ Enjoy the countryside and respect its life and work ☙ Guard against all risk of fire ☙ Fasten all gates ☙ Keep your dogs under close control ☙ Keep to public paths across farmland ☙ Use gates and stiles to cross fences, hedges and walls ☙ Leave livestock, crops and machinery alone ☙ Take your litter home ☙ Help to keep all water clean ☙ Protect wildlife, plants and trees ☙ Take special care on country roads ☙ Make no unnecessary noise

EAST ANGLIA

East Anglia is the ideal 'get away from it all' destination. Here you can play golf, go fishing, follow the region's nature trails or discover the pastoral beauty of Constable country.

Pretty Hertfordshire villages await you, along with the sleepy charms of the Broads, England's newest National Park.

The untamed coastline boasts a number of much-loved seaside resorts like Great Yarmouth, Clacton and Southend-on-Sea while inland, Aldeburgh hosts a famous music festival.

Discover markets, vineyards and the gourmet delights of Cromer crab, Suffolk ham and Colchester oysters, as memorable as the surroundings in which you'll savour them.

FOR MORE INFORMATION CONTACT:
East Anglia Tourist Board
Toppesfield Hall, Hadleigh, Suffolk IP7 5DN
Tel: (01473) 822922 **Fax:** (01473) 823063

Where to Go in East Anglia - see pages 174-177
Where to Stay in East Anglia - see pages 178-196

EAST ANGLIA

Where to Go and What to See

You will find hundreds of interesting places to visit during your stay in East Anglia, just some of which are listed in these pages. The number against each name will help you locate it on the map (page 177). Contact any Tourist Information Centre in the region for more ideas on days out in East Anglia.

1 Wells Walsingham Railway
Stiffkey Road,
Wells-next-the-Sea,
Norfolk NR23 1QB
Tel: (01328) 856506
Four miles of railway. The longest 10 1/4 railway in the World. New locomotive Norfolk Hero now in service, largest of its kind ever built.

2 Thursford Collection
Thursford Green,
Thursford, Fakenham,
Norfolk NR21 0AS
Tel: (01328) 878477
Live musical shows, nine mechanical organs and Wurlitzer show starring Robert Wolfe.

3 Pensthorpe Waterfowl Park
Pensthorpe, Fakenham,
Norfolk NR21 0LN
Tel: (01328) 851465
Large waterfowl and wildfowl collection. Information centre, conservation shop, adventure play area, walks and nature trails. Licensed restaurant.

4 Norfolk Lavender
Caley Mill, Heacham,
King's Lynn, Norfolk PE31 7JE
Tel: (01485) 570384
Lavender is distilled from the flowers and the oil made in to a wide range of gifts. Slide show when distillery not working.

5 Sandringham
Sandringham, King's Lynn,
Norfolk PE35 6EN
Tel: (01553) 772675
Country retreat of HM The Queen. Delightful house and 60-acres of grounds and lakes. Museum of vehicles and royal memorabilia.

6 Banham Zoo
The Grove, Banham,
Norwich, Norfolk NR16 2HE
Tel: (01953) 887771
See some of the world's rare and endangered species.

7 Sainsbury Centre for Visual Arts
University of East Anglia,
Norwich, Norfolk NR4 7TJ
Tel: (01603) 456060
The Robert and Lisa Sainsbury Collection of modern and non modern art is wide-ranging and of international importance. Housed in a building purpose designed by N Foster.

8 Sea Life Centre
Marine Parade, Great Yarmouth,
Norfolk NR30 3AH
Tel: (01493) 330631
Walk under a tropical reef. Shark tank, Ray fish and British sharks, plus 25 themed displays depicting British marine life and local settings.

9 Somerleyton Hall and Gardens
Somerleyton, Lowestoft,
Suffolk NR32 5QQ
Tel: (01502) 730224
Anglo-Italian-style building with state rooms, maze. Garden with azaleas and rhododendrons. Miniature railway, shop, light luncheons and teas.

10 East Anglia Transport Museum
Chapel Road, Carlton Colville, Lowestoft, Suffolk NR33 8BL
Tel: (01502) 518459
A working museum with one of the widest ranges of street transport vehicles on display - and in action!

11 Pleasurewood Hills
Corton, Lowestoft, Suffolk NR32 5DZ
Tel: (01502) 508200
Log flume, chair lift, cine 180, two railways, pirate ship, fort, Aladdin's cave, parrot and sealion shows, roller coasters, waveswinger, Eye in the Sky, Star Ride Enterprise.

12 Otter Trust
Earsham, Bungay, Suffolk NR35 2AF
Tel: (01986) 893470
A breeding and conservation headquarters with the largest collection of otters in the world. Also lakes with collection of waterfowl and deer.

13 Bressingham Steam Museum and Gardens
Bressingham, Diss, Norfolk IP22 2AB
Tel: (01379) 687386
Steam rides through five miles of woodland, garden and nursery.

Mainline locomotives and over 50 steam engines. Alan Bloom's Dell Garden.

14 Sacrewell Farm and Country Centre
Sacrewell, Thornhaugh, Peterborough, Cambridgeshire PE8 6HJ
Tel: (01780) 782222
500-acre farm, with working watermill, farmhouse gardens, shrubberies, nature and general interest trails, 18C buildings, displays of farm, rural and domestic bygones.

15 Ely Cathedral
Chapter House, The College, Ely, Cambridgeshire CB7 4DN
Tel: (01353) 667735
One of England's finest cathedrals. Fine out buildings. Guided tours and tours of Octagon and West Tower. Brass rubbing and stained glass museum.

16 Pakenham Water Mill
Mill Road, Grimestone End, Pakenham, Bury St Edmunds, Suffolk IP3 2NB
Tel: (01787) 247179
18C working water mill on Domesday site, with oil engine and other subsidiary machinery.

17 Framlingham Castle
Framlingham, Woodbridge, Suffolk IP13 9BP
Tel: (01728) 724189
12C curtain walls with 13 towers and Tudor brick chimneys. Built by Bigod family, Earls of Norfolk. Wall walk. 17C almshouses. Home of Mary Tudor in 1553.

18 Imperial War Museum
Duxford Airfield, Duxford, Cambridgeshire CB2 4QR
Tel: (01223) 835000
Over 120 aircraft on display, tanks, vehicles, guns. Ride simulator, adventure playground, shops and restaurant.

19 National Horseracing Museum
99 High Street, Newmarket, Suffolk CB8 8JL
Tel: (01638) 667333
Five permanent galleries telling the story of horseracing. Opened by the Queen in 1983. British sporting art. Temporary Exhibition Gallery.

20 Ickworth House, Park and Gardens
Ickworth, Bury St Edmunds, Suffolk IP29 5QE
Tel: (01284) 735270
Extraordinary oval house with flanking wings begun in 1795. Fine paintings and beautiful collection of Georgian silver. Italian garden and park designed by Capability Brown.

21 Helmingham Hall Gardens

Helmingham,
Suffolk IP14 6EF
Tel: (01473) 890363
Moated and walled garden with many rare roses and possibly the best kitchen garden in Britain. Also highland cattle and safari rides in park to view red and fallow deer.

22 Shuttleworth Collection

Old Warden Aerodrome,
Biggleswade,
Bedfordshire SG18 9ER
Tel: (01767) 627288
Unique historic collection of aircraft from 1909 Bleriot to 1942 Spitfire in flying condition. Cars dating from 1898 Panhard.

23 Audley End House and Park

Saffron Walden,
Essex CB11 4JF
Tel: (01799) 522842
Palatial Jacobean house remodelled in the 18-19C. Magnificent Great Hall. Rooms and furniture by Robert Adam. Park by Capability Brown.

24 Woburn Abbey

Woburn,
Milton Keynes,
Bedfordshire MK43 0TP
Tel: (01525) 290666
18C Palladian mansion altered by Henry Holland, the Prince Regent's architect. Contains a collection of English silver, French and English furniture and an important art collection.

25 Mountfitchet Castle

Stansted Mountfitchet,
Essex CM24 8SP
Tel: (01279) 813237
Reconstructed Norman motte-and-bailey castle and village of Domesday period. Grand Hall, church, prison, seige tower and weapons.

26 Colchester Castle

Colchester,
Essex CO1 1TJ
Tel: (01206) 282931
Norman Keep on foundations of Roman Temple, archaeological material includes much on Roman Colchester.

27 Whipsnade Wild Animal Park

Zoological Society of London,
Dunstable,
Bedfordshire LU6 2LF
Tel: (01582) 872171
Over 2,500 animals set in 600 acres of beautiful parkland. Great Whipsnade Railway. Free animal demonstrations.

28 Hatfield House

Hatfield Park, Hatfield,
Hertfordshire AL9 5NQ
Tel: (01707) 262823
Jacobean house built in 1611 and Old Palace built in 1497. Contains famous paintings, fine furniture and possessions of Queen Elizabeth I. Extensive park and gardens.

29 The Gardens of the Rose

The Royal National Rose Society,
Chiswell Green,
St Albans,
Hertfordshire AL2 3NR
Tel: (01727) 850461
The Royal National Rose Society's Garden, 20 acres of showground and trial grounds for new varieties of rose. 30,000 roses of all types with 1,700 different varieties.

LINCOLNSHIRE

LEICESTER-
SHIRE

Thornhaugh
14
Peterborough
Whittlesey
Yaxley
March

NORTHANTS

Huntingdon
St Ives
Chatteris
Ely **15**

CAMBRIDGESHIRE

St Neots
Cambridge
Bedford   Sandy
Great Shelford
Duxford **18**
Haverhill

BEDFORD-
SHIRE
22
Biggleswade
Letchworth
Stansted
Mountfitchet
23
Saffron Walden

Leighton
Buzzard
24 Woburn
Hitchin
Dunstable
27   Luton

HERTFORD-
SHIRE
25
Bishop's Stortford
Braintree
Harlow
Hertford
Chipping
Ongar
Chelmsford
Hemel
Hempstead
29   **28** Hatfield
St Albans
Brentwood
Ingatestone
Maldon
Watford

BUCKS

BERKS

SURREY

GREATER
LONDON

KENT

Wells-next-the-Sea
1
Fakenham
Pensthorpe **3**
Thursford
2
Sherringham
Cromer
North Walsham
Caister-on-Sea

NORFOLK

King's Lynn
4 **5**
Wisbech
Oxborough
Swaffham
East Dareham
6 **7** Norwich
Wymondham
Attleborough
Somerleyton **9**
Earsham
12
Bungay
8 Great
Yarmouth
10 **11**
Lowestoft
Southwold
Lakenheath
Mildenhall
Bressingham
13 Diss
Halesworth

Bury St Edmunds
Pakenham
Newmarket **19**
20
Ickworth
16
Stowmarket
21
Helmingham
Ipswich
17 Framlingham
Aldeburgh

SUFFOLK

Sudbury
Hadleigh

ESSEX

Harwich
26 Colchester
Coggeshall
Witham
West
Mersea
Clacton-on-Sea
Burnham-on-Crouch

Basildon
Stanford-le-Hope
Grays
Tilbury
Southend-on-Sea

| 0 | 20 Miles |
| 0 | 30 Kms |

FIND OUT MORE

Further information about
holidays and attractions in
East Anglia is available from:
East Anglia Tourist Board,
Toppesfield Hall,
Hadleigh,
Suffolk IP7 5DN.
Tel: (01473) 822922

These publications are available
from the East Anglia Tourist
Board (post free):
■ **Great Escapes** - short breaks
■ **Touring Map** - bed &
breakfast and camping
■ **Freedom Holiday Parks
in Eastern England**

Also available are (prices include
postage and packaging):
■ **East Anglia Guide** £4.50
■ **Gardens to Visit in East
Anglia** £1.99

WHERE TO STAY (EAST ANGLIA)

Accommodation entries in this region are listed in alphabetical order of place name, and then in alphabetical order of establishment. A contact address is given where it differs from the address of the establishment.

Map references refer to the colour location maps at the back of this guide.

Prices shown are weekly per unit.

At-a-glance symbols at the end of each accommodation entry give useful information about services and facilities. A key to symbols can be found inside the back cover flap. Keep this open for easy reference.

ALDEBURGH

Suffolk
Map ref 3C2

A prosperous port in the 16th C, now famous for the Aldeburgh Music Festival held annually in June. The 16th C Moot Hall, now a museum, is a timber-framed building once used as an open market.

62 Crag Path

COMMENDED

Aldeburgh
Contact: Mrs V M Bingham, Cooks Barn, Chillesford Barn, Sudbourne, Woodbridge, Suffolk IP12 2AN
☎ Orford (01394) 450759
Newly converted seafront house on Heritage Coast, with superb sea view. Shower room, bathroom and utility room.
1 self-contained unit; sleeping max 7

Price per week:	£min	£max
Low season	250.00	350.00
High season	400.00	500.00

Magenta

COMMENDED

57 Crag Path, Aldeburgh
Contact: Mrs Vanessa Gorst, 12a Eton Avenue, London NW3 3EH
☎ London (0171) 435 5552 &
Aldeburgh (01728) 452676
Fax (0171) 435 5552
Charming seafront cottage completely refurbished in 1996. Sleeps 4. Close to shops. Wonderful sea views, loads of character and excellent facilities including shower, microwave, washer/dryer and central heating.

1 self-contained unit

Price per week:	£min	£max
Low season	120.00	175.00
High season	200.00	350.00

Telegraph Cottage & Barn

HIGHLY COMMENDED

Warren Hill Lane, Aldeburgh
Contact: Mr Richard John Balls, Gorse Hill, Leiston Road, Aldeburgh, Suffolk IP15 5QD
☎ Aldeburgh (01728) 452162 & 0860 585190
Fax (01728) 452162
Detached self-contained coastal cottage in 3 acres, behind North Warren Reserve and with views to Thorpeness, sea and golf-course. Warm and cosy in winter with wood-burning stove.
2 self-contained units; sleeping 2–4

Price per week:	£min	£max
Low season	245.00	275.00
High season	275.00	330.00

Open March–December

ASHDON

Essex
Map ref 2D1

Whitensmere Farm Cottages

HIGHLY COMMENDED

Whitensmere Farm, Ashdon, Saffron Walden
Contact: Mr & Mrs Graham Ford, Whitensmere Farm, Ashdon, Saffron Walden, Essex CB10 2JQ
☎ Saffron Walden (01799) 584244
Range of converted listed barns on edge of a farm, south-facing and overlooking open countryside.
Wheelchair access category 3
3 self-contained units; sleeping 5–10

Price per week:	£min	£max
Low season	150.00	300.00
High season	200.00	660.00

BADWELL ASH

Suffolk
Map ref 3B2

Driftway Cottage

COMMENDED

Driftway, Badwell Ash, Bury St Edmunds
Contact: Mrs P D Hamilton, Driftway, Badwell Ash, Bury St Edmunds, Suffolk IP31 3DH
☎ Walsham-le-Willows (01359) 259308

Comfortable beamed cottage with open fire, fitted carpets, double glazing, second WC, courtyard garden. Splendid base for touring unspoilt East Anglia. Owner-managed.

| 1 self-contained unit; sleeping max 5 | | |
Price per week:	£min	£max
Low season	155.00	
High season		300.00

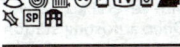

Lodge Cottage

 HIGHLY COMMENDED

Badwell Ash Hall, Badwell Ash, Bury
St Edmunds
Contact: Mrs M Castro, Badwell Ash
Hall, Badwell Ash, Bury St Edmunds,
Suffolk IP31 3JG
☎ Walsham-Le-Willows (01359)
259643

*Beamed country cottage. Central
heating, log fires, 2 bathrooms. Half an
acre of private garden. Games room
and conservatory with indoor barbecue.*
1 self-contained unit; sleeping max 8

Price per week:	£min	£max
Low season	270.00	295.00
High season	345.00	435.00

BARLEY

BARLEY

Hertfordshire
Map ref 2D1

Tree Tops Cottage

COMMENDED

The Old Hall, Barley, Royston
SG8 8JA
☎ Barkway (01763) 848368
Contact: Mrs Caroline Easton
*Comfortable cottage in centre of pretty
village near Cambridge. London 1 hour
by train. Ideal touring centre in
beautiful countryside. Garden with
bantams.*
1 self-contained unit; sleeping max 4

Price per week:	£min	£max
Low season	114.00	
High season	144.00	204.00

> All accommodation in this
> guide has been graded, or is
> awaiting a grading, by a trained
> Tourist Board inspector.

BAYLHAM

Suffolk
Map ref 3B2

Baylham House Annexe &
Baylham House Flat

COMMENDED

Baylham House, Mill Lane, Baylham,
Ipswich
Contact: Mrs Ann Storer, Baylham
House, Mill Lane, Baylham, Ipswich,
Suffolk IP6 8LG
☎ Ipswich (01473) 830264
*Annexe and flat on rare breeds farm
with cattle, sheep, pigs, poultry and
goats. Trout and coarse fishing, good
walking area and touring base for both
inland and coastal Suffolk. Annexe
sleeps 4 plus cot; flat sleeps 2 plus cot.
Both fully equipped to a high standard.*
2 self-contained units; sleeping 2–4

Price per week:	£min	£max
Low season	106.00	172.00
High season	173.00	268.00

BERKHAMSTED

Hertfordshire
Map ref 2D1

Hilltop town on Grand Union Canal
surrounded by pleasant countryside
and a 1200-acre common. It has
remains of an important castle with
earthworks and moat. Birthplace of
William Cowper, the poet.

Holly Tree & Jack's Cottage

COMMENDED

22 & 23 Ringshall, Little Gaddesden,
Berkhamsted
Contact: Mrs D Barrington, 20 & 21
Ringshall, Little Gaddesden,
Berkhamsted, Hertfordshire
HP4 1ND
☎ Little Gaddesden (01442)
843464
Fax (01228) 577442
*Restored, period cottages with all
modern amenities provided, in a village
set in National Trust woodland. London
28 miles.*
2 self-contained units; sleeping 4

Price per week:	£min	£max
Low season	160.00	160.00
High season	185.00	220.00

> Map references apply to
> the colour maps at the
> back of this guide.

BEYTON

Suffolk
Map ref 3B2

Manorflat

HIGHLY COMMENDED

Manorhouse, The Green, Beyton,
Bury St Edmunds
Contact: Mrs Kay Dewsbury,
Manorhouse, The Green, Beyton,
Bury St Edmunds, Suffolk IP30 9AF
☎ Beyton (01359) 270960
Fax (01284) 761611
*Self-contained wing of 15th C listed
farmhouse, refurbished to a high
standard, overlooking village green. 1st
floor double bedroom, en-suite. Linen
and electricity included. Brochure. B &
B also available.*
1 self-contained unit; sleeping max 2

Price per week:	£min	£max
Low season	110.00	130.00
High season	140.00	170.00

BILLERICAY

Essex
Map ref 3B3

Site of both Roman and Saxon
settlements and a popular overnight
stop for Canterbury pilgrims.
Historic links with famous
Mayflower voyage. Now a
flourishing town with a wide variety
of sports, leisure and cultural
activities and some fine examples of
Georgian architecture.

The Pump House
Apartment

DE LUXE

132 Church Street, Great Burstead,
Billericay
Contact: Mrs E R Bayliss, Pump
House, Church Street, Great
Burstead, Billericay, Essex
CM11 2TR
☎ Billericay (01277) 656579
Fax (01277) 631160

*Luxurious apartment on two floors,
equipped and furnished to a very high
standard. Ideal for visiting the South
East and London. Beautiful gardens,
heated outdoor pool (May-September).*
Continued ▶

BILLERICAY
Continued

Personal supervision. Strictly no smoking. Brochure available.
1 self-contained unit; sleeping max 6

Price per week:	£min	£max
Low season	350.00	450.00
High season	475.00	600.00

Cards accepted: Access, Visa

☎ 10 ⊚ ▥ ☉ 🗇 MW 📺 ⊡ 🍳 📻 ((▯
🍴 🚗 P ⚲ ❀ ✈ SP

BLAKENEY
Norfolk
Map ref 3B1

Picturesque village on the north coast of Norfolk and a former port and fishing village. 15th C Guildhall. Marshy creeks extend towards Blakeney Point (National Trust) and are a paradise for naturalists, with trips to the reserve and to see the seals from Blakeney Quay.

The Friary
🔑🔑🔑 APPROVED

Mariners Hill, Blakeney, Holt
Contact: Mrs D Cooke, 31 Bracondale, Norwich NR1 2AT
☎ Norwich (01603) 624827
17th C 4-bedroomed family house with fine views over harbour. Large kitchen/diner, walled garden.
1 self-contained unit; sleeping max 8

Price per week:	£min	£max
Low season	300.00	350.00
High season	475.00	550.00

Open April–October and Christmas
☎ ⊚ ▥ ☉ 🗇 MW 📺 ⊡ 🍳 📻 ((▯
🚗 P ❀ ✈ 🏠

Mariners Hill Cottages
🔑🔑🔑 COMMENDED

Mariners Hill, Blakeney, Holt
Contact: Mrs B Pope, The Lodge, Back Lane, Blakeney, Holt, Norfolk NR25 7NR
☎ Cley (01263) 740477
Fax (01263) 741356
Flint bungalows and converted barns in quiet cul-de-sac facing the harbour amidst mature grounds. Tastefully furnished. Personally supervised by owners. Ideally situated for golf, bird-watching, sailing, riding and walking. Private parking.
4 self-contained units; sleeping 3–8

Price per week:	£min	£max
Low season	190.00	300.00
High season	342.00	562.00

☎ M ⊚ ▥ ☉ 🗇 MW 📺 ⊡ 🍳 ((▯
🚗 P ∪ ❀ ✈ SP

Pye's Farm
🔑🔑 APPROVED

Saxlingham Road, Blakeney, Holt NR25 7PD
☎ Cley (01263) 740738
Contact: Mr Anthony Ette
Comfortable, well-equipped bungalow with idyllic views, within own 40 acres of grass and trees.
1 self-contained unit; sleeping max 5

Price per week:	£min	£max
Low season	150.00	225.00
High season	250.00	300.00

☎ 5 ⊚ ▥ ☉ 🗇 MW 📺 ⊡ 🍳 🚗 🚙
P ❀ SP

BRANCASTER
Norfolk
Map ref 3B1

Thompson Brancaster Farms 🏠
🔑🔑🔑 COMMENDED

Field House, Brancaster, King's Lynn PE31 8AG
☎ (01485) 210261 & (0585) 269538
Fax (01485) 210261
Contact: Mr Jeremy Thompson
Tastefully restored flint and brick farm cottages in beautiful countryside. Fitted kitchens, linen supplied, laundry, TV, patio, barbecue, tennis.
12 self-contained units; sleeping 4–14

Price per week:	£min	£max
Low season	189.00	525.00
High season	357.00	1155.00

☎ ⊚ ▥ ☉ 🗇 📺 ⊡ 🍳 📻 ((▯ 🚗 ✆ ❀
✎ SP

BRISLEY
Norfolk
Map ref 3B1

The Manor Barns
🔑🔑🔑🔑 HIGHLY COMMENDED

Brisley Common, Brisley, East Dereham NR20 5DW
☎ Dereham (01362) 668716
Contact: Mr & Mrs Colin or Jill Dadd
Barn conversion. Heavily beamed home with much character and comfort. Garden with parking. Situated on large common. Convenient for coast and pretty market towns.
1 self-contained unit; sleeping max 4

Price per week:	£min	£max
Low season	180.00	220.00
High season	200.00	290.00

☎ ⊚ ▥ ☉ 🗇 MW 📺 ⊡ 🍳 📻 ((▯ 🚗
P ❀ ✎ SP 🏠

BUCKDEN
Cambridgeshire
Map ref 3A2

Pretty village with several attractive brick houses. Once a posting station and dominated by the remains of the 15th C palace of the Bishops of Lincoln. The local church is noted for its spire and carvings. Nearby is Grafham Water, a reservoir with extensive picnic areas.

Buckden Marina - Lodge 10,13,14 🏠
🔑🔑🔑🔑🔑 HIGHLY COMMENDED

Mill Road, Buckden, St Neots, Huntingdon
Contact: Mr Alex Hayes, The Operation Ltd, Charter House, Latham Close, Bredbury, Stockport, Cheshire SK6 2SD
☎ (0161) 494 1000
Fax (0161) 494 0099

Quality pine lodges in tranquil marina environment. Restaurant and leisure centre on site. Access to River Great Ouse and private boat included.
3 self-contained units; sleeping 4–6

Price per week:	£min	£max
Low season	275.00	395.00
High season	325.00	695.00

☎ ⊚ ▥ ☉ 🗇 MW 📺 ⊡ 🍳 📻 ((▯
🚗 P ⚲ P SP

BUNTINGFORD
Hertfordshire
Map ref 2D1

Southfields Cottages
🔑🔑 APPROVED

Southfields Farm, Throcking, Buntingford SG9 9RD
☎ Cottered (01763) 281224 & (0589) 646759
Fax (01763) 281224
Contact: Mrs I A Murchie
Farm cottages in peaceful countryside, 20 minutes from Stevenage and within easy reach of London and Cambridge.
2 self-contained units; sleeping 5

Price per week:	£min	£max
Low season	110.00	130.00
High season	140.00	200.00

☎ M ⊚ ▥ ☉ 🗇 MW 📺 ⊡ 🍳 ((▯
🚗 ❀ ✈

BURNHAM OVERY STAITHE

Norfolk
Map ref 3B1

Unspoilt scenic village, steeped in naval history, Lord Nelson's playground as a boy. Captain Woodgett of the Cutty Sark once lived here and cargo ships visited the harbour. Wonderful tidal inlet with great variety of natural history. Close to Roman fort at Brancaster and famous Peddars Way.

Flagstaff West, East, Cottage, Barn and Garden House 🐌

COMMENDED

Burnham Overy Staithe, King's Lynn
Contact: Mrs C W Green, Red House Farm, Badingham, Woodbridge, Suffolk IP13 8LL
☎ Badingham (01728) 638637
Fax (01728) 638638

Flagstaff occupies a superb position directly overlooking the picturesque harbour and saltings. Recently converted to self-contained units. Dishwasher in each unit. Free pub bar dinner provided on first night.
5 self-contained units; sleeping 2–12

Price per week:	£min	£max
Low season	210.00	525.00
High season	425.00	625.00

CAMBRIDGE

Cambridgeshire
Map ref 2D1

A most important and beautiful city on the River Cam with 31 colleges forming one of the oldest universities in the world. Numerous museums, good shopping centre, restaurants, theatres, cinema and fine bookshops.
Tourist Information Centre ☎ (01223) 322640

Goose Hall Farm Cottages

APPROVED

Goose Hall Farm, Ely Road, Waterbeach, Cambridge CB5 9PG
☎ (01223) 860235
Fax (01223) 860235
Contact: Mrs Sylvia Lock
Two cottages 4 miles north of

Cambridge on A10 to Ely, 1 mile beyond turn to Waterbeach.
2 self-contained units; sleeping max 5

Price per week:	£min	£max
Low season	125.00	150.00
High season	160.00	200.00

CASTLE ACRE

Norfolk
Map ref 3B1

Remains of castle and priory. Possibly the grandest castle earthworks in England.

Cherry Tree Cottage 🐌

HIGHLY COMMENDED

Back Lane, Castle Acre, King's Lynn
Contact: Mr & Mrs C J Boswell, Wellington House, Back Lane, Castle Acre, King's Lynn, Norfolk PE32 2AR
☎ Swaffham (01760) 755000
Fax (01760) 755000
Charming 4-bedroomed cottage in historic conservation village. Furnished and equipped to a very high standard. Four poster bed. Disabled facilities. Inclusive rates, flexible booking periods.
Wheelchair access category 3 ⚹
1 self-contained unit; sleeping 6

Price per week:	£min	£max
Low season	150.00	180.00
High season	220.00	340.00

Peddars Cottage 🐌

COMMENDED

5 Bailey Gate, Castle Acre, King's Lynn
Contact: Mrs A C Swindell, The Rectory, St Saviour, Jersey, Channel Islands JE2 7NP
☎ Jersey (01534) 27480
Well-equipped cottage-style house situated in centre of historic village. Close to castle, priory and shops.
1 self-contained unit; sleeping 6

Price per week:	£min	£max
Low season	100.00	150.00
High season	200.00	225.00

The National Grading and Classification Scheme is explained in full at the back of this guide.

CHEDGRAVE

Norfolk
Map ref 3C1

On the banks of the River Chet, with its sister village of Loddon on the opposite bank. The church of All Saints has a richly decorated Norman doorway.

Barn Owl Holidays 🐌

COMMENDED

Bryons Green, Big Back Lane, Chedgrave, Norwich NR14 6HB
☎ Loddon (01508) 528786
Fax (01508) 528786
Contact: Mrs R Beattie
18th C barn converted into 3 oak-beamed cottages. Set in grounds of country house. 15 minutes' walk to village, pubs and boat hire. Use of indoor heated swimming pool. Sleeps 2-18 people.
Wheelchair access category 2 ⚹
3 self-contained units; each sleeping 6

Price per week:	£min	£max
Low season	165.00	
High season		430.00

CLEY NEXT THE SEA

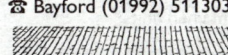

Norfolk
Map ref 3B1

Due to land reclamation the village has not been "next the sea" since the 17th C. Behind the old quay the main street winds between flint-built houses. The marshes between Cley and Salthouse are bird reserves. Cley Windmill is a 160-year-old tower mill converted into a guesthouse.

Archway Cottage 🐌

COMMENDED

Coast Road, Cley next the Sea, Holt
Contact: Mrs V Jackson, 3A Brickendon Lane, Brickendon, Hertford SG13 8NU
☎ Bayford (01992) 511303

18th C flint cottage, fully carpeted, with 4 bedrooms, 2 bathrooms and garage. Near village centre, shops, transport, bird sanctuaries and the sea.

Continued ▶

CLEY NEXT THE SEA
Continued

1 self-contained unit; sleeping max 7

Price per week:	£min	£max
Low season	100.00	200.00
High season	200.00	350.00

🐕 Ⓜ ◎ ▥ ⊙ 🖰 MW 📺 🖵 🖴 🖳 🚗 ❄ SP

2 & 3 Beau Rivage & Saint Margaret's
🔑🔑 COMMENDED

Cley next the Sea, Holt
Contact: Sir David and Lady Hughes,
The Berristead, Wilburton, Ely,
Cambridgeshire CB6 3RP
☎ Ely (01353) 740770
Fax (01353) 741599
Two attractive terraced cottages and a spacious house converted from a 17th C granary adjoining the quay with views of Cley Windmill and salt marshes. Quiet, comfortable, well-equipped. Rent includes electricity. Ample parking, CH and colour TV. Illustrated brochure.
3 self-contained units; sleeping 4–6

Price per week:	£min	£max
Low season	165.00	185.00
High season	330.00	380.00

Open March–December

🐕 ◎ ▥ ⊙ 🖰 📺 🖵 🖴 🚲 🚗 ❄

CLIPPESBY
Norfolk
Map ref 3C1

Clippesby Holidays 🏔
🔑🔑 – 🔑🔑 APPROVED

Clippesby, Great Yarmouth
NR29 3BJ
☎ Great Yarmouth (01493) 369367
Fax (01493) 368181
Contact: Mrs Jean Lindsay
Cottages in Broadlands National Park - a fascinating area of Broads, nature reserves and attractions - close to sea. Country holidays in beautiful surroundings, with lawn tennis, swimming and more in summer. Winner of several awards.
23 self-contained units; sleeping 2–10

Price per week:	£min	£max
Low season	160.00	350.00
High season	180.00	495.00

Cards accepted: Access, Visa, Switch/Delta

🐕 Ⓜ ◎ ▥ ⊙ 📺 🖵 🖴 🖳 P 🐾 🛇 U ✽ SP Ⓣ

COLCHESTER
Essex
Map ref 3B2

Britain's oldest recorded town standing on the River Colne and famous for its oysters. Numerous historic buildings, ancient remains and museums. Plenty of parks and gardens, extensive shopping centre, theatre and zoo.
Tourist Information Centre ☎ (01206) 282920

Mundy
🔑🔑 COMMENDED

The Crescent, West Bergholt,
Colchester
Contact: Mr Brian Hughes, Lynton,
The Crescent, West Bergholt,
Colchester CO6 3DA
☎ Colchester (01206) 240112
Restored timbered cottage. Sleeps 4 (1 double, 1 twin). Lounge, kitchen, garden room. Between Colne and Stour Valleys, close to Constable country. Comfortable, quiet, excellent touring base.
1 self-contained unit

Price per week:	£min	£max
Low season	100.00	150.00
High season	180.00	220.00

🐕 ◎ ▥ 🖰 MW 📺 🖵 🖴 🚗 P ❄ SP 🏠

50 Rosebery Avenue
🔑🔑 COMMENDED

Colchester
Contact: Mrs K Webb, 51 Rosebery Avenue, Colchester, Essex CO1 2UP
☎ Colchester (01206) 866888
Modernised house in quiet town centre location. Castle, park, shops, museums and sports centre within walking distance. Ideal for East Coast.
1 self-contained unit; sleeping max 6

Price per week:	£min	£max
Low season	150.00	170.00
High season	190.00	220.00

🐕 ◎ ▥ ⊙ 🖰 📺 🖵 🖴 🖳 🚗 P ❄ 🛇 SP

CREETING ST MARY
Suffolk
Map ref 3B2

Upper Langdales Farmhouse Holiday Cottages
🔑🔑 COMMENDED

Upper Langdales Farmhouse,
Creeting St Mary, Ipswich IP6 8QF
☎ Needham Market (01449) 720079
Contact: Mr & Mrs B Carter
Well-equipped comfortable cottages, converted from outbuildings, in tranquil

rural setting within grounds of a 16th C thatched farmhouse. Games room, children's play area. Various farm animals and birds.
4 self-contained units; sleeping 2–4

Price per week:	£min	£max
Low season	135.00	185.00
High season	185.00	300.00

🐕 ◎ ▥ ⊙ 🖰 📺 🖵 🖴 🖳 🚗 U ❄ ✗ SP

CRINGLEFORD
Norfolk
Map ref 3B1

The Old Stables and Horseshoe Cottage
🔑🔑 HIGHLY COMMENDED

Pond Farm, Cringleford, Norwich
Contact: Mrs G L Coiley, Pond Farm,
Cringleford, Norwich NR4 6UE
☎ Norwich (01603) 454895

Two attractive cottages converted from former stables. Period character, all modern amenities, garden. In grounds of owners' picturesque thatched farmhouse. All ground floor accommodation. Norwich centre 3 miles. Excellent location for Norfolk coast and Broads.
2 self-contained units; sleeping 2–4

Price per week:	£min	£max
Low season	160.00	260.00
High season	200.00	290.00

🐕 ◎ ▥ ⊙ 📺 🖵 🖴 🖳 🖳 🚗 P ❄ ✗ SP

CROMER
Norfolk
Map ref 3C1

Once a small fishing village and now famous for its fishing boats that still work off the beach and offer freshly caught crabs. Excellent bathing on sandy beaches fringed by cliffs. The town boasts a fine pier, theatre, museum and a lifeboat station.
Tourist Information Centre ☎ (01263) 512497

The Grove 🏔
🔑🔑 – 🔑🔑 COMMENDED

Overstrand Road, Cromer
NR27 0DJ
☎ (01263) 512412
Fax (01263) 513416
Contact: Mrs A Graveling

Converted barn cottages plus fully self-contained bungalow. In 3-acre grounds of adjacent guesthouse with walks to nearby cliffs, woods and golf-course. Washing machine in most units. All fully heated. Linen and towels provided.
6 self-contained units; sleeping 2–6

Price per week:	£min	£max
Low season	153.00	230.00
High season	270.00	465.00

🐎Ⓜ◎∅🖿.☉☐ MW 📺🗑🍳(🍴 🖵✈P▶❄ SP

Kings Chalet Park

🔑🔑 APPROVED

Overstrand Road, Cromer
Contact: Mrs V Bateman, Stenson, 32 Overstrand Road, Cromer, Norfolk NR27 OAJ
☎ Cromer (01263) 511308
Compact chalets, comprising lounge, kitchen/diner and 2 bedrooms. Well-equipped, including sofabed, microwave, colour TV and video.
4 self-contained units; sleeping max 4

Price per week:	£min	£max
Low season	95.00	120.00
High season	140.00	210.00

Open April–October
🐎◎🖿.☉☐ MW 📺🍳(🍴🖵 //∪❄ SP ◎

The Granary 𝔐

🔑🔑 COMMENDED

Priory Farm, Darsham, Saxmundham IP17 3QD
☎ Yoxford (01728) 668459
Contact: Mrs S Bloomfield
Comfortable 17th C granary on family farm. Ideal for exploring Suffolk. Heritage coast 3 miles. Weekly lets or short out-of-season breaks. Cycle hire available.
1 self-contained unit; sleeping max 4

Price per week:	£min	£max
Low season	135.00	185.00
High season	185.00	295.00

🐎Ⓜ◎🖿.☉🍳🖵📺🗑🍳🖵✈ P🐾❄✕🐕 SP 🏠

East Dereham is famous for its associations with the poet William Cowper and also Bishop Bonner, chaplain to Cardinal Wolsey. His home is now a museum. Around the charming market-place are many notable buildings.

Clinton Cottage

🔑🔑 HIGHLY COMMENDED

Clinton House, Well Hill, Clint Green, East Dereham NR19 1RX
☎ (01362) 692079
Contact: Mrs M R Searle
Pretty, detached country cottage 3 miles south of Dereham. Fully equipped kitchen and bathroom. Attractive lounge leading to patio and enclosed garden. Pets welcome. Parking.
1 self-contained unit; sleeping max 4

Price per week:	£min	£max
Low season	85.00	145.00
High season	175.00	240.00

🐎Ⓜ◎🖿.☉☐ MW 📢📺🗑🍳(🍴 🖺//✈P🔍▶❄🐈 SP Ⓣ

The Willows

🔑🔑 COMMENDED

East Dereham
Contact: Ms A Luttman-Johnson, 209a Goldhurst Terrace, London NW6 3ER
☎ (0171) 372 4262
Fax (0171) 372 4262

Comfortable, quiet cottage with mature gardens in historic village north of Dereham. Four bedrooms, 2 bathrooms, open fireplace, west-facing conservatory.
1 self-contained unit

Price per week:	£min	£max
Low season	220.00	310.00
High season	310.00	400.00

🐎◎🖿.☉☐ MW 📢📺🗑🍳✈🖵 ✈P❄✈ SP Ⓣ

The 𝔐 symbol after an establishment name indicates that it is a Regional Tourist Board member.

Dairy Farm Cottages 𝔐

🔑🔑🔑 HIGHLY COMMENDED

Dilham, North Walsham
Contact: Mr & Mrs James & Annabel Paterson, Rumford Limited, Manor Farm, Dilham, North Walsham, Norfolk NR28 9PZ
☎ Smallburgh (01692) 535178 & 536883
Fax (01692) 536723

500-acre mixed farm. Traditional farm buildings converted into cottages. Beautiful, quiet country setting in heart of Broadland. Acres to roam over, including Dilham Islands (Victorian folly). Secure play area, games room, farm animals. Coast 15 minutes. Brochure available.
Wheelchair access category 2♿
6 self-contained units; sleeping 1–4

Price per week:	£min	£max
Low season	195.00	200.00
High season	250.00	410.00

Open March–December
Cards accepted: Visa
🐎Ⓜ◎🖿.☉☐ MW 📺✈🍳(🍴P ❄ SP

Dolphin Lodge 𝔐

🔑🔑🔑 HIGHLY COMMENDED

Roudham Farm, East Harling, Norwich NR16 2RJ
☎ (01953) 717126
Fax (01953) 718593
Contact: Mrs E Jolly

Restored semi-detached cottages with exposed beams, woodburners, Aga, microwave, washing machine, jacuzzi. Each has a large reception room, kitchen, 2 bedrooms, cloakroom and laundry room.

Continued ▶

183

EAST HARLING

Continued

2 self-contained units; sleeping 5

Price per week:	£min	£max
Low season	210.00	260.00
High season	260.00	330.00

🕿 ◎ ⌀ 💻 ⊡ ☉ 🅼 MW ⅂🄴 TV 🗄 🔌 🕿 ♿ P ✎ ✎ ❋ ✕ 🏛

FINCHAM

Norfolk
Map ref 3B1

Chapel

⚷⚷⚷ COMMENDED

St Marys Lodge, High Street,
Fincham, King's Lynn PE33 9EL
🕿 (01366) 347841
Contact: Mrs Brenda Brown
Comfortable two-bedroomed cottage set in beautiful grounds. Ideal as base for visits to west and north Norfolk.
1 self-contained unit; sleeping max 4

Price per week:	£min	£max
Low season	175.00	210.00
High season	210.00	280.00

🕿 ◎ 💻 ☉ 🄴 TV 🔌 P ❋ ✕

FOULSHAM

Norfolk
Map ref 3B1

Handsome village with fine Georgian buildings around the market square dating from Foulsham's prosperous past as a centre for the wool trade. Now a flourishing centre for the local farming community. Public house, restaurant, shop and post office.

Glenmore Cottage

⚷⚷⚷ HIGHLY COMMENDED

High Street, Foulsham, East
Dereham
Contact: Mrs Joan Stevenson, Pound Corner, Thornage, Holt, Norfolk
NR25 7QH
🕿 Melton Constable (01263) 861710
Fax (01263) 861712
3-storey listed Georgian village house, newly renovated. Patio garden with barbecue, 1 single and 2 double bedrooms, cosy lounge, large dining/kitchen.
1 self-contained unit; sleeping max 5

Price per week:	£min	£max
Low season	175.00	200.00
High season	225.00	260.00

🕿 🅼 ◎ 💻 ☉ 🄴 TV 🗄 🔌 ❋ ✎ SP

FOXLEY

Norfolk
Map ref 3B1

Moor Farm Holidays 🍂

⚷⚷⚷ APPROVED

Moor Farm, Foxley, Dereham
Contact: Mr P Davis, Moor Farm,
Foxley, Dereham, Norfolk
NR20 4QN
🕿 Bawdeswell (01362) 688217

Two/three-bed holiday units situated on working farm. Equal distance from Broads, Norwich and coast. Full central heating. Facilities for disabled. Wheelchair access category 3 ♿
7 self-contained units; sleeping 3–7

Price per week:	£min	£max
Low season	135.00	190.00
High season	200.00	340.00

🕿 🅼 ◎ 💻 ☉ 🄴 MW TV 🗄 🔌 🗄 🕿 ♿ P U ✎ ✎ ❋ ✎ SP

GARBOLDISHAM

Norfolk
Map ref 3B2

Burnside

⚷⚷⚷ COMMENDED

Alderwood, Hopton Road,
Garboldisham, Diss IP22 2RQ
🕿 (01953) 688376
Contact: Mrs Connie Atkins
Beautiful Scandinavian-style timber lodge, nestling on its own in wood beside the Little Ouse stream.
1 self-contained unit; sleeping max 4

Price per week:	£min	£max
Low season	175.00	225.00
High season	225.00	295.00

🕿 ◎ 💻 ☉ 🄴 MW TV 🗄 🔌 🗄 🕿 P ❋ SP

GREAT BENTLEY

Essex
Map ref 3B2

The Stable

⚷⚷⚷ HIGHLY COMMENDED

Coppice Farm, Great Bentley,
Colchester
Contact: Mrs Susan Gosling,
Coppice Farm, Great Bentley,
Colchester, Essex CO7 8QZ
🕿 Clacton-on-Sea (01255) 830281
& 0850 682708
Converted stable, sleeps 4 plus cot, in

quiet location on working farm. Essex/Suffolk border. No smoking. Convenient for coast and good walks.
1 self-contained unit; sleeping max 4

Price per week:	£min	£max
Low season	120.00	270.00
High season	120.00	270.00

🕿 ◎ 💻 ☉ 🄴 MW ⅂🄴 TV 🗄 🔌 🗄 ♿ P U ✎ ❋ SP

GREAT DUNMOW

Essex
Map ref 3B2

On the main Roman road from Bishop's Stortford to Braintree. Doctor's Pond near the square was where the first lifeboat was tested in 1785. Home of the Dunmow Flitch trials held every 4 years on Whit Monday.

Old Piggeries 🍂

⚷⚷⚷ COMMENDED

Grange Farm, Little Dunmow,
Dunmow CM6 3HY
🕿 (01371) 820205
Fax (01371) 820205
Contact: Mr J Kirby
Modern facilities in recently converted buildings dating from the 14th C. In a quiet village location convenient for London, Cambridge, Constable country and picturesque north Essex.
3 self-contained units; sleeping 4–6

Price per week:	£min	£max
Low season	120.00	160.00
High season	170.00	360.00

🕿 ◎ 💻 ☉ TV 🗄 🔌 🗄 🕿 ♿ P ✎ U ✎ ✎ ❋ ✎ SP 🏛

GREAT MOULTON

Norfolk
Map ref 3B1

In origin a typical Norfolk wood-pasture village, now a quiet country retreat surrounded by farmland.

Carpenters Cottage

⚷⚷⚷ HIGHLY COMMENDED

Frosts Lane, Great Moulton,
Norwich
Contact: Dr G D Watts, Barn Meadow, Frosts Lane, Great Moulton, Norwich, Norfolk
NR15 2HG
🕿 Tivetshall (01379) 677661
Spacious 17th C timber-framed cottage with recent extension including well-fitted kitchen and bathroom. Peaceful setting in lovely garden with 5 acres of private woodland. Ideal for touring Norfolk and Suffolk.

1 self-contained unit; sleeping 4

Price per week:	£min	£max
Low season	177.00	230.00
High season	298.00	398.00

🐕8Ⓜ🖥⛫.⊙🗄🎱📺🗑💺🎣♨
P❋🍴🏠

GRESHAM

Norfolk
Map ref 3B1

Astalot and Avalon Cottages
🗝🗝 COMMENDED

Gooseberry Alley, Sustead Road,
Lower Gresham, Norwich
Contact: Mrs J J Murray, Mariners
Hard High Street, Cley, Holt,
Norfolk NR25 7RX
☎ Cley (01263) 740404 & 740801
Fax (01263) 740404
*Adjoining flint/brick cottages built over
150 years ago. Completely renovated.
Warm and very comfortable, with small
enclosed gardens. Dogs welcome. Prices
include electricity.*
2 self-contained units; sleeping 3–4

Price per week:	£min	£max
Low season	110.00	180.00
High season	220.00	270.00

🐕🖥⛫.⊙🗄MW📺🗑💺🏠P
♒❋SP

HADLEIGH

Suffolk
Map ref 3B2

Former wool town, lying on a
tributary of the River Stour. The
church of St Mary stands among a
remarkable cluster of medieval
buildings.
*Tourist Information Centre ☎ (01473)
823824*

Stable Cottages 🏔
🗝🗝🗝 — 🗝🗝🗝
HIGHLY COMMENDED

The Granary, Chattisham Place,
Chattisham, Ipswich IP8 3QD
☎ Hintlesham (01473) 652210
Fax (01473) 652210
Contact: Mrs M Langton
*Well-equipped converted stables and
barn in quiet village near Constable
country. Wheelchair facilities, games
room. Swimming and tennis by
arrangement.*
Wheelchair access category 2♿
3 self-contained units; sleeping 2–8

Price per week:	£min	£max
Low season	130.00	220.00
High season	170.00	325.00

Cards accepted: Diners

🐕🖥⛫.⊙🗄MW📺🗑💺📻🎱P
🏹♒U❋🏠

HALESWORTH

Suffolk
Map ref 3C2

Small market town which grew
firstly with navigation on the Blyth
in the 18th C and then with the
coming of the railways in the 19th
C. Opposite the church in a
beautiful 14th C building is the
Halesworth Gallery.

Cornfold and Becks End Cottage
🗝🗝 APPROVED

School Road, Westhall, Halesworth
Contact: Mrs O A Johnson, Beck's
End Farm, Westhall, Halesworth,
Suffolk IP19 8QZ
☎ Brampton (01502) 575239
*Converted village school, overlooking
peaceful countryside. Landscaped
gardens in 1 acre of grounds. Only half
a mile from the village.*
2 self-contained units; sleeping 5–6

Price per week:	£min	£max
Low season	115.00	170.00
High season	185.00	250.00

🐕Ⓜ🖥⛫.⊙🗄📺🎱📻🎣♨

HARTEST

Suffolk
Map ref 3B2

Windrush 🏔
🗝🗝🗝 COMMENDED

Somerton Road, Hartest, Bury St
Edmunds IP29 4NA
☎ Bury St Edmunds (01284)
830327
Contact: Mrs Palmer
*Modern bungalow half-a-mile from the
village green of picturesque Hartest.
Very quiet, many walks - ideal for
country lovers. One-night bookings
accepted.*
1 self-contained unit; sleeping 4

Price per week:	£min	£max
Low season	125.00	150.00
High season	125.00	250.00

🐕🖥⛫.⊙🗄MW📺🎱💺🎣P❋
SP

Information on
accommodation listed in this
guide has been supplied by the
proprietors. As changes may
occur you are advised to check
details at the time of booking.

HEACHAM

Norfolk
Map ref 3B1

The portrait of a Red Indian
princess who married John Rolfe of
Heacham Hall in 1614 appears on
the village sign. Caley Mill is the
centre of lavender growing.

Cedar Springs Chalets
🗝 APPROVED

2,3,4,6,7,8,16,44 & 57, Heacham,
King's Lynn
Contact: Mr & Mrs M Chestney,
35 West Raynham, Fakenham,
Norfolk NR21 7EY
☎ Weasenham-St-Peter (01328)
838341
*2-bedroomed chalets on quiet garden
site 300 yards from beach. No dogs,
please.*
9 self-contained units;
sleeping max 5

Price per week:	£min	£max
Low season	70.00	90.00
High season	95.00	160.00

Open April–September

🐕Ⓜ🖥⛫.🗄📺🗑🎣🍴

Cheney Hollow Cottage
🗝🗝 COMMENDED

Cheney Hollow, 3-5 Cheney Hill,
Heacham, King's Lynn PE31 7BX
☎ Dersingham (01485) 572625
Contact: Mrs Thelma Holland
*Detached carrstone cottage, twin
bedded plus put-up, garden and patio
with furniture. Linen and electricity
included. In private lane with parking.*
1 self-contained unit; sleeping max 2

Price per week:	£min	£max
Low season	130.00	170.00
High season	175.00	200.00

🐕🖥⛫.⊙🗄MW📻📺🗑💺
🎣P❋SP

HELPSTON

Cambridgeshire
Map ref 3A1

The Gate House
🗝🗝🗝 HIGHLY COMMENDED

Helpston House, Helpston,
Peterborough
Contact: Mrs Orton, Helpston
House, Helpston, Peterborough
PE6 7DX
☎ Peterborough (01733) 252190
Fax (01733) 252190
*11th C stone and beamed gatehouse,
fully renovated, with outdoor pool.*
Continued ▶

HELPSTON
Continued

Bicycles and windsurf available. Private mature gardens and garage. Village of poet John Clare.
1 self-contained unit; sleeping 1–5

Price per week:	£min	£max
Low season	190.00	235.00
High season	240.00	270.00

HICKLING
Norfolk
Map ref 3C1

Hickling Broad is one of the largest and most popular of all the Broads and is noted for its birds. Nearby is Sutton Windmill, the tallest in the country.

Cobble Cottage ♙
APPROVED

Stubb Road, Hickling, Norwich NR12 0YS
☎ (01692) 598404
Contact: Mrs L Gibbons
Small, semi-detached cottage simply furnished. One double bedroom, plus bunk beds, lounge with colour TV, kitchen, bathroom. Lawned garden, parking space.
1 self-contained unit; sleeping 4

Price per week:	£min	£max
Low season	90.00	110.00
High season	180.00	220.00

Old Chapel Cottage
HIGHLY COMMENDED

Stubb Road, Hickling, Norwich
Contact: Mrs C Brown, Hollingbery, Guilt Cross, Kenninghall, Norwich NR16 2LJ
☎ Garboldisham (01953) 681314
Traditional Norfolk flint and brick cottage. Sitting room with dining area, kitchen and hall. One double and one twin bedroom. Bathroom with WC. Night storage heaters.
1 self-contained unit; sleeping 4

Price per week:	£min	£max
Low season	210.00	210.00
High season	210.00	210.00

Open March–November

HINGHAM
Norfolk
Map ref 3B1

The Granary ♙
HIGHLY COMMENDED

College Farm, Hingham, Norwich
Contact: Mrs C Dunnett, College Farm, Hingham, Norwich NR9 4PP
☎ Attleborough (01953) 850596
Fax (01953) 851364

Tastefully converted and furnished 18th C granary. Peaceful location on farm with animals. Original beams throughout. Pets galore with children's play area.
1 self-contained unit; sleeping max 6

Price per week:	£min	£max
Low season	150.00	150.00
High season	235.00	275.00

HITCHAM
Suffolk
Map ref 3B2

Jason and Fern Cottages
COMMENDED

Mill House, Water Run, Hitcham, Ipswich IP7 7LN
☎ Bildeston (01449) 740315
Contact: Mrs J M White
Two well-equipped cottages in idyllic 4-acre grounds. Central heating, colour TV, beautiful conservatory. Central for touring. 6 miles from Lavenham.
2 self-contained units; sleeping 2–3

Price per week:	£min	£max
Low season	130.00	155.00
High season	155.00	185.00

The map references refer to the colour maps towards the end of the guide.
The first figure is the map number; the letter and figure which follow indicate the grid reference on the map.

HOLT
Norfolk
Map ref 3B1

Much of the town centre was destroyed by fire in 1708 but has since been restored. The famous Gresham's School founded by Sir Thomas Gresham is sited here.

Carpenters Cottages ♙
UP TO COMMENDED

Carpenters Close, Norwich Road, Holt
Contact: Mr J P Siddall, Fell Dyke Cottage, Well Street, Langham, Oakham, Leicestershire LE15 7JS
☎ Oakham (01572) 756515
Fax (01572) 755279
Attractive 18th C flint and pantile cottages on the edge of a pleasant market town, 4 miles from the coast.
7 self-contained units; sleeping 2–4

Price per week:	£min	£max
Low season	120.00	195.00
High season	165.00	370.00

Poppy Cottage ♙
APPROVED

12 Mill Street, Holt
Contact: Mrs M Morley, South Lea, Bradwell, Sheffield, Yorkshire S30 2JT
☎ Hope Valley (01433) 620873 & 0831 863411
Fax (01433) 621714
Flint-built end-terrace cottage. Cosy and quiet, modern amenities, well maintained. Patio with furniture. Off-street parking.
1 self-contained unit; sleeping max 4

Price per week:	£min	£max
Low season	120.00	130.00
High season	180.00	250.00

Wood Farm Cottages ♙
COMMENDED

Wood Farm, Edgefield, Melton Constable NR24 2AQ
☎ Saxthorpe (01263) 587347
Contact: Mrs Diana Elsby

Recent high quality barn and stable conversions, situated in secluded rural location. Convenient for coast, Broads

---

Please check prices and other details at the time of booking.

and historic Georgian Holt. Two cottages have wheelchair acccess. Launderette facilities for residents' use.
7 self-contained units; sleeping 4–6

Price per week:	£min	£max
Low season	155.00	185.00
High season	335.00	425.00

🐕Ⓜ◎▥·☉🖥MW🔌📺🗄🛁(🖥)🖵
🚗P❄🚭 SP

HORNING

Norfolk
Map ref 3C1

Riverside village and well-known Broadland centre. Occasional glimpses of the river can be caught between picturesque thatched cottages.

Little River View
🔑🔑🔑 HIGHLY COMMENDED

Lower Street, Horning, Norwich
Contact: Mr J L Webb, 20 Rainsford Road, Chelmsford, Essex CM1 2QD
☎ Chelmsford (01245) 284041
Attractive and spacious semi-detached period cottage in Horning's famous Lower Street. Beautiful views over the Bure and sailing club.
1 self-contained unit; sleeping max 4

Price per week:	£min	£max
Low season	135.00	250.00
High season	295.00	395.00

Cards accepted: Visa
🐕Ⓜ◎▥·☉🖥MW🔌📺🗄🛁🖵
🚗P🐕🛶🚭 SP

HUNSTANTON

Norfolk
Map ref 3B1

Seaside resort which faces the Wash. The shingle and sand beach is backed by striped cliffs and many unusual fossils can be found here. The town is predominantly Victorian. The Oasis family leisure centre has indoor and outdoor pools.
Tourist Information Centre ☎ (01485) 532610

Albert House and The Old Victoria Stores ⛰
🔑🔑🔑 COMMENDED

20-22 Church Street, Hunstanton
Contact: Mr Mark Harriman, Hunstanton Holiday Homes, 89 Westgate, Hunstanton, Norfolk PE36 5EP
☎ Hunstanton (01485) 532511
Fax (01485) 532511
Two neighbouring houses near beach and shops. Birdwatching, golf, watersports, riding and touring.

Available separately or together - discount for joint family bookings. Short breaks also available.
2 self-contained units; sleeping 6

Price per week:	£min	£max
Low season	210.00	240.00
High season	350.00	380.00

Cards accepted: Visa
🐕◎▥·☉🖥MW🔌📺🗄🛁🖵
🚗P🛶❄ SP

Brook Bungalow
🔑🔑🔑 COMMENDED

36 Beach Road, Holme next the Sea, Hunstanton
Contact: Mrs J A Whitsed, 16 Thorpe Avenue, Peterborough PE3 6LA
☎ Peterborough (01733) 66696
Spacious, well-appointed 3-bedroomed modern bungalow, standing in own grounds overlooking golf course. Village location, 5 minutes to sea, riding school and bird reserve.
1 self-contained unit; sleeping max 8

Price per week:	£min	£max
Low season	220.00	280.00
High season	300.00	390.00

Open April–October
🐕Ⓜ◎▥·☉🖥MW🔌📺🗄🛁🖵
🚗U❄🗡

Jaskville
🔑🔑🔑 COMMENDED

11 Nene Road, Hunstanton
PE38 5BZ
☎ (01485) 533404
Contact: Mrs Ann Smith
Spacious ground floor flat with enclosed, south-west facing patio, in quiet, but central position. Lovely coastal walks. Ideal for bird-watching, golfing or just relaxing!
1 self-contained unit; sleeping max 2

Price per week:	£min	£max
Low season	90.00	110.00
High season	135.00	175.00

Open February–November
◎🛶☉🖥🔌📺🛁🖵P❄🗡

West Lodge
🔑🔑🔑 HIGHLY COMMENDED

Cole Green, Sedgeford, Hunstanton
Contact: Mrs G Tibbs, Cole Green Cottage, Cole Green, Sedgeford, Hunstanton, Norfolk PE36 5LS
☎ Sedgeford (01485) 571770
Edwardian colonial-style cottage. Furnished in period to a high standard. Garden overlooks woodland valley in conservation village.

1 self-contained unit; sleeping max 3

Price per week:	£min	£max
Low season	120.00	150.00
High season	175.00	250.00

🐕8◎▥·☉🖥MW🔌📺🗄🛁🖵
🚗PU🛶❄🗡🚭 SP🏛

KING'S LYNN

Norfolk
Map ref 3B1

A busy town with many outstanding buildings. The Guildhall and Town Hall are both built of flint in a striking chequer design. Behind the Guildhall in the Old Gaol House the sounds and smells of prison life 2 centuries ago are recreated.
Tourist Information Centre ☎ (01553) 763044

'Fells' Stable/Warehouse
🔑🔑🔑 HIGHLY COMMENDED

5 Market Lane, King's Lynn
Contact: Mrs M Higgins, 1 Langland, Springwood, King's Lynn, Norfolk PE30 4TH
☎ King's Lynn (01553) 772204
Pied a terre in Grade II listed building. Stable/warehouse with sunny patio in historic part of the town.
1 self-contained unit; sleeping max 4

Price per week:	£min	£max
Low season	130.00	
High season	190.00	

Open March–October
🐕Ⓜ◎▥·☉🖥🔌📺🛁🖵🚗❄
🗡🏛

Spring Cottage
🔑🔑🔑 COMMENDED

2A King George V Avenue, King's Lynn
Contact: Mr & Mrs P Main, 17 Extons Place, King's Lynn, Norfolk PE30 5NP
☎ King's Lynn (01553) 764962
Attractive chalet bungalow in quiet residential area, close to town centre. Two double bedrooms, lounge/dining room, kitchen, conservatory, two bathrooms, garage and delightful gardens. Non-smokers only, please.
1 self-contained unit; sleeping 4

Price per week:	£min	£max
Low season	148.00	214.00
High season	227.00	264.00

🐕Ⓜ◎▥·☉🖥MW🔌📺🛁🖵🖵
🚗P🗡

Please mention this guide when making your booking.

KNAPTON

Norfolk
Map ref 3C1

The church is visited for the beauty of its roof and font. The former, dated 1504, is 30 ft wide and adorned with a host of angels. The latter is 13th C, built of Purbeck marble and has an interesting Decorative cover.

The Cottage

APPROVED

Knapton, North Walsham
Contact: Mrs A R Michaels, 23 Lauradale Road, Fortis Green, London N2 9LT
☎ (0181) 444 7678

Charming country home with beams and inglenook. Sheltered sunny garden. In quiet village with views of open countryside less than 2 miles from sea and near the Broads. All bedrooms have fitted basins, two have en-suite showers.
1 self-contained unit; sleeping max 9

Price per week:	£min	£max
High season	350.00	540.00

Open May–October

Suffield Cottage

APPROVED

The Street, Knapton, North Walsham
Contact: Mrs A R Michaels, 23 Lauradale Road, Fortis Green, London N2 9LT
☎ (0181) 444 7678

3-bedroomed attractive traditional Norfolk flint cottage with log fire, in quiet village overlooking fields. Less than 2 miles from the sea and near the Broads.

---

1 self-contained unit; sleeping max 6

Price per week:	£min	£max
Low season	180.00	200.00
High season	200.00	285.00

LAVENHAM

Suffolk
Map ref 3B2

A former prosperous wool town of timber-framed buildings with the cathedral-like church and its tall tower. The market-place is 13th C and the Guildhall now houses a museum.

Bobbin Cottage

COMMENDED

74 High Street, Lavenham, Sudbury
Contact: Mrs G J Clerk, 6 Ropers Court, Lavenham, Sudbury, Suffolk CO10 9PU
☎ Lavenham (01787) 247998

Two-bedroomed cottage with living room, kitchen/diner, bathroom and lobby, leading to enclosed garden with furniture. Set in medieval village. Owner supervised.
1 self-contained unit; sleeping max 4

Price per week:	£min	£max
Low season	120.00	150.00
High season	175.00	210.00

Mews Cottage

COMMENDED

22a High Street, Lavenham, Sudbury
Contact: Mrs Judi Nunn, Brickwall House, 19 Pretoria Road, Halstead, Essex CO9 2EG
☎ Halstead 0378 437944
Delightful Victorian mews cottage in the centre of historic Lavenham. Exquisitely appointed for a restful holiday or peaceful weekend.
1 self-contained unit; sleeping 4

Price per week:	£min	£max
Low season	275.00	
High season	350.00	

Old Wetherden Hall ♏

COMMENDED

Hitcham, Ipswich IP7 7PZ
☎ Bildeston (01449) 740574
Contact: Mrs J Elsden
Recently restored 15th C oak-beamed moated hall, fully modernised. Beautiful secluded setting, large garden, abundance of wildlife.
1 self-contained unit; sleeping max 6

Price per week:	£min	£max
Low season	125.00	200.00
High season	200.00	320.00

LEIGHTON BUZZARD

Bedfordshire
Map ref 2C1

Large market town with many buildings of interest including a fine 15th C market cross, the 17th C Holly Lodge and a number of old inns. The Grand Union Canal is nearby and in Page's Park is a narrow gauge railway.

Foxglove Cottage

COMMENDED

12 High Street, Ivinghoe Aston, Leighton Buzzard
Contact: Mrs D Medlicott, Grove Farm, Ivinghoe Aston, Leighton Buzzard, Bedfordshire LU7 9DF
☎ Ivinghoe Aston (01525) 220631
One of 4 character cottages, the original buildings of the village. Of Brownlow design and built by the Ashridge Estate.
1 self-contained unit; sleeping max 4

Price per week:	£min	£max
Low season	200.00	240.00
High season	240.00	300.00

LITTLE SHELFORD

Cambridgeshire
Map ref 2D1

Little Shelford was developed by academics from nearby Cambridge during Victorian times and there are several old timber-framed buildings.

West Wing

HIGHLY COMMENDED

31 Newton Road, Little Shelford, Cambridge CB2 5HL
☎ Cambridge (01223) 842276
Contact: Mrs D Franklin
Self-contained, comfortable and well-appointed annexe. Bedroom, bathroom, sitting room, kitchen, garden, patio. Linen provided. Country location.

Min and max tariffs below refer to single/double occupancy.

1 self-contained unit; sleeping max 2

Price per week:	£min	£max
Low season	180.00	225.00
High season	180.00	225.00

🐎 10 ◎ 🏛 ⊙ 🗄 🖳 📺 🗄 🍳 🖳 ∥ 🚗 P ✿ ✕ SP

LONG MELFORD

Suffolk
Map ref 3B2

One of Suffolk's loveliest villages, remarkable for the length of its main street. Holy Trinity Church is considered to be the finest village church in England. The National Trust own the Elizabethan Melford Hall and nearby Kentwell Hall is also open to the public.

4 Church Walk
🔑🔑🔑 COMMENDED

Long Melford, Sudbury
Contact: Mr M A Thomas, 33 Patshull Road, Kentish Town, London NW5 2JX
☎ (0171) 2673653
A charming Victorian cottage built in 1838, Grade II listed building, overlooking the village green. Proceed north along A134 from Sudbury - Church Walk is on the left hand side between the Black Lion Hotel and Melford Church.
1 self-contained unit; sleeping 4

Price per week:	£min	£max
Low season	120.00	180.00
High season	180.00	220.00

🐎 ◎ 🌿 🏛 ⊙ 🗄 🖳 📺 🗄 🍳 🖳 🚗 ✕ 🐕 SP

LOWESTOFT

Suffolk
Map ref 3C1

Seaside town with wide sandy beaches. Important fishing port with picturesque fishing quarter. Home of the famous Lowestoft porcelain and birthplace of Benjamin Britten. East Point Pavilion's exhibition describes the Lowestoft story.
Tourist Information Centre ☎ (01502) 523000 or 523057

Kew Cottage
🔑🔑🔑 COMMENDED

44 Church Road, Kessingland, Lowestoft
Contact: Mrs J Gill, 46 St. Georges Avenue, Northampton NN2 6JA
☎ Northampton (01604) 717301 & Answering Machine 791424
Fax (01604) 791424
Modernised 2-bedroomed

---

semi-detached cottage in the middle of village, 10 minutes from the sea.
1 self-contained unit; sleeping max 4

Price per week:	£min	£max
Low season	130.00	
High season		200.00

🐎 ◎ 🏛 ⊙ 🗄 MW 🖳 📺 🍳 🖳 📱 🖳 🚗 ✿ ✕

LUDHAM

Norfolk
Map ref 3C1

Pleasant Broadland village with Womack Broad close by. The centre of the village has some very attractive Georgian houses and the church is outstanding.

Corner Cottage
🔑🔑🔑 APPROVED

Yarmouth Road, Ludham, Great Yarmouth
Contact: Mrs Ann Sparrow, Crown House, Ludham, Great Yarmouth, Norfolk NR29 5QE
☎ St Benets (01692) 678255
Picturesque thatched cottage with exposed beams in centre of delightful Broadland village. Convenient for the coast.
1 self-contained unit; sleeping 4–6

Price per week:	£min	£max
Low season	150.00	170.00
High season	180.00	260.00

🐎 ◎ 🏛 ⊙ 🗄 MW 🖳 📺 🍳 🖳 🚗 P U ✿ SP 🎋

MIDDLETON

Suffolk
Map ref 3C2

Thatched Barn, The Hayloft & Stable Cottage 🏍
🔑🔑🔑 🔑🔑🔑 HIGHLY COMMENDED

Rose Farm, Middleton, Saxmundham
Contact: Mrs Janet Maricic, Rose Farm, Middleton, Saxmundham, Suffolk IP17 3NG
☎ (01728) 648456 & (0585) 194945
On the edge of Middleton village, delightfully furnished and well-equipped converted thatched barn and stables. Close to Aldeburgh, Southwold and Snape. Wheelchair facilities. B&B also available.
3 self-contained units; sleeping 4–6

Price per week:	£min	£max
Low season	200.00	
High season		627.00

Open March–December

🐎 ◎ 🏛 ⊙ 🗄 MW 🖳 📺 🗄 🍳 🖳 📱 🚗 P ✿ ✕ 🎋

NAYLAND

Suffolk
Map ref 3B2

Charmingly located village on the River Stour owing its former prosperity to the cloth trade. The hub of the village is 15th C Alston Court. The altar-piece of St James Church was painted by John Constable.

Gladwins Farm 🏍
🔑🔑🔑 🔑🔑🔑 🔑🔑🔑

HIGHLY COMMENDED

Harpers Hill, Nayland CO6 4NU
☎ (01206) 262261
Fax (01206) 263001
Contact: Mr Robert Dossor

Tastefully converted 15th C timber-framed barn and stables adjacent to owners' farmhouse in rolling Constable countryside. Brochure on request. Heated indoor pool and sauna.
Wheelchair access category 2 ♿
7 self-contained units; sleeping 2–6

Price per week:	£min	£max
Low season	210.00	320.00
High season	390.00	690.00

Cards accepted: Access, Visa, Switch/Delta

🐎 M ◎ 🏛 ⊙ 🗄 MW 📺 🗄 🍳 🖳 📱 ∥ P 🎿 ⚲ U 🎣 🐟 ✿ 🐕 SP 🎋 T

NEWMARKET

Suffolk
Map ref 3B2

Centre of the English horse-racing world and the headquarters of the Jockey Club and National Stud. Racecourse and horse sales. The National Horse Racing Museum traces the history and development of the Sport of Kings.
Tourist Information Centre ☎ (01638) 667200

La Hogue Cottage

ꝑ ꝑ ꝑ ꝑ **DE LUXE**

Chippenham, Ely, Cambridgeshire
Contact: Mr & Mrs J M Tilbrook, La Hogue Hall, Chippenham, Ely, Cambridgeshire CB7 5PZ
☎ Newmarket (01638) 750433
Fax (01638) 712833
Renovated spacious farm cottage, close to many places of historic, scenic and sporting interest.
1 self-contained unit; sleeping max 6

Price per week:	£min	£max
Low season	360.00	425.00
High season	425.00	460.00

ꕔ ◎ ▥ ⊙ 🖵 MW 🗄 TV 🖥 🍴 (🖼 🖵)
✦ P U ✎ ✿ ✕ ⬟

NORFOLK BROADS

See under Clippesby, Hickling, Horning, Lowestoft, Ludham, North Walsham, Norwich, Salle, Sprowston, Stalham

NORTH WALSHAM

Norfolk
Map ref 3C1

Weekly market has been held here for 700 years. 1 mile south of town is a cross commemorating the Peasants' Revolt of 1381. Nelson attended the local Paston Grammar School, founded in 1606 and still flourishing.

The Wolery

ꝑ ꝑ ꝑ ꝑ **HIGHLY COMMENDED**

Bradfield Road, Swafield, North Walsham
Contact: Mr Michael Buckingham, Hill Fruit Farm, Swafield, North Walsham, Norfolk NR28 0PG
☎ North Walsham (01692) 403332
Fax (01692) 403332
Beautifully converted flint barn, ideal for elderly or disabled and families. Full CH, dishwasher, washing machine, tumble dryer. Spring and autumn breaks.

1 self-contained unit; sleeping max 8

Price per week:	£min	£max
Low season	200.00	250.00
High season	350.00	450.00

ꕔ ◎ ▥ ⊙ 🖵 MW TV 🖥 🍴 🔌 🖵 ✦ P
🔍 U ✎ ✿ **SP**

NORWICH

Norfolk
Map ref 3C1

Beautiful cathedral city and county town on the River Wensum with many fine museums and medieval churches. Norman castle, Guildhall and interesting medieval streets. Good shopping centre and market.
Tourist Information Centre ☎ (01603) 666071

Norwich Breaks

ꝑ ꝑ ꝑ ꝑ
HIGHLY COMMENDED

Polly's Cottage, Duke Street, Norwich
Contact: Mr Desmond Wain, Norwich Breaks, 22 Christchurch Road, Norwich, Norfolk NR2 2AE
☎ (01603) 453363
Fax (01603) 259729

A sanctuary in the city centre, near cathedral. Character 2-bedroomed cottage in quiet courtyard. Warm in winter with full central heating, well equipped and attractively furnished. Private parking and telephone. Short breaks. Similar cottages available - ask for colour brochure.
5 self-contained units; sleeping 3–5

Price per week:	£min	£max
Low season	200.00	250.00
High season	260.00	320.00

Cards accepted: Access, Visa, Amex
ꕔ ◎ ▥ ⊙ 🖵 TV 🖥 🍴 (🖼 🖵) ✦ P ✿
✕ **SP** ⊞

Watersides

ꝑ ꝑ ꝑ ꝑ **HIGHLY COMMENDED**

1 Bridge Court, Fishergate, Norwich
Contact: Mrs M E Cockerill, Bush Group, 1 Bridge Court, Fishergate, Norwich, Norfolk NR3 1UF
☎ Norwich (01603) 760255 & 614004
Fax (01603) 761276
2-bedroomed holiday homes with river frontage, near city centre. TV and video,

private parking. Personal supervision. Self-contained flat of similar standard also available.
3 self-contained units; sleeping max 6

Price per week:	£min	£max
Low season	200.00	230.00
High season	230.00	360.00

ꕔ ◎ ▥ ⊙ 🖵 MW TV 🖥 🍴 (🖼 🖵) ✎
✦ P ✎ ✿ **SP**

ORFORD

Suffolk
Map ref 3C2

Once a thriving port, now a quiet village of brick and timber buildings, famous for its castle. Orford comes to life during the summer when boats tie up at the quay.

Daphne Road 41

ꝑ ꝑ ꝑ **COMMENDED**

Orford, Woodbridge
Contact: Mrs Phyllida Flint, Green Lane House, Castle Green, Orford, Woodbridge, Suffolk IP12 2NF
☎ Orford (01394) 450159
Fax (01394) 450827
Very comfortable end of terrace cottage, in village, convenient for a wide variety of local attractions. Open fire and central heating, lovely enclosed garden.
1 self-contained unit; sleeping max 4

Price per week:	£min	£max
Low season	235.00	295.00
High season	340.00	380.00

ꕔ ◎ ▥ ⊙ 🖵 MW 🗄 TV 🖥 🍴 🖵
✦ ⌐ ✿ **SP**

Vesta Cottage

ꝑ ꝑ ꝑ **COMMENDED**

73 Broad Street, Orford, Woodbridge
Contact: Mrs Penny Kay, 74 Broad Street, Orford, Woodbridge, Suffolk IP12 2NP
☎ Woodbridge (01394) 450652
Fax (01394) 450097
Attractive 2 bedroom (double and double-bunk) cottage with garden. Next to medieval friary, near Orford Castle and Quay. Suit sailors, bird-watchers, walkers, etc.
1 self-contained unit; sleeping max 4

Price per week:	£min	£max
Low season	201.00	251.00
High season	293.00	329.00

ꕔ ◎ ▥ ⊙ 🖵 MW 🗄 TV 🖥 🍴 (🖼 🖼
✦ P ✿ ✕ **SP** ⊞

PETERBOROUGH

Cambridgeshire
Map ref 3A1

Prosperous and rapidly expanding cathedral city on the edge of the Fens on the River Nene. Catherine of Aragon is buried in the cathedral. City Museum and Art Gallery. Ferry Meadows Country Park has numerous leisure facilities.
Tourist Information Centre ☎ (01733) 317336

Orchard Cottage
COMMENDED

15 Thorpe Road, Peterborough
Contact: Mrs M Catnach, Orchard Cottage, 15 Thorpe Road, Peterborough PE3 6AB
☎ Peterborough (01733) 65827
Small, detached cottage, well furnished and equipped, in 1 acre garden of Georgian house. Within 5 minutes of main line trains to London, coach station and city centre.
1 self-contained unit; sleeping max 4

Price per week:	£min	£max
Low season	110.00	145.00
High season	110.00	145.00

POLSTEAD

Suffolk
Map ref 3B2

Broom Cottage
APPROVED

C/O Cherrytree Farm, Martens Lane, Polstead, Colchester
Contact: Mrs J S Coulson, Cherrytree Farm, Martens Lane, Polstead, Colchester CO6 5AQ
☎ Nayland (01206) 262387
Large, isolated timber bungalow, set in 34 acres of conservation farm.
1 self-contained unit; sleeping max 6

Price per week:	£min	£max
Low season	100.00	150.00
High season	200.00	

RINGSTEAD

Norfolk
Map ref 3B1

Tumblers and Pickles Patch
HIGHLY COMMENDED

Sedgeford Road Farm, Ringstead, Hunstanton PE36 5JZ
☎ Holme (01485) 525316 & 525530
Contact: Mrs M Greer
Dwellings are converted, ground floor

barns, with original beams, close to Peddars Way, golf-courses, and birdwatching areas. Three miles from coast.
2 self-contained units; sleeping 4–6

Price per week:	£min	£max
Low season	270.00	350.00
High season	350.00	510.00

SAFFRON WALDEN

Essex
Map ref 2D1

Takes its name from the saffron crocus once grown around the town. The church of St Mary has superb carvings, magnificent roofs and brasses. A town maze can be seen on the common. Two miles south-west is Audley End, a magnificent Jacobean mansion owned by English Heritage.
Tourist Information Centre ☎ (01799) 510444

Barn Cottage
APPROVED

Ducketts Farm, Debden Green, Saffron Walden
Contact: Mrs P Winter, Ducketts Farm, Debden Green, Saffron Walden, Essex CB11 3LZ
☎ Thaxted (01371) 830340
Fax (01371) 831440
Small cottage, part of an old Essex barn, very close to historic Thaxted and Saffron Walden. November-April prices include night-storage heating.
1 self-contained unit; sleeping max 4

Price per week:	£min	£max
Low season	140.00	
High season		160.00

22 Fairycroft Road
COMMENDED

Saffron Walden
Contact: Mrs D Helme, Newlands Cottage, Widdington, Saffron Walden, Essex CB11 3SN
☎ Saffron Walden (01799) 540627
Three-bedroomed, semi-detached cottage with own garden in town centre.
1 self-contained unit; sleeping 5

Price per week:	£min	£max
Low season	175.00	185.00
High season	185.00	200.00

The Stables
HIGHLY COMMENDED

Deynes Farm, Debden, Saffron Walden CB11 3LG
☎ (01799) 540128
Contact: Mrs P Swan
150-acre farm. 18th C stables, recently converted but retaining character, on working farm. Large pond with wildlife nearby. Lovely country setting in pretty village.
2 self-contained units; sleeping max 3

Price per week:	£min	£max
Low season	100.00	140.00
High season	150.00	180.00

SALLE

Norfolk
Map ref 3B1

Pronounced "Saul" and famous for the magnificent 15th C church of SS Peter and Paul which is considered to be the finest in the county.

Coachman's Cottage
COMMENDED

Salle Place, Salle, Norwich NR10 5SF
☎ Norwich (01603) 870638
Fax (01603) 872021
Contact: Mrs S R Marshall
Small, typical Norfolk coachman's cottage, in lovely grounds with orchard, wood, lawns, stream and half moat. Wood-burning stove. Heating by night storage heaters. Ideal holiday accommodation.
1 self-contained unit; sleeping max 4

Price per week:	£min	£max
Low season	100.00	150.00
High season	160.00	220.00

Establishments should be open throughout the year, unless otherwise stated.

National gradings and classifications were correct at the time of going to press but are subject to change. Please check at the time of booking.

SANDRINGHAM

Norfolk
Map ref 3B1

Famous as the country retreat of Her Majesty the Queen. The house and grounds are open to the public at certain times.

Folk on the Hill

🔑 🔑 🔑 🔑 DE LUXE

Mill Road, Dersingham, King's Lynn
Contact: Mrs Susan Stevens, Mill Cottage, Mill Road, Dersingham, King's Lynn, Norfolk PE31 6HY
☎ Dersingham (01485) 544411

"Seek peace and pursue it." – Psalm 34:14. By Sandringham, amidst picturesque countryside and with distant sea views, an 18th C barn and stables. Games room, lawned gardens. Children are a focus. Short breaks available.
1 self-contained unit; sleeping 6–7

Price per week:	£min	£max
Low season	285.00	475.00
High season	475.00	550.00

🔖 Ⓜ ◎ ▥ ☉ 🗄 MW 📕 TV 🔅 🔌 📟
🗃 ∥ 🚗 P ℠ U↑ ❀ 🎏 T

SAXMUNDHAM

Suffolk
Map ref 3C2

The church of St John the Baptist has a hammer-beam roof and contains a number of good monuments.

The Granary

🔑 🔑 🔑 COMMENDED

High House Farm, Fristonmoor Lane, Saxmundham IP17 1XD
☎ (01728) 603030
Contact: Mrs S Rawstron
Part of recently restored 16th C farmhouse complex, commended in national conservation awards. Granary has original partitions.
1 self-contained unit; sleeping max 4

Price per week:	£min	£max
Low season	120.00	140.00
High season	160.00	200.00

🔖 ◎ ▥ ☉ 🗄 TV 🔅 🔌 🗃 🚗 P ❀ 🎏

Harvey's Mill

🔑 🔑 COMMENDED

Hill Crest, Main Road, Kelsale, Saxmundham IP17 2RD
☎ (01728) 603212
Contact: Mrs Susan Smith
Delightfully converted windmill providing a high standard of holiday accommodation. Open plan circular ground floor with spiral staircase leading to galleried bedroom. Private garden. Children and pets welcome.
1 self-contained unit; sleeping max 4

Price per week:	£min	£max
Low season	125.00	150.00
High season	200.00	200.00

🔖 Ⓜ ◎ ▥ ☉ 🗄 MW 📕 TV 🔅 🔌
🚗 P ❀ SP 🎏

Snape Maltings Riverside Arts & Activities Centre ⚑

🔑 🔑 COMMENDED

Snape, Saxmundham IP17 1SR
☎ Snape (01728) 688303 & 688304
Fax (01728) 688930
Contact: Mrs G E Gooderham
Victorian maltings on the heritage coast includes a variety of shops, restaurants, world renowned concert hall and 3 tastefully converted cottages.
3 self-contained units; sleeping 2–8

Price per week:	£min	£max
Low season	180.00	290.00
High season	250.00	390.00

Cards accepted: Access, Visa

🔖 ◎ ▥ ☉ 🗄 TV 🔅 🔌 ∥ 🚗 P U
SP 🎏

SHERINGHAM

Norfolk
Map ref 3B1

Holiday resort with Victorian and Edwardian hotels and a sand and shingle beach where the fishing boats are hauled up. The North Norfolk Railway operates from Sheringham station during the summer. Other attractions include museums, theatre and Splash Fun Pool.

Fisherman's Cottage

🔑 🔑 🔑 COMMENDED

1 Barchams Yard, Sheringham
Contact: Mrs B Bennett, 35 Sandilands Road, London SW6 2BZ
☎ (0171) 381 0771

Attractive 200-year-old flint cottage a few yards from the beach in the centre of Sheringham. Furnished to a high standard and with all modern conveniences. Housekeeper will babysit. Pets welcome.
1 self-contained unit; sleeping max 7

Price per week:	£min	£max
Low season	213.00	255.00
High season	272.00	376.00

🔖 ◎ ▥ ☉ 🗄 MW 📕 TV 🔅 🔌 📟
P U↑ ❀ 🚭 SP 🎏

Pebbles

🔑 🔑 🔑 COMMENDED

Flat 2, 9 Westcliff, Sheringham
Contact: Mrs Ann Pope, Ivy Farmhouse, Cranfield Road, Upper Sheringham, Sheringham, Norfolk NR26 8TH
☎ Sheringham (01263) 823471
Ground floor flat with seafront promenade walk from the doorstep. Enjoys excellent sea views. Parking in grounds.
1 self-contained unit; sleeping max 4

Price per week:	£min	£max
Low season	120.00	160.00
High season	160.00	280.00

🔖 Ⓜ ◎ ▥ ☉ 🗄 TV 🔅 🔌 📟 🚗 P ❀
🚭 SP

SNETTISHAM

Norfolk
Map ref 3B1

Village with a superb Decorated church. The 17th C Old Hall is a distinguished-looking house with Dutch gables over the 2 bays. Snettisham Pits is a reserve of the Royal Society for the Protection of Birds. Red deer herd and other animals, farm trails and nature walks at Park Farm.

Cobbe Court

🔑 🔑 🔑 COMMENDED

Snettisham House, Snettisham PE31 7RZ
☎ Dersingham (01485) 543986
Contact: Mr & Mrs James Douglas
Small self-contained cottage for two, including linen and electricity. Parking for 1 car. Microwave oven, electric cooker, fridge.
1 self-contained unit; sleeping 2

Price per week:	£min	£max
Low season	110.00	130.00
High season	140.00	180.00

🔖 ◎ ▥ ☉ 🗄 MW TV 🔅 🔌 📟 🚗 P 🎏

SOUTH MIMMS

Hertfordshire
Map ref 2D1

Best known today for its location at the junction of the M25 and the A1M.
Tourist Information Centre ☎ *(01707) 643233*

The Black Swan

 UP TO COMMENDED

62-64 Blanche Lane, South Mimms, Potters Bar EN6 3PD
☎ Potters Bar (01707) 644180
Contact: Mr W A Marsterson
Cottage and self-contained flats, 16th C listed building. Rail connections at Potters Bar and London Underground at Barnet allow travel to London within 45 minutes.
3 self-contained units; sleeping 2–6

Price per week:	£min	£max
Low season	120.00	180.00
High season	160.00	265.00

🏃♿◎🛏⊙🍴📺 🗄🍳♨P❄ SP 🏠 T

SOUTHWOLD

Suffolk
Map ref 3C2

Pleasant and attractive seaside town with a triangular market square and spacious greens around which stand flint, brick and colour-washed cottages. The parish church of St Edmund is one of the greatest churches in Suffolk.

The Cottage

🔑 🔑 🔑 COMMENDED

11 Elms Lane, Wangford, Beccles
Contact: Mr T Thomas, 28 Lakeside Park Drive, Reydon, Southwold, Suffolk IP18 6YB
☎ Southwold (01502) 723561
Lounge/diner, 1 twin and 1 single bedroom, bathroom, cloakroom, radio and TV. Fully-fitted kitchen with washer/dryer, fridge, freezer and microwave.
1 self-contained unit; sleeping max 6

Price per week:	£min	£max
Low season	145.00	185.00
High season	175.00	225.00

🏃5🔒P✈

SPROWSTON

Norfolk
Map ref 3C1

Holme

🔑 🔑 🔑 APPROVED

3 Recreation Ground Road, Sprowston, Norwich
Contact: Mr H R High, 43 Lowry Cole Road, Sprowston, Norwich NR6 7QT
☎ Norwich (01603) 429517 & 412544
Traditional, 2-bedroomed detached bungalow, 2 miles north of Norwich, 6 miles from the Broads. Enclosed rear garden. All services close by.
1 self-contained unit; sleeping max 4

Price per week:	£min	£max
Low season	110.00	130.00
High season	130.00	170.00

🏃8 M ✏🍳⊙🛏🍴📺🗄🍳🕹🚗 P❄✈ SP

STALHAM

Norfolk
Map ref 3C1

Lies on the edge of the Broads.

144 Broadside Chalet Park

🔑 🔑 APPROVED

Stalham, Norwich
Contact: Mr J Crawford, 5 Collingwood Avenue, Surbiton, Surrey KT5 9PT
☎ (0181) 241 0658
Fax (0181) 241 0658
South-facing, detached chalet on landscaped park, with pleasant lawns for quiet relaxation or where children may play safely. Swimming pool, licensed club and shop. 4 miles from environmentally clean sandy beach. Boat hire and fishing nearby.
1 self-contained unit; sleeping 5

Price per week:	£min	£max
Low season	60.00	110.00
High season	75.00	199.00

Open April–October

🏃🐕 M ◎🍳⊙🛏🍴📺🗄🏊♨ 🚲🎣❄ SP

STIFFKEY

Norfolk
Map ref 3B1

A brick and flint village on the edge of the marshes, famous for cockles.

Primrose Cottage

🔑 🔑 COMMENDED

18 Church Street, Stiffkey, Wells-next-the-Sea
Contact: Mr N Fell, 40 Church Street, Fordham, Ely, Cambridgeshire CB7 5NJ
☎ Newmarket (01638) 721248
Attractive, well presented period cottage, all rooms south-facing. Two bedrooms/bathrooms. Lovely sheltered and secluded situation with good views.
1 self-contained unit; sleeping 4

Price per week:	£min	£max
Low season	125.00	195.00
High season	215.00	395.00

🏃7 M ◎🍳⊙🛏 MW 📺🗄🍳🕹 ♨P❄✈ SP 🏠

STOWLANGTOFT

Suffolk
Map ref 3B2

The Rectory Flat

🔑 🔑 🔑 HIGHLY COMMENDED

Stowlangtoft, Bury St Edmunds
Contact: Mrs J P Godfrey, The Old Rectory, Stowlangloft, Bury St Edmunds, Suffolk IP28
☎ Pakenham (01359) 230857 & Beyton 270536
Fax (01359) 271225

Grade II listed building of exceptional standard. Tranquil garden with tennis and pool. Twin bedroom, bathroom and shower. Fully equipped kitchen, lounge, TV. Superb centre for touring.
1 self-contained unit; sleeping max 2

Price per week:	£min	£max
Low season	95.00	115.00
High season	115.00	230.00

◎🍳⊙🛏📺🗄🍳🕹♨P🎣⚲❄ ✈ SP 🏠

SUDBURY

Suffolk
Map ref 3B2

Former important cloth and market town on the River Stour. Birthplace of Thomas Gainsborough whose home is now an art gallery and museum. The Corn Exchange is an excellent example of early Victorian civic building.
Tourist Information Centre ☎ (01787) 881320

Putts
🔑🔑 COMMENDED

Gt Hickbush, Gt Henny, Sudbury
Contact: Mr & Mrs T E Humphreys, Howe House, Gt Hickbush, Gt Henny, Sudbury, Suffolk CO10 7LU
☎ Twinstead (01787) 269507
Listed 17th C beamed cottage in secluded position in beautiful countryside. Open fire, tastefully furnished and well equipped. Short breaks available.
1 self-contained unit; sleeping max 4

Price per week:	£min	£max
Low season	175.00	200.00
High season	200.00	250.00

🛇7🗲🖬⊙🗒MW▯▱TV🗗🗖🗐🗒🖵
♠P🌣🗡SP🎏

THEBERTON

Suffolk
Map ref 3C2

Orchids Holiday Homes
🔑🔑 COMMENDED

Cakes & Ale Park, Abbey Lane, Theberton, Leiston IP16 4TE
☎ Leiston (01728) 831655
Fax (01473) 736270
Contact: Hilda & Scott Scott
Enjoying private corner location in tranquil grounds of Cakes & Ale Caravan Park, ideal for Minsmere, Dunwich, Aldeburgh and Southwold. Lounge bar, tennis, play areas. Cycling and bird watching.
3 self-contained units; sleeping 2–5

Price per week:	£min	£max
Low season	145.00	240.00
High season	145.00	280.00

Open April–October
🛇🕭🖬⊙🗒MW▯▱TV🗗🗖🗐🖵
♠P🌣🗡SP

The 🅜 symbol after an establishment name indicates that it is a Regional Tourist Board member.

THORNHAM

Norfolk
Map ref 3B1

Oyster Cottage
🔑🔑 COMMENDED

Main Road, Thornham, Hunstanton
Contact: Mrs G Tibbs, Cole Green Cottage, Sedgeford, Hunstanton, Norfolk PE36 5LS
☎ Heacham (01485) 571770 & Royston (Weekdays only) (01763) 208355
Fax (01485) 571770
Traditional period flint and brick cottage, renovated to provide comfortable accommodation. Situated in charming coastal conservation village.
1 self-contained unit; sleeping max 5

Price per week:	£min	£max
Low season	120.00	150.00
High season	175.00	250.00

🛇🅜🖬⊙🗒MW TV🗗🗖🗐🖵U
▶🌣🗡SP🎏

1 West End Cottages

Main Road, Thornham, Hunstanton
Contact: Mrs L K Rigby, 1 West End Cottages, 2 Carlton Court, Castor, Peterborough PE5 7DB
☎ Peterborough (01733) 380399
Small, cosy, terraced cottage, fitted carpets, central heating and open fire. Situated in coastal village. Pretty garden and close to nature reserves.
1 self-contained unit; sleeping max 4

Price per week:	£min	£max
Low season	110.00	150.00
High season	160.00	175.00

🛇🅜🕭🖬⊙🗒▯▱TV🗗🗖♠P
🐾🗡SP

THORPENESS

Suffolk
Map ref 3C2

A planned mock-Tudor seaside resort, built in the early 20th C, with a 65-acre artificial lake. "The House in the Clouds" was built to disguise a water-tower. The windmill contains an exhibition on Suffolk's heritage coast.

The House in the Clouds 🅜
🔑🔑🔑🔑 COMMENDED

The Uplands, Thorpeness, Leiston
Contact: Mrs S Le Comber, 18 Chargrove Close, Marlow Landings, Surrey Quays, London SE16 1AP
☎ (0171) 2520743 & Mobile 0850 851203

Unique, internationally famous "fantasy", unmatched in England, with unrivalled views out to sea and across rolling Suffolk countryside and golf-course.
1 self-contained unit; sleeping max 12

Price per week:	£min	£max
Low season	630.00	800.00
High season	800.00	1300.00

🛇🕭🖬⊙🗒MW▯▱TV🗗🗖🗐
♠P🐾▶🌣🎏

WALSHAM-LE-WILLOWS

Suffolk
Map ref 3B2

Bridge Cottage 🅜
🔑🔑🔑 APPROVED

Grove Road, Walsham-le-Willows, Bury St Edmunds
Contact: Mrs H M Russell, The Beeches, Walsham-le-Willows, Bury St Edmunds, Suffolk IP31 3AD
☎ Walsham-le-Willows (01359) 259227
Fax (01359) 258206

Fully modernised 17th C cottage set in pretty Suffolk village with good shops and pubs. 11 miles north east of Bury St Edmunds.
1 self-contained unit; sleeping 1–5

Price per week:	£min	£max
Low season	180.00	220.00
High season	220.00	250.00

🛇🕭🖬⊙🗒TV🗖🗐🖵♠🛪🗡🔍🌣

TOWN INDEX

This can be found at the back of the guide. If you know where you want to stay, the index will give you the page number listing all accommodation in your chosen town, city or village.

WEST MERSEA

Essex
Map ref 3B3

Weatherboarded and Georgian brick cottages still remain as evidence of the old fishing, oyster and sailing centre and the small museum includes fishing exhibits.

22 Orchid Field Court
Victoria Esplanade, West Mersea, Colchester
Contact: Mrs R Mason, 69 Empress Avenue, West Mersea, Colchester CO5 8BL
☎ Colchester (01206) 382724
Fax (01206) 382724
The flat is only 100 metres from the sea. Facilities include central heating, bathroom with shower, kitchen with dishwasher, refrigerator, washer-dryer and electric cooker.
1 self-contained unit; sleeping max 4

Price per week:	£min	£max
Low season	180.00	200.00
High season	250.00	280.00

Open February–November

WEST RUDHAM

Norfolk
Map ref 3B1

North, South, Bertie's and Sid's Cottages
UP TO COMMENDED
The Grange, West Rudham, King's Lynn PE31 8SY
☎ East Rudham (01485) 528229 & 0860 733766
Fax (01485) 528229
Contact: Mrs A Ringer
Traditional flint cottages, comfortably furnished, in quiet surroundings, 1.5 miles from the village. Bertie's is on edge of village with small garden. Sid's is semi-detached with no enclosed garden and is not suitable for pets.

4 self-contained units; sleeping 4–8

Price per week:	£min	£max
Low season	120.00	300.00
High season	180.00	400.00

WINTERTON-ON-SEA

Norfolk
Map ref 3C1

Transacre Ltd
HIGHLY COMMENDED
Burnley Hall, East Somerton, Great Yarmouth NR29 4DZ
☎ Winterton (01493) 393206
Fax (01493) 393745
Contact: Mrs P Beard
3000-acre mixed & arable farm. Idyllic thatched cottages with gardens on farming estate. Private beach, nature reserve. Near Norfolk Broads. Bicycles and stabling available.
4 self-contained units; sleeping 4–10

Price per week:	£min	£max
Low season	200.00	275.00
High season	295.00	400.00

For ideas on places to visit refer to the introduction at the beginning of this section.

National gradings and classifications were correct at the time of going to press but are subject to change. Please check at the time of booking.

WISBECH

Cambridgeshire
Map ref 3A1

The town is the centre of the agricultural and flower-growing industries of Fenland. Peckover House (National Trust) is an important example of domestic architecture.
Tourist Information Centre ☎ *(01945) 583263*

Carysfort
HIGHLY COMMENDED
Stratton Farm, West Drove North, Walton Highway, Wisbech
Contact: Mrs Sue King, Stratton Farm, West Drove North, Walton Highway, Wisbech, Cambridgeshire PE14 7DP
☎ Wisbech (01945) 880162
Spacious, very well equipped cottage on peaceful farm. 2 en-suite bedrooms. Private garden. Suitable for wheelchair users. Heated swimming pool and carp lake. Smoking not allowed.
1 self-contained unit; sleeping max 4

Price per week:	£min	£max
Low season	195.00	
High season		400.00

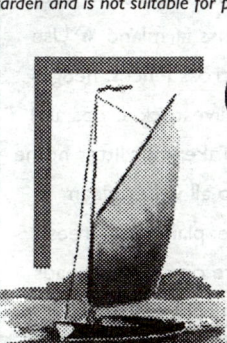

COUNTRY CODE

Always follow the Country Code

Enjoy the countryside and respect its life and work Guard against all risk of fire Fasten all gates Keep your dogs under close control Keep to public paths across farmland Use gates and stiles to cross fences, hedges and walls Leave livestock, crops and machinery alone Take your litter home Help to keep all water clean Protect wildlife, plants and trees Take special care on country roads Make no unnecessary noise

WEST COUNTRY

The West Country is famous for its wildness and beauty, legends and magic... but mostly for the breathtaking variety of its scenery.

From titanic cliffs overlooking sparkling beaches to the vastness of Dartmoor and Exmoor, then on to cosy villages nestling in verdant countryside, this most compelling of regions has inspired generations of writers and artists.

Tintagel Castle, traditionally the home of King Arthur, stares out to sea from the rugged North Cornwall coast. Stonehenge stands silent. Maritime Plymouth waits to welcome its next tide of visitors while elegant Bath and lively Salisbury bustle with life in this land of many mysteries.

FOR MORE INFORMATION CONTACT:
West Country Tourist Board
60 St Davids Hill, Exeter EX4 4SY
Tel: (01392) 425426 **Fax:** (01392) 420891

Where to Go in the West Country -
see pages 198-202
Where to Stay in the West Country -
see pages 203-246

WEST COUNTRY

Where to Go and What to See

You will find hundreds of interesting places to visit during your stay in the West Country, just some of which are listed in these pages. The number against each name will help you locate it on the map (pages 200-201). Contact any Tourist Information Centre in the region for more ideas on days out in the West Country.

1 Great Western Railway Museum
Faringdon Road, Swindon,
Wiltshire SN1 5BJ
Tel: (01793) 493189
Historic Great Western Railway locomotives, wide range of nameplates, models, illustrations, posters and tickets.

2 Dyrham Park
Dyrham,
Chippenham,
Wiltshire SN14 8ER
Tel: (0117) 937 2501
Mansion built between 1691 and 1710 for William Blathwayt. Rooms have been little changed. A herd of deer roams the 263-acre parkland.

3 Bristol Zoo Gardens
Clifton, Bristol BS8 3HA
Tel: (0117) 973 8951
Set in beautiful gardens, the zoo provides a haven for some of the world's most endangered wildlife. Plenty of activities and special events throughout the year.

4 The Exploratory Hands-on Science Centre
Bristol Old Station,
Temple Meads,
Bristol BS1 6QU
Tel: (0117) 925 2008
Exhibition of lights, lenses, lasers, bubbles, bridges, illusions, gyroscopes and much more all housed in Brunel's original engine shed and drawing office.

5 Harveys Wine Museum
12 Denmark Street,
Bristol BS1 5DQ
Tel: (0117) 927 5036
Wine museum in original 13thC cellars displaying artefacts connected with production and enjoyment of wines, especially glass, silver and corkscrews.

6 Bowood House and Gardens
Bowood Estate,
Calne, Wiltshire SN11 0LZ
Tel: (01249) 812102
18thC house by Robert Adam, collections of paintings, watercolours,

Victoriana, Indiana and porcelain. Landscaped park with lake, terraces, waterfall and grottos.

7 Weston-super-Mare Sea Life Centre
Marine Parade,
Weston-super-Mare,
North Somerset BS23 1BE
Tel: (01934) 641603
All aspects of British marine life housed on Britain's first pier for 85 years.

8 Museum of Costume
Assembly Rooms, Bennett Street,
Bath BA1 2QH
Tel: (01225) 477789
Designed by John Wood the Younger in 1769. One of Bath's finest Georgian buildings. Museum of Costume housed in basement.

9 Cheddar Showcaves and Gorge
Cheddar, Somerset BS27 3QF
Tel: (01934) 742343
Beautiful caves located in Cheddar

Gorge. Gough's Cave with its cathedral-like caverns and Cox's Cave with stalagmites and stalactites. Also "The Crystal Quest" fantasy adventure.

10 Secret World
New Road Farm, East Huntspill, Highbridge, Somerset TA9 3PZ
Tel: (01278) 783250
300-year-old farm, many breeds of animals including rare breeds. Old and modern farm machinery on display. Play areas, gardens. Somerset Levels Visitor Centre.

11 Wookey Hole Caves and Papermill
Wookey Hole,
Wells,
Somerset BA5 1BB
Tel: (01749) 672243
Spectacular caves and legendary home of the Witch of Wookey. Working Victorian papermill including Fairground Memories, Old Penny Arcade, Magical Mirror Maze and Cave Diving Museum.

12 Longleat
Warminster,
Wiltshire BA12 7NW
Tel: (01985) 844400
Great Elizabethan house with lived-in atmosphere. Important libraries and Italian ceilings. Capability Brown designed parkland. Safari Park.

13 Stourhead House and Garden
Stourton, Warminster,
Wiltshire BA12 6QH
Tel: (01747) 840348
Landscaped garden laid out in 1741-80, with lakes and temples, rare trees and plants. House begun in 1721 by Colen Campbell contains fine paintings and Chippendale furniture.

14 Wilton House
Wilton, Wiltshire SP2 0BJ
Tel: (01722) 743115
Home of the Earls of Pembroke for nearly 450 years. Famous Double and Single Cube rooms. Art collection. Adventure playground. Woodland walk. Wareham Bears.

15 Salisbury and South Wiltshire Museum
The King's House, 65 The Close, Salisbury, Wiltshire SP1 2EN
Tel: (01722) 332151
Grade 1 listed building. Stonehenge collection, Salisbury Giant, Early man. History of Old Sarum, Salisbury, Romans to Saxons, ceramics, Wedgwood, pictures, costume exhibitions.

16 West Somerset Railway
The Railway Station, Minehead, Somerset TA24 5BG
Tel: (01643) 704996
Preserved steam railway operating between Minehead and Bishops Lydeard, near Taunton. Longest independent railway in Britain (20 miles).

17 Clovelly Village
Clovelly, Bideford,
Devon EX39 5SY
Tel: (01237) 431200
Unspoilt fishing village on North Devon coast with steep cobbled street and no vehicular access. Donkeys and sledges only means of transport. Visitor centre.

18 Dartington Crystal
Linden Close, Torrington,
Devon EX38 7AN
Tel: (01805) 622321
Manufacture of hand-made crystal table glassware by skilled craftsmen. Glass centre and glassware exhibition. Visitors can watch glass blowers "hand blowing" glassware.

19 Rosemoor Garden - Royal Horticultural Society's Garden
Rosemoor, Great Torrington,
Devon EX38 8PH
Tel: (01805) 624067
Garden of rare horticultural interest. Trees, shrubs, roses, alpines and arboretum. Nursery of uncommon and rare plants. 8 acres being expanded to 40 acres.

20 Haynes Motor Museum

Sparkford, Yeovil,
Somerset BA22 7LH
Tel: (01963) 440804
Motor vehicles and memorobilia covering the years from the turn of the century to the present day. Video cinema, exhibition track.

21 Montacute House

Montacute, Yeovil,
Somerset TA15 6XP
Tel: (01935) 823289
Late 16thC house built of local golden Ham stone, by Sir Edward Phelips. The Long Gallery houses a collection of Tudor and Jacobean portraits. Formal gardens and park.

22 Sherborne Castle

Sherborne, Dorset
Tel: (01935) 813182
Built by Sir Walter Raleigh in 1594 to replace the old castle. The Elizabethan Hall and Jacobean Oak Room show two of the many styles of architecture.

24 The Dinosaur Museum

Icen Way,
Dorchester,
Dorset DT1 1EW
Tel: (01305) 269880
Only museum in Britain devoted exclusively to dinosaurs. Fossils, actual-size dinosaur reconstructions, audio-visual, "hands on". Video gallery and computerised displays.

26 Weymouth Sea Life Park

Lodmoor Country Park,
Weymouth, Dorset DT4 7SX
Tel: (01305) 761070
Spectacular displays of British marine life where visitors come face to face with a wide variety of creatures. Also an exciting tropical jungle full of birds.

23 Athelhampton House and Gardens

Athelhampton, Dorset DT2 7LG
Tel: (01305) 848363
Legendary site of King Athelstan's Palace. Family home for five centuries. Fine example of 15thC architecture. Gardens with fountains, pools and waterfalls.

25 Brewers' Quay and Timewalk

Hope Square, Weymouth,
Dorset DT4 8TR
Tel: (01305) 777622
Former brewery now housing The Timewalk, depicting 600 years of Weymouth's history, also The Brewer's Tale exhibition and shopping village with restaurants.

27 Abbotsbury Swannery

New Barn Road, Abbotsbury
Weymouth, Dorset DT3 4JG
Tel: (01305) 871684
The only place in the world where over 600 swans can be visited during the nesting and hatching time (end May-end June). Audio-visual presentation. Ugly duckling trail.

The map shows the South West region of England with numbered locations:

GLOUCESTERSHIRE

SOUTH GLOUCESTERSHIRE

OXFORDSHIRE

BERKSHIRE

WILTSHIRE

HAMPSHIRE

NORTH SOMERSET

BRISTOL

BATH & NORTH EAST SOMERSET

SOMERSET

DORSET (western)

DORSET (eastern)

ISLE OF WIGHT

Towns and locations marked on map:
Portishead, Chipping Sodbury, Malmesbury, Wootton Bassett, Swindon [1], Chippenham [2], Calne [6], Avebury, Kingswood, Western-super-Mare [7], Bristol [3][4][5], Bath [8], Lacock, Banwell, Bradford on Bradford on Avon, Devizes, Burnham-on-Sea, Cheddar [9], Midsomer, Rode, Trowbridge, Wookey Hole [11], Frome, Highbridge [10], Norton Wells, Shepton Mallet, Warminster [12], Amesbury, Bridgwater, Stourton [13], Wilton [14], Taunton, Wincanton, Salisbury [15], Wellington, Yeovil, Sherborne [22], Ilminster [20][21], Crewkerne, Honiton, Beaminster, Athelhampton, Axminster, Bridport, Kingston Maurward [23], Ottery St Mary, Seaton, Lyme Regis, Dorchester [24], Sidmouth, Abbotsbury [27], Weymouth [25][26], Fortuneswell

0 ____ 20 Miles
0 ____ 30 Kms

---

28 Killerton House
Broadclyst, Exeter,
Devon EX5 3LE
Tel: (01392) 881345
18thC house built for the Acland family. Now houses a collection of costumes shown in various room settings. 15 acres of hillside garden with rare trees and shrubs.

29 Babbacombe Model Village
Hampton Avenue, Babbacombe,
Torquay, Devon TQ1 3LA
Tel: (01803) 328669
Hundreds of models and figures laid out in 4 acres of beautiful gardens to represent a model English countryside with modern town, villages and rural areas. Scale to 1/12th.

30 Woodlands Leisure Park
Blackawton, Totnes,
Devon TQ9 7DQ
Tel: (01803) 712598
A full day of variety set in 60 acres of countryside. 12 venture playzones including 500-metre toboggan run, commando course. 34000 sq ft indoor play area, toddlers' areas and animals.

31 Plymouth Dome
The Hoe, Plymouth,
Devon PL1 2NZ
Tel: (01752) 603300
Purpose-built visitor interpretation centre showing the history of Plymouth and its people from Stone Age beginnings to satellite technology. Situated on Plymouth Hoe.

32 Cotehele
St Dominick,
Saltash,
Cornwall PL12 6TA
Tel: (01579) 351346
Medieval granite house. Working watermill. Quay on River Tamar with small shipping museum. Sailing barge "Shamrock". Formal and valley gardens, pools, dovecote. Woodland walks.

33 Newquay Pearl

Southway,
Quintrell Downs,
Newquay,
Cornwall TR8 4LE
Tel: (01637) 872991
A large showroom with every range of pearl and semi-precious stone, with workshops and staff actively working. Pick your own pearl from our oyster tanks.

34 Royal Cornwall Museum

River Street,
Truro,
Cornwall TR1 2SJ
Tel: (01872) 72205
World famous mineral collection, Old Master drawings, ceramics, oil paintings by the Newlyn School and others, including John Opie and Hogarth. Geneaology library.

35 Tate Gallery St Ives

Porthmeor Beach,
St Ives,
Cornwall TR26 1TG
Tel: (01736) 796226
A major new gallery showing changing groups of work from the Tate Gallery's pre-eminent collection of St Ives painting and sculpture.

36 The Minack Theatre and Exhibition Centre

Porthcurno,
Penzance,
Cornwall
Tel: (01736) 810694
Open-air cliffside theatre with breathtaking views, presenting a 16 week season of plays and musicals. Exhibition centre telling the theatre's story.

37 Flambards Village Theme Park

Culdrose Manor,
Helston,
Cornwall TR13 0GA
Tel: (01326) 574549
Life-sized Victorian village with fully stocked shops, carriages and fashions. 'Britain in the Blitz' life-sized wartime street, historic aircraft. Exploratorium.

FIND OUT MORE

Further information about holidays and attractions in the West Country is available from:
West Country Tourist Board,
60 St Davids Hill,
Exeter EX4 4SY.
Tel: (01392) 425426
Fax: (01392) 420891

These publications are available free from the West Country Tourist Board:
- **Great Escapes in England's West Country**
- **Bed & Breakfast Touring Map**
- **West Country Inspected Holiday Homes**
- **Commended Hotels and Guesthouses**
- **Glorious Gardens of the West Country**
- **Camping and Caravan Touring Map**

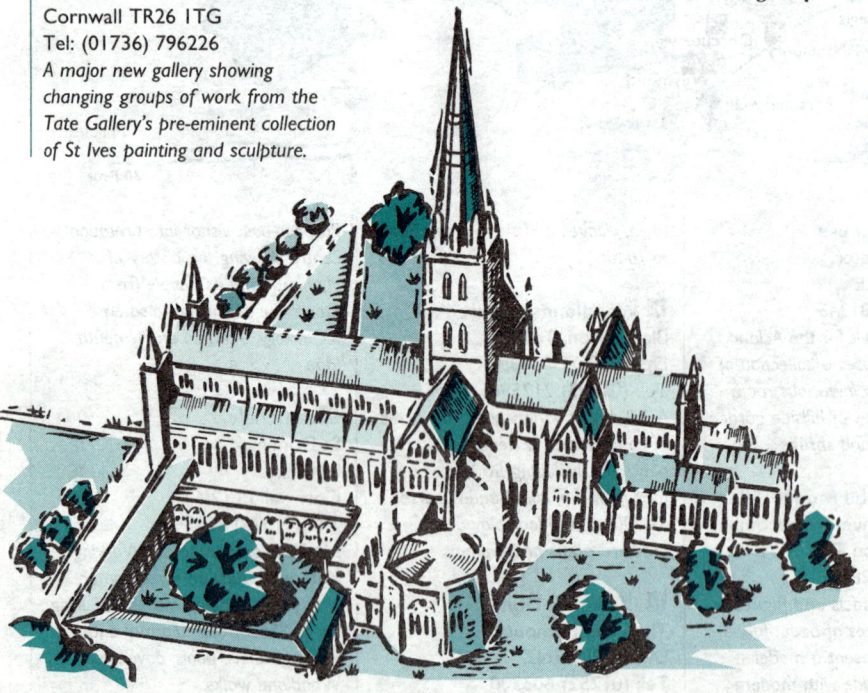

WHERE TO STAY (WEST COUNTRY)

Accommodation entries in this region are listed in alphabetical order of place name, and then in alphabetical order of establishment. A contact address is given where it differs from the address of the establishment.

Map references refer to the colour location maps at the back of this guide.

Prices shown are weekly per unit.

At-a-glance symbols at the end of each accommodation entry give useful information about services and facilities. A key to symbols can be found inside the back cover flap. Keep this open for easy reference.

ABBOTSBURY

Dorset
Map ref 2A3

Beautiful village near Chesil Beach, with a long main street of mellow stone and thatched cottages and the ruins of a Benedictine monastery. High above the village on a hill is a prominent 15th C chapel. Abbotsbury's famous swannery and sub-tropical gardens lie just outside the village.

The Cottage

COMMENDED

Grove Lane, Abbotsbury, Weymouth DT3 4JH
☎ (01305) 871462
Contact: Mrs V Dredge
17th C character cottage with secluded garden. Renovated and equipped with thought and care. Owner supervised. Idyllic setting near sea, swannery and village. Good walking country.
1 self-contained unit; sleeping 5

Price per week:	£min	£max
Low season	115.00	
High season		285.00

ALHAMPTON

Somerset
Map ref 2A2

Village on the River Alham, within easy reach of Castle Cary.

The Truckle

HIGHLY COMMENDED

Langford Farmhouse, Alhampton, Shepton Mallet BA4 6PY
☎ Ditcheat (01749) 860611
Contact: Dr M Labanowska

Cosy, character, self-contained wing of 17th C listed stone farmhouse. Linen and towels provided. Secluded garden with furniture, shared play area. Friendly farmyard animals, complimentary local produce.
1 self-contained unit; sleeping 5

Price per week:	£min	£max
Low season	150.00	
High season		340.00

COLOUR MAPS

Colour maps at the back of this guide pinpoint all places in which you will find accommodation listed.

ALLERFORD

Somerset
Map ref 1D1

Village with picturesque stone and thatch cottages and a packhorse bridge, set in the beautiful Vale of Porlock.

Lynch Country House Holiday Apartments

UP TO HIGHLY COMMENDED

Allerford, Minehead TA24 8HJ
☎ Porlock (01643) 862800
Fax (01643) 862800
Contact: Mr and Mrs B Tacchi
Delightful country house in woodland setting, overlooking moors and sea, tastefully converted to comfortable apartments. Large informal gardens; also cottage within grounds.
8 self-contained units; sleeping 2–8

Price per week:	£min	£max
Low season	135.00	225.00
High season	215.00	495.00

A key to symbols can be found inside the back cover flap.

All accommodation in this guide has been graded, or is awaiting a grading, by a trained Tourist Board inspector.

AMESBURY

Wiltshire
Map ref 2B2

Standing on the banks of the River Avon, this is the nearest town to Stonehenge on Salisbury Plain. The area is rich in prehistoric sites. *Tourist Information Centre ☎ (01980) 622833*

The Stables

HIGHLY COMMENDED

Ivy Cottage, Netheravon, Salisbury SP4 9QW
☎ Stonehenge (01980) 670557
Fax (01980) 670557
Contact: Mrs A Thatcher
Charming cottage, in village, 5 miles north of Stonehenge in Avon valley. Self-catering or half-board, short breaks.
1 self-contained unit; sleeping 5

Price per week:	£min	£max
Low season	230.00	350.00

ASHBURTON

Devon
Map ref 1C2

Formerly a thriving wool centre and important as one of Dartmoor's four stannary towns. Today's busy market town has many period buildings. Ancient tradition is maintained in the annual ale-tasting and bread-weighing ceremony. Good centre for exploring Dartmoor or the south Devon coast.

Wooder Manor

COMMENDED

Widecombe-in-the-Moor, Newton Abbot TQ13 7TR
☎ Widecombe-in-the-Moor (01364) 621391
Contact: Mrs Angela Bell

Cottages nestling in picturesque valley surrounded by woodland, moors and granite tors. Central for touring Devon, exploring Dartmoor and beaches. Clean and well equipped. Easy parking. Gardens.

---

6 self-contained units; sleeping 2–12

Price per week:	£min	£max
Low season	100.00	260.00
High season	160.00	800.00

ASHWATER

Devon
Map ref 1C2

Village 6 miles south-east of Holsworthy, with a pleasant village green dominated by its church.

Blagdon Farm Country Holidays

HIGHLY COMMENDED

Ashwater, Beaworthy EX21 5DF
☎ (01409) 211509 & Mobile (0585) 448625
Fax (01409) 211510
Contact: Mr and Mrs A W Blight
South-facing bungalows overlooking 2.5 acre lake, all set within 38 picturesque and tranquil acres. Many on-site facilities, all wheelchair accessible.
Wheelchair access category 2
4 self-contained units; sleeping 6

Price per week:	£min	£max
Low season	185.00	355.00
High season	355.00	495.00

Braddon Cottages

COMMENDED

Ashwater, Beaworthy EX21 5EP
☎ (01409) 211350 & Mobile 0802 787130
Fax (01409) 211350
Contact: G E and A C Ridge

Cottages equipped to high standard in open west Devon countryside facing south to fishing lake. Tennis court, wood fires, gas central heating, payphones.
8 self-contained units; sleeping 8–12

Price per week:	£min	£max
Low season	75.00	150.00
High season	160.00	530.00

Cards accepted: Access, Visa

BAMPTON

Devon
Map ref 1D1

Riverside market town, famous for its fair each October.

Williams Mill

HIGHLY COMMENDED

Morebath, Tiverton
Contact: Mr Brian Smalley, The Manor, Strete Gate, Dartmouth, Devon TQ6 0RR
☎ Stoke Fleming (01803) 770555
Fax (01803) 770555
Former mill and watermill. Quiet, rural situation. 6 acres of gardens and paddocks, floodlit cascading weirs. Furnished to a very high standard. Cot available.
2 self-contained units; sleeping 8

Price per week:	£min	£max
Low season	670.00	776.00
High season	930.00	1100.00

Wonham Barton

COMMENDED

Bampton, Tiverton EX16 9JZ
☎ (01398) 331312
Fax (01398) 331312
Contact: Mrs A McLean Williams

Savour the tranquil charm of Exe Valley. From this friendly accommodation explore historic Devon; or enjoy country pursuits and 300 acres of pasture, woodland and wildlife near Exmoor.
1 self-contained unit; sleeping 4

Price per week:	£min	£max
Low season	120.00	195.00
High season	195.00	275.00

The symbols in each entry give information about services and facilities. A 'key' to these symbols appears at the back of this guide.

BARNSTAPLE

Devon
Map ref 1C1

At the head of the Taw Estuary, once a ship-building and textile town, now an agricultural centre with attractive period buildings, a modern civic centre and leisure centre. Attractions include Queen Anne's Walk, a charming colonnaded arcade and Pannier Market.
Tourist Information Centre ☎ (01271) 388583 or 388584

Humes Farm Cottages ⚏

UP TO HIGHLY COMMENDED

C/O Bradiford Cottage, Halls Mill Lane, Bradiford, Barnstaple
Contact: Mr and Mrs J A Hare, Bradiford Cottage, Halls Mill Lane, Bradiford, Barnstaple, Devon EX31 4DP
☎ Barnstaple (01271) 45039
Fax (01271) 45039
17th C cottages located in peaceful valley. Spacious, comfortable and secluded base for families and couples to explore Atlantic coast and the moors throughout the year.
5 self-contained units; sleeping 2–12

Price per week:	£min	£max
Low season	107.00	274.00
High season	107.00	690.00

Open February–November

North Hill Cottages ⚏

COMMENDED

North Hill, Shirwell, Barnstaple
Contact: Miss Nicky Faull, Best Leisure, North Hill, Shirwell, Barnstaple, Devon EX31 4LG
☎ Barnstaple (01271) 850611
Fax (01271) 850693
Converted 17th C farm buildings set in 10 acres of secluded gardens and meadows, 10 minutes from Barnstaple town centre.
8 self-contained units; sleeping 2–6

Price per week:	£min	£max
Low season	217.00	308.00
High season	258.00	674.00

For ideas on places to visit refer to the introduction at the beginning of this section.

Willesleigh Farm

HIGHLY COMMENDED

Goodleigh, Barnstaple EX32 7NA
☎ (01271) 43763
Contact: Mrs A Esmond-Cole

86-acre dairy & livestock farm. Charming farmhouse wing and unique gatehouse. Walled gardens, heated indoor swimming pool, peaceful countryside. Family-run farm half a mile from village. West Country Farm Holiday Award winner.
2 self-contained units; sleeping 6

Price per week:	£min	£max
Low season	150.00	
High season		610.00

BATH

Bath & North East Somerset
Map ref 2B2

Georgian spa city beside the River Avon. Important Roman site with impressive reconstructed baths, uncovered in 19th C. Bath Abbey built on site of monastery where first king of England was crowned (AD 973). Fine architecture in mellow local stone. Pump Room and museums.
Tourist Information Centre ☎ (01225) 462831

Greyfield Farm Cottages ⚏

HIGHLY COMMENDED

Greyfield Road, High Littleton, Bristol BS18 5YQ
☎ Mendip (01761) 471132
Contact: Mrs J Merry
Close to Bath, attractive, spacious, fully-appointed 2-bedroomed cottages. Comfortable, cosy, ideal for winter visits. In private peaceful hillside location on edge of village. Excellent touring centre for West Country. Brochure available.
Wheelchair access category 3
5 self-contained units; sleeping 2–4

Price per week:	£min	£max
Low season	135.00	215.00
High season	200.00	335.00

Riverside Cottage

APPROVED

3 High Street, Wick, Bristol
Contact: Mr B Trezise, Riverside Cottage, 1 High Street, Wick, Bristol BS15 5QJ
☎ Bristol (0117) 9372304
Situated in the village with garden running down to a stream. Between Bath and Bristol, giving a good location for touring.
1 self-contained unit; sleeping 5

Price per week:	£min	£max
Low season	125.00	
High season		285.00

Tyning House ⚏

COMMENDED

Freshford, Bath BA3 6DR
☎ (01225) 723288
Fax (01225) 723288
Contact: Mrs P Harward

Attractive country house and coach house in village, 6 miles from Bath. 7 acres organically run with farm and domestic animals. Ideal for children, peaceful.
4 self-contained units; sleeping 4–6

Price per week:	£min	£max
Low season	160.00	280.00
High season	300.00	390.00

Weston Village

COMMENDED

40 Church Road, Weston, Bath
Contact: Mr D Price, 11 Linden Gardens, Bath BA1 2YB
☎ Bath (01225) 426621
Sunny Victorian-style end-of-terrace cottage with part-walled garden. In quiet conservation area, 1.5 miles from centre of Bath.
1 self-contained unit; sleeping 4

Price per week:	£min	£max
Low season	140.00	
High season		250.00

Map references apply to the colour maps at the back of this guide.

BEAMINSTER

Dorset
Map ref 2A3

Old country town of mellow local stone set amid hills and rural vales. Mainly Georgian buildings; attractive almshouses date from 1603. The 17th C church with its ornate, pinnacled tower was restored inside by the Victorians. Parnham, a Tudor manor house, lies 1 mile south.

Greens Cross Farm

APPROVED

Stoke Road, Beaminster DT8 3JL
☎ (01308) 862661
Fax (01308) 863800
Contact: Mr P C Jeanes
Farm buildings converted into 3 well equipped holiday units. Within walking distance of Beaminster in heart of Dorset. Close to coast.
3 self-contained units; sleeping 4

Price per week:	£min	£max
Low season	130.00	175.00
High season	175.00	230.00

Lewesdon Farm Holidays

COMMENDED

Lewesdon Farm, Stoke Abbott, Beaminster DT8 3JZ
☎ Broadwindsor (01308) 868270
Contact: Mrs J Spooncer
Barn conversion, designed with the disabled in mind. All bedrooms en-suite. Blissfully peaceful, glorious country setting. Extremely comfortable. Non-smokers, please.
2 self-contained units; sleeping 6

Price per week:	£min	£max
Low season	160.00	175.00
High season	350.00	425.00

1 The Tanyard

APPROVED

Beaminster
Contact: Reverend R C Butler, The Rectory, Brandram Road, London SE13 5EA
☎ (0181) 852 0633
Fax (0181) 297 2877
Attractive stone cottage, with pretty south-facing garden, in a quiet corner of this small country town.
1 self-contained unit; sleeping 7

Price per week:	£min	£max
Low season	200.00	
High season	300.00	

BEER

Devon
Map ref 1D2

Formerly noted for lace-making and smuggling, this picturesque fishing village lies close to some of Devon's most striking cliff scenery at Beer Head. Smugglers' caves. Quarries to west of village were worked in Roman times.

Tower Country Chalet Park

APPROVED

Seaton Down Hill, Seaton
Contact: Mr and Mrs K M Brooksbank, 1 Netherhay Farm, Netherhay, Beaminster, Dorset DT8 3RH
☎ Broadwindsor (01308) 868872
Fax (01308) 868872
Detached cedarwood chalets on small site about 1 mile from Seaton. Well-placed for touring.
4 self-contained units; sleeping 5–6

Price per week:	£min	£max
Low season	90.00	145.00
High season	200.00	240.00

Open April–October

BELSTONE

Devon
Map ref 1C2

Village in picturesque Dartmoor setting, retaining its stocks and whipping post. Several prehistoric stone circles to be seen in the area.

1 Church Cottages

HIGHLY COMMENDED

Belstone, Okehampton
Contact: Mr and Mrs R S Kingwell, Lowther Cottage, Wymondham Road, Wreningham, Norwich NR16 1AT
☎ Fundenhall (01508) 489757
Comfortable stone cottage in Dartmoor National Park. Situated beside church in centre of Belstone village near Okehampton.
1 self-contained unit; sleeping 4

Price per week:	£min	£max
Low season	150.00	265.00
High season	270.00	320.00

For ideas on places to visit refer to the introduction at the beginning of this section.

Great Down

COMMENDED

Skaigh Lane, Belstone, Okehampton
Contact: Mr A Schuman, Malvern Hills Hotel, Wynds Point, Malvern, Worcestershire WR13 6DW
☎ Colwall (01684) 540690
Fax (01684) 540327
Garden self-contained flatlet with direct access to Dartmoor. Ideal for walkers. Relaxing atmosphere. Easy access to village amenities.
1 self-contained unit; sleeping 2

Price per week:	£min	£max
Low season	125.00	150.00
High season	150.00	180.00

BERRYNARBOR

Devon
Map ref 1C1

Picturesque, old-world village, winner of best-kept village awards, adjoining the lovely, wooded Sterridge Valley. On scenic route between Ilfracombe and Combe Martin.

Wheel Farm Country Cottages

HIGHLY COMMENDED

Berry Down 8, Combe Martin, Ilfracombe EX34 0NT
☎ Combe Martin (01271) 882100
Contact: Mr and Mrs T Massey

Beautiful cottages in water mill and barns. Lovely gardens, peaceful valley views, near beaches and Exmoor. Four-posters, indoor pool, sauna. Home cooking, maid service.
10 self-contained units; sleeping 2–6

Price per week:	£min	£max
Low season	180.00	290.00
High season	330.00	770.00

Open March–October

The National Grading and Classification Scheme is explained in full at the back of this guide.

BIGBURY-ON-SEA

Devon
Map ref 1C3

Small resort on Bigbury Bay at the mouth of the River Avon. Wide sands, rugged cliffs. Burgh Island can be reached on foot at low tide.

Beachdown M

APPROVED

Challaborough Bay, Kingsbridge TQ7 4JB
☎ Kingsbridge (01548) 810089
Contact: Mr and Mrs N Faulkner
Delightful cedarwood bungalows in peaceful 2.5-acre surroundings. 250 yards from sandy beach. Superb cliff walks, golf and heated pool nearby. Ideal for watersports. Dartmoor 30 minutes.
9 self-contained units; sleeping 5–6

Price per week:	£min	£max
Low season	100.00	150.00
High season	175.00	330.00

Open March–October

Touchdown

COMMENDED

Marine Drive, Bigbury-on-Sea, Kingsbridge TQ7 4AS
☎ (01548) 810219
Contact: Mr K Yeomans
Two bedroomed flat, minutes from sandy beaches. Panoramic sea views. Within easy reach of Plymouth, Salcombe, Dartmouth, Dartmoor. No pets.
1 self-contained unit; sleeping 4

Price per week:	£min	£max
Low season	145.00	190.00
High season	190.00	285.00

For ideas on places to visit refer to the introduction at the beginning of this section.

Self-catering agencies which have a selection of holiday homes to let are listed in a special section towards the back of this guide.

BODMIN

Cornwall
Map ref 1B2

County town south-west of Bodmin Moor with a ruined priory and church dedicated to St Petroc. Nearby are Lanhydrock House and Pencarrow House.
Tourist Information Centre ☎ (01208) 76616

Coombe Mill

UP TO HIGHLY COMMENDED

St Breward, Bodmin PL30 4LZ
☎ (01208) 850344
Fax (01208) 850452
Contact: Mr and Mrs D Oldham
Cottages and log cabins in idyllic river valley 30-acre farm park. Red deer, lots of other animals, lake and river fishing. Emphasis on tranquillity. Pets welcome.
18 self-contained units; sleeping 2–8

Price per week:	£min	£max
Low season	145.00	400.00
High season	275.00	755.00

Open March–December
Cards accepted: Access, Visa, Switch/Delta

Penbugle Farm

APPROVED

Penbugle, Bodmin PL31 2NT
☎ (01208) 72844
Contact: Mrs E Tidy
Traditional farm cottage modernised to high standard. Secluded setting with countryside views. Central and convenient location.
1 self-contained unit; sleeping 6

Price per week:	£min	£max
Low season	140.00	
High season		275.00

Treffry Farm Cottages M

HIGHLY COMMENDED

Treffry Farm, Lanhydrock, Bodmin PL30 5AF
☎ (01208) 74405
Fax (01208) 74405
Contact: Mrs P A Smith

Delightful cottages on Cornish dairy farm. Tastefully converted from an old range of traditional farm buildings, retaining much character and charm.
8 self-contained units; sleeping 2–8

Price per week:	£min	£max
Low season	100.00	150.00
High season	150.00	575.00

BOSCASTLE

Cornwall
Map ref 1B2

Small, unspoilt village in Valency Valley. Active as a port until onset of railway era, its natural harbour affords rare shelter on this wild coast. Attractions include spectacular blow-hole, Celtic field strips, part-Norman church. Nearby St Juliot Church was restored by Thomas Hardy.

Cargurra Cottage

COMMENDED

St Juliot, Boscastle
Contact: Mrs G M Elson, Hennet, St Juliot, Boscastle, Cornwall PL35 0BT
☎ Otterham Station (01840) 261206
Comfortable traditional 3-bedroomed cottage with log fires, in peaceful countryside surroundings. Overlooking Valency Valley.
5 self-contained units; sleeping 4–6

Price per week:	£min	£max
Low season	85.00	120.00
High season	130.00	305.00

Courtyard Farm and Cottages M

COMMENDED

Lesnewth, Boscastle PL35 0HR
☎ Otterham Station (01840) 261256
Fax (01840) 261794
Contact: Mr and Mrs David Clough
Cottages converted from the original 17th C corn mill and farm buildings. Set in an attractive courtyard, some overlooking the Valency Valley.
7 self-contained units; sleeping 3–8

Price per week:	£min	£max
Low season	105.00	230.00
High season	295.00	595.00

Cards accepted: Access, Visa

BOSCASTLE

Continued

Paradise Farm Cottage

🔑🔑🔑 COMMENDED

Boscastle PL35 0BL
☎ (01840) 250528
Contact: Mrs D M Hancock
Peaceful sunny cottage on edge of harbour village. Cliff and country walks from the doorstep. Pub and shop close by. Antiques, log fire. Friendly farmyard animals, pony rides. Weekend breaks. Reduction for 2 persons.
1 self-contained unit; sleeping 5

Price per week:	£min	£max
Low season	110.00	170.00
High season	200.00	350.00

🐕 Ⓜ ◎ 🔥 ⊙ 🍴 📺 📻 🖥 📷 🚗 🛏 ❄ 🧺 SP

Wideacres 🏔

🔑🔑🔑🔑🔑🔑 UP TO COMMENDED

Boscastle
Contact: Mrs G Congdon, Tremorle, Boscastle, Cornwall PL35 0BU
☎ Boscastle (01840) 250233
Peaceful, well-equipped bungalows in lovely countryside with sea views. Near coastal path, harbour and Valency Valley walks. Sandy beach 3 miles.
3 self-contained units; sleeping 2–8

Price per week:	£min	£max
Low season	80.00	150.00
High season	150.00	500.00

🐕 Ⓜ ◎ 🔥 ⊙ 🍴 📺 📻 🖥 📷 🚗 P ❄ SP

BOVEY TRACEY

Devon
Map ref 1D2

Standing by the river just east of Dartmoor National Park, this old town has good moorland views. Its church, with a 14th C tower, holds one of Devon's finest medieval rood screens.

Warmhill Farm

🔑🔑🔑 HIGHLY COMMENDED

Hennock, Newton Abbot
TQ13 9QH
☎ (01626) 833229
Contact: Mr W B Marnham
100-acre dairy farm. Superb thatched farmhouse in Dartmoor National Park. Ideal for moor and sea. Spacious and comfortable.
1 self-contained unit; sleeping 12

Price per week:	£min	£max
Low season	250.00	550.00
High season	550.00	980.00

🐕 ◎ 🔥 ⊙ 🍴 MW 🍽 📺 📻 🖥 📷 (🖥) 📷 P ∪ ⑂ ❄ SP 📮 T

BRADFORD-ON-AVON

Wiltshire
Map ref 2B2

Huddled beside the river, the buildings of this former cloth-weaving town reflect continuing prosperity from the Middle Ages. There is a tiny Anglo-Saxon church, part of a monastery. The part-14th C bridge carries a medieval chapel, later used as a gaol.
Tourist Information Centre ☎ (01225) 865797

The Flat Martins

🔑 APPROVED

Whitehill, Bradford-on-Avon
BA15 1SQ
☎ (01225) 863253
Contact: Mrs D Young
First-floor flat with superb south-facing views, 5 minutes' walk to town centre and very well placed for all public transport. Peaceful location.
1 self-contained unit; sleeping 2

Price per week:	£min	£max
Low season		85.00
High season	90.00	130.00

Ⓜ 🛁 🔥 🍴 📺 📷 📷 P ∪ ❄ ✕

BRATTON

Somerset
Map ref 1D1

Hamlet on the edge of the Exmoor National Park, close to the resort of Minehead.

Woodcombe Lodges 🏔

🔑🔑🔑 COMMENDED

Bratton Lane, Minehead TA24 8SQ
☎ Minehead (01643) 702789
Contact: Mr M Simons
Cottages/timber lodges in beautiful 3-acre gardens with wonderful views of the countryside, on edge of Exmoor National Park. Minehead 1.25 miles.
Wheelchair access category 3 ⚹
6 self-contained units; sleeping 2–5

Price per week:	£min	£max
Low season	95.00	135.00
High season	175.00	345.00

🐕 Ⓜ ◎ 🔥 ⊙ 🍴 MW 📺 📷 (🖥) 📷 🚗 P ∪ ❄ 🧺 SP

The National Grading and Classification Scheme is explained in full at the back of this guide.

BRAYFORD

Devon
Map ref 1C1

Village lies 6 miles north-west of South Molton and marks the crossing of the River Bray by one of the main roads from Exmoor to the sea.

Muxworthy Cottage

🔑 APPROVED

Muxworthy Farm, Brayford, Barnstaple EX32 7QP
☎ (01598) 710342
Contact: Mrs G M Bament
Secluded old world cottage 3 miles from the village of Brayford, 11 miles from Barnstaple and surrounded by beautiful countryside, in heart of Exmoor.
1 self-contained unit; sleeping 6

Price per week:	£min	£max
Low season	90.00	100.00
High season	140.00	195.00

🐕 Ⓜ ◎ 🔥 🍴 MW 📺 📷 📷 🥘 🚗 P ∪ ❄ SP

BREAN

Somerset
Map ref 1D1

Caravans and holiday bungalows by sand dunes on the flat shoreline south of Brean Down. This rocky promontory has exhilarating cliff walks, bird-watching and an Iron Age fort.

Hillview Brean Sands

🔑 UP TO COMMENDED

Nos 26, 28 and 29 Hillview, South Road, Brean, Burnham-on-Sea
Contact: Mr and Mrs G Bunting, 10 Malvern Road, Weston-super-Mare BS23 4DF
☎ Weston-super-Mare (01934) 412674
Three holiday bungalows (2 adjoining and 1 opposite) on private site with access to beach. Fully equipped, colour TV, shower room. Private parking.
3 self-contained units; sleeping 4–5

Price per week:	£min	£max
Low season	110.00	150.00
High season	150.00	205.00

Open March–October
🐕 Ⓜ ◎ 🔥 ⊙ 🍴 📺 📷 🚗 P ❄

Establishments should be open throughout the year, unless otherwise stated.

BRIDPORT

Dorset
Map ref 2A3

Market town and chief producer of nets and ropes just inland of dramatic Dorset coast. Old, broad streets built for drying and twisting and long gardens for rope-walks. *Tourist Information Centre ☎ (01308) 424901*

Coniston Holiday Accommodation

🗝🗝🗝 COMMENDED

Coniston House, 69 Victoria Grove, Bridport DT6 3AE
☎ (01308) 424049
Contact: Messrs CA/N Vaughan
Spacious, fully-equipped apartments, formerly a Victorian boarding school, in quaint, historic market town. Rural setting, 5 minutes from town centre.
4 self-contained units; sleeping 4–8

Price per week:	£min	£max
Low season	75.00	165.00
High season	95.00	310.00

Lancombes House ⚲

🗝🗝🗝 UP TO COMMENDED

West Milton, Bridport DT6 3TN
☎ Powerstock (01308) 485375
Contact: Mr and Mrs Mansfield
Pretty cottages in converted barn, with panoramic views to the sea 4 miles away. Pet animals, including ponies, goats and ducks.
4 self-contained units; sleeping 6–8

Price per week:	£min	£max
Low season	230.00	320.00
High season	355.00	440.00

1 Pump Cottages

🗝 APPROVED

West Road, Symondsbury, Bridport
Contact: Miss D Barltrop, 3 Pump Cottages, West Road, Symondsbury, Bridport, Dorset DT6 6AE
☎ Bridport (01308) 424705
19th C modernised country cottage, downstairs living room with double bed-settee, well equipped kitchen area. Upstairs bedroom (twin), bathroom.
1 self-contained unit; sleeping 4

Price per week:	£min	£max
Low season	60.00	85.00
High season	110.00	175.00

Open May–October

Rudge Farm ⚲

🗝🗝 HIGHLY COMMENDED

Chilcombe, Bridport DT6 4NF
☎ (01308) 482630
Fax (01308) 482635
Contact: Mrs S Diment

Peaceful courtyard cottages on working farm in Area of Outstanding Natural Beauty. 2.5 miles from sea.
Wheelchair access category 2
6 self-contained units; sleeping 2–6

Price per week:	£min	£max
Low season	175.00	275.00
High season	275.00	475.00

30 Victoria Grove

🗝 APPROVED

Bridport DT6 3AD
☎ (01308) 424605
Contact: Mrs J Brook
Comfortable, 1-bedroomed Victorian ground floor flat. 2 minutes' walk to town centre, 5 minutes' drive to seaside. Beautiful country walks.
1 self-contained unit; sleeping 3

Price per week:	£min	£max
Low season	80.00	150.00
High season	180.00	180.00

BRISTOL

Map ref 2A2

Famous for maritime links, historic harbour, Georgian terraces and Brunel's Clifton suspension bridge. Many attractions including SS Great Britain, Bristol Zoo, museums and art galleries and top name entertainments. Events include Balloon Fiesta and Regatta. *Tourist Information Centre ☎ (0117) 926 0767*

Avonside

🗝🗝 APPROVED

19 St Edyth's Road, Sea Mills, Bristol BS9 2EP
☎ (0117) 9681967
Contact: Mrs D M Ridout
Comfortable first-floor flat, well-furnished, equipped and maintained to a high standard. Convenient, pleasant residential area 3 miles from city centre. Motorway nearby.

1 self-contained unit; sleeping 4

Price per week:	£min	£max
Low season		180.00

Redland Flat

🗝 APPROVED

Bristol
Contact: Mr H I Jones, Flat 1, Elm Lodge, Elm Grove, London NW2 3AE
☎ (0181) 4506761
Spacious flat with panoramic views over city from south-facing balconies off the lounge and kitchen. City centre 1.5 miles, Durdham Downs 2 minutes.
1 self-contained unit; sleeping 2

Price per week:	£min	£max
Low season		180.00

BRIXHAM

Devon
Map ref 1D2

Famous for its trawling fleet in the 19th C, a steeply-built fishing port overlooking the harbour and fish market. A statue of William of Orange recalls his landing here before deposing James II. There is an aquarium and museum. Good cliff views and walks. *Tourist Information Centre ☎ (01803) 852861*

Devoncourt Holiday Flats

🗝🗝 APPROVED

Berry Head Road, Brixham TQ5 9AB
☎ Torquay (01803) 853748
Fax (01803) 855775
Contact: Mr Robin Hooker

Panoramic sea views from purpose-built flats with private balcony, overlooking Brixham harbour and Torbay. Beach 200 yards. Mini-breaks October-May.
6 self-contained units; sleeping 5–6

Price per week:	£min	£max
Low season	80.00	140.00
High season	180.00	280.00

Cards accepted: Access, Visa, Switch/Delta

BRIXHAM

Continued

Fishcombe Cove Holiday Homes ⛰

🔑🔑🔑 APPROVED

Fishcombe Cove, Brixham
TQ5 8RD
☎ Torquay (01803) 851800
Contact: Mrs B Baker
Modern holiday bungalows in 1.5 acres of garden, with panoramic views of Torbay. All facilities close at hand. Suitable for holidays and short breaks all year round.
8 self-contained units; sleeping 2–6

Price per week:	£min	£max
Low season	150.00	
High season		410.00

Open March–October
Cards accepted: Access, Visa

🔧Ⓜ◎🖥☉ⓉⓋ◎🍴🛏🏧🅿🎣
❄✈🆂🅟Ⓣ◎

BROADHEMPSTON

Devon
Map ref 1D2

Village 4 miles south-east of Ashburton, within easy reach of Dartmoor and the South Devon coast.

4 Borough Court

🔑🔑🔑🔑 HIGHLY COMMENDED

Broadhempston, Totnes
Contact: Mr J W Digweed, 3 Rookery Wood, Sully, Penarth, South Glamorgan CF64 5TD
☎ Cardiff (01222) 530533

Cottage-style house in centre of peaceful village between Newton Abbot and Totnes. 4 bedrooms, 2 bathrooms, 2 receptions, kitchen, cloakroom and double garage. Enclosed rear patio.
1 self-contained unit; sleeping 6

Price per week:	£min	£max
Low season	175.00	225.00
High season	275.00	375.00

🔧◎🖥☉ⓊMW🍴ⓉⓋ◎🛏🏧🅹
🛩🅿❄✈🆂🅿

Map references apply to the colour maps at the back of this guide.

BROADWOODWIDGER

Devon
Map ref 1C2

Village 6 miles north-east of Launceston, with good views across to Dartmoor. The church contains early 13th C work and fine original wagon roofs. Roadford Reservoir north of village.

Barn Cottage

🔑🔑🔑 COMMENDED

Middle West Week, Broadwoodwidger, Lifton PL16 0EU
☎ Ashwater (01409) 211515
Contact: Mrs E M Bury
Spacious self-catering cottage with galleried bedrooms, fully equipped throughout. Conservation area with magnificent views. Private grounds bordering Roadford Lake. Brown trout fishing and sailing.
1 self-contained unit; sleeping 4

Price per week:	£min	£max
Low season	150.00	200.00
High season	240.00	300.00

Open March–December

🔧Ⓜ◎🖥☉ⓊMW🍴ⓉⓋ◎🛏🏧
🅹🛩🅿🎣Ⓤ✈❄🏠

BRUTON

Somerset
Map ref 2B2

Fine old town where an old packhorse bridge, Bruton Bow, spans the narrow valley of the River Brue. A 3-storeyed dovecote on a hill outside the town is all that remains of a 12th C priory (National Trust).

Discove Farm

🔑🔑 COMMENDED

Dropping Lane, Bruton
Contact: Mr A J Eldridge, Discove Farm, Dropping Lane, Bruton, Somerset BA10 0NQ
☎ Bruton (01749) 812284
Two-bedroomed barn conversion and 2 one-bedroomed apartments in peaceful farmland setting. Designed and equipped to a high standard. Especially suitable for elderly or disabled guests.
Wheelchair access category 2 ♿
3 self-contained units; sleeping 3–5

Price per week:	£min	£max
Low season	110.00	220.00
High season	225.00	340.00

🔧Ⓜ◎🖥☉Ⓤ🍴ⓉⓋ◎🛏🏧🅹
🛩🅿❄

BUCKLAND NEWTON

Dorset
Map ref 2B3

Village midway between Sherborne and Puddletown and within easy reach of Dorchester.

Domineys Cottages ⛰

🔑🔑🔑🔑🔑 HIGHLY COMMENDED

Domineys, Buckland Newton, Dorchester DT2 7BS
☎ (01300) 345295
Fax (01300) 345596
Contact: Mrs J D Gueterbock

Peaceful, carefully renovated, comfortable cottages. Furnished, equipped and maintained to highest standard. Heated swimming pool (summer). Lovely countryside for touring and walking. Midway between Dorchester and Sherborne. Babies and children over 5 welcome.
3 self-contained units; sleeping 4

Price per week:	£min	£max
Low season	190.00	240.00
High season	300.00	380.00

🔧5Ⓜ◎🖥☉ⓊMWⓉⓋ◎🛏🏧
🛩🅿🎣Ⓤ✈❄✈🆂🏠

BUDE

Cornwall
Map ref 1C2

Resort on dramatic Atlantic coast. High cliffs give spectacular sea and inland views. Golf-course, cricket pitch, folly, surfing, coarse-fishing and boating. Mother-town Stratton was base of Royalist Sir Bevil Grenville.
Tourist Information Centre ☎ (01288) 354240

Langfield Manor

🔑🔑🔑🔑 ↔ 🔑🔑🔑🔑 UP TO COMMENDED

Broadclose Hill, Bude EX23 8DP
☎ (01288) 352415
Contact: Mr T Farbrother
Quality apartments within fine Edwardian house. Games room including snooker. Sheltered gardens with heated swimming pool. Short walk to shop and beaches.
7 self-contained units; sleeping 2–7

Price per week:	£min	£max
Low season	100.00	
High season		590.00

Open March–October

🏠Ⓜ◎▥⊙▣ MW 📺🗄🚗📻📱
🔌P⌂∪🌸⚲ SP

Trevalgas Farm Cottages 🅜
🔑🔑🔑🔑🔑 COMMENDED

Poughill, Bude EX23 9EX
☎ (01288) 354266
Fax (01288) 354266
Contact: Mrs V Marshall

11 well-appointed cottages offering peace and quiet, set in 22 acres with magnificent views from the grounds. Highly equipped. Indoor heated swimming pool. Well located for touring Cornwall and Devon.
11 self-contained units; sleeping 2–7

Price per week:	£min	£max
Low season	193.00	335.00
High season	330.00	659.00

Open March–December

🏠◎∅▥⊙▣ MW 📺🗄🚗📻📱
P⌂∪🌸⚲ SP

BURNHAM-ON-SEA

Somerset
Map ref 1D1

Small Victorian resort famous for sunsets and sandy beaches, a few minutes from junction 22 of the M5. Ideal base for touring Somerset, Cheddar and Bath. Good sporting facilities, championship golf-course. *Tourist Information Centre* ☎ (01278) 787852

Prospect Farm Guest House and Holiday Cottages
🔑🔑 COMMENDED

Strowlands, East Brent, Highbridge TA9 4JH
☎ Brent Knoll (01278) 760507
Contact: Mrs G D Wall

17th C tastefully restored country cottages set amidst flower gardens and surrounded by countryside, 3 miles from Burnham-on-Sea. Variety of small farm animals and pets. Children welcome.

3 self-contained units; sleeping 4–9

Price per week:	£min	£max
Low season	100.00	120.00
High season	156.00	282.00

🏠Ⓜ◎▥⊙🗆📺 📺🗄🚗📻📱🖥 ∥
🚗P∪⌂🌸 SP 🏺◎

CALLINGTON

Cornwall
Map ref 1C2

A quiet market town standing on high ground above the River Lynher. The 15th C church of St Mary's has an alabaster monument to Lord Willoughby de Broke, Henry VII's marshal. A 15th C chapel, 1 mile east, houses Dupath Well, one of the Cornish Holy Wells.

Deer Park Farm
🔑🔑🔑🔑🔑 APPROVED

Luckett, Callington PL17 8NW
☎ (01579) 370292
Contact: Mr B J Howlett
280-acre mixed farm. Traditional barn conversions, rural location, tranquil walks. Stunning views of Dartmoor and Tamar Valley. Kit Hill country park. Coarse fishing on working livestock farm.
3 self-contained units; sleeping 4–5

Price per week:	£min	£max
Low season	165.00	195.00
High season	235.00	265.00

Open March–December

🏠Ⓜ◎▥⊙▣ MW 📺🗄🚗📻📱
🖥🚗P∪🌸⚲✕⚲ SP 🆃

CAMELFORD

Cornwall
Map ref 1B2

Old market town set between the coast and the moorlands on the north-west edge of Bodmin Moor. Tennyson thought of it as Arthur's Camelot. At the northern end of the town a hilly track leads to Cornwall's second-highest hill, Rough Tor. Local history museum, ornamental gardens.

Kenningstock Cottage 🅜
🔑🔑🔑 COMMENDED

Advent, Camelford
Contact: Mrs I L Austin-Smith, Kenningstock Mill, Advent, Camelford, Cornwall PL32 9QP
☎ Camelford (01840) 213538 & 213761
Fax (01840) 213538
Old stone watermill manager's cottage. Surrounded by farmland, overlooking River Camel and Devil's Jump on Bodmin Moor. Rural and peaceful.

1 self-contained unit; sleeping 6

Price per week:	£min	£max
Low season	160.00	200.00
High season	220.00	360.00

🏠Ⓜ◎▥⊙ MW 📺📺🗄🚗📻
🔌🚗P∪🌸⚲✕⚲ SP 🏺

CARDINHAM

Cornwall
Map ref 1B2

Village on the steeply-wooded south-western fringe of Bodmin Moor with its numerous prehistoric sites. Close by is a hilltop earthwork, site of Cardinham Castle, built by medieval Earls of Cornwall.

Glynn Barton Farm Cottages 🅜
🔑🔑🔑🔑🔑 COMMENDED

The Farmhouse, Glynn Barton, Cardinham, Bodmin PL30 4AX
☎ (01208) 821375
Fax (01208) 821375
Contact: Mr and Mrs A J Mindel
Peaceful hamlet amidst breathtaking valley views, surrounded by forestry and farmland. Friendly farm animals. Splendid woodland walks, secluded heated swimming pool. Centrally positioned idyllic location.
6 self-contained units; sleeping 2–6

Price per week:	£min	£max
Low season	125.00	250.00
High season	190.00	485.00

🏠Ⓜ◎▥⊙▣ MW 📺📺🗄🚗📻
🔌P⌂∪🌸⚲✕⚲ SP 🏺🆃◎

CHAGFORD

Devon
Map ref 1C2

Handsome stone houses, some from the Middle Ages, grace this former stannary town on northern Dartmoor. It is a popular centre for walking expeditions and for tours of the antiquities on the rugged moor. There is a splendid 15th C granite church, said to be haunted by the poet Godolphin.

Throwleigh Manor Gamekeepers/Coach House & Pear Tree 🅜
🔑🔑🔑🔑🔑🔑 COMMENDED

Throwleigh, Okehampton EX20 2JF
☎ Whiddon Down (01647) 231630
Contact: Mrs J Smitheram
Cosy cottages set in beautiful 12-acre grounds of country house, within
Continued ▶

CHAGFORD

Continued

Dartmoor National Park. Swimming pool, games room, private lake. Idyllic, peaceful setting.
3 self-contained units; sleeping 2–5

Price per week:	£min	£max
Low season	114.00	225.00
High season	126.00	414.00

CHAPEL AMBLE

Cornwall
Map ref 1B2

Village 2 miles north of Wadebridge and within easy reach of the Camel Estuary and the North Cornwall coast.

Carclaze Farm

HIGHLY COMMENDED

Chapel Amble, Wadebridge
PL27 6EP
☎ Wadebridge (01208) 813886
Contact: Mrs J Nicholls
Situated in idyllic countryside yet only 10 minutes from coast. Quality cottages. Furnished to high standards. Suitable for those seeking something special.
3 self-contained units; sleeping 2–8

Price per week:	£min	£max
Low season	130.00	195.00
High season	395.00	795.00

The Olde House

UP TO HIGHLY COMMENDED

Chapel Amble, Wadebridge
PL27 6EN
☎ Wadebridge (01208) 813219
Fax (01208) 815689
Contact: Mr and Mrs A Hawkey
Cottages in heart of Cornish countryside, on 500-acre working farm. Indoor heated pool, sauna, jacuzzi and solarium, tennis courts. Overseas visitors especially welcome.
37 self-contained units; sleeping 2–8

Price per week:	£min	£max
Low season	200.00	
High season	435.00	

Cards accepted: Access, Visa

CHARD

Somerset
Map ref 1D2

Market town in hilly countryside. The wide main street has some handsome buildings, among them the Guildhall, court house and almshouses. Modern light industry and dairy produce have replaced 19th C lace making which came at decline of cloth trade.
Tourist Information Centre ☎ *(01460) 67463*

Muttleburys Mead

HIGHLY COMMENDED

Chard Street, Thorncombe, Chard TA20 4NB
☎ Winsham (01460) 30651
Contact: Mrs M Smith
Furnished to high standard, set in 2 acres of landscaped gardens in rural village with spectacular views. Double bedroom, lounge/diner, kitchen, bathroom. Full central heating. Winter weekend breaks. Brochure on request.
1 self-contained unit; sleeping 2

Price per week:	£min	£max
Low season	165.00	205.00
High season	205.00	250.00

CHARMOUTH

Dorset
Map ref 1D2

Set back from the fossil-rich cliffs, a small coastal town where Charles II came to the Queen's Arms when seeking escape to France. Just south at low tide, the sandy beach rewards fossil-hunters; at Black Ven an ichthyosaurus (now in London's Natural History Museum) was found.

Higher Pound Farm Holiday Cottages

HIGHLY COMMENDED

Monkton Wyld, Charmouth, Bridport DT6 6DD
☎ Hawkchurch (01297) 678345
Fax (01297) 678730
Contact: Mr and Mrs R Blatchford
Converted barn cottages with extensive views over the picturesque Char Valley. Forestry walks, farm animals, riding and trekking centre on site.
7 self-contained units; sleeping 4–6

Price per week:	£min	£max
Low season	190.00	250.00
High season	350.00	450.00

Open February–November

CHIDEOCK

Dorset
Map ref 1D2

Village of sandstone thatched cottages in a valley near the dramatic Dorset coast. The church holds an interesting processional cross in mother-of-pearl and the manor house close by is associated with the Victorian Roman Catholic church. Seatown has a pebble beach and limestone cliffs.

Laneside

APPROVED

Laneside Cottage, Chideock, Bridport
Contact: Mr J Turner, Thatch Cottage, Chideock, Bridport, Dorset DT6 6JE
☎ Chideock (01297) 489794
Thatched cottage in village centre. Patio, large garden with play area. Gas CH and open fire. Own parking, all linen, pets welcome. Three bedrooms.
1 self-contained unit; sleeping 6

Price per week:	£min	£max
Low season	120.00	200.00
High season	200.00	360.00

Willowhayne Farm

HIGHLY COMMENDED

Chideock, Bridport DT6 6HY
☎ (01297) 489042
Contact: Mr H E Wickes
16-acre mixed farm. Mellow stone mews cottages, all facing south, set on working farm. Large, peaceful gardens overlooking National Trust land. Private fishing, golf. Riding, walking. Half a mile from the sea.
6 self-contained units; sleeping 2–5

Price per week:	£min	£max
Low season	215.00	300.00
High season	330.00	490.00

Open March–December

The National Grading and Classification Scheme is explained in full at the back of this guide.

CHIPPENHAM

Wiltshire
Map ref 2B2

Ancient market town with modern industry. Notable early buildings include the medieval Town Hall and the gabled 15th C Yelde Hall, now a local history museum. On the outskirts Hardenhuish has a charming hilltop church by the Georgian architect John Wood of Bath.
Tourist Information Centre ☎ (01249) 657733

Roward Farm M

ﾊﾟ ﾊﾟ ﾊﾟ HIGHLY COMMENDED

Draycot Cerne, Chippenham
SN15 4SG
☎ (01249) 758147
Fax (01249) 758149
Contact: Mr David Humphrey

Charming stone cottage on a small farm in peaceful countryside. Furnished and equipped to a very high standard. One bedroom (sleeping up to 4) with spacious living room and kitchen/diner.
1 self-contained unit; sleeping max 4

Price per week:	£min	£max
Low season	150.00	175.00
High season	200.00	250.00

ﾊﾞ ◎ 🍳 ⊙ 🛁 MW 🔦 TV 🖥 🛋 🚗 ▣ 🖵 ✈ P U 🏊 ✦ ✂ ⊗ SP

CHUDLEIGH

Devon
Map ref 1D2

Small market town close to main Exeter to Plymouth road. To the south is Chudleigh Rock, a dramatic limestone outcrop containing prehistoric caves.

Coombeshead Farm M

ﾊﾟ ﾊﾟ ﾊﾟ ﾊﾟ UP TO COMMENDED

Coombeshead Cross, Chudleigh,
Newton Abbot TQ13 0NQ
☎ (01626) 853334
Contact: Mrs A Smith

Comfortable holiday cottages converted from stone farm buildings. Quiet but not isolated, between Dartmoor and sea. Owners in residence.
3 self-contained units; sleeping 6–8

Price per week:	£min	£max
Low season	140.00	260.00
High season	290.00	350.00

Open March–December
ﾊﾞ ◎ 🍳 ⊙ 🛁 MW TV 🖥 🛋 🖵 🚗 P U ✦ ✂ ✈ ⊗ SP

CHURCHSTOW

Devon
Map ref 1C3

Village 2 miles north west of Kingsbridge within easy reach of the South Devon coast.

Thatchers End

ﾊﾟ ﾊﾟ COMMENDED

Tithe Hill, Churchstow, Kingsbridge
Contact: Mrs J P Stevens, 25 Station Road, Keyham, Plymouth PL2 1NF
☎ Plymouth (01752) 563532
Charming, comfortably furnished 17th C thatched 1-bedroomed cottage in rural village. Owner's attention between lettings. Glorious beaches 4 miles away. 1 child aged 8 or over welcome.
1 self-contained unit; sleeping 3

Price per week:	£min	£max
Low season	75.00	180.00
High season	180.00	199.00

Open March–October
ﾊﾞ 8 M ◎ 🍳 ⊙ 🛁 MW TV 🛋 🖵 🚗 U ✦ ✂ ✈ 🏠

COLYFORD

Devon
Map ref 1D2

Horriford Farm M

ﾊﾟ ﾊﾟ ﾊﾟ COMMENDED

Colyford, Colyton EX13 6HW
☎ Colyton (01297) 552316
Contact: Mr and Mrs C E Pady
Situated at the end of a Devon lane near a ford. 17th C wing of farmhouse with many original features, oak screen and inglenook fireplace.
1 self-contained unit; sleeping 8

Price per week:	£min	£max
Low season	200.00	250.00
High season	360.00	420.00

ﾊﾞ M ◎ 🍳 ⊙ 🛁 MW 🔦 TV 🖥 🛋 🖵 P ✦ ✂ ⊗ SP 🏠

Map references apply to the colour maps at the back of this guide.

COLYTON

Devon
Map ref 1D2

Surrounded by fertile farmland, this small riverside town was an early Saxon settlement. Medieval prosperity from the wool trade built the grand church tower with its octagonal lantern and the church's fine west window.

Barritshayes Farm

ﾊﾟ ﾊﾟ ﾊﾟ COMMENDED

Northleigh Road, Colyton
EX13 6DU
☎ (01297) 552485
Fax (01297) 552485
Contact: Mrs P C Green
Four self-catering cottages on smallholding, 5 miles from coast in beautiful Coly Valley. Heated pool, tennis court, games room, croquet. Small, friendly animals. Ample parking. Brochure available.
4 self-contained units; sleeping 4–7

Price per week:	£min	£max
Low season	120.00	184.00
High season	260.00	360.00

Open February–November
ﾊﾞ M ◎ 🍳 ⊙ 🛁 TV 🖥 🛋 🖵 P ⇄ 🏊 ✎ U ✦ ✂ ✈

Colyton Cottages

ﾊﾟ ﾊﾟ ﾊﾟ ﾊﾟ COMMENDED

Briar, Coach and Bramble Cottage, Colyton
Contact: Mrs P A Parker, Colyton Cottage, C/O White Cottage Hotel, Dolphin Street, Colyton, Devon
EX13 6NA
☎ Colyton (01297) 552401
Fax (01297) 553897
Peaceful situation close to edge of town in beautiful Coly/Axe valleys. Optional hotel (bar) facilities. Sorry - no children or pets.
2 self-contained units; sleeping 2–4

Price per week:	£min	£max
Low season	160.00	190.00
High season	260.00	305.00

M ◎ 🍳 ⊙ 🛁 MW TV 🖥 🛋 🖵 🚗 P ✦ ✈ ✂ ⊗ SP T

COLYTON

Continued

Smallicombe Farm

⚹⚹ ⚹ — ⚹⚹⚹ COMMENDED

Northleigh, Colyton EX13 6BU
☎ Wilmington (01404) 831310
Contact: Mrs M A Todd

*Meet our prize-winning rare breed pigs
and other friendly farm animals. Idyllic
rural setting yet close to coast, from
Lyme Regis to Sidmouth. ETB England
for Excellence silver award-winner,
1995.*
Wheelchair access category
1 ♿ & 2 ♿
5 self-contained units; sleeping 2–8

Price per week:	£min	£max
Low season	95.00	295.00
High season	295.00	555.00

🗙 M ◎ ▥ ☉ 🗄 M W 📺 🗄 🖥 ⬛ 🖫 🖵
⬥ P ⛟ ✿ 🗙 🗙 SP 🏠 ◎

COMPTON MARTIN

Bath & North East Somerset
Map ref 2A2

Village below the northern slopes of
the Mendip Hills close to Chew
Valley and Blagdon Lakes.

Wrangle Cottage

⚹⚹ ⚹ COMMENDED

Compton Martin, Bristol BS18 6LB
☎ Mendip (01761) 221279
Contact: Mrs Gill Mayers
*Spacious accommodation with garden
in peaceful, rural location in Mendip
Hills. Convenient for Bath, Bristol and
Wells. Magnificent views across Chew
Valley Lake.*
1 self-contained unit; sleeping 2

Price per week:	£min	£max
Low season	160.00	
High season		260.00

Open February–November

◎ ▥ ☉ 🗄 M W 🖻 📺 🗄 🖥 ⬥ P ✿
🗙

The ⚮ symbol after an
establishment name indicates
that it is a Regional
Tourist Board member.

CONSTANTINE BAY

Cornwall
Map ref 1B2

Wide sands backed with tall dunes
looking toward lighthouse on
Trevose Head. Beautiful sand-dune
golf-course has the ruined chapel of
St Constantine whose font can be
seen in St Merryn Church just
inland.

Trevose Golf and Country Club ⚮

Constantine Bay, Padstow PL28 8JB
☎ Padstow (01841) 520208
Fax (01841) 521057
Contact: Mr P O'Shea
*18-hole championship golf-course plus
two 9-hole golf-courses. Clubhouse with
full catering and bar facilities.
Self-catering units include chalets,
bungalows and flats. Daily rates also
available.*
36 self-contained units; sleeping 2–6

Price per week:	£min	£max
Low season	164.50	455.00
High season	350.00	784.00

Cards accepted: Access, Visa,
Switch/Delta

🗙 ◎ ✿ ▥ ☉ 🗄 📺 🖻 🗄 🖥 ⬛ 🖫 P ⛟ ⚹
U ⬥ ✿ SP

CRACKINGTON HAVEN

Cornwall
Map ref 1C2

Tiny village on the North Cornwall
coast, with a small sandy beach and
surf bathing. The highest cliffs in
Cornwall lie to the south.

Bremor Holiday Bungalows

⚹⚹ APPROVED

Crackington Haven, Bude EX23 0JN
☎ St Gennys (01840) 230340
Contact: Mrs P A Rogers
*Tastefully decorated bungalows with
spacious lawns and excellent walks,
near the sea. Colour TV. Dogs welcome
at no extra charge. Open all year
round. Linen provided.*
2 self-contained units; sleeping 6

Price per week:	£min	£max
Low season	105.00	190.00
High season	190.00	370.00

🗙 M ◎ ▥ ☉ 🗄 M W 📺 🗄 🖥 🖫 🖵
U ✿

A key to symbols can be
found inside the back
cover flap.

Crackington Haven Holiday Cottages ⚮

⚹⚹ ⚹ UP TO COMMENDED

Rosecare, St Gennys, Bude
EX23 0BE
☎ St Gennys (01840) 230310
Fax (01840) 230612
Contact: Mrs P Preller

*Well-equipped Cornish cottages, with
own gardens and picnic tables, close to
beach. Home-cooked take-away meals
service.*
3 self-contained units; sleeping 2–5

Price per week:	£min	£max
Low season	85.00	210.00
High season	210.00	399.00

🗙 M ◎ ▥ ☉ 🗄 📺 🖻 🗄 ⬥ P U ✿
SP

CREDITON

Devon
Map ref 1D2

Ancient town in fertile valley, once
prosperous from wool, now active
in cider-making. Said to be the
birthplace of St Boniface. The 13th
C Chapter House, the church
governors' meeting place, holds a
collection of armour from the Civil
War.

Paschoe Cottage ⚮

⚹⚹ ⚹ COMMENDED

Paschoe Estate, Bow, Crediton
Contact: Mrs V C Blake, The Coach
House, Paschoe Estate, Bow,
Crediton, Devon EX17 6JT
☎ Copplestone (01363) 84288

*Grade II listed stone cottage in tranquil
garden setting, on 380-acre dairy farm
5 miles from Crediton. Enjoy the farm
and its variety of wildlife. Heating
throughout. 3 bedrooms plus cot.*
1 self-contained unit; sleeping 5

Price per week:	£min	£max
Low season	110.00	250.00
High season	200.00	375.00

🗙 M ◎ ▥ ☉ 🗄 M W 📺 🗄 🖥 ⬛ 🖫 🖵
⬥ P ⛟ ✿ ✿ 🗙 🗙 SP 🏠

CREWKERNE

Somerset
Map ref 1D2

This charming little market town on the Dorset border nestles in undulating farmland and orchards in a conservation area. Built of local sandstone with Roman and Saxon origins. The magnificent St Bartholomew's Church dates from 15th C; St Bartholomew's Fair is held in September.

End Cottage
APPROVED

11 Beadon Lane, Merriott
Contact: Mr M Clark, Field House, Unity Lane, Misterton, Crewkerne, Somerset TA18 8NA
☎ Crewkerne (01460) 72619
End-of-terrace cottage, recently renovated, on village edge. Close to shops, tennis courts and within easy distance of National Trust properties, gardens, Hardy country and coast.
1 self-contained unit; sleeping 3

Price per week:	£min	£max
Low season	125.00	
High season	185.00	215.00

CROYDE

Devon
Map ref 1C1

Pretty village with thatched cottages near Croyde Bay. To the south stretch Saunton Sands and their dunelands Braunton Burrows with interesting flowers and plants, nature reserve and golf-course. Cliff walks and bird-watching at Baggy Point, west of the village.

Denham Farm Country House
COMMENDED

North Buckland, Croyde, Braunton EX33 1HY
☎ (01271) 890297
Fax (01271) 890297
Contact: Mrs J Barnes
Barn conversion self-catering units on 160-acre farm near sandy beaches. Ideal for those who enjoy peaceful surroundings, green fields and flower-laden hedgerows.
2 self-contained units; sleeping 4–8

Price per week:	£min	£max
Low season	160.00	340.00
High season	340.00	595.00

Cards accepted: Access, Visa

Fig Tree Cottage
HIGHLY COMMENDED

St Mary's Road, Croyde, Braunton
Contact: Mr and Mrs John Woodington, Fig Tree Farmhouse, St Mary's Road, Croyde, Braunton, Devon EX33 1PJ
☎ Croyde (01271) 890204
Fax (01271) 890204
Grade II listed cottage attached to owner's thatched Devon longhouse, on edge of picturesque village. Large tranquil gardens. Dogs welcome.
1 self-contained unit; sleeping 5

Price per week:	£min	£max
Low season	210.00	325.00
High season	325.00	425.00

Cards accepted: Access, Visa

CUCKLINGTON

Somerset
Map ref 2B3

Village on the Somerset/Dorset border, 3 miles south-east of Wincanton. The hills around the village afford lovely views over Blackmore Vale.

Hale Farm
APPROVED

Cucklington, Wincanton BA9 9PN
☎ Wincanton (01963) 33342
Contact: Mrs P David
Fully-equipped, converted farm unit with beams and stone fireplaces. Quiet location, near farm. Central for touring.
2 self-contained units; sleeping 4

Price per week:	£min	£max
Low season		95.00
High season		175.00

DARTMOOR

See under Ashburton, Belstone, Bovey Tracey, Chagford, Holne, Lustleigh, Moretonhampstead, Okehampton, Tavistock, Yelverton

For ideas on places to visit refer to the introduction at the beginning of this section.

The M symbol after an establishment name indicates that it is a Regional Tourist Board member.

DEVIZES

Wiltshire
Map ref 2B2

Old market town standing on the Kennet and Avon Canal. Rebuilt Norman castle, good 18th C buildings. St John's church has 12th C work and Norman tower. Museum of Wiltshire's archaeology and natural history reflects wealth of prehistoric sites in the county. *Tourist Information Centre ☎ (01380) 729408*

The Gate House
HIGHLY COMMENDED

Wick Lane, Devizes SN10 5DW
☎ (01380) 725283 & 726664
Contact: Mrs L Stratton
Home-from-home comfort. Ground floor accommodation. Set in large garden. No meters. Bath and Salisbury 40 minutes' drive.
1 self-contained unit; sleeping 2

Price per week:	£min	£max
Low season	100.00	
High season		180.00

Home Farm Barn and The Derby
COMMENDED

Home Farm, Heddington, Calne SN11 0PL
☎ (01380) 850523
Fax (01380) 850523
Contact: Mrs D Tyler
17th C barn conversion sleeps 5; bungalow-style stable conversion sleeps 2. On large dairy and arable farm with private lake. Downland walks. Brochures available.
2 self-contained units; sleeping 2–5

Price per week:	£min	£max
Low season	150.00	
High season		350.00

The map references refer to the colour maps towards the end of the guide. The first figure is the map number; the letter and figure which follow indicate the grid reference on the map.

DOWNDERRY

Cornwall
Map ref 1C2

11 Buttlegate

COMMENDED

Downderry, Torpoint
Contact: Mr R H Herbert, Ford
Farm, Coleford, Crediton, Devon
EX17 5DG
☎ (01363) 82325
*Modern spilt-level bungalow with large
sun terrace and overlooking
magnificent sea and coastal views.
Close to beach and coastal footpath.
Well placed for holiday activities.*
2 self-contained units;

Price per week:	£min	£max
Low season	195.00	215.00
High season	240.00	430.00

DULVERTON

Somerset
Map ref 1D1

Set among woods and hills of
south-west Exmoor, a busy riverside
town with a 13th C church. The
Rivers Barle and Exe are rich in
salmon and trout. The information
centre at the Exmoor National Park
Headquarters at Dulverton is open
throughout the year.

Draydon Cottages Exmoor

HIGHLY COMMENDED

Dulverton
Contact: Mrs K W Harris, 6 Crabb
Lane, Alphington, Exeter EX2 9JD
☎ Exeter (01392) 433524

*Fabulous barn conversion cottages
offering outstanding accommodation
with friendly, relaxing atmosphere. In
glorious tranquil setting overlooking
picturesque Barle Valley. Idyllic location
for walking, riding, touring, etc.*
7 self-contained units; sleeping 4–6

Price per week:	£min	£max
Low season	135.00	345.00
High season	230.00	370.00

Open January, March–December

DUNSTER

Somerset
Map ref 1D1

Ancient town with views of Exmoor.
The hilltop castle has been
continuously occupied since 1070.
Medieval prosperity from cloth built
16th C octagonal Yarn Market and
the church. A riverside mill,
packhorse bridge and 18th C hilltop
folly occupy other interesting
corners in the town.

Duddings Country Holidays

HIGHLY COMMENDED

Duddings, Timbercombe, Minehead
TA24 7TB
☎ Timbercombe (01643) 841123
& 841536
Fax (01643) 841252
Contact: Mr G Dobson
*Attractive cottages in old stone barns
on small country estate with heated
indoor pool and tennis court. Attentive
resident owners.*
10 self-contained units; sleeping 2–7

Price per week:	£min	£max
Low season	130.00	320.00
High season	220.00	620.00

Open March–December

EAST BRENT

Somerset
Map ref 1D1

Village 3 miles north-east of
Burnham-on-Sea. St Mary's Church
possesses an ancient stone spire,
mainly 15th C, and a fine plaster
ceiling.

Knoll Farm

UP TO HIGHLY COMMENDED

Jarvis Lane, East Brent, Highbridge
TA9 4HS
☎ Brent Knoll (01278) 760227
Contact: Mrs Jeanne Champion
*150-acre mixed farm. Grade II listed
barns, circa 1703, converted into
holiday accommodation. Old world
features retained, with modern facilities
tastefully incorporated.*
2 self-contained units; sleeping 4–6

Price per week:	£min	£max
Low season	110.00	143.00
High season	190.00	286.00

Open April–October

EGLOSHAYLE

Cornwall
Map ref 1B2

Mill Cottage

HIGHLY COMMENDED

Lemail Quinnies, Egloshayle,
Wadebridge
Contact: Mrs Angela Collop, Lemail
Quinnies, Egloshayle, Wadebridge,
Cornwall PL27 6JQ
☎ Wadebridge (01208) 812566
*Superbly equipped stone-built barn
conversion, furnished to high standard,
close to owner's home in peaceful
countryside. Beaches 6 miles.*
1 self-contained unit; sleeping 4

Price per week:	£min	£max
Low season	180.00	280.00
High season	280.00	360.00

EMBOROUGH

Somerset
Map ref 2A2

Small village high in the Mendips,
close to the main Bath to Wells
road. Excellent fishing on the
Emborough Pool.

Whitnell Manor

APPROVED

Binegar, Emborough, Bath BA3 4UF
☎ Oakhill (01749) 840277
Contact: Mrs A E Rich

*Delightful manor house on working
farm, set in peaceful countryside on
edge of pretty Mendip village between
Bath and Wells. Plenty of things to do
and see, gardens to relax in.*
2 self-contained units; sleeping 4–8

Price per week:	£min	£max
Low season	120.00	
High season		330.00

COLOUR MAPS

Colour maps at the back of
this guide pinpoint all places
in which you will find
accommodation listed.

EXFORD

Somerset
Map ref 1D1

Sheltered village on the River Exe close to Exmoor. Attractive old houses, shops and inns face the village green and the Methodist chapel has 2 windows by Burne-Jones. A footpath north-eastward leads to Dunkery Beacon, Exmoor's highest point.

Riscombe Farm Holiday Cottages and Stabling

COMMENDED

Exford, Minehead TA24 7NH
☎ (01643) 831480
Fax (01643) 831480
Contact: Mr and Mrs Brian/Leone Martin

Stone cottages and stables surrounding attractive courtyard. One and a half miles from village. Very peaceful. In centre of Exmoor National Park.
4 self-contained units; sleeping 2–7

Price per week:	£min	£max
Low season	120.00	160.00
High season	160.00	340.00

EXMOOR

See under Allerford, Bratton, Brayford, Dulverton, Dunster, Exford, North Molton, Parracombe, Porlock, Simonsbath, West Anstey, Wheddon Cross, Winsford, Withypool

EXMOUTH

Devon
Map ref 1D2

Developed as a seaside resort in George III's reign, set against the woods of the Exe Estuary and red cliffs of Orcombe Point. Extensive sands, small harbour, chapel and almshouses, a model railway and A la Ronde, a 16-sided house.
Tourist Information Centre ☎ *(01395) 222299*

The Mews Cottage

APPROVED

The Mews, Knappe Cross, Brixington Lane, Exmouth EX8 5DL
☎ (01395) 272198
Contact: Mrs A Loveridge
Three bedroom cottage set in beautiful wooded and secluded position yet near all local amenities.
1 self-contained unit; sleeping 6

Price per week:	£min	£max
Low season	110.00	165.00
High season	205.00	300.00

Open April–October

For ideas on places to visit refer to the introduction at the beginning of this section.

National gradings and classifications were correct at the time of going to press but are subject to change. Please check at the time of booking.

FALMOUTH

Cornwall
Map ref 1B3

Busy port and fishing harbour, popular resort on the balmy Cornish Riviera. Henry VIII's Pendennis Castle faces St Mawes Castle across the broad natural harbour and yacht basin Carrick Roads, which receives 7 rivers.
Tourist Information Centre ☎ *(01326) 312300*

Anchorage Apartments

COMMENDED

Gyllyngvase Beach, Gyllyngvase Road, Falmouth TR11 4DJ
☎ (01326) 312164
Contact: Mrs P E Cain
1 and 2 bedroom apartments with sea views, in much sought-after position, 1 minute from beach. Pets welcome. High customer recommendations.
9 self-contained units; sleeping 2–5

Price per week:	£min	£max
Low season	75.00	105.00
High season	225.00	330.00

FENNY BRIDGES

Devon
Map ref 1D2

Village on the River Otter, 2 miles north-east of Ottery St Mary.

Skinners Ash Farm 🏍

COMMENDED

Fenny Bridges, Honiton EX14 0BH
☎ Honiton (01404) 850231
Contact: Mrs J S Godfrey
Family-run rare breeds farm. Farm walks, pony rides. Converted barn flat equipped to high standard. Send for colour brochure.

Continued ▶

FENNY BRIDGES

Continued

2 self-contained units; sleeping 6–7

Price per week:	£min	£max
Low season	160.00	
High season		270.00

FORD

Wiltshire
Map ref 2B2

Ivy Cottage M

COMMENDED

The Old Coach Road, Ford,
Chippenham
Contact: Mrs R Helps, 3 The Dene,
Ford, Chippenham, Wiltshire
SN14 8RR
☎ Castle Combe (01249) 782008
Fax (01249) 782398

*Secluded, detached 18th C cottage on
quiet farm track with panoramic views
over the Bybrook Cotswold Valley. 1
mile from Castle Combe, 9 miles from
Bath.*
1 self-contained unit; sleeping 6

Price per week:	£min	£max
Low season	250.00	500.00
High season	400.00	600.00

FOWEY

Cornwall
Map ref 1B3

Set on steep slopes at the mouth of
the Fowey River, important clayport
and fishing town. Ruined forts
guarding the shore recall days of
"Fowey Gallants" who ruled local
seas. The lofty church rises above
the town. Ferries to Polruan and
Bodinnick; August Regatta.
Tourist Information Centre ☎ *(01726)
833616*

Fowey Harbour Cottages M

APPROVED

Chy Vounder, Polruan-by-Fowey
Contact: W J B Hill & Son, 3 Fore
Street, Fowey, Cornwall PL23 1AH
☎ Fowey (01726) 832211
Fax (01726) 832901

---

*A character cottage with views of the
harbour. Ideal sailing and walking
location.*

Price per week:	£min	£max
Low season	100.00	225.00
High season	200.00	350.00

FROME

Somerset
Map ref 2B2

Old market town with modern light
industry, its medieval centre
watered by the River Frome. Above
Cheap Street with its flagstones and
watercourse is the church showing
work of varying periods. Interesting
buildings include 18th C wool
merchants' houses.
Tourist Information Centre ☎ *(01373)
467271*

Executive Holidays (Frome) M

HIGHLY COMMENDED

Iron Mill, Iron Mill Lane Oldford,
Frome BA11 2NR
☎ (01373) 452907 & Mobile 0860
147525
Fax (01373) 453253
Contact: Mr R A Gregory
*Mill and cottage each set in their own
individual peaceful grounds near Bath.
Furnished to highest standards. Ideal
centre for touring, walking, fishing.*
2 self-contained units; sleeping 8–12

Price per week:	£min	£max
Low season	494.00	636.00
High season	997.00	1197.00

Cards accepted: Access, Visa

Ad See display advertisement inside
front cover

The M symbol after an
establishment name indicates
that it is a Regional
Tourist Board member.

Self-catering agencies
which have a selection of
holiday homes to let
are listed in a special section
towards the back
of this guide.

GLASTONBURY

Somerset
Map ref 2A2

Market town associated with Joseph
of Arimathea and the birth of
English Christianity. Built around its
7th C abbey said to be the site of
King Arthur's burial. Glastonbury
Tor with its ancient tower gives
panoramic views over flat country
and the Mendip Hills.
Tourist Information Centre ☎ *(01458)
832954*

Copper Beech

 APPROVED

Magdalene Street, Glastonbury
BA6 9EJ
☎ (01458) 832297
Contact: Mrs I D Ford-Young
*18th C house in historic town. Pleasant
walled garden shaded by large copper
beech tree.*
4 self-contained units; sleeping 2–4

Price per week:	£min	£max
Low season	145.00	225.00
High season	150.00	235.00

Middlewick Farm Holiday Cottages M

COMMENDED

Middlewick Farm, Wick Lane,
Glastonbury BA6 8JW
☎ (01458) 832351
Contact: Mrs A A Coles
*Eight delightful cottages with old world
charm and country-style decor. Set in
cottage gardens. Indoor heated
swimming pool.*
8 self-contained units; sleeping 2–7

Price per week:	£min	£max
Low season	174.00	276.00
High season	270.00	490.00

WELCOME HOST

This is a nationally recognised
customer care programme
which aims to promote
the highest standards of
service and a warm welcome.
Establishments who are taking
part in this initiative are
indicated by the 🌸 symbol.

GORRAN HAVEN

Cornwall
Map ref 1B3

Once important in the pilchard fisheries, now a seaside village gathered at the mouth of its valley. A medieval chapel and Methodist church stand among the cottages overlooking the quay and beautiful unspoilt cliffs spread south-west of Dodman Point.

Tregillan

[APPROVED]

Trewollock Lane, Gorran Haven, St Austell PL26 6NT
☎ Mevagissey (01726) 842452
Contact: Mr and Mrs K Pike
Comfortable self-contained holiday apartments. Beautiful rural area. 600 yards from sandy beach and coastal walks. Private parking. Open all year.
2 self-contained units; sleeping 6

Price per week:	£min	£max
Low season	95.00	95.00
High season	270.00	370.00

HARTLAND

Devon
Map ref 1C1

Hamlet on high, wild country near Hartland Point. Just west, the parish church tower makes a magnificent landmark; the light, unrestored interior holds one of Devon's finest rood screens. There are spectacular cliffs around Hartland Point and the lighthouse.

West Titchberry Farm Cottage

[COMMENDED]

Hartland, Bideford EX39 6AU
☎ (01237) 441287
Contact: Mrs Y Heard
Farm cottage on coastal farm near Hartland Point and lighthouse, quiet, unspoilt area. Coastal walks. Clovelly 6 miles, Bideford and Bude 16 miles. Sorry no pets. Wood-burning stove in lounge - logs free of charge. CH downstairs.
1 self-contained unit; sleeping 6

Price per week:	£min	£max
Low season	90.00	
High season		300.00

HELSTONE

Cornwall
Map ref 1B2

Village 2 miles south-west of Camelford, on the edge of Bodmin Moor and Roughtor, the second highest point in Cornwall.

The Elms

[COMMENDED]

Helstone, Camelford PL32 9RL
☎ Camelford (01840) 213729
Contact: Mrs B E Goldsmith
Well-furnished character cottages with panoramic views. Local golf courses, good walking. Sandy beaches easily reached in 20 minutes by car.
2 self-contained units; sleeping 6

Price per week:	£min	£max
Low season	120.00	165.00
High season	225.00	310.00

HEMYOCK

Devon
Map ref 1D2

Celtic name for summer springs (which never run dry), set in peaceful and beautiful Blackdown Hills only 5 miles from M5 junction 26.

Chapel Cottage

[COMMENDED]

Culm Davy, Hemyock, Cullompton
Contact: Mrs Anthea Edwards, Chapel Farm, Culm Davy, Hemyock, Cullompton, Devon EX15 3UR
☎ Hemyock (01823) 680430
Delightfully secluded country cottage. Beautiful views of unspoilt Blackdown Hills. Pleasant enclosed garden. Ideal for relaxing, walking or touring.
1 self-contained unit; sleeping 4

Price per week:	£min	£max
Low season	140.00	190.00
High season	200.00	250.00

Open March–October

ACCESSIBILITY

Look for the symbols which indicate accessibility for wheelchair users. These are described in detail at the front of this guide.

HOLNE

Devon
Map ref 1C2

Woodland village on south-east edge of Dartmoor. Its 15th C church has a painted medieval screen. Charles Kingsley was born at the vicarage. Holne Woods slope to the River Dart.

Stares Nest Cottage

[COMMENDED]

Holne, Newton Abbot
Contact: Mrs Anne Mortimore, Hazelwood, Holne, Newton Abbot, Devon TQ13 7SJ
☎ Poundsgate (01364) 631235
Near Ashburton, period cottage in the village close to church, shop and pub, and on the edge of Dartmoor in the Dartmoor National Park.
1 self-contained unit; sleeping 5

Price per week:	£min	£max
Low season	174.00	
High season		350.00

HOLWELL

Dorset
Map ref 2B3

Barnes Cross Cottage

[APPROVED]

Holwell, Sherborne DT9 5LA
☎ Bishops Caundle (01963) 23546
Contact: Ms Diana Bath
Well-restored 8-roomed stone cottage with modern kitchen and bathroom and fine views, set in open country.
1 self-contained unit; sleeping 6

Price per week:	£min	£max
Low season	150.00	200.00
High season	200.00	250.00

Open May–October

Establishments should be open throughout the year, unless otherwise stated.

All accommodation in this guide has been graded, or is awaiting a grading, by a trained Tourist Board inspector.

HOLWORTH

Dorset
Map ref 2B3

2 North Holworth Cottage

COMMENDED

Holworth, Dorchester
Contact: Mrs C Thorne, 1 North
Holworth Cottage, Holworth,
Dorchester, Dorset DT2
☎ Warmwell (01305) 852922 &
852282
*Very peaceful cottage in lovely position,
near beaches and coastal walks. Ideal
base for sight-seeing.*
1 self-contained unit; sleeping 5

Price per week:	£min	£max
Low season	165.00	245.00
High season	240.00	335.00

Open April–October

HOPE COVE

Devon
Map ref 1C3

Sheltered by the 400-ft headland of
Bolt Tail, Hope Cove lies close to a
small resort with thatched cottages,
Inner Hope. Between Bolt Tail and
Bolt Head lie 6 miles of beautiful
National Trust cliffs.

Thornlea Mews Holiday Cottages

COMMENDED

Hope Cove, Kingsbridge TQ7 3HB
☎ Kingsbridge (01548) 561319
Contact: Mr J W Blanch

*Attractive cottages 400 yards from safe
sandy beaches. Lovely views, pretty
garden with 1 acre play area. Ample
parking. Pets welcome. Resident
owners.*
10 self-contained units; sleeping 2–7

Price per week:	£min	£max
Low season	50.00	320.00
High season	110.00	400.00

Open March–December

> You are advised to confirm
> your booking in writing.

HORSINGTON

Somerset
Map ref 2B3

Lois Farm

COMMENDED

Horsington, Templecombe
BA8 0EW
☎ Templecombe (01963) 370496
Fax (01963) 370496
Contact: Mr and Mrs P Constant
*90-acre livestock farm. Two light and
spacious recently converted barns on a
peaceful sheep farm in the Blackmore
Vale. Ideal base for touring, walking and
cycling.*
2 self-contained units; sleeping 4–6

Price per week:	£min	£max
Low season	199.00	235.00
High season	239.00	289.00

ILMINSTER

Somerset
Map ref 1D2

Former wool town with modern
industry, set in undulating, pastoral
country. Fine market square of
mellow Ham stone and Elizabethan
school house. The 15th C church
has a handsome tower and lofty,
light interior with notable brass
memorials. Nearby is an art centre
with theatre and gardens.

Myrtle House

APPROVED

Higher Horton, Ilminster
Contact: Mr G E Denman, 51
Halford Road, Ickenham, Uxbridge,
Middlesex UB10 8QA
☎ Uxbridge (01895) 235358

*Comfortable and spacious renovated
19th C farmhouse with some features
dating back to 17th C. Log fire
available. Adjoins fields in quiet village,
convenient for countryside and coast.*
1 self-contained unit; sleeping 8

Price per week:	£min	£max
Low season	200.00	
High season		470.00

Cards accepted: Access, Visa

ISLES OF SCILLY

Map ref 1A3

Picturesque group of islands and
granitic rocks south-west of Land's
End. Peaceful and unspoilt, they are
noted for natural beauty, romantic
maritime history, silver sands, early
flowers and sub-tropical gardens on
Tresco. Main island is St Mary's.
Tourist Information Centre ☎ *(01720)
422536*

Hell Bay Hotel

COMMENDED

Bryher, Isles of Scilly TR23 0PR
☎ Scillonia (01720) 422947
Fax (01720) 423004
Contact: Mrs S M Atkinson
*Beautiful small island location.
Comfortable, well-equipped apartments
opening on to delightful gardens.
Adjacent sandy beaches. Hotel facilities
available to guests.*
4 self-contained units; sleeping 2–4

Price per week:	£min	£max
Low season	175.00	
High season		525.00

Cards accepted: Access, Visa,
Switch/Delta

Holy Vale Holiday Houses

COMMENDED

Holy Vale Farmhouse, St Mary's,
Isles of Scilly TR21 0NT
☎ Scillonia (01720) 422429
Fax (01720) 422429
Contact: Mr and Mrs J R Banfield
*Well-furnished flats, bungalows and
maisonettes in picturesque valley.
Central to St Mary's, a short distance
from bus route, nature trails and
beaches.*
6 self-contained units; sleeping 2–4

Price per week:	£min	£max
Low season	165.00	200.00
High season	246.00	320.00

Open March–October

Standing Stone Terrace

UP TO HIGHLY COMMENDED

Bant's Carn, St Mary's, Isles of Scilly
Contact: Mrs J May, Seaways Flower
Farm, St Mary's, Isles of Scilly
TR21 0NF
☎ Scillonia (01720) 422845
Fax (01720) 423224
*Beautiful recently converted farm
building on the edge of farmland just
by the sea. Very secluded with stunning
views.*

4 self-contained units; sleeping 4–6

Price per week:	£min	£max
Low season	335.00	350.00
High season	555.00	780.00

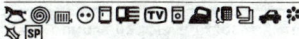

IVYBRIDGE

Devon
Map ref 1C2

Town set in delightful woodlands on the River Erme. Brunel designed the local railway viaduct. South Dartmoor Leisure Centre. *Tourist Information Centre ☎ (01752) 897035*

Strashleigh Annexe

🔑 🔑 COMMENDED

Strashleigh, Ivybridge PL21 9JP
☎ Plymouth (01752) 892226
Fax (01752) 892226
Contact: Mrs P R Salter
Perfectly set, one level self-contained wing of farmhouse on working farm. Fitted kitchen, 1 double en-suite room and cot. Easy access.
1 self-contained unit; sleeping 2

Price per week:	£min	£max
Low season	160.00	160.00
High season	240.00	240.00

Open April–September

KING'S NYMPTON

Devon
Map ref 1C1

Village 3 miles north of Chulmleigh. The church is famous for its fine roofs and rood screen and below the village is Junction Pool which features in "Tarka the Otter" by Henry Williamson.

Collacott Farm

🔑 🔑 ⊸ 🔑 🔑 UP TO COMMENDED

King's Nympton, Umberleigh
EX37 9TP
☎ South Molton (01769) 572491
Fax (01769) 574615
Contact: Mr and Mrs T Sherar
Tasteful, well-equipped barn conversions with heating, fires, private gardens and beautiful views. Tennis, BHS approved riding, swimming, games room, play area.
8 self-contained units; sleeping 4–12

Price per week:	£min	£max
Low season	150.00	367.00
High season	268.00	820.00

Venn Farm Holidays 🏔

🔑 🔑 🔑 UP TO COMMENDED

Venn Farm, King's Nympton, Umberleigh EX37 9TR
☎ South Molton (01769) 572448
Contact: Mrs I Martin
Cottages converted from old stone barn situated on small working farm with views over beautiful countryside to Exmoor and Dartmoor.
5 self-contained units; sleeping 2–7

Price per week:	£min	£max
Low season	120.00	150.00
High season	300.00	450.00

Open March–December

KINGSBRIDGE

Devon
Map ref 1C3

Formerly important as a port, now a market town overlooking head of beautiful, wooded estuary winding deep into rural countryside. Summer art exhibitions; Cookworthy Museum. *Tourist Information Centre ☎ (01548) 853195*

Reads Farm

🔑 🔑 COMMENDED

Loddiswell, Kingsbridge TQ7 4RT
☎ (01548) 550317
Contact: Mrs A Pethybridge
Flats are part of farmhouse in an Area of Outstanding Natural Beauty. Farmland adjoins River Avon. Fishing. Heated swimming pool.
2 self-contained units; sleeping 4–6

Price per week:	£min	£max
Low season	90.00	150.00
High season	150.00	310.00

Open April–September

KINGSKERSWELL

Devon
Map ref 1D2

Village between Newton Abbot and Torquay. St Mary's Church dates from the 15th C.

Barters Old Farmhouse 🏔

🔑 🔑 🔑 COMMENDED

North Whilborough, Kingskerswell
Contact: Mr Tim Hedges, Barters Old Farmhouse, Moradia 2. Lote 4.1.2/7, 8125. Vilamoura, Algarve, Portugal
☎ Portugal (00351) 89321076
Fax (00351) 89321076

Old world farmhouse with delightful gardens. Country hamlet near Torbay, town and beaches. Well furnished and equipped. Three bedrooms, 2 bathrooms.
1 self-contained unit; sleeping 7

Price per week:	£min	£max
Low season	285.00	335.00
High season	335.00	550.00

Open April–October

LANREATH-BY-LOOE

Cornwall
Map ref 1C2

Village 5 miles north-west of Looe. Folk and farm museum in the village tithe barn and Shillamill Lakes nearby.

The Old Rectory 🏔

🔑 🔑 🔑 APPROVED

Lanreath-by-Looe, Looe PL13 2NU
☎ Lanreath (01503) 220247
Fax (01503) 220247
Contact: Mr R W Potts
Gracious Georgian mansion converted into spacious flats, in beautiful secluded gardens on the edge of Lanreath village.
6 self-contained units; sleeping 3–7

Price per week:	£min	£max
Low season	100.00	200.00
High season	180.00	420.00

Establishments should be open throughout the year, unless otherwise stated.

Information on accommodation listed in this guide has been supplied by the proprietors. As changes may occur you are advised to check details at the time of booking.

LAUNCESTON

Cornwall
Map ref 1C2

Medieval "Gateway to Cornwall", county town until 1838, founded by the Normans under their hilltop castle near the original monastic settlement. This market town, overlooked by its castle ruin, has a square with Georgian houses and an elaborately-carved granite church. *Tourist Information Centre ☎ (01566) 772321 or 772333*

Higher Bamham Farm 🏔

UP TO HIGHLY COMMENDED

Launceston PL15 9LD
☎ (01566) 772141
Fax (01566) 775266
Contact: Mrs J A Chapman

Cottages in beautiful countryside, half a mile from Launceston. Magnificent heated indoor swimming pool complex, sauna, solarium, satellite TV, laundry room, private fishing, children's play area.
8 self-contained units; sleeping 4–8

Price per week:	£min	£max
Low season	140.00	195.00
High season	340.00	595.00

LISKEARD

Cornwall
Map ref 1C2

Former stannary town with a livestock market and light industry, at the head of a valley running to the coast. Handsome Georgian and Victorian residences and a Victorian Guildhall reflect the prosperity of the mining boom. The large church has an early 20th C tower and a Norman font.

Beechleigh Cottage Tregondale Farm

HIGHLY COMMENDED

Menheniot, Liskeard PL14 3RG
☎ (01579) 342407
Fax (01579) 342407
Contact: Mrs S Rowe
Just imagine a charming character cottage, fully equipped to a high standard. Double glazed, night stores,

woodburner, tennis court, woodland walks with beautiful wild flowers - just come and explore.
1 self-contained unit; sleeping 4

Price per week:	£min	£max
Low season	120.00	180.00
High season	200.00	395.00

LITTON CHENEY

Dorset
Map ref 2A3

Village 6 miles east of Bridport with stream running past its yellow stone cottages. St Mary's Church dates from the 15th C and contains many brasses and monuments.

Baglake Barn and Brewery Cottage

HIGHLY COMMENDED

Baglake Farm, Litton Cheney, Dorchester DT2 9AD
☎ Long Bredy (01308) 482222
Contact: Mrs and Mr L Barbour

Delightful, listed thatched cottages. The Barn, with wonderful views of Bride Valley, has 2 bedrooms, is all on ground floor and is suitable for disabled. Brewery Cottage has 2 bedrooms, a large inglenook fireplace and a pretty, sheltered garden with stream.
Wheelchair access category 2⅃
2 self-contained units; sleeping 3–4

Price per week:	£min	£max
Low season	290.00	
High season		450.00

A key to symbols can be found inside the back cover flap.

All accommodation in this guide has been graded, or is awaiting a grading, by a trained Tourist Board inspector.

LOOE

Cornwall
Map ref 1C2

Small resort developed around former fishing and smuggling ports occupying the deep estuary of the East and West Looe Rivers. Narrow winding streets, with old inns; museum and art gallery are housed in interesting old buildings. Shark fishing centre, boat trips; busy harbour.

Brier Cottage

COMMENDED

Princes Square, West Looe, Looe
Contact: Mrs L A Gibson, Fine and Fancy Holiday Homes, Fore Street, Looe, Cornwall PL13 1HH
☎ Looe (01503) 262719
Fax (01503) 263562
In heart of the village, 100 yards from river. Shops, pub and restaurants close by. Very comfortable cottage with CH.
1 self-contained unit; sleeping 4

Price per week:	£min	£max
Low season	85.00	125.00
High season	265.00	305.00

Cards accepted: Access, Visa

Bucklawren Farm 🏔

HIGHLY COMMENDED

St Martins, Looe PL13 1NZ
☎ Widegates (01503) 240738
Fax (01503) 240481
Contact: Mrs J Henly
Delightful stone cottages, tastefully converted. Set in large garden. Beautiful location in unspoilt countryside by the sea.
3 self-contained units; sleeping 2–6

Price per week:	£min	£max
Low season	100.00	200.00
High season	200.00	435.00

Open January, March–December
Cards accepted: Access, Visa

Commonwood Cottages 🏔

UP TO DE LUXE

Commonwood Manor Hotel, St Martins Road, East Looe
Contact: Mr and Mrs T E Foxall, Commonwood Manor Hotel, St Martins Road, Looe, Cornwall PL13 1LP
☎ Looe (01503) 262929
Fax (01503) 262632

Detached holiday cottages in landscaped hotel grounds. Breathtaking views over the Looe River valley yet only 5 minutes' walk to harbour, town and beaches.
3 self-contained units; sleeping 4–5

Price per week:	£min	£max
Low season	210.00	360.00
High season	370.00	660.00

Cards accepted: Access, Visa, Amex, Switch/Delta

Hendra Farm Cottages
HIGHLY COMMENDED
Pelynt, Looe PL13 2LU
☎ Lanreath (01503) 220701
Fax (01503) 220701
Contact: Mrs R Chapman
Converted cottages peacefully set on working farm amidst beautiful countryside. A hidden retreat yet only 4 miles to Looe, Polperro and coastal path. Reduction for 2-person occupancy.
3 self-contained units; sleeping 2–5

Price per week:	£min	£max
Low season	100.00	190.00
High season	200.00	395.00

Lemain Garden Apartments
UP TO COMMENDED
Portuan Road, West Looe, Looe PL13 2DR
☎ (01503) 262073
Fax (01503) 265288
Contact: Mrs M Sampson
Early 20th C turreted building, tastefully converted and modernised. In elevated position with 3 storeys, affording magnificent panoramic coastal and sea views.
12 self-contained units; sleeping 2–8

Price per week:	£min	£max
Low season	110.00	290.00
High season	250.00	420.00

Cards accepted: Access, Visa

Plaidy Beach Holiday Apartments
UP TO COMMENDED
Plaidy Park Road, Plaidy, Looe PL13 1LG
☎ (01503) 262044
Contact: Mr N A Jenkins
Panoramic view of sea, coast and beach. Shark fishing, horse riding and golf 10 minutes away; beach 2 minutes. Pets welcome.
8 self-contained units; sleeping 2–7

Price per week:	£min	£max
Low season	80.00	145.00
High season	170.00	365.00

Rock Towers Apartments
HIGHLY COMMENDED
Hannafore Road, West Looe, Looe
Contact: Mr Clive Dixon, Cornish Collection, 73 Bodrigan Road, Barbican, East Looe, Looe, Cornwall PL13 1EH
☎ Looe (01503) 262736
Fax (01503) 262736
Apartments are situated on the front at West Looe with excellent views of beach, estuary and sea.
10 self-contained units; sleeping 4–8

Price per week:	£min	£max
Low season	150.00	200.00
High season	425.00	695.00

Cards accepted: Access, Visa, Switch/Delta

Tremadart Farm
COMMENDED
Duloe, Liskeard PL14 4PE
☎ (01503) 262855
Contact: Mrs E Julian
Large part of farmhouse, secluded position, with large garden. Three miles from Looe. Golf, fishing, sailing, horse riding. Coastal and country walks close by. Quarter of a mile from local amenities.
1 self-contained unit; sleeping 12

Price per week:	£min	£max
Low season	130.00	
High season		595.00

The National Grading and Classification Scheme is explained in full at the back of this guide.

Sunnyside Farm
COMMENDED
Loscombe, Bridport DT6 3TL
☎ Netherbury (01308) 488481
Contact: Major and Mrs M A Everitt
Detached timber-framed bungalow in garden of main house in conservation Area of Outstanding Natural Beauty. Rural area and views to south. Coast 5 miles.
1 self-contained unit; sleeping 5

Price per week:	£min	£max
Low season	165.00	190.00
High season	190.00	210.00

Cornwall's ancient capital which gained its Royal Charter in 1189. Tin from the mines around the town was smelted and coined in the Duchy Palace. Norman Restormel Castle, with its circular keep and deep moat, overlooks the town.

Lanwithan Farm Cottages
COMMENDED
Lostwithiel PL22 0LA
☎ Bodmin (01208) 872444
Fax (01208) 872444
Contact: Mr H F Edward-Collins

Charming selection of Georgian estate cottages (some riverside) set in 110 acres of parkland running down to Fowey River.
7 self-contained units; sleeping 2–6

Price per week:	£min	£max
Low season	130.00	
High season		515.00

You are advised to confirm your booking in writing.

Please check prices and other details at the time of booking.

LOSTWITHIEL

Continued

Newham Farm Cottages

UP TO DE LUXE

Lostwithiel PL22 OLD
☎ Bodmin (01208) 872262
Fax (01208) 873149
Contact: Mrs P Bolsover
17th C original stone buildings delightfully converted into south-facing cottages with spectacular views over the Fowey Estuary. Excellent fishing on 800 yards of private river frontage. Boats available. Heated swimming pool.
5 self-contained units; sleeping 2–6

Price per week:	£min	£max
Low season	198.00	293.00
High season	325.00	669.00

Tredethick Farm Cottages

HIGHLY COMMENDED

The Guildhouse, Tredethick,
Lostwithiel PL22 OLE
☎ Bodmin (01208) 873618
Fax (01208) 873618
Contact: Mr and Mrs T Reed

Exceptional character cottages in beautiful area on edge of Fowey Valley. Wonderful walks and some of the best beaches on Cornwall's south coast nearby. Cottages are winners of 4 awards for architecture and conservation.
6 self-contained units; sleeping 2–6

Price per week:	£min	£max
Low season	135.00	165.00
High season	250.00	490.00

The map references refer to the colour maps towards the end of the guide.
The first figure is the map number; the letter and figure which follow indicate the grid reference on the map.

LUSTLEIGH

Devon
Map ref 1D2

Riverside village of pretty thatched cottages gathered around its 15th C church. The traditional Mayday festival has dancing round the maypole. Just west is Lustleigh Cleave, where Dartmoor is breached by the River Bovey which flows through a deep valley of boulders and trees.

The Mill

APPROVED

Lustleigh, Newton Abbot TQ13 9SS
☎ (01647) 277357
Contact: Mrs J A Rowe
Spacious self-contained part of riverside millhouse on edge of Dartmoor village. Exposed beams, antique furniture. 12-acre smallholding.
1 self-contained unit; sleeping 4

Price per week:	£min	£max
Low season	150.00	200.00
High season	225.00	250.00

LYME REGIS

Dorset
Map ref 1D2

Pretty, historic fishing town and resort set against the fossil-rich cliffs of Lyme Bay. In medieval times it was an important port and cloth centre. The Cobb, a massive stone breakwater, shelters the ancient harbour which is still lively with boats.
Tourist Information Centre ☎ (01297) 442138

Coram Tower Holiday Flats and Cottages

COMMENDED

Coram Tower, Pound Road, Lyme Regis
Contact: Mr and Mrs M Hoskins, Sandwell Holidays Ltd, Coram Tower, Pound Road, Lyme Regis, Dorset DT7 3HX
☎ Lyme Regis (01297) 442012
Self-contained flats and cottages overlooking Lyme Bay. Clean and well-equipped. Parking, garden. Short walk to beach, shops and transport.
11 self-contained units; sleeping 2–8

Price per week:	£min	£max
Low season	115.00	240.00
High season	160.00	480.00

The Gables Holiday Apartments

UP TO COMMENDED

Church Street, Lyme Regis
DT7 3BX
☎ (01297) 442536
Contact: Mr L B Higgins
Spacious self-contained apartments, equipped to high standards. Resident owners. 150 yards level walk to seafront. Licensed lounge bar. Car park.
10 self-contained units; sleeping 2–6

Price per week:	£min	£max
Low season	100.00	185.00
High season	220.00	395.00

Greystones Flat

HIGHLY COMMENDED

Greystones, View Road, Lyme Regis
DT7 3AA
☎ (01297) 443678
Contact: Mrs J B Gollop
Enjoy Heritage Coast views from comfortable ground-floor flat (unsuitable for wheelchairs). Comfortable base for lazing, walking, touring on Dorset, Devon, Somerset borders.
1 self-contained unit; sleeping 4

Price per week:	£min	£max
Low season	170.00	170.00
High season	170.00	357.00

Westover Farm Cottages

UP TO COMMENDED

Westover Farm, Wootton Fitzpaine, Bridport DT6 6NE
☎ Charmouth (01297) 560451
Contact: Mrs Debby Snook
200-acre dairy farm. Two comfortable, spacious 3-bedroomed cottages on edge of picturesque village. Secluded gardens. Heritage coast, National Trust and sea 1.5 miles.
2 self-contained units; sleeping 6–7

Price per week:	£min	£max
Low season	160.00	185.00
High season	190.00	420.00

MAIDEN NEWTON

Dorset
Map ref 2A3

Lancombe Country Cottages

HIGHLY COMMENDED

Lancombe Farm, Maiden Newton, Dorchester

Contact: Mr S A Banks, Lancombe Country Cottages, Lancombe Farm, Maiden Newton, Dorchester, Dorset DT2 0HU
☎ Maiden Newton (01300) 320562
Cottages of character created from a traditional barn, in a secluded setting with magnificent views. Open all year.
5 self-contained units; sleeping 2–5

Price per week:	£min	£max
Low season	152.00	205.00
High season	265.00	424.00

MARAZION

Cornwall
Map ref 1B3

Old town sloping to Mount's Bay with views of St Michael's Mount and a causeway to the island revealed at low tide. In medieval times it catered for pilgrims. The Mount is crowned by a 15th C castle built around the former Benedictine monastery of 1044.

Trenow Farm Cottages
COMMENDED

Trenow Farm, Perranuthnoe, Penzance TR20 9NY
☎ Penzance (01736) 710421
Contact: Mrs F H Phillips
Coastal cottages with spectacular views of Mount's Bay and St Michael's Mount. Ideal touring base, good walking. Parking facilities.
2 self-contained units; sleeping 5

Price per week:	£min	£max
Low season	110.00	
High season		360.00

Vean and Gwel Tregew
APPROVED

Tregew, Rose Hill, Marazion TR17 0HB
☎ Penzance (01736) 710247
Contact: Mrs J H Pool
Quiet, self-contained flats with magnificent views over Mount's Bay. Few minutes' walk to beach and village. Parking. Personally supervised. Regret no pets.
2 self-contained units; sleeping 2–3

Price per week:	£min	£max
Low season	85.00	150.00
High season	150.00	240.00

The White House, Courtyard Cottage and White House Mews
UP TO COMMENDED

The Square, Marazion
Contact: Mr Peter Hall, The Eaves, Porlock, Minehead, Somerset TA24 8QB
☎ Porlock (24 hours) (01643) 863155
Fax (01643) 862042
Immediately above beaches, by shops and the boats to St Michael's Mount. 95 feet long private terraces.
2 self-contained units; sleeping 2–12

Price per week:	£min	£max
Low season	125.00	155.00
High season	145.00	445.00

MERE

Wiltshire
Map ref 2B2

Small town with a grand Perpendicular church surrounded by Georgian houses, with old inns and a 15th C chantry house. On the chalk downs overlooking the town is an Iron Age fort.
Tourist Information Centre ☎ (01747) 861211

Primrose Cottage
COMMENDED

Castle View, The Fields, Mere, Warminster BA12 6EA
☎ (01747) 860103
Contact: Mrs J Bristow
Comfortable cottage in a quiet road amongst a collection of cottages and only a short walk to shops.
1 self-contained unit; sleeping 4

Price per week:	£min	£max
Low season	100.00	
High season		200.00

WELCOME HOST

This is a nationally recognised customer care programme which aims to promote the highest standards of service and a warm welcome. Establishments who are taking part in this initiative are indicated by the ⚜ symbol.

MEVAGISSEY

Cornwall
Map ref 1B3

Small fishing town, a favourite with holidaymakers. Earlier prosperity came from pilchard fisheries, boat-building and smuggling. By the harbour are fish cellars, some converted, and a local history museum is housed in an old boat-building shed. Handsome Methodist chapel; shark fishing, sailing.

Mevagissey House
COMMENDED

Vicarage Hill, Mevagissey, St Austell
Contact: Mrs G Westmacott, Mevagissey House, Vicarage Hill, Mevagissey, St Austell, Cornwall PL26 6SZ
☎ Mevagissey (01726) 842427
Fax (01726) 842427
Old world cottages in 4-acre woodland setting, fully equipped to a high standard. All-inclusive terms. 6 minutes from harbour and beach.
3 self-contained units; sleeping 2–4

Price per week:	£min	£max
Low season	130.00	230.00
High season	250.00	330.00

Cards accepted: Access, Visa

Treleaven Farm Cottages
HIGHLY COMMENDED

Treleaven Farm, Mevagissey, St Austell PL26 6RZ
☎ (01726) 843558 & 842413
Fax (01726) 843558
Contact: Mr L Hennah
Barn conversions close to village and harbours, safe sandy beaches and coastal walks. Games barn and putting green. Everything you need for a memorable holiday. Ample parking. Sorry, no pets.
3 self-contained units; sleeping 2–6

Price per week:	£min	£max
Low season	165.00	325.00
High season	325.00	550.00

The ⚠ symbol after an establishment name indicates that it is a Regional Tourist Board member.

MEVAGISSEY

Continued

Treloen Holiday Apartments 🏵

[UP TO HIGHLY COMMENDED]

Dept E, Polkirt Hill, Mevagissey, St Austell PL26 6UX
☎ (01726) 842406
Fax (01726) 842406
Contact: Mr and Mrs C J Seamark
Quality apartments in secluded clifftop setting, all with spectacular sea views and private balconies/patios. 500 yards from picturesque harbour, shops and beach.
13 self-contained units; sleeping 2–6

Price per week:	£min	£max
Low season	102.00	150.00
High season	232.00	399.00

MINEHEAD

Somerset
Map ref 1D1

Victorian resort with spreading sands developed around old fishing port on the coast below Exmoor. Former fishermen's cottages stand beside the 17th C harbour; cobbled streets climb the hill in steps to the church. Boat trips, steam railway. Hobby Horse festival 1 May.
Tourist Information Centre ☎ (01643) 702624

Anchor Cottage

[HIGHLY COMMENDED]

21 Quay Street, Minehead
Contact: Mr J C Malin, 3 The Courtyard, Bancks Street, Minehead, Somerset TA24 5DJ
☎ Minehead (01643) 707529
Delightful 17th C fisherman's cottage facing Bristol Channel, with rear patio giving superb views. 2 double bedrooms, attic bedroom, bathroom/WC, fully-equipped kitchen, lounge and downstairs WC.
1 self-contained unit; sleeping 5

Price per week:	£min	£max
Low season	185.00	260.00
High season	265.00	385.00

Open March–December

For ideas on places to visit refer to the introduction at the beginning of this section.

MODBURY

Devon
Map ref 1C3

Attractive South Hams town set in rolling countryside, whose Perpendicular church has a rare Devon spire.

Oldaport Farm Cottages 🏵

[HIGHLY COMMENDED]

Modbury, Ivybridge PL21 0TG
☎ (01548) 830842
Fax (01548) 830998
Contact: Miss C M Evans
Comfortable cottages sited on historic small sheep farm in the beautiful Erme Valley, 8 miles from Dartmoor. Sandy beach nearby.
4 self-contained units; sleeping 2–6

Price per week:	£min	£max
Low season	142.00	220.00
High season	262.00	399.00

MONKLEIGH

Devon
Map ref 1C1

Coachmans Cottage

[COMMENDED]

Staddon House, Monkleigh, Bideford
Contact: Mr and Mrs T M Downie, Staddon House, Monkleigh, Bideford, Devon EX39 5UR
☎ Torrington (01805) 623670
Charming character cottage in courtyard setting, within easy reach of national parks and beaches. Price includes cream tea on arrival and fuel for woodburner.
1 self-contained unit; sleeping 4

Price per week:	£min	£max
Low season	100.00	125.00
High season	125.00	165.00

TOWN INDEX

This can be found at the back of the guide. If you know where you want to stay, the index will give you the page number listing all accommodation in your chosen town, city or village.

MONTACUTE

Somerset
Map ref 2A3

Picturesque village named after its "steep hill" and noted for its splendid Elizabethan mansion of Ham stone. By the church stands the gatehouse of a Cluniac priory, built with stone from the hilltop castle. An 18th C folly now crowns the hill, where the Holy Cross of Waltham Abbey was found.

The Annex

[APPROVED]

Park House, Montacute TA15 6UN
☎ Martock (01935) 822949
Contact: Mrs H D McNab
Annexe of country house set in 2 acres of garden, former home of Powys family (authors) and close to many National Trust properties.
1 self-contained unit; sleeping 6

Price per week:	£min	£max
Low season	120.00	180.00
High season	180.00	220.00

MORETONHAMPSTEAD

Devon
Map ref 1C2

Small market town with a row of 17th C almshouses standing on the Exeter road. Surrounding moorland is scattered with ancient farmhouses, prehistoric sites.

Saxon Cottage

[COMMENDED]

Cross Tree House, Moretonhampstead, Newton Abbot TQ13 8NL
☎ (01647) 440726
Contact: Prof and Mrs S Landor
Period cottage with pretty courtyard garden and wealth of oak beams. Outdoor heated pool at end of the village. In Dartmoor National Park, ideal for touring and walks.
1 self-contained unit; sleeping 4

Price per week:	£min	£max
Low season	100.00	200.00
High season	200.00	300.00

Open March–December

Establishments should be open throughout the year, unless otherwise stated.

MOSTERTON

Dorset
Map ref 2A3

Riverside 𝔐

 APPROVED

Bakers Mill Farm, Mosterton,
Beaminster
Contact: Mrs Wort, Willswood
Farm, Woodlands, Southampton,
Hants SO40 7GA
☎ Southampton (01703) 292224 &
771729
*Bungalow on working farm between
Crewkerne and Beaminster. Access and
facilities for wheelchairs and disabled.
Large sun lounge overlooking fields,
large secure kennel and secure
gardens.*
Wheelchair access category 3♿
1 self-contained unit; sleeping 6

Price per week:	£min	£max
Low season	95.00	100.00
High season	150.00	400.00

MOTHECOMBE

Devon
Map ref 1C3

The Flete Estate Holiday Cottages 𝔐

UP TO COMMENDED

Mothecombe, Holbeton, Plymouth
PL8 1LA
☎ Holbeton (01752) 830253
Fax (01752) 830500
Contact: Miss J Webb

*Privately owned 5,000-acre estate in
beautiful countryside, at the sea's edge.
Spectacular West Country setting,
sandy beaches, a paradise for children.*
5 self-contained units; sleeping 6–12

Price per week:	£min	£max
Low season	270.00	650.00
High season	785.00	955.00

A key to symbols can be
found inside the back
cover flap.

MULLION

Cornwall
Map ref 1B3

Small holiday village with a
golf-course, set back from the coast.
The church has a serpentine tower
of 1500, carved roof and beautiful
medieval bench-ends. Beyond
Mullion Cove, with its tiny harbour,
wild untouched cliffs stretch
south-eastward toward Lizard Point.

Polpeor Holiday Apartments and Cottages 𝔐

COMMENDED

Mullion Cove, Helston TR12 7EU
☎ (01326) 240315
Contact: Mr M Raftery

*Completely self-contained apartments
and cottages set in 2.5 acres of
grounds, overlooking Mullion Cove and
adjoining National Trust land.*
6 self-contained units; sleeping 2–6

Price per week:	£min	£max
Low season	110.00	170.00
High season	235.00	495.00

Open February–December

NEWQUAY

Cornwall
Map ref 1B2

Popular resort spread over dramatic
cliffs around its old fishing port.
Many beaches with abundant sands,
caves and rock pools; excellent surf.
Pilots' gigs are still raced from the
harbour and on the headland stands
the stone Huer's House from the
pilchard-fishing days.
Tourist Information Centre ☎ *(01637)
871345*

Fistral Court 𝔐

COMMENDED

Pentire Avenue, Newquay TR7 1PD
☎ (01637) 876890
Fax (01637) 852606
Contact: Mrs C Siveter

Map references apply to
the colour maps at the
back of this guide.

*Small, purpose-built complex on
beautiful Pentire headland, overlooking
beach, coastline and golf course. Ideally
situated for touring or beach holidays.*
19 self-contained units; sleeping 2–8

Price per week:	£min	£max
Low season	140.00	235.00
High season	245.00	695.00

Cards accepted: Access, Visa

NEWTON FERRERS

Devon
Map ref 1C3

Hillside village overlooking wooded
estuary of the River Yealm, with
attractive waterside cottages and
yacht anchorage.

Upwood

COMMENDED

Court Road, Newton Ferrers,
Plymouth PL8 1DA
☎ Plymouth (01752) 872286
Contact: Mrs A M Stackhouse
*Ground floor flat, equipped to high
standard. Easy reach of sea, moors,
National Trust coastline. Sailing, riding,
walking. Cot available.*
1 self-contained unit; sleeping 5

Price per week:	£min	£max
Low season		125.00
High season		225.00

Open January–November

WELCOME HOST

This is a nationally recognised
customer care programme
which aims to promote
the highest standards of
service and a warm welcome.
Establishments who are taking
part in this initiative are
indicated by the ✿ symbol.

NEWTON POPPLEFORD

Devon
Map ref 1D2

Interesting riverside village whose 13th C development as an agricultural settlement can still be traced. Today's thatched cottages date from the 17th C. In the centre is a Victorian church.

Langsford Farm and Cottages

COMMENDED

High Street, Newton Poppleford, Sidmouth EX10 0DU
☎ Colaton Raleigh (01395) 568249 & Mobile 0860 890855
Fax (01395) 568969
Contact: Mr Nigel Hunt
Cottages tastefully converted from an 1874 courtyard of farm buildings in Otter Valley (Area of Outstanding Natural Beauty). RSPB reserve 1 mile.
6 self-contained units; sleeping 2–6

Price per week:	£min	£max
Low season	130.00	180.00
High season	230.00	375.00

Open April–September and Christmas

NORTH MOLTON

Devon
Map ref 1C1

Village on the southern slopes of Exmoor, a centre for local copper mines in the 19th C. A 17th C monument in the church shows the effigies of a mining landlord and his family.

Lambscombe Farm

HIGHLY COMMENDED

North Molton, South Molton EX36 3JU
☎ (01598) 740558
Contact: Mr John Dodds

Grade II listed farmhouse and barns with 16th C origins, providing a delightful period setting 1.5 miles from village on southern edge of Exmoor.
5 self-contained units; sleeping 2–12

Price per week:	£min	£max
Low season	158.00	230.00
High season	377.00	548.00

West Millbrook Farm

UP TO COMMENDED

West Millbrook, Twitchen, South Molton EX36 3LP
☎ (01598) 740382
Contact: Mrs R J Courtney
Farm bordering Exmoor in beautiful, peaceful surroundings. Ideal for touring Exmoor and North Devon/Somerset coast and beaches. Games room. Brochure available.
3 self-contained units; sleeping 3–9

Price per week:	£min	£max
Low season	60.00	
High season		270.00

OKEHAMPTON

Devon
Map ref 1C2

Busy market town near the high tors of northern Dartmoor. The Victorian church, with William Morris windows and a 15th C tower, stands on the site of a Saxon church. A Norman castle ruin overlooks the river to the west of the town. Museum of Dartmoor Life in a restored mill.

Poltimore

UP TO COMMENDED

Ramsley, South Zeal, Okehampton EX20 2PD
☎ (01837) 840209
Contact: Mr P Wilkens
Well-equipped character holiday homes for 2-8 persons, providing direct access to Dartmoor. Close to local shops and pubs.
4 self-contained units; sleeping 2–8

Price per week:	£min	£max
Low season	90.00	185.00
High season	120.00	285.00

Cards accepted: Access, Visa, Amex

PADSTOW

Cornwall
Map ref 1B2

Old town encircling its harbour on the Camel Estuary. The 15th C church has notable bench-ends. There are fine houses on North Quay and Raleigh's Court House on South Quay. Tall cliffs and golden sands along the coast and ferry to Rock. Famous 'Obby 'Oss Festival on 1 May.
Tourist Information Centre ☎ (01841) 533449

Hollyhocks

COMMENDED

4/5 Highlanes Cottages, Padstow
Contact: Mr and Mrs C Riddle, Molesworth House, Royal Cornwall Showground, Wadebridge, Cornwall PL27 7JE
☎ Wadebridge (01208) 812183
Fax (01208) 812713
Delightful and very well furnished Georgian cottage. Beamed ceilings, heating plus log fire, video, bathroom with sunken bath. Three bedrooms plus cot. Garden.
1 self-contained unit; sleeping 6

Price per week:	£min	£max
Low season	210.00	280.00
High season	320.00	400.00

St Ervan Country Cottages

COMMENDED

St Ervan, Rumford, Wadebridge PL27 7TA
☎ Rumford (01841) 540255
Contact: Mrs M E Lloyd
Cottages in grounds of old rectory set in 4 acres. Easy reach of sea and golf courses. Also 2 apartments in main house.
4 self-contained units; sleeping 4–6

Price per week:	£min	£max
Low season	100.00	200.00
High season	250.00	400.00

Open February–November

All accommodation in this guide has been graded, or is awaiting a grading, by a trained Tourist Board inspector.

National gradings and classifications were correct at the time of going to press but are subject to change. Please check at the time of booking.

PAIGNTON

Devon
Map ref 1D2

Lively seaside resort with a pretty harbour on Torbay. Bronze Age and Saxon sites are occupied by the 15th C church, which has a Norman door and font. The beautiful Chantry Chapel was built by local landowners, the Kirkhams.
Tourist Information Centre ☎ (01803) 558383

Torbay Holiday Motel ⚠

🔑 🔑 🔑 APPROVED

Totnes Road, Paignton TQ4 7PP
☎ Torquay (01803) 558226
Fax (01803) 663375
Contact: Mr G H Booth
On the A385 in peaceful countryside, close to all amenities of Torbay. Ideal base for touring Devon.
42 self-contained units; sleeping 4–7

Price per week:	£min	£max
Low season	189.00	378.00
High season	252.00	504.00

Cards accepted: Access, Visa, Amex

🐟🐾📶🍽️📺📠📧☕🚲∥🚗P
🎣🏊⛵☀️ SP T

PARRACOMBE

Devon
Map ref 1C1

Pretty village spreading over the slopes of a river valley on the western edge of Exmoor.

Voley Farm

🔑 🔑 🔑 🔑 HIGHLY COMMENDED

Parracombe, Barnstaple EX31 4PG
☎ (01598) 763315
Fax (01598) 763315
Contact: Mrs Amanda Chadwick
50-acre livestock farm. Exmoor. Two comfortable farm cottages in secluded valley. Original Victorian barn features. Fully equipped with central heating and woodburners. Beautiful walks. Near coast.
2 self-contained units; sleeping 6

Price per week:	£min	£max
Low season	150.00	210.00
High season	260.00	390.00

Open March–December

🐟🖥️📶🍽️📺MW📺📠📧☕🛒
🚗PU♪☀️✈️ SP 🏠

For ideas on places to visit refer to the introduction at the beginning of this section.

PENDEEN

Cornwall
Map ref 1A3

Small village on the beautiful coast road from Land's End to St Ives. A romantic landscape of craggy inland cliffs covered with bracken shelving to a rocky shore. There are numerous prehistoric sites, disused tin mines, a mine museum at Geevor and a lighthouse at Pendeen.

Trewellard Manor Farm

🔑 🔑 🔑 COMMENDED

Pendeen, Penzance TR19 7SU
☎ St Just (01736) 788526
Fax (01736) 788526
Contact: Mrs M Bailey
Two attractive cottages converted from stables. Situated across courtyard from owner's farmhouse on edge of village. Easy reach beaches and coast path. Special winter short breaks.
2 self-contained units; sleeping max 4

Price per week:	£min	£max
Low season	150.00	225.00
High season	225.00	325.00

🐟🖥️📶🍽️📺📠📧☕🚗🌲☀️🚫
SP

PENTEWAN

Cornwall
Map ref 1B3

Tiny 19th C port with a pretty square, hidden from the main road, overlooked by a Regency terrace with luxuriant flower gardens and a Methodist chapel. Separated by the River Winnick from a broad, sandy beach.

Crofters End

🔑 🔑 🔑 COMMENDED

3 Glentowan Road, Pentewan, St Austell
Contact: Mrs J D Clemo, Rescorla Farm, Rescorla, St Austell, Cornwall PL26 8YT
☎ St Austell (01726) 850168
Fax (01726) 850168
Pretty cottage situated just off the village square, 5 minutes' walk from the beach. Cliff walks and cycle trail from the village.
1 self-contained unit; sleeping 4–6

Price per week:	£min	£max
Low season	120.00	
High season		380.00

Cards accepted: Access, Visa

🐟🖥️📶🍽️📺MW📺📠📧☕
P☀️ SP

PENZANCE

Cornwall
Map ref 1A3

Resort and fishing port on Mount's Bay with mainly Victorian promenade and some fine Regency terraces. Former prosperity came from tin trade and pilchard fishing. Grand Georgian style church by harbour. Georgian Egyptian building at head of Chapel Street and Morrab Gardens.
Tourist Information Centre ☎ (01736) 62207

Saint Pirans Cottages ⚠

🔑 🔑 🔑 COMMENDED

Perranuthnoe, Penzance
Contact: Mrs Jill Gresswell, Appletree Cottage, Charters Road, Sunningdale, Ascot, Berkshire SL5 0DE
☎ Ascot (01344) 21220 & Mobile 0860 551834
Fax (01344) 872458
Comfortable cottages 400 metres from sandy cove in pretty village, 5 miles east of Penzance. Ideal for family holidays and excellent centre for walkers.
6 self-contained units; sleeping 2–5

Price per week:	£min	£max
Low season	100.00	200.00
High season	250.00	330.00

🐟🖥️📶🍽️📺MW📺📺📠📧☕
🚗P☀️✈️🚫 SP

PERRANPORTH

Cornwall
Map ref 1B2

Small seaside resort developed around a former mining village. Today's attractions include exciting surf, rocks, caves and extensive sand dunes.

Blue Seas Holiday Caravans

Perranporth
Contact: Mr and Mrs B A Caple, Dunroamin, Newquay Road, Goonhavern, Truro, Cornwall TR4 9QD
☎ Truro (01872) 572176 & Mobile 0836 604373

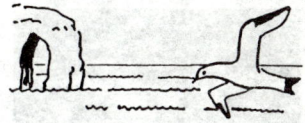

Caravans all with sea and beach views
Continued ▶

PERRANPORTH

Continued

on quiet family park, 10 minutes' walk on pavement to beach and shops.
12 self-contained units; sleeping 4–6

Price per week:	£min	£max
Low season	75.00	245.00
High season	275.00	320.00

Open April–October

4 Eureka Vale
COMMENDED

Perranporth
Contact: Mr and Mrs J A Cuthill, 27 St George's Hill, Perranporth, Cornwall TR6 0JS
☎ Truro (01872) 573624
Early Victorian cottage in a quiet, private location with a sheltered garden, 1150 metres from a sandy surfing beach. Close to all amenities.
1 self-contained unit; sleeping 6

Price per week:	£min	£max
Low season	140.00	295.00
High season	305.00	425.00

Hendra Farm
COMMENDED

Rose, Truro TR4 9PS
☎ Truro (01872) 572273
Contact: Mr Janet Symons
160-acre dairy & livestock farm. Spacious old farmhouse with pretty garden, on family dairy and sheep farm. Private coarse fishing, close to glorious beaches.
1 self-contained unit; sleeping 7

Price per week:	£min	£max
Low season	200.00	325.00
High season	325.00	550.00

Leycroft Country Club Ltd
UP TO COMMENDED

Leycroft House, Perrancoombe, Perranporth TR6 0JQ
☎ Truro (01872) 573044
Fax (01872) 571440
Contact: Mr Martin Gaunt

Naturally attractive 15-acre estate, 1.5 miles from sea. Well-appointed lodges and cottage-style bungalows set in wooded valley. Shallow stream and pond, abundant wildlife and flora.
29 self-contained units; sleeping 2–8

Price per week:	£min	£max
Low season	95.00	225.00
High season	195.00	500.00

Open March–December
Cards accepted: Access, Visa

Mansar Holiday Flats
COMMENDED

Lamorne Close, St Michaels Road, Perranporth TR6 0HQ
☎ Truro (01872) 573313
Contact: Mrs Bea Green
Comfortable self-catering flats with panoramic views of beach, sea and golf-course. Approximately half a mile to beach and shops.
2 self-contained units; sleeping 5

Price per week:	£min	£max
Low season	110.00	175.00
High season	200.00	350.00

Sand Bay Holiday Flats
UP TO HIGHLY COMMENDED

St Pirans Road, Perranporth TR6 0BH
☎ Truro (01872) 572081
Contact: Mr J Mansfield
High-class flats and villas adjacent to Perranporth's 3 miles of golden sands and surf. Level 2 minute walk to shops.
21 self-contained units; sleeping 6–10

Price per week:	£min	£max
Low season	120.00	150.00
High season	375.00	495.00

PEWSEY

Wiltshire
Map ref 2B2

The Cottage
COMMENDED

The Old Manor, Manningford Bruce, Pewsey
Contact: Mr Chris Sangster, The Old Manor, Manningford Bruce, Pewsey, Wiltshire SN9 6JW
☎ Marlborough (01672) 563479
Fax (01672) 563356
Thatched cottage with private garden and country views in grounds of 17th C timbered manor house. Two miles south of Pewsey, off A345.
1 self-contained unit; sleeping 4

Price per week:	£min	£max
Low season	165.00	200.00
High season	200.00	270.00

Open March–October

PIDDLEHINTON

Dorset
Map ref 2B3

Whites Dairy House
APPROVED

16 High Street, Piddlehinton, Dorchester
Contact: Mrs C M Kelsey, Quaives Farm, Wickhambreaux, Canterbury, Kent CT3 1RY
☎ Canterbury (01227) 721217

Delightful, well-equipped 17th C stone/thatched house. Sheltered garden with stream. Lovely walking area. 1 double and 2 twin bedrooms.
1 self-contained unit; sleeping 6

Price per week:	£min	£max
Low season	150.00	
High season		390.00

PLYMOUTH

Devon
Map ref 1C2

Devon's largest city, major port and naval base. Old houses on the Barbican and ambitious architecture in modern centre, with aquarium, museum and art gallery, the Dome - a heritage centre on the Hoe. Superb coastal views over Plymouth Sound from the Hoe.
Tourist Information Centre ☎ (01752) 264849 or 266031 or 266030

Coombe Farm
COMMENDED

Wembury Road, Plymstock, Plymouth PL9 0DE
☎ (01752) 401730
Contact: Mrs S J MacBean
A warm, cosy holiday base on a working dairy farm. Central for touring the moors, coast and city.
1 self-contained unit; sleeping 5

Price per week:	£min	£max
Low season	100.00	
High season		340.00

Hoeside Holiday Flats

🗝🗝🗝🗝 COMMENDED

10 Athenaeum Street, Plymouth
Contact: Mrs D Seymour, The Old
Rectory, 20 Penlee Way, Stoke,
Plymouth PL3 4AW
☎ Plymouth (01752) 563504
Fax (01752) 563504
*Pleasant self-contained flats, centrally
situated on Plymouth Hoe. Athenaeum
Street flats have car park and all have
colour TV, microwave. Linen supplied.*
9 self-contained units; sleeping 2–8

Price per week:	£min	£max
Low season	130.00	190.00
High season	220.00	350.00

Open May–October and Christmas

🖼 M ◎ ▥ ⊙ 🛏 MW 🖵 TV ☕ 🛍 ▣
P SP

Cornwall
Map ref 1C3

Picturesque fishing village clinging to
steep valley slopes about its
harbour. A river splashes past
cottages and narrow lanes twist
between. The harbour mouth,
guarded by jagged rocks, is closed by
heavy timbers during storms.

Osprey Cottage and Harbour View Cottage ⋀

🗝🗝🗝🗝 COMMENDED

Talland Hill, Polperro, Looe
PL13 2RX
☎ (01503) 272819
Fax (01503) 272670
Contact: Mrs M Ferguson
*Harbourside cottages, all south-facing,
with magnificent harbour/sea views.
Convenient for village centre. Parking.*
3 self-contained units; sleeping 4–8

Price per week:	£min	£max
Low season	160.00	250.00
High season	300.00	495.00

🖼 M ◎ ▥ ⊙ 🛏 MW TV ☕ 🛍 ▣ ◰ ☕
P U ❋ 🎿 SP 🏠

WELCOME HOST

This is a nationally recognised
customer care programme
which aims to promote
the highest standards of
service and a warm welcome.
Establishments who are taking
part in this initiative are
indicated by the ✿ symbol.

Somerset
Map ref 1D1

Village set between steep Exmoor
hills and the sea at the head of
beautiful Porlock Vale. The narrow
street shows a medley of building
styles. South westward is Porlock
Weir with its old houses and tiny
harbour and further along the shore
at Culbone is England's smallest
church.

Hunters Rest

🗝🗝🗝🗝 COMMENDED

Mill Lane, Hawkcombe, Porlock,
Minehead TA24 8QW
☎ (01643) 862349
Contact: Mr B West

*Totally self-contained, very spacious
apartment in secluded setting, 10
minutes' walk from Porlock. Lovely
views and direct access to superb
woodland and moorland walks.*
1 self-contained unit; sleeping 4

Price per week:	£min	£max
Low season	140.00	200.00
High season	200.00	280.00

🖼 M ◎ ▥ ⊙ 🛏 🖵 TV ☕ ▣ ❋ SP

Cornwall
Map ref 1B2

Small village sheltering in a narrow
inlet on the dramatic north Cornish
coast. In the 19th C the shingle
beach was a loading site for slate
from the nearby Delabole quarry.

Green Door Cottages ⋀

🗝🗝🗝🗝 COMMENDED

Port Gaverne, Port Isaac PL29 3SQ
☎ Bodmin (01208) 880244 &
Freephone 0500 657867
Fax (01208) 880151
Contact: Mrs M Ross
*Restored 18th C self-contained Cornish
fishermen's cottages built around
enclosed sheltered courtyard in
picturesque cove half a mile from Port
Isaac.*
6 self-contained units; sleeping 3–8

Price per week:	£min	£max
Low season	220.00	265.00
High season	375.00	475.00

Cards accepted: Access, Visa, Diners,
Amex, Switch/Delta

🖼 ◎ ◿ ▥ ⊙ 🛏 TV ☕ 🛍 ▣ P ➤ ❋ SP
🏠

Cornwall
Map ref 1B2

Old fishing port of whitewashed
cottages, twisting stairways and
narrow alleys. A stream splashes
down through the centre to the
harbour. Nearby stands a 19th C
folly, Doyden Castle, with a
magnificent view of the coast.

Trevathan Farm ⋀

🗝🗝🗝🗝🗝 — 🗝🗝🗝🗝🗝

UP TO HIGHLY COMMENDED

St Endellion, Port Isaac PL29 3TT
☎ Bodmin (01208) 880248
Fax (01208) 880248
Contact: Mrs H Symons
*300-acre mixed farm. Cottages with
beautiful countryside views, on working
farm. Very friendly animals to feed.
Tennis court, games room, fitness room
on farm. Water sports, sandy beaches,
golf, riding 3 miles. Also large period
house sleeping 12 + cots. Overlooking
wooded valley.*
10 self-contained units;
sleeping 2–12

Price per week:	£min	£max
Low season	120.00	300.00
High season	320.00	910.00

🖼 M ◎ ▥ ⊙ 🛏 MW 🖵 TV ☕ 🛍
▣ ☕ P ◈ U ↑ ❋ SP 🏠

Dorset
Map ref 2B3

Joined by a narrow isthmus to the
coast, a stony promontory sloping
from the lofty landward side to a
lighthouse on Portland Bill at its
southern tip. Villages are built of the
white limestone for which the "isle"
is famous.

Greenhill Cottage

🗝🗝🗝🗝 APPROVED

1 Greenhill Terrace, Portland
Contact: Mrs M Blues, Fallow Wood,
12 Oak Road, Cobham, Surrey
KT11 3AZ
☎ Cobham (01932) 862788
*Cosy Victorian stone cottage in quiet
cul-de-sac overlooking Chesil Beach.
Extensive views across Lyme Bay.
Modern facilities include dishwasher
and microwave. Bedlinen and towels
supplied. Private parking.*

Continued ▶

PORTLAND
Continued

1 self-contained unit; sleeping 4

Price per week:	£min	£max
Low season	250.00	
High season		325.00

🛏🎧◎🚿☺🍴MW📺🔲🧺🍽🖥P❄✈SP

The Old Higher Lighthouse
COMMENDED

Portland Bill, Portland
Contact: Mrs F E Lockyer, The Old Higher Lighthouse, Portland Bill, Portland, Dorset DT5 2JT
☎ Portland (01305) 822300

Beautiful cottage with all the modern comforts of home, set in decorative gardens and totally surrounded by the sea and coastal views. All welcome to our lighthouse tower and swimming pool.
1 self-contained unit; sleeping 6

Price per week:	£min	£max
Low season	180.00	270.00
High season	300.00	400.00

🛏🎧◎🚿☺🍴MW📺🔲🧺🖥P➡🛒♿❄✈SP🏢

PORTSCATHO
Cornwall
Map ref 1B3

Coastal village spreading along low cliffs of Gerrans Bay on the eastern side of the Roseland Peninsula. Seaside buildings show a variety of styles from late Georgian houses to small, interestingly-designed modern blocks.

Anchorage and Chapel Cottages
HIGHLY COMMENDED

The Anchorage, Portscatho, Truro TR2 5HE
☎ (01872) 580492
Fax (01872) 580933
Contact: Mrs D A Cohen
Unspoilt fishing village. Waterside cottages of character with gardens, terraces, beside coastal path. Lovely beaches, excellent walking. One cottage has two bathrooms, both have baths and showers. Well-equipped kitchens. Near shops.

2 self-contained units; sleeping 4

Price per week:	£min	£max
Low season	140.00	
High season		405.00

🛏🎧◎🚿☺🍴MW📺🔲🧺🖥🚗P❄✈SP🏢

PRAA SANDS
Cornwall
Map ref 1B3

Small village named after the long, sandy bathing beach to the south. Picturesque Prussia Cove, a former haunt of smugglers, lies to the west and is sheltered by Cudden Point. A tower of the 16th C Pengersick Castle remains.

Sea Meads Holiday Homes ⓜ
COMMENDED

Sea Meads Lodge Sea Meads Estate, Praa Sands, Penzance
Contact: Miss Nicky Faull, Best Leisure, North Hill, Shirwell, Barnstaple, Devon EX31 4LG
☎ Barnstaple (01271) 850611
Fax (01271) 850693
Detached, well-equipped houses with gardens. Yards from beach. Superb sub-tropical-like setting, sea views. Ideal for family holidays.
5 self-contained units; sleeping 5–8

Price per week:	£min	£max
Low season	189.00	202.00
High season	292.00	707.00

🛏🎧◎🚿☺🍴MW📺🔲🧺🖥🚗P♿🎵❄SPⓉ

ST AUSTELL
Cornwall
Map ref 1B3

Leading market town, the meeting point of old and new Cornwall. One mile from St Austell Bay with its sandy beaches, old fishing villages and attractive countryside. Ancient narrow streets, pedestrian shopping precincts. Fine church of Pentewan stone and Italianate Town Hall.

Poltarrow Farm
UP TO HIGHLY COMMENDED

St Mewan, St Austell PL26 7DR
☎ St Austell (01726) 67111
Contact: Mrs J D Nancarrow
45-acre mixed farm. Charming, very comfortable, well-equipped cottages on working farm with pets and ponies for children. Peaceful countryside near the sea, central for touring.
Wheelchair access category 3♿
3 self-contained units; sleeping 2–6

Price per week:	£min	£max
Low season	100.00	200.00
High season	200.00	450.00

Cards accepted: Access, Visa

🛏🎧◎🚿☺🍴MW📺🔲🧺🖥🚗P♿❄SP

ST CLETHER
Cornwall
Map ref 1C2

Small village in woods on the slope of a rocky river valley, at the northern edge of Bodmin Moor. Romantically set amid sheep pasture beneath the valley's crags is the 15th C baptistry of St Clether's holy well.

Ta Mill Holidays
UP TO COMMENDED

St Clether, Launceston PL15 8PS
☎ Lifton (01566) 784232 & Otterham Station (01840) 261797
Fax (01840) 261797
Contact: Mr and Mrs M F Shopland
Stone and slate cottages, log cabins and cedar lodges, set in a sheltered valley. Tranquil location twixt moorland and coast.
12 self-contained units; sleeping 2–10

Price per week:	£min	£max
Low season	120.00	400.00
High season	330.00	540.00

🛏🎧◎☺🍴MW📺🔲🧺🖥🍽❄SP

ST COLUMB MAJOR
Cornwall
Map ref 1B2

Old market town of slate-hung houses and a grand church overlooking the wooded valley at one end of the main street. Notable brass monuments in the church commemorate the Arundells of Lanherne. On Shrove Tuesday the ancient game of hurling takes place in the streets of the town.

Higher Polgrain ⓜ
COMMENDED

St Wenn, Bodmin PL30 5PR
☎ St Columb (01637) 880637
Contact: Mrs C Vaughan
Peaceful country barn conversion. Fitted and furnished to a high standard. Heated indoor plunge pool. Inclusive rates. Linen provided. Brochure on request.

4 self-contained units; sleeping 2–4

Price per week:	£min	£max
Low season	175.00	335.00
High season	305.00	475.00

Open January, March–December

🛁🐾💻⌨☉🗄MW 📺🎞🍳💼👜 🛋⛽
P 🏊❄✈ SP

ST IVES

Cornwall
Map ref 1B3

Old fishing port, artists' colony and holiday town with good surfing beach. Fishermen's cottages, granite fish cellars, a sandy harbour and magnificent headlands typify a charm that has survived since the 19th C pilchard boom. Tate Gallery opened in 1993.
Tourist Information Centre ☎ (01736) 796297

The Studio

🗝🗝🗝 APPROVED

St Peters Street, St Ives
Contact: Lady C A Holland, Little Parc Owles, Carbis Bay, St Ives, Cornwall TR26 2RQ
☎ Penzance (01736) 793015
Fax (01736) 793258
This 2 storey converted sail loft has a spacious living room, kitchen, 5 bedrooms, 1 bathroom/WC, 1 shower/WC, generous heating and hot water.
1 self-contained unit; sleeping 9

Price per week:	£min	£max
Low season	125.00	280.00
High season	390.00	445.00

🛁M💻⌨☉🗄MW 📺🎞🍳💼🛋🏠

ST MAWES

Cornwall
Map ref 1B3

Small resort and yachting centre in a pretty estuary setting on the Roseland Peninsula. Enclosed by fields and woods of the Percuil River, it is said to be the warmest winter resort in Britain.

Prydes Cottage

🗝🗝🗝 HIGHLY COMMENDED

20 Marine Parade, St Mawes, Truro
Contact: Mrs M Lumby, Poachers Reach, Feock, Truro, Cornwall TR3 6SQ
☎ Devoran (01872) 864400
Waterfront cottage with panoramic views over sailing waters of Carrick Roads and beyond. Spacious and light with private patio at rear. Ideal for birdwatchers, walkers and artists. Woodburner makes it cosy all year.

Cottages on Restronguet Creek and at Perranwell also available.
1 self-contained unit; sleeping 6

Price per week:	£min	£max
Low season	270.00	340.00
High season	340.00	530.00

🛁🐾💻⌨☉🗄MW ⚡📺🎞🍳💼👜
🛋🚗❄✈ SP

ST MAWGAN

Cornwall
Map ref 1B2

Pretty village of great historic interest, on wooded slopes in the Vale of Lanherne. At its centre, an old stone bridge over the River Menahyl is overlooked by the church with its lofty buttressed tower. Among ancient stone crosses in the churchyard is a 15th C lantern cross with carved figures.

Polgreen Farm

🗝🗝🗝 APPROVED

St Mawgan-in-Pydar, Newquay TR8 4AG
☎ St Mawgan (01637) 860700
Contact: Mrs J A Wake, NDD
Rural cottage adjoining traditional Cornish farmhouse, the residence of landscape artist Judith Wake, N.D.D., and her ornithologist husband Robin Wake. Halfway between Mawgan Porth beach (1 mile) and the attractive village of St Mawgan, with views of beautiful Vale of Lanherne. Painting, bird-watching, riding, golf, badminton. Home-grown produce, including culinary herbs.
1 self-contained unit; sleeping 5

Price per week:	£min	£max
Low season	175.00	200.00
High season	250.00	362.00

Open April–October

🛁M💻⌨☉🗄📺🎞🍳💼🛋🚗P U
🏳❄ SP 🏠

Retorrick Mill 🅼

🗝🗝🗝 APPROVED

St Mawgan, Newquay TR8 4BH
☎ St Mawgan (01637) 860460
Contact: Mr and Mrs R A Alexander
Set in 9 acres in the Lanherne Valley. Quiet and secluded, yet 1 mile from large sandy beach, 6 miles from Newquay and 10 miles from the fishing port of Padstow.
7 self-contained units; sleeping 2–5

Price per week:	£min	£max
Low season	85.00	130.00
High season	145.00	290.00

Open April–October

🛁M💻⌨☉🗄📺🍳P U❄ SP

ST TUDY

Cornwall
Map ref 1B2

Colesent Cottages 🅼

🗝🗝🗝 APPROVED

St Tudy, Wadebridge
Contact: Mrs S Zamaria, Colesent Cottages, St Tudy, Bodmin, Cornwall PL30 4QX
☎ St Tudy (01208) 850112
Traditional stone cottages, well appointed. Quiet location, views of Camel Valley and Bodmin Moor. Late night shop/garage 2 miles away.
2 self-contained units; sleeping 5–7

Price per week:	£min	£max
Low season	150.00	195.00
High season	385.00	415.00

Cards accepted: Access, Visa, Diners, Amex

🛁🐾💻⌨☉🗄📺🍳💼👜🛋🚗P❄♀
SP T

SALCOMBE

Devon
Map ref 1C3

Sheltered yachting resort of whitewashed houses and narrow streets in a balmy setting on the Salcombe Estuary. Palm, myrtle and other Mediterranean plants flourish. There are sandy bays and creeks for boating.
Tourist Information Centre ☎ (01548) 843927

Coxswain's Watch 🅼

🗝🗝🗝 COMMENDED

59 Fore Street, Salcombe
Contact: Mrs S Hannah, Robert Oulsnam & Co, 79 Hewell Road, Barnt Green, Birmingham B45 8NL
☎ (0121) 445 3311
Fax (0121) 445 6026

Well-appointed 3-bedroomed apartment, enjoying beautiful views, near harbour, shops and ferry. Motor-boat and indoor swimming pool.
1 self-contained unit; sleeping 6

Price per week:	£min	£max
Low season	400.00	
High season		910.00

🛁💻⌨☉🗄MW 📺🎞🍳💼👜🏊
❄✈

SALCOMBE

Continued

Rock House Marine Apartment Hotel ▲

🔑🔑 ━ 🔑🔑🔑 **UP TO COMMENDED**

Thurlestone Sands, Kingsbridge
TQ7 3JY
☎ Kingsbridge (01548) 561285
Fax (01548) 562085
Contact: Mr A Ferris

Rock House Marine is in countryside adjoining award-winning sandy beach. Flats and cottages. Bar/restaurant, swimming pool, games and play rooms.
14 self-contained units; sleeping 4–9

Price per week:	£min	£max
Low season	100.00	200.00
High season	330.00	665.00

Cards accepted: Access, Visa

🔌🐾Ⓜ◎🔥·⊙🗂TV🖭⌖🍳📠P➳
🍴❋❄SP T

SALISBURY PLAIN

See under Amesbury, Winterbourne Stoke

SEATON

Devon
Map ref 1D2

Small resort lying near the mouth of the River Axe. A mile-long beach extends to the dramatic cliffs of Beer Head. Annual art exhibition in July.
Tourist Information Centre ☎ *(01297) 21660 or 21689*

West Ridge Bungalow

🔑🔑 **COMMENDED**

Harepath Hill, Seaton EX12 2TA
☎ (01297) 22398
Fax (01297) 22398
Contact: Mr E P Fox

Comfortably-furnished bungalow on elevated ground in 1.5 acres of lawns and gardens. Panoramic views of Axe Estuary and sea.

---

1 self-contained unit; sleeping 5

Price per week:	£min	£max
Low season	125.00	225.00
High season	255.00	315.00

Open March–October

🐾🖌🖆⊙🗂TV🖭⌖🍳📠P∪⼁❋
SP T

SENNEN COVE

Cornwall
Map ref 1A3

Jubilee Cottage

🔑🔑🔑 **APPROVED**

Sennen Cove, Penzance
Contact: Mr J Nicholas, Harbour View, Sennen Cove, Penzance, Cornwall TR19 7DE
☎ Penzance (01736) 871206
Delightful cottage with panoramic views to the harbour and Whitsand Bay. Easy reach of Land's End and open-air Minack Theatre. Sennen Cove has been awarded a Blue Flag and is a good surfing beach.
1 self-contained unit; sleeping 5

Price per week:	£min	£max
Low season	100.00	200.00
High season	230.00	380.00

🐾Ⓜ◎🔥⊙🗂MW TV🖭⌖🍳🚗
P❋

SHALDON

Devon
Map ref 1D2

Pretty resort facing Teignmouth from the south bank of the Teign Estuary. Regency houses harmonise with others of later periods; there are old cottages and narrow lanes. On the Ness, a sandstone promontory nearby, a tunnel built in the 19th C leads to a beach revealed at low tide.

Badgers Brook Holiday Cottages ▲

🔑🔑🔑 **COMMENDED**

Stoke-in-Teignhead, Newton Abbot
Contact: Mr and Mrs T W Aisthorpe, Badgers Brook, Higher Gabwell, Stoke-in-Teignhead, Newton Abbot, Devon TQ12 4QW
☎ Torquay (01803) 327398
Peaceful rural location between Teignmouth and Torbay. Beaches half a mile. Stone barn conversions, set in 3 acres.
3 self-contained units; sleeping 6

Price per week:	£min	£max
Low season	140.00	185.00
High season	225.00	325.00

🐾Ⓜ◎🖌🔥⊙🗂MW TV🖭⌖🍳
🚗P❋❄SP

SHEPTON MALLET

Somerset
Map ref 2A2

Important, stone-built market town beneath the south-west slopes of the Mendips. Thriving rural industries include glove and shoe making, dairying and cider making; the remains of a medieval "shambles" in the square date from the town's prosperity as a wool centre.

Knowle Farm Cottages ▲

🔑🔑🔑 **COMMENDED**

West Compton, Shepton Mallet
BA4 4PD
☎ Pilton (01749) 890482
Fax (01749) 890405
Contact: Mrs J A Boyce
Cottages converted from old farm buildings, set in a pleasant garden in quiet, unspoilt countryside. Ideal for touring.
4 self-contained units; sleeping 2–8

Price per week:	£min	£max
Low season	155.00	350.00
High season	220.00	375.00

🐾Ⓜ🖌🔥⊙🗂TV🖭⌖🍳🍴❋❄🐾
SP ♨

SHERBORNE

Dorset
Map ref 2B3

Dorset's "Cathedral City" of medieval streets, golden Hamstone buildings and great abbey church, resting place of Saxon kings. Formidable 12th C castle ruins and Sir Walter Raleigh's splendid Tudor mansion and deer park. Street markets, leisure centre, many cultural activities.
Tourist Information Centre ☎ *(01935) 815341*

Dairy Cottages

🔑🔑🔑 **HIGHLY COMMENDED**

Holebrook Farm, Lydlinch, Sturminster Newton
Contact: Mr Charles Wingate-Saul, Holebrook Farm, Lydlinch, Sturminster Newton, Dorset DT10 2JB
☎ Hazelbury Bryan (01258) 817348
126-acre mixed farm. The cottages are situated on one side of courtyard, south-east facing, in 19th C barn originally used for hand-milking cattle. Peaceful, centrally heated, superbly comfortable. To the east of Sherborne (15 minutes by car).

4 self-contained units; sleeping 2

Price per week:	£min	£max
Low season	150.00	
High season		405.00

🌊🅜🏢💻☺🛢 MW 📺📷 🚗🛗🛍🎞
🅿🔧❄🛠🚫 SP 🎡

SHERFORD

Devon
Map ref 1C3

Mabins Court Barn

🔑🔑 COMMENDED

Sherford, Kingsbridge TQ7 2AT
☎ Kingsbridge (01548) 531380
Contact: Mrs J Dorey
*Barn newly converted to high standard,
in quiet village with open outlook to
fields. Close to Kingsbridge and
Salcombe Estuary and other beaches.*
1 self-contained unit; sleeping 4

Price per week:	£min	£max
Low season	150.00	175.00
High season	200.00	275.00

🌊🛢💻☺🛢 MW 🎛📺 🚗🛗🛍🅿
❄ SP

SIDMOUTH

Devon
Map ref 1D2

*Charming resort set amid lofty red
cliffs where the River Sid meets the
sea. The wealth of ornate Regency
and Victorian villas recalls the time
when this was one of the south
coast's most exclusive resorts.
Museum; August International
Festival of Folk Arts.*
Tourist Information Centre ☎ *(01395)
516441*

Drupe Farm 🏔

🔑🔑🔑 HIGHLY COMMENDED

Colaton Raleigh, Sidmouth
EX10 0LE
☎ (01395) 568838
Fax (01395) 567882
Contact: Miss G Elliott

*Farmstead converted to quality holiday
cottages in Otter Valley. Only 3 miles to
coast. Linen, electricity and heating
included. Short breaks available.*
14 self-contained units; sleeping 4–7

Price per week:	£min	£max
Low season	148.00	190.00
High season	338.00	455.00

🌊🌀🅜🏢☺🛢 📺📷 🚗🛍🛍🅿🔧❄
SP 🎡

Leigh Farm 🏔

🔑🔑➖🔑🔑🔑🏔
UP TO HIGHLY COMMENDED

Weston, Sidmouth EX10 0PH
☎ (01395) 516065
Fax (01395) 579582
Contact: Mrs M Goddard
*Comfortable cottage and bungalows,
150 yards from coastal path through
National Trust land to sea. Spectacular
views. Excellent walking and touring
area, peaceful location.*
5 self-contained units; sleeping 2–6

Price per week:	£min	£max
Low season	120.00	140.00
High season	290.00	320.00

Cards accepted: Access, Visa
🌊🅜🏢🏢☺🛢📺📷🚗🛍🛍🛗🅿
❄🚫 SP T

SIMONSBATH

Somerset
Map ref 1C1

*Village beside the beautiful River
Barle, deep in Exmoor. From the
Middle Ages until the 19th C this
was stag-hunting country.*

Wintershead Farm

🔑🔑➖🔑🔑🔑🔑 HIGHLY COMMENDED

Simonsbath, Minehead TA24 7LF
☎ Exford (01643) 831222
Fax (01643) 831628
Contact: Mr and Mrs B Styles
*Tastefully converted cottages with
panoramic views, in the heart of
Exmoor. Ideal base for walking.
Children and pets welcome. Phone or
write for colour brochure.*
5 self-contained units; sleeping 2–6

Price per week:	£min	£max
Low season	110.00	240.00
High season	140.00	440.00

🌊🛢🏢☺🛢📺📷🚗🛍🛍🛗🅿❄
🚫 SP 🎡

SOUTHWICK

Wiltshire
Map ref 2B2

The Coach House 🏔

🔑 COMMENDED

The Old House, Southwick,
Trowbridge
Contact: Mrs Dorothy Davison, The
Old House, Frome Road, Southwick,
Trowbridge, Wiltshire BA14 9QF
☎ Trowbridge (01225) 752761

*Period coach house providing charming
and unusual accommodation. Laundry
room, secluded garden, garage.
Convenient for Bath, Cotswolds and
West Country.*
1 self-contained unit; sleeping 2

Price per week:	£min	£max
Low season	120.00	150.00
High season	175.00	225.00

🌊🅜🏢🏢☺🛢 MW 📺📷🚗🛗🛍
🅿🛗🔧❄🛠🚫 SP 🎡

SPREYTON

Devon
Map ref 1C2

Wyncot Cottage

🔑🔑 APPROVED

Spreyton, Crediton EX17 5AF
☎ Whiddon Down (01647) 231385
Contact: Mrs M E Hodge
*Two-storey, 3-bedroomed stone house
with slate roof, in rural surroundings
half a mile from the village of Spreyton.
Central for touring. 5 miles from
Dartmoor National Park, 3 miles from
A30.*
1 self-contained unit; sleeping 4

Price per week:	£min	£max
Low season	80.00	
High season		170.00

Open April–October
🅜🏢🏢☺🛢📺🚗🛍🚗❄

STARCROSS

Devon
Map ref 1D2

*Small village on the western shore
of the Exe Estuary, with a harbour
and 19th C seaside villas.
Powderham Castle and Park, just
north, make a pleasant excursion
and a pedestrian ferry crosses the
water to Exmouth.*

Cofton Country Cottage
Holidays 🏔

🔑🔑🔑🔑 COMMENDED

Starcross, Exeter EX6 8RP
☎ (01626) 890111
Fax (01626) 891572
Contact: Mr and Mrs W G Jeffery

*100-year-old farm buildings tastefully
converted into self-contained cottages.
Lush, green woodland surroundings.*

Continued ▶

STARCROSS

Continued

Colour TV, video, microwave, dishwasher, etc. Use of park amenities during season.
5 self-contained units; sleeping 4–6

Price per week:	£min	£max
Low season	160.00	395.00
High season	420.00	490.00

Cards accepted: Access, Visa

[symbols]

STEEPLE ASHTON

Wiltshire
Map ref 2B2

Old village dominated by its magnificent Perpendicular church, built at a time of prosperity from the medieval wool trade.

Jasmine Cottage M

COMMENDED

1 High Street, Steeple Ashton, Trowbridge
Contact: Mr N A Sharples, 4 St Margarets, Little Aston, Sutton Coldfield, West Midlands B74 4HU
☎ Sutton Coldfield (0121) 353 5258

Delightful, sympathetically modernised character cottage in one of Wiltshire's most picturesque villages. Free supply of logs for blazing fires. Convenient for Bath, Stonehenge and Longleat House. Brochure available.
1 self-contained unit; sleeping 6

Price per week:	£min	£max
Low season	169.00	
High season		349.00

[symbols]

STOKE ST GREGORY

Somerset
Map ref 1D1

Holly Farm M

HIGHLY COMMENDED

Stoke St Gregory, Taunton
Contact: Mr W R Hembrow, Holly Cottage, Stoke St Gregory, Taunton, Somerset TA3 6HS
☎ Taunton (01823) 490828
Barn converted to high standard, with

---

own gardens, in peaceful Somerset Levels. Golf, fishing, cycling, etc. and good pubs within easy reach.
4 self-contained units; sleeping 4–6

Price per week:	£min	£max
Low season	160.00	230.00
High season	215.00	350.00

[symbols]

SYDLING ST NICHOLAS

Dorset
Map ref 2B3

The Stock Barn

COMMENDED

East Street, Sydling St Nicholas, Dorchester
Contact: Mrs P A Gill, The Old Manor, Stratton, Dorchester, Dorset DT2 9RY
☎ Dorchester (01305) 263475
Small barn conversion, comfortably furnished, in quiet village setting. Good centre for Hardy country.
1 self-contained unit; sleeping 6

Price per week:	£min	£max
Low season	100.00	200.00
High season	250.00	295.00

[symbols]

TAUNTON

Somerset
Map ref 1D1

County town, well-known for its public schools, sheltered by gentle hill-ranges on the River Tone. Medieval prosperity from wool has continued in marketing and manufacturing and the town retains many fine period buildings.
Tourist Information Centre ☎ (01823) 336344

Meare Court Farm

UP TO COMMENDED

Wrantage, Taunton TA3 6DA
☎ Hatch Beauchamp (01823) 480570
Contact: Mrs E J Bray
Recently converted historic barn with character, spacious and comfortable. Also ground floor wing of listed farmhouse. On family dairy farm in peaceful surroundings with beautiful views.
2 self-contained units; sleeping 4–6

Price per week:	£min	£max
Low season	180.00	250.00
High season	200.00	300.00

[symbols]

TAVISTOCK

Devon
Map ref 1C2

Old market town beside the River Tavy on the western edge of Dartmoor. Developed around its 10th C abbey, of which some fragments remain, it became a stannary town in 1305 when tin-streaming thrived on the moors. Tavistock Goose Fair, October.
Tourist Information Centre ☎ (01822) 612938

Dartmoor Country Holidays Magpie Leisure Park M

COMMENDED

Bedford Bridge, Horrabridge, Yelverton PL20 7RY
☎ Yelverton (01822) 852651
Contact: Mr Bidder

Pine lodges in peaceful woodland setting next to River Walkham in Dartmoor National Park. Unspoilt countryside, ideal for walkers, lovers of nature, etc. Available winter/summer.
4 self-contained units; sleeping 2–7

Price per week:	£min	£max
Low season	130.00	
High season		440.00

[symbols]

Higher Chaddlehanger Farm

APPROVED

Tavistock PL19 0LG
☎ Mary Tavy (01822) 810268
Contact: Mrs R Cole
Holiday flatlet in farmhouse on beef and sheep farm, close to moors. Own entrance, private garden.
1 self-contained unit; sleeping 4

Price per week:	£min	£max
High season	100.00	120.00

Open April–October
[symbols]

All accommodation in this guide has been graded, or is awaiting a grading, by a trained Tourist Board inspector.

TINCLETON

Dorset
Map ref 2B3

The Dairy House

⚷⚷ ⚷⚷ APPROVED

Tincleton Farm, Tincleton,
Dorchester DT2 8QP
☎ Puddletown (01305) 848 280
Contact: Mrs S B Selby
*Well-equipped, 4-bedroomed cottage.
Hardy country. Working dairy farm.
Private garden, patio, barbecue, parking
for 2. Fishing nearby.*
1 self-contained unit; sleeping 6

Price per week:	£min	£max
Low season	140.00	
High season		260.00

🌣 M ◎ ▦ ⊙ 🗖 MW 📺 🗖 🖳 🚗
P ❄ ✄

TINTAGEL

Cornwall
Map ref 1B2

Coastal village near the legendary
home of King Arthur. There is a
lofty headland with the ruin of a
Norman castle and traces of a
Celtic monastery are still visible in
the turf.

Tregeath Cottage

⚷ APPROVED

Tregeath Lane, Tintagel
Contact: Mrs E M Broad, Davina,
Trevillett, Tintagel, Cornwall
PL34 0HL
☎ Camelford (01840) 770217 &
770279
*Modernised, detached stone and slate
farm cottage on quiet road. 3
bedrooms, 2 night storage heaters and
coal grate.*
1 self-contained unit; sleeping 5

Price per week:	£min	£max
Low season	100.00	
High season		350.00

🌣 M ◎ ▦ ⊙ 🗖 MW 📺 🗖 🖳 🚗 U
❄

Westwood House ⚭

⚷⚷ ⚷⚷ COMMENDED

Fore Street, Tintagel PL34 0DA
☎ Camelford (01840) 770430
Contact: Mr A J Lee
*Two apartments, each suitable for 2
people, in heart of village. Ideal base
for swimmers, walkers, golfers, riders
and fishermen.*
2 self-contained units; sleeping 2

Price per week:	£min	£max
Low season	140.00	160.00
High season	250.00	275.00

Cards accepted: Access, Visa, Diners,
Amex, Switch/Delta

🌣 ◎ ▦ ⊙ 🗖 MW 📢 📺 🗖 🖳 🗲
P ✈ ✄ ⊠ SP

TIVERTON

Devon
Map ref 1D2

Busy market and textile town,
settled since the 9th C, at the
meeting of 2 rivers. Town houses,
Tudor almshouses and parts of the
fine church were built by wealthy
cloth merchants; a medieval castle is
incorporated into a private house;
Blundells School.
*Tourist Information Centre ☎ (01884)
255827*

Cider Cottage

⚷⚷ ⚷⚷ HIGHLY COMMENDED

Great Bradley Farm, Withleigh,
Tiverton EX16 8JL
☎ (01884) 256946
Contact: Mrs S Hann
*Charming, comfortable, well-furnished
cottage on 150-acre dairy farm,
overlooking beautiful, unspoilt
countryside in the heart of Devon.*
1 self-contained unit; sleeping 5

Price per week:	£min	£max
Low season	135.00	200.00
High season	200.00	325.00

🌣 M ◎ ▦ ⊙ 🗖 📺 🗖 🖳 🚗 P ❄
✄ ⊠ SP ▦

Lilac Cottage

⚷⚷ ⚷ COMMENDED

Battens Farm, Sampford Peverell,
Tiverton EX16 7EE
☎ (01884) 820226
Contact: Mrs R J Venner
*Secluded, tastefully furnished cottage.
Three bedrooms, large farm kitchen,
cosy beamed lounge. Large walled
country garden, ideal for dogs. Grand
Western Canal runs through farm, with
pleasant walks.*
1 self-contained unit; sleeping 7

Price per week:	£min	£max
Low season	150.00	200.00
High season	250.00	315.00

🌣 M ◎ ▦ ⊙ 🗖 📺 🗖 🖳 🚗 U ❄

Self-catering agencies
which have a selection of
holiday homes to let
are listed in a special section
towards the back
of this guide.

TOLPUDDLE

Dorset
Map ref 2B3

Southover Cottages ⚭

⚷⚷ ⚷⚷ APPROVED

Lawrences Farm, Southover,
Tolpuddle, Dorchester DT2 7HF
☎ Puddletown (01305) 848460
Fax (01305) 849060
Contact: Mrs Mary Slocock
*Cottages on beautiful 150-acre estate,
with excellent trout fishing. Another
cottage in mainly thatched village 1.5
miles away. Sandy beaches within easy
reach.*
3 self-contained units; sleeping 5–6

Price per week:	£min	£max
Low season	200.00	215.00
High season	320.00	340.00

🌣 M ◎ ▦ ⊙ 🗖 MW 📢 📺 🗖
▣ 🖳 🚗 P ⚓ ❄ ✄ SP

TORCROSS

Devon
Map ref 1D3

Pretty little fishing village on Slapton
Sands, 6 miles east of Kingsbridge
and 6 miles south of Dartmouth.

Torcross Apartment Hotel
(Ref: ET) ⚭

⚷⚷ ⚷⚷ UP TO COMMENDED

Torcross Village, Kingsbridge
TQ7 2TQ
☎ Kingsbridge (01548) 580206
Contact: Mrs F J Signora

At the water's edge on Slapton Sands,
well-appointed apartments. Some
ground floor flats. Superb sea views.
Waterside restaurant and village inn.
Lift to all floors.
18 self-contained units;
sleeping 3–12

Price per week:	£min	£max
Low season	97.00	240.00
High season	275.00	488.00

Open February–October
Cards accepted: Access

🌣 ◎ ▦ ⊙ 🗖 MW 📺 🗖 🖳 ▣ 🗲
P SP ▦ T

TORQUAY

Devon
Map ref 1D2

Devon's grandest resort, developed from a fishing village. Smart apartments and terraces rise from the seafront and Marine Drive along the headland gives views of beaches and colourful cliffs.
Tourist Information Centre ☎ *(01803) 297428*

The Corbyn
🔑🔑🔑🔑 **DE LUXE**
Torbay Road, Torquay
Contact: Mrs S Stamp, Brights of Nettlebed, The Corbyn, Torbay Road, Torquay, Devon TQ2 6RH
☎ Torquay (01803) 215595
Fax (01803) 200568
New concept in quality suite accommodation. 1995 "England for Excellence" Self Catering Holiday of the Year award winners. Colour brochure and/or loan video available.
Wheelchair access category 2♿
17 self-contained units; sleeping 2–8

Price per week:	£min	£max
Low season	216.00	414.00
High season	492.00	1000.00

Cards accepted: Access, Visa, Diners, Amex

Maxton Lodge Holiday Apartments
🔑🔑🔑 **COMMENDED**
Rousdown Road, Chelston, Torquay TQ2 6PB
☎ (01803) 607811
Fax (01803) 200592
Contact: Mr G Paris
Well-appointed and located apartments offering indoor/outdoor pools, spa, sauna, gym, licensed restaurant/snacks. Autumn to spring breaks.
24 self-contained units; sleeping 3–6

Price per week:	£min	£max
Low season	130.00	235.00
High season	250.00	575.00

Cards accepted: Access, Visa

No 5 Bungalow
🔑🔑🔑 **COMMENDED**
No 5 Locks Hill, Babbacombe, Torquay
Contact: Mr A Hedges, Barters Old Farmhouse, Moradia 2. Lote 4,1.2/7, 8125. Vilamoura, Algarve, Portugal
☎ Portugal (00351) 89321076
Bright sunny bungalow. Wide sea views.

Sheltered garden. Near beaches and town. Comfortable and well equipped. Two double bedrooms.
1 self-contained unit; sleeping 5

Price per week:	£min	£max
Low season	190.00	200.00
High season	220.00	405.00

Woodfield Holiday Flats
Lower Woodfield Road, Torquay TQ1 2JY
☎ (01803) 295974
Contact: Mr T W Gaylard

Grade II listed neo-Gothic villa of architectural and historic interest. Views over Torquay harbour. Convenient for all amenities, 600 yards to harbour and town. Free car parking. Family-run business, resident proprietors.
9 self-contained units; sleeping 1–7

Price per week:	£min	£max
Low season	45.00	130.00
High season	90.00	290.00

TORRINGTON

Devon
Map ref 1C1

Perched high above the River Torridge, with a charming market square, Georgian Town Hall and a museum. The famous Dartington Crystal Factory, Rosemoor Gardens and Plough Arts Centre are all located in the town.

Orford Mill
🔑🔑🔑 **HIGHLY COMMENDED**
Torrington
Contact: Miss Nicky Faull, Best Leisure, North Hill, Shirwell, Barnstaple, Devon EX31 4LG
☎ Barnstaple (01271) 850611
Fax (01271) 850693
Converted manor house, corn and timber mill and barns. Set in 3 acres of Tarka Otter land, with the River Torridge running alongside.
8 self-contained units; sleeping 4–7

Price per week:	£min	£max
Low season	196.00	280.00
High season	258.00	502.00

Southview Cottage
🔑🔑🔑 **COMMENDED**
2 Southview, Frithelstock, Torrington
Contact: Mrs J Toogood, 1 Southview, Frithelstock, Torrington, Devon EX38 8JJ
☎ Torrington (01805) 624243
Quiet, semi-detached farmworker's cottage, set in open countryside. Especially suitable for children, with garden and play area. Central for National Parks, beaches and rural cycleway.
1 self-contained unit; sleeping 8

Price per week:	£min	£max
Low season	200.00	
High season		320.00

Stowford Lodge
🔑🔑🔑🔑 **HIGHLY COMMENDED**
Langtree, Torrington EX38 8NU
☎ Langtree (01805) 601540
Fax (01805) 601487
Contact: Mrs S Milsom
Charming cottages with lots of character, converted from Victorian stone farm buildings. Peaceful location in glorious countryside. Heated indoor swimming pool. Pets welcome.
6 self-contained units; sleeping 4–6

Price per week:	£min	£max
Low season	180.00	200.00
High season	240.00	400.00

Week Farm Flat
🔑🔑🔑 **COMMENDED**
Torrington EX38 7HU
☎ (01805) 623354
Contact: Mrs M M Bealey
Spacious with well-equipped kitchen/diner and lounge with colour TV. Room with double bed, room with twin beds. 1 mile from Great Torrington with swimming pool, golf, Tarka Trail, Dartington Glass and RHS Rosemoor Garden. No smoking.
1 self-contained unit; sleeping 5

Price per week:	£min	£max
Low season	95.00	
High season		210.00

The symbol after an establishment name indicates that it is a Regional Tourist Board member.

TOTNES

Devon
Map ref 1D2

Old market town steeply built near the head of the Dart Estuary. Remains of medieval gateways, a noble church, 16th C Guildhall and medley of period houses recall former wealth from cloth and shipping, continued in rural and water industries.
Tourist Information Centre ☎ (01803) 863168

10 The Malthouse
COMMENDED

The Plains, Totnes
Contact: Mrs E Veale, 8 Woodbrook Road, Bridgetown, Totnes, Devon TQ9 5AS
☎ (01803) 865464
Flat in converted old malthouse on the banks of the River Dart, only 3 minutes' level walk from the historic town centre. Ideally placed for moors and coast.
1 self-contained unit; sleeping 4

Price per week:	£min	£max
Low season	150.00	150.00
High season	185.00	285.00

TREGONY

Cornwall
Map ref 1B3

Old village, once a significant port and market town, rising from the River Fal. An inscribed stone of the 6th C forms a cornerstone of the church, which stands above the village and was almost entirely rebuilt in 1899.

The Bolt Hole
HIGHLY COMMENDED

3 Mill Lane, Tregony, Truro
Contact: Ms B F Hunt, The Pines, Lower Golf Links Road, Broadstone, Dorset BH18 8BG
☎ Broadstone (01202) 693817
18th C cottage, fully refurbished and equipped. Tastefully furnished. Vaulted ceiling and beams, delightful garden. Amenities 3 minutes' walk. Quiet. Coastal path nearby, glorious scenery.
1 self-contained unit; sleeping max 2

Price per week:	£min	£max
Low season	170.00	
High season		300.00

WASHFORD

Somerset
Map ref 1D1

Village 2 miles west of Williton and a good centre for many interesting walks. On the edge of the village is Cleeve Abbey, founded in the 13th C by the Cistercians, and with remarkably complete dormitory and refectory.

Meadstone
HIGHLY COMMENDED

Station Road, Washford, Watchet
Contact: Mr J K Westcott, Stonebank, 14 West Street, Chickerell, Weymouth, Dorset DT3 4DY
☎ Weymouth (01305) 760120
Fax (01305) 760871
Comfortable house in ideal touring centre between Exmoor and the Quantocks. Three bedrooms, 3 bathrooms, central heating, garden and parking.
1 self-contained unit; sleeping 6

Price per week:	£min	£max
Low season	200.00	320.00
High season	360.00	460.00

WATCHET

Somerset
Map ref 1D1

Small port on Bridgwater Bay, sheltered by the Quantocks and the Brendon Hills. A thriving paper industry keeps the harbour busy; in the 19th C it handled iron from the Brendon Hills. Cleeve Abbey, a ruined Cistercian monastery, is 3 miles to the south-west.

Beach Cottages
HIGHLY COMMENDED

16 and 17 Market Street, Watchet
Contact: Miss M Williams, Beeches Holiday Park, Blue Anchor Bay, Minehead, Somerset TA24
☎ Washford (01984) 40391
Fax (01984) 640391
2 and 3-bedroomed cottages overlooking the sea, situated in the heart of Watchet. Steps away from beach of this pretty little harbour town. Ideal for touring Exmoor and many famous beauty spots.
2 self-contained units; sleeping 4–6

Price per week:	£min	£max
Low season	177.00	290.00
High season	325.00	355.00

Cards accepted: Access, Visa

WEST ANSTEY

Devon
Map ref 1D1

Dunsley Farm
COMMENDED

West Anstey, South Molton EX36 3PF
☎ Anstey Mills (01398) 341246
Contact: Mrs I M Robins
Bordering Exmoor, 16th C farm holiday cottage offering comfort and cleanliness. Ideal for quiet, relaxing holiday on a working farm with coarse fishing and panoramic views.
1 self-contained unit; sleeping 5

Price per week:	£min	£max
Low season	90.00	
High season		350.00

WEST BEXINGTON

Dorset
Map ref 2A3

Tamarisk Farm ⛰
APPROVED

West Bexington, Dorchester DT2 9DF
☎ Burton Bradstock (01308) 897784
Fax (01308) 897892
Contact: Mrs Josephine Pearse
One 3-bedroomed and two 2-bedroomed cottages, all in own gardens, in hamlet above Chesil Beach. Magnificent sea views. On organic farm. Children and pets welcome. Walking, fishing, touring.
3 self-contained units; sleeping 5–6

Price per week:	£min	£max
Low season	150.00	
High season		450.00

Open March–December

WELCOME HOST

This is a nationally recognised customer care programme which aims to promote the highest standards of service and a warm welcome. Establishments who are taking part in this initiative are indicated by the ◉ symbol.

WEST BUCKLAND

Devon
Map ref 1C1

Taddiport Cottage

COMMENDED

West Buckland, Barnstaple
EX32 0SL
☎ Filleigh (01598) 760287
Contact: Mrs M Hawkins
*Comfortable and well-equipped
converted stone barn. In large
attractive gardens next to country
house amid peaceful valleys and hills.*
1 self-contained unit; sleeping 4

Price per week:	£min	£max
Low season	100.00	
High season		250.00

WEST HARPTREE

Bath & North East Somerset
Map ref 2A2

Pretty red-stone village, with old
manor houses, set under the
northern slopes of the Mendips. It is
well placed for exploring the hills or
the Somerset coast.

Ridge Cottage

APPROVED

Ridge Lane, West Harptree, Bristol
Contact: Mrs J B Moore, Gournay
Court, West Harptree, Bristol
BS18 6EB
☎ Mendip (01761) 221323
*Detached old stone cottage with
beamed ceiling and inglenook fireplace,
in quiet lane close to shop.*
1 self-contained unit; sleeping 8

Price per week:	£min	£max
Low season	155.00	190.00
High season	210.00	245.00

WEYMOUTH

Dorset
Map ref 2B3

Ancient port and one of the south's
earliest resorts. Curving beside a
long, sandy beach, the elegant
Georgian esplanade is graced with a
statue of George III and a cheerful
Victorian Jubilee clock tower.
*Tourist Information Centre ☎ (01305)
765221 or 785747*

Belvidere House Holiday Flats

COMMENDED

119 The Esplanade, Weymouth

Contact: Mrs V J Brown, 16
Nottington Lane, Weymouth,
Dorset DT3 5DF
☎ Weymouth (01305) 814152
*Centre of Weymouth's Georgian
esplanade, 20 yards from beach.
Two-bedroomed self-contained holiday
flats, most with panoramic sea views.*
5 self-contained units; sleeping 6

Price per week:	£min	£max
Low season	150.00	185.00
High season	320.00	400.00

Moonfleet Manor Cottages

HIGHLY COMMENDED

Moonfleet Manor, Weymouth
Contact: Mr B Hemingway,
Moonfleet Manor, Fleet Road,
Weymouth, Dorset DT3 4ED
☎ Weymouth (01305) 786948
Fax (01305) 774395
*Coach house cottages in 17th C listed
building. All facilities of adjoining
Moonfleet Manor hotel are available,
including indoor bowls, indoor pool,
tennis, squash, snooker, children's play
area.*
3 self-contained units; sleeping 4

Price per week:	£min	£max
Low season	130.00	200.00
High season	200.00	600.00

Cards accepted: Access, Visa, Amex

Sunnywey Apartments

COMMENDED

27 Kirtleton Avenue, Weymouth
DT4 7PS
☎ (01305) 781767
Contact: Mrs L Bond
*Attractive Victorian property tastefully
converted into apartments. In a quiet
avenue approximately 450 yards to
seafront, country park and shops.*
7 self-contained units; sleeping 2–7

Price per week:	£min	£max
Low season	100.00	190.00
High season	240.00	470.00

Wellington Court Flats
28,29,30,31,33,40

COMMENDED

Barrack Road, Nothe Peninsula,
Weymouth
Contact: Mrs J Lundy, Peacock
Homes Ltd, 57 Church Street,
Epsom, Surrey KT17 4PX
☎ Epsom (01372) 740071
Fax (01372) 729397
*Six stylish flats in elegant Georgian
buildings near Weymouth harbour.*

*Other cottages available, mainly in
converted listed buildings. Send for
colour brochure.*
6 self-contained units; sleeping 3–5

Price per week:	£min	£max
Low season	155.00	330.00
High season	275.00	605.00

Open February–November

WHEDDON CROSS

Somerset
Map ref 1D1

Crossroads hamlet in the heart of
Exmoor National Park.

Little Quarme Country Cottages

UP TO DE LUXE

Wheddon Cross, Minehead, Exmoor
TA24 7EA
☎ Timberscombe (01643) 841249
Fax (01643) 841249
Contact: Mrs Tammy
Cody-Boutcher

*Six stone cottages standing amid 18
acres in the heart of Exmoor National
Park. Lovely gardens, outstandingly
peaceful situation with panoramic
views. Sheep and horse farm. Quality,
comfort, cleanliness.*
6 self-contained units; sleeping 2–6

Price per week:	£min	£max
Low season	80.00	185.00
High season	265.00	450.00

Open March–December

WHIMPLE

Devon
Map ref 1D2

LSF Holiday Cottages

APPROVED

Whimple, Exeter EX5 2PG
☎ (01404) 822989
Contact: Mrs P A Penfold
*Farmhouse and cottages in 4 acres,
surrounded by beautiful countryside.
Plenty of space for children to play in.*
4 self-contained units; sleeping 6

Price per week:	£min	£max
Low season	111.00	150.00
High season	195.00	285.00

WIDEMOUTH BAY

Cornwall
Map ref 1C2

Small resort on the north Cornwall
coast, with spectacular beaches.
Good surfing centre.

Kennacott Court

UP TO DE LUXE

Widemouth Bay, Bude EX23 0ND
☎ (01288) 361766 & 361683
Fax (01288) 361434
Contact: Mr and Mrs R H Davis
*Cottages in 75 acres. Leisure centre
with indoor swimming pool, sauna,
solarium, snooker, tennis, golf-course.
Spectacular sea views.*
18 self-contained units;
sleeping 2–10

Price per week:	£min	£max
Low season	150.00	1200.00
High season	240.00	1350.00

WILLITON

Somerset
Map ref 1D1

Large village on the edge of the
Quantock Hills. The 19th C church
contains the remains of a chapel
built by Reginal Fitz Urse, one of the
murderers of Thomas a Becket.
Cleeve Abbey is 2 miles west.

Daisy Cottage

COMMENDED

14 Bridge Street, Williton, Taunton
Contact: Mrs A Bishop, 6 North
Street, Williton, Taunton, Somerset
TA4 4SL
☎ Williton (01984) 632657
Fax (01984) 632657
*16th C thatched cottage with exposed
beams and inglenook. Warm and
comfortable in winter with gas central
heating. Garden and parking.
Convenient for exploring the
Quantocks and Exmoor. Short winter
breaks.*
1 self-contained unit; sleeping 5

Price per week:	£min	£max
Low season	150.00	200.00
High season	200.00	350.00

WINSFORD

Somerset
Map ref 1D1

Small village on the River Exe in
splendid walking country under
Winsford Hill. On the other side of
the hill is a Celtic standing stone,
the Caratacus Stone, and nearby
across the River Barle stretches an
ancient packhorse bridge, Tarr Steps,
built of great stone slabs.

The Old Timber Store

HIGHLY COMMENDED

Winsford, Minehead
Contact: Mrs Bridget Ryle, Jasmine
Cottage, Winsford, Minehead,
Somerset TA24 7JE
☎ Winsford (01643) 851317
*Newly converted cottage with 2 twin
bedrooms in the centre of Winsford in
Exmoor National Park. Beautiful views,
lovely moor and riverside walks nearby.*
1 self-contained unit; sleeping 4

Price per week:	£min	£max
Low season	180.00	180.00
High season	200.00	230.00

WINTERBOURNE STEEPLETON

Dorset
Map ref 2B3

Sunny Acres Chalet

COMMENDED

Bridport Road, Winterbourne
Steepleton, Dorchester DT2 9DX
☎ Martinstown (01305) 889396
Contact: Mrs K Hardwick
*On ideally situated 5-acre smallholding
near Weymouth and West Bay. 5 miles
to Chesil Beach, excellent walks and
scenery.*
1 self-contained unit; sleeping 3

Price per week:	£min	£max
Low season	120.00	
High season		185.00

WINTERBOURNE STOKE

Wiltshire
Map ref 2B2

Scotland Lodge

APPROVED

Winterbourne Stoke, Salisbury
SP3 4TF
☎ Shrewton (01980) 620943 &
Mobile 0860 272599
Fax (01980) 620943
Contact: Mrs J Armfelt-Singleton
*Well-appointed and comfortable
self-contained unit within a country
house. Ideal touring base near
Stonehenge and Salisbury. Bed and
breakfast also available.*
1 self-contained unit; sleeping 2

Price per week:	£min	£max
Low season	120.00	150.00
High season	150.00	200.00

WITHYPOOL

Somerset
Map ref 1D1

Pretty village high on Exmoor near
the beautiful River Barle. On
Winsford Hill (National Trust) are
Bronze Age barrows known as the
Wambarrows.

Landacre Bungalow

APPROVED

Landacre Farm, Withypool,
Minehead TA24 7SD
☎ Exford (01643) 831223 & 831487
Contact: Mrs P G Hudson
*Warm, clean, quiet, comfortable and
well equipped bungalow, in an area of
outstanding beauty. Situated on farm
overlooking the moors and the river.*
3 self-contained units; sleeping 4

Price per week:	£min	£max
Low season	95.00	125.00
High season	125.00	200.00

TOWN INDEX

This can be found at the back
of the guide. If you know
where you want to stay, the
index will give you the page
number listing all
accommodation in your
chosen town, city or village.

WOOLACOMBE

Devon
Map ref 1C1

Between Morte Point and Baggy Point, Woolacombe and Mortehoe offer 3 miles of the finest sand and surf on this outstanding coastline. Much of the area is owned by the National Trust.

Beachcroft Holiday Apartments

🔑🔑🔑 APPROVED

Beach Road, Woolacombe
EX34 7BT
☎ (01271) 870655
Contact: Mrs G Barr
Well-equipped, self-contained apartments 2 minutes' walk from beach and shops. Pets welcome. Private parking.
4 self-contained units; sleeping 3–8

Price per week:	£min	£max
Low season	90.00	150.00
High season	230.00	375.00

🖾 Ⓜ ◎ ▥ ☺ 🗇 MW TV 🗪 🞖 🞖
P ❋ SP

The Old Vicarage ⚞

🔑🔑 COMMENDED

Mortehoe, Woolacombe EX34 7ED
☎ (01271) 870598
Contact: Mr S Wood

18th C former vicarage with 2 self-contained cottages adjoining. In good order, well-equipped and continuously updated, centrally heated and with double glazing. In village, 1 mile from beach. Private parking. Small children's play area.

2 self-contained units; sleeping 4–6

Price per week:	£min	£max
Low season	100.00	
High season		335.00

🖾 Ⓜ ⌀ ▥ ☺ 🗇 MW 🗪 TV 🗪 🞖
🞖 P Ս ❋ ✂ 🞖 SP

YELVERTON

Devon
Map ref 1C2

Village on the edge of Dartmoor, where ponies wander over the flat common. Buckland Abbey is 2 miles south-west, while Burrator Reservoir is 2 miles to the east.

Blowiscombe Barton ⚞

🔑🔑🔑🔑—🔑🔑 COMMENDED

Milton Combe, Yelverton PL20 6HR
☎ (01822) 854853
Fax (01822) 854853
Contact: Mrs Pauline Fisk

Farmhouse wing and flat. Beautiful countryside, garden and heated swimming pool. Close village pub and Dartmoor National Park. Plymouth/Tavistock 8 miles.

2 self-contained units; sleeping 3–7

Price per week:	£min	£max
Low season	130.00	250.00
High season	250.00	480.00

Open April–October
Cards accepted: Access, Visa

🖾 Ⓜ ◎ ▥ ☺ 🗇 MW TV 🞖 🗪 🞖
🞖 P ⅃ Ս ⎋ ❋ SP

Scyttel ⚞

🔑🔑🔑🔑 COMMENDED

Sheepstor, Yelverton PL20 6PF
☎ (01822) 852295
Contact: Mrs L M Saunders
Converted stone stables within Dartmoor National Park. Woodland, brook, extensive grounds. Secluded, idyllic, ideal for nature lovers, walkers, children and birdwatchers.
2 self-contained units; sleeping 4

Price per week:	£min	£max
Low season	160.00	185.00
High season	215.00	325.00

Open March–December

🖾 Ⓜ ◎ ▥ ☺ 🗇 MW 🗪 TV 🞖 🗪 🞖
🞖 P Ս ♪ ❋ ✂ SP 🞖

YETMINSTER

Dorset
Map ref 2A3

Manor House Cottage

🔑🔑 COMMENDED

Manor House, High Street, Yetminster, Sherborne DT9 6LF
☎ (01935) 872616
Contact: Mr and Mrs J S Manaton
Well-equipped, 2-bedroomed cottage at rear of 15th C house in centre of village. Large quiet garden. Resident owners. Brochure available.
1 self-contained unit; sleeping 4

Price per week:	£min	£max
Low season	120.00	145.00
High season	185.00	235.00

Open March–October

🖾 Ⓜ ◎ ▥ ☺ 🗇 TV 🞖 🗪 🞖 🞖 🞖 🞖
P ❋

All accommodation in this guide has been graded, or is awaiting a grading, by a trained Tourist Board inspector.

classic **cottages**

Choose your cottage from the finest coastal and country cottages in the West Country.
A pretty fishermans cottage overlooking the harbour in Cornwall; a delightful 17th Century longhouse in Devon; a lovely barn conversion in Somerset; a converted brewhouse to an old vicarage in Dorset – find them all in our 118 page colour brochure.

Honeysuckle Cottage
Newquay, Cornwall

Classic Cottages, Leslie House (1)
Lady Street, Helston, Cornwall, TR13 8NA

Telephone **01326 565555**

Facsimile **01326 565554**

email   classic@classic.co.uk

Farm&Cottage HOLIDAYS

FAMILY HOLIDAYS WITH A DIFFERENCE

★ Choose from over 200 quality self catering cottages throughout the West Country
★ All properties personally inspected ★ Pets accepted ★ Coastal & Rural
★ High quality comfort & cleanliness at an affordable price.
★ Superb half board accommodation also available ★

A HOLIDAY FOR FOUR
INCLUDING LINEN
FROM ONLY **£116 PER WEEK**

FREE Colour Brochure Dept. WTS
12 Fore Street, Northam, Bideford, Devon EX39 1AW

Tel: 01237 479698

ENQUIRY COUPONS

To help you obtain further information about advertisers and accommodation featured in this guide you will find enquiry coupons at the back. Send these directly to the establishments in which you are interested. Remember to complete both sides of the coupon.

COUNTRY CODE

Always follow the Country Code
✿ Enjoy the countryside and respect its life and work ✿ Guard against all risk of fire ✿ Fasten all gates ✿ Keep your dogs under close control ✿ Keep to public paths across farmland ✿ Use gates and stiles to cross fences, hedges and walls ✿ Leave livestock, crops and machinery alone ✿ Take your litter home
✿ Help to keep all water clean
✿ Protect wildlife, plants and trees
✿ Take special care on country roads
✿ Make no unnecessary noise

USE YOUR *i*'s

There are more than 550 Tourist Information Centres throughout England offering friendly help with accommodation and holiday ideas as well as suggestions of places to visit and things to do. There may well be a centre in your home town which can help you before you set out. You'll find the address of your nearest Tourist Information Centre in your local Phone Book.

AT-A-GLANCE SYMBOLS

Symbols at the end of each accommodation entry give useful information about services and facilities. A key to symbols can be found inside the back cover flap.

Keep this open for easy reference.

CHECK THE MAPS

The colour maps at the back of this guide show all the cities, towns and villages for which you will find accommodation entries.

Refer to the town index to find the page on which it is listed.

SOUTH OF ENGLAND

The South of England is a region of contrast and fascination. While the New Forest and Chiltern Hills offer mile upon mile of unspoilt countryside, there is much to please those who prefer town life - not to mention smart little Thameside villages crammed with antiques shops, quaint tea shops and exclusive boutiques.

Historic Oxford, Winchester and Windsor fall within the region, as does Henley, home of the famous Regatta.

The bucolic charms of Dorset await - along with the delightful seaside resorts of Poole, Weymouth and Bournemouth. And don't overlook the pretty Isle of Wight, just a ferry ride away.

FOR MORE INFORMATION CONTACT:
Southern Tourist Board
40 Chamberlayne Road, Eastleigh,
Hampshire SO50 5JH
Tel: (01703) 620555 **Fax:** (01703) 620010

Where to Go in the South of England -
see pages 248-251
Where to Stay in the South of England -
see pages 252-268

SOUTH OF ENGLAND

Where to Go and What to See

You will find hundreds of interesting places to visit during your stay in the South of England, just some of which are listed in these pages. The number against each name will help you locate it on the map (page 251). Contact any Tourist Information Centre in the region for more ideas on days out in the South of England.

1 Broughton Castle
Banbury, Oxfordshire OX15 5EB
Tel: (01295) 262624
Medieval moated house built in 1300 and enlarged between 1550-1600. The home of Lord and Lady Saye and Sele and family home for 600 years. Civil War connections.

2 Blenheim Palace
Woodstock,
Oxfordshire OX20 1PX
Tel: (01993) 811091
Birthplace of Sir Winston Churchill, designed by Vanbrugh. Park designed by Capability Brown. Adventure play area, maze, butterfly house and Churchill exhibition.

3 The Oxford Story
6 Broad Street, Oxford OX1 3AJ
Tel: (01865) 728822
Heritage centre depicting eight centuries of history in sights, sounds, personalities and smells. Visitors are transported in moving desks with commentary of their choice.

4 Didcot Railway Centre
Great Western Society, Didcot,
Oxfordshire OX11 7NJ
Tel: (01235) 817200
Living museum recreating the golden age of the Great Western Railway. Steam locomotives and trains, engine shed and small relics museum.

5 Bekonscot Model Village
Warwick Road, Beaconsfield,
Buckinghamshire HP9 2PL
Tel: (01494) 672919
A complete model village of the 1930's, with outdoor gauge 1 model railway. Zoo, cinema, minster, cricket match and 1,400 inhabitants.

6 Beale Park
The Child-Beale Wildlife Trust
Lower Basildon,
Berkshire RG8 9NH
Tel: (01734) 845172
Established 38 years ago, the park features wildfowl, pheasants,

highland cattle, rare sheep, llamas, narrow guage railway and pet corner.

7 Windsor Castle
Windsor, Berkshire SL4 1NJ
Tel: (01753) 868286
Official residence of HM The Queen and royal residence for nine centuries. State apartments, Queen Mary's Dolls' House, exhibition of The Queen's presents and carriages.

8 Legoland Windsor
Winkfield Road, Windsor,
Berkshire SL4 4AY
Tel: (0990) 626375
A unique family park with hands-on activities, rides, themed playscapes and more Lego bricks than you ever dreamed possible.

9 Museum of Army Flying
Middle Wallop,
Hampshire SO20 8DY
Tel: (01980) 674421
Award-winning and unique collection of flying machines and

displays depicting the role of army flying since the late 19thC.

10 Jane Austen's House
Chawton, Hampshire GU34 1SD
Tel: (01420) 83262
17thC house where Jane Austen lived from 1809-1817, and wrote or revised her six great novels. Letters, pictures, memorabilia, garden.

11 Winchester Cathedral
5 The Close, Winchester,
Hampshire SO23 9LS
Tel: (01962) 853137
Originally Norman with 16thC additions. Old Saxon site adjacent. Tombs, library and medieval wall paintings.

12 The Sir Harold Hillier Gardens and Arboretum
Jermyns Lane, Ampfield,
Hampshire SO51 0QA
Tel: (01794) 368787
The largest collection of trees and shrubs of its kind in the British Isles planted within an attractive landscape of over 166 acres.

13 Marwell Zoological Park
Colden Common, Winchester,
Hampshire SO21 1JH
Tel: (01962) 777407
Set in 100 acres of parkland
surrounding Marwell Hall. Venue suitable for all age groups including disabled.

14 Broadlands
Romsey, Hampshire SO51 9ZD
Tel: (01794) 517888
Home of the late Lord Mountbatten. Magnificent 18thC house and contents. Superb views across River Test. Mountbatten exhibition and audio-visual presentation.

15 Paultons Park
Ower, Romsey,
Hampshire SO51 6AL
Tel: (01703) 814442
A whole day out for all the family in beautiful surroundings. Over 40 different attractions including rides, museums, birds, animals and entertainment.

16 Exbury Gardens
Exbury, Southampton SO4 1AZ
Tel: (01703) 891203
Over 200 acres of woodland garden, including the Rothschild collection of rhododendrons, azaleas, camellias and magnolias.

17 Tudor House Museum
St. Michael's Square, Bugle Street,
Southampton SO14 2AD
Tel: (01703) 332513
Large half-timbered Tudor house with exhibitions on Tudor, Georgian, and Victorian domestic and local history. Unique Tudor garden.

18 Royal Signals Museum
Blandford Camp,
Blandford Forum,
Dorset DT11 8RH
Tel: (01258) 482248
History of Army communication from Crimean War to Gulf War. Vehicles, uniforms, medals and badges on display.

19 The New Forest Owl Sanctuary
Crow Lane, Crow,
Ringwood,
Hampshire BH24 1EA
Tel: (01425) 476487
All the barn owls are destined to be released into the wild. The sanctuary includes an incubation room, hospital unit and 100 aviaries of various size.

20 National Motor Museum
Beaulieu,
Hampshire SO42 7ZN
Tel: (01590) 612345
Motor museum with over 200 exhibits showing history of motoring from 1895. Palace House, Wheels Experience, abbey ruins with a display of monastic life.

Collection of paintings. 250 acres wooded park, herd of Devon cattle.

26 Brownsea Island
Poole Harbour, Poole,
Dorset BH15 1EE
Tel: (01202) 707744
An island of 500 acres of woodland with beaches, glades and nature reserve. Site of Lord Baden Powell's first scout camp.

27 Compton Acres
Canford Cliffs Road,
Canford Cliffs, Poole,
Dorset BH13 7ES
Tel: (01202) 700778
Nine separate and distinct gardens of the world. The gardens include Italian, Japanese, sub tropical glen, rock, water and heather garden. Collection of statues.

28 Poole Pottery
The Quay, Poole,
Dorset BH15 1RF
Tel: (01202) 666200
Factory tour, self-guided commentary includes museum, cinema, factory and craft area. 'Have-a-go area', craft village, throwing, painting, plus craft demonstrations.

29 Corfe Castle
Corfe Castle, Wareham,
Dorset BH20 5EZ
Tel: (01929) 481294
Ruins of former Royal Castle seiged and "slighted" in 1646 by Parliamentary forces.

30 The Tank Museum
Bovington Camp, Wareham,
Dorset BH20 6JG
Tel: (01929) 405096
Largest and most comprehensive museum collection of armoured fighting vehicles in the world. Over 300 vehicles on show with supporting displays and video theatres.

21 HMS Victory
Portsmouth Historic Ships,
HM Naval Base,
Portsmouth PO1 3LJ
Tel: (01705) 839766
Vice Admiral Lord Nelson's flagship at Trafalgar. See his cabin, the "cockpit," where he died. Memorable tours of the sombre gun decks where men lived.

22 Osborne House
East Cowes,
Isle of Wight PO32 6JY
Tel: (01983) 200022
Queen Victoria and Prince Albert's seaside holiday home. Swiss Cottage where royal children learnt cooking and gardening. Victorian carriage service to Swiss Cottage.

23 Carisbrooke Castle
Newport,
Isle of Wight PO30 1XY
Tel: (01983) 522107

A splendid Norman castle, where Charles I was imprisoned. Governors' lodge houses the county museum, wheelhouse operated by donkeys.

24 Alice in Wonderland Maze and Family Park
Merritown Farm, Hurn,
Christchurch, Dorset BH23 6BA
Tel: (01202) 483444
Hedge maze, Mad Hatter's tea garden, Queen of Heart's croquet lawn, Cheshire Cat's adventure playground, Duchess' rose and herb garden, rare breeds farmyard and bouncy colour maze.

25 Kingston Lacy
Wimborne Minster,
Dorset BH21 4EA
Tel: (01202) 883402
17thC house designed for Sir Ralph Bankes by Sir Roger Pratt, altered by Sir Charles Barry in the 19thC.

HEREFORD & WORCESTER

WARWICKSHIRE

NORTHANTS

BEDS

GLOUCESTERSHIRE

BUCKINGHAM-SHIRE

OXFORDSHIRE

BERKSHIRE

WILTSHIRE

SURREY

HAMPSHIRE

WEST SUSSEX

DORSET (eastern)

ISLE OF WIGHT

Cropredy

1 Banbury

Newport Pagnell
Wolverton
Milton Keynes
Buckingham
Bletchley

Chipping Norton

Bicester

2 Woodstock

Witney
Oxford **3**

Aylesbury
Wendover
Chesham
Thame
Princes Risborough
High Wycombe
Beaconsfield **5**

Abingdon
Faringdon
Wallingford
Wantage
Didcot **4**
Henley on-Thames
Marlow
Slough
Maidenhead
7 **8**
Windsor
Lower Basildon **6**
Twyford
Reading
Hungerford
Newbury
Wokingham
Bracknell

Stratfield Saye
Farnborough
Fleet
Aldershot

Basingstoke

Alton
9 Middle Wallop
Chawton **10**

11 Winchester

Liss

Ampfield
Colden Common
Petersfield

14 **15** Romsey
12 Eastleigh
13 Southampton
Totton **16**
17 Waterlooville
Lyndhurst
Fawley
Locks Heath
Lee-on-the-Solent
Ringwood **19**
Brockenhurst
20
Gosport
21 Portsmouth
Blandford **18** Forum
Wimborne Minster **25**
West Moors
Beaulieu
East Cowes **22**
Ryde
Lymington
Poole **26** **27** **28**
24
Christchurch
Newport **23**
Gillingham
Shaftesbury
Fordingbridge

29 **30**
Wareham
Bournemouth
Yarmouth
Sandown
Shanklin
Ventnor
Swanage
Freshwater

0   20 Miles
0   30 Kms

FIND OUT MORE

Further information about holidays and attractions in the South of England is available from:

Southern Tourist Board,
40 Chamberlayne Road,
Eastleigh,
Hampshire SO50 5JH.
Tel: (01703) 620555

WHERE TO STAY (SOUTH OF ENGLAND)

Accommodation entries in this region are listed in alphabetical order of place name, and then in alphabetical order of establishment. A contact address is given where it differs from the address of the establishment.

Map references refer to the colour location maps at the back of this guide.

Prices shown are weekly per unit.

At-a-glance symbols at the end of each accommodation entry give useful information about services and facilities. A key to symbols can be found inside the back cover flap. Keep this open for easy reference.

ABINGDON

Oxfordshire
Map ref 2C1

Attractive former county town on River Thames with many interesting buildings, including 17th C County Hall, now a museum, in the market-place and the remains of an abbey.
Tourist Information Centre ☎ (01235) 522711

The Old School
⚷⚷⚷⚷ COMMENDED
16 High Street, Drayton, Abingdon OX14 4JL
☎ (01235) 531557
Contact: Mrs C A Radburn
Part of 19th C village school, now skilfully converted to provide a spacious, well-equipped and tastefully furnished maisonette. Ideal base for exploring the Thames Valley, Cotswolds and Oxford. Fast train service to London from nearby Didcot station.
1 self-contained unit; sleeping 4–5

Price per week:	£min	£max
Low season	155.00	
High season	195.00	245.00

☎ 7 M ◎ ▥ ⊙ ▣ M W ⊏ TV ⓢ ▱
⬛ ♠ P U ⸙ ❋ ✕ ⟍ SP ⌂

Information on accommodation listed in this guide has been supplied by the proprietors. As changes may occur you are advised to check details at the time of booking.

ALTON

Hampshire
Map ref 2C2

Pleasant old market town standing on the Pilgrim's Way, with some attractive Georgian buildings. The parish church still bears the scars of bullet marks, evidence of a bitter struggle between the Roundheads and the Royalists.
Tourist Information Centre ☎ (01420) 88448

Woodside Farm Annexe ▲
⚷⚷⚷⚷ APPROVED
Gosport Road, Privett, Alton
Contact: Miss V A Crisp & Mrs P Newman, Woodside Farm, Gosport Road, Privett, Alton, Hampshire GU34 3NJ
☎ Privett (01730) 828359
Fully equipped accommodation, including colour TV. Many places of interest nearby. Groceries delivered. Brochure available.
1 self-contained unit; sleeping max 5

Price per week:	£min	£max
Low season	165.00	185.00
High season	170.00	220.00

☎ M ◎ ▥ ▦ ⊙ ▣ TV ⓢ ▱ ⬛ ♠ P U ❋

ALVERSTOKE

Hampshire
Map ref 2C3

28 The Avenue
⚷⚷⚷ APPROVED
Alverstoke, Gosport

Contact: Mr Martin Lawson, 18 Upper Paddock Road, Watford, Hertfordshire WD1 4DZ
☎ Watford (01923) 244042
3-bedroomed house with pleasant garden, 10 minutes from uncrowded beach. Opportunities for fishing, sailing and windsurfing. Close to Portsmouth, Southampton and New Forest.
1 self-contained unit; sleeping max 6

Price per week:	£min	£max
Low season	230.00	270.00
High season	270.00	300.00

☎ ◎ ▥ ⊙ ▣ ⊏ TV ⬛ ▱ ⬛ ♠ P ❋

AMERSHAM

Buckinghamshire
Map ref 2D1

Old town with many fine buildings, particularly in the High Street. There are several interesting old inns.

Cherry Tree Cottage
⚷⚷⚷⚷ COMMENDED
Fagnall Lane, Winchmore Hill, Amersham
Contact: Mr D Frankland, Rose Cottage, Woodside Lane, Gallowstree Common, Reading, Berkshire RG4 9DL
☎ Reading (0118) 972 3630
Fax (0118) 972 4585
Well-equipped bungalow in pretty village location. Convenient for London, Windsor, Oxford and the Thames Valley.
1 self-contained unit; sleeping max 4

Price per week:	£min	£max
Low season	205.00	225.00
High season	225.00	255.00

☎ ◎ ▥ ⊙ ▣ ⊏ TV ⓢ ▱ ⬛ ▥ ⬛ ♠ P ❋ SP

ASHURST

Hampshire
Map ref 2C3

Small village on the A35, on the edge of the New Forest and three miles north-east of Lyndhurst. Easy access to beautiful forest lawns.

Nuthatch Cottage

COMMENDED

Hazel Grove, Woodlands, Southampton
Contact: Mr & Mrs D Cintra, Boltons House, Princes Crescent, Lyndhurst, Hampshire SO43 7BS
☎ Lyndhurst (01703) 282200
Secluded, modern cottage within 3 minutes' walk of open forest. Well furnished, dishwasher, video, etc. Garden and garage. Ideal for relaxed family holidays.
1 self-contained unit; sleeping max 6

Price per week:	£min	£max
Low season	230.00	295.00
High season	330.00	465.00

BANBURY

Oxfordshire
Map ref 2C1

Famous for its cattle market, cakes and nursery rhyme Cross. Founded in Saxon times, it has some fine houses and interesting old inns. A good centre for touring Warwickshire and the Cotswolds.
Tourist Information Centre ☎ *(01295) 259855*

Butler's Cottage

HIGHLY COMMENDED

6 Main Street, Mollington, Banbury
Contact: Mrs R Shahani, Lyttelton House, Stowe, Buckingham, Buckinghamshire MK18 5EH
☎ Buckingham (01280) 822391
Fax (01280) 822769
17th C listed stone cottage under thatched roof. Inglenook fire, low beamed ceiling and four-poster bed. Easy access to Stratford-upon-Avon, Warwick and the Cotswolds.
1 self-contained unit; sleeping max 4

Price per week:	£min	£max
Low season	170.00	
High season		250.00

BARFORD ST. MICHAEL

Oxfordshire
Map ref 2C1

Chapel Cottage

COMMENDED

The Rock, Barford St. Michael, Banbury
Contact: Mrs Penelope Cameron Watt, Yew Tree House, Bucknell, Bicester, Oxfordshire OX6 9LT
☎ Bicester (01869) 249545
Fax (01869) 245203
Delightful, stone 2-bedroomed cottage in pretty village, on edge of Cotswolds, between Oxford and Stratford. Small dog and children welcome (cot available).
1 self-contained unit; sleeping max 6

Price per week:	£min	£max
Low season	165.00	200.00
High season	225.00	375.00

BEAULIEU

Hampshire
Map ref 2C3

Beautifully situated among woods and hills on the Beaulieu river, the village is both charming and unspoilt. The 13th C ruined Cistercian abbey and 14th C Palace House stand close to the National Motor Museum. There is a maritime museum at Bucklers Hard.

Mares Tails Studio

COMMENDED

Mares Tails, Furzey Lane, Beaulieu, Brockenhurst
Contact: Mrs Alice Barber, Mares Tails, Furzey Lane, Beaulieu, Brockenhurst, Hampshire SO42 7WB
☎ Beaulieu (01590) 612160
Modern studio in own secluded garden in grounds of architect's house. One mile from lovely village of Beaulieu, with direct access to open forest. 30 foot conservatory.
1 self-contained unit; sleeping max 2

Price per week:	£min	£max
Low season	220.00	270.00
High season	270.00	320.00

Open May–September

Map references apply to the colour maps at the back of this guide.

BEMBRIDGE

Isle of Wight
Map ref 2C3

Village with harbour and bay below Bembridge Down - the most easterly village on the island. Bembridge Sailing Club is one of the most important in southern England.

Edenmore

COMMENDED

Upper Green Road, St Helens, Ryde
Contact: Mrs R Hickman, Freefolk, Upper Green Road, St Helens, Ryde, Isle of Wight PO33 1UQ
☎ Isle of Wight (01983) 873390
Three-bedroomed house overlooking village green and downland, adjoining owner's period cottage. Near picturesque Bembridge harbour and award-winning beach.
1 self-contained unit; sleeping max 5

Price per week:	£min	£max
Low season	120.00	190.00
High season	220.00	285.00

BICESTER

Oxfordshire
Map ref 2C1

Market town with large army depot and well-known hunting centre with hunt established in the late 18th C. The ancient parish church displays work of many periods. Nearby is the Jacobean mansion of Rousham House with gardens landscaped by William Kent.
Tourist Information Centre ☎ *(01869) 369055*

Pimlico Farm Country Cottages

HIGHLY COMMENDED

Pimlico Farm, Tusmore, Bicester OX6 9SL
☎ Croughton (01869) 810306 & Mobile 0374 940321
Fax (01869) 810306
Contact: Mr & Mrs J Harper

500-acre mixed farm. Cotswold stone barn conversion into 4 top quality cottages, situated in Oxfordshire
Continued ▶

BICESTER

Continued

Cotswolds on a working farm. Free on-farm fishing. Ideal touring base close to Oxford, Stratford and Warwick. Resident owners will make guests welcome.
Wheelchair access category 2♿
4 self-contained units; sleeping 2–6

Price per week:	£min	£max
Low season	155.00	225.00
High season	255.00	420.00

Cards accepted: Access, Visa

BOLDRE

Hampshire
Map ref 2C3

Attractive village with pretty views of the river from the bridge. The white plastered church sits on top of a hill.

Close Cottage ⚃
COMMENDED

Brockenhurst Road, Battramsley, Boldre, Lymington SO41 8PT
☎ Lymington (01590) 675343
Contact: Mr or Mrs C J White
Cosy annexe of period cottage with beamed ceilings and antique decor. French doors to garden, rural views. Ample private parking.
1 self-contained unit; sleeping max 2

Price per week:	£min	£max
Low season	95.00	140.00
High season	160.00	195.00

BONCHURCH

Isle of Wight
Map ref 2C3

Sheltered suburb at the foot of St Boniface Down.

Woodlynch Holiday Flats
COMMENDED

Shore Road, Bonchurch, Ventnor PO38 1RF
☎ Isle of Wight (01983) 852513
Contact: Mr & Mrs C Tasker
Gracious country house in a picturesque seaside village. Self-contained flats convenient for island attractions. Pets by arrangement. Parking.

---

5 self-contained units; sleeping 2–6

Price per week:	£min	£max
Low season	80.00	250.00
High season	135.00	295.00

Open March–October

BOURNEMOUTH

Dorset
Map ref 2B3

Seaside town set among the pines with a mild climate, sandy beaches and fine coastal views. The town has wide streets with excellent shops, a pier, a pavilion, museums and conference centre.
Tourist Information Centre ☎ (01202) 451700

Moonrakers ⚃
COMMENDED

21 St Anthonys Road, Bournemouth BH2 6PB
☎ (01202) 553113
Fax (01202) 553113
Contact: Mr Paul Newsome
Spacious self-contained holiday flats, central, yet quiet. Close to sea, shops, entertainment and Bournemouth International Centre. Fully-equipped. Free parking.
3 self-contained units; sleeping 4–7

Price per week:	£min	£max
Low season	180.00	270.00
High season	280.00	420.00

Open June–September

Saltaire ⚃
UP TO HIGHLY COMMENDED

Sea Road, Southbourne, Bournemouth BH6 4AL
☎ Reservations (01202) 420296 & Brochure (Answerphone) 422875
Fax (01202) 420296
Contact: Mr D H Counter

The majority of flats have sea views and sun balconies. Close to sandy beach and shops, with restaurants nearby. Heated indoor swimming pool, solarium and games room. Free parking. 3-night breaks from £86.

---

40 self-contained units; sleeping 2–8

Price per week:	£min	£max
Low season	115.00	190.00
High season	320.00	598.00

Watersedge ⚃
UP TO HIGHLY COMMENDED

27 Boscombe Overcliff Drive, Boscombe Manor, Bournemouth BH5 1LW
☎ (01202) 300118 & Freefone 0500 300318
Fax (01202) 300118
Contact: Mr Ken Robins
Spacious and well-equipped flats, situated on cliff top with panoramic sea views.
Wheelchair access category 3♿
10 self-contained units; sleeping 2–12

Price per week:	£min	£max
Low season	185.00	405.00
High season	290.00	575.00

Woodview Holiday Apartments
HIGHLY COMMENDED

6 St Anthony's Road, Meyrick Park, Bournemouth BH2 6PD
☎ (01202) 290027 & Mobile 0385 788400
Fax (01202) 295959
Contact: Mr & Mrs Shane Busby
Centrally situated, spacious apartments. Large garden. Convenient for sea, shops, entertainments and conference centre. Ideal touring base. Laundry room and payphone for guests' use.
4 self-contained units; sleeping 2–7

Price per week:	£min	£max
Low season	175.00	225.00
High season	325.00	420.00

Open May–September

BRAISHFIELD

Hampshire
Map ref 2C3

Meadow Cottage & Rosie's Cottage
COMMENDED

Farley Farm, Braishfield, Romsey
Contact: Mrs J W Graham, Farley Farm, Braishfield, Romsey, Hampshire SO51 0QP
☎ Romsey (01794) 368265 & 368513
Fax (01794) 367847
400-acre arable & livestock farm. In unspoilt countryside within easy reach

of New Forest, Romsey, Salisbury, Winchester and the coast. Own transport essential.

2 self-contained units; sleeping max 5

Price per week:	£min	£max
Low season	170.00	
High season		270.00

Open April–October

🛏️ Ⓜ️ 🖥️ ☉ 🛏️ 📺 🍴 ♨️ 🧺 🛍️ 📷 ➹ P ひ ✂️ ❄️

BRIGHSTONE

Isle of Wight
Map ref 2C3

Excellent centre for visitors who want somewhere quiet. Calbourne nearby is ideal for picnics and the sea at Chilton Chine has safe bathing at high tide.

Casses 🏔️
COMMENDED

Main Road, Brighstone
Contact: Mr & Mrs J K Nesbitt, Kerrich House, Peartree Court, Old Orchards, Lymington, Hampshire SO41 3TF
☎ Lymington (01590) 679601

17th C thatched smuggler's cottage in own grounds. Comfortably furnished and fully equipped. Cot available. Non-smokers only, please.

1 self-contained unit; sleeping max 7

Price per week:	£min	£max
Low season	395.00	
High season		765.00

🛏️ 🖥️ 📟 ☉ 🛏️ MW 📺 🍴 ♨️ 🖨️ ➹ P ▶️ ❄️ 🔇 SP 🏮

BRIZE NORTON

Oxfordshire
Map ref 2C1

Village closely associated with the American Air Force. The medieval church is the only church in England dedicated to St Brice, from whom the village takes its name.

Rocky Bank Holiday Cottages
🔑🔑🔑🔑 **COMMENDED**

Rocky Banks, Burford Road, Brize Norton, Oxford OX18 3NT
☎ Carterton (01993) 840770
Contact: Mr & Mrs John Hunt

Stone-built cottages on the edge of the Cotswolds. Oxford and Cheltenham 30 minutes.

2 self-contained units; sleeping 4–8

Price per week:	£min	£max
Low season	165.00	260.00
High season	255.00	385.00

🛏️ Ⓜ️ 🖥️ 📟 ☉ 🛏️ MW 📺 🍴 ♨️ 🧺 🛍️ 📶 P ひ ❄️ ✂️ SP Ⓣ

BROCKENHURST

Hampshire
Map ref 2C3

Attractive village with thatched cottages and a ford in its main street. Well placed for visiting the New Forest.

Flat A Little Prescotes
🔑🔑 **COMMENDED**

Tile Barn Lane, Brockenhurst
Contact: Mrs J H Smith, Little Prescotes, Tile Barn Lane, Brockenhurst, Hampshire SO42 7UE
☎ Lymington (01590) 623352
Spacious, first floor 2-bedroomed flat set in grounds of large country house, with direct access to New Forest.

1 self-contained unit; sleeping 2–4

Price per week:	£min	£max
Low season	220.00	250.00
High season	295.00	330.00

🛏️ Ⓜ️ 🖥️ 📟 ☉ 🛏️ MW 📺 🍴 ♨️ 🖨️ ➹ P ひ ❄️ ✂️

Gorse Cottage
🔑🔑🔑🔑 **COMMENDED**

Balmer Lawn Road, Brockenhurst
Contact: Mrs A Bareford, Whins, Hook Heath Avenue, Woking, Surrey GU22 0HN
☎ Guildford (01483) 760803
Fax (01483) 764227
Cottage/bungalow on open forest road 1 mile from Brockenhurst village. Decorated and furnished to good standard and equipped with many extras. Pets welcome. Fenced garden.

1 self-contained unit; sleeping max 4

Price per week:	£min	£max
Low season	220.00	250.00
High season	320.00	450.00

🛏️ 🖥️ 📟 ☉ 🛏️ MW 🚐 📺 🍴 ♨️ 🖨️ 🛍️ ➹ P ひ ❄️ 🔇 SP

2 Melrose Cottages
🔑🔑🔑 **COMMENDED**

Waters Green, Brockenhurst
Contact: Mrs J H Smith, Little Prescotes, Tile Barn Lane, Brockenhurst, Hampshire SO42 7UE
☎ Lymington (01590) 623352
In the village of Brockenhurst, this pretty, 200-year-old 3-bedroomed

---

cottage overlooks open green where New Forest animals graze.

1 self-contained unit; sleeping max 6

Price per week:	£min	£max
Low season	240.00	285.00
High season	320.00	370.00

🛏️ Ⓜ️ 🖥️ 📟 ☉ 🛏️ MW 🚐 📺 🍴 ♨️ 🖨️ 📶 🛍️ ➹ P ひ ❄️ 🏮

BURFORD

Oxfordshire
Map ref 2B1

One of the most beautiful Cotswold wool towns with Georgian and Tudor houses, many antique shops and a picturesque High Street sloping to the River Windrush.
Tourist Information Centre ☎ *(01993) 823558*

Ael-y-Bryn
🔑🔑🔑🔑 **HIGHLY COMMENDED**

Shipton Road, Fulbrook, Burford OX18 4BU
☎ (01993) 822030
Contact: Mrs Ann Purcell
Cotswold country house in an elevated position. Patio and pretty garden, with superb views of surrounding countryside and Norman church.

1 self-contained unit; sleeping 2–3

Price per week:	£min	£max
Low season	230.00	
High season	230.00	

Open May–September

🛏️ 6 📟 ☉ 🛏️ 📺 🍴 ♨️ 🖨️ 🛍️ 🛍️ ➹ P ❄️ ✂️

High Pound Cottage
🔑🔑🔑 **COMMENDED**

High Pound, Westhall Hill, Fulbrook, Oxford
Contact: Mrs Annette Baker, High Pound, Westhall Hill, Fulbrook, Oxford, Oxfordshire OX18 4BJ
☎ Fulbrook (01993) 822712
Charming, comfortably furnished cottage set in beautiful 2-acre gardens. Only 5 minutes' walk to Burford. Free range eggs.

1 self-contained unit; sleeping 2–6

Price per week:	£min	£max
Low season	210.00	260.00
High season	310.00	360.00

🛏️ 🛍️ P ❄️ SP

Hill View Cottage
🔑🔑 **COMMENDED**

Swinbrook, Oxford OX18 4EF
☎ (01993) 823440
Contact: Miss Patricia Regnart
Adjoining owner's home in peaceful garden setting, this comfortable,

Continued ▶

BURFORD

Continued

*well-equipped cottage is ideal for two.
Lovely rural views and local walks.*
1 self-contained unit; sleeping max 3

Price per week:	£min	£max
Low season	135.00	150.00
High season	205.00	210.00

The Mill at Burford

HIGHLY COMMENDED

Witney Street, Burford OX18 4RX
☎ (01993) 822379
Fax (01993) 822759
Contact: Mrs Ruth Jennings

*Secluded riverside setting with waterfall
and waterwheel. Five minutes' walk
from the centre of historic Burford,
pubs and antique shops. Excellent base
for Cotswolds, Oxford, Stratford.*
5 self-contained units; sleeping 2–5

Price per week:	£min	£max
Low season	150.00	250.00
High season	220.00	440.00

Cards accepted: Access, Visa

Woodgrove House

HIGHLY COMMENDED

Fulbrook Hill, Fulbrook, Burford
Contact: Mrs J Deaney, The
Sheerings, 18 Amberley Close,
Keinton Mandeville, Somerton,
Somerset TA11 6EU
☎ (01458) 223130
*Attractive accommodation with own
pretty garden, adjoining Woodgrove
House. Views over the Windrush Valley.
Use of outdoor swimming pool.*
1 self-contained unit; sleeping 2–3

Price per week:	£min	£max
Low season		150.00
High season		250.00

For ideas on places to visit
refer to the introduction at
the beginning of this section.

BURLEY

Hampshire
Map ref 2B3

Attractive centre from which to
explore the south-west part of the
New Forest. There is an ancient
earthwork on Castle Hill nearby,
which also offers good views.

Burbush Farm Cottages

COMMENDED

Burbush Farm, Pound Lane, Burley,
Ringwood BH24 4RF
☎ (01425) 403238
Contact: Mr & Mrs D C Hayles
*12-acre mixed farm. Modernised,
picturesque cottages, comfortably
furnished, on a farm in the heart of the
New Forest. Beautiful views and walks
with direct access to forest.*
2 self-contained units;
sleeping max 5

Price per week:	£min	£max
Low season	100.00	200.00
High season	200.00	400.00

CHALFONT ST GILES

Buckinghamshire
Map ref 2D2

Pretty, old village in wooded
Chiltern Hills yet only 20 miles from
London and a good base for visiting
the city. Excellent base for Windsor,
Henley, the Thames Valley, Oxford
and the Cotswolds.

Studio Flat at Applewood

COMMENDED

Mill Lane, Chalfont St Giles
Contact: Mr & Mrs J E Newcombe,
Applewood, Mill Lane, Chalfont St
Giles, Buckinghamshire HP8 4NX
☎ Chalfont St Giles (01494)
873343
*Very comfortable, self-contained studio
flat, attached to owner's house and
overlooking attractive garden. Quiet
and fully equipped, including private
telephone. Convenient for Oxford,
Windsor, Henley and Cotswolds.*
1 self-contained unit; sleeping max 2

Price per week:	£min	£max
Low season	160.00	170.00
High season	170.00	180.00

CHARLBURY

Oxfordshire
Map ref 2C1

Large Cotswold village with
beautiful views of the Evenlode
Valley just outside the village and
close to the ancient Forest of
Wychwood.

Banbury Hill Farm Cottages

HIGHLY COMMENDED

Banbury Hill Farm, Charlbury,
Oxford
Contact: Mrs Angela Widdows,
Banbury Hill Farm, Charlbury,
Oxford, Oxfordshire OX7 3JH
☎ Charlbury (01608) 810314
Fax (01608) 811891
*54-acre mixed farm. Farm cottages well
situated for touring the Cotswolds,
Oxford and Stratford. Many bridleways
and footpaths, delightful scenery
overlooking Evenlode Valley and the
famous Wychwood Forest.*
7 self-contained units; sleeping 2–6

Price per week:	£min	£max
Low season	180.00	195.00
High season	280.00	295.00

Barn Annexe

COMMENDED

Rooks Nest House, Spelsbury Road,
Charlbury, Oxford OX7 3LR
☎ (01608) 810409
Contact: Mr & Mrs Selwyn Wyatt
*Converted barn adjoining early 19th C
house, in open countryside. Large
galleried sitting room, double bedroom,
kitchen and shower. Off-road parking.*
1 self-contained unit; sleeping 2–4

Price per week:	£min	£max
Low season	155.00	175.00
High season	175.00	195.00

Open April–October

Nine Acres Cottage

HIGHLY COMMENDED

Thames Street, Charlbury, Oxford
Contact: Mrs D V Lunney, Glebe
House, Thames Street, Charlbury,
Oxford, Oxfordshire OX7 3QL
☎ Charlbury (01608) 810864
Fax (01608) 811429

Cotswold-stone 3-bedroomed cottage, recently refurbished, with large garden laid mainly to lawn in the front. Views across the valley to Wychwood Forest. Convenient for Oxford, Blenheim Palace.
1 self-contained unit; sleeping max 6

Price per week:	£min	£max
Low season	180.00	280.00
High season	285.00	325.00

🐕🦽◎💻⊙📺 MW 📺🗄 🛋🖇🚗
P❄ SP T

CHARNEY BASSETT

Oxfordshire
Map ref 2C2

Small village set in beautiful open countryside, 11 miles south-west of Oxford.

Charncote Cottage
🔑🔑 COMMENDED
30 New Road, Charney Bassett, Wantage
Contact: Mrs Bernice Sweetman, 119 Sandgate High Street, Folkestone, Kent CT20 3BZ
☎ (01303) 249686
Semi-detached stone Gothic-style cottage, originally part of the Pusey Estate. Restored to a high standard, comfortably furnished, fully equipped. Open fire for warm and cosy winters, conservatory with relaxing atmosphere.
1 self-contained unit; sleeping max 5

Price per week:	£min	£max
Low season	255.00	300.00
High season	355.00	400.00

🐕◎🍃🦽💻 MW 📺🗄 🛋🖇🚗 P
❄ SP 🏠

CHILWORTH

Hampshire
Map ref 2C3

Rose Cottage 🄜
🔑🔑 COMMENDED
5 Chilworth Old Village, Chilworth, Romsey
Contact: Mrs Gwendolyn Young, 61 Clifton Road, Regents Park, Southampton, Hampshire SO15 4GY
☎ Southampton (01703) 771729
Beautiful, listed thatched cottage, ideally situated for exploring New Forest, Isle of Wight and South Coast.

1 self-contained unit; sleeping max 5

Price per week:	£min	£max
Low season	100.00	
High season		325.00

🐕🄜◎🦽💻🗄📺🗄🛋🖇🚗P❄
🍴 SP

CHIPPING NORTON

Oxfordshire
Map ref 2C1

Old market town set high in the Cotswolds and an ideal touring centre. The wide market-place contains many 16th C and 17th C stone houses and the Town Hall and Tudor Guildhall.
Tourist Information Centre ☎ (01608) 644379

Heath Farm Holiday Cottages
🔑🔑🔑 HIGHLY COMMENDED
Heath Farm, Swerford, Chipping Norton OX7 4BN
☎ Great Tew (01608) 683270 & 683204
Contact: Mr & Mrs David Barbour

70-acre arable and mixed farm. Stone cottages set around stunning courtyard and water garden in 70 acres of farm and woodland. Near Chipping Norton and convenient for Cotswolds, Oxford, Stratford, Warwick. Non-smoking establishment. Prices shown are for 2 people per unit - add £30 per extra person.
4 self-contained units; sleeping 2–4

Price per week:	£min	£max
Low season	200.00	280.00
High season	275.00	388.00

◎🦽⊙💻 MW 📺📺🗄 🛋🖇🚗
P🖐⚓❄🍴 SP 🏠

CHRISTCHURCH

Dorset
Map ref 2B3

Tranquil town lying between the Avon and Stour just before they converge and flow into Christchurch Harbour. A fine 11th C church and the remains of a Norman castle and house can be seen.
Tourist Information Centre ☎ (01202) 471780

The Causeway 🄜
🔑🔑 APPROVED
32-34 Stanpit, Mudeford, Christchurch BH23 3LZ
☎ Bournemouth (01202) 470149
Contact: Mrs Maria Cory
Ideally situated midway between town and harbour of Christchurch and Mudeford quay and beaches.
3 self-contained units, 2 non-self-contained units; sleeping 1–4

Price per week:	£min	£max
Low season	75.00	110.00
High season	110.00	190.00

🐕◎🦽⊙💻 MW 📺🛋🖇🚗P🍴
SP

CORFE CASTLE

Dorset
Map ref 2B3

One of the most spectacular ruined castles in Britain. Norman in origin, the castle was a Royalist stronghold during the Civil War and held out until 1645. The village had a considerable marble-carving industry in the Middle Ages.

Rose Cottage 🄜
🔑🔑 COMMENDED
42 West Street, Corfe Castle, Wareham
Contact: Mr & Mrs Douglas Doughty, 21 Dundale Road, Tring, Hertfordshire HP23 5BS
☎ Tring (01442) 823336
Listed Purbeck-stone cottage, near village centre but quiet. Sleeps 5 in 2 bedrooms, plus cot. Comfortable lounge with gas fire in inglenook. CH, colour TV, video, radio, telephone. Well-equipped kitchen, secluded patio garden, private parking.
1 self-contained unit; sleeping max 5
Continued ▶

Please mention this guide when making your booking.

CORFE CASTLE

Continued

Price per week:	£min	£max
Low season	200.00	265.00
High season	240.00	385.00

Open April–October

⚇ ⌀ �🁢 ⊙ 🛢 M W 💺 TV 🛋 ♨ P ✿ SP 🏠

Scoles Manor

🗝🗝🗝 HIGHLY COMMENDED

Kingston, Corfe Castle BH20 5LG
☎ (01929) 480312
Fax (01929) 481237
Contact: Mr & Mrs Peter Bell

The Scoles Manor barns were converted in 1990 into 3 high quality dwellings. They are in a superb setting with spectacular views over Corfe Castle and the Purbeck countryside.
3 self-contained units; sleeping 4–10

Price per week:	£min	£max
Low season	175.00	300.00
High season	400.00	800.00

🗝 M ◎ 🁢 ⊙ 🛢 M W 💺 TV 🖥 🛋 📶 🖨 ♨ P U ✿ SP 🏠

COTSWOLDS

See under Brize Norton, Burford, Charlbury, Chipping Norton, Minster Lovell, Witney
See also Cotswolds in Heart of England region

DENMEAD

Hampshire
Map ref 2C3

Comparatively modern town, south-west of the original settlement.

Flint Cottage

🗝🗝🗝 HIGHLY COMMENDED

c/o High Trees, Ashling Close, Denmead, Waterlooville
Contact: Mr & Mrs John & Sheila Knight, High Trees, Ashling Close, Denmead, Waterlooville, Hampshire PO7 6NQ
☎ Waterlooville (01705) 266345
Small, flint and slate roofed, early 19th C coach house. Completely modernised to provide comfortable, self-contained double bedded accommodation, suitable for 1/2 adults only.

1 self-contained unit; sleeping max 2

Price per week:	£min	£max
Low season	150.00	
High season	200.00	

◎ 🁢 ⊙ 🛢 M W 💺 TV 🛋 📶 🖨 ♨ P ✖ SP

FORDINGBRIDGE

Hampshire
Map ref 2B3

On the north-west edge of the New Forest. A medieval bridge crosses the Avon at this point and gave the town its name. A good centre for walking, exploring and fishing.

Warren Park Farm

🗝🗝 — 🗝🗝 UP TO HIGHLY COMMENDED

Alderholt, Fordingbridge SP6 3DE
☎ (01425) 653340
Fax (01425) 653340
Contact: Mrs V A Huzzey

150-acre dairy farm. Comfortable holiday lodge in peaceful position overlooking a lake which provides excellent coarse fishing. Within easy travelling of sea and New Forest.
1 self-contained unit; sleeping 5–6

Price per week:	£min	£max
Low season	145.00	230.00
High season	235.00	370.00

🗝 M ◎ 🁢 ⊙ 🛢 M W TV 🛋 📶 🖨 ♨ P U 🗝 ✿ 🁢 SP

FRESHWATER

Isle of Wight
Map ref 2C3

This part of the island is associated with Tennyson, who lived in the village for 30 years. A monument on Tennyson's Down commemorates the poet.

65 Cliff End

🗝🗝 COMMENDED

Monks Lane, Freshwater
Contact: Mrs Helen Long, c/o 12 Hollis Drive, Brighstone, Newport, Isle of Wight PO30 4AF
☎ Isle of Wight (01983) 740651
Delightful, modern holiday bungalow with views across the Solent towards the Needles. Ideal for walking, boating and wildlife.

1 self-contained unit; sleeping max 6

Price per week:	£min	£max
Low season	100.00	
High season		220.00

Open March–October and Christmas

🗝 ⊙ ◎ 🁢 ⊙ 🛢 M W TV 🛋 📷 ♨ P U ✖

GOSPORT

Hampshire
Map ref 2C3

From a tiny fishing hamlet, Gosport has grown into an important centre with many naval establishments, including HMS Dolphin, the submarine base, with the Naval Submarine Museum which preserves HMS Alliance and Holland I.
Tourist Information Centre ☎ (01705) 522944

Captains Folly

🗝🗝 COMMENDED

The Hardway, 69 Priory Road, Gosport
Contact: Mrs Maureen White, 8 Cambridge Road, Lee on the Solent, Hampshire PO13 9DH
☎ Lee on the Solent (01705) 550883
Large, period house, with 3 baths, sleeps 8 comfortably. Overlooks Portsmouth Harbour towards Portchester Castle. Long garden to harbour beach.

1 self-contained unit; sleeping 6–10

Price per week:	£min	£max
Low season	250.00	320.00
High season	360.00	425.00

🗝 ◎ 🁢 ⊙ 🛢 M W 💺 TV 🖥 🛋 📶 🖨 ♨ P ✿ 🁢 SP 🏠 T

GREAT MILTON

Oxfordshire
Map ref 2C1

Views Farm Barns

🗝🗝🗝 HIGHLY COMMENDED

Views Farm, Great Milton, Oxford OX9 7NW
☎ (01844) 279352 & Mobile 0836 273541
Fax (01844) 279362
Contact: Mr & Mrs C O Peers
400-acre arable and mixed farm. Converted stable block forming well-appointed holiday flats. Close to Oxford and the M40. Superb views of the Thame Valley.
6 self-contained units; sleeping 3–5

Price per week:	£min	£max
Low season	160.00	180.00
High season	270.00	290.00

⌂ ◎ ▥ ⊡ 🗆 MW TV 🖥 🍴 🛏 🚗
P 🎣 ❄ ⚲ SP 🏠 T

Hampshire
Map ref 2C3

Set almost at the mouth of the River Hamble, this quiet fishing village has become a major yachting centre.

The Lodge ▲▲
🔑 🔑 COMMENDED

Riverside Park, Satchell Lane, Hamble, Southampton
Contact: Mr Martin Gray, Davidson Country Park Homes, The Larches, Canal Hill, Tiverton, Devon EX16 4JD
☎ Tiverton (01884) 258944
Fax (01884) 258944
High quality holiday lodge with views over River Hamble and marina. Spaciously appointed, tastefully furnished and fully equipped.
1 self-contained unit; sleeping 2–6

Price per week:	£min	£max
Low season	147.00	
High season		420.00

Cards accepted: Access, Visa

⌂ M ◎ 🔥 ▥ ⊡ 🗆 MW 🍴 TV 🖥 🛏
🍴 🚗 P U ❄ ✈ ⚲ SP T

Dorset
Map ref 2B3

Hartgrove Farm
🔑 🔑 🔑 COMMENDED

Hartgrove, Shaftesbury SP7 0JY
☎ Fontmell Magna (01747) 811830
Fax (01747) 811830
Contact: Mrs Susan Smart

140-acre mixed farm. Family farm, 4 miles south of Shaftesbury. Lovely cottages, 1 suitable for disabled. Tennis court, games room. Superb views, magnificent walking and wildlife, pretty thatched village. Half hour to coast.
Wheelchair access category 1 ♿
5 self-contained units; sleeping 2–5

Price per week:	£min	£max
Low season	160.00	250.00
High season	275.00	450.00

Cards accepted: Amex

⌂ ◎ ▥ ⊡ 🗆 MW TV 🖥 🍴 🛏 🚗 P
⛲ ⚲ ❄ SP 🏠

Berkshire
Map ref 2C2

Yaffles
🔑 🔑 🔑 🔑 🔑 🔑
HIGHLY COMMENDED

Red Shute Hill, Hermitage RG18 9QH
☎ (01635) 201100
Fax (01635) 201100
Contact: Mrs Sally Greig
Set in 5.5 acres of woodland, just north of Newbury, these comfortable units are equipped and maintained to a very high standard. Idyllic setting.
2 self-contained units; sleeping 4–6

Price per week:	£min	£max
Low season	180.00	310.00
High season	230.00	360.00

⌂ ◎ ▥ ⊙ 🗆 MW 🍴 TV 🖥 🛏 📻 🍴
🚗 P ❄ ⚲ SP T

See under Bonchurch, Brighstone, Freshwater, Newport, Ryde, Ventnor, Whitwell

Buckinghamshire
Map ref 2D1

Town Farm Holiday Cottage
🔑 🔑 🔑 COMMENDED

Town Farm, Ivinghoe, Leighton Buzzard, Bedfordshire LU7 9EL
☎ Cheddington (01296) 668455
Contact: Mrs Angie Leach
600-acre mixed farm. The cottage has views over Ivinghoe Beacon and is on the B489 outside Ivinghoe.
1 self-contained unit; sleeping 1–7

Price per week:	£min	£max
Low season	240.00	260.00
High season	280.00	300.00

⌂ M ◎ ▥ ⊙ 🗆 MW 🍴 TV 🖥 🛏 🍴
🍴 🚗 P ⚲ U 🎣 ✈ ❄ ⚲ SP 🏠

Berkshire
Map ref 2C2

Attractive village among the Downs on the River Lambourn. Famous for its racing stables.

Lodge Down ▲▲
🔑 🔑 🔑 COMMENDED

The Woodlands, Lambourn, Hungerford
Contact: Mrs Sally Cook, Lodge Down, The Woodlands, Lambourn, Hungerford, Berkshire RG17 7BJ
☎ Marlborough (01672) 540304
Fax (01672) 540304
100-acre arable farm. Cosy self-contained flat, adjoining country house with spacious grounds and views of gallops and garden.
1 self-contained unit; sleeping max 3

Price per week:	£min	£max
Low season	110.00	150.00
High season	150.00	180.00

⌂ ◎ ▥ ⊙ 🗆 TV 🛏 📻 ∥ P ⛲ ⚲ U
❄

Dorset
Map ref 2B3

18th C Purbeck stone village surrounded by National Trust downland, about a mile from the sea and 350 ft above sea level. Excellent walking.

Flat 5 Garfield House
🔑 🔑 COMMENDED

Langton Matravers, Swanage
Contact: Miss Susan Inge, Flat A, 147 Holland Road, London W14 8AS
☎ Office (0171) 477 8002 & Home 602 4945
Situated near top of village, the property has spectacular views over the sea and to the Purbeck hills. Spacious, comfortable flat in old stone house. Easy parking.
1 self-contained unit; sleeping max 4

Price per week:	£min	£max
Low season	140.00	210.00
High season	210.00	280.00

⌂ ◎ ▥ ⊙ 🗆 🍴 TV 🖥 🛏 🍴 🍴 🚗 P
❄ ✈ SP

All accommodation in this guide has been graded, or is awaiting a grading, by a trained Tourist Board inspector.

Establishments should be open throughout the year, unless otherwise stated.

LYMINGTON

Hampshire
Map ref 2C3

Small, pleasant town with bright cottages and attractive Georgian houses, lying on the edge of the New Forest with a ferry service to the Isle of Wight. A sheltered harbour makes it a busy yachting centre.

Corner Cottage

COMMENDED

20 Eastern Road, Lymington
Contact: Mrs Ginny Neath, Bank Cottage, Grove Road, Barton on Sea, New Milton, Hampshire BH25 7DN
☎ New Milton (01425) 613677
Fax (01425) 613677
Superbly equipped town cottage, very quiet and comfortable. Short walk to Isle of Wight ferry, traditional street market and coastal marshes. 5 minutes to New Forest.
1 self-contained unit; sleeping 2–4

Price per week:	£min	£max
Low season	150.00	190.00
High season	190.00	295.00

Fir Tree Cottage

COMMENDED

Lower Buckland Road, Lymington
Contact: Mrs B Saward, 15 White Knights, Barton Court Avenue, New Milton, Hampshire BH25 7HA
☎ New Milton (01425) 617219
Period cottage 1.5 miles from open forest. Enclosed garden, good for pets and children. Traditional furnishings, books, fitted carpets, double glazing, toys.
1 self-contained unit; sleeping max 5

Price per week:	£min	£max
Low season	170.00	215.00
High season	240.00	325.00

TOWN INDEX

This can be found at the back of the guide. If you know where you want to stay, the index will give you the page number listing all accommodation in your chosen town, city or village.

LYNDHURST

Hampshire
Map ref 2C3

The "capital" of the New Forest, surrounded by attractive woodland scenery and delightful villages. The town is dominated by the Victorian Gothic-style church where the original Alice in Wonderland is buried.
Tourist Information Centre ☎ (01703) 282269

Holly Cottage

COMMENDED

Southampton Road, Lyndhurst
Contact: Mr & Mrs F S Turner, Greensward, The Crescent, Woodlands Road, Ashurst, Southampton, Hampshire SO40 7AQ
☎ Ashurst (01703) 292374 & 771593
Modernised, semi-detached cottage, built 1865, with 2 bedrooms, bathroom, dining room, lounge, well-equipped kitchen, garden and patio.
1 self-contained unit; sleeping max 4

Price per week:	£min	£max
Low season	185.00	250.00
High season	265.00	375.00

MAIDENHEAD

Berkshire
Map ref 2C2

Attractive town on the River Thames which is crossed by an elegant 18th C bridge and by Brunel's well-known railway bridge. It is a popular place for boating with delightful riverside walks. The Courage Shire Horse Centre is nearby.
Tourist Information Centre ☎ (01628) 781110

Courtyard Cottages

HIGHLY COMMENDED

Moor Farm, Holyport, Maidenhead
Contact: Mrs Gillian Reynolds, Moor Farm, Ascot Road, Holyport, Maidenhead, Berkshire SL6 2HY
☎ Maidenhead (01628) 33761 & Mobile 0831 678694
Fax (01628) 33761
100-acre mixed farm. Working farm with easy access to Legoland, London, Windsor and Ascot. Courtyard cottages converted from Georgian stables and picturesque barns, near delightful Holyport village.
4 self-contained units; sleeping 2–4

Price per week:	£min	£max
Low season	225.00	295.00
High season	295.00	395.00

MARNHULL

Dorset
Map ref 2B3

Has a fine church and numerous attractive houses.

Trooper Farm

APPROVED

Love Lane, Marnhull, Sturminster Newton DT10 1PT
☎ Sturminster Newton (01258) 820753
Contact: Mr Cyril Bastable
12-acre beef farm. Delightful 17th C cottage in the centre of Hardy's village of Marnhull midway between Shaftesbury and Sherborne. Lovely countryside, 45 minutes to coast. Two double bedrooms, dining room, lounge, colour TV. Lawns and garden.
1 self-contained unit; sleeping max 4

Price per week:	£min	£max
Low season	90.00	110.00
High season	120.00	175.00

MILBORNE ST ANDREW

Dorset
Map ref 2B3

Small village on the main road from Dorchester to Blandford Forum. To the north lies Milton Abbas.

2 Deverel Cottages

COMMENDED

Deverel Farm, Milborne St Andrew, Blandford Forum
Contact: Mrs C Martin, 1 Deverel Cottages, Deverel Farm, Milborne St Andrew, Blandford Forum, Dorset DT11 0HX
☎ Milborne St Andrew (01258) 837195 & Mobile 0973 953644
Fax (01258) 837195
420-acre mixed farm. Recently redecorated and refurbished, semi-detached, three-bedroomed farm cottage, with enclosed rear garden. Bathroom, separate WC, lounge/diner, kitchen and utility room.
1 self-contained unit; sleeping max 6

You are advised to confirm your booking in writing.

Price per week:	£min	£max
Low season	120.00	150.00
High season	170.00	300.00

Open March–September

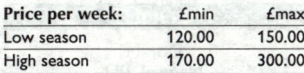

MILFORD-ON-SEA

Hampshire
Map ref 2C3

Victorian seaside resort with shingle beach and good bathing, set in pleasant countryside and looking out over the Isle of Wight. Nearby is Hurst Castle, built by Henry VIII.

Windmill Cottage
HIGHLY COMMENDED

22 Windmill Close, Milford-on-Sea, Lymington
Contact: Mrs S M Perham, Danescourt, Kivernell Road, Milford-on-Sea, Lymington, Hampshire SO41 0PQ
☎ Lymington (01590) 643516

3-bedroomed, Georgian-style house in select residential area close to village, sea and the New Forest.
1 self-contained unit; sleeping max 5

Price per week:	£min	£max
Low season	185.00	205.00
High season	215.00	395.00

MILTON ABBAS

Dorset
Map ref 2B3

Sloping village street of thatched houses. A boys' school lies in Capability Brown's landscaped gardens amid hills and woods where the town once stood. The school chapel, former abbey church, can be visited.

Luccombe Farm
COMMENDED

Milton Abbas, Blandford Forum DT11 0BE
☎ (01258) 880558
Contact: Mr & Mrs Murray & Amanda Kayll

650-acre mixed farm. Sympathetically converted Georgian barns, away from roads in a hidden valley, provide peaceful and comfortable holidays. Many leisure activities and services available.
Wheelchair access category 3
3 self-contained units; sleeping 2–5

Price per week:	£min	£max
Low season	150.00	250.00
High season	250.00	450.00

Open March–December

Primrose Cottage
HIGHLY COMMENDED

29 The Street, Milton Abbas, Blandford Forum
Contact: Mrs G D Garvey, 16 Mole Road, Hersham, Walton-on-Thames, Surrey KT12 4LU
☎ Hersham (01932) 220395

Grade II listed 18th C thatched cob cottage set on The Street, in the unique village of Milton Abbas created by Lord Milton. Centre of Hardy country. Ideal for walkers and romantics.
1 self-contained unit; sleeping max 6

Price per week:	£min	£max
Low season	175.00	195.00
High season	240.00	375.00

MINSTER LOVELL

Oxfordshire
Map ref 2C1

Picturesque village on the River Windrush with thatched cottages and 19th C houses. Minster Lovell Hall, built in the 15th C by the Lovell family, is the subject of several legends and now stands in ruins in a beautiful riverside setting.

Orchard End & The Stable
COMMENDED

Whitehall, Minster Lovell, Oxford

Contact: Mr A A Brodtman, 8 Wymondham Court, St Johns Wood Park, London NW8 6RD
☎ (0171) 586 1716 & Minster Lovell (01993) 775247
In the heart of the countryside, midway between Witney and Burford and within easy reach of Oxford, Cheltenham and many lovely Cotswold villages. The cottages are approached by a private drive from B4047. London 1.5 hours (M40). Attractively furnished and fully equipped. Open fires, hard tennis court, garden.
2 self-contained units; sleeping 4–6

Price per week:	£min	£max
Low season	140.00	210.00
High season	250.00	345.00

NEW FOREST

See under Ashurst, Beaulieu, Boldre, Brockenhurst, Burley, Fordingbridge, Lymington, Lyndhurst, Milford-on-Sea, Ringwood

NEWPORT

Isle of Wight
Map ref 2C3

Commercial capital of the island, lying on the River Medina. Vessels sail into the harbour from Cowes. The town has many historic buildings including the Old Grammar School which was a lodging for Charles II.
Tourist Informatiom Centre ☎ (01983) 525450

Bethel Cottage
COMMENDED

New Road, Porchfield, Newport
Contact: Mrs Bridget Lewis, Channers Ltd, 7 Argyll Street, Ryde, Isle of Wight PO33 3BZ
☎ Isle of Wight (01983) 568995

Charming detached stone-built character country cottage, beautifully restored and maintained, tucked away in attractive garden. 5 miles from Newport. Pub close by.
1 self-contained unit; sleeping max 4

Price per week:	£min	£max
Low season	100.00	
High season		325.00

OLNEY

Buckinghamshire
Map ref 2C1

The Old Stone Barn

HIGHLY COMMENDED

Home Farm, Warrington, Olney
MK46 4HN
☎ Bedford (01234) 711655
Fax (01234) 711855
Contact: Mr & Mrs G Pibworth
Barn conversion on a quiet 800-acre arable farm. Approximately 10 miles from Bedford, Northampton and Milton Keynes.
Wheelchair access category 3

6 self-contained units; sleeping 2–6

Price per week:	£min	£max
Low season	150.00	275.00
High season	190.00	325.00

Cards accepted: Access, Visa

OXFORD

Oxfordshire
Map ref 2C1

Beautiful university town with many ancient colleges, some dating from the 13th C, and numerous buildings of historic and architectural interest. The Ashmolean Museum has outstanding collections. Lovely gardens and meadows with punting on the Cherwell.
Tourist Information Centre ☎ (01865) 726871

8 Anne Greenwood Close

COMMENDED

Iffley, Oxford
Contact: Mr Milan Misina, 91 Divinity Road, Oxford, Oxfordshire OX4 1LN
☎ Oxford (01865) 245740
Fax (01865) 245740
Holiday home situated close to banks of River Thames, in quaint village of Iffley, 1.5 miles from Oxford city centre. Generously furnished throughout. Large garden and garden furniture.
1 self-contained unit; sleeping max 5

Price per week:	£min	£max
Low season	335.00	350.00
High season	365.00	395.00

Cards accepted: Switch/Delta

Chilswell Farm

APPROVED

Boars Hill, Oxford OX1 5EP
☎ (01865) 735223
Contact: Mrs H Farrant
400-acre arable & dairy farm. Completely self-contained part of old farmhouse, 4 miles from Oxford. Car essential. Pleasant walks.
1 self-contained unit; sleeping max 6

Price per week:	£min	£max
Low season	160.00	190.00
High season	190.00	235.00

PANGBOURNE

Berkshire
Map ref 2C2

A pretty stretch of river where the Pang joins the Thames with views of the lock, weir and toll bridge. Once the home of Kenneth Grahame, author of "Wind in the Willows".

Brambly Thatch

COMMENDED

Whitchurch Hill, Pangbourne, Reading
Contact: Mr & Mrs J N Hatt, Merricroft Farming, Goring Heath, Reading, Berkshire RG8 7TA
☎ Pangbourne (0118) 9843121

300-acre mixed farm. Picturebook thatched farm cottage of brick and flint. Well placed for visiting London, the Home Counties, Thames Valley, Chilterns and Cotswolds.
1 self-contained unit; sleeping max 5

Price per week:	£min	£max
Low season	235.00	265.00
High season	255.00	285.00

Map references apply to the colour maps at the back of this guide.

A key to symbols can be found inside the back cover flap.

For ideas on places to visit refer to the introduction at the beginning of this section.

POOLE

Dorset
Map ref 2B3

Tremendous natural harbour makes Poole a superb boating centre. The harbour area is crowded with historic buildings including the 15th C Town Cellars housing a maritime museum.
Tourist Information Centre ☎ (01202) 673322

House

COMMENDED

Poole
Contact: Mrs J A Marchant, 57 Abden Avenue, Kinghorn, Burntisland, Fife KY3 9TE
☎ Kirkcaldy (01592) 890545
3 bedroom house for 5 persons close to town centre. All inclusive except telephone. Lounge/dining room, bathroom/shower, fully-equipped kitchen, parking and sea views. Pets welcome.
1 self-contained unit; sleeping 5–6

Price per week:	£min	£max
Low season	125.00	200.00
High season	150.00	325.00

57 Labrador Drive

COMMENDED

Baiter Park, Poole
Contact: Mr & Mrs R W Stamper, Bowbeck Farm, Bardwell, Bury St Edmunds, Suffolk IP31 1BA
☎ Bury St Edmunds (01359) 269239
Modern 3-bedroom house on Baiter Park, convenient for quay and Poole town centre. Harbour views. Parking, patio, CH, fully-equipped kitchen, TV. Sorry no pets. Non-smokers.
1 self-contained unit; sleeping 6–7

Price per week:	£min	£max
Low season	200.00	
High season		320.00

Open March–December

Woben Luxury Flats

HIGHLY COMMENDED

Rowans, 49 Cliff Drive, Canford Cliffs, Poole BH13 7JF
☎ Canford Cliffs (01202) 708244
Contact: Mrs Rosalind Benham
Beautifully-appointed, 2 bedroom, 2 bathroom flat, with gas central heating, TV, large lounge and dining room, kitchen. Close to sea and shop.

1 self-contained unit; sleeping 4–5

Price per week:	£min	£max
Low season	195.00	275.00
High season	275.00	400.00

🐾Ⓜ◎📶⊙🗄🍴📺🗄🗄📮📱📺
🐾P✈

PORTCHESTER

Hampshire
Map ref 2C3

41 The Keep Ⓜ

🔑🔑🔑 HIGHLY COMMENDED

Portchester, Fareham
Contact: Mrs E L Harris, 14 The
Crossway, Portchester, Fareham,
Hampshire PO16 8PF
☎ Cosham (01705) 371305
*Situated in historic Portchester,
detached house in quiet area with
forecourt and pretty gardens. Near
village centre, buses and station. Sea
and castle close by. Convenient for New
Forest, Meon Valley and Langstone
Harbour.*
1 self-contained unit; sleeping max 4

Price per week:	£min	£max
Low season	150.00	200.00
High season	250.00	325.00

🐾8Ⓜ◎🎱⊙🗄MW🍴📺🗄
🗄📮📱🐾P✈❄ SP

PORTSMOUTH & SOUTHSEA

Hampshire
Map ref 2C3

The first dock was built in 1194.
HMS Victory, Nelson's flagship, is
here and Charles Dickens' former
home is open to the public.
Neighbouring Southsea has a
promenade with magnificent views
of Spithead.
*Tourist Information Centre ☎ (01705)
838635 & 826722*

Atlantic Apartments Ⓜ

🔑🔑🔑 COMMENDED

61-63 Festing Road, Southsea
Contact: Mr F Hamdani, 61A Festing
Road, Southsea, Hampshire
PO4 0NQ
☎ Portsmouth (01705) 735574 &
734233
Fax (01705) 297046
*Situated in one of the most attractive
areas of Southsea, only a few yards
from the canoe lake and seafront. All
apartments are fully self-contained and
a large car park is available.*
6 self-contained units; sleeping 2–7

Price per week:	£min	£max
Low season	100.00	200.00
High season	160.00	250.00

Open June–October

🐾2🎱📶⊙🗄MW📺🗄📮📱📺✎
P🏠📺

PRINCES RISBOROUGH

Buckinghamshire
Map ref 2C1

Old market town with many 16th C
cottages, houses and a brick Market
House at its centre.

Old Callow Down Farm Ⓜ

🔑🔑 COMMENDED

Wigans Lane, Bledlow Ridge, High
Wycombe HP14 4BH
☎ (01844) 344416
Contact: Mrs N E Gee

*37-acre beef farm. Spacious stable
conversion on 16th C small, secluded
livestock farm. Large garden. Ridgeway
path. Conveniently central for Oxford,
Cotswolds, Chilterns. London 45
minutes by rail.*
1 self-contained unit; sleeping max 5

Price per week:	£min	£max
Low season	200.00	250.00
High season	250.00	300.00

🐾◎📶⊙🗄MW🍴📺🗄📮📱
🐾P❄🏠

RINGWOOD

Hampshire
Map ref 2B3

Market town by the River Avon
comprising old cottages, many of
them thatched. Although just
outside the New Forest, there is
heath and woodland nearby and it is
a good centre for horse-riding and
walking.

Glenavon

🔑🔑🔑 COMMENDED

12 Boundary Lane, St Leonards,
Ringwood BH24 2SE
☎ Ferndown (01202) 873868
Contact: Mrs C D Wareham
*Semi-detached bungalow with 3 acres
of grounds available to guests, in
pleasant rural surroundings. Adjacent to
Barnsfield Heath forest, convenient for
exploring the New Forest and Dorset.
One double bedroom with cot, 1 twin.
No smoking, please.*

1 self-contained unit; sleeping 4–5

Price per week:	£min	£max
Low season	145.00	175.00
High season	215.00	255.00

🐾◎📶⊙🗄MW🍴📺🗄📮📱
🐾P❄ SP

Highfield Ⓜ

🔑🔑 APPROVED

Crow Hill, Ringwood BH24 3DQ
☎ (01425) 471372
Contact: Mr & Mrs Derek Harvey
*Cottage adjacent to house, in secluded
area looking towards Bournemouth
over wooded slopes. Not suitable for
very young children.*
1 self-contained unit; sleeping max 4

Price per week:	£min	£max
Low season	55.00	120.00
High season	125.00	185.00

🐾5Ⓜ◎📶⊙🗄🍴📺🗄🗄🐾
P⏰❄

Karelia Holidays Ⓜ

🔑🔑 UP TO HIGHLY COMMENDED

c/o The Studio, Ashley, Ringwood
BH24 2EE
☎ (01425) 478920
Fax (01425) 480479
Contact: Mr R Gleed

*Genuine Finnish log houses in a
beautiful natural setting. Log sauna
with a swimming pool. Full-size snooker
table available.*
5 self-contained units; sleeping 2–10

Price per week:	£min	£max
Low season	100.00	360.00
High season	195.00	585.00

🐾Ⓜ◎📶⊙🗄📺🗄🗄🗄🐾P🎾
⏰❄ SP

RYDE

Isle of Wight
Map ref 2C3

The island's chief entry port, connected to Portsmouth by ferries and hovercraft. 7 miles of sandy beaches with a half-mile pier, esplanade and gardens.
Tourist Information Centre ☎ (01983) 562905

Ashey Valley Holidays Ltd ⋔
APPROVED

Ashey Road, Ryde PO33 4BB
☎ Isle of Wight (01983) 566027
Fax (01983) 616599
Contact: Mrs P A Green
Modern, self-contained, fully equipped and comfortable bungalows, set in peaceful countryside, with large, heated outdoor swimming pool, play area and restaurant.
12 self-contained units; sleeping 4–6

Price per week:	£min	£max
Low season	105.00	
High season		395.00

Cards accepted: Access, Visa, Amex

SHAFTESBURY

Dorset
Map ref 2B3

Hilltop town with a long history. The ancient and cobbled Gold Hill is one of the most attractive in Dorset. There is an excellent small museum containing a collection of buttons for which the town is famous.
Tourist Information Centre ☎ (01747) 853514

The Bungalow
APPROVED

Priors Farm, Semley, Shaftesbury
Contact: Miss Nora Williamson, Priors Farm, Semley, Shaftesbury, Dorset SP7 9BP
☎ East Knoyle (01747) 830218
Roomy bungalow with sunny garden in peaceful countryside. Ideal for touring or walking and 40 minutes' drive from coast.
1 self-contained unit; sleeping max 5

Price per week:	£min	£max
Low season	69.00	99.00
High season	109.00	114.00

Open April–October and Christmas

Dairy Cottage
COMMENDED

Broadlea Farm, Sutton Waldron, Blandford Forum DT11 8NS
☎ Fontmell Magna (01747) 811330
Contact: Mr. R G Gorton
Fully equipped cottage amidst lovely countryside, south of Shaftesbury. 2 bedrooms, spacious lounge/dining room, separate kitchen and bathroom. Easy access to Fontmell Down (National Trust).
1 self-contained unit; sleeping max 4

Price per week:	£min	£max
Low season	110.00	110.00
High season	195.00	195.00

Open April–October

SHILLINGSTONE

Dorset
Map ref 2B3

Village in the River Stour valley.

1, 2 & 3 Newmans Drove ⋔
COMMENDED

Bere Marsh Farm, Shillingstone, Blandford Forum DT11 0QY
☎ Child Okeford (01258) 860284
Contact: Mrs Fiona Idda
400-acre dairy farm. Converted "L"-shaped farm building, beautifully situated in the Blackmoor Vale with commanding views of the surrounding countryside. Easily accessible.
3 self-contained units; sleeping max 6

Price per week:	£min	£max
Low season	120.00	195.00
High season	195.00	325.00

The National Grading and Classification Scheme is explained in full at the back of this guide.

The symbols in each entry give information about services and facilities. A 'key' to these symbols appears at the back of this guide.

SIBFORD GOWER

Oxfordshire
Map ref 2C1

Fairytale village with a number of thatched and stone cottages and a Quaker burial ground.

Cara Mia Cottage
COMMENDED

Sibford Gower, Banbury
Contact: Mrs M E Wealsby, Ryehill Farm, Sibford Gower, Banbury, Oxfordshire OX15 5RU
☎ Swalcliffe (01295) 780371
Old stone, semi-detached cottage in village off the B4035 Banbury-Shipston road. A delightful area for touring and relaxing.
1 self-contained unit; sleeping max 4

Price per week:	£min	£max
Low season	140.00	
High season		210.00

SOUTHAMPTON

Hampshire
Map ref 2C3

One of Britain's leading seaports with a long history, now a major container port. In the 18th C it became a fashionable resort with the assembly rooms and theatre. The old Guildhall and the Wool House are now museums. Sections of the medieval wall can still be seen.
Tourist Information Centre ☎ (01703) 221106

Pinewood Lodge Apartments
COMMENDED

Pinewood Lodge, Kanes Hill, Southampton SO19 6AJ
☎ Bursledon (01703) 402925
Contact: Dr or Mrs S W Bradberry
Double or twin-bedded self-contained apartments, each with separate kitchen, bathroom and lounge. Private verandah or patio.
2 self-contained units; sleeping max 2

Price per week:	£min	£max
Low season		125.00
High season		163.00

SOUTHSEA

Hampshire

See under Portsmouth & Southsea

STEEPLE ASTON

Oxfordshire
Map ref 2C1

Oxfordshire village whose church has one of the finest examples of church embroidery in the world. Nearby is the Jacobean Rousham House which stands in William Kent's only surviving landscaped garden.

The Beeches

HIGHLY COMMENDED

Heyford Road, Steeple Aston, Oxford OX6 3SN
☎ (01869) 340238
Contact: Mrs Angela Marshall
Fully-equipped character flat, in grounds of small country house. Exposed beams. Tranquil country setting. Every comfort, warmest welcome.
1 self-contained unit; sleeping max 3

Price per week:	£min	£max
Low season	150.00	150.00
High season	175.00	200.00

STRATTON AUDLEY

Oxfordshire
Map ref 2C1

Audley Cottage

COMMENDED

Stratton Audley, Bicester
Contact: Mr C R Venner, Upper Tetchwick Farm, Kingswood, Aylesbury, Buckinghamshire HP18 0RD
☎ Grendon Underwood (01296) 770514 & Cellnet 0850 318384
Fax (01296) 770514
Formerly a gate house to Audley Manor. Situated opposite the village church. Four bedrooms, 2 bathrooms, double garage. Ideal base for Oxford and Cotswolds.
1 self-contained unit; sleeping max 8

Price per week:	£min	£max
Low season	275.00	425.00
High season	350.00	625.00

The ᴍ symbol after an establishment name indicates that it is a Regional Tourist Board member.

STUDLAND

Dorset
Map ref 2B3

On a beautiful stretch of coast and good for walking, with a National Nature Reserve to the north. The Norman church is the finest in the country, with superb rounded arches and vaulting. Brownsea Island, where the first scout camp was held, lies in Poole Harbour.

2 Vine Cottage

COMMENDED

Beach Road, Studland, Swanage
Contact: Mrs Janet Bjorkstrand, Maycroft, Old Malthouse Lane, Langton Matravers, Swanage, Dorset BH19 3HH
☎ Swanage (01929) 424305
Spacious well-equipped thatched cottage in quiet position close to beach. Ideal for family holidays or out of season short breaks.
1 self-contained unit; sleeping 2–6

Price per week:	£min	£max
Low season	180.00	325.00
High season	260.00	500.00

STURMINSTER NEWTON

Dorset
Map ref 2B3

Every Monday this small town holds a livestock market. One of the bridges over the River Stour is a fine medieval example and bears a plaque declaring that anyone "injuring" it will be deported.

Yew House Cottages

COMMENDED

Yew House Farm, Marnhull, Sturminster Newton DT10 1PD
☎ Marnhull (01258) 820412
Fax (01258) 821044
Contact: Mrs G M Espley
Timber lodges in secluded position, with superb views of open countryside. Very peaceful, every comfort. One lodge suitable for disabled. Free colour brochure.
3 self-contained units; sleeping 4–5

Price per week:	£min	£max
Low season	95.00	95.00
High season	95.00	290.00

SWANAGE

Dorset
Map ref 2B3

Began life as an Anglo-Saxon port, then a quarrying centre of Purbeck marble. Now the safe, sandy beach set in a sweeping bay and flanked by downs is good walking country, making it an ideal resort.
Tourist Information Centre ☎ (01929) 422885

Cliff Place Cottages ᴍ

UP TO COMMENDED

Cliff Place, off Marshall Row, Swanage
Contact: Dr & Mrs J M Ferrar, Benington Old House, Benington, Stevenage, Hertfordshire SG2 7BT
☎ Stevenage (01438) 869281
Grade II listed cottages (2 or 3 bedrooms) and studio flat in conservation area. Close to sea, shops and Downs. Cottages have fridge/freezers and washer/dryers, 2 have dishwashers, telephone.
5 self-contained units; sleeping 2–6

Price per week:	£min	£max
Low season	60.00	160.00
High season	130.00	345.00

THAME

Oxfordshire
Map ref 2C1

Historic market town on the River Thame. The wide, unspoilt High Street has many styles of architecture with medieval timber-framed cottages, Georgian houses and some famous inns.
Tourist Information Centre ☎ (01844) 212834

Honeysuckle Cottage

COMMENDED

Frogmore Lane, Long Crendon, Aylesbury, Buckinghamshire HP18 9DZ
☎ Long Crendon (01844) 208697
Contact: Mr & Mrs A Lester
Very comfortable, well-equipped, self-contained annexe to cottage with private garden. Off-lane parking.
1 self-contained unit; sleeping max 3

Price per week:	£min	£max
Low season	140.00	160.00
High season		180.00

VENTNOR

Isle of Wight
Map ref 2C3

Town lies at the bottom of an 800-ft hill and has a reputation as a winter holiday and health resort due to its mild climate. There is a pier, small esplanade and Winter Gardens.

Micklepage Holiday Flats ♨

COMMENDED

12 Spring Gardens, Ventnor PO38 1QX
☎ Isle of Wight (01983) 852120
Contact: Mr & Mrs Roy Dicker
Comfortable, well-appointed flats in quiet cul-de-sac. Sea views, car parking. Resident owners. Beautiful Bonchurch village is minutes' walk away.
3 self-contained units; sleeping 2–6

Price per week:	£min	£max
Low season	75.00	150.00
High season	210.00	230.00

🖐 M ◎ 🔥 ▦ ⊙ 🖥 🖼 TV 🛋 ▦🖽 🚗 P

Wight House Luxury Apartments ♨

HIGHLY COMMENDED

Devonshire Terrace, Ventnor
Contact: Mr & Mrs J O Jones, Trewartha, Bath Road, Ventnor, Isle of Wight PO38 1JH
☎ Isle of Wight (01983) 852259
Fax (01983) 852259
As-new apartments with easy access to beach, town and buses. Some have balconies overlooking sea. Dishwasher, microwave, washer/dryer, garden, telephone.
6 self-contained units; sleeping 2–8

Price per week:	£min	£max
Low season	101.00	337.00
High season	158.00	545.00

🖐 M ◎ 🔥 ▦ ⊙ 🖥 MW 🖼 TV 🛋
▦🖽 🚗 P U ⛴ ✿ ✕ ⅂ SP T

WALLINGFORD

Oxfordshire
Map ref 2C2

Site of an ancient ford over the River Thames, now crossed by a 900-ft-long bridge. The town has many timber-framed and Georgian buildings, Gainsborough portraits in the 17th C Town Hall and a few remains of a Norman Castle.
Tourist Information Centre ☎ *(01491) 826972*

The Annexe

HIGHLY COMMENDED

Alders Croft, South Moreton, Didcot OX11 9AD
☎ Didcot (01235) 813104
Contact: Mrs R A Ryder
Single-storey annexe to main house overlooking garden. Convenient for River Thames, Oxford, Cotswolds and Windsor. Good walking on Ridgeway. Third person charged extra.
1 self-contained unit; sleeping 2–3

Price per week:	£min	£max
Low season	140.00	150.00
High season	150.00	160.00

Open April–October
🖐 8 M 🔥 ▦ ⊙ 🖥 TV 🛋 🖼 P ⚲ ✿ ✕

WAREHAM

Dorset
Map ref 2B3

This site has been occupied since pre-Roman times and has a turbulent history. In 1762 fire destroyed much of the town, so the buildings now are mostly Georgian.
Tourist Information Centre ☎ *(01929) 552740*

Dairy Cottage ♨

COMMENDED

Trigon Farm, Wareham
Contact: Mrs G Sturdy, Trigon House, Wareham, Dorset BH20 7PD
☎ Wareham (01929) 552097
1400-acre mixed farm. Picturesque, fully modernised terraced cottage. Near sea, Hardy country, old town, walking, bird-watching.
1 self-contained unit; sleeping max 7

Price per week:	£min	£max
Low season	110.00	
High season		360.00

☎ ◎ ▦ ⊙ 🖥 TV 🛋 ▦🖽 🚗 P ⅃ ✿

WATCHFIELD

Oxfordshire
Map ref 2B2

The Coach House

♨♨ HIGHLY COMMENDED

Old Westmill Farmhouse, Watchfield, Swindon, Wiltshire
Contact: Mrs B M Shephard, Old Westmill Farmhouse, Watchfield, Swindon, Wiltshire SN6 8TH
☎ Swindon (01793) 782321 & (0181) 969 1402

The coach house is about 100 yards from the farmhouse, with its own secluded garden area and use of the main grounds. Both buildings are Grade II listed. Close to river and farmland.
1 self-contained unit; sleeping 4–5

Price per week:	£min	£max
Low season	195.00	270.00
High season	275.00	380.00

Open March–October
🖐 🔥 ▦ ⊙ 🖥 MW 🖼 TV 🛋 🖽 ▦
🚗 P ✿ ✕ ⅃ SP 🏛

WHITWELL

Isle of Wight
Map ref 2C3

West of Ventnor, with interesting church, thatched inn and youth hostel. Good walking area.

Lynbrook

♨ COMMENDED

14 Nettlecombe Lane, Whitwell, Ventnor
Contact: Mrs Linda Bek, 75 Welch Gate, Bewdley, Worcestershire DY12 2AU
☎ Bewdley (01299) 401649
Comfortable, well-equipped, 2-bedroomed detached bungalow in quiet location with private, mature garden, central heating, garage.
1 self-contained unit; sleeping max 6

Price per week:	£min	£max
Low season	130.00	230.00
High season	260.00	325.00

🖐 ◎ ▦ ⊙ 🖥 MW 🖼 TV 🛋 🖽 ▦🖽
🚗 P ✿

WINCHESTER

Hampshire
Map ref 2C3

King Alfred the Great made Winchester the capital of Saxon England. A magnificent Norman cathedral, with one of the longest naves in Europe, dominates the city. Home of Winchester College founded in 1382.
Tourist Information Centre ☎ (01962) 840500 or 848180

Chakrata

COMMENDED

61 Elder Close, Badger Farm, Winchester
Contact: Mr & Mrs Paul Tipple, 9 Mount View Road, Olivers Battery, Winchester, Hampshire SO22 4JJ
☎ Winchester (01962) 861918
Terraced 2-bedroomed bungalow in cul-de-sac on high ground, 2 miles west of Winchester. Garden front and rear.
1 self-contained unit; sleeping max 4

Price per week:	£min	£max
Low season	152.00	180.00
High season	186.00	197.00

WINDSOR

Berkshire
Map ref 2D2

Town dominated by the spectacular castle, home of the Royal Family for over 900 years. Parts are open to the public. There are many attractions including the Great Park, Eton and trips on the river.
Tourist Information Centre ☎ (01753) 852010

9 The Courtyard

HIGHLY COMMENDED

4 High Street, Windsor

Contact: Mrs N J Hitchcock, 1 Agar's Place, Datchet, Slough, Berkshire SL3 9AH
☎ Slough (01753) 545005
Fax (01753) 545005
Attractively furnished modern apartment served by lift. Courtyard setting just off High Street. Well located for Ascot, Henley and London.
1 self-contained unit; sleeping max 4

Price per week:	£min	£max
Low season	295.00	345.00
High season	345.00	375.00

WINFRITH NEWBURGH

Dorset
Map ref 2B3

Village 4 miles south-west of Wool, and within easy reach of Lulworth Cove by car.

Snail's Place

COMMENDED

25 High Street, Winfrith Newburgh, Dorchester
Contact: Mrs Delia Simmons, Brickhill Lodge, Dibden Hill, Chalfont St Giles, Buckinghamshire HP8 4RD
☎ Chalfont St Giles (01494) 872649
Fax (01494) 872649
Intimate, 17th C listed thatched cottage, with exposed beams and large inglenook. Comfortably furnished. Close to sea and glorious walking countryside.
1 self-contained unit; sleeping max 4

Price per week:	£min	£max
Low season		175.00
High season		350.00

WITNEY

Oxfordshire
Map ref 2C1

Town famous for its blanket-making and mentioned in the Domesday Book. The market-place contains the Butter Cross, a medieval meeting place, and there is a green with merchants' houses.
Tourist Information Centre ☎ (01993) 775802

Gleann Cottages ♙

HIGHLY COMMENDED

Woodstock Road, Witney OX8 6UH
☎ (01993) 778007
Fax (01993) 775957
Contact: Mr S Murtagh
Stone-built, self-contained cottages in pleasant landscaped farm surroundings and close to town amenities.
8 self-contained units; sleeping 2–4

Price per week:	£min	£max
Low season	165.00	200.00
High season	215.00	260.00

Willowdene

COMMENDED

11 Back Lane, Ducklington, Witney OX8 7UE
☎ (01993) 702897
Contact: Mrs Josephine McGhee
Just south of Witney, in the attractive village of Ducklington, bounded by the River Windrush. Easy access to Oxford and the Cotswolds.
1 self-contained unit; sleeping max 4

Price per week:	£min	£max
Low season	130.00	165.00
High season	200.00	220.00

COUNTRY CODE

Always follow the Country Code ❧Enjoy the countryside and respect its life and work ❧Guard against all risk of fire ❧Fasten all gates ❧Keep your dogs under close control ❧Keep to public paths across farmland ❧Use gates and stiles to cross fences, hedges and walls ❧Leave livestock, crops and machinery alone ❧Take your litter home ❧Help to keep all water clean ❧Protect wildlife, plants and trees ❧Take special care on country roads ❧Make no unnecessary noise

WOOL

Dorset
Map ref 2B3

On the River Frome with a mainline station. Woolbridge Manor is of interest and occupies a prominent position.

Whitemead Lodge

⚷⚷⚷ APPROVED

East Burton Road, Wool, Wareham
Contact: Mrs B Precey, Frome Cottage, East Burton Road, Wool, Wareham, Dorset BH20 6HG
☎ Bindon Abbey (01929) 462241
Swedish-style, mainly wood bungalow, well furnished, with half-sunken bath. Good centre for coast and country.
1 self-contained unit; sleeping max 5

Price per week:	£min	£max
Low season	115.00	
High season		195.00

Open April–October

🍳 Ⓜ ◎ 🏭 ⊙🖬 TV 🗄 🍖 🏪 ⚓ P ❄ 🐾

WORTH MATRAVERS

Dorset
Map ref 2B3

For centuries the village was one of the main centres for quarrying Purbeck marble. At St Aldhelm's Head, 2 miles away, the cliffs rise to nearly 400 ft and offer magnificent views along the coast.

1 London Row

⚷⚷ COMMENDED

Worth Matravers, Swanage
Contact: Mrs Monica Sanders, 54 Hillway, Highgate, London N6 6EP
☎ (0181) 348 9815
Fax (0181) 347 7124
Listed 18th C Purbeck cottage in conservation area, overlooking village green and with footpath to beach. Sun lounge and patio garden. Walking, biking, bird-watching, swimming, diving, sailing, climbing nearby.
1 self-contained unit; sleeping 5–7

Price per week:	£min	£max
Low season	172.00	230.00
High season	256.00	310.00

🍳 Ⓜ ◎ 🏭 ⊙🖬 MW 🖥 TV 🗄 🍖 🍽 🏠 ⚓ P U ❄ 🐾 SP 🏛

SOUTH EAST ENGLAND

South East England conjures up images of cricket on the village green, traditional village pubs and Sussex cream teas with lashings of home-made jam!

The beauty is, the fantasy is reality. South East England truly is unspoilt.

Visit Kent, the Garden of England, with its oasthouses, abundant vineyards, fruitful orchards and pretty weatherboard cottages.

Wander across the glorious South Downs, the heathland of Surrey, or head for Dover's white cliffs or the buzz of Regency Brighton.

Explore the medieval Cinque Ports and the region's churches, castles, manor houses and gardens. It's all here. As it has been for centuries.

FOR MORE INFORMATION CONTACT:
South East England Tourist Board,
The Old Brew House, Warwick Park,
Tunbridge Wells, Kent TN2 5TU
Tel: (01892) 540766 **Fax:** (01892) 511008

Where to Go in South East England -
see pages 270-273
Where to Stay in South East England -
see pages 274-285

SOUTH EAST ENGLAND

Where to Go and What to See

You will find hundreds of interesting places to visit during your stay in South East England, just some of which are listed in these pages. The number against each name will help you locate it on the map (page 273). Contact any Tourist Information Centre in the region for more ideas on days out in South East England.

1 Royal Engineers Museum
Prince Arthur Road,
Gillingham,
Kent ME4 4UG
Tel: (01634) 406397
The characters, lives and work of Britain's soldier-engineers 1066-1945. Medals, uniforms, scientific and technical equipement. Collection of ethnography and decorative arts.

2 The Historic Dockyard
Chatham, Kent ME4 4TE
Tel: (01634) 812551
Historic 18thC 80 acre dockyard. Museum with seven major attractions including the award-winning 'Wooden Walls' gallery, sail and colour loft, working ropery.

3 Brogdale Horticultural Trust
Brogdale Farm,
Brogdale Road,
Faversham, Kent ME13 8XZ
Tel: (01795) 535286
National Fruit Collection with 4,000

varieties of fruit in 30 acres of orchards: apples, pears, cherries, plums, currants, quinces, medlars and other fruits.

4 Belmont
Belmont Park,
Throwley,
Kent ME13 0HH
Tel: (01795) 890202
Late 18thC country mansion designed by Samuel Wyatt, seat of the Harris family since 1801. Harris clock collection, mementos of connections with India. Gardens and pinetum.

5 Leeds Castle
Leeds, Maidstone,
Kent ME17 1PL
Tel: (01622) 765400
Castle on two islands in lake dating from 12thC. Furniture, tapestries, art treasures. Dog Collar Museum. Gardens, parkland, duckery, aviaries, maze, grotto, small vineyard, greenhouses.

6 The Royal Horticultural Society's Garden
Wisley, Surrey GU23 6QB
Tel: (01483) 224234
World famous RHS garden covering 250 acres of vegetable, fruit and ornamental gardening. Trial grounds, glasshouses, rock garden, ponds. Rose, model and specialist gardens.

7 Guildford Boat House River Trips
Millbrook, Guildford,
Surrey GU1 3XJ
Tel: (01483) 504494
Regular trips from Guildford to St. Catherine's Lock and Farncombe along River Wey. Also 'Alfred Leroy' cruising restaurant. Rowing boats and canoes.

8 Guildford Cathedral
Stag Hill, Guildford,
Surrey GU2 5UP
Tel: (01483) 565287
New Anglican cathedral, foundation

stone laid 1936 and consecrated 1961. Notable glass engravings, embroidered kneelers. Modern furnishings. Brass Rubbing Centre.

9 Loseley House and Park Farm
Loseley Park,
Guildford,
Surrey GU3 1HS
Tel: (01483) 304440
Elizabethan mansion with decorated ceilings, unusual chalk fireplace, period furniture and paintings. Parkland and farm with famous Jersey cows, rare breeds and trailer tours.

10 Denbies Wine Estate
London Road, Dorking,
Surrey RH5 6AA
Tel: (01306) 876616
England's largest wine estate, 250 acres in beautiful countryside. Winery and visitor centre featuring 3-D time-lapse film of vine growing. Viewing and picture galleries.

11 Birdworld and Underwaterworld
Holt Pound, Farnham,
Surrey GU10 4LD
Tel: (01420) 22140
20 acres of garden and parkland with ostriches, flamingoes, hornbills, parrots, emus, pelicans etc. Penguin island, tropical and marine fish. Plant area, seashore walk.

12 Hever Castle and Gardens
Hever, Edenbridge,
Kent TN8 7NG
Tel: (01732) 865224
Moated castle, family home of Anne Boleyn. Restored by Astor family. Fine interior, furniture, paintings and panelling. Gardens, lake, topiary, maze, minature model houses exhibition.

13 Headcorn Flower Centre and Vineyard
Grigg Lane, Headcorn,
Ashford, Kent TN27 9LX
Tel: (01622) 890250
Walk around 6 acres of vines. Reservoir with wildlife. Weekend and group tours visit flowerhouses with chrysanthemums and orchid lilies flowering all year.

14 Dover Castle and Hellfire Corner
Dover, Kent CT16 1HU
Tel: (01304) 201628
One of the most powerful medieval fortresses in Western Europe. St Mary-in-Castro Saxon church. Roman lighthouse, Hellfire Corner, 'All The Queen's Men' exhibition.

15 Groombridge Place Gardens
Groombridge,
Royal Tunbridge Wells,
Kent TN3 9QG
Tel: (01892) 863999
Grade I listed 17thC restored walled gardens. Drunken topiary garden, oriental and sculpture gardens, ancient and mystical woodland with spring-fed pools.

16 Bedgebury National Pinetum
Goudhurst, Kent TN17 2SL
Tel: (01580) 211044
The Forestry Commission's superb collection of specimen conifers in 150 acres with lake and streams. Plus many rhododendrons and azaleas.

17 Leonardslee Gardens
Lower Beeding,
West Sussex RH13 6PP
Tel: (01403) 891212
Rhododendrons and azaleas in a peaceful 240-acre valley garden with seven beautiful lakes. Rock garden, Bonsai exhibition and wallabies.

18 The Bluebell Railway
Sheffield Park,
East Sussex TN22 3QL
Tel: (01825) 722370
9 miles of vintage steam and train railway from Sheffield Park to Horsted Keynes and extension to Kingscote. Largest collection of engines in the south. Victorian stations and museum.

19 Brickwall House and Gardens
Northiam,
East Sussex TN31 6NL
Tel: (01797) 223329
Formal gardens with terracotta entrance gates, 18thC bowling alley, sunken topiary garden, yew hedges, chess garden, arboretum. Jacobean house with 17thC plaster ceilings.

20 Great Dixter House and Gardens
Northiam,
East Sussex TN31 6PH
Tel: (01797) 253107
Fine example of 15thC manor house with antique furniture and needlework. Unique great hall restored by Lutyens who also designed garden – topiary, meadow garden, flower beds.

21 Buckleys Yesterday's World
89-90 High Street, Battle,
East Sussex TN33 0AQ
Tel: (01424) 775378
Over 100,000 exhibits in a Wealden hall house recall shopping and domestic life from 1850 to 1950 with smells and commentaries. Railway station, play village, garden.

22 A Smugglers Adventure At St. Clements Caves
West Hill, Hastings,
East Sussex TN34 3HY
Tel: (01424) 422964
An extensive exhibition of 18thC smuggling, housed in 2000 sq m of caves. Exhibition, museum, video theatre, extensive Adventure Walk incorporating dramatic special effects.

23 Brighton Sea Life Centre
Marine Parade,
Brighton,
East Sussex BN2 1TB
Tel: (01273) 604234
Discover the thrilling world beneath the waves as the Brighton Sea Life Centre takes you on an unforgettable voyage of discovery.

24 Foredown Tower Countryside Centre
Foredown Road, Portslade,
East Sussex BN41 2EW
Tel: (01273) 422540
Water tower housing a camera obscura, an unusual viewing device used by artists and astronomers since the 17thC. Popular entertainment in Victorian times.

25 Charleston Farmhouse
Firle, Lewes, East Sussex BN8 6LL
Tel: (01323) 811265
A 17-18thC farmhouse, home of Vanessa and Clive Bell and Duncan Grant. House and contents decorated by the artists. Restored garden room. Traditional flint-walled garden.

26 Amberley Museum
Houghton Bridge, Amberley,
Arundel, West Sussex BN18 9LT
Tel: (01798) 831370
Open-air industrial history centre in chalk quarry. Working craftsmen, narrow gauge railway, early buses, working machines and many other exhibits. Nature trail and visitor centre.

27 The Wildfowl and Wetlands Centre
Mill Road, Arundel,
West Sussex BN18 9PB
Tel: (01903) 883355
Reserve in 60 acres of watermeadows. Tame swans, ducks, geese and many wild birds. Film theatre and visitor centre with gallery.

28 Weald and Downland Open Air Museum
Singleton,
West Sussex PO18 0EU
Tel: (01243) 811348
Open-air museum of rescued historic buildings from South East England reconstructed on downland. 35 buildings include medieval farmstead and watermill.

29 Pallant House
9 North Pallant, Chichester,
West Sussex PO19 1TJ
Tel: (01243) 774557
Queen Anne townhouse with important works by British and European masters of the 20thC. Antiques include the world's greatest collection of Bow porcelain.

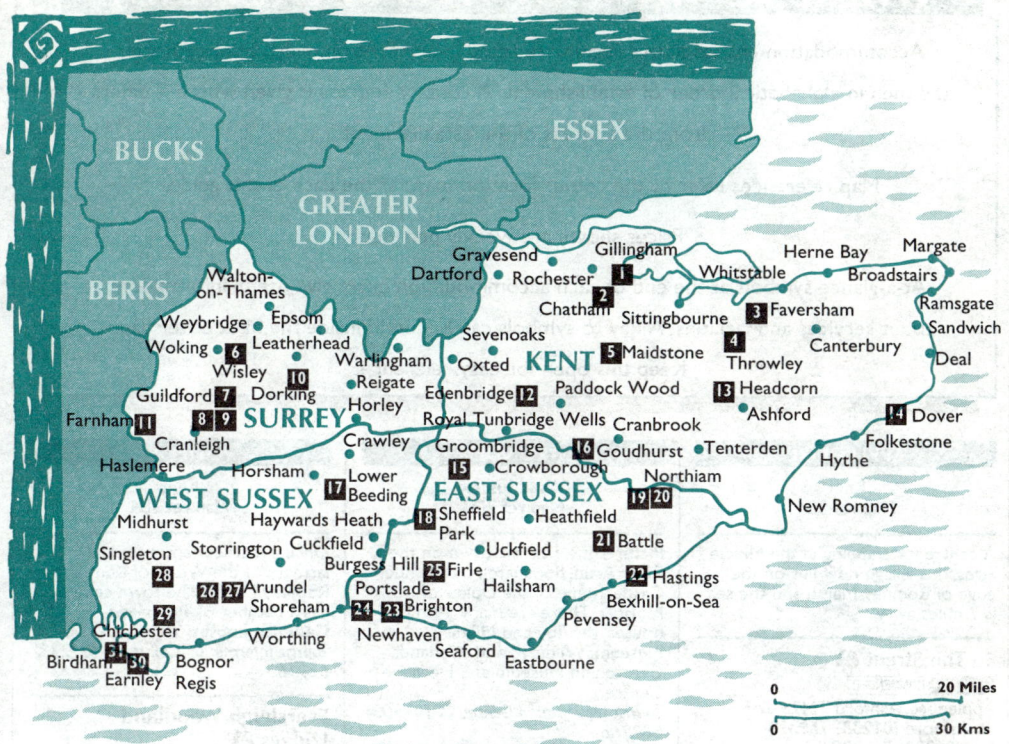

FIND OUT MORE

Further information about holidays and attractions in South East England is available from:
South East England Tourist Board,
The Old Brew House, Warwick Park, Tunbridge Wells, Kent TN2 5TU.
Tel: (01892) 540766

These publications are available free from the South East England Tourist Board:
■ **Great Escapes**
■ **Accommodation Guide**
■ **Events South East**
■ **Bed and Breakfast Touring Map**

■ **Outstanding Churches and Cathedrals**

Also available is (price includes postage and packaging):
■ **South East England Leisure Map** £4
■ **Hundreds of Place to Visit in the South East** £2.80
■ **Villages to Visit** £2.50

WHERE TO STAY (SOUTH EAST ENGLAND)

Accommodation entries in this region are listed in alphabetical order of place name, and then in alphabetical order of establishment. A contact address is given where it differs from the address of the establishment.

Map references refer to the colour location maps at the back of this guide.

Prices shown are weekly per unit.

At-a-glance symbols at the end of each accommodation entry give useful information about services and facilities. A key to symbols can be found inside the back cover flap. Keep this open for easy reference.

APPLEDORE

Kent
Map ref 3B4

A centre for shipping in the Middle Ages, this village now lies on the edge of Romney Marsh and the sea is 7 miles away.

53 The Street M

COMMENDED

Appledore, Ashford TN26 2AF
☎ Ashford (01233) 758320
Fax (01233) 758320
Contact: Mrs A Homewood
Spacious, recently refurbished first floor flat, in centre of village on edge of Romney Marsh. Lounge/diner with colour TV, fully-equipped kitchen, 2 bedrooms with double bed and bunk beds. Cot available. Sorry, no pets.
1 self-contained unit; sleeping max 4

Price per week:	£min	£max
Low season	120.00	140.00
High season	140.00	200.00

A key to symbols can be found inside the back cover flap.

All accommodation in this guide has been graded, or is awaiting a grading, by a trained Tourist Board inspector.

ARUNDEL

West Sussex
Map ref 2D3

Picturesque, historic town on the River Arun, dominated by Arundel Castle, home of the Dukes of Norfolk. There are many 18th C houses, the Toy and Military Museum, Wildfowl and Wetlands Centre and Museum and Heritage Centre.
Tourist Information Centre ☎ (01903) 882268

Village Holidays - Park End/The Hollies/Lion Cottage/Lion House

COMMENDED

The Street, Walberton, Arundel
Contact: Mrs G Pilkington, Village Holidays Re: Park End/The, Hollies/Lion Cottage/Lion House, c/o 22 Down View Road, Yapton, Arundel, West Sussex BN18 0HJ
☎ Yapton (01243) 552414 & 551073
4 adjacent houses with sunny enclosed gardens in attractive village conservation area, 3 miles west of Arundel. Ideal all-season touring base. Central heating, washing machine. Dogs and children welcome.
4 self-contained units; sleeping 4–6

Price per week:	£min	£max
Low season	150.00	250.00
High season	250.00	400.00

ASHFORD

Kent
Map ref 3B4

Once a market centre for the farmers of the Weald of Kent and Romney Marsh. The town centre has a number of Tudor and Georgian houses.
Tourist Information Centre ☎ (01233) 629165

Eversleigh Woodland Lodges M

COMMENDED

Eversleigh House, Hornash Lane, Shadoxhurst, Ashford TN26 1HX
☎ Hamstreet (01233) 733248
Fax (01233) 733248
Contact: Mrs C J Drury
Spacious detached lodges in woodland setting. Heated indoor swimming pool, games room, gymnasium, solarium, gardens. Ideal base for touring: easy access South Coast, London, Canterbury, Channel ports and tunnel.
6 self-contained units; sleeping 4

Price per week:	£min	£max
Low season	230.00	335.00
High season	340.00	445.00

Open February–December
Cards accepted: Access, Visa

The Old Dairy

COMMENDED

Whatsole Street Farm, Elmsted, Ashford TN25 5JW
☎ (01233) 750238
Contact: Mrs June Browning
Converted milking parlour, dating from 18th C with some older parts. M20 to

junction 11, then B2068. After 5 miles turn left for Stowting, after 1 mile turn right for Whatsole Street and Elmsted.
1 self-contained unit; sleeping max 5

Price per week:	£min	£max
Low season	160.00	300.00
High season	310.00	370.00

Open April–November

⌂ Ⓜ 🏠 🏢 ☉ 🍴 MW 📺 🎱 🍽 ⏚
🐾 P ❀ ✕ 🏕

BEACHY HEAD

East Sussex
Map ref 3B4

Black Robin Farm ⋀
COMMENDED

Beachy Head, Eastbourne
BN20 7XX
☎ Eastbourne (01323) 643357 &
Mobile 0973 418654
Contact: Mrs Jane Higgs
1000-acre livestock farm. Peaceful farm bungalows set in middle of South Downs. Excellent views. Close to town, beach and South Downs Way. Dogs and children welcome.
2 self-contained units; sleepinh 6–7

Price per week:	£min	£max
Low season	100.00	
High season		300.00

⌂ Ⓜ ✎ 🏢 ☉ 🍴 📺 🎱 🏕🏕🍽 🐾 P ❀

BEXHILL-ON-SEA

East Sussex
Map ref 3B4

Popular resort with beach of shingle and firm sand at low tide. The De la Warr Pavilion has good entertainment facilities.
Tourist Information Centre ☎ (01424) 212023 or 732208

74 Collington Lane East
COMMENDED

Bexhill-on-Sea

Contact: Mr & Mrs H West, Re. 74 Collington Lane East, 21 Millfield Rise, Bexhill-on-Sea, East Sussex TN40 1QY
☎ Bexhill (01424) 220060
Three bedroomed, detached chalet-style house with garden and 2 bedroom purpose built flat (at separate location) close to seafront.
2 self-contained units; sleeping 4–6

Price per week:	£min	£max
Low season	85.00	145.00
High season	200.00	365.00

⌂ ⊙ 🏢 ☉ 🍴 MW 📣 📺 🎱 🍽
🐾 P ❀

BIRCHINGTON

Kent
Map ref 3C3

Town on the north coast of Kent with sandy beaches and rock pools. Powell Cotton Museum is in nearby Quex Park.

Streete Cottage
COMMENDED

Court Road, St Nicholas at Wade, Birchington
Contact: Mr E B Broadley, Re. Streete Cottage, Streete House, Court Road, St Nicholas at Wade, Birchington, Kent CT7 0NH
☎ Thanet (01843) 847245
17th C semi-detached oak-beamed cottage with pretty garden. Convenient for East Kent, Canterbury, Herne Bay, Margate and Ramsgate.
1 self-contained unit; sleeping max 6

Price per week:	£min	£max
Low season	126.00	150.00
High season	150.00	360.00

⌂ Ⓜ ✎ 🏢 ☉ 🍴 📺 🎱 🍽 P ❀ SP

BRIGHTON & HOVE

East Sussex
Map ref 2D3

Brighton's attractions include the Royal Pavilion, Volks Electric Railway, Sea Life Centre and Marina Village, Conference Centre and "The Lanes" and several theatres. Neighbouring Hove is a resort in its own right.
Tourist Information Centre ☎ (01273) 323755; for Hove (01273) 746100 or 778087

Brighton Marina Holiday Apartments ⋀
HIGHLY COMMENDED

5 Mariners Quay, Brighton Marina Village, Brighton, East Sussex BN2 5UZ
☎ Brighton (01273) 693569
Fax (01273) 693569
Contact: Mrs S B Wills
Brighton Marina waterside apartments, beautifully furnished and with magnificent views overlooking lagoon.
4 self-contained units; sleeping 2–6

Price per week:	£min	£max
Low season	225.00	325.00
High season	295.00	525.00

⌂ ⊙ 🏢 ☉ 🍴 MW 📣 📺 🎱 🍽
🐾 P 🚭 SP

Metropole Court ⋀
HIGHLY COMMENDED

Metropole Hotel, Kings Road, Brighton, East Sussex
Contact: Mr & Mrs Harold & Valerie Williams, Cliff Edge, 28 Marine Drive, Rottingdean, Brighton, East Sussex BN2 7HQ
☎ Brighton (01273) 302431
Fax (01273) 307744
Well-appointed private apartments located above Metropole Hotel with sea and/or town views. Direct access to hotel facilities including free use of indoor swimming pool.

Continued ▶

BRIGHTON & HOVE
Continued

3 self-contained units; sleeping 3–5

Price per week:	£min	£max
Low season	220.00	390.00
High season	320.00	570.00

Cards accepted: Access, Visa

🐕🏠8◎💻⊙🛢📺🛢💼🗂🏊
✖️🗑SP

Seapoint 🏔
🔑🔑🔑🔑 HIGHLY COMMENDED

2 Roedean Terrace, Brighton, East Sussex
Contact: Mr R T Harris, Best of Brighton and, Sussex Cottages, Horseshoe Cottage, 2 Whipping Post Lane, Rottingdean, Brighton, East Sussex BN2 7HZ
☎ Brighton (01273) 308779 &
Mobile 0956 662457
Fax (01273) 300266
Former coastguard's cottage offering unrivalled panoramic views of Brighton Marina and the English Channel. Lovely south-facing garden and patio. One mile from Brighton town centre. Three bedrooms, 2 bathrooms.
1 self-contained unit; sleeping 6–7

Price per week:	£min	£max
Low season	275.00	325.00
High season	355.00	525.00

Cards accepted: Access, Visa

🐕◎🏠⊙🛢MW📺🛢💼🗂
📮P❄SP

BROADSTAIRS
Kent
Map ref 3C3

Popular seaside resort with numerous sandy bays. Charles Dickens spent his summers at Bleak House where he wrote parts of David Copperfield. The Dickens Festival is held in June, when many people wear Dickensian costume.
Tourist Information Centre ☎ (01843) 862242

Fisherman's Cottage 🏔
🔑🔑🔑🔑 HIGHLY COMMENDED

5 Union Square, Broadstairs
Contact: J A McDonnell, 113 Whitstable Road, Canterbury, Kent CT2 8EF
☎ Canterbury (01227) 761352
Fax (01227) 761065

Delightfully converted and equipped 4-storey cottage with spiral staircases. In conservation area by harbour and beaches. Next to Charles Dickens's "Bleak House".
1 self-contained unit; sleeping max 6

Price per week:	£min	£max
Low season	120.00	180.00
High season	300.00	450.00

Cards accepted: Access, Visa

🐕◎🏠⊙🛢MW📺🛢💼🗂
❄✖️SP🏠

CANTERBURY
Kent
Map ref 3B3

Place of pilgrimage since the martyrdom of Becket in 1170 and the site of Canterbury Cathedral. Visit St Augustine's Abbey, St Martin's (the oldest church in England), Royal Museum and Art Gallery and the Canterbury Tales. Nearby is Howletts Wild Animal Park. Good shopping centre.
Tourist Information Centre ☎ (01227) 766567

Curiosity Cottage
🔑🔑 COMMENDED

4 St Paul's Terrace, Canterbury
Contact: Mr R Allcorn, Re. Curiosity Cottage, 115 Whitstable Road, Canterbury, Kent CT2 8EF
☎ Canterbury (01227) 450265
Victorian cottage in a quiet setting, just outside city walls. Furnished to provide a comfortable and enjoyable break or holiday. Leaflet available.
1 self-contained unit; sleeping max 5

Price per week:	£min	£max
Low season	180.00	220.00
High season	220.00	375.00

🐕🏠M◎🗑🏠⊙🛢MW📺🛢💼🗂
🏠❄✖️SP

Ebury Hotel Flat and Bungalows 🏔
🔑🔑🔑🔑 HIGHLY COMMENDED

65/67 New Dover Road, Canterbury CT1 3DX
☎ (01227) 768433
Fax (01227) 459187
Contact: Mr & Mrs Mason
Quiet, comfortable hotel flats and bungalows standing in 3 acres, half a mile from the city centre. Heated indoor pool and spa.

3 self-contained units; sleeping 4–6

Price per week:	£min	£max
Low season	200.00	240.00
High season	300.00	345.00

Cards accepted: Access, Visa, Amex, Switch/Delta

🐕🏔◎🏠⊙🛢📺🛢💼🗂🖊🚗
P🔑🍴❄✖️✕

Haybarn
🔑🔑🔑🔑 HIGHLY COMMENDED

Walnut Tree Farm, Lynsore Bottom, Upper Hardres, Canterbury
Contact: Mrs Shelia Wilton, Re. Haybarn, Walnut Tree Farm, Upper Hardres, Canterbury, Kent CT4 6EG
☎ Stelling Minnis (01227) 709375
Barn conversion to very high standard. All electric with woodburner. Situated on edge of meadow, peaceful, with magnificent views, in the grounds of Walnut Tree Farm, a 14th C thatched house. Canterbury 6 miles, Dover 12 miles.
1 self-contained unit; sleeping 1–4

Price per week:	£min	£max
Low season	180.00	240.00
High season	240.00	300.00

Open March–December

🐕🏔5M◎🏠⊙🛢MW📺🛢💼
🗂🏠📮P🔑❄✖️SP

Henry's of Ash
🔑🔑🔑🔑 COMMENDED

51 The Street, Ash, Canterbury
Contact: Mr P H Robinson, Henry's of Ash, Darrington, Durlock Road, Ash, Canterbury, Kent CT3 2HU
☎ Ash (01304) 812563
Comfortable self-contained maisonette, over central village antiques shop. Double glazing. Handy for touring East Kent and Channel trips.
1 self-contained unit; sleeping max 3

Price per week:	£min	£max
Low season	96.00	116.00
High season	126.00	141.00

🐕🏔M◎🏠⊙🛢📺🛢💼🗂✖️

Old Dairy Farmhouse Annexe
🔑🔑 COMMENDED

Misling Farm, Stelling Minnis, Stone Street, Canterbury CT4 6DE
☎ Stelling Minnis (01227) 709256
Contact: Mrs P Topping
Converted dairy set by paddocks and woodland, comprising kitchen, bathroom, spacious living room, 1 double and 1 family bedroom. Convenient for Channel ports. Suitable for wheelchairs.
Wheelchair access category 2♿
1 self-contained unit; sleeping 4–5

Map references apply to the colour maps at the back of this guide.

Price per week:	£min	£max
Low season	180.00	250.00
High season	280.00	300.00

Open April–September

⌂ M ◎ 🏢 ⊙ 🛢 TV 🛢 🖾 🖳 🔌 P U ✿

Orchard View ⚠

🔑🔑🔑 COMMENDED

Selling Road, Old Wives Lees, Canterbury
Contact: Mr R Darby, Re. Orchard View, 12 Chantry Hurst, Epsom, Surrey KT18 7BW
☎ Epsom (01372) 720723
Fax (01372) 744492
Charming detached cottage on Pilgrims' Way, overlooking orchards, equipped to high standard. Large garden. Sandy beaches 30 minutes away. Cot available.
1 self-contained unit; sleeping 1–5

Price per week:	£min	£max
Low season	195.00	290.00
High season	300.00	440.00

⌂ M ◎ 🏢 ⊙ 🛢 MW TV 🛢 🖾 (🖳)🖳
🔌 P ✿ ✗ 🐾 SP

CHELWOOD GATE

East Sussex
Map ref 2D2

Small village on the edge of the Ashdown Forest.

2 High Weald Cottages Chelwood Farm

🔑🔑🔑 COMMENDED

Nutley, Uckfield
Contact: Mrs N J Howe, Re. High Weald Cottages, Sheffield Park Farm, Uckfield, East Sussex TN22 3QR
☎ Danehill (01825) 790235 & 790267
Fax (01825) 790151
Attractive, semi-detached, traditional farm cottage located on the edge of a working dairy farm, close to the Ashdown Forest.
1 self-contained unit; sleeping 5

Price per week:	£min	£max
Low season	175.00	
High season		350.00

⌂ ◎ 🏢 ⊙ 🛢 TV 🛢 🖾 (🖳)🖳 🔌 P U
✿ ✗ SP 🏠

COLOUR MAPS

Colour maps at the back of this guide pinpoint all places in which you will find accommodation listed.

CHICHESTER

West Sussex
Map ref 2C3

The county town of West Sussex with a beautiful Norman cathedral. Noted for its Georgian architecture but also has modern buildings like the Festival Theatre. Surrounded by places of interest, including Fishbourne Roman Palace and Weald and Downland Open-Air Museum.
Tourist Information Centre ☎ (01243) 775888

Hunston Mill

🔑🔑🔑 HIGHLY COMMENDED

Selsey Road, Hunston, Chichester PO20 6AU
☎ (01243) 783375
Fax (01243) 785179
Contact: Mr & Mrs P T Rist

18th C windmill and adjoining buildings, converted into comfortable holiday homes. In the country between Chichester and the sea.
6 self-contained units; sleeping 2–5

Price per week:	£min	£max
Low season	160.00	210.00
High season	225.00	350.00

Cards accepted: Access, Visa

⌂ ◎ 🏢 ⊘ ⊙ 🛢 🛢 TV 🛢 🖾 🖳 (🖳)🖳 P ⌘
U ✿ SP 🏠 T

CHIDDINGLY

East Sussex
Map ref 2D3

Small village with views over the Weald towards the Downs. Once the home of Sir John Jefferay, Baron of the Exchequer under Queen Elizabeth I.

Pekes ⚠

🔑🔑🔑 – 🔑🔑🔑🔑 COMMENDED

Chiddingly, Hailsham
Contact: Ms Eva Morris, Re. Pekes, 124 Elm Park Mansions, Park Walk, London SW10 0AR
☎ (0171) 352 8088
Fax (0171) 352 8125

Spacious oast house, 2 cottages and wing of Tudor manor in extensive grounds. Hard tennis court, indoor heated pool, sauna, jacuzzi, solarium. Children and pets welcome. Off-peak and short breaks available. Prices below refer to the cottages.
4 self-contained units; sleeping 4–11

Price per week:	£min	£max
Low season	295.00	
High season		560.00

⌂ M ◎ 🏢 ⊙ 🛢 MW 🖪 TV 🛢 🖾 (🖳)
🏠 🔌 🐾 ⌘ ⌘ U ✿ SP 🏠

CHIDDINGSTONE

Kent
Map ref 2D2

Pleasant village of 16th and 17th C, preserved by the National Trust, with an 18th C "castle" and attractive Tudor inn.

Whitepost Farmhouse ⚠

🔑🔑🔑 COMMENDED

Chiddingstone Causeway, Tonbridge TN11 8JE
☎ Penshurst (01892) 870629
Fax (01892) 870629
Contact: Mr & Mrs F W Bradbury
In the charming, quiet grounds of a listed Tudor house, each antique-furnished cottage opens on to its own garden. Close to historic houses and convenient for London.
2 self-contained units; sleeping 3

Price per week:	£min	£max
Low season	160.00	
High season		260.00

⌂ ◎ ⊘ 🏢 ⊙ 🛢 MW TV 🛢 🖾 (🖳)🖳
🔌 P ✿ ✗ 🏠

WELCOME HOST

This is a nationally recognised customer care programme which aims to promote the highest standards of service and a warm welcome. Establishments who are taking part in this initiative are indicated by the ⊛ symbol.

CHILHAM

Kent
Map ref 3B3

Extremely pretty village of mostly Tudor and Jacobean houses. The village rises to the spacious square with the castle and the 15th C church.

Monckton Cottages ⋔

🗝🗝🗝 COMMENDED

Heron Manor, Mountain Street, Chilham, Canterbury CT4 8DG
☎ Canterbury (01227) 730256
Contact: Dr R W Kirwan
Charming self-contained cottages, part of 15th C manor, in 3 acres. Picturesque setting on North Downs Way. Immaculately maintained, each with private garden and fully equipped.
2 self-contained units; sleeping 2–3

Price per week:	£min	£max
Low season	110.00	190.00
High season	170.00	310.00

🗝Ⓜ◎🖭⊙🖵TV🗄🔌🛒P∪♪▶✿🛠🏠

DEAL

Kent
Map ref 3C4

Coastal town and popular holiday resort. Deal Castle was built by Henry VIII as a fort and the museum is devoted to finds excavated in the area. Also the Time-Ball Tower museum. Angling available from both beach and pier.
Tourist Information Centre ☎ (01304) 369576

Scandinavian Style Chalets ⋔

🗝🗝🗝🗝 HIGHLY COMMENDED

45 & 78 Kingsdown Park, Upper Street, Kingsdown, Deal
Contact: Mrs P M Palmer, Scandinavian Style Chalets, c/o 80 Potash Road, Billericay, Essex CM11 1HH
☎ Billericay (01277) 656481
Fax (01277) 656481
Fully-equipped chalets with lounge/dining area, kitchen, 3 bedrooms and bathroom. Heated indoor swimming pool, tennis, site restaurant and bar.
2 self-contained units; sleeping 6

Price per week:	£min	£max
Low season	160.00	210.00
High season	260.00	350.00

Open March–October and Christmas

🗝◎🖭⊙🖵MW🖵TV🗄🔌🏢🗄P▶✿∪♪✿🛠🏠SP

DENTON

Kent
Map ref 3C4

Hamlet of tile-hung houses and a little Early English church reached via a grassy track.

Low Borrans Cottage ⋔

🗝🗝🗝 COMMENDED

Denton, Canterbury CT4 6QZ
☎ Folkestone (01303) 844289
Fax (01303) 844289
Contact: Mr & Mrs P Lucock
17th C country cottage with exposed beams, inglenook fireplace and antique furniture. Centre of small village 8 miles from Canterbury, Folkestone, Dover. Comfortable, warm relaxed atmosphere for winter breaks.
1 self-contained unit; sleeping max 5

Price per week:	£min	£max
Low season	130.00	180.00
High season	180.00	290.00

🗝2Ⓜ◎🖭⊙🖵🍴TV🗄🔌🗄🚗P✿🍴SP🏠

DODDINGTON

Kent
Map ref 3B3

The Old School House

🗝🗝🗝 COMMENDED

Adjacent St Johns Church, Church Hill, Doddington, Sittingbourne
Contact: Mrs J S Stevens, The Pheasantry, Newnham Lane, Eastling, Faversham, Kent ME13 0AT
☎ Faversham (01795) 890484

Fully modernised old school house on 2 levels. Large grounds, beautiful views and countryside.
1 self-contained unit; sleeping max 5

Price per week:	£min	£max
Low season	107.20	175.00
High season	137.20	225.00

🗝4Ⓜ◎🖭⊙🖵MW🖵TV🗄🔌🚗P✿🛠🍴SP

> The National Grading and Classification Scheme is explained in full at the back of this guide.

DORKING

Surrey
Map ref 2D2

Ancient market town and a good centre for walking, delightfully set between Box Hill and the Downs.

Bulmer Farm

🗝🗝🗝—🗝🗝🗝🗝 COMMENDED

Holmbury St Mary, Dorking RH5 6LG
☎ (01306) 730210
Contact: Mrs Gill Hill
30-acre beef farm. Two single-storey units tastefully converted from 17th C farm building. Two-person unit suitable for disabled and four-person unit combine to form attractive courtyard to farmhouse. Village is 5 miles from Dorking.
Wheelchair access category 3♿
2 self-contained units; sleeping 2–4

Price per week:	£min	£max
Low season	140.00	220.00
High season	200.00	290.00

🗝◎🖭⊙🖵TV🗄🔌🗄🚗P✿🏠

DOVER

Kent
Map ref 3C4

A Cinque Port and busiest passenger port in the world. Still a historic town and seaside resort beside the famous White Cliffs. The White Cliffs Experience attraction traces the town's history through the Roman, Saxon, Norman and Victorian periods.
Tourist Information Centre ☎ (01304) 205108

Meggett Farm Cottage ⋔

🗝🗝🗝🗝 HIGHLY COMMENDED

Meggett Farm, Meggett Lane, Dover
Contact: Mr & Mrs S Price, Meggett Farm, Meggett Lane, Alkham, Dover, Kent
☎ Dover (01303) 252764 & Mobile 0831 834094
Fax (01303) 252764

Newly converted farm building on edge of hamlet overlooking the Alkham Valley between Dover and Folkestone.

1 self-contained unit; sleeping max 6

Price per week:	£min	£max
Low season	209.00	278.00
High season	278.00	446.00

☎ ◉ �🖥 ⊙ 🗇 M W 📻 TV 🖹 🎣 🍳
♣ P U ✿

EAST WITTERING

West Sussex
Map ref 2C3

Residential and holiday town with a long sandy beach from which the Nab Tower and Isle of Wight can be seen.

Doves Flutter
HIGHLY COMMENDED

1 Seagate Court, Shore Road, East Wittering, Chichester
Contact: Dr W S Barber, Bishopstone Beehive, Bishopstone Drive, Herne Bay, Kent CT6 6RE
☎ Canterbury (01227) 741028 & Mobile (0589) 596059
Fax (01227) 741046
Superior 3-bedroomed beach-front ground floor flat, level throughout. Private enclosed patio. South-facing to Channel and Isle of Wight. Spectacular sea views, wonderful sunsets.
Wheelchair access category 2 ♿
1 self-contained unit; sleeping 6–8

Price per week:	£min	£max
Low season	350.00	450.00
High season	495.00	650.00

☎ M ◉ ◉ 🖥 ⊙ 🗇 M W 📻 TV 🖹 🎣 (
🈂 ♣ P U ✿ ✕

EASTBOURNE

East Sussex
Map ref 3B4

One of the finest, most elegant resorts on the south-east coast situated beside Beachy Head. Long promenade, plenty of gardens, theatres, Towner Art Gallery, "How We Lived Then" museum of shops and social history.
Tourist Information Centre ☎ (01323) 411400

Courtney House Holiday Flats
COMMENDED

53 Royal Parade, Eastbourne BN22 7AQ
☎ (01323) 732697
Fax (01323) 732697
Contact: Mr & Mrs A Beney
Self-contained holiday flats, ideally situated on seafront, with sea views. Close to all amenities. Unrestricted street parking. Golf and boating nearby.

---

5 self-contained units; sleeping 2–5

Price per week:	£min	£max
Low season	90.00	150.00
High season	200.00	275.00

☎ 6 M ◉ ◉ 🖥 ⊙ 🗇 M W 📻 TV 🖹 🎣 (
🍳 ✕ SP

EASTCHURCH

Kent
Map ref 3B3

Village on the Isle of Sheppey, once an important centre of aviation. The Short brothers built England's first aircraft factory here and there is a stone memorial to C S Rolls and C S Grace - pioneers of flying - opposite the church.

Connetts Farm Holiday Cottages
COMMENDED

Plough Road, Eastchurch, Sheerness ME12 4JL
☎ Isle of Sheppey (01795) 880358
Fax (01795) 880358
Contact: Mrs M A Phipps

Tastefully converted barn on 130-acre working farm, overlooking lawns, ponds and farmland. Near Blue Flag beach, naturist beach and RSPB reserve. London 50 miles, Canterbury 30 miles.
3 self-contained units; sleeping 4–5

Price per week:	£min	£max
Low season	100.00	130.00
High season	170.00	225.00

☎ M ◉ 🛏 ⊙ 🗇 M W TV 🖹 🎣 🍳 ♣ P
U ♪ ✿ SP T

EGHAM

Surrey
Map ref 2D2

In attractive and historic area beside the Thames, adjoining Runnymede and near Windsor, Thorpe Park and Savill Garden. Convenient for Heathrow Airport and good base for London, Wisley and Hampton Court.

Burford
COMMENDED

59 Egham Hill, Egham TW20 0ER
☎ (01784) 432196
Contact: Mr David Coltman
Self-contained apartment on second floor of large Victorian family home

---

with many original features, a wonderful view and beautiful garden.
1 self-contained unit; sleeping max 4

Price per week:	£min	£max
Low season	200.00	240.00
High season	240.00	280.00

☎ 12 ◉ 🛏 ⊙ 🗇 M W 📻 TV 🖹 🎣
♣ P ✿ ✕ T

EPSOM

Surrey
Map ref 2D2

Horse races have been held on the slopes of Epsom Downs for centuries. The racecourse is the home of the world-famous Derby. Many famous old homes are here, among them the 17th C Waterloo House.

7 Great Tattenhams
COMMENDED

Epsom KT18 5RF
☎ Burgh Heath (01737) 354112
Contact: Mrs M K Willis
Modern, spacious, comfortably furnished first floor flat. A good touring centre for London and the south east.
1 self-contained unit; sleeping max 5

Price per week:	£min	£max
Low season	105.00	130.00
High season	150.00	170.00

☎ M ◉ 🛏 🗇 TV 🖹 🎣 (🍳 P U ✕

FAIRWARP

East Sussex
Map ref 2D3

Situated in the Ashdown Forest in an Area of Outstanding Natural Beauty and good walking country.

Bracken Cottage
HIGHLY COMMENDED

Browns Brook, Ashdown Forest, Fairwarp, Uckfield
Contact: Mrs J Clark, Quest Croft, Fairwarp, Uckfield, East Sussex TN22 3BE
☎ Nutley (01825) 712304

In "Pooh" country: 1 of 3 delightful Victorian cottages right on Ashdown Forest. Lovely garden with many unusual plants and shrubs. Log fires in winter.

Continued ▶

FAIRWARP

Continued

1 self-contained unit; sleeping max 4

Price per week:	£min	£max
Low season	225.00	
High season		300.00

🐎12 ◎ 🖥 ⊙ 🗄 📺 🛋 🗞 🎇 🚗
P U ❄ SP 🏠

FAVERSHAM

Kent
Map ref 3B3

Historic town, once a port, dating back to prehistoric times. Abbey Street has more than 50 listed buildings. Roman and Anglo-Saxon finds and other exhibits can be seen in a museum in the Maison Dieu at Ospringe. Fleur de Lis Heritage Centre.
Tourist Information Centre ☎ (01795) 534542

Old Dairy - Shepherds Hill
⚷ ⚷ ⚷ COMMENDED

Shepherds Hill, Selling, Faversham
Contact: Mrs G Falcon, Shepherds Hill, Selling, Faversham, Kent ME13 9RS
☎ Canterbury (01227) 752212
Fax (01227) 752212
22-acre livestock farm. Converted 18th C farm building with 30 ft living room, 2 bedrooms, views over countryside, beams, garden. Very peaceful location. Convenient for Canterbury, coast, days in France, walking, castles.
1 self-contained unit; sleeping max 4

Price per week:	£min	£max
Low season	225.00	
High season		325.00

🐎 ◎ 🖥 ⊙ 🗄 MW 🖥 📺 🛋 🗞
🚗 P ❄ 🔥 SP 🏠

FAWKHAM

Kent
Map ref 2D2

Village with small, pretty church set amongst trees. Nearby is the famous motor-racing circuit of Brands Hatch.

Three Gates Stables ⚐
⚷ ⚷ ⚷ HIGHLY COMMENDED

Speedgate Hill, Fawkham, Longfield DA3 8NJ
☎ New Ash Green (01474) 872739
Fax (01474) 879455
Contact: Mr Thomas Cramer

In beautiful countryside set around a charming stable courtyard. Near motorways, airports, convenient for Channel ports and 40 minutes from London.
5 self-contained units; sleeping 3–6

Price per week:	£min	£max
Low season	220.00	300.00
High season	260.00	340.00

🐎 ◎ 🖥 ⊙ 🗄 MW 📺 🖥 🛋 🗞 🚗
P U ❄ SP

FOLKESTONE

Kent
Map ref 3C4

Popular resort and important cross-channel port. The town has a fine promenade, the Leas, from where orchestral concerts and other entertainments are presented. Horse-racing at Westenhanger Racecourse nearby.
Tourist Information Centre ☎ (01303) 258594

Seafront Holiday Flats ⚐
⚷ ⚷ APPROVED

7 Wellington Terrace, Sandgate, Folkestone CT20 3DY
☎ (01304) 852369
Contact: Mrs N Aherne
South-facing period house. Lovely seafront location. All flats with uninterrupted sea views. 1-3 bedrooms. Near shops, bus stop. Off-season mini-breaks.
3 self-contained units; sleeping 3–7

Price per week:	£min	£max
Low season	85.00	180.00
High season	130.00	250.00

🐎 M ⊘ 🖥 ⊙ 🗄 📺 🛋 📷 🚗 P SP

 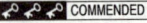
GOUDHURST

Kent
Map ref 3B4

Village on a hill surmounted by a square-towered church with fine views of orchards and hopfields. Achieved prosperity through weaving in the Middle Ages. Finchcocks houses a museum of historic early keyboard instruments.

Risebridge Farm ⚐
⚷ ⚷ ⚷ COMMENDED

Goudhurst, Cranbrook TN17 1HN
☎ (01580) 211775
Fax (01580) 211984
Contact: Mr R Hillier
100-acre mixed farm. Attractive group of 9 cottages/apartments on small farm in beautiful countryside. Leisure facilities include indoor pool, squash, tennis, badminton, gymnasium and horse riding.
9 self-contained units; sleeping 2–8

Price per week:	£min	£max
Low season	225.00	425.00
High season	365.00	755.00

🐎1 M ◎ 🖥 ⊙ 🗄 📺 🖥 🛋 🗞 P ⚡
🎿 U 🚣 ❄ SP 🏠

Three Chimneys Farm ⚐
⚷ ⚷ ⚷ HIGHLY COMMENDED

Bedgebury Road, Goudhurst, Cranbrook TN17 2RA
☎ (01580) 212175
Contact: Mrs Marion Fuller
80-acre mixed farm. Spacious cottages in a beautiful location, very quiet but not isolated.
3 self-contained units; sleeping 2–6

Price per week:	£min	£max
Low season	150.00	250.00
High season	300.00	550.00

🐎 M ◎ 🖥 ⊙ 🗄 MW 🖥 📺 🖥 🛋 🗞
🗞 🚗 P U ❄ 🔥 SP T

HASTINGS

East Sussex
Map ref 3B4

Ancient town which became famous as the base from which William the Conqueror set out to fight the Battle of Hastings. Later became one of the Cinque Ports, now a leading resort. Castle, Hastings Embroidery inspired by the Bayeux Tapestry and Sea Life Centre.
Tourist Information Centre ☎ (01424) 781111

12 The Coastguards
⚷ ⚷ ⚷ COMMENDED

Toot Rock, Pett Level, Hastings

Contact: Mrs J Doyle, Re. 12 The
Coastguards, Merton House,
11 Barrack Street, Bridport, Dorset
DT6 3LX
☎ Bridport (01308) 423180
*Character coastguard cottage near Rye.
On private road in unique sea/country
position. Ideal retreat/touring. Sleeps
4/5. Comfortably furnished. Car
parking.*
1 self-contained unit; sleeping max 5

Price per week:	£min	£max
Low season	155.00	215.00
High season	265.00	315.00

HEATHFIELD

East Sussex
Map ref 2D3

Old Heathfield is a pretty village
which was one of the major centres
of the Sussex iron industry.

Boring House Farm
COMMENDED

Vines Cross, Heathfield TN21 9AS
☎ (01435) 812285
Contact: Mrs A Reed
*90-acre mixed farm. Self-contained
portion of a farmhouse on a working
farm approximately 15 miles from
Eastbourne. Lovely views and walks.*
1 self-contained unit; sleeping max 6

Price per week:	£min	£max
Low season	100.00	120.00
High season	120.00	180.00

Open March–October and
Christmas

HENFIELD

West Sussex
Map ref 2D3

Ancient village with many old
houses and good shopping facilities,
on a ridge of high ground
overlooking the Adur Valley. Views
to the South Downs.

New Hall Cottage & New
Hall Holiday Flat
COMMENDED

New Hall, Small Dole, Henfield
BN5 9YJ
☎ Brighton (01273) 492546
Contact: Mrs M W Carreck
*Self-contained flat and 17th C cottage
attached to manor house. In 3.5 acres
of mature gardens, surrounded by
farmland.*

2 self-contained units; sleeping 3–5

Price per week:	£min	£max
Low season	110.00	220.00
High season	235.00	270.00

HERNE BAY

Kent
Map ref 3B3

Seaside resort which has 7 miles of
shingle beach with excellent bathing,
sailing and sea-angling.
Tourist Information Centre ☎ *(01227)
361911*

Arlington Lodge
COMMENDED

Upper Flat, 27 Wester Esplanade,
Herne Bay
Contact: Mr A F Webb, 47 West
Bank, Dorking, Surrey RH4 3DQ
☎ Dorking (01306) 883238
*Spacious first-floor seafront flat with
balcony in quiet residential area. Own
beach hut.*
1 self-contained unit; sleeping max 5

Price per week:	£min	£max
Low season	200.00	300.00
High season	300.00	400.00

HOVE

East Sussex

See under Brighton & Hove

LAMBERHURST

Kent
Map ref 3B4

Long village street passes over the
River Teise and has retained much
of its ancient character. Scotney
Castle Gardens (National Trust) and
Lamberhurst Vineyards are close by.

Sandhurst Farm
HIGHLY COMMENDED

Clayhill Road, Lamberhurst, Royal
Tunbridge Wells TN3 8AX
☎ (01892) 890595
Fax (01892) 891110
Contact: Mrs S A McGonigal
*230-acre mixed farm. Two
2-bedroomed apartments in a barn on
a working farm, enjoying wide views
over a beautiful and secluded valley. 3
miles from Lamberhurst village, 1
hour's drive to London or the coast.*

2 self-contained units; sleeping 4–5

Price per week:	£min	£max
Low season	150.00	240.00
High season	220.00	345.00

LEWES

East Sussex
Map ref 2D3

Historic county town with Norman
castle. The steep High Street has
mainly Georgian buildings. There is a
folk museum at Anne of Cleves
House and the archaeological
museum is in Barbican House.
Tourist Information Centre ☎ *(01273)
483448*

Duck Barn Holidays
UP TO HIGHLY COMMENDED

Telscombe Village, Lewes
Contact: Mrs A Kennedy, Appletrees,
Firle, Lewes, East Sussex BN8 6LF
☎ Brighton (01273) 858221
*Beautifully converted barn and cottages
in tranquil downland hamlet south of
Lewes and 2 miles from coast. Exposed
beams, old pine furniture, wood-burning
stoves.*
3 self-contained units; sleeping 2–10

Price per week:	£min	£max
Low season	130.00	325.00
High season	265.00	640.00

LEYSDOWN ON SEA

Kent
Map ref 3B3

Small resort complete with holiday
camps, a promenade, seaside
amusements and a stretch of sandy
beach.

Birdwatchers Cottage
HIGHLY COMMENDED

Newhouse Farm, Leysdown on Sea,
Sheerness ME12 4BA
☎ (01795) 510201
Fax (01795) 880379
Contact: Mrs S Marsh

410-acre mixed farm. Idyllic, quality
Continued ▶

LEYSDOWN ON SEA
Continued

cottage on family-run working farm. Touring base and quiet hideaway. Send SAE for leaflet.
1 self-contained unit; sleeping max 8

Price per week:	£min	£max
Low season	165.00	
High season		350.00

🛥️Ⓜ️◎⌀▥☉🛢️MW🖳📺🛢️🔌
🍳🔌🛥️♿P✻✈🚭SP

LOWER BEEDING
West Sussex
Map ref 2D3

Close to St Leonard's Forest, once a royal hunting ground, the area is also well-known for its hammer ponds, used when iron was smelted here. Leonardslee Gardens are especially beautiful in spring and autumn.

Black Cottage
🗝️🗝️🗝️ APPROVED
Newells Farmhouse, Newells Lane, Lower Beeding, Horsham
Contact: Mrs V Storey, Black Cottage, C/O Newells Farmhouse, Newells Lane, Lower Beeding, Horsham, West Sussex RH13 6LN
☎ Horsham (01403) 891326
Fax (01403) 891530
Charming secluded 19th C cottage removed from the farmyard and surrounded by own fields and woods.
1 self-contained unit; sleeping 4

Price per week:	£min	£max
Low season	130.00	145.00
High season	175.00	230.00

🛥️Ⓜ️◎▥☉🛢️🖳📺🛢️🗄️🛥️P
🚣♪✻SP

MAIDSTONE
Kent
Map ref 3B3

Busy county town of Kent on the River Medway has many interesting features and is an excellent centre for excursions. Museum of Carriages, Museum and Art Gallery, Archbishop's Palace, Mote Park.
Tourist Information Centre ☎ (01622) 673581 or 602169

Brook House 📶
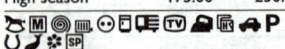
🗝️🗝️🗝️🗝️ HIGHLY COMMENDED
Old Loose Hill, Maidstone
ME15 0BL
☎ (01622) 743703
Fax (01622) 747828
Contact: Mrs Linda Doust

Attractive listed converted heavily beamed barn, in grounds of 16th C listed house situated in conservation village. 2 bedrooms, 1 en-suite bathroom plus 2nd bathroom, sofa bed, luxuriously furnished and fully equipped.
1 self-contained unit; sleeping 2–6

Price per week:	£min	£max
Low season	300.00	400.00
High season	400.00	550.00

🛥️Ⓜ️◎▥☉🛢️MW🖳📺🛢️🛥️🍳
🔌🛥️PU✻✈SP🏠

Lavender Cottage 📶
🗝️🗝️🗝️ APPROVED
Headcorn Road, Grafty Green, Maidstone ME17 2AN
☎ (01622) 850287
Contact: Mr & Mrs Hulm
17th C oak-beamed, two bedroomed cottage. Log fire, fully equipped. In pretty village, close to Leeds Castle, with easy access to M20, Channel ports and London.
1 self-contained unit; sleeping max 3

Price per week:	£min	£max
Low season	120.00	150.00
High season	160.00	200.00

🛥️5Ⓜ️◎▥☉🛢️MW🖳📺🛢️🍳
🛥️P✻SP

MIDHURST
West Sussex
Map ref 2C3

Historic, picturesque town just north of the South Downs, with the ruins of Cowdray House, medieval castle and 15th C parish church. Polo at Cowdray Park. Excellent base for Chichester, Petworth, Glorious Goodwood and the South Downs Way.
Tourist Information Centre ☎ (01730) 817322

Greens Cottage 📶
🗝️🗝️🗝️ HIGHLY COMMENDED
Duck Lane, Midhurst
Contact: Mrs Susan Clark, 9 St Johns Close, Midhurst, West Sussex GU29 9QB
☎ Midhurst (01730) 816488
Fax (01730) 816488
Tastefully furnished, well equipped, first floor apartment forming part of a listed building, in quiet central position. All inclusive and spacious

accommodation for 3 plus cot/child's bed. Short breaks available. Phone for brochure.
1 self-contained unit; sleeping max 3

Price per week:	£min	£max
Low season	100.00	175.00
High season	200.00	350.00

Cards accepted: Access, Visa
🛥️◎▥☉🛢️MW🖳📺🛢️🛥️🍳🔌
🚭SP🏠

NEWHAVEN
East Sussex
Map ref 2D3

Town has the terminal of a car-ferry service to Dieppe in France.

The Granary
🗝️🗝️ COMMENDED
High Barn, Piddinghoe, Newhaven
Contact: Mrs B M Cheeseman, Re. The Granary, High Barn, Piddinghoe, Newhaven, East Sussex BN9 9AW
☎ Newhaven (01273) 514484
Ground floor flat in converted barn, in conservation area in middle of pretty riverside village.
1 self-contained unit; sleeping 2

Price per week:	£min	£max
Low season	120.00	
High season		225.00

Ⓜ️◎▥☉🛢️📺🛢️🗄️🛥️P✻✈🚭
SP🏠

NUTLEY
East Sussex
Map ref 2D3

Richard II had a hunting lodge at Nutley, which he used when hunting in the Ashdown Forest. To the north of the village is Nutley Mill, built in 1690 (open selected days only).

2 Victoria Cottage Hole and Alchorne Farm
🗝️🗝️🗝️ HIGHLY COMMENDED
Bell Lane, Nutley, Uckfield
Contact: Mr P Graves, 2 Victoria Cottage, Hole and Alchorne Farm, Bell Lane, Nutley, Uckfield, East Sussex TN22 3PD
☎ Nutley (01825) 712475
Fax (01825) 712475
60-acre dairy farm. Well-appointed, semi-detached traditional farm cottage with pleasant garden, in beautiful location near Ashdown Forest.
1 self-contained unit; sleeping max 5

Price per week:	£min	£max
Low season	160.00	180.00
High season		280.00

🐕 Ⓜ ◎ ▥ ☉ 🗍 MW 📶 TV 🗄 ➡ 📱
🖫 ♿ ♨ ❋ ✗

White House Farm Holiday Homes Ⓜ

🔑🔑🔑 COMMENDED

White House Farm, Horney Common, Nutley, Uckfield TN22 3EE
☎ Uckfield (01825) 712377 & Mobile 0836 723543
Contact: Mr John Francis
Overlooking Ashdown Forest with panoramic views. Large lounge/dining area, spacious kitchen, small terrace. Pets welcome on this working farm.
Wheelchair access category 3♿
5 self-contained units; sleeping 4–5

Price per week:	£min	£max
Low season	200.00	225.00
High season	265.00	370.00

Cards accepted: Access, Visa

🐕 ◎ ▥ 🗍 MW TV 🗄 ➡ 📱 🖫 P ❋ ✗
SP 🏠

Town dominated by Petworth House (National Trust), the great 17th C mansion, set in 2000 acres of parkland laid out by Capability Brown. The house contains wood-carvings by Grinling Gibbons.
Tourist Information Centre ☎ (01798) 343523

The Cottage Ⓜ

🔑🔑🔑 HIGHLY COMMENDED

Salmonsbridge Farm, River, Petworth
Contact: Mrs Tina Carroll, Salmonsbridge Farm, River, Petworth, West Sussex GU28 9DW
☎ Lodsworth (01798) 861693
Fax (01798) 861693
30-acre livestock farm. Converted 15th C farm building. 2 double bedrooms, dressing room, bathroom, sitting room, large kitchen, wood burner, tennis court.
1 self-contained unit; sleeping max 5

Price per week:	£min	£max
Low season	350.00	400.00
High season	400.00	500.00

Open January–March, May–December

◎ ▥ ☉ 🗍 TV 🗄 ➡ 📱 🐎 ➡ P ☍
🛠 ✗ 🏠

Village standing high above the Kent Weald, with a 17th C church in the centre and a rare medieval domestic house.

Golding Hop Farm Cottage Ⓜ

🔑🔑🔑 HIGHLY COMMENDED

Bewley Lane, Plaxtol, Sevenoaks TN15 0PS
☎ Borough Green (01732) 885432
Contact: Mrs J Vincent
South-facing cottage with garden and all modern conveniences on cobnut farm. Quiet position but not isolated.
1 self-contained unit; sleeping max 5

Price per week:	£min	£max
Low season	140.00	190.00
High season	190.00	270.00

🐕 Ⓜ ◎ ▥ ☉ 🗍 MW TV 🗄 ➡ 📱
➡ P U ❋

Popular holiday resort with good sandy beaches. At Pegwell Bay is replica of a Viking longship. Terminal for car-ferry service to Dunkirk and Ostend.
Tourist Information Centre ☎ (01843) 583333

Ramsgate Holiday Homes Ⓜ

🔑🔑🔑 — 🔑🔑🔑 COMMENDED

21 Avebury Avenue, Ramsgate CT11 8BB
☎ (01843) 592945
Contact: Mrs P J Martin
House and apartments in attractive Georgian terrace near harbour. Also house with nice garden in quiet road on Broadstairs border. Short stays accepted out of season.
3 self-contained units; sleeping 3–6

Price per week:	£min	£max
Low season	115.00	150.00
High season	170.00	330.00

Cards accepted: Access, Visa, Switch/Delta

🐕 Ⓜ ▥ ☉ 🗍 MW 📶 TV 🗄 ➡ 📱
🖫 ➡ P ❋ ✗ 🎙 SP 🏠

The **Ⓜ** symbol after an establishment name indicates that it is a Regional Tourist Board member.

This "Royal" town became famous as a spa in the 17th C and much of its charm is retained, as in the Pantiles, a shaded walk lined with elegant shops. Heritage attraction "A Day at the Wells". Rich in parks and gardens and a good centre for walks. Excellent shopping centre.
Tourist Information Centre ☎ (01892) 515675

Itaris Properties Ⓜ

🔑🔑🔑 — 🔑🔑🔑 COMMENDED

12 Mount Ephraim, Royal Tunbridge Wells
Contact: Mrs Mary Collins, Itaris Properties Ltd, 12 Mount Ephraim, Royal Tunbridge Wells, Kent TN4 8AS
☎ Tunbridge Wells (01892) 511065
Fax (01892) 540171

Self-contained flats and house in Royal Tunbridge Wells.
3 self-contained units; sleeping 2–6

Price per week:	£min	£max
Low season	105.00	200.00
High season	175.00	270.00

🐕 Ⓜ ◎ ▥ ⌀ ▥ ☉ 🗍 MW TV 🗄 ➡ 📱
🖫 ➡ P ❋ ✗

Cobbled, hilly streets and fine old buildings make Rye, once a Cinque Port, a most picturesque town. Noted for its church with ancient clock, potteries and antique shops. Town Model Sound and Light Show gives a good introduction to the town.
Tourist Information Centre ☎ (01797) 226696

Cobble Cottage

🔑🔑 COMMENDED

16 West Street, Rye
Contact: Mr John Thulborn, Brackendene, Five Elms Road, Hayes, Bromley BR2 7AD
☎ (0181) 462 8183 & 676 8099

Continued ▶

RYE

Continued

16th C Grade II* listed cottage in central conservation area. Children welcome. Linen hire. Rental fully inclusive. Pets welcome by arrangement.
1 self-contained unit; sleeping 1–6

Price per week:	£min	£max
Low season	100.00	200.00
High season	175.00	325.00

Cards accepted: Access, Visa, Diners, Amex, Switch/Delta

SANDWICH

Kent
Map ref 3C3

Delightful old market town, once a Cinque Port, now 2 miles from the sea. Many interesting old buildings including the 16th C Barbican and the Guildhall which contains the town's treasures. Several excellent golf-courses.

The Ridgeway Farm Lodge

COMMENDED

Woodnesborough Road, Sandwich
Contact: Mrs B A Durban, The Ridgeway Farm, Woodnesborough Road, Sandwich, Kent CT13 0BA
☎ Sandwich (01304) 612121
40-acre arable farm. Converted chauffeur's lodge, built circa 1900, and 1 acre of garden, on the outskirts of historic Sandwich. Close to Channel ports and Tunnel and several golf-courses.
1 self-contained unit; sleeping max 4

Price per week:	£min	£max
Low season	160.00	180.00
High season	195.00	205.00

A key to symbols can be found inside the back cover flap.

Information on accommodation listed in this guide has been supplied by the proprietors. As changes may occur you are advised to check details at the time of booking.

SEVENOAKS

Kent
Map ref 2D2

Set in pleasant wooded country, with a distinctive character and charm. Nearby is Knole (National Trust), home of the Sackville family and one of the largest houses in England, set in a vast deer park.
Tourist Information Centre ☎ (01732) 450305

Ash Place Farm

COMMENDED

Ash, Sevenoaks
Contact: Mrs Scott, Re. Ash Place Farm, Ash Manor, Ash, Sevenoaks, Kent TN15 7HD
☎ Ash Green (01474) 872238 & Mobile 0589 489380
Upper flat in converted Victorian farmhouse with large garden and splendid views, on 600-acre working farm.
1 self-contained unit; sleeping 4

Price per week:	£min	£max
Low season	150.00	150.00
High season	150.00	220.00

STAPLEHURST

Kent
Map ref 3B4

The Early English/Perpendicular church is notable for the ancient ironwork carried by the south door.

Bramley Cottage 🅜

APPROVED

Harts Heath Farm, Staplehurst, Tonbridge
Contact: Mrs F Tipples, Re. Bramley Cottage, Harts Heath Farm, Staplehurst, Tonbridge, Kent TN12 0HP
☎ Maidstone (01622) 831229
Fax (01622) 833034
Modern detached 3-bedroomed house on 300-acre hop and fruit farm in wooded area between Staplehurst, Marden and Goudhurst, half a mile from Curtisden Green.
1 self-contained unit; sleeping 6–8

Price per week:	£min	£max
Low season	160.00	175.00
High season	175.00	350.00

Open April–October

TENTERDEN

Kent
Map ref 3B4

Most attractive market town with a broad main street full of 16th C houses and shops. The tower of the 15th C parish church is the finest in Kent. Fine antiques centre.

Cromwell Cottage

APPROVED

139 High Street, Tenterden
Contact: Mrs V Ernst, Re. Cromwell Cottage, Aventine, Ingleden Park Road, Tenterden, Kent TN30 6NS
☎ Tenterden (01580) 762958
Listed terraced cottage of historic interest, with 2 bedrooms, bathroom, lounge, kitchen and enclosed paved courtyard. Parking for 1 car. All services included in price.
1 self-contained unit; sleeping max 4

Price per week:	£min	£max
Low season	125.00	170.00
High season	175.00	265.00

Meadow Cottage & Tamworth Cottage 🅜

HIGHLY COMMENDED

Great Prawls Farm, Stone-in-Oxney, Tenterden
Contact: Mrs P Cooke, Great Prawls Farm, Stone-in-Oxney, Tenterden, Kent TN30 7HB
☎ Wittersham (01797) 270539
Lovely bungalow on sheep farm. Peaceful situation with beautiful views. 15 minutes from sea, Rye, Tenterden. Castles, National Trust, steam trains nearby. Accessible Channel Tunnel. Part-weeks low season.
2 self-contained units; sleeping max 5

Price per week:	£min	£max
Low season	125.00	
High season		350.00

Please check prices and other details at the time of booking.

For ideas on places to visit refer to the introduction at the beginning of this section.

Quince Cottage

🗝️🗝️🗝️🗝️ HIGHLY COMMENDED

143 High Street, Tenterden
Contact: Mrs H E Crease, Re.
Quince Cottage, Laurelhurst,
38 Ashford Road, Tenterden, Kent
TN30 6LL
☎ Tenterden (01580) 765636
Fax (01580) 765922

Listed end-of-terrace beamed cottage,
furnished and equipped to a high
standard. 3 bedrooms, cot available.
Rear secluded courtyard. Owner
supervised. Good centre for exploring
Kent and East Sussex.
1 self-contained unit; sleeping max 5

Price per week:	£min	£max
Low season	170.00	240.00
High season	260.00	320.00

🛎️🌀⊙🗑️MW📼📺🗑️🚗📟
🚗P❄️✂️⬇️SP🏡

TONBRIDGE

Kent
Map ref 2D2

Ancient town, built on the River
Medway, has a long history of
commercial importance and is still a
thriving town. Attractive gardens
surround the remains of the
Norman castle. Large new
swimming complex with indoor and
outdoor pools.
Tourist Information Centre ☎ *(01732)*
770929

Ciderpress Cottage/Walnut Tree Cottage 🅼

🗝️🗝️🗝️🗝️ DE LUXE

Goldhill Mill, Golden Green,
Tonbridge

Contact: Mr & Mrs V Cole,
Ciderpress Cottage/Walnut Tree,
Cottage, Goldhill Mill, Golden
Green, Tonbridge, Kent TN11 OBA
☎ Hadlow (01732) 851626
Fax (01732) 851881

*Two beautiful, idyllic period cottages in
tranquil 20-acre grounds of old
watermill. High quality interior decor,
well furnished and fully equipped.
South East England Tourism
Self-Catering Holiday of the Year award
and ETB England for Excellence Silver
award 1994.*
2 self-contained units; sleeping 6

Price per week:	£min	£max
Low season	325.00	425.00
High season	475.00	675.00

🛎️🅼🌀📿🗑️⊙🗑️MW📼📺🗑️🚗
📟🛎️🚗P❄️✂️⬇️✂️🏡T

TUNBRIDGE WELLS

See under Royal Tunbridge Wells

WEST MALLING

Kent
Map ref 3B3

Became prominent in Norman times
when an abbey was established
here.

The Shire

🗝️🗝️🗝️🗝️ HIGHLY COMMENDED

Manor Farm, West Malling
Contact: Mrs R Lambert, Re. The
Shire, Manor Farm, West Malling,
Kent ME19 6RE
☎ West Malling (01732) 842091
Fax (01732) 873784
*Stable conversion in quiet farmyard. 5
minutes from Saxon village, country*

park and pubs. Tennis and table tennis,
swimming and sports complex 2 miles
away.
1 self-contained unit; sleeping max 6

Price per week:	£min	£max
Low season	220.00	
High season	500.00	

🛎️🅼🌀🗑️⊙🗑️MW📼📺🗑️🚗📟
🛎️🚗P❄️✂️🏡

WROTHAM

Kent
Map ref 3B3

Below Wrotham Hill close to the
North Downs Way, the village has
an impressive 14th C church and
several interesting old buildings,
some dating from Elizabethan times.

Butts Hill Farm Country Holidays 🅼

🗝️🗝️🗝️🗝️ HIGHLY COMMENDED

Labour-in-Vain Road, Wrotham,
Sevenoaks TN15 7PA
☎ Sevenoaks (01732) 822415
Fax (01732) 822415
Contact: Mr & Mrs G Morel
*Timber lodges in tranquil woodland
setting. Comfortably furnished and fully
equipped. Ideal for touring Kent, the
South East, London and for access to
Channel ports and tunnel.*
4 self-contained units; sleeping 4–7

Price per week:	£min	£max
Low season	240.00	312.00
High season	384.00	480.00

Cards accepted: Access, Visa

🛎️📿🗑️⊙🗑️MW📼📺🗑️🚗📟🛎️
P∪❄️✂️⬇️✂️SPT

CHECK THE MAPS

The colour maps at the back of this guide show

all the cities, towns and villages for which you will

find accommodation entries.

Refer to the town index to find the page

on which it is listed.

USE YOUR *i*'s

There are more than 550 Tourist Information Centres throughout England offering friendly help with accommodation and holiday ideas as well as suggestions of places to visit and things to do. There may well be a centre in your home town which can help you before you set out. You'll find the address of your nearest Tourist Information Centre in your local Phone Book.

AT-A-GLANCE SYMBOLS

Symbols at the end of each accommodation entry give useful information about services and facilities. A key to symbols can be found inside the back cover flap.

Keep this open for easy reference.

ENQUIRY COUPONS

To help you obtain further information about advertisers and accommodation featured in this guide you will find enquiry coupons at the back. Send these directly to the establishments in which you are interested. Remember to complete both sides of the coupon.

SELF-CATERING AGENCIES

This section of the guide lists agencies which have a selection of holiday homes to let in various parts of the country. Some agencies specialise in a particular area or region while others have properties in all parts of England.

The agencies listed here are grouped first into those who have had *all properties* inspected and quality graded by the English Tourist Board and secondly into those that have *a varying number* of tourist board inspected properties.

To obtain further information on individual properties please contact the agency or agencies direct, indicating the time of year when the accommodation is required, the number of people to be accommodated and any preferred locations. You may find the Accommodation Coupons towards the back of this guide helpful when making contact.

The prices shown in each agency entry are weekly terms per unit.

The symbol T at the end of an agency entry means that accommodation may be booked with that agency through a bona fide travel agent.

ALL PROPERTIES INSPECTED

The following agencies have had *all their properties inspected and quality graded* by the English Tourist Board and are therefore eligible to display the official logo shown above.

Beach & Bracken Exmoor Holidays
Bratton Fliming,
Barnstaple,
Devon EX32 7JL
Tel: Brayford (01598) 710702
An all hours, all season booking service for quality ETB inspected self-catering cottages and farmhouse accommodation at reasonable prices throughout our beautiful coastal Exmoor.
Price range:
low season (October-May)
£105-£440;
high season (May-September)
£220-£695
Short breaks also available.
T Ad See display advertisement on page 217.

Best Leisure
North Hill, Shirwell,
Barnstaple,
Devon EX31 4LG
Tel: Barnstaple (01271) 850611
Fax: (01271) 850693
Superb self-catering holiday homes, cottages and apartments in idyllic surroundings. Sea, river and hill view locations, each with its own special charm, in Devon, Cornwall and the Cotswolds. All furnished and fully equipped to a high standard, sleeping 2-7, close to local amenities. Open all year. Colour brochure available on request.
Price range:
low season £189-£308;
high season £258-£707.
Short breaks also available.

'Heart of the Lakes' and 'Cottage Life'

Rydal Holme,
Rydal, Ambleside,
Cumbria LA22 9LR
Tel: Ambleside (015394) 32321
Fax: (015394) 33251

Wide selection of well presented holiday homes throughout central Lakeland, some with lake views, many with gardens. Rural locations or village centre properties available. Ideal for holidays at any time of the year. Cottages, apartments and houses all shown in fully illustrated brochures.

Price range:
low season (November-March, excluding Christmas and New Year) £125-£550;
high season (April-October, plus Christmas and New Year) £150-£1100.
Short breaks also available (winter only).

Lakeland Cottage Holidays

3 The Heads,
Keswick,
Cumbria CA12 5ES
Tel: Keswick (017687) 71071
Fax: (017687) 75036

The largest local Agency with all its properties ETB Inspected and Quality Graded to help you select your holiday retreat from individual cottages, bungalows and farmhouses all in the heart of England's finest National Park. Enjoy a whole range of outdoor pursuits or just relax in peace amidst magnificent lake and mountain scenery. Log fires make holidays cosy and warm all year round. Many properties welcome children and dogs.

Price range:
low season (November-March excl. Xmas & New Year) £120-£345;
high season (April-October incl. Xmas & New Year) £171-£597.

Powells Cottage Holidays

Dolphin House,
52 High Street, Saundersfoot,
Dyfed SA69 9EJ
Freephone: 0800 378771
Tel: Saundersfoot (01834) 813232
Fax: (01834) 811731

Choose from beautiful properties throughout the West Country, Wales and the Cotswolds. For your free 100-page colour brochure ring freephone 0800 378771.

Price range:
low season (October-December and January-April) £99-£400;
high season (May-September) £150-£900.
Short breaks also available.

T Ad See display advertisement on page 13.

Quality Cottage Holidays

Karinya, Becketts Lane,
Greet, Winchcombe,
Gloucestershire GL54 5NX
Tel: Cheltenham (01242) 602459

Properties from Stratford and the Cotswolds to the West Country. All the properties are personally known and inspected by the Agency's proprietors. A good selection of properties from countryside to town. Helpful service and prompt, personal attention to meet your requirements.

Price range:
low season (October-March) £170-£300;
high season (June-September) £295-£700.
Short breaks also available.

Red Rose Cottages

16 Shawbridge Street,
Clitheroe, Lancashire BB7 1LY
Tel: Clitheroe (01200) 427310
Fax: (01200) 428929

Selected English Tourist Board inspected and graded properties to sleep 2-11, in town, village and countryside in Lancashire and the Pennines, including the Forest of Bowland. Children and pets welcome at most properties. Some suitable for disabled.

Price range:
low season (October-end May excluding half-term weeks, Easter and Spring Bank Holiday) £95-£430;
high season (June-September) £150-£650.
Short breaks also available.

West Country Cottages

The Geminids,
Priory Road,
Abbotskerswell,
Devon TQ12 5PP
Tel: (01626) 333678
Fax: (01626) 336678

English Tourist Board graded cottages (up to Five-Key De Luxe) from Land's End to the New Forest. Coastal and moorland properties in delightful settings. Some have swimming pools, games rooms, four poster beds, golf, fishing, tennis and other sport facilities.

Price range:
low season (January-March) £102-£534;
high season (mid July-end August) £225-£1,269.
Short breaks also available.

The following agencies vary in the number of their properties which are inspected and quality graded by the English Tourist Board. It is advisable to enquire whether the property you choose is ETB inspected or not at the time of booking.

All Recommended Cottage Holidays

Eastgate House,
Eastgate, Pickering,
North Yorkshire YO18 7DW
Tel: Pickering (01751) 475547
Fax: (01751) 475559
Personally inspected, quality properties (cottages, houses, bungalows, converted barns) throughout England, Scotland and Wales, at most competitive prices. Free full colour brochure.
Price range:
low season (September-May)
£99-£567;
high season (June-August)
£161-£737.
Short breaks also available.
T

Apartment Services

2 Sandwich Street,
London WC1H 9PL
Tel: (0171) 388 3558
Fax: (0171) 383 7255
Self-contained, comfortably furnished, fully equipped apartments in central London. Serviced weekly. Convenient for public transport, West End and theatres. Deposit: £100. Cancellation: Deposit is refundable providing at least six weeks' notice is given or property is relet.
Price range:
(January-December) £150-£1500.
Short breaks also available.
Minimum of one week.
T Ad See display advertisement on page 24.

Jean Bartlett Cottage Holidays

7 Fore Street,
Beer, Devon
Tel: Seaton (01297) 23221, for brochure (01297) 20973
Fax: (01297) 23303
Quality cottages, farmhouses and apartments close to the coast and the beautiful East Devon/West Dorset countryside. To suit most tastes and pockets. All inspected and familiar to local family run agency.
Price range:
low season (November-March excluding Xmas & New Year)
£110-£300;
high season (April-October)
£280-£750.
Short breaks also available.
T Ad See display advertisement on page 242.

Best of Brighton and Sussex Cottages

Horseshoe Cottage,
Whipping Post Lane,
Rottingdean,
Sussex BN2 7HZ
Tel: Brighton (01273) 308779
Fax: (01273) 300266
Offering interesting and unusual properties - all personally inspected by the proprietor (Mr RTS Harris) - and located in Brighton and Hove and the country areas of East and West Sussex, but mainly within 15 miles of Brighton. 50 properties sleeping 2-10 people.
Price range:
low season (November-March)
£155-£900;
high season (April-October)
£245-£1,650.
Short breaks also available.
Ad See display advertisement on page 275.

Blakes Country Cottages

Stoney Bank Road,
Earby, Colne,

Lancashire BB8 6PR
Tel: (01282) 445777 for brochure requests;
(01282) 445225 for bookings
Fax: (01282) 841399
2,000 properties throughout the whole of England, sleeping 2-16 people, with a range of cottages, farmhouses, lodges, chalets and even castles. Free colour brochure available by phoning or from any travel agent.
Price range: from £99-£1,695
Short breaks also available.
T

Clark Scott-Harden (English Lakes & Eden Valley)

St Andrew's Churchyard,
Penrith,
Cumbria CA11 7YE
Tel: Penrith (01768) 864541
Fax: (01768) 865578
Varied selection of apartments, cottages and houses in a variety of locations in the Lakes and Eden Valley. Pets are welcome in some. We have properties to suit all needs and requirements.
Price range:
low season (October-pre-Easter, excluding Christmas & New Year) £130-£1,000;
high season (early July-mid September) £180-£1,500.
Short breaks also available.

Classic Cottages

Leslie House,
Lady Street, Helston,
Cornwall TR13 8NA
Tel: Helston (01326) 565656
Fax: (01326) 565554
The specialists for cottages of distinction and quality. Full colour brochure lists 350 selected coastal and country cottages throughout the West Country.
Price range: low season (October-April) £171-£594; high season (July-August) £285-£1,512.

Short breaks also available.
Ad See display advertisement on page 243.

Coast and Country Cottages
Church Street,
Salcombe,
Devon TQ8 8DH
Tel: Salcombe (01548) 843773
Telephone for a free colour brochure. Over 100 self-catering cottages, houses and flats, all personally inspected and approved. Salcombe and surrounding area.
Price range: from £80-£1500.
Please ring for details.

Coast and Country Holidays
15 Town Green,
Wymondham,
Norfolk NR18 0PN
Tel: Wymondham (01953) 604480
Fax: (01953) 606671
Wide selection of properties including cottages, houses, farmhouses, chalets and flats in East Anglia.
Price range:
low season (October-April) £96-£483;
high season (June-September) £206-£854.
Short breaks also available.
Ad See display advertisement on page 195.

Cornish Cottage Holidays
3 Meneage Street,
Helston,
Cornwall TR13 8AA
Tel: Helston (01326) 573808
Fax: (01326) 564992
We let over 200 houses, cottages and apartments all over Cornwall, in coastal or rural locations, specialising in quality accommodation which is either personally or tourist board inspected.
Price range:
low season (October-Easter)

£85-£200;
high season (Easter-October) £200-£800.
Short breaks also available.

Cornish Holiday Cottages
Killibrae,
Maenporth,
Falmouth,
Cornwall TR11 5HP
Tel: Falmouth (01326) 250339
Fax: (01326) 250339
Properties in Falmouth to Helford River area, each with garden and some by the waterside. Personally supervised and maintained to a high standard. Helpful staff available at all times.
Price range:
low season (September-April) £90-£415;
high season (July-September) £110-£1030.
Short breaks also available off-season.

Cornish Riviera Holidays
Westcotts Quay,
St Ives,
Cornwall TR26 2DY
Tel: Penzance (01736) 797891
Over 60 fishermans cottages and flats all in St Ives and near the harbour. All personally inspected and well equipped. Linen, cots and some car spaces available.
Price range:
low season (January-May) £90-£235;
high season (May-September) £220-£600.
Short breaks also available.

Cornish Traditional Cottages
Peregrine Hall,
Lostwithiel,
Cornwall PL22 0HT
Tel: Bodmin (01208) 872559
Fax: (01208) 873548
400 traditional cottages, bungalows and houses in Cornwall.

Price range:
low season (1 October-15 March) £140-£676;
high season (16 March-30 September) £150-£1,050.
Short breaks also available October-April.
T

Cottage in the Country
Forest Gate,
Frog Lane,
Milton-under-Wychwood,
Oxfordshire OX7 6JZ
Tel: (01993) 831495/831743
Fax: (01993) 831095
Personally known properties. Town, village or rural. Traditional cottages to modern luxury apartments. Central middle England - includes Windsor and the Thames Valley, Oxon, The Cotswolds, Worcestershire & Herefordshire, Shropshire & Welsh Borders.
Price range:
low season (November-March) £150-£800;
high season (April-October) £150-£950.
Short breaks also available.
T

Cottages South West
46 Fore Street,
Shaldon,
Devon TQ14 0EA
Tel: Shaldon (01626) 872314
(24 hour answer phone)
Fax: (01626) 872314
Contact us now for a lovely selection of mainly coastal cottages and apartments, many with sea views in picturesque Shaldon and Teignmouth.
Price range:
low season (November-May) £114-£298;
high season (June-September) £130-£430.
Short breaks also available.

Country Cottage Hoildays

Dryden House,
Market Place, Hawes,
North Yorkshire DL8 3RA
Tel: Wensleydale (01969)
667654
Fax: (01969) 667999
*100 cottages in the villages and
glorious countryside of Wensleydale,
Swaledale and Dentdale in the
Yorkshire Dales. Our cottages
feature colour TV, central heating,
open fires, superb views, gardens,
private parking and many allow
pets. Sleep 1-10. Personal callers
very welcome at our offices in the
centre of Hawes.*
Price range:
low season (October-May
excluding school holidays)
£120-£175;
high season (July-August)
£180-£395.
Short breaks also available.
T

Dales Holiday Cottages

Carleton Business Park,
Carleton New Road, Skipton,
North Yorkshire BD23 2DG
Tel: Skipton (01756)
799821/790919
Fax: (01756) 797012
*Over 600 personally inspected
holiday properties for 2-12 people
in Yorkshire, Northumbria, the Lake
District and Cumbria.*
Price range:
low season £140-£420;
high season £230-£750.
Short breaks also available
November-March.
Ad See display advertisement on
page 112.

English Country Cottages

Department E105,
Grove Farm Barns,
Fakenham, Norfolk NR21 9NB
Tel: Fakenham (01328) 851155
for bookings or (01328) 864041
Dial-a-Brochure quoting

reference E105.
*Over 2,300 properties, from
cottages to castles, furnished and
equipped to the highest standards,
in fine coastal and countryside
locations.*
Price range:
low season 1996-1997
(2 November-15 March)
£177-£1,464;
high season 1997
(15 March-1 November)
£183-£1,530;
low season 1997-1998
(1 November-14 March)
£186-£1,611.
Short breaks also available.
Ad See display advertisement on
page 15.

Fairhaven Holiday Cottages

'Derby House',
123 Watling Street,
Gillingham,
Kent ME7 2YY
Tel: Medway (01634) 570157
Fax: (01634) 570157
*Offering an extensive selection of
personally inspected properties of
all shapes and sizes situated
throughout southern England - Kent
and Sussex a speciality - coast,
countryside and town.*
Price range:
low season (October-March)
from £150;
high season (April-September)
£700 max.
Short breaks also available.

Farm and Cottage Holidays

12 Fore Street,
Northam,
Bideford,
Devon EX39 1AW
Tel: Bideford (01237) 479698
Fax: (01237) 421512
*Self-catering or half-board holidays
in Devon, Cornwall and Somerset,
many of them farm-based. Some
with animals to feed, fishing, ponies
and other attractions.*

Price range:
low season from £105;
high season from £138.
Short breaks also available.
T Ad See display advertisement
on page 243.

Freedom Holiday Homes

Frittenden, Cranbrook,
Kent TN17 2EP
Tel: Frittenden (01580) 852251
Fax: (01580) 852455

*Converted barns, granaries, stables,
luxury houses and flats, pretty
cottages - all sizes, all prices -
throughout Kent and Sussex.*
Price range:
low season (November-April)
£75-£340;
high season (May-October)
£85-£650.
Short breaks also available.

Harrogate Holiday Cottages

The Old Post Office,
Kettlesing,
Harrogate,
North Yorkshire
Tel: Harrogate (01423) 772700
Fax: (01423) 772359
*We offer over 70 properties -
apartments, cottages, some with
swimming pools, in a variety of
locations in and around Harrogate,
York, Thirsk and the Dales.
Excellent value. Sleeping from 2-30
people.*
Price range:
low season (January-March and
October-December) £128-£305;
high season (July-August)
£142-£555.
Short breaks also available.
T

Helpful Holidays
Coombe, Ref 9,
Chagford,
Devon TQ13 8DF
Tel: Chagford (01647) 433593
Fax: (01647) 433694
Tremendous variety of over 400 cottages, houses, apartments - seaside, moorland, farmland - throughout Devon, Cornwall and Somerset, regularly inspected, fully described and personally star-rated in the free colour brochure which many say is the best.
Price range:
low season (October-June)
£87-£2,405;
high season (June-September)
£118-£2,707.
Short breaks available off-season.
T

Hideaways
Chapel House, Luke Street,
Berwick St John,
Shaftesbury,
Dorset SP7 0HQ
Tel: Donhead (01747) 828000
for brochures, (01747) 828170
for bookings
Fax: (01747) 829090
Wide range of high quality cottages, farmhouses, country homes and apartments, many of period character, in rural and coastal settings and in historic towns throughout the heart of England, south, south-east and south-west. Sleeping from 2-12 people.
Price range:
low season (November-April)
£140-£785;
high season (May-October)
£180-£1,400.
Short breaks also available.
T Ad See display advertisement on page 15.

Holidays
101 Coventry Road,
Coleshill,
Warwickshire B46 3EX

Tel: Coleshill (01675) 463588
A small selection of comfortable self-catering holiday cottages, houses and flats in beautiful North Cornwall. Seaside, town, and country locations. Mini breaks available out-of-season.
Price range:
low season (October-March)
£85-£250;
high season (July-August)
£175-£735.

Holidays In Lakeland
Stock Park Estate,
Newby Bridge,
Ulverston, Cumbria LA12 8AY
Tel: Newby Bridge (015395)
31549
Fax: (015395) 31591
A wide selection of properties situated throughout the Lake District National Park. Free colour brochure.
Price range:
low season (October-April)
£105-£560; high season
(May-September) £145-£760.
Short breaks also available off-season.

Hoseasons Holidays Ltd
H19, Sunway House,
Lowestoft,
Suffolk NR32 2LW
Tel: Lowestoft (01502) 500500
Wide range of fully equipped accommodation, in over 200 quiet locations or all-action holiday villages, seaside or countryside. Many open all year round, all to Hoseasons' high standards.
Price range: £65-£750.
Short breaks also available.
T

Ingrid Flute Holiday Accommodation Agency
Established since 1970
White Cottage,
Ravenscar,
Scarborough,

North Yorkshire YO13 0NE
Tel: Scarborough (01723)
870703
Fax: (01723) 870703
For the largest selection of carefully chosen holiday cottages in North Yorkshire, including Scarborough, Whitby, Robin Hood's Bay and Ryedale contact us for a free brochure. Properties available all year. Yorkshire and Humberside Tourist Board Member.
Price range:
low season (November-March)
£100-£500;
high season (July-August)
£170-£750.
Short breaks also available
November-March.

Keys Holidays
18 Station Road,
Sheringham, Norfolk NR26 8RE
Tel: Sheringham (01263) 823010
Fax: (01263) 821449
Selection of cottages, houses and bungalows for self-catering holidays. Sheringham and Cromer areas.
Price range:
low season (March-May)
£110-£220;
high season (July-September)
£185-£400.

Lakeland Cottage Company
Waterside House,
Newby Bridge,
Ulverston, Cumbria LA12 8AN
Tel: Newby Bridge (015395)
30024
Fax: (015395) 31932
South Lakes area - fine hand-picked properties, sleeping 2-18, including 17thC farmhouses, large house with four-poster, sauna and whirlpool bath, and house with lakeside gardens. All thoughtfully prepared and welcoming, with many extra services available. Help provided in choosing properties, with care taken in meeting individual needs. Open all year. Phone for brochure.

Price range: low season
(October-May) from £200;
high season (June-September)
£250-£1,200.
Short breaks also available.

Lyme Bay Holidays
Stanley House (TB12),
The Street, Charmouth,
Bridport, Dorset DT6 6PN
Tel: Charmouth (01297) 560755
(24 hours)
Fax: (01297) 560415
*Quality West Country cottages,
houses, flats etc, many in and
around Lyme Regis and Charmouth.
Close to the sea, stunning
countryside and famous for fossils.
Free brochure.*
Price range:
low season (October-April)
£120-£350; high season
(July-August) £200-£600 plus.
Out-of-season and short break
holidays available.

Mackay's Agency
30 Frederick Street,
Edinburgh EH2 2JR
Tel: Bookings (0131) 225 3539
24 hours brochure line
(0131) 226 4364
Fax: (0131) 226 5284
*A selection of cottages, houses and
farmhouses throughout the North
of England and the Borders.
Personally inspected properties,
ideal for family holidays.*
Price range:
low season (November-April)
£120-£225;
high season (May-October)
£175-£495.
Short breaks also available.
T

Manor Cottages
Village Farm,
Little Barrington, Burford,
Oxon OX18 4TE
Tel: Cotswold (01451) 844643
Fax: (01451) 844607

*A selection of country cottages and
town houses, furnished and
equipped to a high standard,
located throughout the
Gloucestershire and Oxfordshire
Cotswolds. Airport collection and
local car hire available.*
Price range:
low season (October-April)
£150-£650;
high season (May-September)
£200-£1,000.
Short breaks also available.
Ad See display advertisement on
page 128.

Meridian Holiday Homes
PO Box 9,
Thirsk,
North Yorkshire YO7 2YZ
Tel: Thirsk (01845) 597660
Fax: (01845) 597630
*Cottages throughout Yorkshire
including the city of York. Over 70
privately owned and cared for
cottages and houses, less than 1
hour travelling from York, some
within the city itself. All with central
heating, modern equipment and
tasteful furnishings. Full colour
brochure.*
Price range:
low season (November-March)
£155-£360;
high season (April-October and
Christmas) £175-£560.
Short breaks also available.

Miles & Son
Railway House,
2 Rempstone Road,
Swanage,
Dorset BH19 1DW
Tel: Swanage (01929) 423333
Fax: (01929) 427533
*Wide range of over 100 self-
catering fully equipped Houses,
Cottages, Bungalows and Flats
sleeping 2-14 in Swanage and the
surrounding areas of the Isle of
Purbeck. Visit beautiful Dorset with
its many places of interest.*

*Telephone for FREE colour
brochure.*
Price range:
low season (October-April)
£95-£800;
high season (May-September)
£135-£1,200.
Short breaks available out of
season.

Milkbere Cottage Holidays
Milkbere House,
14 Fore Street,
Seaton,
Devon EX12 2LA
Booking line: (01297) 20729
Brochure line: (01297) 22925
*Pretty cottages, modern bungalows,
seafront apartments and houses,
rustic farmhouses, excellently
situated on the Devon/Dorset
border, both coast and countryside.*
Price range:
low season (September-April)
£97-£260;
high season (May-August)
£120-£580.
Short breaks also available.
T Ad See display advertisement
on page 244.

Mrs Jane Good Ltd
Blandings,
Hasketon, Woodbridge,
Suffolk IP13 6JA
Tel: Woodbridge (01394)
382770
Fax: (01394) 380914
*A good selection of self-catering
houses, cottages and flats in Suffolk
and North Essex. All well equipped
and furnished to a high standard
and carefully maintained by the
individual owners.*
Price range:
low season (November-March)
£95-£400;
high season (April-October)
£140-£750.
Short breaks also available.
Ad See display advertisement on
page 196.

Norfolk Country Cousins
Point House, Ridlington,
North Walsham,
Norfolk NR28 9TY
Tel: Walcott (01692) 650286
Fax: (01692) 650180
Relaxing cottages chosen for their
charm and location as well as
comfort. Coastal and countryside in
Norfolk, sleeping 2-12. Guided boat
trip on Broads available and bike
hire too. An afternoon with an
English family can be arranged.
Price range:

low season (October-April)
£110-£550;
high season £165-£900.
Short breaks available out of
season.

Perfect Places - London
53 Margravine Gardens,
London W6 8RN
Tel: (0181) 748 6095
Fax: (0181) 741 4213
One and two bedroom apartments

located in Chelsea, Knightsbridge,
Kensington and Westminster. Linen
and towels included. Cots and extra
beds available at a small additional
charge.
Price range:
low season (November-March)
£400-£600;
high season (April-October)
£450-£1200.
Short breaks also available.
T

COUNTRY CODE

Always follow the Country Code
Enjoy the countryside and respect
its life and work   Guard against all
risk of fire   Fasten all gates   Keep
your dogs under close control   Keep
to public paths across farmland   Use
gates and stiles to cross fences, hedges
and walls   Leave livestock, crops and
machinery alone   Take your litter home
Help to keep all water clean
Protect wildlife, plants and trees
Take special care on country roads
Make no unnecessary noise

ENQUIRY COUPONS

To help you obtain further information
about advertisers and accommodation featured in
this guide you will find enquiry coupons at the back.
Send these directly to the establishments
in which you are interested.
Remember to complete both sides of the coupon.

INFORMATION PAGES

National Grading and Classification Scheme   296

General Advice and Information   297

About the Guide Entries   299

Events for 1997   301

Enquiry Coupons   307

Town Index   313

Index to Advertisers   317

Mileage Chart   318

Reader Survey   319

Location Maps   321

InterCity Rail Map   335

NATIONAL GRADING AND CLASSIFICATION SCHEME

Sure Signs

The Tourist Boards in Britain operate a National Quality Grading and Classification Scheme for all types of accommodation. The purpose of the scheme is to identify and promote those establishments that the public can use with confidence. The system of facility classification and quality grading also acknowledges those that provide a wider range of facilities and services and higher quality standards.

Over 30,000 places to stay are inspected under the scheme and offer the reassurance of a national grading and classification.

For self-catering holiday homes there are five classification bands: ONE to FIVE KEY. Quite simply, the more Keys, the wider the range of facilities and equipment provided.

Quality Grading

To help you find accommodation that offers even higher standards than those required for a Key rating, there are four levels of quality grading, using the terms DE LUXE, HIGHLY COMMENDED, COMMENDED and APPROVED.

Wherever you see a national grading and classification sign, you can be sure that a Tourist Board inspector has been there before you, checking the place on your behalf - and will be there again, because every place with a national rating is inspected annually.

Quality grades are based on an assessment of a wide variety of items, ranging from the appearance of the building and tidiness of the garden to the quality of the furnishings, fittings and floor coverings. Everything that impinges on the experience of a guest is included in the assessment.

Tourist Board inspectors receive careful training to enable them to apply the quality standards consistently and fairly. Only those facilities and services provided are assessed, and due consideration is given to the style and nature of the establishment.

All types of establishment, whatever their Key classification, can achieve a high quality grade if the facilities and services they provide, however limited in range, are to a high quality standard.

The quality grade that is awarded to an establishment is a reflection of the overall standard, taking everything into account. It is a balanced view of what is provided and, as such, cannot acknowledge individual areas of excellence.

Quality grades are not intended to indicate value for money. A high quality product can be over-priced; a product of modest quality, if offered at a low price, can represent good value. The information provided by the combination of the classification and quality grade will enable you to determine for yourself what represents good value for money.

All Inspected

All holiday homes listed in this guide have been inspected or are awaiting inspection under the National Grading and Classification Scheme. The ratings that appear in the accommodation entries were correct at the time of going to press but are subject to change. If no rating appears in that entry it means that the inspection had not been carried out by the time of going to press.

An information leaflet giving full details of the National Grading and Classification Scheme - which also covers hotels, motels, guesthouses, inns, B&Bs, farmhouses, motorway lodges and caravan, chalet and camping parks - is available from any Tourist Information Centre.

GENERAL ADVICE AND INFORMATION

Making a Booking

When enquiring about accommodation, make sure you check prices and other important details. You will also need to state your requirements, clearly and precisely - for example:

• **Arrival and departure dates,** with acceptable alternatives if appropriate.

• **The accommodation you need.**

• **Number of people in your party,** and the ages of any children.

• **Special requirements,** such as ground-floor bathroom, garden, cot.

Booking by letter

Misunderstandings can easily happen over the telephone, so we strongly advise you to confirm your booking in writing if there is time.

If you decide to enquire in writing in the first place, you might find it helpful to use the Accommodation Coupons on pages 307-310, which can be cut out and posted to the places of your choice.

Remember to include your name and address, and a stamped self-addressed envelope, or an international reply coupon if you are writing from outside Britain.

Please note that the English Tourist Board does not make reservations - you should write direct to the accommodation.

Deposits

When you book your self-catering holiday, the proprietor will normally ask you to pay a deposit immediately, and then to pay the full balance before your holiday date.

The reason for asking you to pay in advance is to safeguard the proprietor in case you decide to cancel at a late stage, or simply do not turn up. He or she may have turned down other bookings on the strength of yours, and may find it hard to re-let if you cancel.

Cancellations

Legal contract

When you accept accommodation that is offered to you, by telephone or in writing, you enter a legally binding contract with the proprietor.

This means that if you cancel your booking, fail to take up the accommodation or leave early, you will probably forfeit your deposit, and may expect to be charged the balance at the end of the period booked if the place cannot be re-let.

Where you have already paid the full amount before cancelling, the proprietor is likely to retain the money. If the accommodation is re-let, the proprietor will make a refund, normally less the amount of the deposit.

And remember, if you book by telephone and are asked for your credit card number, you should check whether the proprietor intends charging your credit card account should you later cancel your reservation. A proprietor should not be able to charge your credit card account with a cancellation unless he or she has made this clear at the time of your booking and you have agreed. However, to avoid later disputes, we suggest you check with the proprietor whether he or she intends to charge you credit card account if you cancel.

Insurance

There are so many reasons why you might have to cancel your holiday, which is why we strongly advise people to take out a cancellation insurance policy. In fact, many self-catering agencies now insist their customers take out a policy when they book their holiday.

Code of Conduct

All the places featured in this guide have agreed to observe the following Codes of Conduct:

1 To ensure high standards of courtesy and cleanliness, catering and service appropriate to the type of establishment.

2 To describe fairly to all visitors and prospective visitors the amenities, facilities and services provided by the establishment, whether by advertisement, brochure, word of mouth or any

other means. To allow visitors to see accommodation, if requested, before booking.

3 To make clear to visitors exactly what is included in all prices quoted, including service charges, taxes and other surcharges. Details of charges, if any, for heating or additional service of facilities should also be made clear.

4 To adhere to, and not to exceed, prices current at time of occupation for accommodation or other services.

5 To advise visitors at the time of booking, and subsequently of any change, if the accommodation offered is in an unconnected annexe, or similar, or by boarding out; and to indicate the location of such accommodation and any difference in comfort or amenities from accommodation in the main establishment.

6 To give each visitor, on request, details of payments due and a receipt if required.

7 To deal promptly and courteously with all enquiries, requests, reservations, correspondence and complaints from visitors.

8 To allow an English Tourist Board representative reasonable access to the establishment, on request, to confirm that the Code of Conduct is being observed.

Comments and Complaints

Information
The proprietors themselves supply the descriptions of their establishments and other information for the listings, and they pay to have their entries included in the guide. They have

all signed a declaration that their information conforms to the Trade Description Acts 1968 and 1972. All the places featured in the guide have also been inspected or have applied for inspection under the National Grading and Classification Scheme.

The English Tourist Board cannot guarantee accuracy of information in this guide, and accepts no responsibility for any error or misrepresentation. All liability for loss, disappointment, negligence or other damage caused by reliance on the information contained in this guide, or in the event of bankruptcy or liquidation or cessation of trade of any company, individual or firm mentioned, is hereby excluded.

We strongly recommend that you carefully check prices and other details when you book your accommodation.

Problems
Of course, we hope you will not have cause for complaint, but problems do occur from time to time.

If you are dissatisfied with anything, make your complaint to the management immediately. Then the management can take action at once to investigate the matter and put things right. The longer you leave a complaint, the harder it is to deal with it effectively.

In certain circumstances, the English Tourist Board may look into complaints. However, the Board has no statutory control over establishments or their methods of operating. The Board

cannot become involved in legal or contractual matters.

Feedback Questionnaire
We find it very helpful to receive your comments about the places featured in *Where to Stay* and your suggestions on how to improve the guide. Please send us your views using the Customer Feedback Questionnaire on pages 319-320 - we would like to hear from you.

Return it to: Department AS, English Tourist Board, Thames Tower, Black's Road, Hammersmith, London W6 9EL.

ABOUT THE GUIDE ENTRIES

Locations

Places to stay are listed under the town, city or village where they are located. If a place is out in the countryside, you will find it listed under the nearest village or town.

Town names are listed alphabetically within each regional section of the guide, along with the name of the county they fall under, and their map reference.

Map references
These refer to the colour location maps at the back of the guide. The first figure shown is the map number, the following letter and figure indicate the grid reference on the map.

Some entries were included just before the guide went to press, so they do not appear on the maps.

Addresses
County names, which appear in the town headings, are not normally repeated in the entries. When you are writing, you should of course make sure you use the full address and postcode.

Telephone Numbers
Telephone numbers are listed below the accommodation address for each entry. Area codes are shown in brackets, and the exchange name is also included (before the code) if it differs from that of the town under which a place is listed.

Price

The prices shown in *Where to Stay 1997* are only a general guide; they were supplied to us by proprietors in summer 1996. Remember, changes may occur after the guide goes to press, so we strongly advise you to check prices when you book your accommodation.

Prices are shown in pounds sterling and include VAT where applicable. The prices shown are per unit per week.

Also remember that prices may be higher in summer and during school holidays, and lower in the autumn, winter and spring.

Opening Period

All places should be open all year, except where a specific opening period is indicated in an entry.

Symbols

The at-a-glance symbols included at the end of each entry show many of the facilities and equipment available at each place.

You will find the key to these symbols on the back cover flap.

Open out the flap and you can check the meanings of the symbols as you go.

Smoking

Some places prefer not to accommodate smokers and in such cases the listing information makes this clear.

Pets

Many places accept guests with pets, but we do advise you to check this when you book, and ask about any extra charges or any rules about exactly where your pet is allowed.

Some establishments do not accept dogs at all, and these places are marked with the symbol ✖.

Visitors from overseas must not bring pets of any kind into Britain, unless they are prepared for the animals to go into lengthy quarantine. Because of the continuing threat of rabies, the penalties for ignoring these regulations are extremely severe.

Credit and Charge Cards

The credit and charge cards accepted by a place are listed immediately above the line of symbols at the end of each entry. The abbreviations used are:
Access - Access/Eurocard/ Mastercard
Visa - Visa/Barclaycard
Diners - Diners
Amex - American Express
Switch/Delta - Direct debit cards
If you do plan to pay by card, check that the establishment will take your card before you book.

Some proprietors will charge you a higher rate if you pay by credit card rather than cash or cheque. The difference is to cover the percentage paid by the proprietor to the credit card company.

If you are planning to pay by credit card, you may want to ask whether it would, in fact, be cheaper to pay by cheque or cash. When you book by telephone, you may be asked for your credit card number as

'confirmation'. But remember, the proprietor may then charge your credit card account if you cancel your booking. See under Cancellations on page 297.

CHECK THE MAPS

The colour maps at the back of this guide show all the cities, towns and villages for which you will find accommodation entries.

Refer to the town index to find the page on which it is listed.

USE YOUR *i*'s

There are more than 550 Tourist Information Centres throughout England offering friendly help with accommodation and holiday ideas as well as suggestions of places to visit and things to do. You'll find the address of your nearest Tourist Information Centre in your local Phone Book.

ENQUIRY COUPONS

To help you obtain further information about advertisers and accommodation featured in this guide you will find enquiry coupons at the back. Send these directly to the establishments in which you are interested. Remember to complete both sides of the coupon.

EVENTS FOR 1997

This is a selection of the many cultural, sporting and other events that will be taking place throughout England during 1997. Dates marked with an asterisk* were provisional at the time of going to press.

January 1997

2-13 January*
43rd London International Boat Show
Earls Court Exhibition Centre,
Warwick Road, London SW5
Contact: (01784) 473377

6 January
Old Custom: Haxey Hood Game
The Village, Haxey,
North Lincolnshire
Contact: (01427) 752845

9-12 January
Autosports International
National Exhibition Centre,
Birmingham, West Midlands
Contact: (0171) 402 2555

February 1997

7-16 February
Great St Valentine's Fair
City Centre,
Leeds, West Yorkshire
Contact: (0113) 247 4293

9 February*
Chinese New Year Celebrations: Year of the Ox
Centered on Gerrard Street
and Leicester Square,
London, WC2
Contact: (0171) 734 5161

9 February-16 March
Wildlife Photographer of the Year 1995
Lancaster City Museum,
Market Square,
Lancaster, Lancashire
Contact: (01524) 841692

9-14 February*
The Wordsworth Winter School
Dove Cottage & Wordsworth
Museum, Town End,
Grasmere, Cumbria
Contact: (015394) 35544

20-23 February
Harrogate Antique and Fine Art Fair
Royal Baths Assembly Rooms,
Crescent Road, Harrogate,
North Yorkshire
Contact: (01823) 323363

March 1997

6-9 March
Crufts Dog Show
National Exhibition Centre,
Birmingham, West Midlands
Contact: (0171) 4936651

7-9 March
Working Days
Abbeydale Industrial Hamlet,
Abbeydale Road South,
Sheffield
Contact: (0114) 236 7731

11-13 March
Cheltenham Gold Cup National Hunt Racing Festival
Cheltenham Racecourse,
Cheltenham, Gloucestershire
Contact: (01242) 513014

13 March-6 April
Daily Mail Ideal Home Exhibition
Earls Court Exhibition Centre,
Warwick Road,
London SW5
Contact: (01895) 677677

22 March-6 April
Easter Activities
Salford Museum & Art Gallery,
Peel Park, The Crescent,
Salford, Greater Manchester
Contact: (0161) 736 2649

28 March
Old Custom: Pace Egg Plays
Various venues in and around
Hebden Bridge,
West Yorkshire
Contact: (01422) 843831

29 March*
Oxford and Cambridge Boat Race
River Thames, London

April 1997

3-5 April
Grand National Meeting
Aintree Racecourse,
Ormskirk Road,
Aintree, Merseyside
Contact: (0151) 523 2600

4 April
Birkenhead Park 150th Anniversary
Birkenhead Park, Merseyside

8 April
Old Custom: World Coal Carrying Championship
Royal Oak Public House,
Owl Lane, Ossett,
West Yorkshire

11-13 April
2nd North East Knitting and Needlecraft Exhibition
Leeds University Exhibition
& Conference Centre,
Willow Terrace Road,
Leeds, West Yorkshire
Contact: (0117) 970 1370

11-13 April
County Spring Flower Show - 100th Anniversary
The Lost Gardens of Heligan,
Heligan, Pentewan, Cornwall
Contact: (01872) 74057

13 April*
London Marathon
Greenwich Park,
London SE10
Contact: (0171) 620 4117

19-20 April
Bike Expo 97
Sheffield Arena,
Broughton Lane,
Sheffield, South Yorkshire
Contact: (01484) 605555

26-27 April
Centennial Orchid Society
The Floral Halls,
Marine Parade, Southport,
Merseyside

26-27 April
Rainbow Craft Fair
Meols Hall, Churchtown,
Southport, Merseyside
Contact: (01704) 28326

27 April
Three Peaks Race
Playing Field,
Horton-in-Ribblesdale,
North Yorkshire
Contact: (0113) 258 5586

May 1997

2-3 May
Nottinghamshire County Show
Newark and Notts Show Ground,
Winthorpe, Nottinghamshire
Contact: (01636) 610642

2-4 May
Cleethorpes Beer Festival
Winter Gardens, Kingsway,
Cleethorpes,
North East Lincolnshire
Contact: (01472) 692925

3 May
Gawthorpe Maypole Procession
High Street, Gawthorpe,
Ossett, West Yorkshire

3-5 May*
Rochester Sweeps Festival
Various venues,
Rochester, Kent
Contact: (01634) 843666

3-5 May*
Spalding Flower Parade and Springfields Country Fair
Springfields Show Gardens,
Spalding, Lincolnshire
Contact: (01775) 724843

3-25 May
Brighton International Festival
Various venues,
Brighton, East Sussex
Contact: (01273) 676926

4-5 May
Kids International
Telford Town Park,

Telford, Shropshire
Contact: (01952) 203009

8-11 May
Living Crafts Exhibition
Hatfield House, Hatfield,
Hertfordshire
Contact: (01582) 761235

10-25 May
Bournemouth International Festival
Various venues,
Bournemouth, Dorset
Contact: (01202) 297327

16-18 May
Keswick Jazz Festival
Keswick, Cumbria
Contact: (01900) 602122

17 May
Football: FA Challenge Cup Final
Wembley Stadium, London
Contact: (0171) 402 7151

20-23 May
Chelsea Flower Show
Royal Hospital Chelsea,
Royal Hospital Road,
London SW3

24-25 May
Air Fete 97
RAF Mildenhall, Suffolk

24 May-9 June
Salisbury Festival
Various venues,
Salisbury, Wiltshire
Contact: (01722) 323883

25-26 May
Southend Air Show
Western Esplanade,
Southend-on-Sea, Essex

25-26 May*
**North Shields Fishquay
Festival**
North Shields, Tyne and Wear
Contact: (0191) 257 5544

26 May
**Northumberland County
Show**
Tynedale Park Rugby Ground,
Corbridge, Northumberland
Contact: (01434) 344443

26 May
Surrey County Show
Stoke Park, Guildford, Surrey
Contact: (01483) 414651

28-29 May
**Corpus Christi Carpet of
Flowers and Floral Festival**
Cathedral of Our Lady
and St Philip Howard,
Cathedral House,
Arundel, West Sussex
Contact: (01903) 882297

28-31 May
**The Royal Bath
and West Show**
The Royal Bath & West
Showground,
Shepton Mallet, Somerset
Contact: (01749) 822200

29-31 May*
Dickens Festival
Various venues,
Rochester, Kent
Contact: (01634) 843666

30 May-1 June
**Great Garden and
Countryside Festival**
Holker Hall and Gardens,
Cark in Cartmel, Cumbria
Contact: (015395) 58838

June 1997

1 June*
**229th Royal Academy
Summer Exhibition**
Royal Academy of Arts,
Burlington House, Piccadilly,
London W1
Contact: (0171) 494 5615

5-7 June
**South of England
Agricultural Show**
South of England Showground,
Ardingly, West Sussex
Contact: (01444) 892048

8 June
Open Day
Myerscough College,
Bilsborrow, Lancashire
Contact: (01995) 640611

13-29 June
**50th Aldeburgh Foundation
of Music and the Arts**
Snape Maltings Concert Hall,
Snape, Suffolk
Contact: (01728) 452935

14 June*
Durham Regatta
River Wear, Durham
Contact: (0191) 383 1594

14 June*
**Trooping the Colour - The
Queen's Birthday Parade**
Horse Guards Parade,
London SW1
Contact: (0171) 414 2479

25-26 June
Royal Norfolk Show 97
The Showground, Dereham Road,
Norwich, Norfolk
Contact: (01603) 748931

28-29 June
Middlesex Show
Uxbridge Showground,
Park Road, Uxbridge, London
Contact: (01895) 252131

28-29 June
**Royal Air Force Waddington
Air Show**
RAF Waddington, Lincolnshire
Contact: (01522) 726100

28-29 June
Vintage Vehicle Rally
Meols Hall, Churchtown,
Southport, Merseyside
Contact: (01704) 28326

30 June-3 July
The Royal Show
National Agricultural Centre,
Stoneleigh Park, Warwickshire
Contact: (01203) 696969

July 1997

1-31 July*
Hull International Festival
Various venues, Hull,
Kingston-upon-Hull
Contact: (01482) 615623

2-6 July
Henley Royal Regatta
Henley-on-Thames, Oxfordshire
Contact: (01491) 572153/4

3-20 July
The Exeter Festival
Various venues, Exeter, Devon
Contact: (01392) 265118

5-6 July
International Kite Festival
Northern Playing Fields,
Washington, Tyne and Wear
Contact: (0191) 514235

6-22 July
Chichester Festivities
Various venues,
Chichester, West Sussex
Contact: (01243) 785718

8-10 July
Great Yorkshire Show
Great Yorkshire Showground,
Harrogate, North Yorkshire
Contact: (01423) 561536

9-12 July
Claremont Fete Champetre
Claremont Landscape Garden,
Portsmouth Road,
Esher, Surrey
Contact: (01372) 453401

11-13 July*
British Grand Prix 97
Silverstone,
Northamptonshire
Contact: (01327) 857271

11, 12, 13 July
Swanage Jazz Festival
Various venues,
Swanage, Dorset
Contact: (01929) 422885

11-20 July
**"Ways with Words"
Literature Festival**
Dartington Hall,
Dartington, Devon
Contact: (01803) 867311

12-13 July
Durham County Show
Clondyke Garden Centre,
Lambton Park,
Chester-Le-Street, Durham
Contact: (0191) 3885459

15-26 July
The Royal Tournament
Earls Court Exhibition Centre,
Warwick Road,
London SW5
Contact: (0171) 370 8202

19 July
Cumberland County Show
Rickerby Park,
Carlisle, Cumbria
Contact: (01228) 560364

19-20 July
Holkham Country Fair
Holkham Hall,
Wells-next-the-Sea, Norfolk
Contact: (01328) 830367

19-27 July
Whitstable Oyster Festival
Whitstable Harbour, Kent
Contact: (01227) 273570

19 July-2 August
King's Lynn Festival 97
King's Lynn Arts Centre,
King Street,
King's Lynn, Norfolk
Contact: (01553) 774725

25 July
**Horse Racing: Glorious
Goodwood**
Goodwood Racecourse,
Goodwood, West Sussex
Contact: (01243) 774107

26-27 July
Cumbria Steam Gathering
Cark Airfield, Flookburgh,
Cumbria
Contact: (015242) 71584

26-31 July*
**Teesside International
Eisteddfod**
Middlesbrough Festival Town
Centre,
Middlesbrough,
Tees Valley
Contact: (01642) 327088

1-8 August
**43rd Sidmouth International
Festival of Folk Arts**
The Arena and other Venues,
Sidmouth, Devon

2-9 August
Cowes Week
Cowes, Isle of Wight
Contact: (01983) 293303

2-17 August
**International Gilbert and
Sullivan Festival**
Buxton Opera House,
Water Street,
Buxton, Derbyshire
Contact: (01422) 359161

6-7 August
167th Bakewell Show
The Showground, Coombs Road,
Bakewell, Derbyshire
Contact: (01629) 812736

8-10 August
**Bristol International Balloon
Fiesta**
Ashton Court Estate,
Long Ashton, Bristol
Contact: (0117) 953 5884

8-10 August
**Lowther Horse Driving
Trials and Country Fair**
Lowther Castle,
Lowther, Cumbria
Contact: (01931) 712378

9-16 August*
**Billingham International
Folklore Festival**
Queensway, Billingham,
Tees Valley
Contact: (01642) 558212

15-16 August
Shrewsbury Flower Show
Quarry Park, Shrewsbury,
Shropshire
Contact: (01743) 364051

15-17 August
**International Birdwatching
Fair**
Egleton Reserve, Rutland Water,
Oakham, Leicestershire
Contact: (01572) 770651

15-17 August
**Northampton Hot Air
Balloon Festival**
Northampton Racecourse,
St. George's Avenue,
Northampton, Northamptonshire
Contact: (01604) 233500

16-22 August
Whitby Folk Week
Various venues,
Whitby, North Yorkshire
Contact: (01757) 708424

20 August
Weymouth Carnival
The Seafront, Weymouth, Dorset
Contact: (01305) 772444

20-22 August
**Ladies British Amateur
Stroke Play Championships**
Silloth-on-Solway Golf Club,
The Clubhouse, Silloth, Cumbria
Contact: (016973) 31304

21-26 August
**International Beatles
Festival**
Various venues,
Liverpool, Merseyside
Contact: (0151) 236 9091

22-25 August
Clacton Jazz Festival
Various venues,
Clacton-on-Sea, Essex
Contact: (01255) 425501

23-30 August
Bude Jazz Festival
Various venues, Bude, Cornwall
Contact: (01684) 566956

24 August
**Leicester International Air
Display**
Leicester Airport, Gartree Road,
Leicester, Leicestershire
Contact: (0116) 259 2360

24-25 August
Eye Show
Eye Show Ground, Dragon Hill,
Eye, Suffolk
Contact: (01379) 870224

25 August
Mathew Street Festival
Cavern Quarter,
Liverpool City Centre,
Mathew Street,
Liverpool
Contact: (0151) 236 9091

27-31 August
Great Dorset Steam Fair
South Down,
Tarrant Hinton, Dorset
Contact: (01258) 860361

28 August
**Buckinghamshire County
Show**
Weedon Park, Weedon,
Aylesbury, Buckinghamshire
Contact: (01296) 83734

28 August
**Muncaster Country Fair and
Sheepdog Trials**
Muncaster, Ravenglass,
Cumbria
Contact: (01229) 717608

29-31 August
Shepway Festival
The Leas, Folkestone, Kent
Contact: (01303) 852321

30 August
**Hesket Newmarket
Agricultural Show**
Hog House Field, Hudscales,
Hesket Newmarket, Cumbria
Contact: (016974) 78663

September 1997

4 September
**The Blenheim International
Horse Trials**
Blenheim Palace,
Woodstock, Oxfordshire
Contact: (01993) 813335

5-7 September
Swanage Folk Festival
Various venues,
Swanage, Dorset
Contact: (01929) 427490

6-7 September
Chatsworth Country Fair
Chatsworth House and Garden,
Bakewell, Derbyshire
Contact: (01328) 830367

6-7 September
**Kirby Lonsdale Victorian
Fair**
Kirkby Lonsdale,
Cumbria
Contact: (015242) 71237

13 September
Romsey Show
Broadlands Park,
Romsey, Hampshire
Contact: (01794) 517521

13-14 September
**Essex Steam Rally and
Craft Fair**
Barleylands Farm Museum,
Billericay, Essex
Contact: (01268) 532253

13-15 September*
Stanhope Agricultural Show
Unthank Park,
Stanhope, Durham
Contact: (01833) 650879

13-21 September
**Southampton International
Boat Show**
Western Esplanade,
Southampton, Hampshire
Contact: (01784) 473377

14-20 September
**Egremont Crab Fair
and Sports**
Baybarrow, Egremont, Cumbria
Contact: (01946) 821554

20-21 September
**Newbury and Royal County
of Berkshire Show**
Newbury Showground,
Chieveley, Berkshire
Contact: (01635) 247111

28 September
Urswick Rushbearing
Urswick Church, Urswick,
Ulverston, Cumbria

October 1997

1-5 October
Horse of the Year Show
Wembley Arena, Empire Way,
Wembley, London
Contact: (01203) 693088

9-19 October
**Norfolk and Norwich
Festival 97**
Various venues,
Norwich, Norfolk
Contact: (01603) 614921

10-18 October*
Hull Fair
Walton Street Fairground, Hull,
Kingston-upon-Hull
Contact: (01482) 615623

10-19 October
**Cheltenham Festival of
Literature**
Town Hall, Imperial Square,
Cheltenham, Gloucestershire
Contact: (01242) 521621

11-25 October
Canterbury Festival
Various venues,
Canterbury, Kent
Contact: (01227) 455600

12 October
**World Conker
Championships**
The Village Green,
Ashton, Northamptonshire

16-26 October
The London Motor Show
Earls Court Exhibition Centre,
Warwick Road, London SW5

19 October
**Trafalgar Day Parade -
The Sea Cadet Corps**
Trafalgar Square, London WC2
Contact: (0171) 928 8978

November 1997

1 November
Grand Firework Spectacular
Leeds Castle, Leeds, Kent
Contact: (01622) 765400

1 November
Firework Displays
Christchurch Park,
Ipswich, Suffolk

1 November
**Bonfire and Firework
Display**
Meols Hall, Churchtown,
Southport, Merseyside
Contact: (01704) 28326

6 November
**Bridgwater Guy Fawkes
Carnival**
Town Centre,
Bridgwater, Somerset
Contact: (01278) 425344

8 November
Lord Mayor's Show
City of London
Contact: (01992) 505306

20 November
**Biggest Liar in the World
Competition**
Bridge Inn, Wasdale,
Santon Bridge, Cumbria
Contact: (01946) 67575

December 1997

18-22 December
**Olympia International
Showjumping Championships**
Olympia, Hammersmith Road,
London W14
Contact: (0171) 370 8202

30 December*
**Carlisle Races Christmas
Meet**
Carlisle Racecourse,
Durdar, Cumbria
Contact: (016973) 42634

31 December
Allendale Baal Festival
Market Square, Allendale,
Northumberland
Contact: (01434) 683763

ACCOMMODATION COUPONS

► *Complete this coupon and mail it direct to the establishment in which you are interested. Do not send it to the English Tourist Board. Remember to enclose a stamped addressed envelope (or international reply coupon).*

► *Tick as appropriate and complete the reverse side if you are interested in making a booking.*

❏ *Please send me a brochure or further information, and details of prices charged.*
❏ *Please advise me, as soon as possible, if accommodation is available as detailed overleaf.*

Name: _____ (BLOCK CAPITALS)

Address: _____

_____

_____ Postcode: _____

Telephone number: _____ Date: _____

Where to Stay 1997
Self-Catering Holiday Homes

► *Complete this coupon and mail it direct to the establishment in which you are interested. Do not send it to the English Tourist Board. Remember to enclose a stamped addressed envelope (or international reply coupon).*

► *Tick as appropriate and complete the reverse side if you are interested in making a booking.*

❏ *Please send me a brochure or further information, and details of prices charged.*
❏ *Please advise me, as soon as possible, if accommodation is available as detailed overleaf.*

Name: _____ (BLOCK CAPITALS)

Address: _____

_____

_____ Postcode: _____

Telephone number: _____ Date: _____

Where to Stay 1997
Self-Catering Holiday Homes

ACCOMMODATION COUPONS

▶ **Complete this side if you are interested in making a booking.**

▶ **Please read the information on pages 297–300 before confirming any booking.**

Please advise me if accommodation is available as detailed below.

From (date of arrival): _____   To (date of departure): _____

or alternatively from: _____   To: _____

Adults _____   Children _____   (ages _____)
Please give the number of people and ages of children

Accommodation required: _____

_____

Meals required: _____

Other/special requirements: _____

▶ **Please enclose a stamped addressed envelope (or international reply coupon).**

▶ **Complete this side if you are interested in making a booking.**

▶ **Please read the information on pages 297–300 before confirming any booking.**

Please advise me if accommodation is available as detailed below.

From (date of arrival): _____   To (date of departure): _____

or alternatively from: _____   To: _____

Adults _____   Children _____   (ages _____)
Please give the number of people and ages of children

Accommodation required: _____

_____

Meals required: _____

Other/special requirements: _____

▶ **Please enclose a stamped addressed envelope (or international reply coupon).**

ACCOMMODATION COUPONS

► *Complete this coupon and mail it direct to the establishment in which you are interested. Do not send it to the English Tourist Board. Remember to enclose a stamped addressed envelope (or international reply coupon).*

► *Tick as appropriate and complete the reverse side if you are interested in making a booking.*

❏ *Please send me a brochure or further information, and details of prices charged.*
❏ *Please advise me, as soon as possible, if accommodation is available as detailed overleaf.*

Name: _____ (BLOCK CAPITALS)

Address: _____

_____

_____

Postcode: _____

Telephone number: _____ Date: _____

Where to Stay 1997
Self-Catering Holiday Homes

English Tourist Board

► *Complete this coupon and mail it direct to the establishment in which you are interested. Do not send it to the English Tourist Board. Remember to enclose a stamped addressed envelope (or international reply coupon).*

► *Tick as appropriate and complete the reverse side if you are interested in making a booking.*

❏ *Please send me a brochure or further information, and details of prices charged.*
❏ *Please advise me, as soon as possible, if accommodation is available as detailed overleaf.*

Name: _____ (BLOCK CAPITALS)

Address: _____

_____

_____

Postcode: _____

Telephone number: _____ Date: _____

Where to Stay 1997
Self-Catering Holiday Homes

English Tourist Board

309

ACCOMMODATION COUPONS

► *Complete this side if you are interested in making a booking.*

► *Please read the information on pages 297-300 before confirming any booking.*

Please advise me if accommodation is available as detailed below.

From (date of arrival): _____   To (date of departure): _____

or alternatively from: _____   To: _____

Adults _____   Children _____   (ages _____)
Please give the number of people and ages of children

Accommodation required: _____

_____

_____

Meals required: _____

Other/special requirements: _____

► *Please enclose a stamped addressed envelope (or international reply coupon).*

► *Complete this side if you are interested in making a booking.*

► *Please read the information on pages 297-300 before confirming any booking.*

Please advise me if accommodation is available as detailed below.

From (date of arrival): _____   To (date of departure): _____

or alternatively from: _____   To: _____

Adults _____   Children _____   (ages _____)
Please give the number of people and ages of children

Accommodation required: _____

_____

_____

Meals required: _____

Other/special requirements: _____

► *Please enclose a stamped addressed envelope (or international reply coupon).*

ADVERTISEMENT COUPONS

► **Complete this coupon and mail it direct to the advertiser from whom you would like to receive further information. Do not send it to the English Tourist Board.**

To (advertiser's name): _____

Please send me a brochure or further information on the following, as advertised by you in the English Tourist Board's **Where to Stay 1997** Guide:

_____

_____

► **Complete this coupon and mail it direct to the advertiser from whom you would like to receive further information. Do not send it to the English Tourist Board.**

To (advertiser's name): _____

Please send me a brochure or further information on the following, as advertised by you in the English Tourist Board's **Where to Stay 1997** Guide:

_____

_____

► **Complete this coupon and mail it direct to the advertiser from whom you would like to receive further information. Do not send it to the English Tourist Board.**

To (advertiser's name): _____

Please send me a brochure or further information on the following, as advertised by you in the English Tourist Board's **Where to Stay 1997** Guide:

_____

_____

ADVERTISEMENT COUPONS

Name: _____ (BLOCK CAPITALS)

Address: _____

_____

Postcode: _____

Telephone Number: _____ Date: _____

Where to Stay 1997
Self-Catering Holiday Homes

English Tourist Board

Name: _____ (BLOCK CAPITALS)

Address: _____

_____

Postcode: _____

Telephone Number: _____ Date: _____

Where to Stay 1997
Self-Catering Holiday Homes

English Tourist Board

Name: _____ (BLOCK CAPITALS)

Address: _____

_____

Postcode: _____

Telephone Number: _____ Date: _____

Where to Stay 1997
Self-Catering Holiday Homes

English Tourist Board

TOWN INDEX

The following cities, towns and villages all have accommodation listed in this guide.

If the place where you wish to stay is not shown, the location maps (starting on page 321)

will help you to find somewhere suitable in the same area.

A — page no

Abberley *Hereford and Worcester*	118
Abbotsbury *Dorset*	203
Abingdon *Oxfordshire*	252
Akeld *Northumberland*	62
Alcester *Warwickshire*	118
Aldeburgh *Suffolk*	178
Alderton *Gloucestershire*	118
Aldsworth *Gloucestershire*	119
Alford *Lincolnshire*	156
Alhampton *Somerset*	203
Alkmonton *Derbyshire*	156
Allendale *Northumberland*	62
Allerford *Somerset*	203
Alnmouth *Northumberland*	62
Alnwick *Northumberland*	63
Alston *Cumbria*	32
Alstonefield *Staffordshire*	119
Altham *Lancashire*	84
Alton *Hampshire*	252
Alverstoke *Hampshire*	252
Ambleside *Cumbria*	32
Amersham *Buckinghamshire*	252
Amesbury *Wiltshire*	204
Amotherby *North Yorkshire*	94
Ampleforth *North Yorkshire*	94
Appleby-in-Westmorland *Cumbria*	34
Appledore *Kent*	274
Appleton-le-Moors *North Yorkshire*	94
Arundel *West Sussex*	274
Ashbourne *Derbyshire*	156
Ashburton *Devon*	204
Ashdon *Essex*	178
Ashford *Kent*	274
Ashford in the Water *Derbyshire*	158
Ashurst *Hampshire*	253
Ashwater *Devon*	204
Aslockton *Nottinghamshire*	158
Atherstone *Warwickshire*	119
Aysgarth *North Yorkshire*	95

B — page no

Badwell Ash *Suffolk*	178
Bailey *Cumbria*	34
Bakewell *Derbyshire*	158
Bamburgh *Northumberland*	63
Bamford *Derbyshire*	159
Bampton *Devon*	204
Banbury *Oxfordshire*	253
Barford St. Michael *Oxfordshire*	253
Barlaston *Staffordshire*	119
Barley *Hertfordshire*	179
Barnard Castle *Durham*	64
Barningham *Durham*	65
Barnstaple *Devon*	205

Barrasford *Northumberland*	65
Barton-le-Willows *North Yorkshire*	95
Bassenthwaite *Cumbria*	34
Bath *Bath & North East Somerset*	205
Bay Horse *Lancashire*	84
Baylham *Suffolk*	179
Bayton *Hereford and Worcester*	119
Beachy Head *East Sussex*	275
Beadnell *Northumberland*	65
Beaminster *Dorset*	206
Beamish *Durham*	65
Beaulieu *Hampshire*	253
Beer *Devon*	206
Belford *Northumberland*	65
Bellingham *Northumberland*	66
Belper *Derbyshire*	159
Belstone *Devon*	206
Bembridge *Isle of Wight*	253
Bentham *North Yorkshire*	95
Berkhamsted *Hertfordshire*	179
Berrynarbor *Devon*	206
Berwick-upon-Tweed *Northumberland*	66
Bewdley *Hereford and Worcester*	119
Bexhill-on-Sea *East Sussex*	275
Beyton *Suffolk*	179
Bibury *Gloucestershire*	120
Bicester *Oxfordshire*	253
Bigbury-on-Sea *Devon*	207
Billericay *Essex*	179
Birchington *Kent*	275
Birchover *Derbyshire*	159
Birmingham *West Midlands*	120
Birmingham Airport *West Midlands* (See under Birmingham, Coventry)	
Bishop Auckland *Durham*	66
Bishop's Castle *Shropshire*	120
Blakeney *Norfolk*	180
Blanchland *Northumberland*	67
Blankney *Lincolnshire*	160
Blockley *Gloucestershire*	120
Bodmin *Cornwall*	207
Bolam *Durham*	67
Boldre *Hampshire*	254
Bolton Abbey *North Yorkshire*	95
Bonchurch *Isle of Wight*	254
Borrowdale *Cumbria*	35
Boscastle *Cornwall*	207
Bosley *Cheshire*	84
Bourne *Lincolnshire*	160
Bournemouth *Dorset*	254
Bourton-on-the-Water *Gloucestershire*	121
Bovey Tracey *Devon*	208
Brackley *Northamptonshire*	160
Bradford-on-Avon *Wiltshire*	208
Braishfield *Hampshire*	254
Braithwaite *Cumbria*	35
Brampton *Cumbria*	35

Brancaster *Norfolk*	180
Bratton *Somerset*	208
Brayford *Devon*	208
Brean *Somerset*	208
Bridgnorth *Shropshire*	122
Bridport *Dorset*	209
Brighstone *Isle of Wight*	255
Brighton & Hove *East Sussex*	275
Brimfield *Hereford and Worcester*	122
Brisley *Norfolk*	180
Bristol	209
Brixham *Devon*	209
Brize Norton *Oxfordshire*	255
Broad Campden *Gloucestershire*	122
Broadhempston *Devon*	210
Broadstairs *Kent*	276
Broadway *Hereford and Worcester*	123
Broadwoodwidger *Devon*	210
Brockenhurst *Hampshire*	255
Brompton-by-Sawdon *North Yorkshire*	95
Bromsgrove *Hereford and Worcester*	123
Bromyard *Hereford and Worcester*	123
Broughton-in-Furness *Cumbria*	35
Broxholme *Lincolnshire*	160
Bruton *Somerset*	210
Buckden *Cambridgeshire*	180
Buckland Newton *Dorset*	210
Bude *Cornwall*	210
Buntingford *Hertfordshire*	180
Burford *Oxfordshire*	255
Burley *Hampshire*	256
Burnham-on-Sea *Somerset*	211
Burnham Overy Staithe *Norfolk*	181
Burwarton *Shropshire*	123
Bury *Greater Manchester*	84
Buttermere *Cumbria*	36
Buxton *Derbyshire*	160

C — page no

Caldbeck *Cumbria*	36
Callington *Cornwall*	211
Calver *Derbyshire*	161
Cambridge *Cambridgeshire*	181
Camelford *Cornwall*	211
Canon Frome *Hereford and Worcester*	124
Canterbury *Kent*	276
Cardinham *Cornwall*	211
Carleton *Cumbria*	36
Carlisle *Cumbria*	37
Carlton-in-Coverdale *North Yorkshire*	95
Carsington *Derbyshire*	161
Cartmel *Cumbria*	37
Castle Acre *Norfolk*	181

Castle Carrock *Cumbria* 37
Castleside *Durham* 67
Chagford *Devon* 211
Chalfont St Giles
Buckinghamshire 256
Chapel Amble *Cornwall* 212
Chapel-en-le-Frith *Derbyshire* 161
Chard *Somerset* 212
Charlbury *Oxfordshire* 256
Charlton Kings *Gloucestershire* 124
Charmouth *Dorset* 212
Charney Bassett *Oxfordshire* 257
Chathill *Northumberland* 67
Chedgrave *Norfolk* 181
Chedworth *Gloucestershire* 124
Chelmarsh *Shropshire* 124
Cheltenham *Gloucestershire* 124
Chelwood Gate *East Sussex* 277
Chester *Cheshire* 85
Chesterfield *Derbyshire* 161
Chichester *West Sussex* 277
Chiddingly *East Sussex* 277
Chiddingstone *Kent* 277
Chideock *Dorset* 212
Chilham *Kent* 278
Chilworth *Hampshire* 257
Chippenham *Wiltshire* 213
Chipping *Lancashire* 85
Chipping Campden
Gloucestershire 126
Chipping Norton *Oxfordshire* 257
Christchurch *Dorset* 257
Chudleigh *Devon* 213
Church Stretton *Shropshire* 126
Churchstow *Devon* 213
Cirencester *Gloucestershire* 126
Clearwell *Gloucestershire* 127
Cleator *Cumbria* 37
Cley next the Sea *Norfolk* 181
Clippesby *Norfolk* 182
Clitheroe *Lancashire* 85
Cloughton *North Yorkshire* 96
Coberley *Gloucestershire* 127
Cockermouth *Cumbria* 37
Colchester *Essex* 182
Coleford *Gloucestershire* 127
Colwall *Hereford and Worcester* 127
Colyford *Devon* 213
Colyton *Devon* 213
Compton Abdale *Gloucestershire* 127
Compton Martin *Bath & North East
Somerset* 214
Coniston *Cumbria* 38
Consett *Durham* 68
Constantine Bay *Cornwall* 214
Corbridge *Northumberland* 68
Corfe Castle *Dorset* 257
Cotherstone *Durham* 68
Cotswolds: *Heart of England*
(See under Aldsworth, Bibury,
Blockley, Bourton-on-the-Water,
Broad Campden, Broadway,
Chedworth, Cheltenham, Chipping
Campden, Cirencester, Coberley,
Compton Abdale, Daglingworth,
Lechlade, Minchinhampton,
Miserden, Moreton-in-Marsh,
Naunton, Nympsfield, Owlpen,
South Cerney, Stanton,
Stow-on-the-Wold, Stroud, Tetbury,
Tewkesbury, Winchcombe,
Witcombe, Wotton-under-Edge)

Cotswolds: *South of England*
(See under Brize Norton, Burford,
Charlbury, Chipping Norton,
Minster Lovell, Witney)
Coventry *West Midlands* 128
Crackington Haven *Cornwall* 214
Crakehall *North Yorkshire* 96
Craswall *Hereford and Worcester* 128
Crediton *Devon* 214
Creeting St Mary *Suffolk* 182
Cressbrook *Derbyshire* 162
Crewkerne *Somerset* 215
Crich *Derbyshire* 162
Cringleford *Norfolk* 182
Cromer *Norfolk* 182
Crookham *Northumberland* 69
Crooklands *Cumbria* 39
Cropton *North Yorkshire* 96
Croston *Lancashire* 86
Croyde *Devon* 215
Cucklington *Somerset* 215
Cullercoats *Tyne and Wear* 69
Cutthorpe *Derbyshire* 162

D page no

Daglingworth *Gloucestershire* 128
Darsham *Suffolk* 183
Dartmoor
(See under Ashburton, Belstone,
Bovey Tracey, Chagford, Holne,
Lustleigh, Moretonhampstead,
Okehampton, Tavistock, Yelverton)
Deal *Kent* 278
Denholme *West Yorkshire* 96
Denmead *Hampshire* 258
Dent *Cumbria* 39
Denton *Kent* 278
Derby *Derbyshire* 162
Dereham *Norfolk* 183
Devizes *Wiltshire* 215
Digby *Lincolnshire* 162
Dilham *Norfolk* 183
Doddington *Kent* 278
Donington on Bain *Lincolnshire* 162
Dorking *Surrey* 278
Dorrington *Lincolnshire* 163
Dover *Kent* 278
Downderry *Cornwall* 216
Droitwich *Hereford and
Worcester* 128
Dulverton *Somerset* 216
Dunster *Somerset* 216
Durham *Durham* 69
Dymock *Gloucestershire* 129

E page no

Eardisley *Hereford and Worcester* 129
Earl Sterndale *Derbyshire* 163
East Brent *Somerset* 216
East Butterwick *North Lincolnshire* 96
East Harling *Norfolk* 183
East Wittering *West Sussex* 279
Eastbourne *East Sussex* 279
Eastchurch *Kent* 279
Ebberston *North Yorkshire* 96
Eckington *Hereford and Worcester* 129
Edith Weston *Rutland* 163
Edmundbyers *Durham* 69

Eggleston *Durham* 69
Egham *Surrey* 279
Egloshayle *Cornwall* 216
Elkesley *Nottinghamshire* 163
Ellesmere *Shropshire* 129
Elmley Castle *Hereford and
Worcester* 129
Elterwater *Cumbria* 39
Embleton *Northumberland* 70
Emborough *Somerset* 216
Ennerdale *Cumbria* 40
Epperstone *Nottinghamshire* 163
Epsom *Surrey* 279
Eskdale *Cumbria* 40
Evesham *Hereford and Worcester* 130
Ewyas Harold *Hereford and
Worcester* 130
Exford *Somerset* 217
Exmoor
(See under Allerford, Bratton,
Brayford, Dulverton, Dunster,
Exford, North Molton, Parracombe,
Porlock, Simonsbath, West Anstey,
Wheddon Cross, Winsford,
Withypool)
Exmouth *Devon* 217
Eyam *Derbyshire* 164

F page no

Fairwarp *East Sussex* 279
Falmouth *Cornwall* 217
Faversham *Kent* 280
Fawkham *Kent* 280
Fenny Bridges *Devon* 217
Filey *North Yorkshire* 96
Fincham *Norfolk* 184
Folkestone *Kent* 280
Ford *Wiltshire* 218
Fordingbridge *Hampshire* 258
Forest of Dean
(See under Clearwell, Coleford,
Gatcombe, Newent, Parkend,
Tidenham)
Foulsham *Norfolk* 184
Fourstones *Northumberland* 70
Fowey *Cornwall* 218
Foxholes *North Yorkshire* 97
Foxley *Norfolk* 184
Frampton-on-Severn
Gloucestershire 130
Freshwater *Isle of Wight* 258
Frome *Somerset* 218
Frosterley *Durham* 70
Fylingdales Moor *North Yorkshire* 97

G page no

Garboldisham *Norfolk* 184
Garrigill *Cumbria* 40
Garstang *Lancashire* 86
Gatcombe *Gloucestershire* 130
Glaisdale *North Yorkshire* 97
Glastonbury *Somerset* 218
Glenridding *Cumbria* 40
Goathland *North Yorkshire* 97
Gorran Haven *Cornwall* 219
Gosport *Hampshire* 258
Goudhurst *Kent* 280
Grange-over-Sands *Cumbria* 41

Grasmere *Cumbria* 41
Gratton Dale *Derbyshire* 164
Grayrigg *Cumbria* 42
Great Ayton *North Yorkshire* 98
Great Bentley *Essex* 184
Great Carlton *Lincolnshire* 164
Great Dunmow *Essex* 184
Great Hucklow *Derbyshire* 164
Great Langdale *Cumbria* 42
Great Milton *Oxfordshire* 258
Great Moulton *Norfolk* 184
Greenfield *Greater Manchester* 86
Gresham *Norfolk* 185
Grewelthorpe *North Yorkshire* 98
Greystoke *Cumbria* 42

H page no

Hadleigh *Suffolk* 185
Halesworth *Suffolk* 185
Haltwhistle *Northumberland* 70
Hamble *Hampshire* 259
Hamsterley *Durham* 71
Hamsterley Forest *Durham* 71
Harrogate *North Yorkshire* 98
Hartest *Suffolk* 185
Hartgrove *Dorset* 259
Hartington *Derbyshire* 165
Hartland *Devon* 219
Harwood *Durham* 71
Hastings *East Sussex* 280
Hathersage *Derbyshire* 165
Hawes *North Yorkshire* 99
Hawkshead *Cumbria* 42
Haworth *West Yorkshire* 99
Haydon Bridge *Northumberland* 71
Hayfield *Derbyshire* 165
Heacham *Norfolk* 185
Heathfield *East Sussex* 281
Hebden Bridge *West Yorkshire* 100
Helmsley *North Yorkshire* 100
Helpston *Cambridgeshire* 185
Helstone *Cornwall* 219
Hemyock *Devon* 219
Henfield *West Sussex* 281
Hereford *Hereford and Worcester* 131
Hermitage *Berkshire* 259
Herne Bay *Kent* 281
Hexham *Northumberland* 71
Hickling *Norfolk* 186
High Lorton *Cumbria* 43
Hingham *Norfolk* 186
Hitcham *Suffolk* 186
Hoarwithy *Hereford and Worcester* 131
Holbeach *Lincolnshire* 166
Holmbridge *West Yorkshire* 100
Holne *Devon* 219
Holt *Norfolk* 186
Holwell *Dorset* 219
Holworth *Dorset* 220
Holy Island *Northumberland* 72
Hope *Derbyshire* 166
Hope Cove *Devon* 220
Horncastle *Lincolnshire* 166
Horning *Norfolk* 187
Horsington *Somerset* 220
Horsley Woodhouse *Derbyshire* 166
Horton-in-Ribblesdale *North Yorkshire* 100

Hove *East Sussex*
(See under Brighton & Hove)
Hovingham *North Yorkshire* 101
Hunstanton *Norfolk* 187
Huntley *Gloucestershire* 132
Hutton-le-Hole *North Yorkshire* 101

I page no

Ilmington *Warwickshire* 132
Ilminster *Somerset* 220
Ingleby Greenhow *North Yorkshire* 101
Ireby *Cumbria* 43
Ironbridge *Shropshire* 132
Isle of Wight
(See under Bonchurch, Brighstone,
Freshwater, Newport, Ryde,
Ventnor, Whitwell)
Isles of Scilly 220
Ivinghoe *Buckinghamshire* 259
Ivybridge *Devon* 221

K page no

Kendal *Cumbria* 43
Keswick *Cumbria* 44
Kettleshulme *Greater Manchester* 86
Kielder Forest *Northumberland*
(See under Bellingham, West
Woodburn)
King's Lynn *Norfolk* 187
King's Meaburn *Cumbria* 46
King's Nympton *Devon* 221
Kingsbridge *Devon* 221
Kingskerswell *Devon* 221
Kington *Hereford and Worcester* 132
Kirk Ireton *Derbyshire* 167
Kirkby Fleetham *North Yorkshire* 101
Kirkby Lonsdale *Cumbria* 46
Kirkby Stephen *Cumbria* 47
Knapton *Norfolk* 188
Knaresborough *North Yorkshire* 101
Knutsford *Cheshire* 86

L page no

Lamberhurst *Kent* 281
Lambley *Nottinghamshire* 167
Lambourn *Berkshire* 259
Langdale *Cumbria* 47
Langton Matravers *Dorset* 259
Lanreath-by-Looe *Cornwall* 221
Launceston *Cornwall* 222
Lavenham *Suffolk* 188
Lazonby *Cumbria* 47
Leadenham *Lincolnshire* 167
Lealholm *Devon* 219
Lealholm *North Yorkshire* 102
Leamington Spa *Warwickshire* 133
Lechlade *Gloucestershire* 133
Ledbury *Hereford and Worcester* 133
Leek *Staffordshire* 134
Leighton Buzzard *Bedfordshire* 188
Leominster *Hereford and Worcester* 134
Lewes *East Sussex* 281
Leyburn *North Yorkshire* 102
Leysdown on Sea *Kent* 281
Leysters *Hereford and Worcester* 134

Lincoln *Lincolnshire* 167
Liskeard *Cornwall* 222
Little Shelford *Cambridgeshire* 188
Litton *Derbyshire* 168
Litton Cheney *Dorset* 222
Lockton *North Yorkshire* 102
Loftus *Tees Valley* 72
London 23
Long Melford *Suffolk* 189
Longsleddale *Cumbria* 47
Longtown *Hereford and Worcester* 134
Looe *Cornwall* 222
Lorton *Cumbria* 47
Loscombe *Dorset* 223
Lostwithiel *Cornwall* 223
Louth *Lincolnshire* 168
Lower Beeding *West Sussex* 282
Lower Benefield *Northamptonshire* 168
Lowestoft *Suffolk* 189
Loweswater *Cumbria* 48
Lowick *Northumberland* 72
Ludham *Norfolk* 189
Ludlow *Shropshire* 135
Lullington *Derbyshire* 168
Lustleigh *Devon* 224
Lyme Regis *Dorset* 224
Lymington *Hampshire* 260
Lyndhurst *Hampshire* 260

M page no

Macclesfield *Cheshire* 86
Madley *Hereford and Worcester* 135
Maiden Newton *Dorset* 224
Maidenhead *Berkshire* 260
Maidstone *Kent* 282
Malvern *Hereford and Worcester* 136
Manchester Airport
(See under Knutsford, Stockport)
Marazion *Cornwall* 225
Marnhull *Dorset* 260
Masham *North Yorkshire* 102
Matlock *Derbyshire* 168
Mayfield *Staffordshire* 136
Mere *Wiltshire* 225
Mevagissey *Cornwall* 225
Mickleton *Durham* 72
Middleton *Suffolk* 189
Middleton- by-Youlgreave *Derbyshire* 168
Middleton-in-Teesdale *Durham* 72
Midhurst *West Sussex* 282
Milborne St Andrew *Dorset* 260
Milford-on-Sea *Hampshire* 261
Millom *Cumbria* 48
Milton Abbas *Dorset* 261
Milwich *Staffordshire* 136
Minchinhampton *Gloucestershire* 137
Mindrum *Northumberland* 73
Minehead *Somerset* 226
Minster Lovell *Oxfordshire* 261
Minsterley *Shropshire* 137
Miserden *Gloucestershire* 137
Modbury *Devon* 226
Monkleigh *Devon* 226
Montacute *Somerset* 226
Moreton-in-Marsh *Gloucestershire* 137
Moretonhampstead *Devon* 226

Mosterton *Dorset* 227
Mothecombe *Devon* 227
Much Cowarne *Hereford and Worcester* 138
Much Wenlock *Shropshire* 138
Mullion *Cornwall* 227
Mungrisdale *Cumbria* 48
Munslow *Shropshire* 138
Mytholmroyd *West Yorkshire* 102

N — page no

Nantwich *Cheshire* 87
Naunton *Gloucestershire* 138
Nayland *Suffolk* 189
Neasham *Durham* 73
Nenthead *Cumbria* 49
Neston *Cheshire* 87
New Forest
(See under Ashurst, Beaulieu, Boldre, Brockenhurst, Burley, Fordingbridge, Lymington, Lyndhurst, Milford-on-Sea, Ringwood)
Newcastle upon Tyne *Tyne and Wear* 73
Newent *Gloucestershire* 138
Newhaven *East Sussex* 282
Newmarket *Suffolk* 190
Newport *Isle of Wight* 261
Newquay *Cornwall* 227
Newton-by-the-Sea *Northumberland* 74
Newton Ferrers *Devon* 227
Newton-on-Rawcliffe *North Yorkshire* 103
Newton Poppleford *Devon* 228
Newton upon Derwent *East Riding of Yorkshire* 102
Norfolk Broads
(See under Clippesby, Hickling, Horning, Lowestoft, Ludham, North Walsham, Norwich, Salle, Sprowston, Stalham)
North Molton *Devon* 228
North Scarle *Lincolnshire* 169
North Walsham *Norfolk* 190
Northallerton *North Yorkshire* 103
Norwich *Norfolk* 190
Nutley *East Sussex* 282
Nympsfield *Gloucestershire* 139

O — page no

Oakham *Leicestershire* 169
Okehampton *Devon* 228
Olney *Buckinghamshire* 262
Orford *Suffolk* 190
Oswestry *Shropshire* 139
Oundle *Northamptonshire* 169
Ovington *Northumberland* 74
Owlpen *Gloucestershire* 139
Oxford *Oxfordshire* 262

P — page no

Padstow *Cornwall* 228
Paignton *Devon* 229
Pangbourne *Berkshire* 262

Parkend *Gloucestershire* 139
Parracombe *Devon* 229
Pateley Bridge *North Yorkshire* 103
Patterdale *Cumbria* 49
Peak District
(See under Ashbourne, Ashford in the Water, Bakewell, Bamford, Birchover, Buxton, Calver, Chapel-en-le-Frith, Cressbrook, Earl Sterndale, Eyam, Gratton Dale, Great Hucklow, Hartington, Hathersage, Hayfield, Hope, Litton, Thorpe, Tideswell, Winster)
Pembridge *Hereford and Worcester* 139
Pendeen *Cornwall* 229
Penrith *Cumbria* 49
Pentewan *Cornwall* 229
Penzance *Cornwall* 229
Perranporth *Cornwall* 229
Peterborough *Cambridgeshire* 191
Petworth *West Sussex* 283
Pewsey *Wiltshire* 230
Pickering *North Yorkshire* 103
Piddlehinton *Dorset* 230
Plaxtol *Kent* 283
Plymouth *Devon* 230
Polperro *Cornwall* 231
Polstead *Suffolk* 191
Poole *Dorset* 262
Porlock *Somerset* 231
Port Gaverne *Cornwall* 231
Port Isaac *Cornwall* 231
Portchester *Hampshire* 263
Portland *Dorset* 231
Portscatho *Cornwall* 232
Portsmouth & Southsea *Hampshire* 263
Potterhanworth *Lincolnshire* 169
Praa Sands *Cornwall* 232
Preston *Lancashire* 87
Princes Risborough *Buckinghamshire* 263

R — page no

Ramsgate *Kent* 283
Redmile *Leicestershire* 169
Reeth *North Yorkshire* 103
Ringstead *Norfolk* 191
Ringwood *Hampshire* 263
Ripponden *West Yorkshire* 104
Robin Hood's Bay *North Yorkshire* 104
Ropsley *Lincolnshire* 169
Ross-on-Wye *Hereford and Worcester* 140
Rothbury *Northumberland* 74
Royal Tunbridge Wells *Kent* 283
Rydal *Cumbria* 49
Ryde *Isle of Wight* 264
Rye *East Sussex* 283

S — page no

Saddleworth *Greater Manchester* 87
Saffron Walden *Essex* 191
St Austell *Cornwall* 232
St Clether *Cornwall* 232
St Columb Major *Cornwall* 232
St Ives *Cornwall* 233

St Mawes *Cornwall* 233
St Mawgan *Cornwall* 233
St Tudy *Cornwall* 233
Salcombe *Devon* 233
Salisbury Plain
(See under Amesbury, Winterbourne Stoke)
Salle *Norfolk* 191
Saltburn-by-the-Sea *Tees Valley* 75
Sandringham *Norfolk* 192
Sandwich *Kent* 284
Satterthwaite *Cumbria* 49
Sawrey *Cumbria* 50
Saxmundham *Suffolk* 192
Scarborough *North Yorkshire* 104
Scotch Corner *North Yorkshire* 105
Seahouses *Northumberland* 75
Seathwaite *Cumbria* 50
Seaton *Devon* 234
Sedbergh *Cumbria* 50
Sedbusk *North Yorkshire* 105
Sedgeberrow *Hereford and Worcester* 141
Selston *Nottinghamshire* 170
Sennen Cove *Cornwall* 234
Settle *North Yorkshire* 105
Sevenoaks *Kent* 284
Shaftesbury *Dorset* 264
Shaldon *Devon* 234
Sheffield *South Yorkshire* 105
Shepton Mallet *Somerset* 234
Sherborne *Dorset* 234
Sherford *Devon* 235
Sheringham *Norfolk* 192
Sherwood Forest
(See under Epperstone)
Shillingstone *Dorset* 264
Shrewsbury *Shropshire* 141
Sibford Gower *Oxfordshire* 264
Sidmouth *Devon* 235
Simonsbath *Somerset* 235
Sinnington *North Yorkshire* 106
Skipton *North Yorkshire* 106
Slaley *Northumberland* 75
Slingsby *North Yorkshire* 106
Snettisham *Norfolk* 192
South Cerney *Gloucestershire* 141
South Mimms *Hertfordshire* 193
Southampton *Hampshire* 264
Southport *Merseyside* 87
Southsea *Hampshire*
(See under Portsmouth & Southsea)
Southwick *Wiltshire* 235
Southwold *Suffolk* 193
Spark Bridge *Cumbria* 50
Spilsby *Lincolnshire* 170
Spreyton *Devon* 235
Sprowston *Norfolk* 193
Staithes *North Yorkshire* 106
Stalham *Norfolk* 193
Stamford Bridge *East Riding of Yorkshire* 106
Stanton *Gloucestershire* 142
Stanton-on-the-Wolds *Nottinghamshire* 170
Staplehurst *Kent* 284
Starcross *Devon* 235
Staveley *Cumbria* 50
Steeple Ashton *Wiltshire* 236
Steeple Aston *Oxfordshire* 265
Stiffkey *Norfolk* 193
Stiperstones *Shropshire* 142

Stockport *Greater Manchester* 88
Stoke-on-Trent *Staffordshire* 142
Stoke St Gregory *Somerset* 236
Stow-on-the-Wold *Gloucestershire* 142
Stowlangtoft *Suffolk* 193
Stratford-upon-Avon *Warwickshire* 144
Stratton Audley *Oxfordshire* 265
Stroud *Gloucestershire* 145
Studland *Dorset* 265
Sturminster Newton *Dorset* 265
Stutton *North Yorkshire* 107
Sudbury *Suffolk* 194
Summer Bridge *North Yorkshire* 107
Sutton-in-Craven *North Yorkshire* 107
Sutton on the Hill *Derbyshire* 170
Swanage *Dorset* 265
Sydling St Nicholas *Dorset* 236
Symonds Yat *Hereford and Worcester* 145
Symonds Yat West *Hereford and Worcester* 146

T page no

Taunton *Somerset* 236
Tavistock *Devon* 236
Tebay *Cumbria* 50
Telford *Shropshire* 146
Temple Normanton *Derbyshire* 170
Tenterden *Kent* 284
Tetbury *Gloucestershire* 146
Tetford *Lincolnshire* 170
Tewkesbury *Gloucestershire* 146
Thame *Oxfordshire* 265
Theberton *Suffolk* 194
Theddlethorpe All Saints *Lincolnshire* 171
Thirsk *North Yorkshire* 107
Thornham *Norfolk* 194
Thornthwaite *Cumbria* 51
Thornton Dale *North Yorkshire* 107
Thorpe *Derbyshire* 171
Thorpeness *Suffolk* 194
Threlkeld *Cumbria* 51
Thursby *Cumbria* 51
Tidenham *Gloucestershire* 146
Tideswell *Derbyshire* 171
Tincleton *Dorset* 237
Tintagel *Cornwall* 237
Tiverton *Devon* 237
Todmorden *West Yorkshire* 108
Tolpuddle *Dorset* 237
Tonbridge *Kent* 285
Torcross *Devon* 237
Torquay *Devon* 238
Torrington *Devon* 238
Totnes *Devon* 239
Tow Law *Durham* 76
Tregony *Cornwall* 239
Troutbeck *Cumbria* 51
Tunbridge Wells
(See under Royal Tunbridge Wells)

U page no

Ullswater *Cumbria* 52
Ulverston *Cumbria* 52
Uppingham *Leicestershire* 171

Upton-upon-Severn *Hereford and Worcester* 147

V page no

Ventnor *Isle of Wight* 266

W page no

Wakefield *West Yorkshire* 108
Wallingford *Oxfordshire* 266
Walsham-le-Willows *Suffolk* 194
Wareham *Dorset* 266
Warkworth *Northumberland* 76
Warwick *Warwickshire* 147
Wasdale *Cumbria* 52
Washford *Somerset* 239
Watchet *Somerset* 239
Watchfield *Oxfordshire* 266
Wearhead *Durham* 76
Welbury *North Yorkshire* 108
Wellesbourne *Warwickshire* 147
Wellington *Shropshire* 147
Welton *Cumbria* 52
Wem *Shropshire* 148
West Anstey *Devon* 239
West Bexington *Dorset* 239
West Buckland *Devon* 240
West Felton *Shropshire* 148
West Harptree *Bath & North East Somerset* 240
West Malling *Kent* 285
West Mersea *Essex* 195
West Rudham *Norfolk* 195
West Scrafton *North Yorkshire* 109
West Woodburn *Northumberland* 76
Weston Rhyn *Shropshire* 148
Weymouth *Dorset* 240
Whatstandwell *Derbyshire* 171
Wheddon Cross *Somerset* 240
Whimple *Devon* 241
Whitby *North Yorkshire* 109

Whitwell *Isle of Wight* 266
Widemouth Bay *Cornwall* 241
Williton *Somerset* 241
Winchcombe *Gloucestershire* 148
Winchester *Hampshire* 267
Windermere *Cumbria* 53
Windsor *Berkshire* 267
Winfrith Newburgh *Dorset* 267
Winsford *Somerset* 241
Winster *Derbyshire* 171
Winterbourne Steepleton *Dorset* 241
Winterbourne Stoke *Wiltshire* 241
Winterton-on-Sea *Norfolk* 195
Wirral *Merseyside*
(See under Neston)
Wisbech *Cambridgeshire* 195
Witcombe *Gloucestershire* 149
Witherslack *Cumbria* 55
Withypool *Somerset* 241
Witney *Oxfordshire* 267
Wolsingham *Durham* 76
Wolverley *Hereford and Worcester* 149
Wool *Dorset* 268
Woolacombe *Devon* 242
Wooler *Northumberland* 77
Wootton *Staffordshire* 149
Worcester *Hereford and Worcester* 149
Worth Matravers *Dorset* 268
Wotton-under-Edge *Gloucestershire* 149
Wrotham *Kent* 285
Wye Valley
(See under Hereford, Ross-on-Wye, Symonds Yat, Symonds Yat West)
Wythall *Hereford and Worcester* 150

Y page no

Yelverton *Devon* 242
Yetminster *Dorset* 242
York 110

MILEAGE CHART

The distances between towns on the mileage chart are given to the nearest mile, and are measured along routes based on the quickest travelling time, making maximum use of motorways or dual-carriageway roads. The chart is based upon information supplied by the Automobile Association.

From \ To	Aberdeen	Aberystwyth	Barnstaple	Birmingham	Brighton	Bristol	Cambridge	Cardiff	Carlisle	Carmarthen	Colchester	Dorchester	Dover	Edinburgh	Exeter	Fort William	Glasgow	Gloucester	Guildford	Holyhead	Hull	Inverness	Kendal	Leeds	Lincoln	Liverpool	Maidstone	Manchester	Middlesbrough	Newcastle	Norwich	Nottingham	Oxford	Penzance	Perth	Plymouth	Sheffield	Southampton	Stranraer	Taunton	York
Aberystwyth	468																																								
Barnstaple	603	211																																							
Birmingham	431	123	178																																						
Brighton	606	285	206	171																																					
Bristol	514	128	100	.88	169																																				
Cambridge	462	214	267	97	120	171																																			
Cardiff	534	117	129	108	203	46	205																																		
Carlisle	232	236	372	196	375	282	257	302																																	
Carmarthen	517	50	190	169	264	107	266	67	285																																
Colchester	515	289	291	171	112	195	48	229	310	290																															
Dorchester	596	203	94	170	121	62	180	121	364	182	208																														
Dover	586	325	272	207	81	206	124	239	401	300	116	201																													
Edinburgh	125	335	471	296	474	382	334	401	99	384	387	463	458																												
Exeter	587	195	55	161	176	84	251	113	356	174	276	54	244	455																											
Fort William	156	446	582	406	584	492	467	511	209	495	520	574	611	133	566																										
Glasgow	147	332	468	293	471	379	354	398	96	381	407	461	498	47	452	102																									
Gloucester	479	111	126	53	155	36	150	66	247	127	170	118	192	346	110	457	343																								
Guildford	564	222	174	128	44	106	91	139	332	200	103	98	97	431	147	541	428	100																							
Holyhead	460	105	341	165	344	251	260	206	228	155	334	333	370	327	325	438	324	216	301																						
Hull	361	227	321	134	260	231	139	251	170	312	192	313	264	232	305	380	266	196	239	218																					
Inverness	106	494	630	455	633	540	516	560	258	543	569	622	659	157	614	65	173	505	591	485	428																				
Kendal	279	190	326	150	329	236	245	256	47	239	319	318	355	146	310	257	143	201	286	181	164	305																			
Leeds	328	173	309	115	262	220	146	239	122	299	199	302	271	199	293	332	219	185	220	165	59	318	72																		
Lincoln	387	201	276	99	208	187	88	206	182	267	141	245	212	258	260	392	278	152	166	204	47	440	176	72																	
Liverpool	358	111	234	99	277	184	193	204	216	188	264	219	398	284	110	153	179	71	129	160	118																				
Maidstone	547	283	233	168	50	167	85	200	362	261	77	162	41	419	206	572	458	153	58	330	225	620	316	233	173	264															
Manchester	352	131	262	86	264	172	160	191	120	180	213	254	291	220	246	360	216	137	222	122	98	378	74	44	85	35	249														
Middlesbrough	276	244	359	172	319	269	199	288	95	293	252	351	323	148	343	281	191	234	277	235	89	308	84	64	123	141	281	114													
Newcastle	234	274	389	202	350	300	229	319	59	323	282	381	354	105	373	238	153	265	307	266	142	266	101	95	154	175	311	145	39												
Norwich	487	276	329	159	169	233	63	267	282	328	59	242	173	359	313	492	378	212	161	321	150	540	176	172	103	240	131	185	223	254											
Nottingham	393	160	235	53	195	145	86	164	188	226	139	227	218	264	219	398	284	110	153	179	71	129	160	118																	
Oxford	503	159	170	68	109	74	81	107	271	168	124	115	146	370	154	481	367	48	67	239	189	529	225	171	130	173	106	161	227	257	161	103									
Penzance	697	305	110	271	288	194	361	223	466	284	386	166	356	565	110	675	561	219	259	433	414	724	419	403	369	367	317	355	451	482	423	328	264								
Perth	86	382	518	343	521	428	379	448	146	431	432	510	504	42	502	102	61	393	479	237	114	193	245	304	272	462	266	193	151	404	311	418	612								
Plymouth	628	236	61	202	219	125	292	154	397	214	317	97	287	496	45	606	492	150	190	364	345	655	350	334	300	298	248	286	382	413	354	259	195	78	543						
Sheffield	366	167	272	86	233	183	122	202	162	263	175	265	247	238	257	371	258	148	191	158	65	420	125	36	47	79	204	38	103	133	147	44	141	366	283	297					
Southampton	570	221	140	213	167	139	137	139	338	200	158	547	434	99	48	306	256	596	299	237	196	240	112	227	293	324	193	170	66	221	484	152	207								
Stranraer	239	342	478	303	481	388	363	408	106	391	417	470	507	133	462	186	84	353	438	333	276	265	153	229	288	232	465	226	201	163	389	295	378	572	153	503	268	444			
Taunton	555	162	50	129	158	51	218	80	323	141	243	45	224	422	34	533	419	77	126	291	272	581	277	260	227	225	184	212	309	340	280	186	121	144	469	75	223	91	429		
York	321	201	316	129	276	226	156	245	117	250	209	308	280	193	300	323	213	191	234	192	38	375	91	25	81	102	238	72	50	88	181	87	184	410	238	341	60	251	223	267	
London	545	238	216	120	59	120	60	153	314	214	62	129	78	413	200	523	409	102	30	281	187	572	267	199	136	215	38	203	254	285	115	131	56	310	460	241	168	80	419	167	211

CUSTOMER FEEDBACK QUESTIONNAIRE

We hope you have found this guide useful in selecting accommodation in England which suits your needs.

It is very helpful to the English Tourist Board to receive comments about establishments in *Where to Stay* and suggestions on how to improve the guide, and also on the National Grading and Classification Schemes.

We would like to hear from you. If you wish to do so, you can send us your views using this questionnaire. You need not name the establishment concerned.

Q1 Did you use the *Where to Stay* guide to find:
Holiday accommodation ☐
Business accommodation ☐
Both ☐

Q2 Did you use the establishment's Quality Grading/Crown or Key Classification to help you in making your choice?
Yes ☐
No ☐

Q3 If you did, was it the Quality Grading (Approved, Commended, Highly Commended or De Luxe) or the number of Crowns or Keys for facilities that influenced you most?
The Quality Grading ☐
The number of Crowns/Keys ☐
Both ☐

Q4 What was the Quality Grading and Crown or Key Classification of the establishment you chose?

....

Q5 Do you find the National Grades and Classifications:
Very easy to understand ☐

Fairly easy to understand ☐
Difficult to understand ☐
If you find them difficult to understand, please specify why:

....
....

Q6 Was the accommodation you used:
Hotel ☐
Guesthouse ☐
Farmhouse ☐
Bed & Breakfast ☐
Self-Catering Holiday Home ☐

Q7 Did the establishment chosen:
Exceed your expectations ☐
Meet your expectations ☐
Fail to meet your expectations ☐
If it failed to meet your expectations, please specify how:

....
....

Q8 Would you say the establishment offered good value for money?
Yes ☐
No ☐

Q9 Was there any feature of your stay that you would particularly praise or criticise (please specify):

....
....
....

Q10 Have you bought a *Where to Stay* guide before?

Yes ☐
No ☐

If yes, how long ago:

Last year ☐
2 years ago ☐
More than 2 years ago ☐

Q11 Did you find the *Where to Stay* guide:

Very easy to use ☐
Fairly easy to use ☐
Difficult to use ☐

Q12 Are there any aspects of the *Where to Stay* guide that you would particularly praise or criticise (please specify):

....
....
....

Q13 Is there any additional information not already featured in this guide that you would find helpful (please specify):

....
....
....

Please would you give us a few details about yourself:

Q14 Are you:

Married ☐
Single ☐

Q15 Do you have dependent children?

Yes ☐
No ☐
If yes, how many ☐

Q16 Into which age group do you fall?

17-24 ☐
25-34 ☐
35-44 ☐
45-54 ☐
55+ ☐

Q17 Are you an overseas visitor (i.e. from outside the UK visiting this country)?

Yes ☐
No ☐

Q18 Did you travel alone or with a party?

Alone ☐
Party of people ☐
of which   were adults
and   children

Q19 How long did you stay in the establishment?
                                                    nights

Q20 Do you plan to use the guide to book any further stays this year?

Yes ☐
No ☐
If yes, how many ☐

Q21 What other sources of information did you use in selecting your accommodation (please specify):

....
....
....

Q22 Did you obtain your copy of *Where to Stay* from

Bookshop ☐
Tourist Information Centre ☐
Other (please specify) ☐

Thank you for giving us your views. Please return this questionnaire to: Department AS, English Tourist Board, Thames Tower, Black's Road, Hammersmith, London W6 9EL.

LOCATION MAPS

Every place name featured in the accommodation listings pages of this *Where to Stay* guide has a map reference to help you locate it on the maps which follow. For example, to find Colchester, Essex, which has 'Map ref 3B2', turn to Map 3 and refer to grid square B2.

All place names in the listings pages are shown in black type on the maps. This enables you to find other places in your chosen area which may have suitable accommodation - the Town Index (preceding pages) gives page numbers.

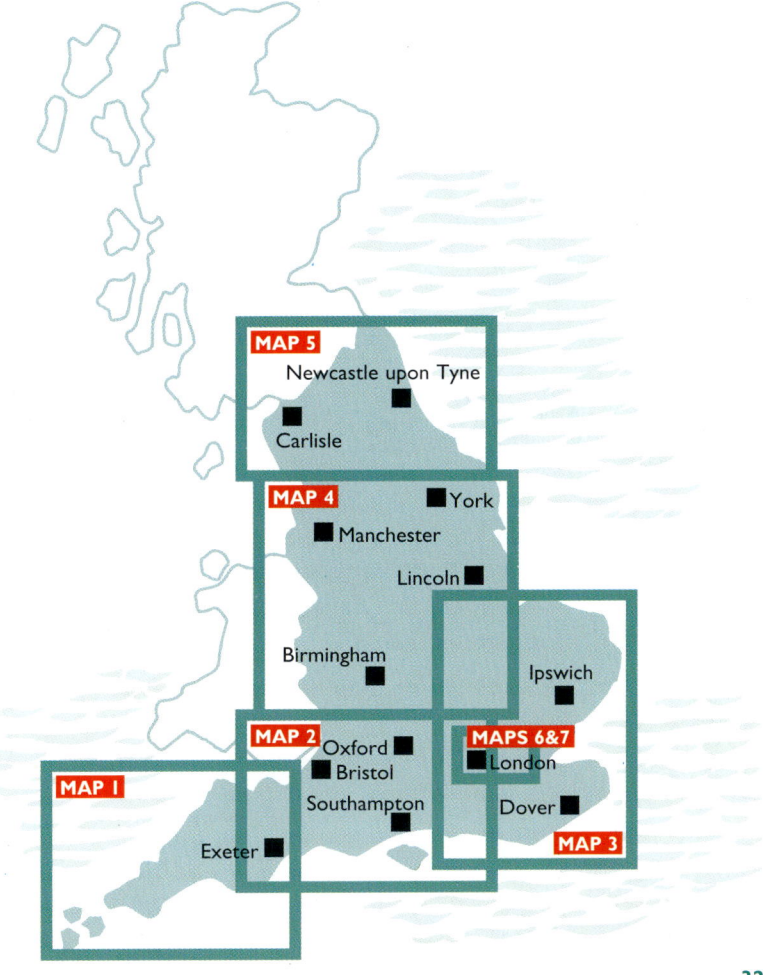

A

B

1

2

3

Boscastle
Tintagel
Camelford
Helstone
Port Isaac
Port Gaverne
Chapel Amble
St Tudy
Constantine Bay
Padstow
A39
A30
St Mawgan
Egloshayle
Cardinham
Newquay
St Columb Major
Bodmin
Newquay
Lostwithiel
A392
A30
A391
A390
Perranporth
St Austell
Fowey
A39
Pentewan
Truro
Mevagissey
A390
Tregony
Gorran Haven
St Ives
A30
Camborne
A39
Portscatho
Pendeen
A394
Falmouth
Penzance
Marazion
St Mawes
Sennen Cove
Praa Sands
Isles of Scilly
Mullion
Isles of Scilly (St. Mary's)

MAP I

C   D

M4

A48

NORTH SOMERSET

Weston-super-Mare

Brean

A370
A38

East Brent
Burnham-on-Sea

M5

Ilfracombe

Woolacombe

Croyde

Berrynarbor

Parracombe

Porlock
Allerford

Bratton
Minehead
Dunster
Watchet

A39

EXMOOR

Exford

Simonsbath

Brayford

Withypool

Winsford

Wheddon
Cross

Washford

Williton

A39

Bridgwater

A39

SOMERSET

A39

NATIONAL PARK

West
Buckland

North
Molton

Dulverton

A396

West
Anstey

Bampton

Taunton

Stoke
St Gregory

Barnstaple

Bideford

Hartland

Monkleigh

Torrington

A361

King's
Nympton

A38

A358

A377

Tiverton

DEVON

Hemyock

A303

Ilminster

Crewkerne

Bude

Widemouth
Bay

Crackington
Haven

A39

A386

A386

A396

Crediton

M5

A373

A30

Chard

A30

Axminster

A35

Whimple

Fenny
Bridges

A30

Charmouth

Colyton

Seaton

Lyme
Regis

Chideock

St Clether

Launceston

A395

Ashwater

Broadwoodwidger

Okehampton

Belstone

Spreyton

A30

Chagford

Moretonhampstead

Exeter

Exeter

Newton
Poppleford

Sidmouth

Beer

A376

Starcross

Exmouth

A30

CORNWALL

A388

DARTMOOR

NATIONAL PARK

Lustleigh

Chudleigh

Bovey Tracey

A38

Teignmouth

Tavistock

Yelverton

A386

Ashburton

Holne

Newton
Abbot

Shaldon

A380

Callington

A390

A388

Kingskerswell

Broadhempston

Torquay

Plymouth City

Ivybridge

A38

A38

Totnes

A385

Paignton

A3022

Brixham

Liskeard

A38

Lanreath-
by-Looe

Downderry

Looe

Polperro

PLYMOUTH

Newton
Ferrers

A379

Modbury

Mothecombe

Churchstow

Bigbury-on-Sea

Kingsbridge

Hope Cove

Salcombe

A3122

Sherford

Torcross

Roscoff

Santander

N

25 Miles

40 Kilometres

Produced by COLIN EARL Cartography

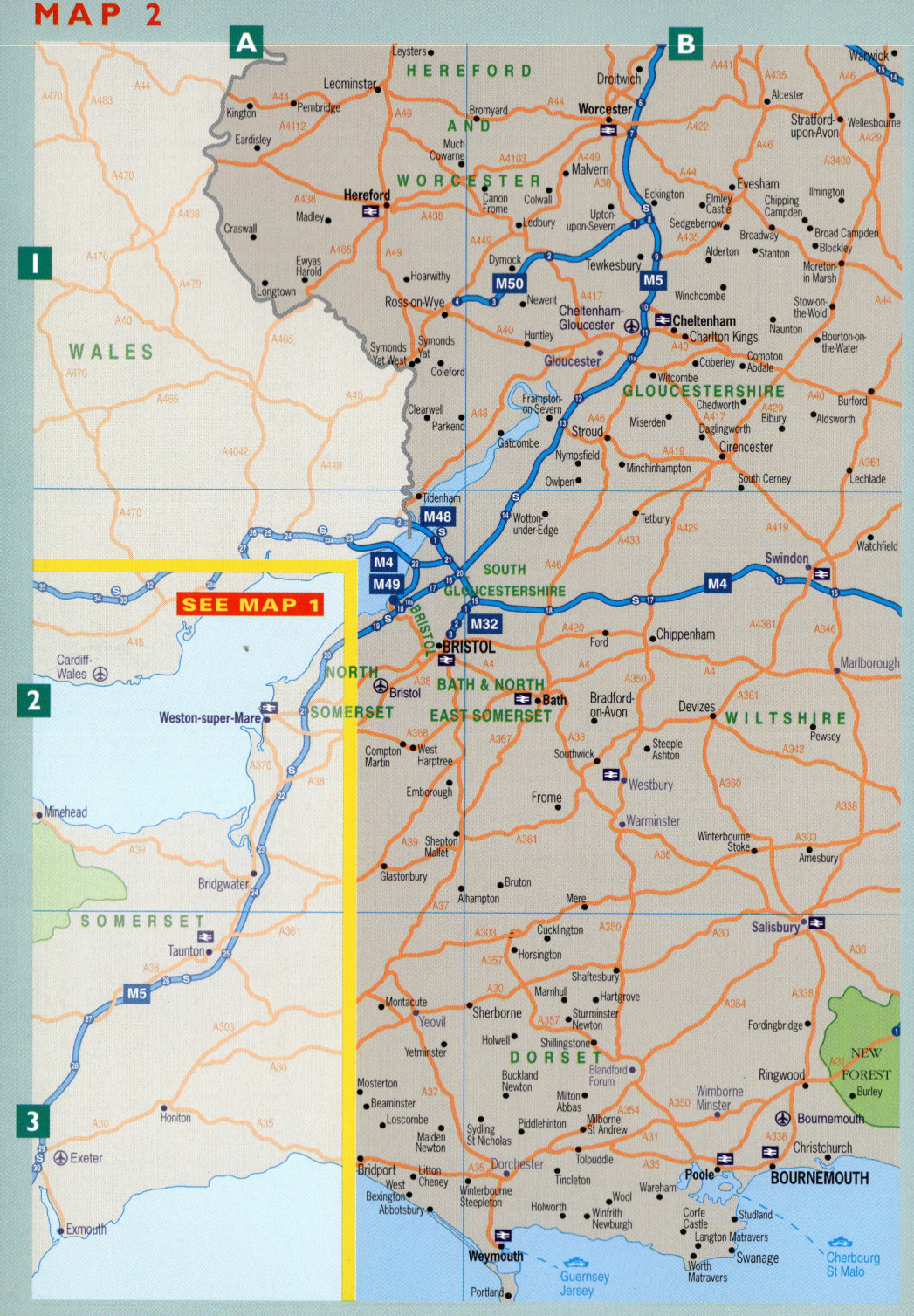

MAP 2

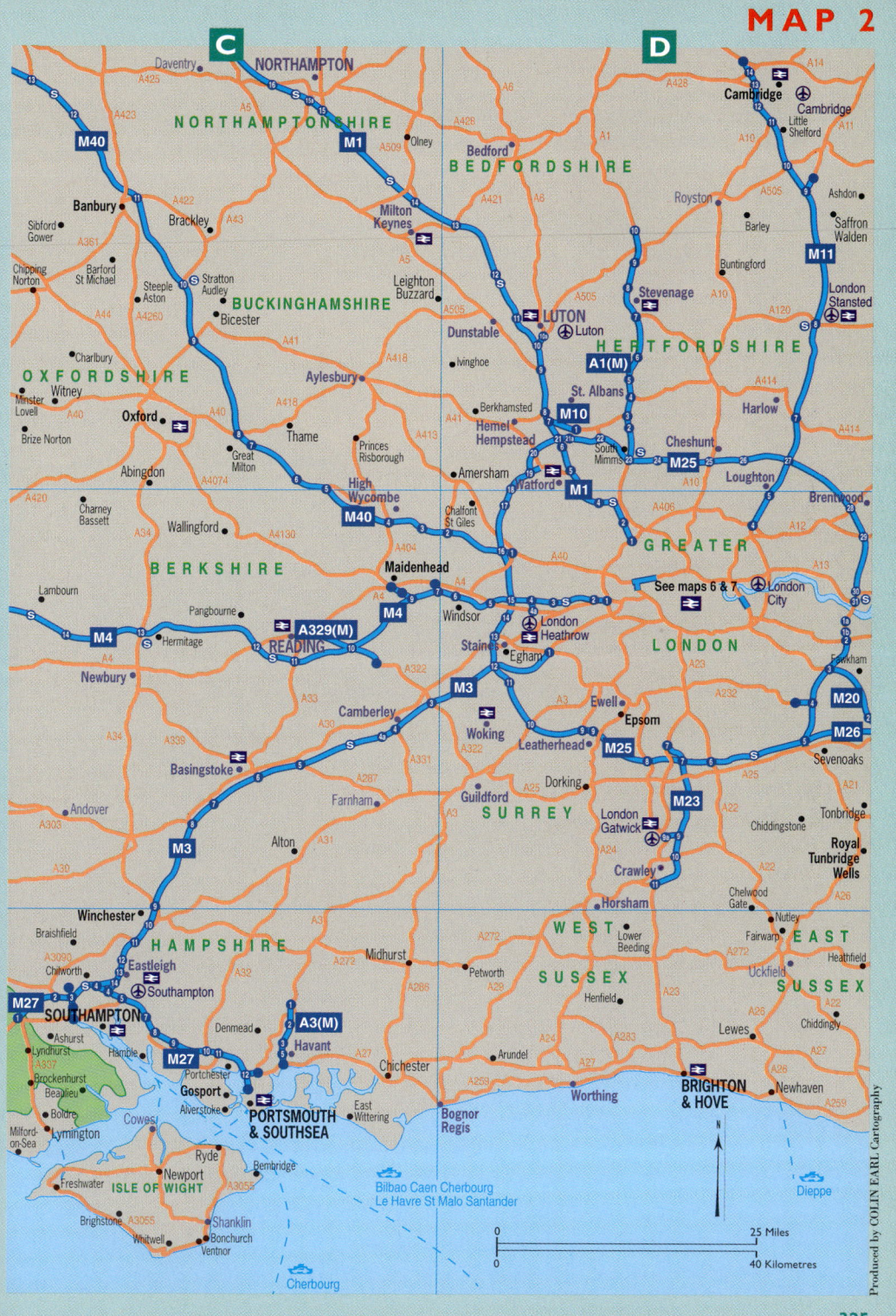

MAP 2

MAP 3

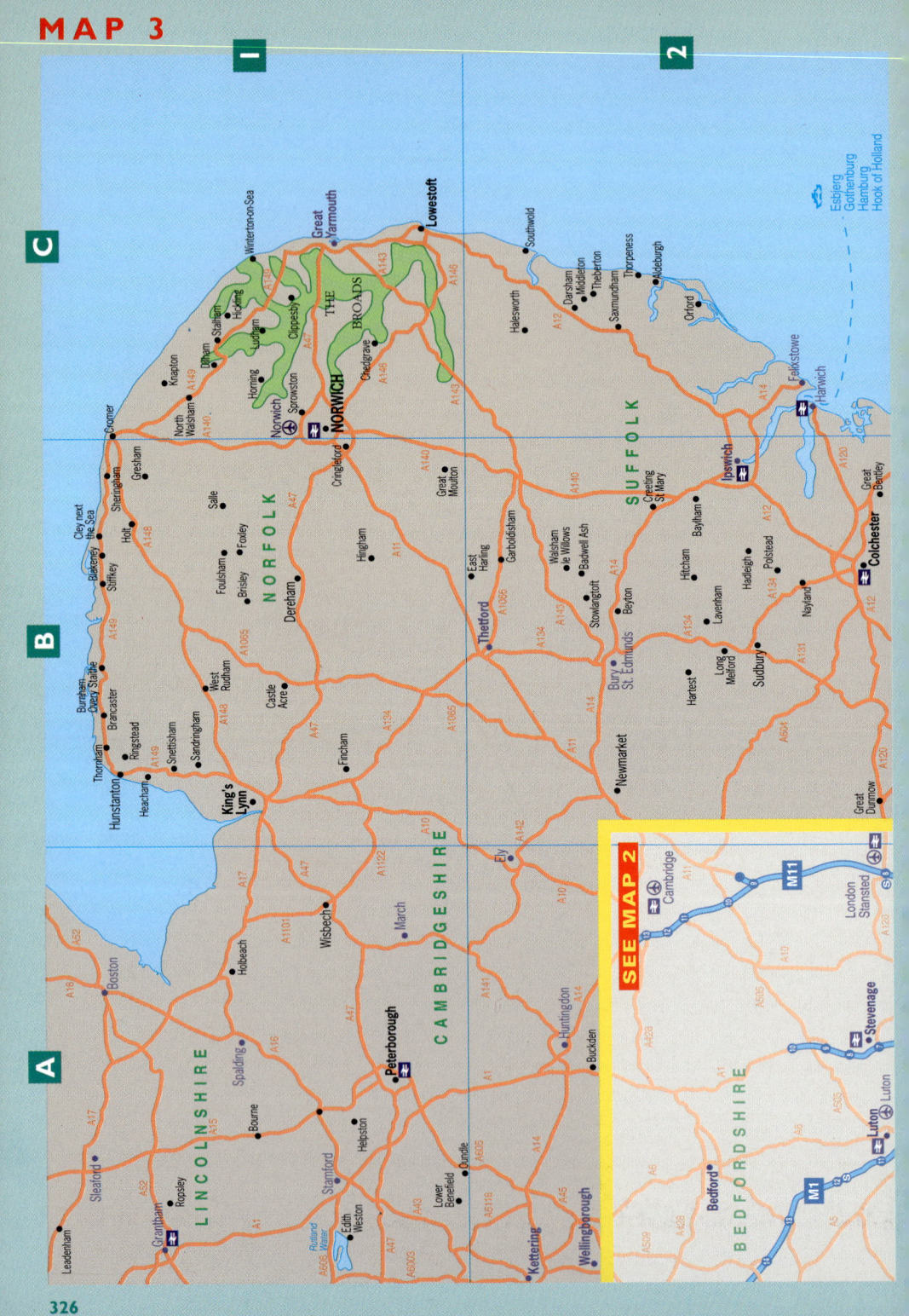

Produced by COLIN EARL Cartography

MAP 4

C D

329

Produced by COLIN EARL Cartography

MAP 5

C

D

0 _____ 25 Miles
0 _____ 40 Kilometres

N

Amsterdam
Bergen
Esbjerg
Gothenburg
Hamburg
Haugesund
Stavanger

Bamburgh
Seahouses
Beadnell
Chathill
Newton-
by-the-Sea
Embleton
Alnwick
Alnmouth
Warkworth

A1
A1068
A697
A1
A189
A696

Whitley Bay
Cullercoats
Tynemouth
Newcastle   NEWCASTLE
               UPON TYNE
                          South
                          Shields
               TYNE
               AND WEAR
A692   A19   SUNDERLAND
Beamish   Washington
A691   A690
Durham
A167   A690
A88   A688   A1(M)
       Bishop
       Auckland   A689
Bolam   Redcar
          Stockton-   TEES VALLEY   Saltburn-by-the-Sea
          on-Tees   Loftus
          Darlington   MIDDLESBROUGH Staithes
                       A171
          Tees-side   Whitby
A66   Great Ayton
          Neasham   Ingleby   Robin
          A172   Greenhow   Hood's Bay
                      Lealholm
A66   Glaisdale
       Scotch   NORTH YORK MOORS
       Corner   NATIONAL PARK   Goathland
A1   Welbury   Fylingdales
       Kirkby   Moor
       Fleetham A684   A189   A171   Cloughton
A684 Crakehall Northallerton
                       Hutton-   Scarborough
                       le-Hole
                  Appleton-le-Moors Newton-on-Rawcliffe
          Thirsk   Helmsley Cropton Lockton
                       A170 Sinnington Ebberston Filey
NORTH YORKSHIRE Masham   Pickering Thornton
       Grewelthorpe   Dale Brompton- Foxholes
                  Ampleforth   by-Sawdon
                  Hovingham Slingsby   A64   A165
Pateley A61 A168 Amotherby
Bridge Summer A19
        Bridge A1(M)   Bridlington
                       Barton-   A614
                       le-Willows

Produced by COLIN EARL Cartography

331

MAP 6

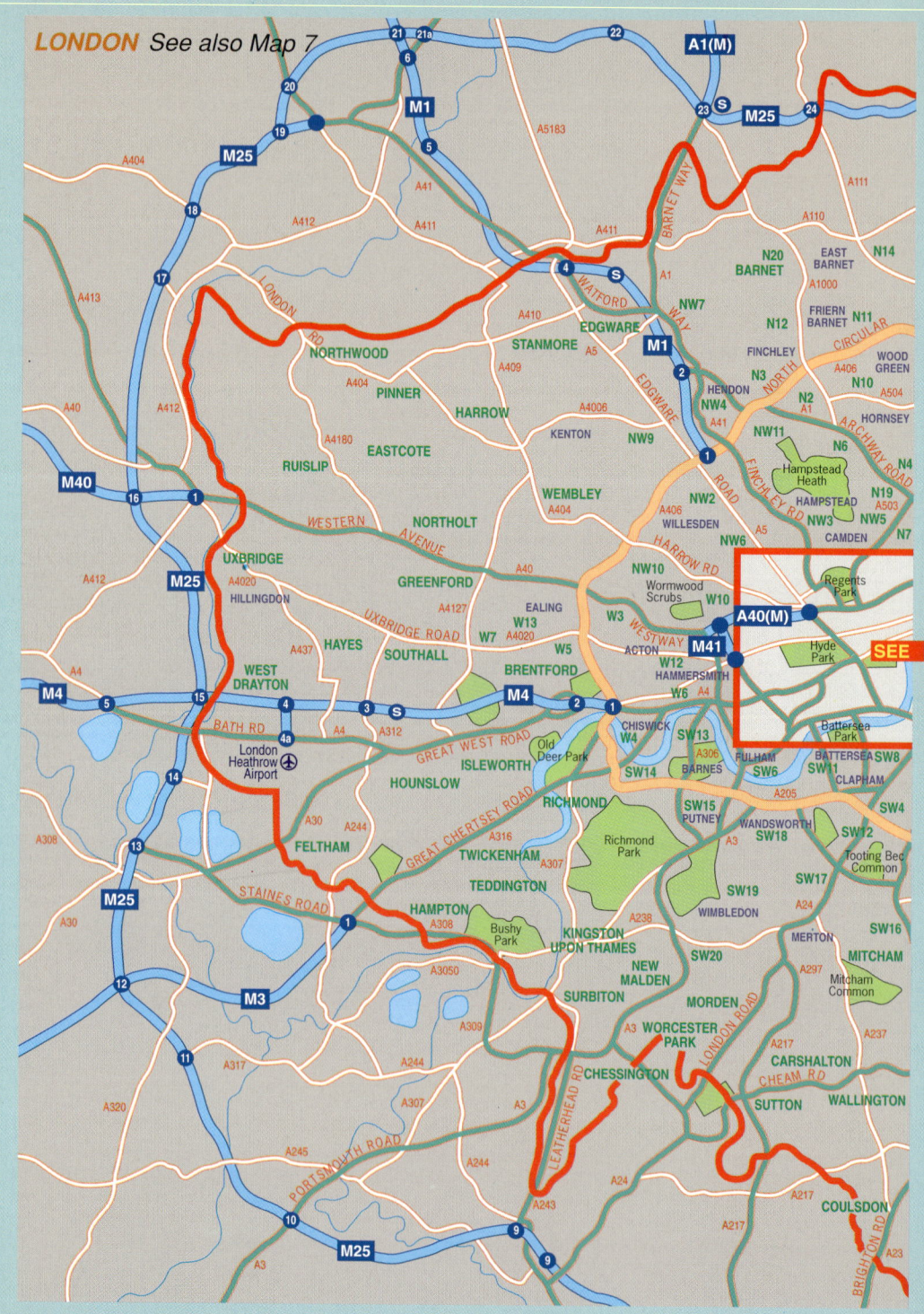

LONDON *See also Map 7*

MAP 6

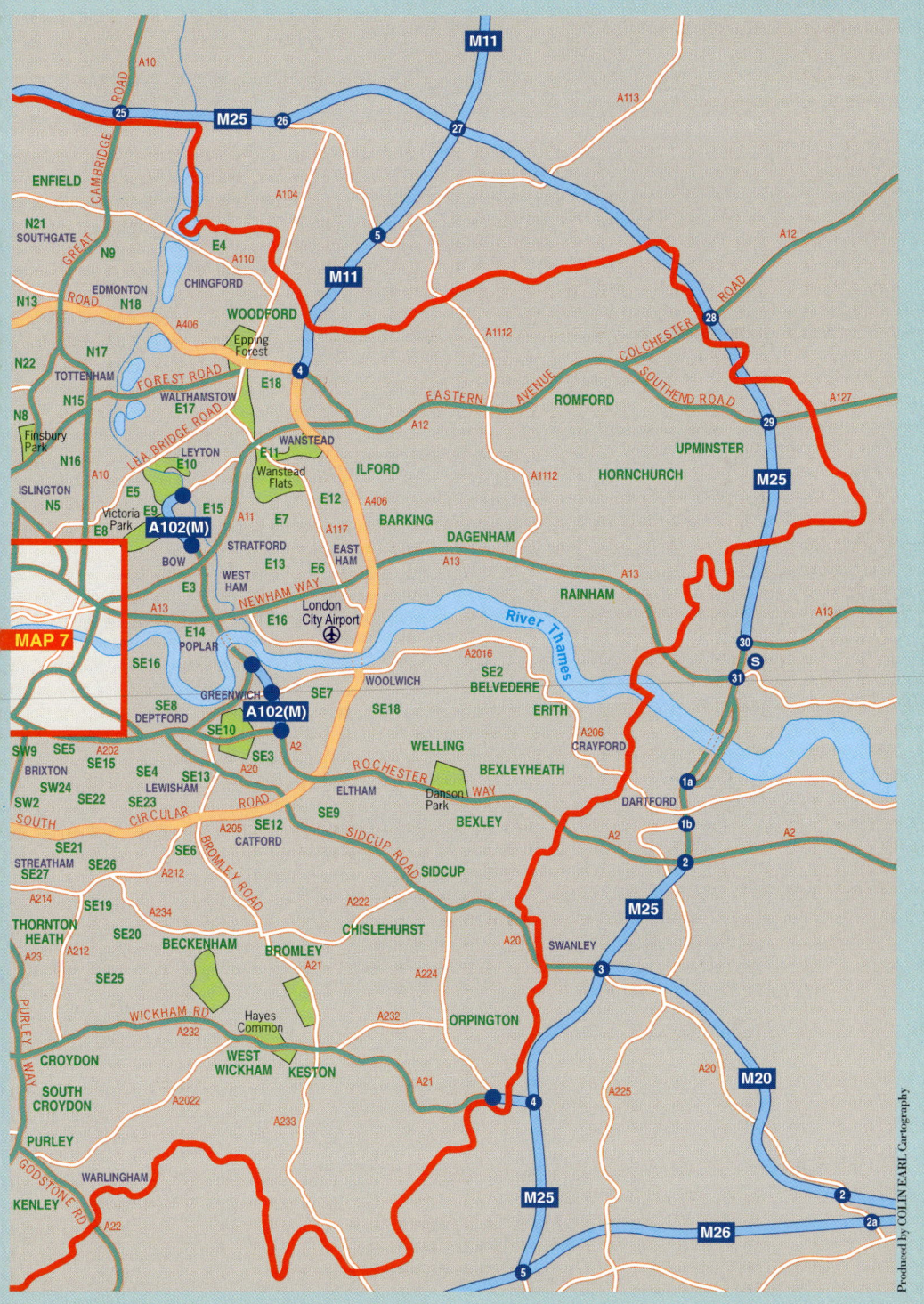

MAP 7

Produced by COLIN EARL Cartography

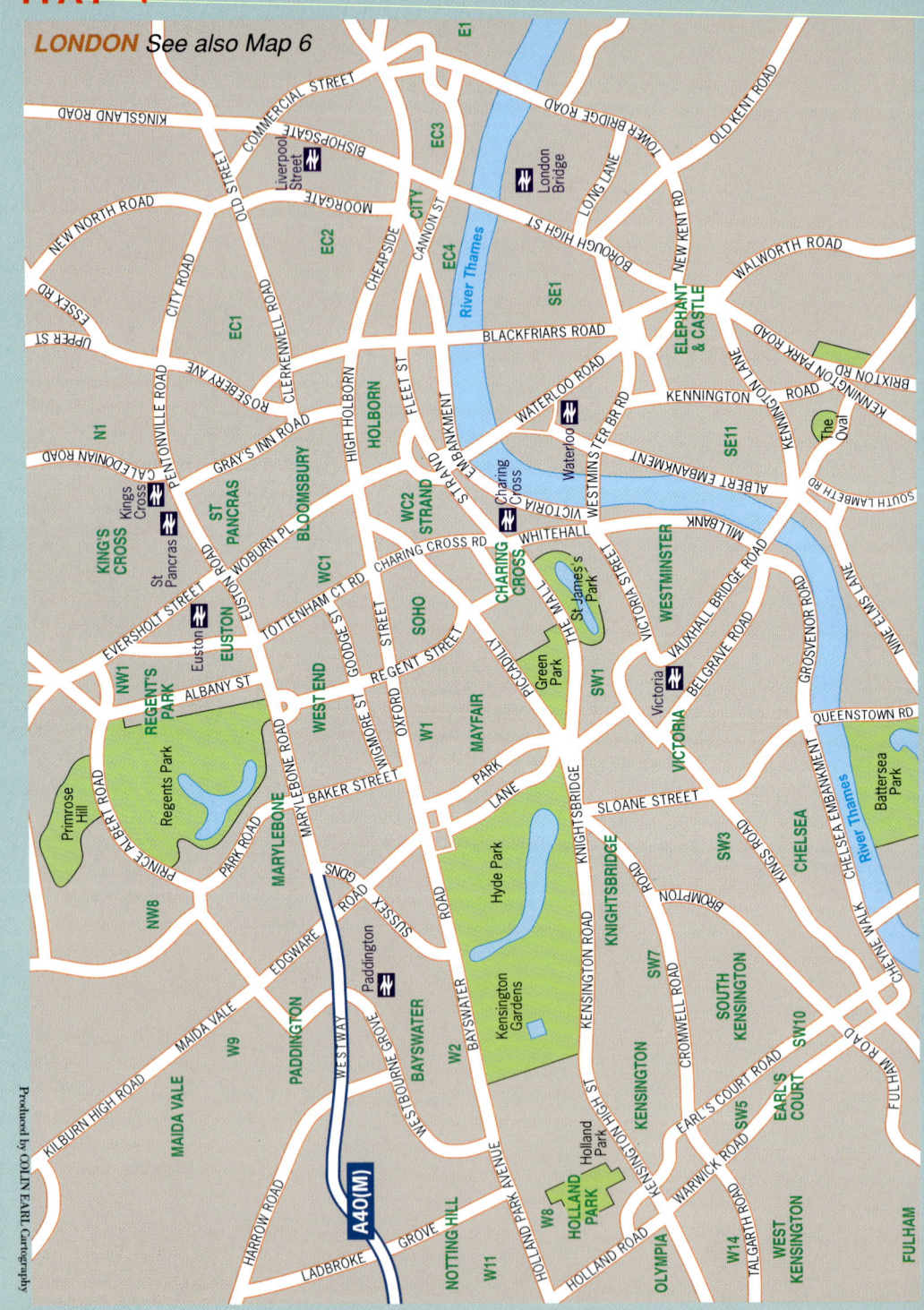

LONDON *See also Map 6*

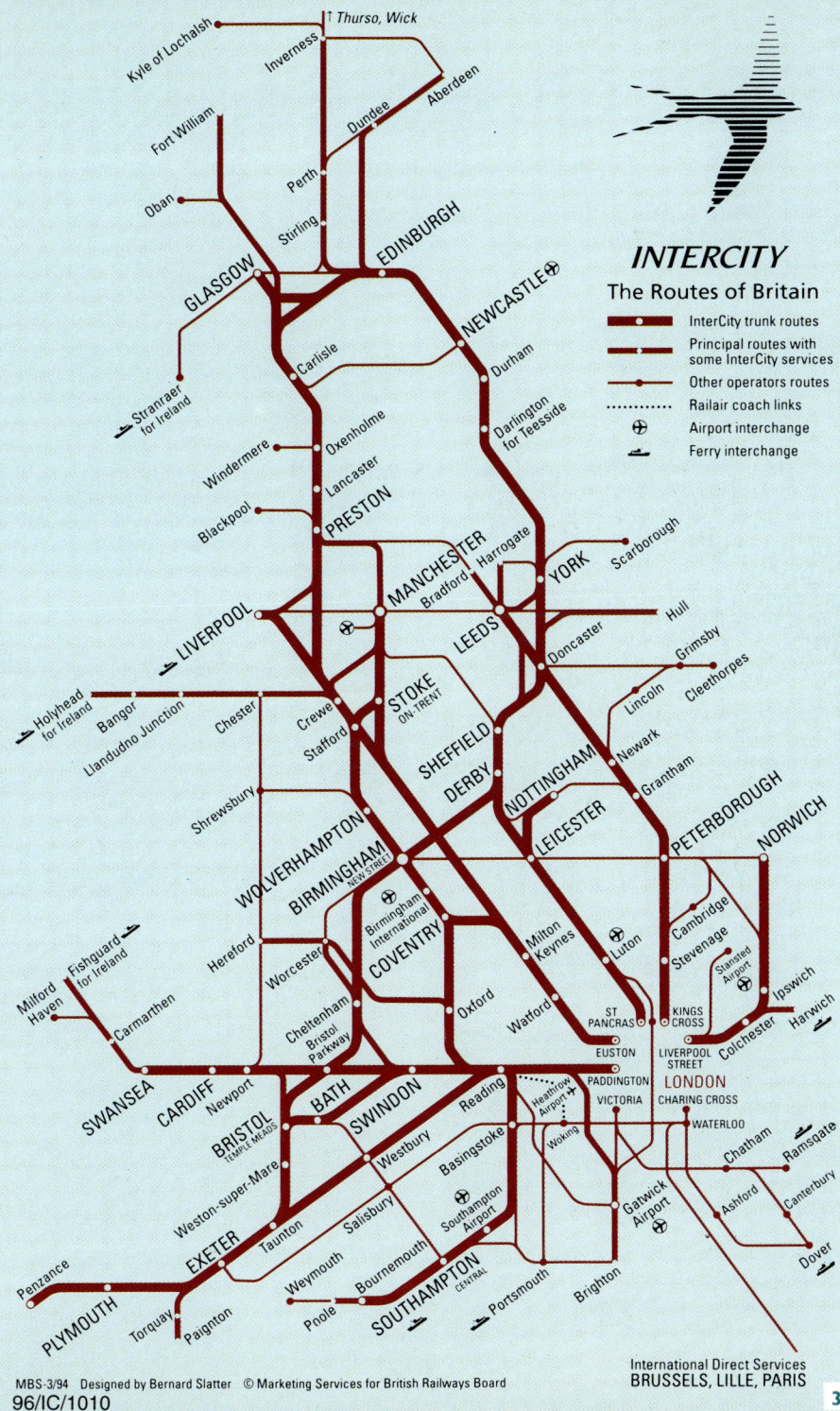

INTERCITY

The Routes of Britain

- ●━━━● InterCity trunk routes
- ━━━━ Principal routes with some InterCity services
- ●━━● Other operators routes
- ·········· Railair coach links
- ✈ Airport interchange
- ⛴ Ferry interchange

↑ Thurso, Wick

Kyle of Lochalsh
Inverness
Fort William
Aberdeen
Dundee
Oban
Perth
Stirling
GLASGOW
EDINBURGH
Stranraer for Ireland
Carlisle
NEWCASTLE ✈
Durham
Darlington for Teesside
Windermere
Oxenholme
Lancaster
Blackpool
PRESTON
MANCHESTER
Bradford
Harrogate
YORK
Scarborough
LIVERPOOL ⛴
LEEDS
Hull
Holyhead for Ireland
Bangor
Doncaster
Grimsby
Llandudno Junction
Chester
Crewe
STOKE ON-TRENT
Lincoln
Cleethorpes
Stafford
SHEFFIELD
Newark
Shrewsbury
DERBY
NOTTINGHAM
Grantham
WOLVERHAMPTON
BIRMINGHAM NEW STREET
LEICESTER
PETERBOROUGH
NORWICH
Hereford
Birmingham International
COVENTRY
Milton Keynes
Cambridge
Stevenage
Stansted Airport
Worcester
Ipswich
Cheltenham
Bristol Parkway
Oxford
Luton ✈
Harwich ⛴
Milford Haven
Fishguard for Ireland
Watford
Colchester
Carmarthen
ST PANCRAS
KINGS CROSS
SWANSEA
CARDIFF
Newport
BATH
SWINDON
Reading
EUSTON
LIVERPOOL STREET
LONDON
BRISTOL TEMPLE MEADS
Heathrow Airport ✈
PADDINGTON
VICTORIA
CHARING CROSS
Weston-super-Mare
Westbury
Basingstoke
Woking
WATERLOO
Chatham
Ramsgate
EXETER
Taunton
Salisbury
Southampton Airport ✈
Gatwick Airport
Ashford
Canterbury
Penzance
Weymouth
Bournemouth
SOUTHAMPTON CENTRAL
Portsmouth
Brighton
Dover ⛴
PLYMOUTH
Torquay
Paignton
Poole

International Direct Services
BRUSSELS, LILLE, PARIS

MBS-3/94   Designed by Bernard Slatter   © Marketing Services for British Railways Board
96/IC/1010

335

YOUR QUICK GUIDE

Where to Stay makes it quick and easy to find a place to stay that offers the standard of quality and facilities you're looking for.

The TOWN INDEX (starting on page 313) and the LOCATION MAPS (starting on page 321) show all cities, towns and villages with accommodation listings in this guide.

1 Town Index

If the place you plan to visit is included in the town index, turn to the page number given to find accommodation available there. Also check that location on the colour maps to find other places nearby which also have accommodation listings in this guide.

1	
Batley West Yorkshire	158
Battlesbridge Essex	317
Beadnell Northumberland	100
Bedale North Yorkshire	158
Bedford Bedfordshire	317
Belford Northumberland	100
Bellingham Northumberland	100
Belper Derbyshire	285
Belton Leicestershire	286
Berkhamsted Hertfordshire	318
Berrynarbor Devon	372
Berwick-upon-Tweed Northumberland	100
Bexhill-on-Sea East Sussex	509
Bexleyheath Greater London	43
Bibury Gloucestershire	217

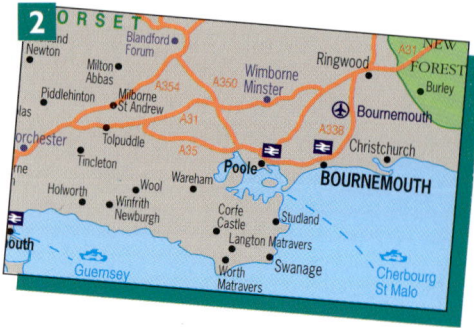

2 Location Maps

If the place you want is not in the town index - or you only have a general idea of the area in which you wish to stay - use the colour location maps to find places in the area which have accommodation listings in this guide.

When you have found suitable accommodation, check its availability with the establishment and also confirm any other information in the published entry which may be important to you (price, whether bath and/or shower available, children/dogs/credit cards welcome, months open, etc).

If you are happy with everything, make your booking and, if time permits, confirm it in writing.